# Statistics

FOURTH EDITION

**Frank Owen · Ron Jones**

*An imprint of* **Pearson Education**

Harlow, England · London · New York · Reading, Massachusetts · San Francisco
Toronto · Don Mills, Ontario · Sydney · Tokyo · Singapore · Hong Kong · Seoul
Taipei · Cape Town · Madrid · Mexico City · Amsterdam · Munich · Paris · Milan

Pearson Education Limited
Edinburgh Gate
Harlow
Essex CM20 2JE
England

and Associated Companies throughout the world    *519.5*

*Visit us on the World Wide Web at:*
http://www.pearsoneduc.com

© Longman Group UK Limited 1990, 1994

First edition 1977
Second edition 1982
Third edition 1990
Fourth edition 1994

**British Library Cataloguing in Publication Data**
Owen, Frank, 1922–1982
    Statistics. – 4th ed
    I. Title    II. Jones, Ron, 1939–
    519.5

ISBN 0–273–60320–5

10   9   8   7
04   03   02   01   00

Typeset by Mathematical Composition Setters Ltd, Salisbury, Wiltshire
Produced by Pearson Education Asia Pte Ltd
Printed and bound in Singapore (COS)

*The Publishers' policy is to use paper manufactured from sustainable forests.*

# Contents

# Preface

In surveying the literature, it seemed to us that although there were many excellent books on statistical methods, there was a marked deficiency of textbooks designed to cover the first year syllabus of the major professional bodies. It is this gap that the first edition of this book was intended to fill. The book is also suitable for BTEC HND and HNC courses, and the Business Statistics courses in Business Studies Degrees.

All authors know that their books are never entirely their own work. We owe a great deal to the comments and criticism of our colleagues at Liverpool John Moores University; and to those who have so willingly allowed us to use their past examination questions.

This new edition has been brought fully up to date and contains a new chapter on Simulation.

Detailed solutions to the exercises, where appropriate, have been given in the *Lecturer's Guide*, which is available to lecturers adopting this textbook.

RON JONES

# Acknowledgements

We would like to express our thanks to the following examination bodies who have allowed us to make such a liberal use of their past examination questions.

The Association of Chartered Certified Accountants (ACCA)

The Chartered Institute of Secretaries and Administrators (ICSA)

The Chartered Institute of Management Accountants (CIMA)

The Association of International Accountants (AIA)

The Chartered Institute of Public Finance and Accountancy (CIPFA)

The Institute of Chartered Accountants in England and Wales (ICAEW)

# The electronic spreadsheet

The electronic spreadsheet is an extremely useful tool for the statistician. Spreadsheets can be used to produce diagrams, and have built-in statistical functions that can be used to remove much of the drudgery involved in statistical computations. However, there are two problems involved in using the spreadsheet: to be used effectively, they demand a fairly high degree of knowledge of how a spreadsheet works – knowledge that you may not have. Second, the statistical functions supplied with the spreadsheet tend to be rather limited.

With this new edition, the opportunity has been taken to make available a number of pre-written spreadsheet templates. These templates are available on request from the publisher. The templates automate much of the graphics drawing procedures of the spreadsheet and extend the statistical functions to cover the main concepts introduced in this book. The aim in producing these templates has been not primarily to produce templates that are elegant and efficient, but to mirror as closely as possible the procedures used within this text.

The fact that these spreadsheet templates are available should not be taken to mean that their use is essential – far from it. *If you elect not to use the templates, then your understanding of statistics will in no way be impaired.* You should consider the templates as an optional extra (albeit an extremely useful optional extra). They are there if you want to use them – it's entirely up to you. If you do not intend to use the templates, then you should proceed directly to Chapter 1. If you would like to use the templates, then there are a number of points you must consider.

## What will you need?

First, the hardware requirements. You will need an IBM PC or near compatible. Second, if you wish to use commercial software, the requirements are:

> *either* Lotus 1–2–3
>
> *or* Borland Quattro configured to run in Lotus mode.

We realise that both of these applications are rather expensive and may indeed be beyond what you are prepared to pay. As an alternative, and on the same disk, the templates have been converted to run using the shareware spreadsheet ASEASYAS. This spreadsheet is available from shareware distributors at an extremely low price – some distributors sell it for as little as £1.75. Shareware distributors advertise in those magazines dedicated to personal computing, and you can find such magazines on sale in large, High Street newsagents.

## What will you need to know?

Some knowledge of personal computing is expected. In particular, you must know how to boot up the system and how to load your spreadsheet application. It would obviously help if you had some knowledge of a spreadsheet and how it works, though this is not essential. You must, however, be able to retrieve a spreadsheet file.

When you receive the disk, you should immediately make a copy of it to use as a working disk. You should then keep the original in a safe place and never use it in case it should become accidentally corrupted. The files on the disk are stored in two subdirectories, and the subdirectory and files that you will use depends upon which spreadsheet application you are using. There are two batch files that will copy the appropriate files to the root directory. With the disk in drive A, type:

LOTUS  if you are using Lotus 1–2–3 or Quattro, or

ASEASY if you are using ASEASYAS version 4.0 or later.

Your disk will now be ready to use.

If you are using a hard disk machine, then you might like to copy the files to the same directory as that containing your spreadsheet application. If you change to this directory and type GO, then the use of the templates is completely automated.

# 1 The organisation of data

The modern business world has a great hunger for facts and data. Well organised data improves our understanding of problems, and helps us to take decisions wisely. Badly organised data is little better than worthless. Unfortunately, you will all-too-often come across data that is not organised – most firms have filing cabinets full of data that someone intends to organise 'one day'. In this chapter we will suggest methods by which data can be organised for meaningful analysis – we will take our first steps in the rewarding (though often confusing) world of statistics.

Most people are vaguely aware that Statistics is concerned with figures in one way or another. Equally, we think, most people are rather distrustful of the statistics that they see quoted in the press or on television. We must admit that we ourselves have some sympathy for the shoppers who are told on the news one evening that the cost of living has gone up by only 2% this month, and then find in the shops next morning that everything they buy has, in fact, risen in price by between 5% and 10%. When this sort of thing happens it is no wonder that people get the impression that statistics can be made to prove anything. And yet – if our figures are accurate and the information is presented properly – how can this be so? We would like you to believe right from the start that no genuine statistician will ever deliberately misrepresent information or use it to mislead people. It can be done of course. In life many people are unscrupulous, and later in this course we will tell you how they misrepresent information, with the strict warning that *you* must never do it.

The great weakness of Statistics is that, to the man in the street who has never studied it, the methods used by statisticians are a closed book. We hope that as you work through this course your own personal book will be opened and that you will understand the dilemma in which our shoppers find themselves.

## Data types

Before we begin to think of the techniques you will use and the calculations you will perform, let us stop for a minute to consider the raw material you will be dealing with.

Suppose that the student union in your school or college wishes to obtain information about its members – their age, sex, home area, whether they live in a flat, or at home, or in lodgings and so on. How would the union secretary go about collecting this information? The most obvious way is for each student to be issued with a questionnaire, posing the relevant questions, and asking for it to be returned to the secretary's office. No doubt some of the forms will be incorrectly completed; some students may genuinely misunderstand the questions; some may refuse to answer certain questions which they regard as personal; doubtless some, in the fashion of the great petitions of the nineteenth century, will be signed by Queen Victoria or Karl Marx. Yet, with all its faults, this mass of completed questionnaires is the basic raw material for the statistical report that the union secretary wishes to produce.

Raw material such as this, collected at first hand, in response to specific questions is known as *primary data*; its characteristics are that it is obtained directly for the purpose of the survey which is being undertaken, and is, as yet, unanalysed.

Now, if your union secretary is lucky, he may also be able to obtain a great deal of information from the college administration, who, using enrolment forms as their primary data, may already have produced for their own purposes a fair amount of statistical information about students. Such information will, of course, have been produced for college purposes and may not be exactly what the union wants, but it is often useful additional information. Such data, which has already been collected for another, and different purpose, we know as *secondary data*. Usually it is of less use than primary data since it has already been processed and the original questionnaire is unlikely to have asked all the questions you would like to have asked. But whether it is primary or secondary, there can be very little statistical information which was not at one time to be found only in a pile of completed forms or questionnaires.

We said earlier that the most obvious way for the union secretary to collect his data was to issue a questionnaire to each and every student. The results of his enquiry would cover every single student in the college – it will refer to what statisticians call the *population* of students. Beware of this term population. In statistics it does not mean the number of people living in a particular area. What it implies is that we have examined or obtained information about every single member of a particular group we are investigating. Thus we can talk of a population of telegraph poles, a population of shaggy-haired dogs, a population of ball-bearings and so on.

But is there any need for us to examine the population of students attending the college? If we wish to save time and money, can we not do as so many public opinion polls do and take a sample of students? We could issue the questionnaire to, say, 60 or 70 students only, or perhaps to every tenth student, and so reduce our raw data considerably. The *sample results* we obtain can then be applied to the population of students: if 12% of the sample live at home, we will argue that about 12% of all students in the college live at home.

Now, you may well argue that this can lead to wildly inaccurate results; and if you consider some of the results of public opinion polls in recent years it is apparent that things can, and do, go wrong. The sample chosen may be too small; it may not be representative of the population; the error arising as a result may mislead us. At this stage we will merely point out that in taking a sample we are in good company: an extremely high percentage of government statistics such as the statistics of Household Expenditure are based on samples which, on the face of it, appear to be ludicrously small.

The main task of any writer on Statistics is to explain what the statistician does with his raw data between collecting it and presenting his report. So let us go back to your union secretary.

It is obvious that no-one would sit down and write a report in the form:

> 'Mary Smith is 17, lives in Durham, and is in lodgings here; Susan Yeung comes from Singapore and is in lodgings here ...'

We might as well hand over the completed forms to anyone who is interested since all that this type of report does is list the information which is already given in detail on the questionnaire.

We can get a clue about the next stage of the analysis if we ask ourselves what it is that the union really wants to know. Surely the sort of information that is really wanted is how many students are 16 years old, how many are 17 and so on; what percentage of students live at home; what proportion of students come from overseas. It is not the individual we are interested in so much as total numbers in given categories. The categories in this investigation may be age, sex, type of residence, number of hours a week spent on study and so on. Within each category students will vary. Some are 16; others are 17; some live at home; others in lodgings. We call each of these categories a *variable* because within each category students will vary. So we may now say that we are interested in a number of variables such as age, and more specifically in the value we can assign to each student within the range of values over which the variable extends. We may find, for example, that when we consider the variable 'age', 267 students are aged 17, 164 are aged 18 and so on up to the eldest student. The numbers of students whom we can place at each value of the variable we will call the *frequency*, because it tells us how often we will come across a student with this particular characteristic (that is, aged 18, or doing 27 hours a week private study, or travelling more than 15 miles to college). Thus the first step we must take is to decide what aspects of student life we are interested in and count up how many students are found within each of these categories. In so doing we are simplifying our data – reducing it to a more manageable form. In the process some detail is lost. We no longer know how old Brenda Jones is; but if we are interested we still have her completed questionnaire. On the other hand we do know that 267 students are aged 17 as well as a great deal of other general information.

## Statistical tabulations

Once we have reached this stage we are in a position to summarise our results in the form of a table and our work begins to look more like that of a statistician. Probably as a first tentative step we would produce a simple table dealing with only one variable. It might appear like this:

**Age of students attending ABC College**

| Age (the variable) | Number of students (the frequency) |
|---|---|
| 17 | 267 |
| 18 | 164 |
| 19 | 96 |
| 20 | 74 |
| 21 and over | 23 |
| | 624 |

There is nothing wrong with our producing 15 or 20 tables like this, each concerned with a single variable, but surely it is better for presentation purposes if we could produce a small number of compound tables each showing several variables at once. Thus we could construct a double table showing the two variables, age and sex of students at the same time.

We have constructed this table by listing one of our variables vertically (age) and the other horizontally (sex). There is no golden rule, but it generally looks better if we tabulate the variable with the greater number of values vertically and that with the smaller number of values horizontally. Notice too that we have totalled both the vertical and the horizontal columns and that this adds to our information. We not only have the age distribution of male students and of female students but also the age distribution of the entire student population, and the total number of male and female students.

| Age | Number of students | | |
|---|---|---|---|
| | Male | Female | Total |
| 17 | 151 | 116 | 267 |
| 18 | 98 | 66 | 164 |
| 19 | 70 | 26 | 96 |
| 20 | 52 | 22 | 74 |
| 21 + | 18 | 5 | 23 |
| Total | 389 | 235 | 624 |

You may of course still argue that the table is still concerned with only one variable, age, and that all we have is two age distributions. Let us then extend our table to consider three variables, age, sex and type of accommodation. Obviously now we must further subdivide either the horizontal or the vertical columns. Again it is a good general guide to say that we believe it better to subdivide the horizontal rather than the vertical columns. But in doing this the variable in the vertical column tends to become the more important. So we must consider which is the most important variable, and this often depends on what we are trying to show. Let us suppose that in this case we are aiming to show that the type of accommodation a student occupies depends on his or her age. In this case we will list the ages vertically and subdivide the horizontal columns. Our table may now appear like this:

| Age | Number of students | | | | | | Total |
|---|---|---|---|---|---|---|---|
| | At home | | In lodgings | | In flat | | |
| | M | F | M | F | M | F | |
| 17 | 112 | 92 | 16 | 20 | 23 | 4 | 267 |
| 18 | 64 | 42 | 24 | 16 | 10 | 8 | 164 |
| 19 | 31 | 12 | 28 | 7 | 11 | 7 | 96 |
| 20 | 8 | 4 | 16 | 10 | 28 | 8 | 74 |
| 21 + | 2 | 3 | 3 | 1 | 13 | 1 | 23 |
| Total | 217 | 153 | 87 | 54 | 85 | 28 | — |
| | 370 | | 141 | | 113 | | 624 |

You will readily appreciate what a vast amount of information a table such as this can give us: the number of students who live at home, subdivided into male and female and classified according to age, as well as the same information for those who are living in lodgings or living in a flat. You can understand too how much more information could be incorporated if we subdivided further the horizontal axis as well as some subdivision of the vertical axis such as the area of origin followed in each case by the age range.

There is one problem – the more we subdivide, the more complicated our table becomes, and there comes a time when it is so difficult to read it and understand it that we find that clarity has been lost rather than gained. It is true that one treble table, such as the one above, is better than three single tables. It is equally true that if we are considering eight or nine variables, three treble tables are better than one very complex one. And if you are wondering why clarity is so important think again about what we have been doing. We have collected primary data, simplified it and classified it, and are now trying to present it to our union executive in a readily digestible form. How much notice do you think the executive will take of us if they cannot understand what our tables are all about?

Just in case you are ever in the position of having to construct tables to present the raw material you have collected, there are several points you should bear in mind. Let us call them the 'Principles of Good Tabulation'.

- Every table should have a short explanatory title at the head. At the end you should put a note of the source of the information you have used, whether it is based on your own survey or secondary data.

- The unit of measurement should be clearly stated, and if necessary defined in a footnote. Not many people, for example, would know off-hand what a metric tonne is. In addition the heading to every column should be clearly shown.

- Use different rulings to break up a larger table – double lines or thicker lines add a great deal to the ease with which a table is understood.

- Whenever you feel it useful, insert both column and row totals.

- If the volume of data is large, two or three simple tables are better than one cumbersome one.

- Before you start to draft a table, be quite sure what you want it to show. Remember that although most people read from left to right, most people find it easier to absorb figures which are in columns rather than rows.

As with most things practice is the best way of learning, and these principles will soon become second nature after you have drafted a few tables for yourself.

You might well ask at this stage whether this is all there is in the subject of Statistics. If it were, you would all end up with distinctions. But the most important part of the work is still to come. No statisticians (or students) worth their salt are content with a mere list of figures. They now begin to ask questions, the most important of which is 'What do the figures tell us?' We now begin to analyse the figures, and statistical techniques are largely methods of extracting the utmost possible information from the data we have available. We could, for example, calculate the average age of students living at home, and compare it with the average age of students living in flats to try to determine whether we are right in assuming that the younger student will tend to live at home and the older students tend to be flat-dwellers. We can do the same thing for both male and female students to see if they behave differently. Let us say that there are many questions that the statistician can ask, even from the simple data we have used so far.

If you think back now to the questions we suggested that you might ask about what our tables can tell us, you will realise that most of them involve a more detailed study of one variable only – the age of females living at home, the age of males living in flats, etc. When we do begin to analyse, you will appreciate that this is usual. The table presents several variables at once, but we extract just one of them at a time for further examination. In a few cases we will use two variables at once, when we are asking if there is a relationship between them such that one affects the other or that both move in sympathy. But in this foundation course we will never ask you to get involved in the analysis of three or more variables at once – which is indeed a complex matter.

## The grouped frequency distribution

Let us examine again the table showing the age of students attending the ABC College:

| Age (x) | Number of students (f) |
|---------|------------------------|
| 17 | 267 |
| 18 | 164 |
| 19 | 96 |
| 20 | 74 |
| 21 and over | 23 |
| | 624 |

Such a table is called a *frequency distribution*. It shows how many students (f) have the stated age (x). For example, it tells us that 96 students are 19 years old. We stated that this table was ideal for summarising data dealing with only one variable – in this case, age. However, it is not always convenient to arrange single variable data into a table like this. Suppose, for example, that a scrap metal dealer buys a job lot of metal pipes. To get some idea of the lengths of pipes he selects 100 and carefully measures them. Now it is highly likely that no two pipes will have *exactly* the same length. It is no use then arranging the data into a distribution like the one we had for the ages of students. It might well be a table consisting of 100 rows. It would be far more sensible to *group* the lengths together into classes like this:

**Lengths of 100 copper pipes**

| Length (cm) | | Frequency |
|---|---|---|
| 10 but under | 20 | 3 |
| 20 | 30 | 7 |
| 30 | 40 | 10 |
| 40 | 50 | 16 |
| 50 | 60 | 34 |
| 60 | 70 | 13 |
| 70 | 80 | 7 |
| 80 | 90 | 6 |
| 90 | 100 | 4 |

A table such as this is known as a *grouped frequency distribution*.

Certain points about this distribution can be noted.

1  There is no ambiguity about the way the classes have been stated. We are left in no doubt about the class to which a pipe belongs. For example, a pipe with a length of exactly 20 cm would go into the second class, i.e. 20 but under 30. However, if we were to state the classes like this:

   10–20
   20–30

into which class would we then put the pipe?

2  Although it is certainly more convenient to put the lengths of pipes into this distribution (much more convenient than a list of 100 lengths), we have lost something. For example, without going back to the original data, we would have no idea of the *actual* lengths of (say) the three pipes in the group 10 but under 20. We have sacrificed detail for the sake of presenting a picture which can be absorbed fairly easily. It might seem, of course, that the use of class intervals will prevent our using the frequency distribution as a basis for further work. Naturally, it does create a problem, and to overcome it we must make an assumption. We will assume that all three pipes in the class 10 but under 20 have lengths precisely at the centre of this class. Now, the smallest length that could be in the class is exactly 10 cm, and the largest length is 19.9999 cm. The centre then (or the *mid-point* as it is called) is:

$$\frac{10 + 19.9999}{2} = 15$$

3 We stated that the largest pipe in the first group could have a length of 19.9999 cm and this throws light on the nature of the data we are dealing with. This data is what statisticians call *continuous* data – it can take any value within a particular group. There is, however, no reason why the data should have *particular* values within a group. It may well be that the scrap metal dealer, when taking measurements, has recorded only certain values. He might, for example, have recorded only to the nearest half centimetre, 11.0, 11.5, 13.5 and so on. But this way of measuring has been decided by the dealer and not by the *nature* of the data. The pipes may still have any length within the group, no matter how that length has been recorded. Generally speaking, any data that is obtained by measuring rather than by counting is continuous data, and, as we have said, should be listed in classes arranged in the form:

x and under y

4 Let us now turn to another example. Suppose we count the number of telephone calls made by 100 firms on a particular day. Clearly this is not continuous data as the number of telephone calls made cannot take any value within a group. Thus, in the group 10 and under 20, we cannot make 10.2 or 14.3 telephone calls. The number of calls made can increase only in uniform steps of one. Such data is called *discrete* data,[*] and it is usual to arrange it in a frequency distribution like this:

| No. of calls | No. of firms |
|:---:|:---:|
| 10–19 | 9 |
| 20–29 | 14 |

There is no ambiguity in stating the classes in this way as we cannot have 19.1, 19.2, 19.3, etc. calls. Again we have no precise idea of the exact number of calls made by firms in any particular class, and we assume that all firms have made a number of calls equal to the mid-point of the class, i.e.:

$$\frac{10+19}{2} = 14.5 \text{ calls.}$$

Now you may think that this is nonsense. After all, we have just stated that the number of calls must be a whole number, so how can we assume that nine firms each made 14.5 calls? Well, don't let this worry you. This is something we assume merely for convenience of calculation.

---

[*] The uniform stepped increase for discrete data need not be one – shoe sizes increase by $\frac{1}{2}$, hat sizes by $\frac{1}{8}$, and money (in pounds sterling) by £0.01.

At this stage it would be useful to give a few words of warning about using continuous and discrete data. We have implied that it is better to use classes of the type

10 and under 20
20 and under 30   for continuous data (Type A)

and

10–19
20–29   for discrete data (Type B).

Now although it would be wrong to use Type B for continuous data, there is nothing wrong with using Type A for discrete data, though it does create problems. Suppose we had arranged our data on telephone calls like this:

10 but under 20   9
20 but under 30   14

The unwary student might be tempted to say that the mid-point of the first class is $(10 + 20)/2 = 15$; but we know it is really 14.5. To avoid problems like this, never assume that data is continuous merely because it is in a Type A distribution. Read the heading at the top of the table and decide what is the smallest and what is the largest possible value in each class. The mid-point is then:

$$\frac{\text{smallest} + \text{largest}}{2}$$

Another warning we must give you concerns *rounded* data (i.e. data given to the nearest whole number, the nearest 10, etc.). Suppose, for example, that the scrap metal dealer had rounded his measurements to the nearest centimetre. Now we know this data is continuous, so we may be tempted to use the Type A distribution:

10 but under 20
20 but under 30

However, suppose we have a pipe with an actual length of 19.6 cm, this would be rounded up to 20 and put into the second class *even though, really, it should be in the first class*. Problems such as this can be avoided if classes are carefully stated. It would not occur if, in this case, we had stated the classes as:

9.5 but under 19.5
19.5 but under 29.5

The pipe with a length of 19.6 would be rounded up and (correctly) placed in the second class. Now, admittedly, many people use a Type B distribution for rounded data, but the implication of doing this is that the class limits are 9.5 to 19.5 – another reason for reading carefully the heading at the top of the table and deciding for yourself whether the data is continuous or discrete.

A final warning concerns the class interval used in a frequency distribution. If it is a Type A distribution, say:

10 but under 20

then this of course covers a (continuous) range of 10 numbers and the class interval is 10.

If it is a Class B distribution, say:

10–19
20–29

you must remember that the groups cover 10 discrete values (10 to 19 inclusive) and the class interval is also 10 in this case.

Finally, you will find, if you look at any published statistical tables, that in many cases no limits are given for the first and last classes. An income distribution showing annual income might begin merely with 'Under £660' and end up with the group 'Over £50 000'. Such open-ended classes create problems and we will give you a few hints on how to handle them later.

One of the most difficult problems you will have in building up a frequency distribution from raw data is to decide on what class intervals to use. Obviously, a great deal will depend on the data you have available, but a few general guidelines may help.

- Try not to choose class intervals which will reduce the number of groups below five or six. If you do the data will be so compressed that no pattern emerges. Naturally the rule is not infallible – the European Community (EC) has published statistics of farm sizes giving only three classes. These three, however, correspond to a generally accepted international definition of small, medium and large farms. Our advice is that you should try not to emulate the EC.

- At the other extreme, do not have too many classes. About 15 or 16 is the maximum. The problem here is not only the difficulty of absorbing lengthy tables, but also the fact that each group will have a very low, or in some cases, even a zero frequency. And this leads to another point.

- At the upper end of the table, if you stick slavishly to a single class interval you may well find that several consecutive groups have no members while a higher group has a frequency of two or three. In these circumstances you should sacrifice the idea of equal class widths and combine the several classes into a single wider class.

● A good general guide is to take the difference between the minimum and maximum value of the variable (which we call the *range*), and divide by 10. This will give you the right class width (or thereabouts) for the majority of classes, provided that you realise that a class width of five or 10 or 50 is better than one of four, or seven or 62, and provided that you take care with the extreme values of the variable.

Before we leave this brief description of the frequency distribution it would be an advantage if we show you how to tackle examination questions which ask you to construct a frequency distribution from a mass of figures. For this purpose we will look at a typical examination question.

| EXAMPLE |

The following is a record of the percentage marks gained by candidates in an examination:

```
65  57  57  55  20  54  52  49  58  52
86  39  50  48  83  71  66  54  51  27
30  44  34  78  36  63  67  55  40  56
63  75  55  15  96  51  54  52  53  42
50  25  85  27  75  40  37  46  42  86
16  45  12  79  50  46  46  59  57  50
56  74  50  68  52  61  40  38  57  31
35  93  54  26  67  62  51  52  54  61
93  84  28  66  62  57  45  43  47  33
45  25  77  80  91  67  53  55  51  36
```

Tabulate the marks in the form of a frequency distribution, grouping by suitable intervals.

Looking at the figures we find that there are 100 marks given ranging from 12 to 96. We have laid down a principle of aiming at somewhere in the region of 10 classes in our frequency distributions and it certainly seems that the best class width in this example would be 10 marks. If we were to use five mark intervals we would end up with some 18 classes which is too many; if we use 15 mark intervals we end up with only six classes which is too few.

We now have to find out how many of these marks fall within each class, and we recommend that you should do this in this way. First list every class vertically; now take each candidate's marks in turn, and place a dash or a one, or some other suitable mark against the class into which it falls.

Having done this for every mark we can now take each class in turn and add up how many candidates fall into each class. Your rough working will appear something like this. You will notice that for ease of counting we have divided our dashes into groups of five:

| | | |
|---|---|---|
| 10–19 | III | 3 |
| 20–29 | ⌗ II | 7 |
| 30–39 | ⌗ ⌗ | 10 |
| 40–49 | ⌗ ⌗ ⌗ I | 16 |
| 50–59 | ⌗ ⌗ ⌗ ⌗ ⌗ ⌗ IIII | 34 |
| 60–69 | ⌗ ⌗ III | 13 |
| 70–79 | ⌗ II | 7 |
| 80–89 | ⌗ I | 6 |
| 90–99 | IIII | 4 |
| | | 100 |

The first thing we notice about this data is that it is a list of examination marks. There are extremely few examinations where marks are recorded in anything but whole numbers, and we may safely say that this data is discrete. We will, therefore, use what we called earlier a Type B distribution.

Before you do anything else now, check that the total frequency (i.e. the number of dashes) in your rough working is the same as the number of items given in the question. Having done this, you are now ready to construct your frequency distribution. Remember, though, all the things that are necessary: the heading of the table, the column headings and the source, if it is available. Getting the table correct is only one part of the answer, although it is an important part. Your final frequency distribution will appear something like this:

**Marks gained by candidates in an examination (%)**

| Marks awarded | No. of candidates |
|---|---|
| 10–19 | 3 |
| 20–29 | 7 |
| 30–39 | 10 |
| 40–49 | 16 |
| 50–59 | 34 |
| 60–69 | 13 |
| 70–79 | 7 |
| 80–89 | 6 |
| 90–99 | 4 |
| | 100 |

Source: *Examiners' Report*

## The stem and leaf diagram

Consider again the percentage marks gained by candidates in an examination. The marks could be placed in ascending order thus:

```
12  15  16  20  25  25  26  27  27  28
30  31  33  34  35  36  36  37  38  39
40  40  40  42  42  43  44  45  45  45
46  46  46  47  48  49  50  50  50  50
50  51  51  51  51  52  52  52  52  52
53  53  54  54  54  54  54  55  55  55
55  56  56  57  57  57  57  57  58  59
61  61  62  62  63  63  65  66  66  67
67  67  68  71  74  75  75  77  78  79
80  83  84  85  86  86  91  93  93  96
```

A glance at this data shows that there are three marks between 10 and 19 (12, 15 and 16), there are seven marks between 20 and 29 (20, 25, 25, 26, 27, 27 and 28), etc.

This data can be represented in a *stem and leaf diagram* thus:

| Stem | Leaf |
|------|------|
| 10 | 2 5 6 |
| 20 | 0 5 5 6 7 7 8 |
| 30 | 0 1 3 4 5 6 6 7 8 9 |
| 40 | 0 0 0 2 2 3 4 5 5 5 6 6 6 7 8 9 |
| 50 | 0 0 0 0 0 1 1 1 1 2 2 2 2 2 3 3 4 4 4 4 4 5 5 5 5 6 6 7 7 7 7 7 8 9 |
| 60 | 1 1 2 2 3 3 5 6 6 7 7 7 8 |
| 70 | 1 4 5 5 7 8 9 |
| 80 | 0 3 4 5 6 6 |
| 90 | 1 3 3 6 |

For any number in this diagram, the *stem* is its tens value, and the *leaf* is the unit value. Thus, the mark 27 has a stem value of 20 and a leaf value of 7. Such diagrams can be considered as an alternative to a grouped frequency distribution. They have the advantage of showing the actual values of the data items, but are only suitable for a small volume of data which has a limited range of values.

## The time series

All frequency distributions and stem and leaf diagrams have one thing in common: they tell us the magnitude of a variable at a given moment in time. There are times, however, when we will need to look at the way the magnitude of a variable changes over fairly long time periods – for example we may be considering the way in which the volume of British imports from Hong Kong has changed year by year since 1980. Such a table is called a *time series*. It follows from the nature of the times series that it consists of a series of time periods: years quarters, months or even days, with the value of the variables given against each time period. As an example, consider the following data which refer to road casualties in Great Britain.

**Road casualties in Great Britain (thousands)**

| *1990* | 1st quarter | 81 |
| | 2nd quarter | 85 |
| | 3rd quarter | 87 |
| | 4th quarter | 89 |
| *1991* | 1st quarter | 70 |
| | 2nd quarter | 78 |
| | 3rd quarter | 82 |
| | 4th quarter | 82 |

Source: *Monthly Digest*

In much statistical work a time series of this nature may extend over many years, and you will be surprised what such a series can tell us.

If you have followed carefully the argument of this chapter it should now be apparent that we are concerned with the collection, simplification, presentation and analysis of information which can be expressed quantitatively. If you do your work well you will get an accurate picture of the data you are studying. There will still be some of you who may claim that figures can be made to prove anything, and, to be fair, if the data is misused this may be true. If you ignore parts of the data, and conveniently forget to include calculations and information which is inconvenient or does not support your preconceived ideas, most things are possible. But if you follow your analysis through to the bitter end, using all the information which is available, keeping an open mind and interpreting only what your figures throw up, you cannot but be somewhere near the truth. In a world in which so much reliance is placed on the work of statisticians, where government policy often depends on their findings, and where industrial decisions involving millions of pounds are taken on the basis of statistical analysis, it is important to remember that whether you like what your figures show or not, your task is to interpret what the available data tells us as honestly as you are able.

## Using the spreadsheet

Forming frequency distributions from raw data can be tedious, and so on the distribution disk there is a template that will do this for you. If your machine has a hard disk and you have copied the templates to the subdirectory containing your spreadsheet application, you should change to that subdirectory and type GO. Otherwise, load up your spreadsheet application (Lotus 1–2–3, Quattro or ASEASYAS) and from the distribution disk retrieve the template called MENU.

**Lotus users**

Your screen should now look something like this:

| Descriptive statistics | | Analytical statistics | | Quit | |
|---|---|---|---|---|---|
| Frequency | Diagrams | Time series | | Index numbers | |
| A | B | C | D | E | F |
| 1 | | | | | |
| 2 | | | | | |
| 3 | | | | | |
| 4 | | | | | |
| 5 | | | Main Menu | | |
| 6 | | | – – – – – | | |
| 7 | | | | | |

Descriptive statistics is highlighted, and a list of available templates is displayed, i.e. Frequency, Diagrams, Time series and Index numbers. These are the templates associated with Descriptive statistics. Press the right arrow and Analytical statistics is highlighted, with the associated templates listed on the second line thus:

| Descriptive statistics | | Analytical statistics | | Quit | | | |
|---|---|---|---|---|---|---|---|
| Probability | Control charts | Estimation | | Significance tests | | Regression | |
| A | B | C | D | E | F | G | H |
| 1 | | | | | | | |
| 2 | | | | | | | |
| 3 | | | | | | | |
| 4 | | | | | | | |
| 5 | | | Main Menu | | | | |
| 6 | | | – – – – – | | | | |
| 7 | | | | | | | |

The first template we wish to use is under Descriptive statistics. Press the left arrow to highlight Descriptive statistics and press Enter. Your screen should look like this:

```
Frequency     Diagrams      Time series      Index numbers
New data      Ogive     Polygon      Statistics
         A          B          C          D          E
1
2
3
4
5                                  Main Menu
6                                  – – – – –
7
8
```

Frequency is highlighted. Press Enter to load this template.

```
New data      Ogive      Polygon      Statistics      Hardcopy      File      Quit
Enter new frequency distribution
         A          B          C          D          E          F
1               * * * * * * Frequency Distribution * * * * * *
2
3
4
5
```

The top line gives the list of options associated with this template. The first option – New data – is the option associated with forming a frequency distribution from raw data. This option is highlighted, so press Enter to reveal:

```
         A          B          C          D          E          F          G          H
1                        FREQUENCY DISTRIBUTION
2
3
4      Lower    Upper
5      Bound    Bound
6
7                                   Enter boundaries of frequency distribution
8
9                                   Press ALT and S when finished
10
11
```

You should skip the next section and move to the section headed 'Entering data'.

**ASEASYAS users**

Your screen should now look something like this:

Descrip. is highlighted, and a list of available templates is displayed, i.e. Frequency, Diagrams, Time series and Index numbers. These are the templates associated with Descriptive statistics. Press the down arrow and Analytical is highlighted, with the associated templates listed on the second top line thus:

The first template we wish to use is under Descriptive statistics.

Press the up arrow to highlight Descrip. and press Enter.

Your screen should look like this:

Frequency is highlighted. Press Enter to load this template.

The box on the left gives the list of options associated with this template. The first option – New data – is the option associated with forming a frequency distribution from raw data. This option is highlighted, so press Enter to reveal:

```
        A        B        C        D        E        F        G        H
  1              FREQUENCY DISTRIBUTION
  2
  3
  4     Lower    Upper
  5     Bound    Bound
  6
  7                                Enter boundaries of frequency distribution
  8
  9                                Press ALT and S when finished
 10
 11
```

*Entering data*

The cursor is positioned in cell A6, and you are requested to fill in the lower class and upper class boundaries of the frequency distribution that you wish to form. Let us suppose that we wish to enter continuous data ranging between 10 and 59: we could enter the class boundaries like this:

```
        A        B        C        D        E        F        G        H
  1              FREQUENCY DISTRIBUTION
  2
  3
  4     Lower    Upper
  5     Bound    Bound
  6       10       20
  7       20       30              Enter boundaries of frequency distribution
  8       30       40
  9       40       50              Press ALT and S when finished
 10       50       60
 11
 12
```

We tell the template that we have finished entering the class boundaries by holding down the ALT key and pressing S. Your screen would now look like this:

|   | A | B | C | D | E | F | G | H |
|---|---|---|---|---|---|---|---|---|
| 1 |  | < – – – Enter data here or enter frequencies |  |  |  |  |  |  |
| 2 |  |  | starting at cell C6 |  |  |  |  |  |
| 3 |  |  |  |  |  |  |  |  |
| 4 | Lower | Upper | Frequency |  |  |  |  |  |
| 5 | Bound | Bound |  |  | Press ALT with R when finished |  |  |  |
| 6 | 10 | 20 | 0 |  |  |  |  |  |
| 7 | 20 | 30 | 0 |  |  |  |  |  |
| 8 | 30 | 40 | 0 |  |  |  |  |  |
| 9 | 40 | 50 | 0 |  |  |  |  |  |
| 10 | 50 | 60 | 0 |  |  |  |  |  |
| 11 | Total Frequency = |  | 0 |  |  |  |  |  |
| 12 |  |  |  |  |  |  |  |  |

The cursor jumps to cell A1 ready to receive your data. You can now enter numbers within the range of the frequency distribution and watch the frequency build up. You should hit the Enter key after typing in each number. Notice that numbers which are less than 10, or 60 or more, are ignored as they would be outside the range of the frequency distribution.

The template can distinguish between discrete and continuous data. For example, in the distribution above, the data is assumed to be continuous, and if you entered the number 20 in cell A1 then the frequency in the second class would increment by one. However, had you entered the classes like this:

|   | A | B |
|---|---|---|
| 1 |  |  |
| 2 |  |  |
| 3 |  |  |
| 4 | Lower | Upper |
| 5 | Bound | Bound |
| 6 | 11 | 20 |
| 7 | 21 | 30 |
| 8 | 31 | 40 |

and so on, then the data would be assumed discrete and entering 20 in cell A1 would increment the frequency of the first class by one.

There is one problem with using this template: it will error if one of the class limits is zero. This error can be overcome if a zero class limit is entered as 1E–30.

When you have finished entering the data press ALT and R and the menu returns.

You can now either:

1 Select New data and form another frequency distribution.

2 Select Hardcopy and send the frequency distribution formed to a connected printer.

3 Select File, which will store the frequency distribution formed for later use, and return to the main menu, or

4 Select Quit, which will return to the main menu without saving the frequency distribution.

The other options in the menu list will be used in later chapters. The options Hardcopy, File and Quit are available on all the templates and have the same function in each.

To exit, select Quit or File, and select Quit from the main menu.

## Summary

The use of the spreadsheet templates can be summarised thus:

1 All spreadsheet templates should be accessed by first loading the menu template.

2 All templates are listed under two groups: Descriptive statistics and Analytical statistics.

3 On loading the menu template, the Descriptive statistics templates are displayed. To display the Analytical statistics templates, use the arrow key to highlight 'Analytical statistics' ('Analytical' in ASEASYAS).

4 The menu structure is shown in Fig 1.1.

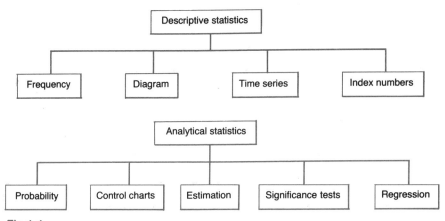

Fig 1.1

Hence, to access the spreadsheet dealing with probability, you would highlight Analytical statistics and press Enter and then highlight Probability and press Enter. Generally, to select an option, simply use the arrow keys to highlight it and press Enter, or press the first letter of the option. The advantage of using the first method is that by highlighting an option, a brief description of the option is displayed on the second line.

## QUESTIONS

**1.1**  Describe in detail the steps in a statistical investigation; include in your description a brief summary of the various methods of presenting conclusions. Illustrate your answer with examples of statistical investigations that might be carried out in a business environment.

**1.2**  (a) Distinguish carefully between discrete and continuous data, giving examples of each.

(b)  State three methods of presenting the results of such an investigation.

**1.3**  What is the difference between primary and secondary data? Why is it important that statisticians should make a distinction in their use of these categories of data?

**1.4**  **Average weekly earnings of certain professional workers (£) 1988–92**

| Year | Hotel and catering | Transport and communications | Banking, finance and insurance |
|------|------|------|------|
| 1988 | 178.8 | 229.6 | 260.1 |
| 1989 | 197.1 | 248.3 | 284.6 |
| 1990 | 214.0 | 266.3 | 317.7 |
| 1991 | 230.3 | 288.4 | 336.9 |
| 1992 | 243.5 | 310.9 | 357.1 |

Source: *New Earnings Survey,* 1992

Write a short report in which you bring out the main features of the data above. Include any appropriate derived statistics.

**1.5**  In 1980, 753 000 persons received unemployment benefit; 1 197 000 received sickness benefits; 9 108 000 received state retirement pensions and 14 000 received widows' benefit. In 1990, the corresponding figures were 331 000 for unemployment benefit, 1 516 000 for sickness benefits, 10 180 000 for state retirement pensions and 13 000 for widows' benefit. Source: *Monthly Digest of Statistics.*

Tabulate this data. Calculate appropriate secondary statistics and include these statistics in your tabulations. Comment briefly on, and give reasons for the changes in benefit payments between the two years.

**1.6** An inquiry into the population of a town showed that the total was 297 500 persons of whom 60% were females and 40% males. 50 000 females were aged 30 and under, 60 000 were aged from 31 to 60 and the remainder were over 60 years of age. The corresponding figures for males were 60 000, 39 000 and 20 000. The average family size was 3.5, 75% of the female population lived in the northern area of the town and the remainder in the southern area. Of the males, 20% lived in the southern area.

Tabulate the data given showing the analysis of each class of person into areas and age groups. Include actual figures and percentages. Show also the number of families for the town in total.

**1.7** The Saturn Finance Company wishes to study for several years (19X1, 19X2, 19X3, 19X4) the distribution of loans according to the size of its loans (under £1000, £1000 and under £2500, £2500 and under £5000, £5000 and over) and the purpose of the loan (home improvement, car purchase, durable household goods, other).

(a) Prepare a table in which the data can be classified by year, size of loan and purpose of loan. Include summary rows and insert columns for all classifications given.

(b) Insert the following figures in the appropriate cells:

- In 19X2, 42.7% of all loans made for home improvements were for £1000 and under £2500.

- In 19X1, 31.4% of all loans made for the purchase of cars were for £2500 and under £5000.

- In 19X4, 29.7% of all loans were under £1000.

**1.8** While the population of the United Kingdom grew from 38.2 m in 1901 to an estimated 57.4 m in 1990, the increase was not uniform between the regions. In 1901, the south-east was the most populous region with 10.5 m. In 1990 its estimated population was 17.4 m. Both the West Midlands and East Midlands have also grown quickly; the former from 3.0 m to 5.2 m and the latter from 2.1 m to 4.0 m. During the same period, East Anglia's population grew from 1.1 m to 2.0 m, while the south-west increased from 2.6 m to 4.6 m.

Despite its generally high birth rate, Northern Ireland's population, while growing from 1.2 m in 1901 to 1.6 m in 1990, fell as a proportion of total UK population. A similar trend is revealed in other economically depressed regions, and both Wales and Scotland, because of losses due to migration, have grown much more slowly than average, Wales from 2.0 m to 2.9 m and Scotland from 4.5 m to 5.1 m.

(Source: *New Society and Social Trends* (modified). Note: not all regions have been included.)

Arrange the above data in a suitable table, providing additional columns, in blank, appropriately headed, in which could be inserted derived statistics enabling comparisons to be made.

**1.9**  The total number of employees of Core and Peel Ltd. at 31 December 19X1 was 10 590, of which 6721 were men, 3106 women and the rest juniors. During 19X1 108 men resigned and 74 men were engaged. The corresponding figures for women were 29 and 87 and for juniors 17 and 23. 1386 men, 976 women and 16 juniors were absent some time during the year due to illness, 509 men, 876 women due to domestic circumstances and 366 men, 272 women and three juniors due to other causes. The average weekly wage rate paid to men was £320, to women £201.30 and to juniors £182.50. The company worked 50 weeks in the year.

Tabulate these details showing suitable totals and sub-totals. Include also:

(a) the numbers employed at 1st January 19X1.

(b) an estimate of the total annual wages paid per grade of labour and for the employees in total.

**1.10**  The Family Expenditure Survey gives details of Gross Household Weekly Income. In 1990, of the households interviewed, in 3349 cases the head of the household was not classified as 'employed'. In 699 of such households, the occupation of the head of the household was 'self-employed'; 39 earned less than £100 per week, 146 earned £100 but less than £225 per week, 315 earned £225 but less than £475 per week, 139 earned £475 but less than £800 per week.

In 1876 of such households, the head of the household was retired. 816 earned less than £100 per week, 660 earned £100 but less than £225 per week, 328 earned £225 but less than £475 per week, 60 earned £470 but less than £800 per week.

Of the remaining households with the head not classified as 'occupied', the head of the household was classified as 'unoccupied'; 317 earned less than £100 per week, 248 earned £100 but less than £225 per week, 152 earned £225 but less than £475 per week, 46 earned £475 but less than £800 per week.

Tabulate this data.

**1.11**  In a certain country, in 1970, 19 000 houses were built with a local authority mortgage (total sum advanced = $418 m), 40 000 were built with loans from insurance companies ($1400 m advanced) while the building societies lent $14 200 m to 460 000 purchasers. These figures compare with 56 000 ($1456 m), 34 000 ($1428 m), 504 000 ($18 648 m) in 1980 and 44 000 ($1364 m), 32 000 ($1664 m), 540 000 ($22 880 m) in 1990.

(a) Arrange the above data in concise tabular form.

(b) Prepare a blank table with suitable headings in which could be inserted derived statistics from the above figures which would facilitate the making of comparisons.

**1.12** (a) List clearly the steps taken in forming a frequency distribution from a set of about 1000 observations giving reasons where necessary.

(b) Construct a frequency distribution using the following observations:

**Lives of electric light bulbs, in hours, to the last complete hour.**

```
690  701  722  684  662  699  715  742  726  716
728  705  693  691  688  706  707  691  701  713
740  662  676  738  714  703  695  692  699  685
698  687  703  726  699  692  714  724  664  689
694  705  717  682  717  707  696  697  681  708
712  733  705  673  694  716  745  692  719  701
679  680  654  691  669  685  725  704  724  714
689  702  710  696  697  709  721  677  680  671
685  724  736  696  688  692  728  656  690  695
702  696  708  698  710  682  694  676  700  663
```

**1.13** The following is a record of the heights in centimetres of a sample of 85 servicemen:

```
169  179  183  186  166  181  177  173  167  193  176  183  162  170  186  174
188  165  168  174  170  176  186  177  185  175  179  166  190  182  182  180
194  177  184  175  168  181  180  172  178  192  175  189  180  175  183  191
172  188  180  176  185  178  179  173  165  170  178  181  181  189  187  191
179  196  179  182  171  169  171  184  198  182  175  190  187  176  164  187
167  185  177  184  178
```

Tabulate the above data in the form of a frequency distribution, using as intervals 160 cm and under 165 cm, 165 cm and under 170 cm, 170 cm and under 175 cm, etc.

**1.14** The lengths of telephone calls from a certain office were noted and the results are shown below giving the times in seconds.

```
141   43  203  104   82   63   24   84   41   86   47   43
100   53  139  147  137  186  214  106  150  109  170  172
194  124  175  177  162  129  128  219   40  105   48   65
105  154  154   35  149   54  104  109  119   74  140  104
168  127  191   30  109   88  104  207   38  164  182  120
166   53  145   29  112  143   49  199  130   52  109   77
142   75  146  105  125  112   40  126   67   49   90  140
132  118  134  133  159  123  161  112  157  104   92  112
151   98  156  117  156  190  122  135  116   96  163  116
186  155  106  153   69  105  136  106  131  118   94  121
```

Arrange these figures in a grouped frequency distribution using the intervals 0–19, 20–39, etc.

**1.15**  The data below are the times for completion, rounded to the nearest hour, of a sample of 50 houses.

911 902 900 867 897 915 945 940 917 883 874 880 932 919 899 903 872
901 874 925 886 928 917 906 925 913 898 888 912 896 921 908 933 903
920 885 901 892 931 902 893 887 928 907 916 895 907 864 891 890

Classify this data into a frequency distribution. Construct a stem and leaf diagram.

**1.16**  The following is a record of marks scored by candidates in an examination.

77 59 84 73 51 43 50 81 61 53 69
37 58 63 67 61 90 61 50 60 84 56
77 57 42 43 41 49 37 21 24 35 34
50 11 52 30 16 33 67 87 64 47 59
37 92 88 30 38 22 22 49 46 50 64
23 73 73 48 26 36 51 85 71 57 45

Tabulate the marks in the form of a frequency distribution, grouping by suitable intervals. Construct a stem and leaf diagram.

**1.17**  A person's socio-economic status can be classified as either A, B, C1, C2, D or E in descending order. A random sample of 60 individuals gave the following information on weekly earnings (£) in relation to socio-economic class:

| | | | | |
|---|---|---|---|---|
| 245 (B) | 220 (E) | 216 (D) | 261 (C2) | 218 (E) |
| 232 (C2) | 222 (C2) | 264 (C1) | 262 (C1) | 233 (D) |
| 249 (D) | 228 (C1) | 260 (C2) | 274 (B) | 250 (C2) |
| 249 (C2) | 264 (B) | 233 (D) | 229 (C2) | 221 (E) |
| 224 (C1) | 248 (C2) | 223 (D) | 227 (C2) | 226 (E) |
| 226 (D) | 237 (C2) | 285 (A) | 218 (C1) | 242 (C2) |
| 243 (C1) | 237 (C2) | 267 (B) | 219 (E) | 222 (D) |
| 217 (C2) | 217 (C2) | 219 (D) | 223 (D) | 250 (C2) |
| 266 (C1) | 274 (C1) | 217 (E) | 237 (C2) | 255 (C1) |
| 252 (C2) | 237 (C2) | 226 (D) | 242 (C1) | 240 (C2) |
| 279 (B) | 223 (E) | 224 (D) | 231 (D) | 244 (C1) |
| 215 (E) | 218 (E) | 240 (C2) | 265 (C1) | 217 (E) |

(a) Compile a frequency distribution of earnings with intervals of a suitable width.

(b) By considering earnings to fall into one of three groups of less than £225, £225–245, and more than £245 compile a two-way table showing the frequencies in each earnings group/socio-economic class combination.

(c) Describe the main features of the data as observed from the table compiled in answer to (b) above.

(d) Construct a stem and leaf diagram.

# 2 The presentation of data I

Numerical data, however well organised, can often fail to fulfil one of its prime functions – to communicate information. This is because many people have a positive hatred of numbers. Be honest – how often have you read a newspaper article and simply skipped over any tables it contains? It is not enough to organise data well: it must also be well presented. One of the main jobs of a statistician is to identify the main features of information given by data, and to present them in such a way that they become intelligible and interesting. In this chapter, we will examine some of the graphs and diagrams that the statistician uses to achieve this end.

Watch any television education programme and almost certainly one of the first things to strike you will be the number of devices used to present information in a vivid and interesting fashion. Graphs, diagrams, animated cartoons – all play their part in putting the subject over.

Of course, television is the ideal medium for this type of visual presentation, and one of the more important developments of the second half of the twentieth century may well turn out to be the impact of television as a means of imparting information. Yet, in all this, the television producer is doing little more than statisticians have already been doing for a considerable period of time. The scale is larger; the impact is probably many times greater; but the techniques are the same.

We would like, at this point, to be able to say to you that we are going to give you a few simple rules which will enable you to master the technique of presenting diagrammatic information quickly and easily. It is not, however, as simple as that. The diagram you draw depends in part on the information you have, and what you are trying to stress. If you are trying to stress how much the government is spending annually, you will produce a very different diagram from one which sets out to examine what the government spends the money on. It might also depend on the readers you are aiming at. A diagram suitable for the readers of a mass circulation daily newspaper will be very different from one in an accounting journal; a diagram intended to extol the qualities of a particular brand of soap powder will be far removed from one designed to show the changing composition of agricultural output in the European Community (EC). Effective presentation is a question of flair and experience, and there is only one guideline: does the diagram present clearly and vividly the information it is designed to present?

We cannot pretend that the way in which we illustrate the presentation of particular information is the only way. You may, in fact, think it is not the best way. What we will do is to indicate the weapons you have available. The rest is up to you!

## The bar chart

One of the most common of all techniques for presenting data is the use of the bar chart, in which the length of the bar is proportional to the size of the items we are considering. Suppose we are considering the estimated population of some EC countries in the year 2000; we could be presented with a table like this:

|          | Population (million) |             | Population (million) |
|----------|----------------------|-------------|----------------------|
| France   | 57                   | Denmark     | 5                    |
| Belgium  | 10                   | UK          | 59                   |
| Germany* | 61                   | Netherlands | 16                   |
| Italy    | 58                   |             |                      |

Now, shut your eyes, and without reference to the table state which country has the highest population, which is the lowest, and where the UK comes in the league table. If you have played fair we are prepared to bet that a high proportion of you cannot answer all three questions correctly. Why? Simply because experience shows that people do not absorb lists of figures. A very different result would be obtained if we presented the same information in the form of a bar chart (see Fig 2.1).

The immediate impression we get is of four giant members accompanied by a number of very small members; and it hits the eye that the UK is a giant, second only to Germany.

You will notice that the bar diagram has a heading, as should all diagrams. It is no use presenting information unless the reader knows what the information is. Note, too, that the source of the information is given as we are using secondary data. This enables the reader, if he is interested, to go back to the original figures and delve more deeply.

Here we are looking at one variable factor at a particular point in time, but we may equally use the bar diagram to show how the value of something varies over time. This is done in Fig 2.2, which shows the number of applications for refugee status or asylum in the UK during the 1980s.

---

* Excludes former East Germany.

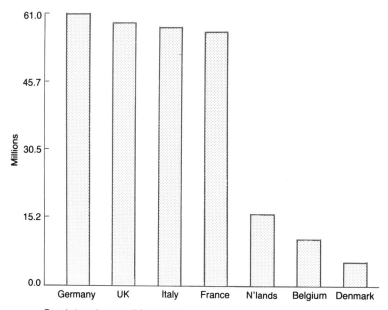

*Population of certain EC countries*
Source: Statistics Office, European Community

**Fig 2.1**

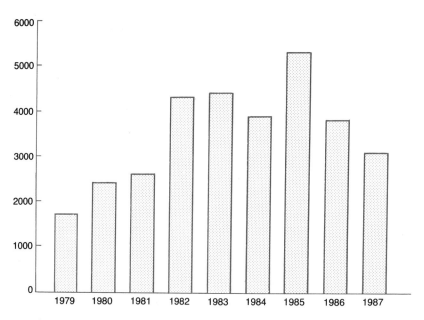

*Applications for refugee status or asylum in the United Kingdom 1979–87*
Source: *Social Trends*, 1991

**Fig 2.2**

Here you will notice that the bars are separated – this is a matter of personal preference. It is probably neater, but many statisticians say that it is more difficult to compare the height of the bars. Looking at Fig 2.2, 1985 stands out as a year with an abnormally large number of applications. This reflects the persecution of minorities in Sri Lanka and Iran.

The bar chart is a most versatile instrument and capable of adaptation to almost any data. Three further modifications will, we think, convince you of this versatility.

Often the data we are examining includes negative figures. Profits in one year, for example, might be converted into losses the next; the balance of payments may be in surplus or deficit. Such negative figures can be represented on the bar chart quite simply by extending the bar below the zero base line as in Fig 2.3. This diagram clearly brings out the deterioration in the UK Balance of Payments during the 1980s.

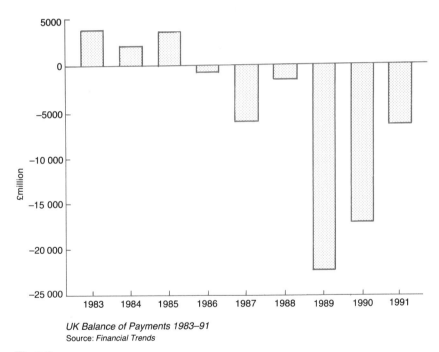

UK Balance of Payments 1983–91
Source: *Financial Trends*

**Fig 2.3**

Sometimes, of course, we may be less interested in an absolute total than we are in the way that total is made up. We may wish to find out how the final cost of production is made up, where sales revenue goes to, what the government does with the money it collects. Again the bar chart proves itself equal to the task, since we can always subdivide the bar as shown in Fig 2.4.

*Grants of asylum into UK, 1979–89*
Source: *Social Trends,* 1991

**Fig 2.4**

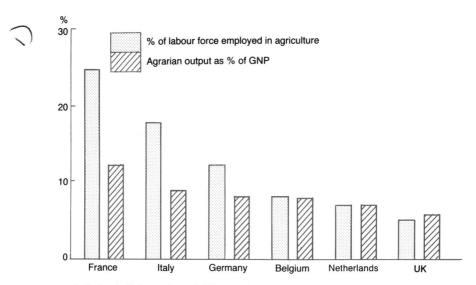

*Agricultural efficiency of certain EC countries*
Source: *EC Reports*

**Fig 2.5**

Such a chart is called a *compound* or *component* bar chart, since it illustrates the components that go to make a total. In this example, percentages have been used, though there is no reason why the actual numbers granted asylum could not have been used.

As a final example of the use of the bar chart we will try to show how it can be used to derive information which is not immediately obvious. A burning question within the European Community is agricultural efficiency. But how can efficiency be measured? It is fair to say that if 30% of the total labour force is engaged in agriculture but the agrarian output is 10% of the Gross National Product, that country's agriculture is inefficient compared with a country for which the figures are 10% and 12% respectively, and this will be the criterion we will use.

We think you will agree that, using our criterion of efficiency, of the seven countries shown in Fig 2.5, only three – the Netherlands, Belgium and the UK – can be said to be efficient producers in the agricultural sector, and this may well be a factor in the problems facing the common agricultural policy of the EC.

## The pie chart

The pie, or circular diagram is a device beloved of those who present statistical data for the general public. It is a rare report, and a still rarer copy of the *Economist* magazine, which does not contain several such diagrams. In fact, we firmly believe that the extent to which this technique is used grossly exaggerates its utility.

This diagram has only one real use – to show the relative size of the component parts of a total. A complete circle represents the total and this circle is divided into segments the size of which represents the relative importance of each constituent of the total. Thus, if we were trying to show the nature of road accidents in a particular area, we might find that of 300 accidents occurring last year, 57 involved motor cycles. We now have to mark off a segment of the circle corresponding in size to the proportion of accidents involving motor cycles, that is, 57/300 or 19/100. Since there are 360 degrees in a circle the appropriate segment must subtend an angle of $19/100 \times 360$ degrees at the centre, i.e. an angle of 68.4 degrees. Our complete pie diagram will appear something like Fig 2.6.

Even with this single simple example you should find it easy to spot the weaknesses of the pie diagram:

1   It involves cumbersome calculations.

2   It is more difficult to compare segments of a circle in a pie diagram than to compare heights in a bar diagram.

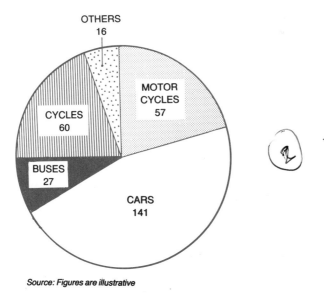

*Source: Figures are illustrative*

**Fig 2.6   Analysis of road accidents**

3  It gives no information as to absolute magnitude unless figures are inserted in each segment, whereas the bar diagram is scaled against a single axis.

Our own advice is not to use this method of presentation unless it is forced upon you.

## Plotting the frequency distribution – the histogram

You will remember that the frequency distribution examines the frequency of occurrence of different values of a variable at a given point of timé, and that sometimes the values of the variable are combined together into classes of a predetermined size. It is this type of distribution that the histogram represents. The histogram is so similar to the bar chart that students often assume that they are one and the same thing. There is, however, a major difference between them. In the bar chart we are interested in only one factor, say output, the magnitude of which can be represented by the height of a bar. It does not matter how wide the bars are (as long as they are all of the same width); we look only at the height. In a histogram, however, we are interested in two factors – the width of the bar (which represents the value of the variable) and the height of the bar (which represents the frequency). In the histogram, then, it is the *area* of the bar that is important.

We will now illustrate the histogram with a simple example. Suppose we examined a batch of cars at the end of the production line, and counted the number of faults per car. The following results were obtained.

| Number of faults | Number of cars |
|---|---|
| 1 | 18 |
| 2 | 25 |
| 3 | 19 |
| 4 | 8 |
| 5 | 3 |
| 6 or more | 0 |
| | 73 |

The histogram showing these results appears in Fig 2.7.

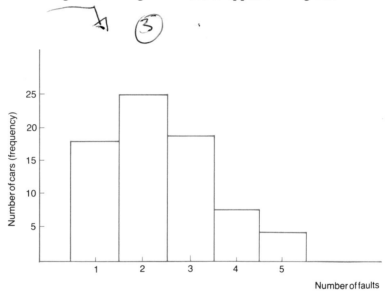

Fig 2.7 Number of faults observed in motor cars

Notice that the rectangles are drawn to 'enclose' the value of the variable (the rectangle representing one fault runs from 0.5 to 1.5, the rectangle representing two faults runs from 1.5 to 2.5, etc.). This prevents any ambiguity. Notice also that the area of the rectangles ($1 \times 18$ square units, $2 \times 25$ square units, etc.) is proportional to the frequencies.

Let us now examine how we would draw the histogram of a grouped frequency distribution. In Chapter 1 we examined a scrap metal dealer who bought a large job lot of metal pipes. To obtain some idea of the lengths of pipes he selected a sample of 100, measured them, and recorded the results in a frequency distribution.

**Lengths of 100 metal pipes**

| Length (cm) | Frequency |
|---|---|
| 10 but under 20 | 3 |
| 20 but under 30 | 7 |
| 30 but under 40 | 10 |
| 40 but under 50 | 16 |
| 50 but under 60 | 34 |
| 60 but under 70 | 13 |
| 70 but under 80 | 7 |
| 80 but under 90 | 6 |
| 90 but under 100 | 4 |

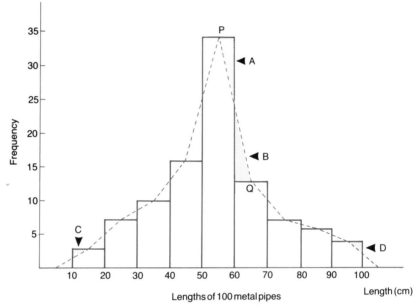

Lengths of 100 metal pipes

**Fig 2.8**

The histogram of this data is shown in Fig 2.8. Here, the rectangles are drawn to enclose the class limits, so the width of each rectangle is the same as the class interval. Notice again that the areas of the rectangles $(10 \times 3$ sq. units, $10 \times 7$ sq. units, etc.) is in the same proportion as the frequencies. The dotted line superimposed on the histogram is called the *frequency polygon*, which converts the histogram into a simple graph. It is drawn in such a fashion that the area under the frequency polygon is the same as the area under the histogram. Take, for example, the part of the frequency polygon marked PQ. The area under the histogram (but not under the polygon) which is marked A is the same as the area under the frequency polygon (but not under the histogram) which is marked B. We can obtain a frequency polygon for a distribution by joining the mid-points at the top of each rectangle as *long as the class width is constant*. To compensate for the loss of areas C and D, we must start the frequency polygon at 5 (the mid-point of the group 0 and under 10) and end it at 105 (the mid-point of the group 100 and under 110).

Drawing the histogram and frequency polygon for unequal class intervals is rather more awkward. Suppose, for example, our scrap metal dealer had obtained the following distribution:

| Length (cm) | Frequency |
|---|---|
| 10 but under 20 | 4 |
| 20 but under 30 | 6 |
| 30 but under 40 | 8 |
| 40 but under 50 | 11 |
| 50 but under 60 | 10 |
| 60 but under 70 | 9 |
| 70 but under 80 | 8 |
| 80 but under 100 | 7 |
| 100 but under 130 | 6 |
| 130 but under 170 | 4 |

Lengths of metal pipes                         Length (cm)

**Fig 2.9**

The histogram of the distribution is shown in Fig 2.9. The first seven classes present us with no problems as the class width is a constant 10. The rectangles of the first seven classes have areas of 40, 60, 80, 110, 100, 90, and 80 square units respectively. Now let us turn to the eighth class. This class is for those pipes that have lengths greater than 80 cm but less than 100 cm – a class width of 20. To be in line with other classes, the rectangle representing this class should have an area of 70 square units. As the rectangle must have a width of 20, its height must be $70/20 = 3.5$. In other words, if we double the class width, we must divide the frequency by two to give us a rectangle with an area representative of the frequency. Can you see what we have implied by drawing the rectangle in this way? We know that there are seven pipes with lengths between 80 and 100 cm, and we have assumed that 3.5 pipes are in the group 80 but under 90, and 3.5 are in the group 90 but under 100. However, we do not draw a line down the middle of this rectangle – this would be quite wrong as it would imply that there are *exactly* 3.5 pipes in the group 80 but under 90 and *exactly* 3.5 pipes in the group 90 but under 100. We can deal with the remaining classes in a similar fashion. The ninth class (which has a width of 30) contains six pipes. We must assume that two pipes are in the group 100 but under 110, two in the group 110 and under 120 and two in the group 120 and under 130, so we draw a rectangle with a height of two. Finally, can you see that the correct height for the last rectangle is one?

Let us now examine the effect of unequal class intervals on the frequency polygon. For the first six classes there is no problem – we proceed as before joining the mid-points at the top of the rectangles. Problems arise when we reach point A. If we join point A to the mid-point at the top of the rectangle representing the group 80 but under 100, then the area under the polygon would be greater than the area under the histogram. We can overcome this by drawing the line so it passes through the mid-point of CD. The line should pass through the midpoint of EF, GH and IJ. This assures that the histogram and frequency polygon enclose equal areas.

Before we leave the histogram, we must have a few words to say about grouped, discrete frequency distributions. Often you will see the classes arranged like this:

**Number of telephone calls made by 100 firms on a particular day**

| Number of calls | Number of firms |
|-----------------|-----------------|
| 10–19 | 9 |
| 20–29 | 14 |
| 30–39 | 18 |
| 40–49 | 27 |
| 50–59 | 12 |
| 60–69 | 10 |
| 70–79 | 6 |
| 80–89 | 4 |
| | 100 |

Fig 2.10 shows the histogram of this distribution. Notice that the rectangles are drawn from the points 9.5, 19.5, 29.5 etc. The reason for this is that the class width is 10 (10 to 19 inclusive is 10 numbers). However, if we draw the rectangles from 10 to 19, from 20 to 29, etc., then the class width would only be nine.

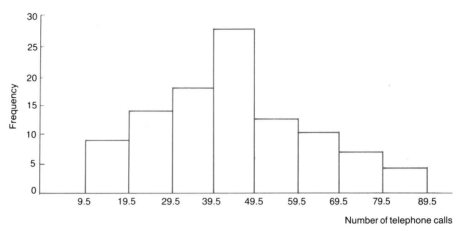

**Fig 2.10   Number of telephone calls made by 100 firms**

## The ogive

It is often useful to present the frequency distribution in a different way altogether. Instead of considering the frequency of each class, we may consider the frequency with which the variable falls *below* a particular value. Consider again the distribution of lengths of 100 metal pipes.

| *Length (cm)* | *Frequency* |
|---|---|
| 10 but under  20 | 3 |
| 20 but under  30 | 7 |
| 30 but under  40 | 10 |
| 40 but under  50 | 16 |
| 50 but under  60 | 34 |
| 60 but under  70 | 13 |
| 70 but under  80 | 7 |
| 80 but under  90 | 6 |
| 90 but under 100 | 4 |

Examining this frequency distribution, we can conclude that

  3 pipes have lengths less than 20 cm
10 pipes have lengths less than 30 cm (i.e. 3 + 7)
20 pipes have lengths less than 40 cm (i.e. 3 + 7 + 10)

Continuing in this way, we obtain what is called the cumulative frequency distribution:

| Length (cm) | Cumulative frequency |
|---|---|
| Under 20 | 3 |
| Under 30 | 10 |
| Under 40 | 20 |
| Under 50 | 36 |
| Under 60 | 70 |
| Under 70 | 83 |
| Under 80 | 90 |
| Under 90 | 96 |
| Under 100 | 100 |

As we shall see later, the cumulative frequency distribution can be used to derive certain summary statistics. Plotting the cumulative frequency distribution gives the diagram called the *ogive* (see Fig 2.11).

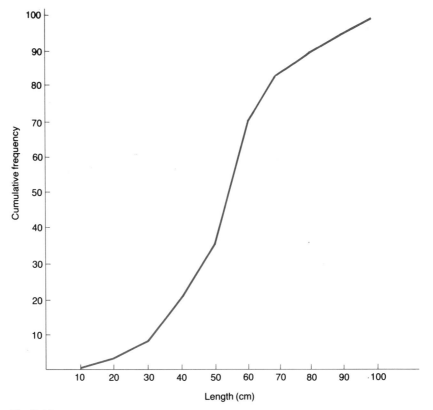

**Fig 2.11**

The first thing you will notice is that we have joined the points on the ogive by straight lines rather than the smooth curve that you are probably more used to. The reason for this is that we do not know how the items in any group are scattered between the upper and lower limits; so we make the only reasonable assumption that we can – that the items in any group are distributed evenly across the group. It may be a false assumption. We may find, in the group 40 and under 50 cm all 16 pipes have lengths of 49 cm, but it is not likely. Assuming an even distribution across each class should not materially affect our results.

## Plotting the time series

You will remember from the last chapter that much data is given in the form of a time series, in which we take a variable and show how its magnitude has varied over a period of time. We have obtained from the United Kingdom *Annual Abstract of Statistics* the following table showing how consumer expenditure at constant prices varied during the period 1979 to 1989.

**Consumer expenditure at 1985 prices (£billion)**

| | | | |
|---|---|---|---|
| *1979* | 195 | *1985* | 218 |
| *1980* | 196 | *1986* | 232 |
| *1981* | 196 | *1987* | 244 |
| *1982* | 198 | *1988* | 262 |
| *1983* | 207 | *1989* | 272 |
| *1984* | 210 | | |

Source: *Annual Abstract of Statistics*, 1991

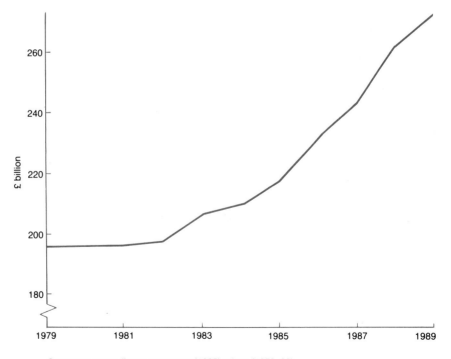

*Consumer expenditure at constant (1985) prices (1979–89)*

**Fig 2.12**

Perhaps you will agree that these figures, involving thousands of millions of pounds, mean very little; if we are honest probably very few of you even read the figures in detail. But suppose we now draw a graph of these figures!

We are sure that even a quick glance at Fig 2.12 will leave you with a strong impression of the way in which consumer expenditure has been changing.

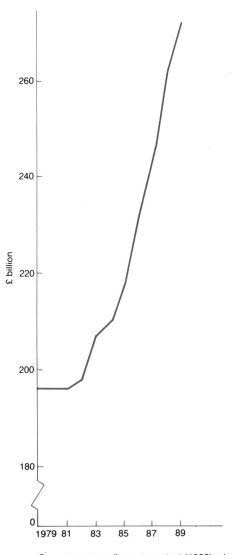

*Consumer expenditure at constant (1985) prices (1979–89)*

**Fig 2.13**

With the exception of the period 1979–82, consumer expenditure grew steadily. Since we have plotted expenditure at constant prices, this represents a rising consumption of goods, i.e. a rising standard of living (it may of course be at the expense of past saving).

You will have noticed the break in Fig 2.12 on the vertical axis and the sudden jump from 0 to 180. This is a device used by statisticians when every figure is high and we do not want to crush our graph into a small space at the top of the graph paper. Remember too that we could have left you with a very different impression of the behaviour of consumer expenditure by adjusting the scales on the axis. Try it for yourself by doubling the scale on the vertical axis and halving the horizontal scale; or halving the vertical scale and doubling the horizontal. We have altered the scales in Figs 2.13 and 2.14. After looking at three graphs of consumer expenditure, can you really draw any conclusions as to the rate at which consumer expenditure has been rising? We know it has gone up – and that is about all.

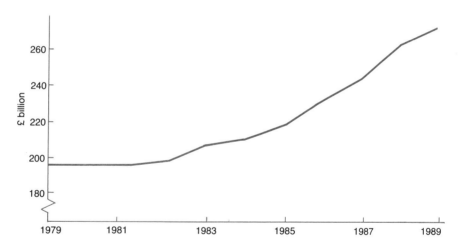

*Consumer expenditure at constant (1985) prices (1979–89)*

**Fig 2.14**

Now, this is all very well, but our friends, the economists, will immediately want to know what we have been spending more on. Are we buying more food and clothes, buying more houses, or wasting our resources in riotous living? For their sakes, and for yours, in Fig 2.15 we include the way in which consumption of four sub-categories of our expenditure have been behaving in the same period.

**Consumer expenditure (£billion) at 1985 prices**

| | Expenditure (£billion) | | | |
| | Food | Alcohol | Clothing | Rent, rates and water |
| --- | --- | --- | --- | --- |
| 1979 | 30.4 | 16.1 | 9.4 | 25.1 |
| 1980 | 30.4 | 15.5 | 9.6 | 25.4 |
| 1981 | 30.2 | 14.9 | 9.6 | 27.7 |
| 1982 | 30.3 | 14.5 | 9.9 | 26.1 |
| 1983 | 30.8 | 15.1 | 10.6 | 26.8 |
| 1984 | 30.3 | 15.4 | 11.1 | 27.1 |
| 1985 | 30.7 | 15.7 | 12.1 | 27.5 |
| 1986 | 31.7 | 15.7 | 13.3 | 27.9 |
| 1987 | 31.9 | 14.0 | 14.1 | 27.3 |
| 1988 | 32.1 | 16.4 | 14.6 | 28.6 |
| 1989 | 32.2 | 16.3 | 14.3 | 29.0 |

Source: *Blue Book*, 1991

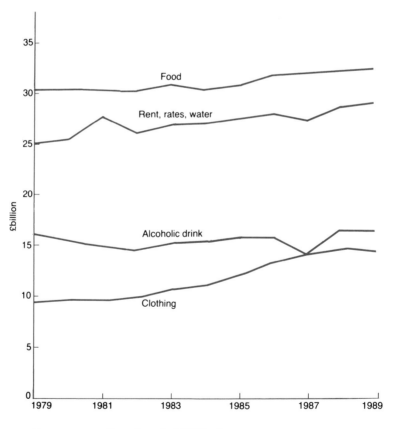

*Consumer expenditure at constant (1985) prices*
Source: *Blue Book*, 1991

**Fig 2.15**

Whenever we wish to compare the way in which several variables have been behaving over a period of time, it is perfectly permissible to draw as many as four or five time series on the same axes, as long as we clearly distinguish the different graphs and the diagram is not too difficult to interpret.

You can see from Fig 2.15 how the pattern of expenditure is changing. The proportion of income spent on food has been remarkably stable, as has been the proportion spent on housing (with the exception of 1981). The proportion spent on alcohol has tended to decline, while the proportion spent on clothing has tended to increase.

## The strata graph

Do you remember when we discussed the bar chart we showed how it could be used to illustrate the constituents of a given total? Now, there are times when we want to illustrate how these constituents have varied over time. It may be, for example, that over the course of years road accidents involving bicycles have been forming a smaller and smaller part of total road accidents, while accidents involving motor cars have been gradually forming an increasing proportion of total accidents. There is nothing to stop us from drawing three or four different time series, one for each type of vehicle showing the number of accidents involving that type of vehicle. We could even draw a number of graphs showing the percentage of accidents involving each type of vehicle, and we have no doubt that the diagrams would bring out the changing pattern. For this type of analysis it is far better to use a special type of diagram, the *strata graph*, or, if you are dealing in percentages, the *percentage strata graph*. We must, however, keep the number of constituents reasonably few since otherwise the diagram may become difficult to interpret. The great advantage of this type of presentation is, as you will see, that the lines showing the magnitude of each constituent can never cross. Figure 2.16 is a typical strata graph, showing the constitution of road accidents over a period of time in a large city. In order to stress the points that we would like to bring out, the figures are purely imaginary, so do not think that your own town is abnormal if the pattern of accidents is different from the one we have represented.

The principle of the strata graph is that our totals are successively cumulated. Thus the height of line A represents the number of accidents involving motor cars each year. When we consider those accidents involving bicycles we add together for each year those accidents involving motor cars and those involving bicycles to produce line B, the height of which for any year tells us the number of accidents involving (motor cars + bicycles). In the same way line C is the graph of the number of accidents involving (motor cars + bicycles + motor cycles). Finally when we add to these figures those accidents involving mopeds, we arrive at line D, which is the total

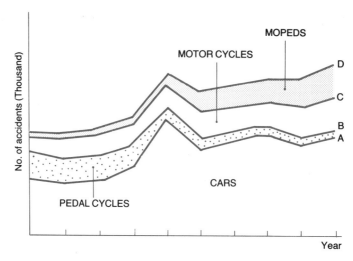

*Number of road accidents 19 . . to 19 . . analysed by type of vehicle*

**Fig 2.16**

number of accidents for all vehicles. You will have realised already that the distance between each line represents those accidents involving a particular vehicle. Thus the gap between A and B shows us accidents involving bicycles and the gap between B and C those involving motor cycles. It is, of course, desirable to distinguish each type of vehicle by distinctive shading to give the diagram clarity, but we think you will agree that such a diagram is relatively easy to interpret. Even a cursory glance tells us that the total number of road accidents have been on the increase, but within this total three distinct trends are apparent. Bicycle accidents, which were quite numerous in the early years, have dwindled away and are now very few; conversely, moped accidents, which were very few in the early years, probably because there were few moped owners, are now becoming quite an important constituent of total accidents: car accidents have increased, and although it is difficult to judge, probably remain much the same proportion of an increased total. Motor cycle accidents, it is apparent, have remained fairly constant over the years.

If we wish to draw a percentage strata graph, it is just as easy, although the initial calculations, converting our figures into percentages, are very cumbersome. Can you see that the line D in such a graph would be a horizontal straight line at 100%?

## Using the spreadsheet

Spreadsheets have the ability to produce statistical diagrams very effectively. We will now examine how the spreadsheet can be used to reproduce the diagrams introduced in this chapter.

**Drawing pie charts and bar chars**

Retrieve the menu template, select Descriptive statistics and then select Diagrams.

If you are using Lotus, your opening screen will look like this:

If you are using ASEASYAS, your opening screen will be:

The menu option Pie-Bar is used to draw pie charts or bar charts. Select this option.

It is strongly recommended that you do not attempt to draw a diagram with more than eight attributes, otherwise your diagram will look very cluttered. Suppose we wished to draw the pie chart and bar chart of the population of certain EC countries, as discussed in this chapter. The data would be entered like this:

```
............ A/ .......... B/ .......... C/ .......... D/ ......... E/ ......... F/.
 1  Attribute     Value
 2  France         57
 3  Belgium        10        Enter data
 4  Germany        61        (at most eight attributes)
 5  Italy          58
 6  Denmark         5        Press ALT P for Piechart
 7  UK             59
 8  N'lands        16        Press ALT B for Barchart
 9
10                           Press ALT M for menu
11
12
```

Now press ALT and P together and the pie chart is drawn. Press ALT and B together and the bar chart is drawn. When the bar chart is revealed, you may well find that the titles run into each other. Press ALT and M together and the menu returns. You may then select Pie-Bar again to enter fresh data. Press File or Quit when you have finished with the template.

If you are using ASEASYAS, then the menu contains a PLOT option. Selecting this option will produce a hard copy of the last diagram on an Epson compatible printer.

**Drawing the frequency polygon and ogive**

To draw a frequency polygon or ogive, select Descriptive statistics and then Frequency from the main menu (this is the same template used in the last chapter). Once the template has loaded, select New data.

In other words, we have the same screen as we had with the template used in the last chapter. Suppose we wanted to draw the frequency polygon and ogive of the distribution of the number of telephone calls considered in this chapter, we would enter data like this:

|   | A | B | C | D | E | F | G | H |
|---|---|---|---|---|---|---|---|---|
| 1 |   |   | FREQUENCY DISTRIBUTION |   |   |   |   |   |
| 2 |   |   |   |   |   |   |   |   |
| 3 |   |   |   |   |   |   |   |   |
| 4 | Lower | Upper |   |   |   |   |   |   |
| 5 | Bound | Bound |   |   |   |   |   |   |
| 6 | 10 | 19 |   |   |   |   |   |   |
| 7 | 20 | 29 |   | Enter boundaries of frequency distribution |   |   |   |   |
| 8 | 30 | 39 |   |   |   |   |   |   |
| 9 | 40 | 49 |   | Press ALT and S when finished |   |   |   |   |
| 10 | 50 | 59 |   |   |   |   |   |   |
| 11 | 60 | 69 |   |   |   |   |   |   |
| 12 | 70 | 79 |   |   |   |   |   |   |
| 13 | 80 | 89 |   |   |   |   |   |   |
| 14 |   |   |   |   |   |   |   |   |

Now press ALT and S and you will notice that you are given the option of entering raw data in cell A1, or the frequencies starting in cell C6. As we know the frequencies, move cursor to cell C6 and enter them directly like this:

|   | A | B | C | D | E | F | G |
|---|---|---|---|---|---|---|---|
| 1 |   | < – – – Enter data here or enter frequencies |   |   |   |   |   |
| 2 |   | starting at cell C6 |   |   |   |   |   |
| 3 |   |   |   |   |   |   |   |
| 4 | Lower | Upper | Frequency |   |   |   |   |
| 5 | Bound | Bound |   |   | Press ALT with R when finished |   |   |
| 6 | 10 | 19 | 9 |   |   |   |   |
| 7 | 20 | 29 | 14 |   |   |   |   |
| 8 | 30 | 39 | 18 |   |   |   |   |
| 9 | 40 | 49 | 27 |   |   |   |   |
| 10 | 50 | 59 | 12 |   |   |   |   |
| 11 | 60 | 69 | 10 |   |   |   |   |
| 12 | 70 | 79 | 6 |   |   |   |   |
| 13 | 80 | 89 | 4 |   |   |   |   |
| 14 | Total Frequency = |   | 100 |   |   |   |   |
| 15 |   |   |   |   |   |   |   |

Now press ALT and R and the menu returns.

Highlight Polygon and press Enter for the frequency polygon. Press any key to return to the menu. Now highlight Ogive and press Enter for the ogive. Again press Enter to return to the menu. If you are using

ASEASYAS, then selecting Plot from the menu will send the last diagram drawn to an Epsom compatible printer.

You should note that although the diagram for the ogive is reliable for all frequency distributions, the diagram of the frequency polygon assumes that the class widths are constant.

To exit the template press either File or Quit, depending upon whether or not you wish to save the data.

QUESTIONS

**2.1**   Describe the purpose and construction of a pie chart, illustrating your answer with a simple example of your own invention.

**2.2**   (a)   What are the advantages of using charts and graphs in statistical investigations?

(b)   Describe clearly the methods to be employed in constructing:

- a pie chart;
- a histogram.

(c)   State the kind of diagram you consider most suitable to illustrate:

- daily hours of sunshine for a period of one month;
- the number of workers, male and female, employed in a factory at each of three dates.

Briefly give your reasons for your choice in each case.

**2.3**   Discuss the suitability of a compound bar chart and a pie chart, for the presentation of data to:

(a)   top management,

(b)   lower management,

(c)   the public.

Give examples of data which could be satisfactorily presented by each of these charts. (Do not draw the charts.)

**2.4**   A daily count of the number of rejects from the assembly line of a local manufacturer has yielded the following data:

```
138  164  150  132  144  125  149  157
146  158  140  147  136  148  152  144
168  126  138  176  163  119  154  165
146  173  142  147  135  153  140  135
161  145  135  142  150  156  145  128
```

(a) Using the data, construct a frequency distribution table and from that sketch the corresponding frequency curve.

(b) Comment on the shape of the frequency curve you have obtained and compare it with the sketched shapes of two others with which you are familiar.

**2.5** The set of figures below shows the ages at which 50 employees were appointed to a certain grade.

```
28  27  30  27  28  28  26  27  28  28
26  28  29  31  27  28  27  29  27  29
28  27  31  27  27  29  30  27  28  28
28  29  28  29  27  30  27  28  27  29
28  27  28  29  29  28  28  28  28  27
```

(a) Write the data in the form of a frequency table and draw the frequency curve.

(b) Draw also the cumulative relative frequency curve.

**2.6** The table below gives the destinations of British holidaymakers taking foreign holidays in 1989.

| Destination | % | Destination | % |
|---|---|---|---|
| Austria/Switzerland | 5 | Netherlands | 3 |
| Belgium | 1 | Italy | 4 |
| France | 18 | Spain | 28 |
| West Germany | 3 | United States | 6 |
| Greece | 8 | Other | 21 |
| Irish Republic | 3 | | |

Source: *Social Trends*, 1991

Represent this data in a suitable diagram.

**2.7** The following is a record of marks scored by candidates in an examination:

```
77  59  84  73  51  43  50  81  61  53  69
37  58  63  67  61  90  61  50  60  84  56
77  57  42  43  41  49  37  21  24  35  34
50  11  52  30  16  33  67  87  64  47  59
37  92  88  30  38  22  22  49  46  50  64
23  73  73  48  26  36  51  85  71  57  45
```

(a) Tabulate the marks in the form of a frequency distribution, grouping by suitable intervals.

(b) Construct a histogram from your frequency distribution.

(c) Explain the essential differences between a histogram and a bar chart.

**2.8**

| | Expenditure (£m) | |
|---|---|---|
| Year | Overseas visitors in UK | UK residents abroad |
| 1985 | 5442 | 4871 |
| 1986 | 5553 | 6083 |
| 1987 | 6260 | 7280 |
| 1988 | 6184 | 8216 |
| 1989 | 6945 | 9357 |
| 1990 | 7785 | 9916 |
| 1991 | 7168 | 9834 |

Source: *Monthly Digest of Statistics*, November 1992

Draw a diagram of this data and comment on the main features it reveals.

**2.9** **Household expenditure (£b) 1988**

| | |
|---|---|
| Food | 37 |
| Alcoholic drink | 19 |
| Tobacco | 8 |
| Clothing | 20 |
| Housing | 43 |
| Fuel and Power | 12 |
| Household goods and services | 19 |
| Transport and communications | 50 |
| Entertainment | 26 |
| Other | 49 |

Source: *Social Trends*, 1990

Draw a chart, graph or diagram to represent household expenditure in units of actual money spent. Draw a second chart, graph or diagram to represent household expenditure in percentage terms.

**2.10**

*Families receiving Family Income*
*Supplement (thousands)*

| Month | All families | One-parent families | Two-parent families |
|---|---|---|---|
| 1989 Jan | 286 | 177 | 108 |
| April | 313 | 195 | 118 |
| July | 314 | 192 | 122 |
| Oct | 299 | 180 | 119 |
| 1990 Jan | 314 | 192 | 121 |
| April | 326 | 200 | 126 |
| July | 326 | 197 | 129 |
| Oct | 315 | 189 | 126 |
| 1991 Jan | 341 | 210 | 131 |
| April | 355 | 222 | 133 |
| July | 349 | 214 | 135 |
| Oct | 349 | 214 | 136 |
| 1992 Jan | 349 | 214 | 136 |
| April | 389 | 234 | 155 |

Source: *Monthly Digest of Statistics*, December 1992

(a)  Prepare a suitable graph or chart to represent the data given above.

(b)  Write a short report on the main features revealed by your diagram.

**2.11**  Fuel used by the public electricity supply system, 1992 (million tons of coal or coal equivalent)

| | Coal | Oil | Nuclear | Hydro | Total |
|---|---|---|---|---|---|
| January | 4.04 | 0.47 | 1.34 | 0.15 | 6.00 |
| February | 4.33 | 0.47 | 1.31 | 0.11 | 6.22 |
| March | 4.87 | 0.50 | 1.72 | 0.19 | 7.29 |
| April | 3.53 | 0.37 | 1.22 | 0.12 | 5.24 |
| May | 3.12 | 0.34 | 1.23 | 0.11 | 4.80 |
| June | 3.72 | 0.39 | 1.44 | 0.05 | 5.60 |
| July | 3.12 | 0.39 | 0.96 | 0.04 | 4.51 |
| August | 2.78 | 0.30 | 1.10 | 0.06 | 4.31 |
| September | 3.81 | 0.39 | 1.39 | 0.08 | 5.91 |

Source: Department of Trade and Industry

Prepare a suitable graph or chart to show the data above relating to fuel used by the public electricity supply system. Write a short report on the main points revealed by your diagram, using derived statistics where appropriate.

**2.12**

| | Recipients of Social Security benefits (thousands) | | |
|---|---|---|---|
| Year | Unemployment benefit | Sickness benefit | Widows' benefit |
| 1982 | 1041 | 1198 | 433 |
| 1983 | 987 | 1202 | 426 |
| 1984 | 926 | 1044 | 420 |
| 1985 | 901 | 1098 | 414 |
| 1986 | 956 | 1141 | 398 |
| 1987 | 811 | 1168 | 380 |
| 1988 | 630 | 1278 | 388 |
| 1989 | 381 | 1395 | 371 |
| 1990 | 331 | 1516 | * |

Source: DSS

*Figures not yet available.

(a) Prepare a suitable graph or chart to represent the data given above.

(b) Write a short report on the main features revealed by the table and your graph or chart, using derived figures where appropriate.

**2.13**

| | Families receiving Child Benefit (thousands) | | |
|---|---|---|---|
| | | Number of children | |
| Year | One | Two | Three or more |
| 1984 | 2970 | 2939 | 1188 |
| 1985 | 2963 | 2901 | 1172 |
| 1986 | 2962 | 2851 | 1164 |
| 1987 | 2948 | 2817 | 1164 |
| 1988 | 2956 | 2788 | 1179 |
| 1989 | 2872 | 2699 | 1124 |

Source: DSS

Prepare a suitable graph or chart to show the data given above relating to Child Benefit claims in Great Britain. Write a short report on the main points revealed by your graph, using derived figures where appropriate.

**2.14**  **Subjects studied at Britannia College of Commerce 1992**

| Subject | Number of students |
|---|---|
| Professional: | |
| Management | 240 |
| Banking | 120 |
| Accountancy | 980 |
| Languages: | |
| Spanish | 20 |
| French | 220 |
| German | 100 |
| BTEC: | |
| General | 350 |
| National | 225 |
| Higher | 115 |

(a)  Depict the data given above in the form of:

- a simple bar chart,

- component bar chart (actuals),

- a percentage component bar chart,

- a pie chart.

(b)  Comment on the effectiveness of using the pie chart and the component bar chart as a means of illustrating data classification.

# 3

# The presentation of data II

The diagrams that we have examined so far are in fairly common usage. In fact we would be prepared to bet that, with the exception of strata graphs, you will have already seen all of the diagrams in the previous chapter. Basically, all of these diagrams are attempting to show the relative quantities in the data in an interesting and easily grasped manner. Yet some diagrams show much more than just the relative sizes, and we will now turn our attention to such diagrams. The chapter is concluded with a discussion on how diagrams can be made to misrepresent data.

## Logarithmic graphs

As we have seen, one of the problems with ordinary graphs is that they tend to give a false impression of the way in which figures are changing. Using a vertical scale of 1 inch = 100 units, a change from 100 to 200 units is represented by the same upward movement as a change from 1000 to 1100 units, even though it is 100% change as compared with a 10% change. The slope of the graph is the same – yet the rate of change is very different. Now, in most cases this does not matter. We may be interested only in the swings of the absolute figures; or the range of the figures may be such that the difference in the rates of change is negligible. If this is the case, we can get all we need from the graphs we have drawn. However, if we are considering inflation, for example, it is the rate at which prices are rising which is important, rather than the actual price increases.

Fortunately, if we plot the logarithms of our figures rather than the figures themselves, we can produce a graph the slope of which represents the real rate of change. Why should this be so?

Consider a case in which prices are rising by 20% a year. We can easily construct a table to show what happens to prices.

| Period | Price | Log of price | Difference of logs |
|--------|-------|--------------|--------------------|
| 1 | 100 | 2.0000 | |
| 2 | 120 | 2.0792 | 0.0792 |
| 3 | 144 | 2.1584 | 0.0792 |
| 4 | 172.8 | 2.2375 | 0.0792 |
| 5 | 207.36 | 2.3167 | 0.0792 |

Don't you find it rather frightening that an inflation rate less than that of Britain in the mid-1970s will more than double prices in five years?

As you can see, the log of each price rises by 0.0792 irrespective of the magnitude of the price change, and hence we obtain a straight line graph if we plot the logarithms. This of course tells us that the rate of change of prices is constant. It does not tell us what the rate of change is, but merely enables us to compare rates of change over time.

Strictly such a graph is known as a *semi-logarithmic* graph, as we plot logarithms only on the vertical axis. On the horizontal axis we do not plot the logarithms of the time periods.

As you can see from Fig 3.1, if we plot the prices themselves the slope of the curve gets steeper and the fact that the rate of change is the same is completely hidden.

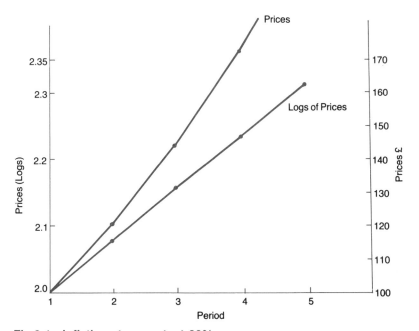

Fig 3.1  Inflation at a constant 20%

Often a logarithmic graph can be used also when the figures with which we are concerned range so widely that it is inconvenient to use a normal graph. Such a situation would occur if we tried to plot German price movements during the great inflation of the 1920s when prices were increasing by hundreds of times each month.

Now, although few students find difficulty in mastering the principles involved in the construction of semi-logarithmic graphs, this is such a common question in examinations that we would strongly recommend you to work through the following example with us, making sure that you understand each step.

---

**EXAMPLE**

Sales of two companies

|  | Sales (£000) | |
| --- | --- | --- |
| Year | Company A | Company B |
| 19X0 | 2240 | 980 |
| 19X1 | 2460 | 1082 |
| 19X2 | 2680 | 1205 |
| 19X3 | 2915 | 1289 |
| 19X4 | 3136 | 1382 |
| 19X5 | 3362 | 1476 |
| 19X6 | 3590 | 1580 |
| 19X7 | 3821 | 1687 |
| 19X8 | 4049 | 1787 |
| 19X9 | 4280 | 1891 |

(a) Plot the time series on (i) an arithmetic scale graph, and (ii) a semi-logarithmic graph.

(b) Interpret the results.

Well, the first part of this question will cause you no difficulty at all. As you well know, an arithmetic scale graph is a normal graph, in which we let a given distance (usually a centimetre) represent a given change in the magnitude of the variable on both the horizontal and the vertical axes. We then plot the figures given in the question according to the scale we have used. Thus, in Fig 3.2 on the horizontal axis we could let 2 cm represent one year, while on the vertical axis it represents £500 000 sales. We have plotted the graphs showing the variation in the sales of the two companies in the normal way.

When we now come to consider the semi-logarithmic graphs, we have to be careful. In some examinations you will be issued only with the normal graph paper we have used so far; in others with graph paper already designed for semi-logarithmic use. Let us suppose first that you have been issued only with the normal arithmetic scale graph paper. In this case, as you know, we will plot the years along the horizontal axis as normally, but along the vertical axis you will have to plot the logarithms of the sales figure for each year. Our first step then must be to obtain these logarithms. We strongly advise you to do this as part of the answer and not on a piece of scrap paper. It is easy to make a mistake, and if you do examiners are far more inclined to be generous if they can trace easily

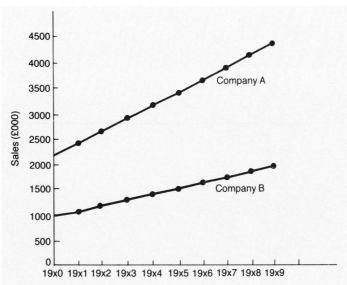

**Fig 3.2**

where the mistake has arisen. So we proceed as follows:

| Year | Company A Sales (£000) | Log | Company B Sales (£000) | Log |
|------|------------------------|--------|------------------------|--------|
| 19X0 | 2240 | 3.3502 | 980  | 2.9912 |
| 19X1 | 2460 | 3.3909 | 1082 | 3.0342 |
| 19X2 | 2680 | 3.4281 | 1205 | 3.0810 |
| 19X3 | 2915 | 3.4646 | 1289 | 3.1103 |
| 19X4 | 3136 | 3.4964 | 1382 | 3.1405 |
| 19X5 | 3362 | 3.5266 | 1476 | 3.1691 |
| 19X6 | 3590 | 3.5551 | 1580 | 3.1987 |
| 19X7 | 3821 | 3.5822 | 1687 | 3.2271 |
| 19X8 | 4049 | 3.6073 | 1787 | 3.2521 |
| 19X9 | 4280 | 3.6314 | 1891 | 3.2767 |

Although this seems to be a cumbersome process, almost any of the small pocket calculators you are normally allowed to use will give you the logarithms you require in a matter of seconds. All you have to do now is to scale the vertical axis to accommodate the logarithms you have obtained, and draw the graphs. We have done this in Fig 3.3, but you will notice that we have also inserted on the vertical axis on the right some of the absolute values of the sales. While modern management is well aware of the use of semi-logarithmic graphs they also wish to be able to see at a glance the value of the sales turnover without having to refer to a book of log tables.

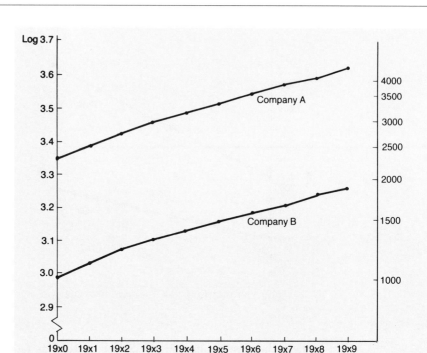

**Fig 3.3**

Even a quick glance at Figs 3.2 and 3.3 brings out the advantages of the semi-logarithmic graph. The graphs of the sales figures on arithmetic scale imply that the two companies increased their sales at a steady rate throughout the whole period. But as you are aware, such graphs show absolute changes, not *rates* of change, and equal absolute increases imply a declining *rate* of increase. This is well brought out in the semi-logarithmic graphs, where a close look at company A shows a marked tendency of the rate of change to fall.

More importantly, the two graphs give completely different impressions of the relative performance of the two companies. The arithmetic scale graph implies that company A is expanding more rapidly than company B because the slope of the graph of the former's sales is steeper. But again the use of absolute figures is deceptive. The semi-logarithmic graphs show that company B's performance is at least as good as that of company A in that it is expanding at the same rate, while on a very close examination we find that the rate of growth over the whole period is marginally better than that of company A, and from 19X3 onwards growth certainly seems to be steadier and more sustained than that of company A. Thus, we may come to the conclusion that, although both companies have grown substantially in the period, company B, although smaller, appears to have done marginally better.

Now this is all very well, but suppose you are issued with semi-logarithmic graph paper already ruled. The great advantage of this paper is that you can insert the *absolute* figures of sales on the graph without first having to look up the logarithms. Probably, however, few of you have had the opportunity yet of seeing semi-logarithmic graph paper, so let us explain the principles on which it is ruled. One axis is ruled normally, in centimetres and millimetres (after all, it is *semi*-logarithmic). But the other axis is quite differently ruled. It is drawn on the basis that equal distances represent equal percentage changes rather than equal absolute changes. Thus, if 1 cm represents a change from 10 to 100 (an increase of 10 times), the next centimetre will represent a change from 100 to 1000 (also an increase of 10 times).

There is more to it than this, however. No-one would expect you to calculate the percentage change for each figure that you have to plot on the graph. We have merely stated the obvious – that one axis of the semi-logarithmic graph paper is scaled logarithmically. Let us take it further. If we take the first centimetre on the vertical scale to represent an increase of one unit (from 1 to 2), the next centimetre would represent an increase from 2 to 4. We could have obtained exactly the same effect by plotting logarithms. The log of 1 is 0.0, so you will realise that the logarithmic graph can range upwards only from an absolute value of 1 (not 0 as can the arithmetic scale graph). Now the logarithm of 2 is 0.30103, and the logarithm of 4 is 0.60206. Similarly the logarithm of 8 is 0.90309. Can you see that, in allowing each centimetre to represent the same proportional increase in the absolute figures, we are scaling according to the logarithms of the numbers? In this case 1 cm represents an increase in the logarithm of 0.30103; and when we add 0.30103 to a logarithm, we are in fact multiplying the previous number by 2. So each successive centimetre represents an increasing change in the absolute figures – 2, 4, 8, 16, etc.

But the logarithmic scale is not drawn in centimetres as is the arithmetic axis. Suppose once again that we take the first vertical division on the graph paper to be 1 cm long (whether it is or not depends on the graph paper with which you are issued). We can let this centimetre represent any absolute magnitude that we wish. Let us again assume that it represents an increase from 1 to 2. The next main division on our graph paper will also represent an absolute increase of one unit, from 2 to 3, but this division will not be a centimetre deep. We have already said that the second centimetre represents an increase in absolute values from 2 to 4, so you would naturally expect the second division representing an increase from 2 to 3 to be less than a centimetre deep. It will in fact be about 0.585 cm deep only. Thus each successive unit increase on the logarithmic axis will entail a smaller and smaller vertical rise, and the vertical scaling will look something like Fig 3.4.

**Fig 3.4**

**Fig 3.5**

In practice, of course, the graph paper you will be given will have each main division subdivided as normal graph paper is into 10 subsections to enable you to plot the intermediate figures. If you have not seen such graph paper before, we strongly recommend that you immediately study carefully Fig 3.5 where we have drawn the two graphs we are concerned with on semi-logarithmic paper, and, most important, obtain a stock of such paper of your own and practise drawing semi-logarithmic graphs using the exercises at the end of this chapter.

## The Lorenz curve

If you look at statistics of income one of the first things that strikes you is the inequality in the distribution of incomes in most countries. Not only is the range of incomes wide, from under £5000 a year to £100 000 a year and more in the United Kingdom, but we also find that a very small percentage of the income recipients at the top of the scale receive a disproportionately large share of total income. Equally, the very large percentage of low income earners receive in total a very small percentage of the total income. You must, at some time in your life, have met such statements as 'the top 5% of income recipients receive over 70% of total income'.

Now any economist will tell you that one purpose of our taxation system, or any taxation system which is progressive, is to reduce the inequality of incomes, and naturally we would all like to know how far the system is succeeding in this objective. Statisticians have derived a diagram, the *Lorenz curve*, which enables us to show graphically the extent of inequality, not only of incomes, but also of many other things.

In Fig 3.6, considering income distribution, we measure on the horizontal axis the percentage of population, and on the vertical axis the percentage of income.

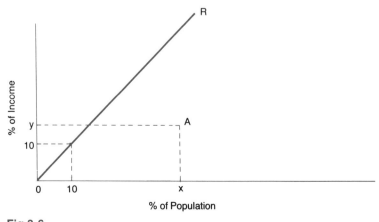

**Fig 3.6**

Now, obviously, if incomes are distributed equally, the bottom 10% of income earners will receive 10% of total income, the bottom 20% of income earners will receive 20% of total income and so on. The graph representing such a distribution of income will be the straight line OR passing through the origin and at 45 degrees (provided, that is, that the horizontal and vertical scales are the same), and any divergence from this line will indicate some degree of inequality. The point A for example would be interpreted as 'the bottom $x$% of income earners receive $y$% of total income', and, since $x$ is greater than $y$, would be derived from a situation such as 'the bottom 65% of income earners receive only 32% of total income'.

Let us illustrate the use of Lorenz curves by applying them to the following income statistics of the United Kingdom:

| | No. of taxpayers | | Pre-tax income | | Post-tax income | |
|---|---|---|---|---|---|---|
| *Annual income* | *(00 000)* | *%* | *£b* | *%* | *£b* | *%* |
| Less than 8 000 | 44.0 | 22.7 | 45.0 | 11.4 | 41.4 | 13.9 |
| 8 000– 12 000 | 53.3 | 27.5 | 62.6 | 15.9 | 45.8 | 15.4 |
| 12 000– 20 000 | 57.7 | 29.8 | 88.4 | 22.4 | 75.8 | 25.4 |
| 20 000– 30 000 | 22.1 | 11.4 | 52.9 | 13.4 | 44.1 | 14.8 |
| 30 000–100 000 | 10.9 | 5.6 | 46.7 | 11.8 | 26.3 | 8.8 |
| Over 100 000 | 5.5 | 2.8 | 99.3 | 25.1 | 64.9 | 21.8 |
| | 193.5 | 100.0 | 394.9 | 100.0 | 298.3 | 100.0 |

Source: *Inland Revenue (1988/9 survey)*

The first step in the construction of our diagram is to calculate the percentages appropriate to each group and each column. Thus the 5.33 million people in the group £8000–£12 000 comprise 27.5% of all income earners, and received 15.9% of pre-tax income. The next step is to cumulate the percentages in this way:

| *Income earners (%)* | | *Pre-tax income (%)* | *Post-tax income (%)* |
|---|---|---|---|
| 22.7 | receive | 11.4 | 13.9 |
| 50.3 | | 27.2 | 29.2 |
| 80.1 | | 49.6 | 54.6 |
| 91.5 | | 63.0 | 69.4 |
| 97.2 | | 74.9 | 78.2 |
| 100.0 | | 100.0 | 100.0 |

It is now easy to draw the Lorenz curves relating to pre-tax and post-tax income (see Fig 3.7).

Now any divergence from our straight line of equal distribution of income indicates that there is inequality in the distribution of incomes, and the further the Lorenz curve is from this line of reference, the greater is the degree of inequality. It is worth noting that if the Lorenz curve is below the straight line the inequality is in favour of the upper income groups in that a high percentage of low income earners receive a small percentage of income.

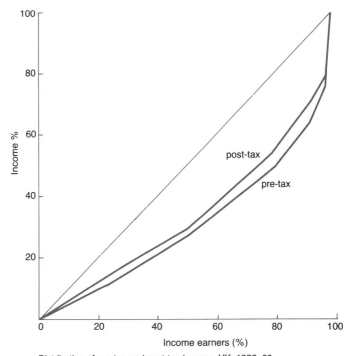

*Distribution of pre-tax and post-tax income, UK, 1988–89*

**Fig 3.7**

If, on the other hand, the Lorenz curve is above the straight line, it implies that a given percentage of the bottom income earners receive a higher percentage of total income; the inequality, that is, works in favour of the poor.

Looking at Fig 3.7, it is apparent that at that time there was a great deal of inequality in the income structure of the United Kingdom. Although the taxation system did reduce it, the reduction seems to have been minimal. We have not, however, asked what was done with the tax revenue. Much of it was returned to the lower income groups in the form of social benefits – child benefit, supplementary benefits, subsidised housing and so on. It may well be that when we allow for this transfer of income, the effects of taxation would appear very different.

## The Z chart

A diagram which is often used in industry and commerce, although it seems to be less popular among statisticians, is the Z chart, so called because the completed diagram takes the form of the letter Z. This is merely a device to enable management to show concisely three different aspects of a time series plotted on the one graph. On the bottom bar of the Z we plot the time series of monthly (or weekly) sales, or output, or whatever variable we are considering. On the diagonal bar of the Z we plot the cumulative total to date, that is, the total sales or output we have achieved since the beginning of the year. Finally on the top bar of the Z we plot the total sales achieved in the last year: the first or January figure is the total sales achieved during the period 1 February last to 31 January this year; the February figure is the total from last March until the end of February this year, etc.

We will illustrate by plotting the figures of output for the firm ABC Ltd. The figures are simplified to enable you to follow the calculations more easily. Obviously, although we are plotting figures for the current year only, if we are to obtain a running total of sales over the last 12 months we will need the figures for two years.

**Output – ABC Limited**

|  | Last year | Current year | Cumulative total | Moving annual total |
|---|---|---|---|---|
| January | 9 | 11 | 11 | 146 |
| February | 8 | 14 | 25 | 152 |
| March | 9 | 12 | 37 | 155 |
| April | 13 | 15 | 52 | 157 |
| May | 14 | 16 | 68 | 159 |
| June | 18 | 19 | 87 | 160 |
| July | 16 | 18 | 105 | 162 |
| August | 15 | 14 | 119 | 161 |
| September | 12 | 14 | 133 | 163 |
| October | 10 | 13 | 146 | 166 |
| November | 9 | 11 | 157 | 168 |
| December | 11 | 15 | 172 | 172 |

A glance at Fig 3.8 shows what a vast amount of information is given by this simple diagram. The cumulative total tells us performance to date, and it is a simple matter to superimpose on the diagram a line showing planned or expected performance. Thus we can see at a glance whether our plans are being realised or whether we are falling behind. The moving annual total enables us to compare performance this year with that at a comparable time last year. If this chart is rising it means that figures in that month are higher than they were in the same month last year. Thus we have the means of making a direct comparison with last year. Finally the monthly total enables us to keep a direct check on what is happening now; and if we are falling behind our plan we can usually spot a month with low figures which has caused this and so discover why. Is it any wonder, with this wealth of information to be had, that the Z chart is so popular in industry?

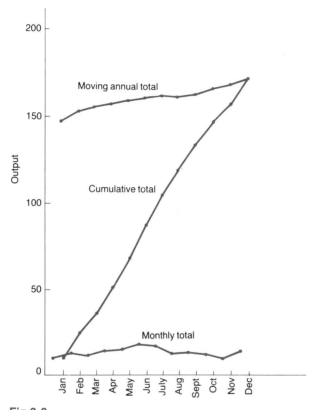

**Fig 3.8**

## The scatter diagram

The final diagram we will introduce you to is not a graph at all. It looks at first glance rather like a series of dots placed haphazardly on a sheet of graph paper. But it is anything but haphazard, as we will see. The basic aim underlying the scatter diagram is to try to ascertain if there is a relationship between two factors, such that when one is high the other is high, when one is low the other is low. Or perhaps the relationship is inverse – when one variable is low, the other is high and vice versa. Suppose we are examining the relationship between the level of employment and the level of industrial investment, see Fig 3.9(a), (b) and (c).

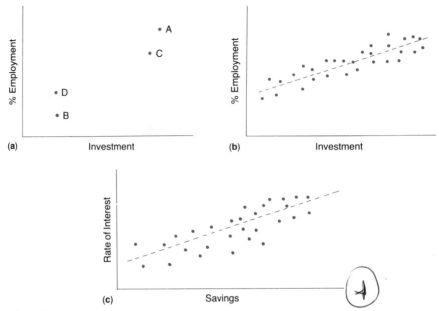

**Fig 3.9**

First we will have figures over a considerable period of time giving us the level of industrial investment and the percentage employment rate associated with that level of investment. Let us take just four of those pairs of figures. The first pair tells us that the level of investment was high and associated with it was a high level of employment. This position is indicated by point A in Fig 3.9(a). Another pair of figures tells us that when investment was slightly lower employment was considerably lower – point C. Still a third pair of figures tells us that at a time when investment was low, employment was also low. This is indicated by point B. If we examine the last figures we find that although investment was the same as before, the level of employment was, in fact, very much higher – point D. If we plot sufficient pairs of figures we may well get a series of dots such as those on Fig 3.9(b) which show a pattern. Generally the higher the level of investment the higher the level of employment, and this we have indicated by inserting freehand a dotted line rising upwards from left to right. The same sort of pattern is seen when we examine savings and the rate of interest in Fig 3.9(c). Of course, as you can see from the scatter of the points the relationship is not perfect. We cannot forecast the exact level of employment from the level of investment. It would be fine if we could do this, but at the moment all we are interested in is the general tendency. Before you leave the scatter diagram, experiment for yourself. Draw a scatter diagram showing the relationship between investment and *un*employment. You should get an inverse relationship – the points *falling* from left to right. And finally, try to draw a scatter diagram in which there is no clear relationship shown between two variables.

## Some examples of bad practice

We must not leave the subject of graphs and diagrams without giving you some advice on what not to do. Unfortunately you will find examples every day of diagrams which illustrate what we are about to say should not happen.

A device beloved of advertisers today is to represent their information in the form of little pictures or ideograms. The sales of a particular brand of beer may be represented by the size of a foaming tankard, the amount of washing-up liquid you get for a penny by the height of liquid in a test-tube. Now, many advertisers using this technique are merely doing their job to the best of their ability; but some advertisements we have seen seem designed to mislead the reader.

Look at Fig 3.10 which represents the sales of 'Whizz' by varying the size of the packets. There is nothing wrong with this technique – it can put over the idea of increasing sales forcibly and effectively. But look at the size of the packets. Doubling the dimensions of a packet does not indicate, of course, that sales have doubled. The volume of the second packet is in fact eight times that of the first, and the volume of the last packet is, believe it or not, 64 times that of the first. Thus, in spite of the writing saying that sales are doubling every year, the reader is left with a completely false impression of the rate at which they are rising.

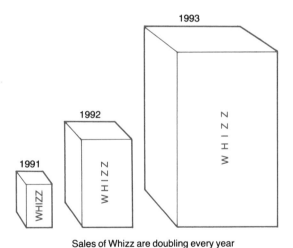

Sales of Whizz are doubling every year

**Fig 3.10**

Even more unpardonable, in our opinion, is the situation shown in Fig 3.11. You know that before you draw any graph, you should clearly mark the scales on the axis. Before you indignantly retort that this is an obvious point and will never be forgotten, you must realise that many people do quite deliberately omit the scales, intending to mislead. You must have seen this situation in television commercials. A mysterious line runs across the screen – showing absolutely nothing, but still leaving the impression that sales are skyrocketing and that we are missing the chance of a lifetime by not buying the product. Couple this with the statement that this is the housewives' choice and we are caught. No-one likes to be out of step with one's friends and neighbours.

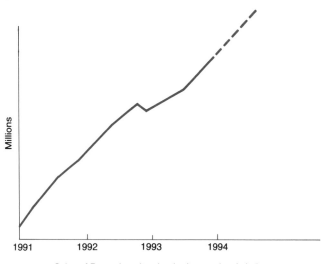

Sales of Bang show it to be the housewives' choice

**Fig 3.11**

Equally bad, if not worse, is the invention of units that do not exist. The scales should tell us something; they should use units that are real and that can be understood. But look at Fig 3.12.

Imagine this graph on your television screen, and the smooth voice of the announcer 'proving' by pointing to the graph that daily brushing with Gritto is bound to make your teeth whiter. But what is a unit of brightness? We are afraid that we do not know, and we very much suspect that the advertising agencies do not know either.

Students often ask us which is the best diagram to use, for a particular purpose. There is no real answer to this and we suggest that you do not waste time looking for one. Any diagram should present the salient features of the data simply and vividly. Equally, if the reader has to spend a great deal of time 'sorting out' what a diagram means, it is a bad diagram.

But do not let it stop here. Certain features of the data should be obvious from the diagram. Now ask questions. Why has the variable behaved in this manner? Why has A behaved differently from B? Is there a relationship between C and D, and, if so, what is this relationship? Only by asking questions such as these will you get full value from your diagrams.

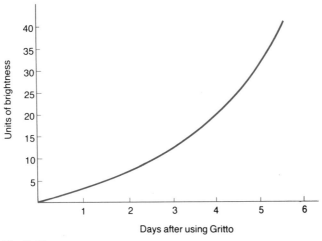

Fig 3.12

## Using the spreadsheet

The menu structure of the spreadsheet template which accompanies this chapter can be seen in Fig 3.13. The option Plot is not available with Lotus 1–2–3. Hence, to draw a Lorenz curve select the options Descriptive statistics, Diagrams (to retrieve the template) then select Lorenz. The data is entered from the cursor position. The following tables show how the data should be entered for the three examples used in this chapter.

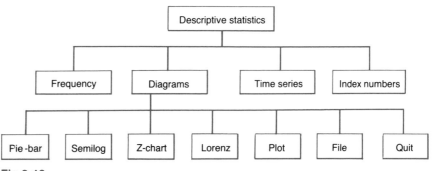

Fig 3.13

**Semi-log graph**

| | A | B | C | D | E | F | G |
|---|---|---|---|---|---|---|---|
| 1 | Data | | | | | | |
| 2 | 2240 | | | | | | |
| 3 | 2460 | | | | | | |
| 4 | 2680 | | | | | | |
| 5 | 2915 | | | | Input data | | |
| 6 | 3136 | | | | | | |
| 7 | 3362 | | | | Press ALT L when finished | | |
| 8 | 3590 | | | | | | |
| 9 | 3821 | | | | | | |
| 10 | 4049 | | | | | | |
| 11 | 4280 | | | | | | |

After pressing ALT L, the template counts the number of data items input and draws the semi-log graph.

**Z chart**

| | A | B | C | D | E | F | G | H |
|---|---|---|---|---|---|---|---|---|
| 1 | | Last | Current | | | | | |
| 2 | | Year | Year | | | | | |
| 3 | Jan | 9 | 11 | | | | | |
| 4 | Feb | 8 | 14 | | Enter data | | | |
| 5 | Mar | 9 | 12 | | | | | |
| 6 | Apr | 13 | 15 | | Press ALT F when finished | | | |
| 7 | May | 14 | 16 | | | | | |
| 8 | Jun | 18 | 19 | | | | | |
| 9 | Jul | 16 | 18 | | | | | |
| 10 | Aug | 15 | 14 | | | | | |
| 11 | Sep | 12 | 14 | | | | | |
| 12 | Oct | 10 | 13 | | | | | |
| 13 | Nov | 9 | 11 | | | | | |
| 14 | Dec | 11 | 15 | | | | | |
| 15 | | | | | | | | |

After pressing ALT F, the cumulative totals and moving annual totals are shown. Pressing Enter reveals the Z chart.

**Lorenz curve – Lotus**

|   | A | B | C | D | E | F | G | H |
|---|---|---|---|---|---|---|---|---|
| 1 | X-value | Y-value | | | | | | |
| 2 | 44.0 | 45.0 | | | | | | |
| 3 | 53.3 | 62.6 | | Enter data | | | | |
| 4 | 57.7 | 88.4 | | | | | | |
| 5 | 22.1 | 52.9 | | Press ALT S when finished | | | | |
| 6 | 10.9 | 46.7 | | | | | | |
| 7 | 5.5 | 99.3 | | | | | | |
| 8 | | | | | | | | |
| 9 | | | | | | | | |
| 10 | | | | | | | | |
| 11 | | | | | | | | |

After pressing ALT S the Lorenz curve is drawn. Columns E and F in the table give the cumulative percentages for X and Y.

## QUESTIONS

### 3.1

**Transport in Great Britain**

|  | Vehicles currently licensed (000s) | Billion vehicle kilometres |
|---|---|---|
| 1982 | 19 762 | 284 |
| 1983 | 20 209 | 288 |
| 1984 | 20 765 | 303 |
| 1985 | 21 157 | 310 |
| 1986 | 21 699 | 325 |
| 1987 | 22 152 | 350 |
| 1988 | 24 196 | 403 |

Source: Department of Transport

(a) The table of transport in Great Britain given above contains two sets of data expressed in different terms. By means of a ratio-scale graph show how these two sets of data may be compared. Use natural scale paper.

(b) Comment on the situation revealed by your graph.

### 3.2 (a) Describe four diagrammatic methods of presenting numerical data.

(b) The following hypothetical data shows the state of weather in London on ten consecutive days.

| Day | 1 | 2 | 3 | 4 | 5 | 6 | 7 | 8 | 9 | 10 |
|---|---|---|---|---|---|---|---|---|---|---|
| Noon temp. (°C) | 19 | 18 | 17 | 20 | 21 | 19 | 18 | 20 | 22 | 19 |
| | C | W | W | S | S | C | W | S | S | C |

(C = cloudy, W = wet and S = sunny)

By using appropriate diagrammatic methods, illustrate:

(i)  the proportion of days which were cloudy, wet and sunny; and

(ii) how the noon temperature varied from day to day.

**3.3** (a) Plot the following two series on the same diagram using semi-logarithmic graph paper to show their relative movements and comment on the results.

(b) How could a similar comparison be achieved without using semi-logarithmic paper?

**Growth of a company**

| | 19X0 | 19X1 | 19X2 | 19X3 | 19X4 |
|---|---|---|---|---|---|
| Turnover (£) | 70 000 | 400 000 | 1 200 000 | 1 800 000 | 4 100 000 |
| Cost of materials (£) | 30 000 | 160 000 | 500 000 | 750 000 | 1 400 000 |

**3.4** (a) For what reasons do we use semi-logarithmic or ratio-scale graph paper rather than the more usual arithmetic scale paper?

(b) Plot the data given below, on semi-logarithmic paper.

(c) Comment briefly on what your graph shows.

**Consumer expenditure in the UK in £billion at current prices 1980–1989**

| | 1980 | 1983 | 1986 | 1989 |
|---|---|---|---|---|
| Total | 46.318 | 61.204 | 74.791 | 98.686 |
| Food | 23.655 | 28.058 | 33.070 | 39.181 |
| Rent and rates | 16.153 | 24.024 | 30.173 | 40.003 |
| Motor vehicles | 6.510 | 9.112 | 11.548 | 19.502 |

Source: Central Statistical Office

**3.5**   The following table shows civil aviation revenues (£m) between 1982 and 1991.

|      | Overseas passenger revenue £m | Freight on UK exports £m |
|------|------|------|
| 1982 | 1119 | 129 |
| 1983 | 1304 | 146 |
| 1984 | 1560 | 175 |
| 1985 | 1749 | 180 |
| 1986 | 1653 | 209 |
| 1987 | 1991 | 230 |
| 1988 | 1932 | 236 |
| 1989 | 2304 | 280 |
| 1990 | 2656 | 285 |
| 1991 | 2363 | 211 |

Source: *CSO Pink Book*, 1992

Graph this data on a semi-logarithmic scale, and use your graph to compare passenger and freight revenues over the period.

**3.6**   **Consumer expenditure on certain items at 1985 prices (£b)**

|      | Food (£b) | Engery products (£b) | Durable goods (£b) |
|------|------|------|------|
| 1979 | 21.0 | 17.5 | 16.2 |
| 1980 | 23.7 | 17.3 | 15.4 |
| 1981 | 25.0 | 17.3 | 15.7 |
| 1982 | 26.5 | 17.4 | 16.5 |
| 1983 | 28.1 | 17.4 | 19.4 |
| 1984 | 29.3 | 17.7 | 19.3 |
| 1985 | 30.7 | 18.5 | 20.3 |
| 1986 | 33.1 | 19.3 | 22.2 |
| 1987 | 34.5 | 19.6 | 24.5 |
| 1988 | 36.6 | 20.3 | 27.7 |
| 1989 | 39.2 | 20.1 | 29.3 |

Source: Central Statistical Office

Using semi-logarithmic graphs, compare expenditure on the three classes of goods over the period.

**3.7**   (a)   Plot the following data using arithmetic scale graph paper.

| Period | 1 | 2 | 3 | 4 | 5 | 6 | 7 | 8 |
|--------|-----|-----|-----|------|------|------|------|------|
| Data   | 200 | 320 | 640 | 1180 | 2080 | 4050 | 6480 | 9030 |

(b) Describe two methods of drafting a semi-logarithmic curve when no semi-logarithmic graph paper is available. Using one of those methods plot the data and state the advantages and disadvantages of using the semi-log scale over the more usual arithmetic scale.     CIMA

**3.8**     **Stoppages of work due to industrial disputes**

|  | Number of stoppages | Aggregate working days lost in these stoppages (to nearest thousand) |
|---|---|---|
| Under 250 days | 1200 | 125 |
| 250 and under 500 | 453 | 161 |
| 500 and under 1 000 | 402 | 282 |
| 1 000 and under 5 000 | 592 | 1250 |
| 5 000 and under 25 000 | 180 | 1844 |
| 25 000 and under 50 000 | 24 | 859 |
| 50 000 days and over | 22 | 2625 |

Illustrate the above data by means of a Lorenz curve. Why is this form of graph the most suitable for displaying the above information?

**3.9** (a) Construct a Lorenz curve in respect of the following data concerning the net output of manufacturing industry X:

**Manufacturing industry X**

| Average number of employees | Number of firms | Net output (£m) |
|---|---|---|
| 25 and under 100 | 205 | 16 |
| 100 and under 300 | 200 | 60 |
| 300 and under 500 | 35 | 18 |
| 500 and under 750 | 30 | 26 |
| 750 and under 1000 | 20 | 26 |
| 1000 and under 1500 | 10 | 54 |

(b) Explain the purpose of presenting information in the form of the Lorenz curve, and comment on your answer to (a) above.     ACCA

**3.10**   A sales department of a firm might plot a Z chart to check or monitor the annual performance of its sales staff. Describe such a chart with an example and explain how it is used.                                                                                    ACCA

**3.11**   The production figures for a company were as follows:

|      | *Jan*   | *Feb*   | *Mar*   | *Apr*   | *May*   | *June*  |
|------|---------|---------|---------|---------|---------|---------|
| 1987 | 60 746  | 57 071  | 63 621  | 66 014  | 71 736  | 80 213  |
| 1988 | 68 123  | 58 983  | 60 693  | 61 247  | 67 778  | 76 567  |

|      | *July*  | *Aug*   | *Sept*  | *Oct*   | *Nov*   | *Dec*    |
|------|---------|---------|---------|---------|---------|----------|
| 1987 | 91 780  | 92 314  | 76 770  | 67 123  | 71 512  | 87 490   |
| 1988 | 92 124  | 99 632  | 104 210 | 99 634  | 88 241  | 107 870  |

(a)   Round the above production figures to the nearest thousand.

(b)   Use the rounded figures to produce a Z chart for 1988.

(c)   Comment on your chart.

**3.12**       **Road vehicles in Great Britain: new registrations (thousands)**

|           | 1990 (000s) | 1991 (000s) |
|-----------|-------------|-------------|
| January   | 242.0       | 191.2       |
| February  | 204.3       | 147.1       |
| March     | 253.9       | 204.3       |
| April     | 201.2       | 152.0       |
| May       | 212.2       | 147.0       |
| June      | 176.7       | 123.9       |
| July      | 64.7        | 52.1        |
| August    | 498.8       | 420.8       |
| September | 189.1       | 154.4       |
| October   | 161.9       | 125.7       |
| November  | 148.7       | 123.7       |
| December  | 84.5        | 79.3        |

Source: *Monthly Digest of Statistics*

From the information given, construct a Z chart for 1991. Explain when you might find such charts used and comment briefly on the advantages of representing data in this way.

**3.13**      **Tonnage and service speed of passenger liners of the X-Y Company**

| Gross tonnage | Service speed (knots) |
|---|---|
| 26 000 | 25.0 |
| 21 700 | 24.0 |
| 26 000 | 25.0 |
| 21 630 | 24.0 |
| 20 300 | 19.4 |
| 15 020 | 21.6 |
| 15 010 | 21.6 |
| 20 100 | 20.0 |
| 26 300 | 24.6 |
| 21 660 | 20.5 |
| 10 470 | 19.4 |
| 20 450 | 22.2 |
| 11 730 | 20.1 |
| 12 150 | 19.9 |
| 16 990 | 19.6 |
| 19 930 | 19.4 |
| 14 440 | 19.0 |
| 19 420 | 19.3 |

(a) What is the purpose of analysing data by means of a scatter diagram?

(b) Draw a scatter diagram to illustrate above figures.

(c) Comment on what the diagram reveals.

# 4 Approximation and error

Does it surprise you that in a course on Statistics we should devote a whole chapter to the subject of error? Surely the aim of a course such as this should be to teach you about accuracy, not about errors. You may believe, in fact, that we should devote our time to teaching you how to avoid error.

This apparently strange chapter becomes less strange if we consider what we mean by error. To the majority of people trained in answering mathematical problems, the very idea of error implies that we have made a mistake. Certainly, if we say that $4 + 3 - 2 = 6$, we have made an error in our calculations, and our answer is wrong. It would be futile to pretend that this sort of thing does not happen in statistical work. No-one is perfect, and even writers of textbooks sometimes make mistakes that would cause a first-year student to feel ashamed.

Even if our calculations are accurate, our answers may still be wrong because of deficiencies in our raw material. We doubt very much if even the Census of Population taken, in the United Kingdom, every 10 years, can claim to be completely accurate. The investigator might not ask the right questions; the respondent may tick the wrong answer; the statistician might analyse the data wrongly, or he might misread his figures, writing 796 instead of 769 when constructing his frequency distributions. There are so many possible mistakes that can be made that one sometimes wonders whether any statistician can ever guarantee 100% accuracy.

When, however, we talk of statistical error, it is not in this sense that we are using the word. Often it is inconvenient, or impossible, to give figures which are correct to the last unit. When we say that 1.7 m children die every year in a particular area, we obviously do not mean that exactly 1 700 000 children die every year. What we are saying is that approximately 1.7 m children die, and a note at the head of our table will tell us the extent of our approximation. It is very likely that a figure such as this would be accurate to the nearest 0.1 of a million. The annual number of deaths, that is, could be anything between 1 650 000 and 1 750 000. In quoting 1.7 m, we could be as far as 50 000 different from the absolutely accurate figure. It is this difference between the approximate figure and the true figure that the statistician calls 'error'. It is, then, a very different concept from that of a mistake. When we make a mistake we do not know the amount by which our results are wrong; when we speak of error we are qualifying the degree of accuracy of our result. Then, too, a mistake is usually involuntary and something to be avoided; approximations are made to improve the presentation of our figures and in this sense the creation of statistical error is deliberate. So useful is the idea of approximation that you will find very few statistical tabulations which give figures with absolute accuracy, and this is understandable. Which of the following statements do you think that you could remember more easily? 'The output of steel was 110 m tonnes' or 'The output of steel was 109 764 397 tonnes'. The widespread use of approximations, however, means that any conclusions drawn from our figures are themselves subject to error, and we must look very carefully at the effects of approximating our figures.

## Approximation

Suppose we come across a table telling us the number of cattle in our country at a particular date. We might find the heading of the column in which we are interested reads '*No. of cattle (million)*'. What does this mean precisely? The fact that we have 'million' in brackets tells us that the person who has constructed the table has approximated his figures to the nearest million. Thus, if he tells us that the number of cattle in the country was 25 m, we know that the true figure must lie between 24 500 000 and 25 500 000. If it were any less than 24 500 000 the approximated figure would be 24 m, if it were any more than 25 500 000 the approximated figure would be 26 m. A problem arises of course if the true figure were exactly 24.5 or exactly 25.5 m. Do we raise or lower the figure in order to approximate? A good general rule is to look at the number of millions, and if it is an odd number raise it, if it is an even number lower it.

If we were approximating to the nearest thousand we would naturally look to see whether we had an even or odd number of thousands, and so on.

In tabular work it is often enough to put the degree of approximation in brackets like this: (millions). For other purposes it may be much more convenient to give the approximated figure and append to it the maximum amount of the possible error. Thus we could express exactly the same information as before in the form:

No. of cattle = 25 m ± 500 000

Occasionally too it is convenient to express the error in percentage form, and we could say:

No. of cattle = 25 m ± 2%

Each of these three statements say exactly the same thing. It makes little difference which way you put it. What is important is that whenever you approximate you should indicate clearly the basis of your approximation.

If you are approximating a number of figures and then totalling them, a peculiar result may arise. It is possible that when you add the approximated figures you do not get the same result as when you approximate the exact total. For example:

|  | *Actual output*<br>*(tonnes)* | *Output*<br>*(million tonnes)* |
|---|---|---|
| Firm A | 102 428 621 | 102 |
| Firm B | 204 364 147 | 204 |
| Firm C | 673 424 961 | 673 |
|  | 980 217 729 | 980 not 979 |

You can see that, because of the approximation, the addition of the approximated totals is only 979. But the total output to the nearest million tonnes is 980 m. This is the figure that goes in the total of the approximated figures and you must *never* adjust it merely to make your additions seem to be right.

## Biassed and unbiassed errors

When we are dealing with a number of figures that we are totalling, the amount of error in our total depends to a very large extent on the way in which we are approximating. If we are approximating to the *nearest* hundred (or thousand, or million), some of our approximated figures will be too high, others will be too low. But the excesses and the deficits will tend to cancel each other out and the aggregate error will probably be very small. In fact, the greater the number of items we consider, the smaller is the total error likely to be relative to the actual total. Such an error is said to be *unbiassed*, because it is not consistently in the same direction. Suppose we are approximating the following figures:

|  | *Actual figures* | *To nearest thousand* | *Error* |
|---|---|---|---|
|  | 81 171 | 81 | −171 |
|  | 316 | 0 | −316 |
|  | 3 521 | 4 | +479 |
|  | 2 638 | 3 | +362 |
|  | 34 451 | 34 | −451 |
|  | 5 467 | 5 | −567 |
|  | 95 711 | 96 | +289 |
|  | 90 501 | 91 | +499 |
|  | 842 | 1 | +158 |
| Total | 314 618 | 315 | +382 |

As you can see, the error in the approximated total is only $+382$ in a total of 315 000, an error of only 0.12%; it is equally apparent that the reason for such a small error is that the positive and negative errors offset each other.

But suppose we were to approximate to the nearest thousand above, or to the nearest thousand below. Here the picture is very different. Far from offsetting each other, the errors are all in the same direction and the aggregate error is cumulative. We can see what a tremendous difference it makes to the error in our total if we use the same figures as above, but approximate them differently:

| | *Approximation to the nearest thousand* | |
|---|---|---|
| *Actual figures* | *Above* | *Below* |
| 81 171 | 82 | 81 |
| 316 | 1 | 0 |
| 3 521 | 4 | 3 |
| 2 638 | 3 | 2 |
| 34 451 | 35 | 34 |
| 5 467 | 6 | 5 |
| 95 711 | 96 | 95 |
| 90 501 | 91 | 90 |
| 842 | 1 | 0 |
| 314 618 | 319 | 310 |
| Error | $+4382$ | $-4618$ |
| Percentage error | $+1.39\%$ | $-1.46\%$ |

This type of error is known as a *biassed* error – for obvious reasons, and, as you can see, the aggregate error is dramatically larger than the aggregate unbiassed error. Why, then, should we ever concern ourselves with biassed errors? Often, when we are collecting statistics, an element of error may creep into every figure we collect. Many people argue, for example, that if we are collecting ages every woman will tend to understate her age. Whether this is correct or not, it is certainly true that if we are recording temperature or atmospheric pressure on an instrument which is recording wrongly, we will consistently overstate or understate the true reading. The error that results in any of these cases will be a biassed error, and we must learn to be aware of it.

You should also beware of data that has built-in biassed error – this is not as rare as you might think. There are many examples of data expressed correct to the last complete unit – age is expressed correct to the last completed year, the electricity and telephone companies bill us to the last complete unit consumed.

## Absolute and relative error

You will have noticed that in the last section we said that the unbiassed error in the figures we were discussing was $+382$ or $+0.12\%$. When we state it as $+382$ we are measuring the arithmetic difference between the actual total and the approximated total, and this we call the *absolute* error. Unfortunately, the size of the absolute error does not give us any indication of the importance of the error involved. An error of five in a total of 50 is of much greater importance relatively than an error of 500 in a total of 50 000. To enable us to compare the extent of the error when widely differing totals are involved, the relative error is used. This is merely the absolute error expressed as a percentage of the approximated total.

## Calculations involving error

In both theory and practice we often have to make calculations in which error is present. We might wish to know the number of children likely to be born next year in our local town in order to plan maternity services. But the population statistics may well be available only to the nearest thousand, and the birth rate only accurate to one place of decimals. Similarly if we are planning the building of schools two or three years ahead, we need to know the number of children likely to be born in the relevant years, and also the number of those who will die before reaching school age. We will also want to know the number of children who will move out of the area with their parents, and the number of children who will move into the area. All these figures are usually available, but every one of them is approximate, and the potential amount of error involved in any calculation can be very large.

Fortunately, provided we know the amount of error involved in each of our figures, it is simple to calculate the probable degree of error arising in the final result.

**Addition and subtraction**

Let us look first at the simple processes of addition and subtraction. Suppose we are adding together 50 000 correct to the nearest 1000 and 3600 correct to the nearest 100:

that is, $(50\,000 \pm 500) + (3600 \pm 50)$

The maximum result we could possibly obtain would be when we added together the two largest figures, i.e. $50\,500 + 3650 = 54\,150$. The smallest results we could get is when we add together the two smallest numbers, i.e. $49\,500 + 3550 = 53\,050$. Thus, our result would lie between $53\,050$ and $54\,150$ which we may state as $53\,600 \pm 550$.

Let us now subtract $727 \pm 15$ from $926 \pm 20$. Here the maximum result is obtained when we subtract the smallest total from the largest: $946 - 712 = 234$. The minimum result is obtained when we subtract the largest figure that 727 could reach from the smallest figure that 926 could reach: $906 - 742 = 164$. Our result lies between 234 and 164, and again we can express this as $199 \pm 35$.

We will now put these two results together and look at them carefully:

$$(50\,000 \pm 500) + (3600 \pm 50) = 53\,600 \pm 550$$

$$(\ \ \ 926 \pm \ \ 20) - (\ 727 \pm 15) = \ \ \ 199 \pm \ \ 35$$

It is apparent that when we are adding or subtracting we perform the normal arithmetic process ignoring the fact that the figures are approximated, and that the maximum possible error to which this total is subject is plus or minus the sum of the individual *absolute* errors. Be careful when performing this calculation. You will often find that one or more errors are given as relative errors, but the rule applies only to the sum of the absolute errors.

The result could be of importance to any manufacturer, especially during a time when his costs are likely to vary. Suppose that a garment manufacturer wishes to know what price he should quote for cotton shirts to be delivered in six months' time. He knows that his average fixed cost will be 35p per shirt but that his supplies of cotton may cost up to 20% more or 20% less than the current cost of 85p per shirt. Similarly, his wage cost will be £1.20 ± 5p per shirt depending on changes in productivity and wage rates. His total cost per shirt would be:

$$[35 + (85 \pm 20\%) + (120 \pm 5)] \text{ p or } [35 + (85 \pm 17) + (120 \pm 5)] \text{ p and}$$
this equals £2.40 ± 0.22.

He could not then be sure of making a profit unless he sold his shirts at a price greater than £2.62 each. Of course, if all went extremely well he might be able to break even if he sold at a price as low as £2.18, but he cannot be sure of this. You will notice that in his calculation, in the case in which a percentage error was given we immediately changed it into the absolute error.

**Multiplication and division**

When we come to multiplication and division we find that the assessment of error in the answer is not quite as simple. We find that the error that arises in one direction is different, and often very different, from that arising in the other. Suppose we are multiplying $40 \pm 10\%$ by $20 \pm 5\%$. The result is 800 plus and minus an error. The largest figure we could get is

$44 \times 21 = 924$, an error of $+124$ or $+15.5\%$. To our surprise, however, when we calculate the smallest figure it is $36 \times 19 = 684$, an error of only $-116$ or $-14.5\%$.

When multiplying two approximate values, it is customary to state the *largest* error that could occur, so the result above would be given as $800 \pm 15.5\%$. The same thing is true when we are dividing. If we are dividing $1000 \pm 50$ by $100 \pm 10$ the quotient is $10$. The largest error that could occur is when the result of our division is a maximum, and this occurs when we divide the largest dividend by the smallest possible divisor, i.e. $1050 \div 90 = 11.667$. Thus the largest error could be $+1.667$ or $+16.67\%$, and our result is stated as:

$$(1000 \pm 50) \div (100 \pm 10) = 10 \pm 16.67\%$$

You should not try to remember the formulae for these operations devised by some earlier writers. Remember the basic principle – the maximum error is always possible and it is this, therefore, that should be quoted. Remember too that no amount of juggling with figures can increase accuracy when you are dealing with approximated figures. The accuracy of your result can never be better than, and can seldom be even as good as, the least accurate of the figures used in your calculation.

Let us conclude this chapter by looking at an exercise set by the Institute of Statisticians.

---

EXAMPLE

A motorist whose car has a broken mileage recorder and who measures distance travelled by map reading, wishes to assess his petrol consumption in miles per gallon, on a European trip. His petrol gauge indicates his fuel consumption in litres with an error of $\pm 10\%$. He also uses approximate conversion figures of 1 gallon = 4.5 litres and 1 mile = 1.6 kilometres instead of the more accurate 1 gallon = 4.55 litres and 1 mile = 1.61 kilometres.

Estimate his total fuel consumption in miles per gallon if he claims to be getting 31 miles per gallon after a trip of exactly 615 miles.

Notice that here only the amount of petrol consumed is subject to error in the sense in which we have been discussing it. The remaining errors are errors in converting litres into gallons and kilometres into miles. So first let us eliminate the errors made when converting metric into Imperial measurement.

When our motorist says that he has travelled 615 miles, he is in fact saying that he has travelled $615 \times 1.6 = 984$ kilometres. But, of course, this is not really 615 miles since he used the wrong conversion factor. The distance travelled in miles is really $984 \div 1.61 = 611.18$.

Now a motorist who says he is getting a petrol consumption of 31 miles per gallon on a trip of 615 miles, is saying that he has used $615 \div 31 = 19.84$ gallons of petrol, or, as his gauge reads in litres, $19.84 \times 4.5$ litres of petrol, or 89.28 litres. We know, however, that this reading is subject to a 10% error, so the true petrol consumption lies somewhere between $89.28 + 8.928$ litres, and $89.28 - 8.928$, between 98.208 and 80.352 litres. In gallons then his petrol consumption for the journey of 611.18 miles lay somewhere between $98.208 \div 4.55$ and $80.352 \div 4.55$ gallons, between 21.584 and 17.66 gallons.

We now have the motorist's true mileage and the true limits of his petrol consumption. Thus his fuel consumption lies between $611.18 \div 21.584$ and $611.18 \div 17.66$ miles per gallon, or between 28.32 and 34.61 miles per gallon.

This seems to be quite a wide range and is possibly not a very satisfactory answer to our problem. What you must remember is that when we say between 28.32 and 34.61 we are quoting extreme limits. It does not seem half as bad if we put the solution as $31.465 \pm 3.145$ miles per gallon. Here the implication given is that the motorist will get about 31.5 miles to the gallon subject to a small error of about three miles per gallon either way. The concentration is switched from extreme figures and quite a wide range to a central figure with only about 10% error.

Enough has been said in this chapter to warn you against reading too much into published statistics. In all but a few cases, figures are quoted approximately and hence are subject to error. You can imagine the size of the error in your conclusions if you begin to calculate using figures approximated to the nearest hundred million. Fortunately, as you will see, most calculations of error in statistics do not involve magnitudes as great as this, and the calculation of the probable error in our results can indeed be extremely useful.

## QUESTIONS

**4.1** Write an essay on the importance of accuracy and approximation when using statistics.

**4.2** (a) Explain what is meant by the term 'error' in statistics and the circumstances in which it may arise.

(b) 2.91; 3.473; 8.2; 4.005.

    (i) Add the above rounded figures and state the answer as accurately as possible, showing the limits of error.

    (ii) Calculate the percentage relative error in (i).

(c) (i) The death rate of the population of a certain town was stated to be 15.5 per thousand when the population was known to be 22 000 expressed to the nearest thousand. Calculate, as accurately as possible, the number of deaths during the year.

    (ii) Calculate the percentage relative error in (i).

**4.3** An inventor plans to set up a business to manufacture and market a product which incorporates his recently patented device. He considers the product will sell for £10 and that in the first year 120 000 plus or minus 20% will be sold. The cost of the materials in the product is estimated at £4, a figure which is considered to be correct to within 10%, similarly, the labour cost is estimated at £1.50 but it is thought that it could increase by 20%. The first year's fixed costs are expected to be £100 000 plus or minus 5%. You are required to calculate for the first year:

(a) the estimated profit,

(b) the minimum expected profit, and

(c) the maximum expected profit.                                                  AIA

**4.4** A builder has a plot of land on which he can build 350 houses. His costs are estimated as follows:

|           | £                                      |
|-----------|----------------------------------------|
| Land      | 10 000 000                             |
| Materials | 3 750 000 to the nearest £10 000       |
| Labour    | 5 000 000 ± 2%                         |
| Overheads | 3 000 000 ± 5%                         |

He intends to sell the houses at £79 000 ± £1250 each. Assuming he sells all the houses, estimate his profit from the contract (express the answer in the form of £x ± error).

**4.5** Statistical data is frequently rounded in some way before calculations begin or schedules compiled.

(a) What advantages are obtained from rounding?

(b) Explain what is meant by the terms: unbiassed error, biassed error, absolute error, relative error, and illustrate each by using the following actual figures:

| | |
|---|---|
| 56 321 | 998 |
| 1 465 | 15 431 |
| 43 501 | 9 702 |
| 2 786 | 11 100 |
| 12 157 | 7 009 |

CIMA

**4.6**     **Return of 12 American banks at 31 December 19X9**

| | |
|---|---|
| Total advances | $2.830 million |
| Ratio of advances to deposits | 25.8% |
| Ratio of cash to deposits | 12.4% |

Given that the above figures are correct to three significant figures, estimate (a) the amount of deposits and (b) the amount of cash. State the limits of error in each case.

**4.7**  Calculate the answers required in each of the following cases. Give the limits of error. The degree of approximation is given.

(a)  (i)  $(283 \pm 3\%) + (146 \pm 1\%)$

(ii)  $(490 \pm 3\%) - (230 \pm 1\%)$

(b)  Total bank advances £984m.
Ratio of advances to deposits 15.5%.
Both figures are correct to three significant figures.
Estimate the amount of deposits.

(c)  Area sown 3 982 000 to the nearest 500 hectares.
Yield per hectare 0.5 tonnes correct to the nearest tonne.
Estimate the total yield in tonnes.

**4.8**  (a)  If $A = 5600$ to the nearest hundred and $B = 120$ to the nearest ten, calculate (i) $A + B$, and (ii) $A - B$, giving the absolute and relative errors in both cases.

(b)  Using logarithms or a calculator find the value of each of the following correct to three significant figures.

(i)  $$\frac{11 \times 136 - 3 \times 5}{\sqrt{[(11 \times 167 - 3^2)(11 \times 148 - 5^2)]}}$$

(ii)  $\sqrt[4]{(268 \times 343 \times 496 \times 534)}$

**4.9**  Imports of motor cars and motor cycles into a country in 19X9

|  | Unit | No. of units imported | Total value (£m) |
|---|---|---|---|
| Motor cars | thousands | 10.3 | 86 |
| Motor cycles | thousands | 42.6 | 28 |

Each entry is correct to the number of figures given in the table. Calculate the average import price per vehicle of each type and state the limits of error.

**4.10**  (a) What are the advantages of using approximate amounts?

(b) The total output of 86 businesses amounted to 3 829 000 tonnes. Estimate the possible error in the figure if, in arriving at the total:

(i) the output of each business had been rounded off to the nearest thousand tonnes;

(ii) the output of each business had been rounded off to the nearest thousand tonnes above the actual figure.

(c) (i) Factory A produced 28 m tonnes in 1973. The number of workers was 206 000. Calculate the average output per worker and indicate the possible absolute error of your answer if it is suspected that both of the values have been rounded off.

(ii) Factory B produces 1250 (to the nearest 10) tins of pink powder per batch and 2700 (to the nearest 10) tins of white powder per batch. Each tin contains between 80 and 100 grams of powder. Calculate the total weight of powder in a consignment of two batches of pink powder and one batch of white powder sent to a customer. Show the relative error of your total.

**4.11**  Value of UK exports of chemicals and related products, 1991

|  | £m |
|---|---|
| Organic chemicals | 324.0 |
| Inorganic chemicals | 88.3 |
| Dyeing, tanning and colouring materials | 101.1 |
| Medicinal and pharmaceutical products | 239.2 |
| Essential oils and perfume materials, toilet, polishing and cleansing materials | 132.2 |
| Fertilisers | 7.9 |
| Plastics in primary form | 109.5 |
| Plastics in non-primary form | 67.5 |
| Others | 165.7 |
| Total | 1235.4 |

Source: *Monthly Digest of Statistics*, November 1992

    (a)  Approximate the above data to

        (i)  the nearest million;

        (ii)  the nearest 10 million.

    (b)  Estimate the absolute and percentage relative error of the totals obtained in (a).

**4.12**  A firm's estimated sales for 1993 are 83 000 units at a price of £5 each. These figures are liable to errors of 1% and 5% respectively. The estimated costs are:

    Wages £72 500 ± 2%
    Materials £125 000 ± 4%
    Other expenses £41 500 ± 3%.

    (a)  Calculate the approximate net profit for the year giving the limits of possible error.

    (b)  Calculate the relative errors in the estimate of net profit.

**4.13**      **Personal incomes UK, 1991**

| | £000m | % |
|---|---|---|
| Consumer expenditure | | |
|   Food | 44 | 8.6 |
|   Other | 324 | 63.7 |
| Income tax | 64 | 12.6 |
| National Insurance | 37 | 7.3 |
| Savings | 40 | 7.8 |
| Total personal income | 509 | 100.0 |

Source: *National Income and Expenditure*, 1992

The data given in the table are rounded to the nearest £1000 m. Calculate, giving the error in each case:

    (a)  Consumer expenditure

    (b)  Income after tax

    (c)  The aggregate amount saved given total personal incomes and % savings

    (d)  Percentage savings given aggregated savings and total personal incomes.

**4.14**  The following data show the value of UK exports in 1991 to the European Community and to the rest of Western Europe.

| European Community | £m |
|---|---|
| France | 10 885.8 |
| Belgium and Luxembourg | 5 648.6 |
| Netherlands | 5 716.6 |
| FRG | 13 226.4 |
| Italy | 5 612.8 |
| Irish Republic | 5 311.5 |
| Denmark | 1 413.7 |
| Greece | 682.9 |
| Spain | 3 750.1 |
| Portugal | 1 033.3 |

| Rest of Western Europe | £m |
|---|---|
| Norway | 1 289.8 |
| Sweden | 2 712.8 |
| Finland | 1 041.7 |
| Switzerland | 2 258.5 |
| Austria | 705.9 |
| Turkey | 606.8 |
| Other | 323.0 |

Source: Department of Trade and Industry

(a)  Obtain totals for both the European Community and the Rest of Western Europe.

(b)  Round off each figure in an unbiassed sense to the nearest £10 million and again obtain the totals.

(c)  Calculate the relative error in total resulting from your rounding for the European Community.

(d)  If you wish to take the difference between exports to the European Community and exports to the rest of Western Europe, how would you round your totals if you wished your rounding errors at that stage to be compensatory?

**4.15**  A company is marketing a new product to sell at £5. The sales for the first year are expected to be 50 000 ± 10%. The costs are calculated to be:

Fixed overheads £40 000 ± 5%
Variable costs £3 per unit sold.

Calculate:

(a)  the net profit which can be obtained, giving the limits;

(b)  the rate of net profit to sales and the limits;

(c)  the net profit if there were no variation?

**4.16**   (a)   Define the terms:

     (i)    absolute error,
     (ii)   relative error,
     (iii)  compensating error.

    (b)   A firm works a nominal 40-hour week but with overtime and short time its actual working week varies by as much as half an hour from the nominal figure. The firm produces $(50 \pm 1)$ articles per hour. If the production costs and selling prices are £2.00 and £3.00 respectively per unit rounded off to the nearest 10p, estimate:

     (i)   the weekly profit;

     (ii)  the percentage profit, based on cost price, per unit sold (to the nearest 0.5%).

**4.17**   (a)   Use logarithms or a calculator to find the value of each of the following, correct to three significant figures.

     (i)    $\sqrt{468} + (24.3)^2$

     (ii)   $1 - \dfrac{6 \times 728}{16(16^2 - 1)}$

     (iii)  $37.5 + \dfrac{117 - 89}{83} \times 4$

    (b)   If $x = 90.8956$, write the value of $x$ correct to

     (i)    four significant figures,

     (ii)   three decimal places,

     (iii)  the nearest integer,

     (iv)   the nearest tenth.

# 5 The averaging of data

So far, we have concentrated our attention on organising and presenting data. What we shall now do is attempt to summarise the data at our disposal into a single statistic. This will certainly ease the task of making comparisons, though we must always remember that summarising data is bound to mean that something will be lost.

If you think carefully about it, you will realise that statisticians spend a great deal of their time making comparisons, and the conclusions they reach are often of fundamental importance to every one of us. Comparing income today with income 10 years ago is an indicator of how our living standards have changed. Comparing incomes between regions helps the government in its regional policies. Comparing how our prices are changing over time in relation to price changes abroad indicates how competitive our industries are, and comparing our balance of payments over time indicates our ability to pay our way in the world.

Many of the comparisons made present no problems, as we are comparing a single figure value. For example, we can state that ICI earned a certain profit in 1988, and compare this with the profit earned in 1989. Any problems involved in this comparison will be concerned with the calculation of the profit and the rate of inflation, and no-one will dispute that it is legitimate to compare profit in 1988 with profit in 1989 as long as inflation is taken into account. In some cases, however, the things we are trying to compare vary in themselves. Suppose, for example, we attempt to compare incomes on Merseyside with incomes in London: not only is there a variation between the regions, but also a variation within each region. In a previous chapter you saw that we could put raw data into a frequency distribution, and present it in the form of a histogram, etc. No doubt we could draw histograms, showing the distribution of incomes in London and Merseyside, and this would enable us to state that incomes earned in London exceeded incomes earned on Merseyside. But is this good enough?

You can probably identify two problems in the statement above. First, do we mean that *all* incomes in London exceed *all* incomes on Merseyside? Obviously not! Many people on Merseyside will earn much more than, say, a porter on the London Underground. Second, given that incomes earned in London exceed incomes earned on Merseyside, we would wish to know by how much. In other words, we wish to *quantify* the differences in income, and we certainly will not be able to do this by just looking at a frequency distribution or a histogram. What we need is some figure that is *representative* of income in London. We can then obtain a representative figure for Merseyside incomes, compare them, and draw some conclusions as to the size of the difference in incomes.

How are we going to obtain this representative figure? You have probably guessed already, especially in the current economic climate with our preoccupation with income levels. The TV newscaster does not state that incomes have risen by 10% over the last 12 months: he states that *average* incomes have risen. We are given information on *average* hourly rates of pay, *average* rainfall levels, batting and bowling *averages*, the *average* amount we spend on drink – and so on. The advertising men are very fond of telling us what the *average man* buys, where he goes for his holidays, and what he does with his leisure.

Three conclusions can be drawn from this last paragraph.

- An average is obviously meant to tell us something about the matter under consideration, and unless it is representative of the data, it obviously cannot do this efficiently.

- The word 'average' is one that we meet daily in our conversation, and is a word that is used in a very loose manner. How many times have you heard people use such remarks as 'I *think* that on average I use *about* five gallons of petrol per week'? Here the idea of an average and an *estimate* are shading into each other. We must avoid this at all costs. An average is capable of being calculated from data, and so it is precise.

- Averages are used to describe a wide variety of data, and we must be really sure that we know what an average is. In fact there are many types of average, and we must be sure to select the right one for the right job. If we don't do this, then there is a great danger that the average we quote will not be representative of the data.

## The arithmetic mean

Most people will tell you to calculate an average something like this: total all the numbers in the group and divide by how many numbers there are in the group. So the average of 5, 7, 9, and 10 is:

$$\frac{5+7+9+10}{4} = 7.75$$

In fact, it is easier to demonstrate how to calculate an average than it is to explain how to calculate it. Now mathematicians have developed two useful symbols to overcome this problem. Suppose we put this group of figures we wish to average in a column, and give this column a heading $x$. The group we considered above would look like this:

$x$
5
7
9
10

If we wish to total these figures, the mathematician would state $\Sigma x$ – meaning take the sum of the column headed $x$. ($\Sigma$ is a Greek capital letter pronounced *sigma*.) Also, we state that there are $n$ figures in the column (in this case $n = 4$). So the expression:

$$\frac{\Sigma x}{n}$$

tells us precisely how to calculate the average. We stated earlier that there are many forms of average, and the average we have just calculated is called the *arithmetic mean*. Statisticians use the symbol $\bar{x}$ (pronounce it 'x-bar') to stand for the arithmetic mean, so we can write:

$$\bar{x} = \frac{\Sigma x}{n}$$

The arithmetic mean is certainly the most widely used average, both by statisticians and laymen. It will be useful, then, to examine in what sense it is representative. Returning to our example, we have:

$$x = 5, 7, 9, 10 \qquad \bar{x} = 7.75$$

Notice that the arithmetic mean represents not one single item in the group, so it cannot be representative in the sense that it is typical. It follows, then, that 'representative' means something other than typical. If we subtract the mean from each of the items in the group, we have:

$$-2.75, -0.75, +1.25, +2.25$$

We call each of these differences a *deviation* from the arithmetic mean. Notice that the sum of these deviations is zero. Using the sigma notation we have:

$$\Sigma(x - \bar{x}) = 0$$

So the arithmetic mean tells us the point about which the values in the group cluster ('mean' in fact means centre, and statisticians call averages measures of central tendency). This is what we imply when we state that the mean is representative. So we now have a definition of the arithmetic mean – a measure chosen such that the sum of the deviations from it is zero.

For the moment, we shall postpone judging whether this meaning of representative is valid, and concentrate on the important definition of the mean. In fact, the definition enables us in many cases to simplify our calculations of the arithmetic mean. Suppose we guess a value for the arithmetic mean (call this guess $x_0$). Now if our guess is correct, then the sum of the deviations from $x_0$ would be zero. If it isn't, then our guess was wrong, and we can adjust our guess to give the true value of the mean. Suppose, for example, we wish to find the arithmetic mean of the group:

$$100.1, 100.2, 100.4, 100.8$$

If we guess the mean to be 100, then the deviations are:

$$+0.1, +0.2, +0.4, +0.8, \quad \text{sum} = 1.5$$

Clearly, our guess was too low, and we must adjust our guess by:

$$\frac{+1.5}{4} = +0.375$$

so the true value of the mean is:

$$100 + 0.375 = 100.375$$

(You should check this value by calculating the mean directly.) We can again use the sigma sign to show precisely how to use this method to calculate the arithmetic mean:

$$\bar{x} = x_0 + \frac{\Sigma(x - x_0)}{n}$$

In other words, the arithmetic mean is the assumed mean plus a correction factor.

Now let us examine another factor of the arithmetic mean which will simplify calculations. We can multiply or divide the group of numbers we wish to average, and find the average of this adjusted group. We can then adjust the average we have calculated to the true value. Suppose, for example, we want to find the arithmetic mean of the group:

$$0.0002, 0.0005, 0.0012, 0.0015$$

Multiplying this group by 10 000 we have:

2, 5, 12, 15

which has a mean of 8.5. To obtain a true value for the mean, we now divide by 10 000 giving:

$\bar{x} = 0.00085$

Of course, in many cases we would not bother to use either of the simplifications mentioned – especially as you probably have access to an electronic calculator. Later, though, we shall meet cases where they speed up our calculations considerably, and also lessen the risk of arithmetic error.

## The arithmetic mean of a frequency distribution

Earlier we recommended that you put raw data into frequency distributions wherever possible, so we must now examine how to find their arithmetic mean. If we consult the General Household Survey, we would learn that 1000 couples married eight years ago would be expected to have the following number of children now:

| Number of children | 0 | 1 | 2 | 3 | 4 |
| --- | --- | --- | --- | --- | --- |
| Number of families | 364 | 362 | 226 | 44 | 4 |

We require to know the mean number of children per family. First, we will write the data into two columns, one headed $x$ (the number of children – this is our variable) and the other headed $f$ (frequency). If we multiply the columns together ($fx$) this will give the total number of children for each family size. So, for example, we see that there are a total of 132 children from three-children families:

| $x$ | $f$ | $fx$ |
| --- | --- | --- |
| 0 | 364 | 0 |
| 1 | 362 | 362 |
| 2 | 226 | 452 |
| 3 | 44 | 132 |
| 4 | 4 | 16 |
| | 1000 | 962 |

Adding up the $fx$ column, there are a total of 962 children in the 1000 families, which gives an average of $\frac{962}{1000} = 0.962$ children per family. Now we know that $\Sigma f$ means total the column headed $f$ (this gives the total number of families) and $\Sigma fx$ means total the column headed $fx$ (which gives the total number of children). So we now know how to find the arithmetic mean of a discrete frequency distribution:

$$\bar{x} = \frac{\Sigma fx}{\Sigma f}$$

Now this is all very well, but much of the data is in the form of a grouped frequency distribution. Suppose we wished to find the average length of the metal pipes that we considered in Chapter 1. The distribution was:

| Length (cm) | Frequency |
|---|---|
| 10–20 | 3 |
| 20–30 | 7 |
| 30–40 | 10 |
| 40–50 | 16 |
| 50–60 | 34 |
| 60–70 | 13 |
| 70–80 | 7 |
| 80–90 | 6 |
| 90–100 | 4 |
| | 100 |

Now we have a problem here: look at the group 10–20. Within this group, there are three pipes, but we have no idea what their *actual* lengths are. We are going to have to make some assumption about their actual lengths. Probably the most sensible assumption to make is that the three pipes in this group have an average length of 15 cm – the mid-point of the group. If we do this for all groups, then we can use the formula we obtained earlier to calculate the arithmetic mean:

| Mid-point $x$ | Frequency $f$ | $fx$ |
|---|---|---|
| 15 | 3 | 45 |
| 25 | 7 | 175 |
| 35 | 10 | 350 |
| 45 | 16 | 720 |
| 55 | 34 | 1870 |
| 65 | 13 | 845 |
| 75 | 7 | 525 |
| 85 | 6 | 510 |
| 95 | 4 | 380 |
| | 100 | 5420 |

$$\bar{x} = \frac{\Sigma fx}{\Sigma f} = \frac{5420}{100} = 54.2 \text{ cm}$$

So the average length of the metal pipes is 54.2 cm.

Let us now see if we can simplify the arithmetic involved in these calculations. Just as we did earlier, we can take an assumed mean (in this case we take 55) and calculate the deviations of the items $x$ from 55. Notice that all the deviations are divisible by 10, and if we do this we have the column headed $d$:

| $x$ | $(x - 55)$ | $d$ | $f$ | $fd$ |
|-----|-----------|-----|-----|------|
| 15 | $-40$ | $-4$ | 3 | $-12$ |
| 25 | $-30$ | $-3$ | 7 | $-21$ |
| 35 | $-20$ | $-2$ | 10 | $-20$ |
| 45 | $-10$ | $-1$ | 16 | $-16$ |
| 55 | 0 | 0 | 34 | 0 |
| 65 | 10 | 1 | 13 | 13 |
| 75 | 20 | 2 | 7 | 14 |
| 85 | 30 | 3 | 6 | 18 |
| 95 | 40 | 4 | 4 | 16 |
| | | | 100 | $-8$ |

So the average deviation from the mean is $-8/100 = -0.08$ cm. But as we have divided the deviations by 10, we must multiply the average deviation by 10 to give $-0.8$ cm. In other words, our value for the assumed mean is 0.8 *greater* than the true value for the mean. So the true value for the mean is:

$$55 - 0.8 = 54.2 \text{ cm}$$

which agrees with the value we obtained previously.

Now if we say that $d$ is the deviation from the assumed mean divided by a constant $c$ then we can write a formula for our simplified method like this:

$$\bar{x} = x_0 + \frac{c\Sigma fd}{\Sigma f}$$

Notice that the constant $c$ is normally equal to the class width, though you can choose any value for $c$ which is convenient.

It will be interesting to examine the accuracy of the two means we have calculated. Considering first the mean number of children per family, the distribution gave us the exact number of children in each of the 1000 families. So our calculation of the mean number of children gave us the exact value for the mean: the same result would have been obtained if we had used the frequency distribution or the raw data. However, this is not so with the mean lengths of metal pipes as we did not know the exact lengths of the individual pipes. In fact, for the members of each class we found it necessary to make an assumption about their lengths, so we cannot guarantee the accuracy the mean. You should realise that although it is much more convenient to consider grouped frequency distributions than raw data, the price we pay for the convenience is the loss of accuracy. In most cases, however, the loss of accuracy is not too serious.

So far, we have considered frequency distributions with constant class widths. Now let us examine a case where the class width is uneven.

**Estimated distribution of weekly earnings of male manual workers in Ruritania**

| Weekly income ($) | Frequency (million) | Mid-point (x) |
|---|---|---|
| 80–100 | 0.2 | 90 |
| 100–120 | 0.4 | 110 |
| 120–140 | 0.5 | 130 |
| 140–160 | 0.6 | 150 |
| 160–180 | 0.7 | 170 |
| 180–200 | 0.7 | 190 |
| 200–250 | 1.2 | 225 |
| 250–300 | 0.6 | 275 |
| 300–350 | 0.3 | 325 |
| 350–400 | 0.1 | 375 |
| 400–500 | 0.1 | 450 |

In this case, we will take an assumed mean of 190 and simplify the deviations by dividing by five.

| x | (x – 190) | d | f | fd |
|---|---|---|---|---|
| 90 | – 100 | – 20 | 0.2 | – 4.0 |
| 110 | – 80 | – 16 | 0.4 | – 6.4 |
| 130 | – 60 | – 12 | 0.5 | – 6.0 |
| 150 | – 40 | – 8 | 0.6 | – 4.8 |
| 170 | – 20 | – 4 | 0.7 | – 2.8 |
| 190 | 0 | 0 | 0.7 | 0.0 |
| 225 | 35 | 7 | 1.2 | 8.4 |
| 275 | 85 | 17 | 0.6 | 10.2 |
| 325 | 135 | 27 | 0.3 | 8.1 |
| 375 | 185 | 37 | 0.1 | 3.7 |
| 450 | 260 | 52 | 0.1 | 5.2 |
| | | | 5.4 | 11.6 |

$$\bar{x} = 190 + 5 \times 11.6/5.4 = \$200.74$$

Sometimes, it is not practical to use the simplified method (it probably wasn't in the example above), and you should always weigh up carefully whether it is worth the effort involved. After all, modern cheap electronic calculators have taken all the drudgery out of multiplication.

# Limitations on the use of the arithmetic mean

Earlier, we postponed judgement on just how representative was the arithmetic mean. We simply stated that 'representative' certainly doesn't mean typical. The time has now come to put the arithmetic mean through a series of tests, and see how it performs.

If you examine sources of published statistics, you will be surprised how often frequency distributions have 'open-ended' classes. We reproduce below a frequency distribution showing the estimated wealth of individuals in Great Britain in 1989.

| Wealth | Frequency (thousands) |
|---|---|
| Not over £25 000 | 5518 |
| £25 000– £50 000 | 3372 |
| £50 000– £100 000 | 4010 |
| £100 000– £200 000 | 1846 |
| £200 000– £500 000 | 576 |
| £500 000–£1 000 000 | 76 |
| Over £1 000 000 | 22 |

Source: Inland Revenue, 1991

When we calculated the mean from a frequency distribution, we had to make assumptions about the values of the items in each class. We took the mid-point as the representative value of each class. But what assumptions can we make about the average wealth of individuals in the final class? It would be a brave man indeed who would estimate the upper limit for this group. Likewise, what would be a reasonable lower limit to put on the first class? Unless we have adequate information about the first and last groups, we cannot calculate the mean for this type of distribution. To obtain a mean, we must refer to the raw data (and this just is not available for government published statistics). Clearly, we need a measure that does not depend upon the adequate knowledge of extreme values of the distribution. This problem of open-ended statistics is one you will meet continually in analysis of published statistics – in fact we had quite a job finding distributions that were not open-ended! Before we leave this point, however, it should be stated that if you *must* estimate the missing limit for open-ended distributions, make sure that the frequencies in the open-ended classes are small in relation to other frequencies. Any inaccuracies due to estimates shouldn't, then, be too serious.

The second point about the arithmetic mean is that it often produces results that are not suitable from a communication viewpoint. Earlier, we found that the average number of children per family was 0.962. Most people would consider this to be a ridiculous statement. In situations like this, people expect an integer (i.e. a whole number) to be representative of the number of children per family. If we are going to ensure that all averages are integers, then we must change our idea of an average.

The third point is perhaps the most important of all: the mean is highly sensitive to extreme values. Consider the case of Fred, who at an interview for a job is told that the average income of salesmen in the company is £18 000 per year. He accepts the job as he considers the firm to be very progressive with excellent prospects for himself. Although his starting salary is only £12 000 a year, his salary will obviously climb very quickly. You could imagine how cheated Fred felt when he found that the sales force consisted of just five men: the sales director on £40 000 a year and four salesmen on £12 500 a year! The extreme value (in this case the sales director's salary) has caused the arithmetic mean to be most unrepresentative. To examine this point further, let us return again to the distribution of earnings of male manual workers. The cumulative frequency distribution would look like this:

**Estimated distribution of weekly earnings of male manual workers in Ruritania**

| Weekly income ($) | Cumulative frequency (million) |
|---|---|
| less than 100 | 0.2 |
| less than 120 | 0.6 |
| less than 140 | 1.1 |
| less than 160 | 1.7 |
| less than 180 | 2.4 |
| less than 200 | 3.1 |
| less than 250 | 4.3 |
| less than 300 | 4.9 |
| less than 350 | 5.2 |
| less than 400 | 5.3 |
| less than 500 | 5.4 |

Consulting this distribution we see that 3.1 m people earn less than the average wage of $200 (approx) which represents nearly 58% of all workers in this category. On this basis, many would claim that the mean is not representative of this data. Had we taken *all* incomes rather than weekly incomes of male manual workers then the average would have been much higher (and hence even more unrepresentative). This is the reason that so many people scoff at the average income figures that are quoted from time to time.

Before we search for an alternative to the arithmetic mean, we must say something in its defence. The main redeeming feature of the arithmetic mean is that its calculation involves the use of *all* the data. We will see later that this is not a characteristic of alternatives to the arithmetic mean. In other words, the weaknesses of the arithmetic mean are also its strengths. Because all the data is used, and because the arithmetic mean is capable of precise calculation, most statisticians still prefer it to other measures. In fact the arithmetic mean is capable of, and is the basis for, advanced analysis. Any alternative to the arithmetic mean cannot be used for advanced analysis, so their uses are descriptive rather than analytical.

## The median

Suppose we arranged a group of numbers in ascending order, then the median would be the value of the item in the middle. So the median of the group $3, 4, 7, 8, 11$ is 7. Notice that the median is quite unaffected by extremities at either end of the group. Take the case of the sales force considered earlier: the incomes are

$$£12\ 500, £12\ 500, £12\ 500, £12\ 500, £40\ 000$$

and the median income is £12 500. The actual size of the director's income makes no difference whatsoever to the median: if the director's salary was doubled or halved then the median would still remain £12 500. So the median is quite insensitive to extreme values in the group or distribution, and certainly overcomes the major objections to the arithmetic mean. If you arrange a group of $n$ items in ascending order, then the value of the $\frac{(n+1)}{2}$ th item is the value of the median. If we had an even number of items, then there will be *two* middle items. Conventionally, we take the median to be the arithmetic mean of the two middle items. So the mean of $4, 9, 13, 17, 30, 32$ is $\frac{13+17}{2} = 15$. Now if $n$ is large, the difference between $\frac{(n+1)}{2}$ and $\frac{n}{2}$ is negligible – so take $\frac{n}{2}$ in such cases. Finally, then, we can see that half the items in a distribution will have a greater value than the median, and half the items a smaller value.

Look again at the cumulative frequency distribution of weekly incomes of male manual workers in the previous section. There are 5.4 m workers, so if we wish to find the median income, this will involve finding the income of the 2.7 millionth worker.

Figure 5.1 shows the ogive of this cumulative frequency distribution. Reading off the income of this worker from the ogive, we find that the median income is $189, compared with a mean income of $200.74. You would probably find that most people would accept the median as being more representative than the arithmetic mean.

It is often quite difficult to read off the value of the median from the ogive, and to overcome this problem it is useful to magnify that part of the ogive containing the median. From the cumulative frequency distribution, we can see that 2.4 m people earn less than \$180 per week, and 3.1 m earn less than \$200 per week. So the median lies somewhere between \$180 and \$200 per week. We can plot these points on a graph and join them with a straight line. Reading off from Fig 5.2, we see that the median income is \$188.5.

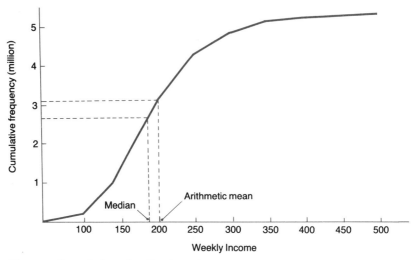

Fig 5.1  **Cumulative distribution of earnings of male manual workers**

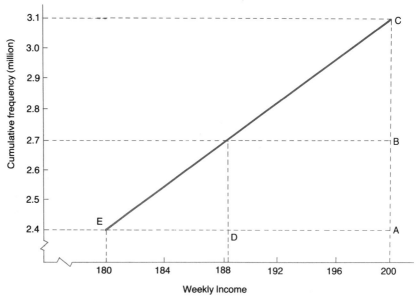

Fig 5.2  **Cumulative distribution of earnings of male manual workers**

If you look carefully at Fig 5.2, you will realise that it is possible to calculate rather than read off the value of the median. Do you remember the similar triangle theorems? If you do, then you will realise that:

$$\frac{AB}{AC} = \frac{ED}{AE}$$

so   $ED = \frac{AB \times AE}{AC}$

Now we can see that $ED$ is the amount by which the median exceeds $180 so the median is:

$$180 + \frac{AB \times AE}{AC}$$

$$= 180 + \frac{0.3 \times 20}{0.7}$$

$$= \$188.57$$

It might be useful to see how we could obtain these figures directly from the cumulative frequency distribution. The relevant parts of this distribution are:

|  | Cumulative frequency |
| --- | --- |
| Under $180 | 2.4 |
| Under $200 | 3.1 |

so we see that the median is in the group $180–$200 and the median is:

$$180 + \frac{0.3 \times 20}{0.7}$$

Clearly, 180 represents the lower class boundary (LCB) of the median group, and $AE$ represents the class interval of this group. The quantity $AC$ is the frequency of the median group 3.1–2.4 and the quantity $AB$ is the median item minus cumulative frequency up to the median group 2.7–2.4. So we can calculate the median like this:

$$\text{LCB} + \frac{\text{class interval} \times \left( \left[ \frac{n+1}{2} \right] - \text{cum. frequency to median group} \right)}{\text{frequency of median group}}$$

Now let us see if we can calculate the median directly, i.e. without reference to graphs.

**Wealth of individuals in Great Britain (1989)**

| Wealth | | Frequency (thousands) | Cumulative frequency |
|---|---|---|---|
| Not over | £25 000 | 5 518 | 5 518 |
| £25 000– | £50 000 | 3 372 | 8 890 |
| £50 000– | £100 000 | 4 010 | 12 900 |
| £100 000– | £200 000 | 1 846 | 14 746 |
| £200 000– | £500 000 | 576 | 15 322 |
| £500 000– | £1 000 000 | 76 | 15 398 |
| Over | £1 000 000 | 22 | 15 420 |
| | | 15 420 | |

Source: Inland Revenue, 1991

We wish to find the median wealth, i.e. the wealth of the $15\,420/2 = 7710$ thousandth person in the frequency distribution. The median person is in the group £25 000–£50 000 which contains 3372 thousand individuals. Hence, the median is

$$£25\,000 + \frac{25\,000 \times (7710 - 5518)}{3372}$$

$= £41\,250$ (to nearest £50).

Notice how difficult it would be to calculate the arithmetic mean of this distribution. It would be extremely difficult to put a lower limit on the first group, or an upper limit on the last group. The median, then, has decided advantages over the arithmetic mean; it can cope with open-ended distributions and is unaffected by extremities at either end of the distribution. Its disadvantage is that it ignores the bulk of the data presented to us, and this disadvantage really is critical! We would like to emphasise again that you should always attempt to use the mean rather than the median, especially if there is not much difference between them. In fact, the difference between them depends on the skewness of the distribution (this is illustrated in Fig 5.3). The median splits the area under the frequency curve into two halves. If the distribution is symmetrical, then the mean and median will coincide. With a negatively skewed distribution the median exceeds the mean, and with a positively skewed distribution the mean exceeds the median. The more pronounced is the skew, the greater will be the difference between the mean and median. Let us now attempt to summarise this into a simple rule: if you require a representative measure and the distribution is markedly skew, use the median – otherwise use the mean.

One final problem concerned with the median is that we cannot pool two medians to find an overall median. If we know that a factory employs 100 Grade B employees at a median wage of £175 per week and 200 Grade A employees at a median wage of £250 per week, we cannot calculate the median wage for all workers without consulting the raw data. But this is not the case with the arithmetic mean. Suppose the data referred to mean rather than median wages, then the total wages earned by Grade B employees would be $£175 \times 200 = £35\,000$, and the total wages earned by Grade A employees would be $£250 \times 100 = £25\,000$. So the labour force of 300 earns $£60\,000$, which gives an average wage of $£60\,000/300 = £200$ per week. This ability to pool means can be very useful.

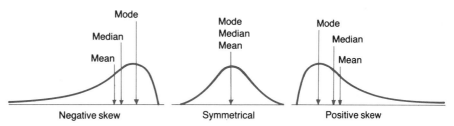

**Fig 5.3**

## The mode

The mode is the value or attribute that occurs most often, so is an extremely simple concept. Look again at the incomes of the sales force described earlier: $£12\,500$, $£12\,500$, $£12\,500$, $£12\,500$, $£40\,000$. You will realise that the modal income is $£12\,500$. Straight away, though, we can see a snag with the mode: if all the numbers in the group are different, then we cannot have a modal value.

With a frequency distribution, the mode is the value with the greatest frequency. Let us examine again the distribution of the number of children of 1000 young married couples:

| *Number of children* | 0 | 1 | 2 | 3 | 4 |
|---|---|---|---|---|---|
| *Number of families* | 364 | 362 | 226 | 44 | 4 |

The mean number of children per family we calculated to be 0.962, and the median number of children is one (i.e. the number of children in the 500th family). But the modal number of children is zero, because more families are childless than have any other number of children.

To find the mode of a grouped frequency distribution, we must first identify the class containing the greatest number of items. Look again at the frequency distribution of length of metal pipes (*see* page 98): the class with the greatest number of items is 50–60 cm, and we call this the modal class. If we wanted to estimate the mode more precisely than this, then we notice that the class preceding the modal class has a frequency greater than the class following the modal class. This could be taken to imply that the mode might be nearer to 50 cm than to 60 cm. Its actual value can be estimated from the histogram in Fig 5.4.

**Fig 5.4**

The mode has the same weaknesses as the median: it ignores the bulk of the data and is not capable of being pooled. We have also seen that it is quite possible for a group of numbers all to have different values, and under such circumstances a mode would not exist. Also, in some distributions it is possible to have more than one mode – a distribution like the one in Fig 5.5 is called *bimodal*. To quote two modes is just clouding the issue! Finally, if you have a frequency distribution with unequal class intervals, it is possible that you will not be able to identify the modal class and so be unable to estimate the mode. A good example of this is the distribution of earnings of male manual workers that we considered earlier in this chapter.

Although the group $200–$250 has the greatest frequency we cannot assume it is the modal class, because the previous class is much narrower. The great strength of the mode is that conceptually it is so easy to understand. Also, it is particularly useful when describing attributes – when we state that the average family cleans their teeth with 'Gritto' we mean that more families use Gritto than any other toothpaste. You can readily understand why the mode is so popular with market researchers!

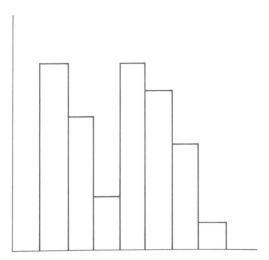

**Fig 5.5   A bimodal distribution**

Before we conclude measures of central tendency, there is one final point we should consider. Why did we call the mean the *arithmetic* mean? This surely implies that there are other means we could consider. This is indeed the case, and if we calculate a mean, we must be absolutely certain that we are using the right one! Let us, therefore, consider some alternative means (called minor means) and discuss their appropriate usage.

## The harmonic mean

Suppose a motorist told you that he travelled from Liverpool to Manchester at an average speed of 40 kph, and returned at an average speed of 50 kph. If then he claimed that his overall average speed was 45 kph, you would probably agree with him, wouldn't you? However, you would be quite wrong. Let us examine the problem in more detail. The distance from Liverpool to Manchester is 55 km, so the time taken at 40 kph is $\frac{55}{40} = \frac{11}{8}$ hours, and the time taken at 50 kph is $\frac{55}{50} = \frac{11}{10}$ hours. The time taken for both journeys is:

$$\frac{11}{8} + \frac{11}{10} = \frac{99}{40} \text{ hours}$$

and the total distance travelled is 110 km. Now we know that average speed is distance divided by time, so the average speed for the round journey is:

$$110 \times \frac{40}{99} = 44 \tfrac{4}{9} \text{ kph}$$

So you see that averaging the two speeds simply by adding them and dividing by two gives us the wrong answer. Why is the arithmetic mean not appropriate here? Well the reason is that the different speeds are maintained for the same *distance* and not the same *time*. If they were maintained for the same time then the arithmetic mean would have been appropriate. What we should have used here is the *harmonic mean*, which is used for averaging rates and prices. We calculate the harmonic mean as follows:

$$HM = \frac{n}{\sum \frac{1}{x}}$$

or using our example:

$$\text{Average speed} = \frac{2}{\frac{1}{40} + \frac{1}{50}}$$

$$= \frac{2 \times 200}{9}$$

$$= 44\tfrac{4}{9} \text{ kph}$$

Now let us examine an example using prices. Suppose we made a mixture using four ingredients costing £1, £2, £3 and £4 per kilogram respectively, and spent an equal amount on each ingredient, then the price per kilogram of the mix is:

$$\frac{4}{1 + \frac{1}{2} + \frac{1}{3} + \frac{1}{4}} = £1.92 \text{ per kilo}$$

However, had we mixed equal quantities of ingredients, then the price would have been £2.50 per kilo. You should check these conclusions by direct calculation.

## The geometric mean

Let us suppose we invest £100 at 10% per annum compound interest. At the end of the first year we would have £100 + £10 = £110 invested. At the end of the second year we would have £110 + 10% of £110 = £121 invested. Now we can continue in this fashion and calculate the sum available at the end of each year for 10 years. The graph of the sum available against time is shown in Fig 5.6.

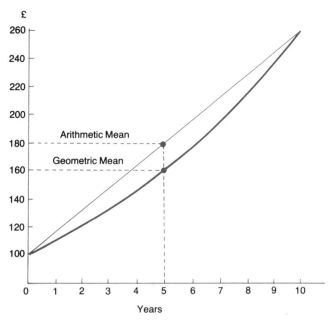

**Fig 5.6   Growth of £100 invested at 10% per annum compound**

The sum available at the end of the tenth year is £259.37. Now suppose we knew the sum available after 10 years, could we use the arithmetic mean to estimate the sum available after five years? The arithmetic mean would be:

$$\frac{100 + 259.37}{2} = £179.69$$

which, as you can see from the graph, is a rotten estimate. Once again, we have used the wrong mean. The arithmetic mean would have given a good estimate had the sum invested earned a constant *amount*. In other words, it would have worked if the sum invested had earned simple interest – the graph would have been a straight line. In this case, however, the sum invested increases by a constant *proportion*, and a much better estimate is achieved if we use the *geometric mean*.

$$GM = \sqrt[n]{x_1 \times x_2 \times \cdots \times x_n}$$

This simply states that we multiply the $n$ numbers together, and then take the $n$th root. So our estimate of the sum available after five years is:

$$\sqrt{100 \times 259.37}$$
$$= £161.05$$

which agrees exactly with the value obtained from the graph.

This method of estimating a 'mid-point' value by using an average is called *interpolation*. To attempt to clarify which mean should be used, consider this problem: suppose you started work earning £4000 per year, and you were told what your salary would be in 10 years' time. You want to estimate your salary after five years. If your salary rises by constant annual increments, then the arithmetic mean would be appropriate, but if it rises by a constant percentage of the previous year's salary, you would have to use the geometric mean. Again, a census is taken in the UK every 10 years, and it would be useful to use these figures to estimate the population on the five-year intervals. As populations do not grow by constant amounts, the geometric mean would give a better estimate. But even using a geometric mean might not give a good estimate: can you think why this might be so?

Now a word or two in conclusion. We have seen that there are many forms of 'average', and it is vitally important that you choose the right one for the job. We must state, though, that the arithmetic mean is by far the most important and is most commonly used in preference to other alternatives. As you work through this book, you will meet the arithmetic mean over and over again (from now on we shall refer to it simply as the mean) – but always bear in mind that it does have limitations.

## Using the spreadsheet

In Chapter 1 we introduced a spreadsheet template that would create a frequency distribution. The same template was used in Chapter 2 to draw a frequency polygon and an ogive. The template also has the capability to calculate the arithmetic mean and the median of a frequency distribution.

Retrieve this template by selecting Descriptive statistics then Frequency from the main menu. Again, you must enter the lower and upper bounds of the classes first. Select the 'New data' option and enter the lower and upper bounds of the classes of the estimated distribution of earnings of male manual workers used in this chapter and then press ALT S.

As before, you have the option of entering the observations directly in cell A1 or the actual frequencies starting at cell C6. As we know the actual frequencies, move the cursor to cell C6, enter the frequencies in the column and press ALT R to retrieve the menu. Select the 'Statistics' option and your screen should look something like this:

| | A | B | C | D | E | F | G |
|---|---|---|---|---|---|---|---|
| 1 | | | | | | | |
| 2 | Input 0 if frequencies exact, 1 if frequencies rounded | | | | | | |
| 3 | | | | | | | |
| 4 | Lower | Upper | Frequency | | | | |
| 5 | Bound | Bound | | | | | |
| 6 | 80 | 100 | 0.2 | | | | |
| 7 | 100 | 120 | 0.4 | | | | |
| 8 | 120 | 140 | 0.5 | | | | |
| 9 | 140 | 160 | 0.6 | | | | |
| 10 | 160 | 180 | 0.7 | | | | |
| 11 | 180 | 200 | 0.7 | | | | |
| 12 | 200 | 250 | 1.2 | | | | |
| 13 | 250 | 300 | 0.6 | | | | |
| 14 | 300 | 350 | 0.3 | | | | |
| 15 | 350 | 400 | 0.1 | | | | |
| 16 | 400 | 500 | 0.1 | | | | |
| 17 | Total Frequency = | | 5.4 | | | | |
| 18 | | | | | | | |
| 19 | | | | | | | |

The calculation of the median from the data you have input will depend upon whether the frequencies are rounded or exact. In this case, the frequencies are rounded (i.e. expressed correct to the nearest million) so type 1 and press enter. The mean and median are now displayed, and the menu is also displayed. The meaning of Q1, Q3, Variance, Stdev and CoV will be explained in a later chapter.

If the frequencies are exact, then the median is the value of the $(n + 1)/2$ th item, but if the frequencies are rounded, then the median is the value of the $n/2$ th item.

Let us now look at the tabulations performed by the template in order to derive these statistics. Press the F5 key, then type I1.

- Column J gives the mid-point of the classes.

- Column K is a copy of the frequencies, with the total frequency (5.4) positioned just under the word 'Freq'.

- Column L calculates the cumulative frequencies.

- Column M calculates the $fx$ values from row 6 downward. The value 1084 represents $\Sigma fx$. The value of the mean is produced at the top of this column.

- Column N is the cumulative frequencies, dropped down one line. This is necessary to find the median.

- Column O contains the expressions necessary to find the median. The value in the cell K2 is the median item.

If you want to see the actual expressions used move the cursor to cell J6 and the expression is reproduced on line 1. Now move the cursor to the right and watch the expressions change. Most of these expressions you should be able to follow if you have mastered the techniques introduced in this chapter. However, the expression in cell O6 is particularly complicated!

When you have finished looking at the expressions, press the home key, press ALT M to retrieve the menu. If you wish to save the data within the template, then select File; otherwise select Quit.

## QUESTIONS

**5.1** Explain why it is frequently necessary to summarise masses of data by using representative or typical values. Describe two such measures and their methods of calculation.                                                                          ACCA

**5.2** If we examine the batting average table for Coalshire we find that Fred Sloggin has an average of 51 runs, and DEM Bones has an average of 39 runs. Would you conclude that Sloggin was the more effective batsman?

Sloggin's average of 51 runs has been obtained in 39 innings. The next innings will be his last of the season. How many runs must he score in the last innings if his final average is to be at least 55 runs?

**5.3** Given that $\Sigma(x - \bar{x}) = 0$, show that $\bar{x} = \dfrac{\Sigma x}{n}$

**5.4**

**No. of children per 1000 families in which couples were married**

| No. of children | 0 | 1 | 2 | 3 | 4 | 5 | 6+ |
|---|---|---|---|---|---|---|---|
| Frequency (%) | 5.3 | 5.2 | 55.4 | 11.4 | 18.9 | 1.5 | 2.3 |

Source: *General Household Survey*

Calculate the median.

Calculate the mean number of children per family for the above data, given that the average size of a family with six or more children is 6.5.

**5.5**   A company employing 60 people found that the number of sick days taken by its employees last year were as follows:

| | | | | | | | | | |
|---|---|---|---|---|---|---|---|---|---|
| 10 | 5 | 12 | 0 | 2 | 35 | 11 | 12 | 4 | 9 |
| 12 | 17 | 3 | 7 | 8 | 8 | 8 | 10 | 11 | 29 |
| 44 | 4 | 9 | 3 | 6 | 6 | 7 | 13 | 18 | 4 |
| 15 | 25 | 5 | 2 | 7 | 20 | 9 | 16 | 10 | 9 |
| 5 | 2 | 31 | 6 | 0 | 7 | 10 | 9 | 22 | 1 |
| 3 | 1 | 23 | 9 | 12 | 18 | 6 | 9 | 31 | 0 |

Group the above figures into intervals of five days. Calculate the mean. Draw the cumulative frequency curve of the distribution and comment on the distribution.

**5.6**      **Orders Received**

| Value of order (£00) | Number of orders received |
|---|---|
| 0 and under  5 | 20 |
| 5 and under 10 | 51 |
| 10 and under 15 | 139 |
| 15 and under 20 | 116 |
| 20 and under 25 | 31 |
| 25 and under 30 | 14 |
| 30 and over | 5 |
| | 376 |

(a)   From the above table of orders received calculate the mean value of orders received.

(b)   Comment briefly on your results for (a).

(c)   Suppose the value of the median to be less than the mean. What would this indicate?

**5.7**   A sample of 120 houses was valued for Council Tax as follows:

| Value (£) | Number of houses |
|---|---|
| 40 000– 52 000 | 3 |
| 52 000– 68 000 | 15 |
| 68 000– 88 000 | 30 |
| 88 000–120 000 | 36 |
| 120 000–160 000 | 18 |
| 160 000–320 000 | 12 |
| Over     320 000 | 6 |

Assuming that the mid-point of the last group is £400 000, estimate the average value of the sample of houses.

**5.8** The table below gives the age distribution of the management of a large company.

| Age | Frequency |
|---|---|
| Under 20 | 2 |
| 20–29 | 12 |
| 30–39 | 31 |
| 40–49 | 39 |
| 50–59 | 26 |
| Over 60 | 10 |

Calculate the mean of the distribution. List the assumptions you made in carrying out the calculation and explain why you think you were justified in making them.

**5.9**

**Age distribution of the members of a golf club**

| Age (in completed years) | No. of members |
|---|---|
| 10–19 | 185 |
| 20–29 | 263 |
| 30–39 | 325 |
| 40–49 | 442 |
| 50–59 | 368 |
| 60–69 | 134 |
| 70 and over | 83 |

(a) Calculate the arithmetic mean age for the data. (Use mid-value of Group 40–49 as a working origin.)

(b) Define and distinguish between discrete and continuous variables.

**5.10** The frequency table gives the age distribution of the estimated male population of Northern Ireland on 30 June 1989. Calculate the arithmetic mean for this distribution.

| Age | Number (000's) |
|---|---|
| 0–9 | 137.7 |
| 10–19 | 134.8 |
| 20–29 | 136.6 |
| 30–39 | 101.8 |
| 40–49 | 90.1 |
| 50–59 | 71.7 |
| 60–69 | 59.3 |
| 70–79 | 36.1 |
| 80 and over | 12.3 |

Source: *Monthly Digest of Statistics*, June 1992

**5.11**    Distinguish between discrete and continuous data. The data below shows the number of local telephone calls made by 75 subscribers during a certain interval of time.

| No. of calls made | No. of subscribers |
|---|---|
| 1–10 | 9 |
| 11–15 | 12 |
| 16–20 | 24 |
| 21–25 | 16 |
| 26–40 | 14 |
|  | 75 |

(a)  Calculate the average number of calls made per subscriber.

(b)  Calculate the maximum error in your average due to grouping in the data given.

**5.12**    **Mileages recorded by 60 commercial travellers in the course of one week**

| | | | | | |
|---|---|---|---|---|---|
| 515 | 611 | 530 | 557 | 586 | 528 |
| 533 | 516 | 519 | 560 | 572 | 509 |
| 520 | 543 | 556 | 532 | 512 | 605 |
| 559 | 549 | 539 | 609 | 589 | 537 |
| 524 | 521 | 513 | 541 | 581 | 618 |
| 544 | 545 | 535 | 568 | 583 | 521 |
| 555 | 552 | 579 | 581 | 558 | 539 |
| 562 | 578 | 563 | 598 | 594 | 560 |
| 595 | 507 | 562 | 532 | 590 | 578 |
| 526 | 533 | 574 | 531 | 584 | 543 |

(a)  From this data tabulate directly a grouped frequency distribution using equal class intervals and starting with 500–519.

(b)  What is the direction of skew of this distribution?

(c)  Calculate the arithmetic mean of the grouped frequency distribution.

(d)  Explain why the arithmetic mean of the ungrouped data would be different from the mean obtained in (c).

**5.13**    Values of orders taken by representatives employed by a wholesale firm on a certain day. The values are rounded off to the nearest £1.

| Value of order (£) | No. of orders |
|---|---|
| 5– 9 | 85 |
| 10–19 | 120 |
| 20–29 | 225 |
| 30–49 | 135 |
| 50–99 | 105 |
| 100 and over | 20 |

(a)  Illustrate the data by means of a histogram.

(b)  Calculate the median and mark it on your histogram.

**5.14** The following table shows the age distribution of employees in two factories, A and B. Estimate the median age in each factory using an appropriate graph and check the results by calculation.

| Age of Employees | Number of Employees A | B |
|---|---|---|
| 16–19 | 79 | 5 |
| 20–24 | 98 | 23 |
| 25–29 | 128 | 58 |
| 30–34 | 83 | 104 |
| 35–39 | 39 | 141 |
| 40–44 | 19 | 98 |
| 45–49 | 11 | 43 |
| 50–54 | 7 | 19 |
| 55–59 | 3 | 6 |

**5.15** The table below gives the earnings (to the nearest £) of 150 employees in a large factory.

| Income (£) | Frequency |
|---|---|
| 14 500–14 999 | 20 |
| 15 000–15 499 | 42 |
| 15 500–15 999 | 38 |
| 16 000–16 499 | 34 |
| 16 500–16 999 | 8 |
| 17 000–17 499 | 4 |
| 17 500–17 999 | 2 |
| 18 000–18 499 | 1 |
| 18 500–18 999 | 0 |
| 19 000–19 499 | 1 |

(a) What are the class boundaries of the class with frequency 8?

(b) Draw the cumulative frequency curve of the distribution.

(c) What percentage of the group earns less than £16 200?

(d) Calculate the median as accurately as you can.

(e) Under what circumstances is the median a better measure of central tendency than the mean?

**5.16**   Distribution of weekly earnings (males)

| Weekly earnings (£) | Frequency (%) |
|---|---|
| Less than 150 | 10.5 |
| 150–170 | 3.3 |
| 170–200 | 12.3 |
| 200–230 | 14.1 |
| 230–270 | 18.1 |
| 270–300 | 11.5 |
| 300–360 | 14.6 |
| 360–420 | 7.9 |
| 420–480 | 3.6 |
| 480–600 | 2.8 |
| Over 600 | 1.3 |
| | 100.0 |

Source: *New Earnings Survey*, 1992

(a)   Obtain the cumulative frequencies and plot the ogive.

(b)   A firm proposes to market a household product in two qualities – standard and de luxe – which it expects to sell to the income brackets £330–£410 and £410–£470 respectively. If each 1% of the survey can be taken to represent 180 000 households in the population, estimate the market size for the two grades of product.

**5.17**   Distribution of male hourly earnings

| Hourly rate (pence) | Frequency (%) |
|---|---|
| Less than 340 | 6.7 |
| 340– 420 | 9.6 |
| 420– 480 | 12.7 |
| 480– 540 | 13.9 |
| 540– 600 | 12.8 |
| 600– 700 | 17.3 |
| 700– 800 | 11.6 |
| 800– 900 | 7.3 |
| 900–1100 | 6.0 |
| 1100–1400 | 1.6 |
| Over 1400 | 0.5 |
| | 100.0 |

Source: *New Earnings Survey*, 1992

(a)   Obtain the cumulative frequencies.

(b)   By calculation or graphically, obtain the median.

(c)   Would you expect the arithmetic mean of the distribution to be greater than, equal to, or less than the median? Explain your answer. (Do not carry out any further calculations.)

**5.18** (a) Define the median, mean, and mode, listing the advantage and disadvantages attributable to each.

(b) (i) Calculate the median, mean and mode for the following:

| Wage groups (hourly rate in pence) | Number of employees |
|---|---|
| 200 and under 300 | 5 |
| 300 and under 400 | 25 |
| 400 and under 500 | 134 |
| 500 and under 600 | 85 |
| 600 and under 700 | 69 |
| 700 and under 800 | 43 |
| 800 and under 900 | 34 |

(ii) Illustrate a use for each of the three statistics calculated.

**5.19** The marks scored by students in an examination are shown below. (Marking is in whole marks only.)

| Mark scored | 10–19 | 20–29 | 30–39 | 40–49 | 50–59 | 60–69 | 70–79 | 80–89 | 90–99 |
|---|---|---|---|---|---|---|---|---|---|
| No. of students | 4 | 12 | 23 | 37 | 43 | 32 | 19 | 8 | 2 |

(a) Draw a histogram to illustrate the above distribution.

(b) What are the class boundaries of the modal class?

(c) Estimate by calculation the median mark.

(d) If $16\frac{2}{3}\%$ of the pupils are to be given a pass with distinction, what mark will be necessary to achieve this?

(e) What proportion would fail if the pass mark were 48?

**5.20** The following figures give the age of a sample of 100 students taking BTEC National Business Studies examinations. The ages are rounded to the next lowest complete month.

| Years | Months | Years | Months | Years | Months | Years | Months | Years | Months |
|-------|--------|-------|--------|-------|--------|-------|--------|-------|--------|
| 17 | 7 | 18 | 4 | 17 | 0 | 16 | 5 | 18 | 8 |
| 18 | 2 | 18 | 3 | 17 | 11 | 18 | 8 | 18 | 7 |
| 17 | 9 | 17 | 3 | 17 | 10 | 18 | 9 | 17 | 3 |
| 16 | 5 | 17 | 1 | 18 | 9 | 17 | 2 | 17 | 10 |
| 19 | 2 | 18 | 9 | 19 | 5 | 16 | 10 | 18 | 1 |
| 17 | 9 | 17 | 8 | 17 | 3 | 17 | 3 | 18 | 4 |
| 17 | 3 | 18 | 11 | 17 | 4 | 16 | 9 | 17 | 11 |
| 16 | 11 | 19 | 0 | 18 | 0 | 16 | 8 | 18 | 0 |
| 18 | 5 | 19 | 8 | 17 | 9 | 17 | 1 | 18 | 3 |
| 18 | 4 | 16 | 4 | 17 | 11 | 18 | 4 | 18 | 1 |
| 17 | 11 | 16 | 10 | 16 | 10 | 19 | 0 | 16 | 10 |
| 17 | 10 | 18 | 1 | 17 | 2 | 18 | 11 | 16 | 11 |
| 18 | 3 | 17 | 8 | 17 | 2 | 17 | 11 | 17 | 2 |
| 16 | 9 | 17 | 7 | 17 | 1 | 18 | 0 | 17 | 3 |
| 17 | 2 | 16 | 11 | 17 | 7 | 17 | 10 | 17 | 8 |
| 18 | 0 | 17 | 3 | 16 | 10 | 17 | 3 | 17 | 11 |
| 17 | 0 | 18 | 2 | 18 | 3 | 16 | 9 | 18 | 2 |
| 17 | 8 | 18 | 11 | 17 | 2 | 16 | 6 | 17 | 10 |
| 17 | 9 | 17 | 5 | 17 | 3 | 17 | 5 | 17 | 10 |
| 18 | 1 | 18 | 5 | 17 | 9 | 17 | 8 | 18 | 3 |

(a)  From these figures compile a frequency distribution table. You are advised to work in half-yearly class intervals, paying particular attention to the way you select these intervals and their class boundaries.

(b)  Draw a histogram to represent the frequency distribution.

(c)  From the histogram find a value for the modal age.

**5.21**  A random sample of the accounts of 50 construction companies gave the following frequency distribution of profit.

| Profit (£m) | Number of companies |
|-------------|---------------------|
| −10 and under −5 | 2 |
| −5 and under 0 | 0 |
| 0 and under 5 | 2 |
| 5 and under 10 | 4 |
| 10 and under 15 | 8 |
| 15 and under 20 | 11 |
| 20 and under 25 | 13 |
| 25 and under 30 | 6 |
| 30 and under 35 | 4 |

Construct an ogive of the cumulative frequency distribution and use it to estimate:

(a)  the median profit,

(b)  the profit exceeded by 75% of companies,

(c) the number of companies out of 500 similar ones whose profit for that year was between eight and 18 million pounds. ACCA

**5.22** (a) Place the arithmetic mean, median and mode in order of merit as averages for the following frequency distributions, and briefly explain your rankings in each case.

(1) Incomes, taken from a wages survey.

(2) Ladies' shoe sizes, based on sales data.

(3) Percentage of defective products, based on batches examined.

(b) The following table shows the number of hours of sunshine recorded during July at a certain seaside town.

| Hours of sunshine | Number of days |
|---|---|
| 0 and under 1 | 1 |
| 1 and under 2 | 2 |
| 2 and under 3 | 4 |
| 3 and under 4 | 11 |
| 4 and under 5 | 24 |
| 5 and under 6 | 35 |
| 6 and under 7 | 43 |
| 7 and under 8 | 49 |
| 8 and under 9 | 54 |
| 9 and under 10 | 31 |
| 10 and under 11 | 15 |
| 11 and under 12 | 10 |
| | 279 |

Calculate:

(1) the mean number of hours of sunshine; and

(2) the median number of hours of sunshine. ACCA

**5.23** The table below gives the distribution of marks of a group of candidates taking a statistics examination.

**Examination Results**

| Mark | Number of candidates |
|---|---|
| 30 and under 40 | 2 |
| 40 and under 50 | 5 |
| 50 and under 60 | 7 |
| 60 and under 70 | 13 |
| 70 and under 80 | 15 |
| 80 and under 90 | 5 |
| 90 and under 100 | 3 |

You are required to:

(a) calculate the mean and the median marks, and

(b) explain what the values calculated in your answer to (a) indicate about the distribution of examination results, particularly with reference to the difference between the mean and median values.                                    ACCA

**5.24**  In a survey of the value of orders received, a manufacturing company obtained the following grouped frequency table:

| Value of orders (£) | Number of orders |
|---|---|
| 100 and up to but less than 200 | 169 |
| 200 and up to but less than 300 | 176 |
| 300 and up to but less than 400 | 75 |
| 400 and up to but less than 500 | 32 |
| 500 and up to but less than 600 | 8 |

Draw the histogram for this distribution and from this, or by other means, find the value of the modal order, to the nearer £1. Calculate the mean value of orders, and thus estimate the total value of all the orders.                                    CISA

**5.25**  By taking random samples over a period, information has been collected giving the following age distribution of young persons attending a sport and recreation centre.

| Age in years | Number of young persons |
|---|---|
| 12 and under 13 | 3 |
| 13 and under 14 | 11 |
| 14 and under 15 | 29 |
| 15 and under 16 | 99 |
| 16 and under 17 | 203 |
| 17 and under 18 | 258 |
| 18 and under 19 | 247 |

(a) Calculate to the nearest month the arithmetic mean age and the median age of young persons attending the centre.

(b) Find the modal age to the nearest month of young persons attending the centre.

Discuss the relative merits and possible uses of these three measures of central position.

**5.26**    Total income before tax, 1988–89, UK

| Income range (£) | Number (thousands) | Total income (£m) |
|---|---|---|
| Less than 3 000 | 557 | 1 560 |
| 3 000–  5 000 | 3 369 | 13 310 |
| 5 000–  7 000 | 3 275 | 19 660 |
| 7 000– 10 000 | 4 350 | 36 900 |
| 10 000– 15 000 | 5 220 | 64 100 |
| 15 000– 20 000 | 2 940 | 50 500 |
| 20 000– 50 000 | 3 067 | 84 300 |
| 50 000–100 000 | 232 | 15 300 |
| 100 000 and over | 55 | 9 930 |

Source: Board of Inland Revenue, 1991

Find the arithmetic mean and median of total incomes. Which, in your opinion, is the better indicator of average income?

**5.27**  (a)  Discuss the importance of averages in statistical analysis, and describe the characteristics and methods of calculation of two *commonly* used averages.

(b)  Using the geometric mean, calculate the average annual ratio of change in family income from the data in the following table.

| Year | Family income as a ratio of preceding year's income |
|---|---|
| 1985 | 1.05 |
| 1986 | 1.17 |
| 1987 | 1.33 |
| 1988 | 1.25 |

(c)  Explain the use of the geometric mean as an average and what your answer indicates about the change in family income over the period.          ACCA

**5.28**  Given that the population of the United Kingdom in 1977 was 49 440 000 and in 1987 was 50 243 000 estimate the population in 1982. Comment on your estimate given that the population in 1982 was 49 601 000.

**5.29**  Suppose we decided to make a general-purpose fertiliser by mixing together in equal values five ingredients costing £1, £5, £6, £9 and £11 per kilo. Find the cost per kilo of the mixture.

**5.30**  Prove that the sum of squares of the deviations of the items from the arithmetic mean is a minimum (you will need a knowledge of differential calculus to be able to show this).

# 6

# The time series – analysis of trend

## The components of a time series

If Plumpton Rovers were drawn against Arsenal in the third round of the FA Cup, there is no doubt who would be expected to win. Past records show that non-league clubs seldom win against First Division teams. If, however, the non-league club had won such a tie on 18 out of the last 19 meetings, then in spite of their relative strength we would expect Arsenal to lose. We tend to base our forecast of the match result on what has happened in the past. This is as true of the accountant as it is of the football fan. In trying to budget for the cost of raw materials or for labour costs in the immediate future, he will look carefully in the first instance at what has happened in the recent past – expecting that the past behaviour of costs will be carried forward into the future.

The statistical series which tells us how data has been behaving in the past is the *time series*. It gives us the value of the variable we are considering at various points in time – each year for the last 15 years; each quarter for the last five years. Yet, when you look at a typical time series, the data fluctuates so much that it seems unlikely that it can help us a great deal. Let us take a series, then, and begin by assessing the factors which cause this fluctuation in the value of the data.

**Imports of Raw Material into Ruritania**
(19-0 = 100)

| Year | *Quarter* 1 | 2 | 3 | 4 |
|------|------|------|------|------|
| 19-2 | 114 | 142 | 155 | 136 |
| 19-3 | 116 | 150 | 153 | 140 |
| 19-4 | 128 | 158 | 169 | 159 |
| 19-5 | 137 | 180 | 192 | 172 |
| 19-6 | 145 | 194 | | |

The figures are given in index number form, and they are plotted as a graph in Fig 6.1.

Look carefully at this diagram. Although the figures are fluctuating quarter by quarter two things are immediately apparent. There is a general upward *trend* in the figures as a whole. It is not an exceptional rise, but it is quite marked. Apart from the third quarter of 19-3, the figures in any quarter are higher than those in the same quarter of the previous year.

**Fig 6.1**

Secondly, although the figures fluctuate, there is a pattern. The index of imported raw materials is always highest in the third quarter of the year, and always lowest in the first quarter. There is, then, a very marked *seasonal fluctuation* in the figures.

Although it is not apparent in the graph, there is likely to be a third influence on the data. We would not expect import figures to remain unaffected by day-to-day happenings such as disputes in the docks, exchange rate fluctuations or fuel shortages. It is probably something of this nature that has reduced the figure for the third quarter of 19-3. Thus, our data is likely to be affected by what we can call *residual* or *random influences* which cannot be foreseen or pinpointed without a great deal of outside knowledge – but which may be of great importance.

The series we are looking at is, of course, a short one. We could link the trend perhaps to a general expansion of the economy during the upward phase of the trade cycle. If we were to extend the series and consider a far longer period, the upward expansion might reach a peak and the trend would begin to turn downwards as the economy moves towards depression.

Thus, the series we examine might be affected to a great extent by *cyclical influences* resulting in a trend such as that in Fig 6.2.

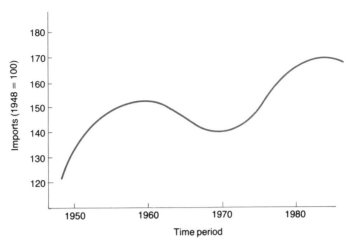

**Fig 6.2   A trend line showing cyclical influences**

Thus, data such as this which fluctuates quite markedly over time, may be responding to any, or all, of four sets of forces:

1   The **trend** or general way in which the figures are moving. It is important to distinguish between a trend resulting from cyclical influences on the economy and one resulting from, for example, a change in tastes or consumer buying habits. It is likely that there would have been a downward trend in the sales of black-and-white television sets, even though the economy as a whole was expanding and the sales of all television sets (including colour) were rising.

2   **Seasonal variations**. It is common knowledge that the value of many variables depends in part on the time of year we are considering. Everyone knows that the price of flowers rises as we approach Mothers' Day; or that the price of tomatoes is higher in winter than it is in summer. You can multiply these examples indefinitely from your own experience, and anyone concerned with planning must take account of them.

3   **Residual influences**. These are random external events which affect our variables. Sometimes the effect is negligible; at other times it is great; some occurrences will increase our figures; others will reduce them. We cannot see what is going to happen in the future, and so we cannot forecast such events. It is, however, reasonable to assume that in the long run they will tend to cancel each other out, and that in our analysis we may initially ignore their impact.

4 **Cyclical influences**. As the economy expands during a period of boom we would expect to find that such data as sales, output or consumer expenditure also show a rising trend; and during a period of slump we would expect them to show a downward trend. Thus a wavelike motion may be observed in the pattern of our data. If we were to take a sufficiently long period, covering several cycles, we might even find a trend superimposed on the cyclical pattern – each cycle being generally higher, or lower, than the last.

Now, it is one thing to identify the factors which may cause the fluctuations in our data: it is quite another matter to disentangle one from the other and to measure its influence. We will try, in the next section, to isolate and measure the trend.

## The calculation of the trend

In Fig 6.1 we have drawn a straight line through the middle of the series and said that the trend is rising 'something like this'. For serious statistical work, however, it is no use proceeding by guesswork. If we are going to use the trend figures we must calculate them, not guess them.

Now there are several methods of calculating trend, but the method we will explain first is a general all-purpose method – the method of *moving averages*. We will illustrate this method by calculating the trend in sales of capital goods in Ruritania during a 16-year period.

**Sales of capital goods: Ruritania**

| Year | Sales ($b) | 5-year total | 5 year moving average = Trend |
|---|---|---|---|
| 1 | 1.3 | | |
| 2 | 1.1 | | |
| 3 | 1.2 | 7.1 | 1.42 |
| 4 | 1.4 | 8.0 | 1.60 |
| 5 | 2.1 | 8.5 | 1.70 |
| 6 | 2.2 | 8.8 | 1.76 |
| 7 | 1.6 | 9.4 | 1.88 |
| 8 | 1.5 | 9.8 | 1.96 |
| 9 | 2.0 | 9.2 | 1.84 |
| 10 | 2.5 | 9.0 | 1.80 |
| 11 | 1.6 | 9.0 | 1.80 |
| 12 | 1.4 | 9.4 | 1.88 |
| 13 | 1.5 | 9.3 | 1.86 |
| 14 | 2.4 | 10.1 | 2.02 |
| 15 | 2.4 | | |
| 16 | 2.4 | | |

A moving average is a simple arithmetic mean. We select a group of numbers at the start of the series, in this case the first five, and average them to obtain our first trend figure:

$$(1.3 + 1.1 + 1.2 + 1.4 + 2.1) \div 5 = 7.1 \div 5 = 1.42$$

This trend figure is placed opposite the centre of the group of five numbers, that is, opposite year 3.

To obtain our second trend figure we drop the first number of this initial group (1.3) and include the next number in the series (2.2). So our second group of five numbers is:

$$1.1 + 1.2 + 1.4 + 2.1 + 2.2 = 8.0$$

and our second trend figure is:

$$8.0 \div 5 = 1.60$$

which is placed opposite Year 4. We now drop the figure for Year 2 (1.1) and include that for Year 7 (1.6), giving us a third trend figure of 1.70. We carry on in this way until all our data is exhausted.

You will notice that, using this method, there is no trend figure for the first two years nor for the last two. Do not forget this if you are asked to plot the original data and the trend on the same graph. Look carefully at Fig 6.3 where the data has been plotted.

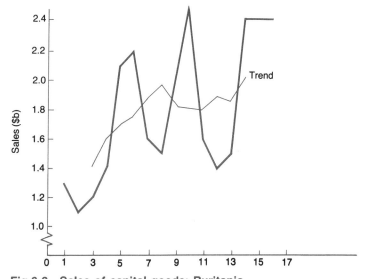

**Fig 6.3   Sales of capital goods: Ruritania**

The trend is probably not as smooth as you thought it would be. True, the large scale fluctuations have been eliminated, and up to Year 8 it is fairly smooth; but from this point on there is no clear indication of which way the trend is moving. The trend may have been influenced by government policy (e.g. to counter inflation).

You are probably wondering why we chose a five-year moving average rather than a three-year or a seven-year one. There is no infallible rule you can follow. The correct time period to use is the one that gives the smoothest trend. A good working rule, however, is to look at the peaks and the troughs in the series. Troughs occur in Years 2, 8 and 12; peaks occur in Years 6, 10 and 14 to 16. It looks as if sales of capital goods are subject to a five-year cycle, and, in fact, economists confirm that this frequently is so. Hence we chose a five-year moving average.

## The trend of a quarterly series

A great deal of the data statisticians deal with is given quarterly or monthly, rather than annually. We saw in the previous section that one of the characteristics of such a series is that peaks usually occur in the same quarter of every year, as do the troughs; so the correct moving average to use is the four-quarterly moving average. This does not demand any new concepts, but it does raise a practical problem. When we calculate the four-quarterly moving average and it is placed opposite the mid-point of the group of numbers to which it refers, it falls *between* the second and third figures. Thus we cannot relate our figures of trend to any particular quarter. To see how we overcome this let us calculate the trend of the quarterly series of Imports of Raw Material into Ruritania.

| Year | Quarter | Imports | Moving annual total | Moving pair total | Trend |
|------|---------|---------|---------------------|-------------------|-------|
| 19-2 | 1 | 114 | | | |
| | 2 | 142 | | | |
| | | | 547 | | |
| | 3 | 155 | | 1096 | 137.0 |
| | | | 549 | | |
| | 4 | 136 | | 1106 | 138.25 |
| | | | 557 | | |
| 19-3 | 1 | 116 | | 1112 | 139.0 |
| | | | 555 | | |
| | 2 | 150 | | 1114 | 139.25 |
| | | | 559 | | |
| | 3 | 153 | | 1130 | 141.25 |
| | | | 571 | | |
| | 4 | 140 | | 1150 | 143.75 |
| | | | 579 | | |
| 19-4 | 1 | 128 | | 1174 | 146.75 |
| | | | 595 | | |
| | 2 | 158 | | 1209 | 151.125 |
| | | | 614 | | |
| | 3 | 169 | | 1237 | 154.625 |
| | | | 623 | | |
| | 4 | 159 | | 1268 | 158.5 |
| | | | 645 | | |
| 19-5 | 1 | 137 | | 1313 | 164.125 |
| | | | 668 | | |
| | 2 | 180 | | 1349 | 168.625 |
| | | | 681 | | |
| | 3 | 192 | | 1370 | 171.25 |
| | | | 689 | | |
| | 4 | 172 | | 1392 | 174.0 |
| | | | 703 | | |
| 19-6 | 1 | 145 | | | |
| | 2 | 194 | | | |

Notice that when we add up in groups of four, the total is placed midway between the relevant quarters. In itself there is little wrong with this, but it prevents any comparison between the level of imports and the trend – a comparison we will have to make if we are to continue the analysis. To eliminate the problem, we use a technique known as centring. At present we have a trend figure of $547 \div 4 = 136.75$ placed opposite Quarter $2\frac{1}{2}$, and one of 137.25 placed opposite Quarter $3\frac{1}{2}$. If we take the average of these two it would be placed opposite Quarter 3, and we have centred the trend so as to relate it to a specific quarter, i.e.:

$$\frac{136.75 + 137.25}{2} = 137.0$$

The easiest way to do this in practice is to total successive pairs of four quarterly totals (e.g. $547 + 549$; $549 + 557$) and divide the resultant totals by eight to give the trend. This is done in the last two columns of the table.

## Exponential smoothing

In our analysis so far, we have used moving averages to 'smooth out' fluctuations in our data and obtain a trend line. Now moving averages have three great disadvantages. First, we do not have a trend value corresponding to each item of data. If, for example, we are calculating a five-year moving average trend or a four-quarterly, centred moving average trend we will not have trend values corresponding to the first two nor the last two items. Secondly, each moving average is calculated over a limited number of periods only, and all earlier data is ignored. To appreciate that this is so, suppose that the data items for seven years were $X_1, X_2, X_3, X_4, X_5, X_6$ and $X_7$, and that we wish to calculate a five-year moving average trend. The first trend value is:

$$\frac{X_1 + X_2 + X_3 + X_4 + X_5}{5}$$

The second trend value is:

$$\frac{X_2 + X_3 + X_4 + X_5 + X_6}{5}$$

The third trend value is:

$$\frac{X_3 + X_4 + X_5 + X_6 + X_7}{5}$$

So we see that the first value $X_1$ has no effect on the second, third and all following trend values. Likewise, the second value $X_2$ has no effect on the third and all following trend values. The third disadvantage with moving averages is that we must choose a suitable period as a basis for calculation. We suggested earlier that if peaks or troughs appeared at regular intervals, then this would seem the most suitable period to select. However, some series show no apparent cyclical or seasonal pattern, and the choice of a suitable period will be extremely difficult.

*Exponential smoothing* is an alternative method of determining the trend that goes a long way to meeting the objections to the moving average. It also has the added advantage that it is very much easier to calculate! This method starts by setting the first trend value equal to the value of the data for the first period. All subsequent trend values are calculated like this:

Trend for current period $= \alpha$ (actual value for current period) $+ (1 - \alpha)$ (trend value for last period).

The value $\alpha$ is called the *smoothing constant* and can take any value between zero and one.

Notice that the value for the current trend depends on the trend for the previous period. Hence, unlike with moving averages, all individual items of data in the past affect the current trend value. However, the contribution of any individual value in the past to the value of the current trend becomes less at each successive time period. The speed at which the effect of historical data is reduced depends much on the size of the smoothing constant $\alpha$. For values of $\alpha$ near to one, then the effect of any item in the past falls quickly.

The theory of selecting the 'best' smoothing constant involves a more than elementary knowledge of mathematics, however some general remarks can be made. Look again at the expression for the exponentially smoothed trend and you will realise that a large value for the smoothing constant will give more weight to the current period than to past data – after all when $\alpha$ is large, $(1 - \alpha)$ will be small. When the data under consideration is subject to large random fluctuations, then we would like to even out the effects of the random fluctuations quickly. Hence, we would wish to give more weight to the previous trend than to any current item that might be abnormal: we would select a small smoothing constant. However, for data not subject to large random fluctuations the reverse would be true and we would select a large smoothing constant.

---

EXAMPLE

The following example illustrates these points. It is concerned with the average price of a security over a 30-week period. The price of the security shows rather large random fluctuations, and three smoothing methods have been employed: a five-week moving average, an exponentially smoothed trend using a smoothing constant of $\alpha = 0.1$ and an exponentially smoothed trend using a smoothing constant of $\alpha = 0.5$.

| Week | Security price | Moving average trend | Exponentially smoothed trend with $\alpha = 0.1$ | $\alpha = 0.5$ |
|---|---|---|---|---|
| 1 | 172 | | 172.00 | 172.00 |
| 2 | 171 | | 171.90 | 171.50 |
| 3 | 170 | 169.4 | 171.71 | 170.75 |
| 4 | 169 | 168.2 | 171.44 | 169.88 |
| 5 | 165 | 168.6 | 170.80 | 167.44 |
| 6 | 166 | 170.4 | 170.32 | 166.72 |
| 7 | 173 | 171.8 | 170.58 | 169.86 |
| 8 | 179 | 174.0 | 171.43 | 174.43 |
| 9 | 176 | 176.0 | 171.88 | 175.21 |
| 10 | 176 | 175.6 | 172.29 | 175.61 |
| 11 | 176 | 175.0 | 172.67 | 175.80 |
| 12 | 171 | 175.0 | 172.50 | 173.40 |
| 13 | 176 | 174.8 | 172.85 | 174.70 |
| 14 | 176 | 175.4 | 173.16 | 175.35 |
| 15 | 175 | 178.6 | 173.35 | 175.18 |
| 16 | 179 | 180.0 | 173.91 | 177.09 |
| 17 | 187 | 180.0 | 175.22 | 182.04 |
| 18 | 183 | 179.8 | 176.00 | 182.52 |
| 19 | 176 | 178.6 | 176.00 | 179.26 |
| 20 | 174 | 176.0 | 175.80 | 176.63 |
| 21 | 173 | 174.0 | 175.52 | 174.82 |
| 22 | 174 | 174.4 | 175.37 | 174.41 |
| 23 | 173 | 176.4 | 175.13 | 173.70 |
| 24 | 178 | 178.2 | 175.42 | 175.85 |
| 25 | 184 | 179.8 | 176.28 | 179.93 |
| 26 | 182 | 182.4 | 176.85 | 180.96 |
| 27 | 182 | 184.0 | 177.36 | 181.48 |
| 28 | 186 | 184.2 | 178.23 | 183.74 |
| 29 | 186 | | 179.00 | 184.87 |
| 30 | 185 | | 179.60 | 184.94 |

The five-week moving average has been calculated in the usual way, i.e.:

$$\text{First trend value} = \frac{172 + 171 + 170 + 169 + 165}{5} = 169.4$$

$$\text{Second trend value} = \frac{171 + 170 + 169 + 165 + 166}{5} = 168.2$$

To find the exponentially smoothed trend, we set the trend for the first week equal to the price in the first week (172) in each case.

With $\alpha = 0.1$ the trend value for the second week is:

$$0.1 \times 171 + (1 - 0.1) \times 172 = 171.9$$

With $\alpha = 0.5$ the trend value for the second week is:

$$0.5 \times 171 + (1 - 0.5) \times 172 = 171.5$$

With $\alpha = 0.1$ the trend value for the third week is:

$$0.1 \times 170 + (1 - 0.1) \times 171.9 = 171.71$$

With $\alpha = 0.5$ the trend value for the third week is:

$$0.5 \times 170 + (1 - 0.5) \times 171.5 = 170.75$$

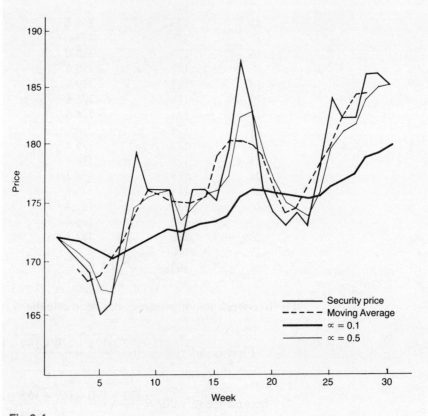

**Fig 6.4**

The actual prices and the three trends are drawn in Fig 6.4. All three trend lines are smoother than the original data, however the exponentially smoothed trend with $\alpha = 0.1$ is by far the most stable. This latter trend, although undershooting the original data for much of the time, does give a clearer indication of what is happening to the price of the security, and it would seem sensible to employ a small value for $\alpha$ when smoothing this data. You should *not* however take this to be a generalisation as the best size for $\alpha$ will vary according to the data.

## Using the spreadsheet

The menu structure of the spreadsheet template to accompany this chapter appears in Fig 6.5.

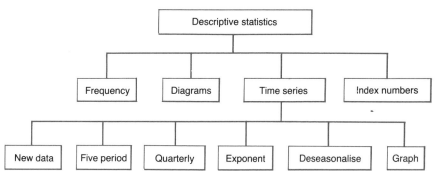

**Fig 6.5**

You should now retrieve this template. Select 'New data' and enter the data in the column starting from the cursor position. Press ALT G when you have finished entering the data. You should now select 'Five period' option and a five-period moving average trend is calculated (you must, of course, input more than five data items before such a trend is produced). Select 'Graph' to view the graph of the original data and trend line. (If you wish to see how the trend line was obtained, press Esc and move the cursor to cell C10. You should recognise the expression produced on the top of the screen. Press ALT M to bring back the menu.)

Now select the 'Quarterly' option and a four-quarter, centred trend is produced. Select 'Graph' to view the graph of the data and the trend line. Moving the cursor to cell C10 will reveal the expression used to calculate the trend line. Finally, select 'Exponential' and you will be prompted to input a smoothing constant. Input a suitable value (e.g., 0.1) and the exponentially smoothed trend line is produced. Select 'Graph' to view the original data and exponentially smoothed trend. It is now extremely easy to determine the effect of changing the smoothing constant. Press Esc and move the cursor to cell G4 (if it isn't already there). Type in another value for the smoothing constant and press Enter. The trend values are altered immediately. Press F10 to view the effects of the change. When you have finished experimenting, press ALT M to retrieve the menu. Selecting Hardcopy will send the output to the printer and (if you are using ASEASYAS) selecting 'Plot' will print out the graph of the data.

## QUESTIONS

**6.1** Describe the components into which statistical data relating to business and economic events may be analysed by the use of time series analysis.

**6.2** Specify and describe the various movements which may be identified when analysing economic and business statistics over a long time span.

**6.3** In the analysis of a time series:

(a) explain what is meant by a trend line and describe very briefly the method of calculating it;

(b) explain what is meant by residual variations and why they are important;

(c) sketch a graph of a time series which shows a trend and also cyclical and seasonal movements. ACCA

**6.4** The table shows the number of parcels carried by Rapid Carriage Plc to destinations within the United Kingdom:

| | *Number of parcels carried (000s)* | | | |
| | | *Quarters* | | |
| *Year* | *1* | *2* | *3* | *4* |
| 19-5 | | | | 800 |
| 19-6 | 690 | 1580 | 2250 | 940 |
| 19-7 | 830 | 1900 | 2670 | 1130 |
| 19-8 | 1040 | 2160 | 3070 | 1360 |
| 19-9 | 1190 | 2580 | | |

Plot the data and obtain the moving average trend. Plot the trend line on the same graph. What conclusions may be deduced from your graph?

**6.5**  (a)  State four components of a time series.

(b)  The following table shows the quarterly sales of a company in thousands of tonnes for a period of four years:

| | Sales | | | |
| | Quarter | | | |
| Year | 1 | 2 | 3 | 4 |
|---|---|---|---|---|
| 1 | 70 | 41 | 52 | 83 |
| 2 | 78 | 44 | 48 | 85 |
| 3 | 83 | 54 | 51 | 96 |
| 4 | 85 | 49 | 54 | 89 |

You are required to use the information given above to:

(a)  plot on a graph the quarterly sales;

(b)  derive and plot the appropriate moving average.

**6.6**  A traffic census taken at the same time each day during July on a busy road approaching a holiday resort revealed that the number of vehicles passing per hour was as follows (to nearest 10).

| | No. of vehicles | | | | |
| | Week 1 | Week 2 | Week 3 | Week 4 | Week 5 |
|---|---|---|---|---|---|
| Monday | | 840 | 840 | 830 | 820 |
| Tuesday | | 860 | 860 | 830 | |
| Wednesday | | 1190 | 1200 | 1220 | |
| Thursday | | 840 | 830 | 840 | |
| Friday | | 970 | 1020 | 1080 | |
| Saturday | 1800 | 1860 | 1950 | 2100 | |
| Sunday | 1460 | 1480 | 1520 | 1550 | |

(a)  Plot the data on a graph.

(b)  Calculate a suitable moving average and plot the trend line. Explain your choice of time period.

(c)  If the survey had been carried out in say, November, what do you think the figures would have looked like then? (You may illustrate by a rough sketch or by providing possible figures for one or two weeks.)

**6.7**

| Year | Cost of raw materials (£ per tonne) |
|------|------|
| 1 | 3.38 |
| 2 | 4.11 |
| 3 | 4.17 |
| 4 | 3.87 |
| 5 | 3.26 |
| 6 | 3.81 |
| 7 | 3.89 |
| 8 | 4.45 |
| 9 | 4.30 |
| 10 | 3.65 |
| 11 | 5.00 |

(a) Construct a five-year moving average, graphing the trend line against the original data. Comment on your results. If the interval for the moving average had not been suggested, how would you have determined it? What is the purpose of a moving average?

(b) With which characteristic movement of a time series would you mainly associate each of the following?

(i) a minor fire delaying production for three weeks;

(ii) an increase in unemployment during the winter months;

(iii) the increasing demand for small cars;

(iv) a recession.

**6.8** Unemployment as a percentage of total employees

| Year | March | June | September | December |
|------|-------|------|-----------|----------|
| 1 | 2.3 | 2.4 | 2.6 | 2.6 |
| 2 | 2.9 | 3.2 | 3.6 | 3.7 |
| 3 | 3.9 | 3.5 | 3.6 | 3.2 |
| 4 | 2.8 | 2.6 | 2.4 | 2.1 |
| 5 | 2.4 | 2.5 | | |

(a) Smooth this time series by means of a centred four-quarterly moving average.

(b) Plot the original and the moving average figures on the same graph.

(c) Discuss whether this moving average has any value for forecasting future percentage unemployment.

**6.9** For the data in Questions 6.4 to 6.8, obtain exponentially smoothed trend lines, with $\alpha = 0.2$. If you are using the spreadsheet template, try varying values of $\alpha$ and obtain the smoothest trend lines that you can.

# 7 The time series – deseasonalisation and forecasting

## The calculation of seasonal variation

In the last chapter, we looked at methods of detecting any underlying trend within time series data. In this chapter, we will attempt to remove any seasonal elements within a time series (a technique called 'deseasonalisation') and examine elementary forecasting methods.

We have defined seasonal variation as an upswing and downswing in the value of our data. If we are to measure the magnitude of these fluctuations we must have a point of reference from which to measure. After all, when we say a mountain is 1000 metres high, what we really mean is that it is 1000 metres *above sea level*. It seems logical that we should measure the magnitude of the seasonal swing as the deviation from our calculated trend figure. So seasonal variation is not merely an upswing and downswing – it is a swing around the trend line. Armed with this definition we can now calculate the quarterly variation in imports from our figures. The variation in any particular quarter will be:

(Original data MINUS calculated trend)

In the last chapter, we found the trend of raw material imports into Ruritania. We will now calculate the quarterly variation for this data:

| Year | Quarter | Imports | Trend | Deviation from trend |
|------|---------|---------|---------|---------------------|
| 19-2 | 1 | 114 | | |
| | 2 | 142 | | |
| | 3 | 155 | 137.0 | + 18.0 |
| | 4 | 136 | 138.25 | − 2.25 |
| 19-3 | 1 | 116 | 139.0 | −23.0 |
| | 2 | 150 | 139.25 | +10.75 |
| | 3 | 153 | 141.25 | +11.75 |
| | 4 | 140 | 143.75 | − 3.75 |
| 19-4 | 1 | 128 | 146.75 | −18.75 |
| | 2 | 158 | 151.125 | + 6.875 |
| | 3 | 169 | 154.625 | +14.375 |
| | 4 | 159 | 158.5 | + 0.5 |

| Year | Quarter | Imports | Trend | Deviation from trend |
|------|---------|---------|--------|----------------------|
| 19-5 | 1 | 137 | 164.125 | −27.125 |
|      | 2 | 180 | 168.625 | +11.375 |
|      | 3 | 192 | 171.25 | +20.75 |
|      | 4 | 172 | 174.0 | − 2.00 |
| 19-6 | 1 | 145 | | |
|      | 2 | 194 | | |

The meaning of the deviations we have calculated in the last column is that in that particular quarter seasonal and other influences have caused imports to vary from trend by the calculated amount. Thus, in the third quarter of 19-2 these influences cause imports to rise 18.0 points above trend; in the third quarter of 19-3, 11.75 points above trend; in the third quarter of 19-4, 14.375 points above and so on. Why should the deviations be so different in the same quarter of the year? The answer lies in the fact that seasonal and *other* influences have been at work. The deviations have been caused by both seasonal and residual influences.

While we cannot separate these two influences, it is reasonable to believe that while seasonal influences will always operate in the same direction, residual influences will sometimes raise the figures and at other times will lower them. If, then, we take a sufficiently long series and take the *average* deviation for any particular quarter, the residual influences will tend to offset each other and we will be left with the purely seasonal variation. This is the rationale behind the calculation of seasonal variation, and the reason why it is often called *average seasonal variation*.

We will now pick up the quarterly deviations from trend and tabulate them in order to calculate seasonal variation:

| | | | Quarter | | |
|---------|---------|---------|---------|---------|---------|
| Year | *1* | *2* | *3* | *4* | |
| 19-2 | | | +18.0 | −2.25 | |
| 19-3 | −23.0 | +10.75 | +11.75 | −3.75 | |
| 19-4 | −18.75 | + 6.875 | +14.375 | +0.5 | |
| 19-5 | −27.125 | +11.375 | +20.75 | −2.0 | |
| Total | −68.875 | +29.0 | +64.875 | −7.5 | |
| Average | −22.958 | + 9.667 | +16.219 | −1.875 | = +1.053 |
| Adjust | − 0.263 | − 0.263 | − 0.263 | −0.263 | |
| | −23.221 | + 9.404 | +15.956 | −2.138 | |
| SV | −23 | +9 | +16 | −2 | |

There are several things to note about this table.

- You will see that there are four deviation figures for the third and fourth quarters, but only three for the first and second. This is common and depends simply on the lengths of the series we are examining, but we must not forget it when we are calculating the average quarterly deviation.

● The total of the average deviations should be zero (remember the definition of the arithmetic mean). In fact, the total is +1.053, and since we know it should be zero an adjustment is necessary. We do not know where the difference springs from, so we adjust each quarterly average by the same amount, 0.263 (i.e. 1.053 ÷ 4). Since the total deviations are too many we will have to subtract 0.263 from each quarterly average.

● When we have made all these adjustments, we are left with average deviations correct to three places of decimals. Now this is silly! In the course of our calculations we have made a number of assumptions. Each one is a logical, reasonable assumption, but we must not pretend to a degree of accuracy we cannot guarantee. Since the original data is given in integers only, it is better to give average seasonal variation in integers also. So we will quote the seasonal variation as −23, +9, +16, −2. Notice that the total still comes to zero.

What do these figures mean? Using the figures for the first quarter as an example, it merely says that economic conditions are such that the index of imports will tend to fall below the trend, and that on average it will be 23 points below. On the other hand, in the second quarter of the year, the economic climate is different, imports tend to rise above trend and on average are nine points above it.

## Series with seasonal variation eliminated

Useful as a knowledge of seasonal variation may be to a firm planning for the future, there is little doubt that the constant fluctuations tend to hide the underlying behaviour of the variable. Comparisons and assessments of performance over time are difficult to make. When a particular salesman returns with a full order book, is it because he has made a superhuman effort, or merely because the seasonal swing is in his favour. The need to make assessments of this nature has resulted more and more in data being produced 'deseasonalised', 'seasonally adjusted', or 'with seasonal variation eliminated'.

Adjusting data to eliminate seasonal variation is a relatively simple matter. If seasonal variation is +23, we are, in effect, saying that our data is 23 points above the trend because of seasonal influences, and we must, therefore, reduce our figures by 23 to eliminate these influences. Similarly, if seasonal variation is − 23, we must add 23 to our figures. If we remember that (− −) = (+), we may formulate the rule that:

Series with seasonal variation eliminated = original data − seasonal variation

Applying this rule to the data we are analysing:

| Year | Quarter | Import index | Seasonal variation | Series with seasonal variation eliminated |
|------|---------|--------------|--------------------|-------------------------------------------|
| 19-2 | 1 | 114 | −23 | 137 |
|      | 2 | 142 | + 9 | 133 |
|      | 3 | 155 | +16 | 139 |
|      | 4 | 136 | − 2 | 138 |
| 19-3 | 1 | 116 | −23 | 139 |
|      | 2 | 150 | + 9 | 141 |
|      | 3 | 153 | +16 | 137 |
|      | 4 | 140 | − 2 | 142 |
| 19-4 | 1 | 128 | −23 | 151 |
|      | 2 | 158 | + 9 | 149 |
|      | 3 | 169 | +16 | 153 |
|      | 4 | 159 | − 2 | 161 |
| 19-5 | 1 | 137 | −23 | 160 |
|      | 2 | 180 | + 9 | 171 |
|      | 3 | 192 | +16 | 176 |
|      | 4 | 172 | − 2 | 174 |
| 19-6 | 1 | 145 | −23 | 168 |
|      | 2 | 194 | + 9 | 185 |

We now have three different series obtained from the same data, the original figures, the trend and the series with seasonal variation eliminated. When you eliminate the seasonal variation, you might, of course, expect to be left with a series approximating to trend. Do not forget, however, that residual influences will still be found in this series, and the more important the residual influence, the more the series will differ from trend.

In Fig 7.1 we have plotted the three series on the same graph. What conclusions can we draw? First, the trend shows us that there has been a steady and unbroken rise in the volume of imports over the whole period, which shows little signs of ceasing. This may be a result of an expanding industry requiring more and more raw materials, or it may be a result of the domestic consumer buying more and more foreign consumer goods. The graph will not tell us why something happens − but it will lead us to ask the questions.

Secondly, the trend and the series with seasonal variation eliminated tend to run closely together. There are differences, but they are small. So we can come to the conclusion that residual influences are fairly unimportant and do not drastically affect the level of imports. These may seem strange, but in fact events such as a dock strike which largely cuts off the flow of goods are very rare.

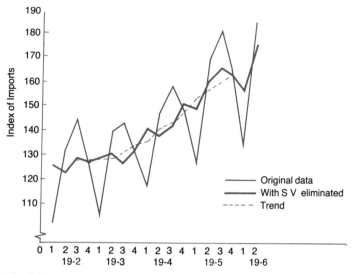

**Fig 7.1**

Nor do such residual influences as there are always work in one direction. Sometimes they raise the level of imports above trend; at other times they lower them; and the pattern is regular. In fact, so regular is the pattern that one can speculate that residuals here have a double effect. At first they slow down the level of imports, but fairly quickly a back-log of orders builds up, and as a result, in the next quarter imports have to rise as the back-log is cleared.

## The importance of residuals

You can find out a great deal about residual influences from a graph such as Fig 7.1, but it does not tell us why residual influences are important.

All planning, whether financial or not, is based on forecasting, and if the forecast cannot be relied on planning is a waste of time. Now, the characteristic of a residual is that it cannot be included in our forecast, so, when its influence is felt, the forecast is upset. In analysing our series of imports we have already discovered that the influence of residuals is fairly small. So, it is probable that though our forecast may be upset, we will not be very far wrong. On the other hand, if the residual influence is great, our forecasts may be badly upset.

Before we come to any decisions, however, we must obtain a quantitative measure of the extent of residual variations. We know that the original data is composed of:

Trend + Seasonal variations + Residual variations

and it follows then that:

Residuals = Original data − Trend − Seasonal variations

Let us, then, bring together the calculations we have made so far:

| Year | Quarter | Imports | Trend | Seasonal variation | Residual Absolute | Residual As % of imports |
|------|---------|---------|-------|-----------|----------|----------|
| 19-2 | 1 | 114 |         | −23 |       |      |
|      | 2 | 142 |         | + 9 |       |      |
|      | 3 | 155 | 137.0   | +16 | +2    | 1.3  |
|      | 4 | 136 | 138.25  | − 2 | −0.25 | 0.18 |
| 19-3 | 1 | 116 | 139.0   | −23 | 0.0   | —    |
|      | 2 | 150 | 139.25  | + 9 | +1.75 | 1.17 |
|      | 3 | 153 | 141.25  | +16 | −4.25 | 2.78 |
|      | 4 | 140 | 143.75  | − 2 | −1.75 | 1.25 |
| 19-4 | 1 | 128 | 146.75  | −23 | +4.25 | 3.32 |
|      | 2 | 158 | 151.125 | + 9 | −2.125 | 1.34 |
|      | 3 | 169 | 154.625 | +16 | −1.625 | 0.96 |
|      | 4 | 159 | 158.5   | − 2 | +2.5  | 1.57 |
| 19-5 | 1 | 137 | 164.125 | −23 | −4.125 | 3.01 |
|      | 2 | 180 | 168.625 | + 9 | +2.375 | 1.32 |
|      | 3 | 192 | 171.25  | +16 | +4.75 | 2.47 |
|      | 4 | 172 | 174.0   | − 2 | 0.0   | —    |
| 19-6 | 1 | 145 |         | −23 |       |      |
|      | 2 | 194 |         | + 9 |       |      |

Our calculations confirm what we suspected from the graph. The residual influence never affects our figures by more than 4.75 points, and, what is more important, on only two occasions is there more than a 3% influence. Thus, if our forecast is otherwise accurate, we would expect it to be correct to within 3% in spite of the residual influences.

## Forecasting from the time series

The key words in the last paragraph are 'if our forecast is otherwise accurate'. Naturally, in looking to the future, absolute accuracy is difficult to attain, but nevertheless, very good forecasts can be made.

**Projecting the trend**

The basis of the forecasting we will do lies in our knowledge of the behaviour of trend. The trend will not suddenly change direction. As you can see, in Fig 7.2 the trend is beginning to rise rather more slowly.

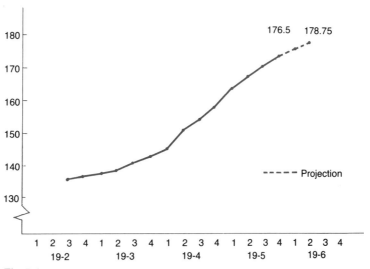

**Fig 7.2**

Over the next few quarters the rate of rise may continue to fall and eventually the trend will reach a maximum and perhaps begin to fall. Or it may slowly change direction upwards with an accelerated rate of rise. The point is that it is not going to change *suddenly*. So, we can extend (or project) the trend forward over the next two or three quarters, confident that our projection will be fairly accurate. The further we project the trend, of course, the greater is the possibility of inaccuracy, and great care is needed in making the projection.

In Fig 7.2 the trend is drawn and a suggested projection made, extending over the next two quarters. We make no claim, of course, that this projection is perfect, and you may make a far more accurate one yourself. Our new trend values are:

$$
\begin{array}{lll}
\text{19-6 Quarter 1} & & 176.5 \\
2 & & 178.75
\end{array}
$$

To understand just how we can use these figures we will go back to the calculation of trend and reproduce the last part of the calculations:

| Year | Quarter | Imports Col. 1 | Moving annual total Col. 2 | Moving pair total Col. 3 | Trend Col. 4 |
|------|---------|----------------|----------------------------|--------------------------|--------------|
| 19-5 | 3 | 192 | 681 | 1370 | 171.25 |
|      | 4 | 172 | 689 | 1392 | 174.0 |
| 19-6 | 1 | 145 | 703 | $(8x = 1412)$ | $(x = 176.5)$ |
|      | 2 | 194 | $(8x - 703 = 709)$ | $8y =$ | $(y = 178.75)$ |
|      | 3 | $(a = 198)$ |  |  |  |
|      | 4 | $b =$ |  |  |  |

We will call the forecast values for 19-6, Quarter three, $a$, and that for Quarter 4, $b$. Suppose the trend value we read from the graph is $x$. This is placed in Column 4. But we obtain $x$ by dividing Column 3 by eight, so in Column 3 we must place $8x$. In its turn this $8x$ is the sum of 703 plus an unknown number, which will have therefore a value $8x - 703$, which is the next figure in Column 2. Column 2 is the sum of four import indices and $8x - 703 = 145 + 172 + 194 + a$. It follows then that:

$$a = 8x - 703 - 172 - 145 - 194 = 8x - 1214$$

Since $x = 176.5$

$$a = (8 \times 176.5) - 1214 = 1412 - 1214 = 198$$

This seems to be a reasonable forecast since the third quarter is always slightly higher than the second quarter (which was 194). The values we have calculated have been placed in the appropriate columns in the table. Now, using these figures, and given that the value of the trend $y$ is 178.75, calculate for yourself the value of the import index for the fourth quarter of 19-6.[*] The answer is given in the footnote, and you will probably agree that the two figures we have forecast are entirely consistent with the pattern of the series.

Forecasting by projecting the trend of an annual series is exactly the same as for a quarterly series. Suppose we are taking a five-year moving average, and the last few rows of our calculations are:

| Year | Output | 5-year total | Trend |
|------|--------|--------------|-------|
| 19-2 | 15 | 70 | 14.0 |
| 19-3 | 18 | 74 | 14.8 |
| 19-4 | 13 | 76 | 15.2 |
| 19-5 | 14 | ? | ? |
| 19-6 | 16 |  |  |
| 19-7 | ? |  |  |

[*] Answer: $y = 178.75$  $b = 8y - 709 - 145 - 194 - 198 = 8y - 1246 = 1428 - 1246 = 182$

The first step in forecasting a value for 19-7 would be to project the trend forward. We could then read a value for 19-5. Suppose this value of the projected trend were 15.6. This figure is the average of a five-year total in the previous column, so that total must be $5 \times 15.6 = 78$. This in itself is the sum of $18 + 13 + 14 + 16 +$ (output in 19-7). Thus output in 19-7 would be forecast as:

$$78 - 18 - 13 - 14 - 16 = 17.$$

**The average rate of change**

The problem with projecting the trend by eye is that forecasts made using this method will not be consistent. If you ask a number of people to use this method, then it is almost certain that there will be variations in the forecasts made because opinions will vary as to the future position of the trend. What we require is a method that will achieve a consistent forecast, and this can be done by considering the *average rate of change of the trend*. Consider the trend values for the index of imports:

| Year | Quarter | Trend |
|------|---------|----------|
| 19-2 | 3 | 137.0000 |
|      | 4 | 138.2500 |
| 19-3 | 1 | 139.0000 |
|      | 2 | 139.2500 |
|      | 3 | 141.2500 |
|      | 4 | 143.7500 |
| 19-4 | 1 | 146.7500 |
|      | 2 | 151.1250 |
|      | 3 | 154.6250 |
|      | 4 | 158.5000 |
| 19-5 | 1 | 164.1250 |
|      | 2 | 168.6250 |
|      | 3 | 171.2500 |
|      | 4 | 174.0000 |

For the period over which trend values are available, the trend has increased by $174 - 137 = 37$ units. Over this same period, the trend has changed 13 times (one less than the number of trend values). Hence the average rate of change in trend is $37/13 = 2.846$ units.

Future trend values can be predicted by adding the average rate of change to the previous values. So, for example:

Forecast trend for 19-6 quarter 1 is $174.000 + 2.846 = 176.846$
Forecast trend for 19-6 quarter 2 is $176.846 + 2.846 = 179.692$
Forecast trend for 19-6 quarter 3 is $179.692 + 2.846 = 182.538$
Forecast trend for 19-6 quarter 4 is $182.538 + 2.846 = 185.384$

Forecasts for these periods can now be made by adding the appropriate value for seasonal variation.

| Year | Quarter | Forecast trend | Seasonal variation | Forecast index |
|------|---------|----------------|--------------------|----------------|
| 19-6 | 1 | 176.846 | $-23$ | $153.846 = 154$ |
|      | 2 | 179.692 | $+ 9$ | $188.692 = 189$ |
|      | 3 | 182.538 | $+16$ | $198.538 = 199$ |
|      | 4 | 185.384 | $- 2$ | $183.384 = 183$ |

We have the actual values for the import index for the first two quarters of 19-6, and they can be used to check the accuracy of our forecasts. The actual value for the first quarter is 145 (compared with the 154 forecast) and the actual value for the second quarter is 194 (compared with the 189 forecast).

Many statisticians would argue that finding the average rate of change of the trend over the whole period for which data is available may not be a valid method of predicting the future value of the trend. The most recent data may be the more valid, and some statisticians think that the last three trend values only should be used to estimate the future trend value.

| 19-5 | 1 | 164.1250 |
|------|---|----------|
|      | 2 | 168.6250 |
|      | 3 | 171.2500 |
|      | 4 | 174.0000 |

Using this method for the import index data, the change in trend over the last three trend values is $174 - 168.625 = 5.375$, and as two changes in trend values have occurred over this period, the average rate of change is $5.375/2 = 2.6875$. Again, future trend values can be predicted by adding the average rate of change to the previous values.

Forecast trend for 19-6 quarter 1 is $174.0000 + 2.6875 = 176.6875$
Forecast trend for 19-6 quarter 2 is $176.6875 + 2.6875 = 179.3750$
Forecast trend for 19-6 quarter 3 is $179.3750 + 2.6875 = 182.0625$
Forecast trend for 19-6 quarter 4 is $182.0625 + 2.6875 = 184.7500$

| Year | Quarter | Forecast trend | Seasonal variation | Forecast index |
|------|---------|----------------|--------------------|----------------|
| 19-6 | 1 | 176.6875 | $-23$ | $153.6875 = 154$ |
|      | 2 | 179.3750 | $+ 9$ | $188.3750 = 188$ |
|      | 3 | 182.0625 | $+16$ | $198.0625 = 198$ |
|      | 4 | 184.7500 | $- 2$ | $182.7500 = 183$ |

In this example, both methods produce essentially similar results, though this will not always be the case.

Of course, it would be perfectly possible to use the trend values forecast from the average rate of change and then 'work backward' as was done when the trend position was estimated by eye. Using the trend values forecast from the last three periods this would be done as follows:

| Year | Quarter | Imports | Moving annual total | Moving pair total | Trend | |
|------|---------|---------|---------------------|-------------------|-------|--|
| 19-5 | 3 | 192 | | | | |
| | | | 689 | | | |
| | 4 | 172 | | 1392 | 174.000 | Actual |
| | | | 703 | | | |
| 19-6 | 1 | 145 | | 1413(.5) | 176.6875 | Forecast |
| | | | 710 | | | |
| | 2 | 194 | | 1435 | 179.3750 | |
| | | | 725 | | | |
| | 3 | 199 | | | | |
| | 4 | 187 | | | | |

The advantage of using the last three trend values for estimating the trend and then working backward is that emphasis is placed on the most recent data. The disadvantage is that if the most recent data is not typical of the series, then forecasts will be distorted.

## Additive or multiplicative model?

In our analysis of time series, we have assumed that:

Actual data = Trend + seasonal variation (+ residuals)

This is the so-called *additive model*: it assumes that there is a constant absolute difference between the actual data and the trend, and we call this difference the seasonal variation. Now most statisticians think this is not a reasonable assumption: it does not seem reasonable to adjust every (say) first quarter by adding or subtracting a constant amount. It would be much better to adjust every corresponding quarter by a constant percentage. This gives the more satisfactory *multiplicative model*:

Actual data = Trend × seasonal variation (+ residuals)

Instead, then, of taking seasonal variation to be the average of the (actual − trend) values, we will take it to be the average of the (actual/trend) values. Let us rework our example of the import index, this time using the multiplicative model. The trend is calculated in exactly the same manner as for the additive model – by using a four-quarter, centred, moving average.

| Year | Quarter | Import index | Trend | Actual/<br>Trend |
|------|---------|--------------|---------|--------|
| 19-2 | 1 | 114 | | |
| | 2 | 142 | | |
| | 3 | 155 | 137.000 | 1.1313 |
| | 4 | 136 | 138.250 | 0.9837 |
| 19-3 | 1 | 116 | 139.000 | 0.8345 |
| | 2 | 150 | 139.250 | 1.0771 |
| | 3 | 153 | 141.250 | 1.0831 |
| | 4 | 140 | 143.750 | 0.9739 |
| 19-4 | 1 | 128 | 146.750 | 0.8722 |
| | 2 | 158 | 151.125 | 1.0454 |
| | 3 | 169 | 154.625 | 1.0929 |
| | 4 | 159 | 158.500 | 1.0031 |
| 19-5 | 1 | 137 | 164.125 | 0.8347 |
| | 2 | 180 | 168.625 | 1.0674 |
| | 3 | 192 | 171.250 | 1.1211 |
| | 4 | 172 | 174.000 | 0.9885 |
| 19-6 | 1 | 145 | | |
| | 2 | 194 | | |

| | | Quarter | | |
|------|--------|--------|--------|--------|
| Year | 1 | 2 | 3 | 4 |
| 19-2 | | | 1.1313 | 0.9837 |
| 19-3 | 0.8345 | 1.0771 | 1.0831 | 0.9739 |
| 19-4 | 0.8722 | 1.0454 | 1.0929 | 1.0031 |
| 19-5 | 0.8347 | 1.0674 | 1.1211 | 0.9885 |
| Total | 2.5414 | 3.1899 | 4.4284 | 3.9492 |
| Average | 0.8471 | 1.0633 | 1.1071 | 0.9873 |

We would predict the total of the average ratios to be four, whereas it is 4.0048. So we must adjust the averages by multiplying each average ratio by $\frac{4}{4.0048}$ to give seasonal variation ratios:

| | Quarter | | |
|------|------|------|------|
| 1 | 2 | 3 | 4 |
| 0.846 | 1.062 | 1.106 | 0.986 |

If we wish to find a deseasonalised series, we would divide the actual data by the seasonal variation.

| Year | Quarter | Index | Seasonal ratio | Deseasonalised index |
|------|---------|-------|----------------|----------------------|
| 19-2 | 1 | 114 | 0.846 | 135 |
|      | 2 | 142 | 1.062 | 134 |
|      | 3 | 155 | 1.106 | 140 |
|      | 4 | 136 | 0.986 | 138 |
| 19-3 | 1 | 116 | 0.846 | 137 |
|      | 2 | 150 | 1.062 | 141 |
|      | 3 | 153 | 1.106 | 138 |
|      | 4 | 140 | 0.986 | 142 |
| 19-4 | 1 | 128 | 0.846 | 151 |
|      | 2 | 158 | 1.062 | 149 |
|      | 3 | 169 | 1.106 | 153 |
|      | 4 | 159 | 0.986 | 161 |
| 19-5 | 1 | 137 | 0.846 | 162 |
|      | 2 | 180 | 1.062 | 169 |
|      | 3 | 192 | 1.106 | 174 |
|      | 4 | 172 | 0.986 | 174 |
| 19-6 | 1 | 145 | 0.846 | 171 |
|      | 2 | 194 | 1.062 | 183 |

Finally, if seasonal ratios are to be used for forecasting, then forecast trend values are multiplied by the seasonal ratios to give the actual forecasts. Again, using the import index example, if the trend is forecast using the average rate of change of the trend for the whole period for which data is available, then the import index would be forecast thus:

| Year | Quarter | Forecast trend | Seasonal ratio | Forecast index |
|------|---------|----------------|----------------|----------------|
| 19-6 | 1 | 176.846 | 0.864 | 149.612 = 150 |
|      | 2 | 179.692 | 1.062 | 190.833 = 191 |
|      | 3 | 182.538 | 1.106 | 201.884 = 202 |
|      | 4 | 185.384 | 0.986 | 182.789 = 183 |

## Using the spreadsheet

The menu structure of the spreadsheet template to accompany this chapter is shown in Fig 7.3.

Select 'New data' and enter quarterly data. Press ALT G and the menu returns. Now select 'Quarterly' option: the template outputs the trend. Now select 'Deseasonalise' and you are presented with the option to use either the additive or multiplicative model. Whichever model is selected, the template outputs seasonal variation and deseasonalised data, together with a prediction for the last two quarters of the current data and the next two quarters. You should note that the extrapolated trend is obtained by taking the average rate of change for the whole period for which trend data is available.

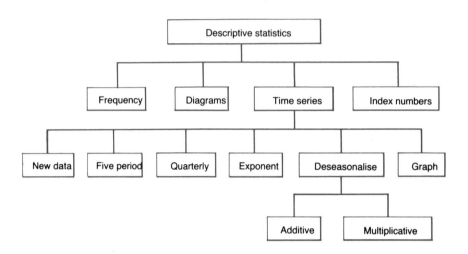

**Fig 7.3**

QUESTIONS

**7.1** The number of prescriptions dispensed by chemists under the National Health Service in England and Wales during a five-year period is shown in the table below.

*NHS prescriptions (millions)*

| Year | 1 | 2 | 3 | 4 |
|------|-----|-----|-----|-----|
| 1 |     |     | 60 | 71 |
| 2 | 69 | 67 | 62 | 69 |
| 3 | 73 | 66 | 62 | 68 |
| 4 | 72 | 66 | 65 | 67 |
| 5 | 75 |     |     |     |

(a) Plot the data on a graph.

(b) Calculate and plot on the same graph a suitable moving average.

(c) Using the additive model, obtain the average seasonal variation.

**7.2**

| | *Percentage Turnover of Labour Force* | | | |
|---|---|---|---|---|
| | | *Quarter* | | |
| *Year* | *1* | *2* | *3* | *4* |
| 19-0 | 11 | 23 | 16 | 8 |
| 19-1 | 14 | 29 | 16 | 9 |
| 19-2 | 18 | 34 | 17 | 9 |
| 19-3 | 19 | 42 | 23 | 12 |

(a) Smooth this time series by means of a centred four-quarterly moving average.

(b) Calculate the average seasonal variations. (Use the additive model.)

(c) Using the average rate of change of trend for the whole period and seasonal variations calculated in (b), forecast the turnover for the first two quarters of 19-4.

**7.3**

| | *Quarterly Sales (£000)* | | | |
|---|---|---|---|---|
| | | *Quarter* | | |
| *Year* | *1* | *2* | *3* | *4* |
| 19-0 | 19 | 30 | 63 | 8 |
| 19-1 | 20 | 32 | 67 | 16 |
| 19-2 | 23 | 35 | 74 | 14 |

Find the quarterly trend values. Using the average rate of change of trend for the last three periods, and 'working backward', forecast sales for the first two quarters of 19-3.

**7.4**

| | *Number of houses completed in England and Wales* | | | |
|---|---|---|---|---|
| | | *Quarter* | | |
| *Year* | *1* | *2* | *3* | *4* |
| 19-0 | 32 458 | 32 881 | 35 049 | 39 462 |
| 19-1 | 33 310 | 31 953 | 33 628 | 35 983 |
| 19-2 | 30 808 | 27 935 | 27 526 | 30 946 |
| 19-3 | 28 674 | | | |

(a) Rewrite the number of houses completed to the nearest hundred.

(b) Using the rounded data: (i) calculate, by means of four-quarterly moving averages, the trend of the series; (ii) calculate the seasonal variations (use the multiplicative model).

(c) State the main factors affecting a time series.

**7.5** The following data gives the index numbers for cost of labour for a small firm during the period 19-5 to 19-8. By calculating an appropriate moving average obtain the trend and hence the seasonal factors for each quarter (use the multiplicative model). Using the average rate of change of trend for the whole period and seasonal factors calculated, obtain a forecast of the index for the fourth quarter of 19-8.

|        |        | Quarter |       |       |
| Year   | 1      | 2       | 3     | 4     |
| --- | --- | --- | --- | --- |
| 19-5   |        |         |       | 103.5 |
| 19-6   | 102.2  | 101.2   | 95.1  | 103.5 |
| 19-7   | 99.1   | 103.8   | 96.8  | 109.0 |
| 19-8   | 112.1  | 110.5   | 105.2 |       |

**7.6**

Supplies and deliveries of
crude steel (thousand tonnes)

|        |      | Quarter |      |      |
| Year   | 1    | 2       | 3    | 4    |
| --- | --- | --- | --- | --- |
| 19-5   | 480  | 520     | 466  | 526  |
| 19-6   | 541  | 541     | 440  | 510  |
| 19-7   | 538  | 544     | 493  | 531  |

(a) Calculate the average seasonal variation for this data (use the additive model)

(b) Deseasonalise the series.

(c) Briefly comment on your findings.

**7.7**

|        |      | Quarter |      |      |
| Year   | 1    | 2       | 3    | 4    |
| --- | --- | --- | --- | --- |
| 19-0   |      | 110     | 120  | 140  |
| 19-1   | 110  | 124     | 130  | 154  |
| 19-2   | 123  | 134     | 143  | 176  |
| 19-3   | 139  |         |      |      |

The above data gives the index numbers for the total value of sales in catering in Great Britain for the years 19-0 to 19-3. By calculating an appropriate moving average obtain the trend and hence the seasonal factors for each quarter (use the multiplicative model). Deseasonalise the quarters of 19-2.

**7.8**

| | | Days lost due to industrial accidents | | |
|---|---|---|---|---|
| | | | Quarter | |
| Year | 1 | 2 | 3 | 4 |
| 19-4 | 152 | 204 | 134 | 213 |
| 19-5 | 187 | 198 | 311 | 299 |
| 19-6 | 210 | 257 | 231 | 323 |
| 19-7 | 201 | 225 | 236 | 318 |
| 19-8 | 180 | | | |

From the data given in the table calculate the average seasonal variation in days lost in the years 19-4 to 19-7 inclusive (use the multiplicative model). Deseasonalise the data.

**7.9**

| | | No. of visitors (hundreds) | | |
|---|---|---|---|---|
| | | | Quarter | |
| Year | 1 | 2 | 3 | 4 |
| 19-2 | 58 | 85 | 97 | 73 |
| 19-3 | 64 | 96 | 107 | 89 |
| 19-4 | 76 | 102 | 115 | 94 |

The above table shows the number of visitors (in hundreds) to an hotel during a period of three years. By using the method of moving averages, rewrite the series without seasonal variations (use the multiplicative model).

Using the average rate of change of trend for the last three periods, and 'working backward', forecast visitors for the first two quarters of 19-5.

**7.10** The following table gives the sales (in hundreds) of components manufactured by Company A.

| | | Quarterly sales in hundreds | | |
|---|---|---|---|---|
| | | | Quarter | |
| Year | 1 | 2 | 3 | 4 |
| 19-2 | | | | 13 |
| 19-3 | 14 | 16 | 9 | 14 |
| 19-4 | 16 | 17 | 12 | 17 |
| 19-5 | 18 | 20 | 13 | |

Calculate the seasonal fluctuations and rewrite the series with the seasonal variations removed (use the multiplicative model).

Draw a graph of the trend values and project it into 19-6. Calculate the expected sales for the next four quarters.

**7.11** Quarterly production at a paper making plant was reported as follows:

|  | Quarterly production (000 tonnes) | | | |
| --- | --- | --- | --- | --- |
|  | Quarter | | | |
| Year | 1 | 2 | 3 | 4 |
| 19-2 | 38.8 | 41.3 | 39.0 | 45.6 |
| 19-3 | 44.7 | 45.2 | 42.0 | 49.9 |
| 19-4 | 46.7 | 48.2 | 44.5 | 51.3 |
| 19-5 | 50.1 | 54.6 | | |

Using the method of moving averages, find the average seasonal deviations (use the multiplicative model).

Using the average rate of change of trend for the whole period and seasonal ratios calculated, forecast production for the last two quarters of 19-5.

# 8 Index numbers

In Chapter 5, we explored at some depth the meaning of the word average, and we were at pains to point out that an average is not necessarily representative of the data it describes. In this chapter, we are going to concern ourselves with averages at work – especially in an economic context. Make no mistake about it, averages do play a very important part in our lives – especially those that try to describe economic data. Now statisticians have constructed a device which attempts to measure the magnitude of economic changes over time – a device called an *index number*. This device is also used for international comparisons of economic data. Almost certainly, the Index of Retail Prices is the most widely quoted of all index numbers. Let us now examine just how important this index is to all of us.

You will realise that the Index of Retail Prices attempts to measure the change in the price of a whole range of goods and services that we regularly buy. So you can see that it is attempting to measure the cost of living – something that vitally concerns us all. In times of inflation, the retail price index is probably more important than at any other time in its existence. The United Kingdom government has a policy to keep inflation under strict control and this index is used as a yardstick of its success.

Its importance does not stop here. Increases in the cost of living have been accepted as justification for an increase in pay, and the Index of Retail Prices has often been used as a basis for wages negotiations. In fact, under the last Labour administration in the 1970s many million workers obtained an automatic 40p rise per week for each one-point rise in the cost of living index – the so-called threshold payments. Due to government pressure, it is no longer fashionable to link wage rates to the cost of living directly, but any incomes policy that ignores the index altogether seems doomed to failure. As further examples of the importance of this index we could note that the government has introduced an index-linked issue of savings certificates, the value of which will rise with the cost of living. Also, it is government policy to make pensions index-linked. If we are willing to accept index linking as desirable, we should be sure that we know what an index is, how it is calculated and what its limitations are.

Without doubt, an index is an extremely fashionable statistical tool. Open any copy of the Annual Abstract of Statistics and you are sure to be impressed by the number of indexes (or indices, if you prefer this form of the plural) that are calculated by the government statisticians. In fact, no self-respecting government department would fail to produce at least one index! We do not wish you to get the impression that all index numbers are generated by government departments – the *Financial Times* Ordinary Share Index, and the *Economist*'s Key Indicators are notable indexes generated by the private sector. With the great number of indexes available, and the fact that they are used as a basis for taking decisions of national importance, it is worrying to be told that some statisticians doubt their validity. Now we cannot subscribe to this view. Index numbers are an invaluable tool in the decision-taking process – provided that they are treated with caution!

## An expenditure index

An index number is merely a device to measure the change in some economic variable over time. One particular time period is chosen (called the *base* period) and the variable for that period is given an arbitrary value of 100. An *index* is then calculated for the remaining periods on the assumption that the base period has a value of 100. An index, then, gives the percentage change that has occurred since that base period.

**EXAMPLE**

Al Coholic throws a (rather unusual) party each Christmas for his friends. Details of his expenditure on food and drink are as follows:

|  | 1992 | | 1993 | |
|  | price | quantity | price | quantity |
|  | $p_0$ | $q_0$ | $p_n$ | $q_n$ |
|---|---|---|---|---|
| Lager (per bottle) | £1.00 | 40 | £1.15 | 50 |
| Crisps (per packet) | £0.20 | 100 | £0.27 | 90 |
| Cake | £2.00 | 1 | £2.20 | 1 |

In 1992, Al spent $£1.00 \times 40 + £0.20 \times 100 + £2.00 \times 1 = £62.00$ and in 1993 he spent $£1.15 \times 50 + £0.27 \times 90 + £2.20 \times 1 = £84.00$. If we call expenditure in 1992 100, then expenditure in 1993 would be:

$$\frac{84}{62} \times 100 = 135.4$$

which shows that his expenditure in 1993 was 35.4% higher than in 1992.

As you might expect, the index we have calculated is called an *expenditure index*. If we call base year prices and quantities $p_0$ and $q_0$, and current year prices and quantities $p_n$ and $q_n$, then we can calculate any expenditure index like this:

$$\frac{\Sigma p_n q_n}{\Sigma p_0 q_0} \times 100$$

## A price index

Now one reason for the change in expenditure incurred by Al Coholic is the change in the price of the goods he has bought. It would be interesting to construct an index number to measure the extent of the change in price. Now expenditure is made up of two components, price and quantities bought, and any change in either (or both) of these components will cause a change in expenditure. So it must follow that if we hold quantities constant, then any change in expenditure must be due to price changes.

**EXAMPLE**

We know that the total expenditure incurred by Al in 1992 was:

$$1.00 \times 40 + 0.20 \times 100 + 2.00 \times 1 = £62$$

If Al had bought the same quantities in 1993 then his total expenditure would have been:

$$1.15 \times 40 + 0.27 \times 100 + 2.20 \times 1 = £75.20$$

As we have held the quantities constant, the change in outlay must be entirely due to the change in price. If we call the price index for 1992 100, then the index for 1993 is:

$$\frac{75.20}{62} \times 100 = 121.3$$

i.e. prices have increased by 21.3%.

**Laspeyre's Index** Using the same symbols as before, we can calculate this index by taking:

$$\frac{\Sigma p_n q_0}{\Sigma p_0 q_0} \times 100$$

It shows what the cost of goods in the nth year would be, assuming that we bought the same quantities as in the base year, and assuming that we call the base year price 100. An index calculated in this way is called *Laspeyre's Index*.

Now you may well complain that we have made a bit of a meal of calculating a price index. We could argue that the cost of 'one of each' in 1992 was £1.00 × £0.20 + £2 = £3.20, and the cost of 'one of each' in 1993 was £1.15 + £0.27 + £2.20 = £3.62. With 1992 as base year, the price index for 1993 is:

$$\frac{3.62}{3.20} \times 100 = 113.1$$

An index calculated in this way is called a *simple aggregative index* and it has two major faults. First, the value of the index will depend upon the pricing unit used – if we had quoted the price of lager as '£12 per case of 12' for 1992 and '£13.80 per case of 12' for 1993 we would have obtained a very different answer – even though we have not changed the price per bottle. The second drawback of this method is that it assumes that the items bought have the same significance to us, as it takes no account of the quantities bought. Surely, a 50% increase in the price of lager will have more significance to Al than a 50% increase in the price of cake? After all, he buys 40 bottles of lager but only one cake! Fortunately, Laspeyre's Index suffers from neither of these defects. By taking into account the quantities bought, it recognises that some items bought have more significance to us than others. Using the statistician's jargon, Laspeyre's Index gives a *weighting* to the individual items to show their relative importance, using the quantities bought in the base year as weights.

Before we judge the efficiency of Laspeyre's Index we should note that in practice it is not usually calculated in the way we have done – it is more usual to use *price relatives*. Price relatives refer to individual items in the index, and simply show the change in price per item since the base year. So the price relatives are calculated like this:

$$\frac{p_n}{p_0} \times 100$$

| EXAMPLE |
|---|

The price relatives for the items bought by Al Coholic would be:

|  | *Price in* | | *Price relative* |
|---|---|---|---|
|  | *1992* | *1993* |  |
|  | $p_0$ | $p_n$ |  |
| Lager | £1.00 | £1.15 | 115.0 |
| Crisps | £0.20 | £0.27 | 135.0 |
| Cake | £2.00 | £2.20 | 110.0 |

To calculate the price index, we must now weight the price relatives, and the appropriate weights for Laspeyre's Index is expenditure in the base year.

|  | 1992 Price $p_0$ | Quantity $q_0$ | Expenditure (weight) | Relative | Weight $\times PR$ |
|---|---|---|---|---|---|
| Lager | £1.00 | 40 | 40 | 115.0 | 4600 |
| Crisps | £0.20 | 100 | 20 | 135.0 | 2700 |
| Cake | £2.00 | 1 | 2 | 110.0 | 220 |
|  |  |  | 62 |  | 7520 |

The price index is now found by taking:

$$\frac{\Sigma(\text{price relative} \times \text{weight})}{\Sigma(\text{weights})} \times 100$$

$$\frac{7520}{62} = 121.3$$

So we have a choice of two methods for calculating Laspeyre's Index. If we wish to use base-year quantities as weights, then we must use actual prices to calculate our price index. However, if we use base-year expenditures as weights, then we use price relatives to calculate the index. As stated earlier, it is more usual in practice to use expenditure as weights. The reason is quite simply that it is easier to obtain data on expenditure (cost of living weights are obtained by the Survey of Household Expenditure – that is, by sampling). Also, we can consider occasions when 'quantities' wouldn't make sense – how can one define 'quantities' of public transport? However, it would be quite possible to obtain details of personal expenditure on public transport.

Let us summarise what we have done so far. We have calculated an index called Laspeyre's Index, which tells us what we would have paid in year $n$ for a collection of goods assuming we bought base-year quantities. This description is true whether we use expenditure or quantities as weights. The point is that Laspeyre's Index uses base-year statistics as weights.

**Paasche's Index**  Many statisticians doubt the validity of taking base-year weights, as it implies that the quantities we buy do not vary over time. In many cases this will not be true. Suppose we have a cost of living index based on 1970, and one of the items included is potatoes. The index for 1976 would assume that we bought the same quantity of potatoes as in 1970. But the period 1975–1976 saw a dramatic increase in the price of potatoes, and one consequence of this was a fall in demand. Without doubt, people consumed considerably fewer potatoes and turned to substitutes, so because of this fall in quantity purchased the Laspeyre Index tends to *overstate* increases in price. Another problem is that tastes tend to change fairly markedly over time, so weights that were appropriate for 1970 will not be appropriate for today. For example, few colour television sets were bought in 1970 in preference to monochrome, but today this situation is completely reversed.

In an attempt to overcome these problems, many statisticians have suggested that current-year quantities should be used as weights. Our index now becomes:

$$\frac{\Sigma p_n q_n}{\Sigma p_0 q_n} \times 100$$

and such an index is called a *Paasche Index*. The approach here is quite different: we ask what would be the total outlay in the base year if we bought current-year quantities, and compare this with current year outlay.

---

**EXAMPLE**

Paasche's Price Index for the data supplied by Al Coholic is:

|  | 1992 | 1993 |  |  |  |
|---|---|---|---|---|---|
|  | $p_0$ | $p_n$ | $q_n$ | $p_0 q_n$ | $p_n q_n$ |
| Lager | £1.00 | £1.15 | 50 | 50 | 57.5 |
| Crisps | £0.20 | £0.27 | 90 | 18 | 24.3 |
| Cake | £2.00 | £2.20 | 1 | 2 | 2.2 |
|  |  |  |  | 70 | 84.0 |

$$\text{Paasche's Price Index} = \frac{84}{70} \times 100 = 120$$

---

This certainly overcomes the main objections to the Laspeyre Index, but does tend to raise problems of its own. First, the Paasche Index is not a pure price index as it also takes into account changes in quantities bought. Just, then, as the Laspeyre Index tends to overstate the effect of rising prices, the Paasche Index tends to understate the effects. Secondly, it can be a long and expensive job calculating the values for weights with a Paasche Index. This must be done for every period, while with a Laspeyre Index this is done for the base year only. The current cost of living index is a compromise between the two: the index is published monthly and the weights are adjusted annually by the Survey of Consumer Expenditure.

## A volume index

So far, we have assumed that the change in expenditure incurred by Al Coholic has been due to price changes, and we have attempted to measure the extent of the price change with a price index. However, the change in expenditure could be due to changes in quantities bought, and we can measure the extent of these changes by a *volume index*. We have been comparing Al Coholic's expenditure at two moments of time. If we keep the quantities bought the same, then any variation in outlay must be due to changes in price, so we can calculate a price index. If, however, we keep the prices the same, then any variation in outlay must be due to changes in quantities bought, so we can calculate a volume index. If, then, we use quantities as weights we obtain a price index, but if we use prices as weights then we obtain a volume index. Again, we have the choice between current-year and base-year weighting, so we have:

$$\text{Laspeyre's Volume Index} \quad \frac{\Sigma p_0 q_n}{\Sigma p_0 q_0} \times 100$$

$$\text{Paasche's Volume Index} \quad \frac{\Sigma p_n q_n}{\Sigma p_n q_0} \times 100$$

Let us now calculate both indexes for the data supplied by Al Coholic.

EXAMPLE

|  | 1992 | | 1993 | | | | | |
|---|---|---|---|---|---|---|---|---|
|  | Price | Quantity | Price | Quantity | | | | |
|  | $p_0$ | $q_0$ | $p_n$ | $q_n$ | $p_0q_0$ | $p_0q_n$ | $p_nq_0$ | $p_nq_n$ |
| Lager | 1.00 | 40 | 1.15 | 50 | 40 | 50 | 46.0 | 57.5 |
| Crisps | 0.20 | 100 | 0.27 | 90 | 20 | 18 | 27.0 | 24.3 |
| Cake | 2.00 | 1 | 2.20 | 1 | 2 | 2 | 2.2 | 2.2 |
|  |  |  |  |  | 62 | 70 | 75.2 | 84.0 |

$$\text{Laspeyre's Volume Index} = \frac{70}{62} \times 100 = 112.9$$

$$\text{Paasche's Volume Index} = \frac{84.0}{75.2} \times 100 = 111.7$$

## Selecting a suitable base period

One of the main problems in constructing index numbers is the choice of a suitable base period. We wish really to choose a base when the price is as 'normal' as possible, i.e. when the price is not unduly high or unduly low. Otherwise, the index will move away from the base figure too quickly and show very large deviations from it. Suppose, for example, the price of a particular stock at certain periods of time was:

| | | |
|---|---|---|
| April | 125p | (takeover rumour) |
| July | 69p | (takeover unsuccessful, poor dividends announced) |
| Dec | 95p | (quite good dividends forecast) |

then the price index for this particular stock could be:

| | *April = 100* | *July = 100* | *Dec. = 100* |
|---|---|---|---|
| April | 100 | 181.2 | 131.6 |
| July | 55.2 | 100 | 72.6 |
| Dec | 76 | 137.7 | 100 |

The best base to choose is probably December, because this minimises the greatest deviation from the base (31.6). Does this matter? Well, there is evidence to show that people are more likely to understand and appreciate smaller percentage changes than larger ones. This is one of the reasons that statisticians tend to update the bases that they use. Another reason is that bases in the not-too-distant past tend to be much more meaningful to the users of the index. It would be much more reasonable to compare prices now with prices 10 years ago than it would be to compare them with prices in 1949.

This problem of choosing a suitable base can also be illustrated if we are constructing an index to measure the volume of production. If we take as our base a month in which there is a major strike, then the index in the following months would be bound to show a substantial increase and give a misleading impression of the prosperity of the industry. If we were constructing an index of motor-car sales, which do you think would be the *worst* month to choose as a base?

An alternative to updating the base period is to use instead a *chain-based system*, where the base used is the previous period. This method has found particular favour in the United States. To illustrate the difference between the chain-based and fixed-base system, consider the following example which refers to the average price of a certain security over six months.

| Month | Price (p) | Price index (chain-based, previous month = 100) | Price index (fixed-based, August = 100) |
|---|---|---|---|
| August | 155 | | $\frac{155}{155} \times 100 = 100$ |
| September | 143 | $\frac{143}{155} \times 100 = 92.3$ | $\frac{143}{155} \times 100 = 92.3$ |
| October | 144 | $\frac{144}{143} \times 100 = 100.7$ | $\frac{144}{155} \times 100 = 92.9$ |
| November | 139 | $\frac{139}{144} \times 100 = 96.5$ | $\frac{139}{155} \times 100 = 89.7$ |
| December | 140 | $\frac{140}{139} \times 100 = 100.7$ | $\frac{140}{155} \times 100 = 90.3$ |
| January | 131 | $\frac{131}{140} \times 100 = 93.6$ | $\frac{131}{155} \times 100 = 84.5$ |

Consider the price in (say) January. Using the chain-base numbers, we can see that the price was 6.4% lower than the previous month and using the fixed-base numbers we can see that the price was 15.5% lower than in August. We can see, then, that chain-based index numbers are particularly suited for period-by-period comparisons, but if we are to compare the movement of prices over time then the fixed-based indexes are much easier to interpret.

## Fisher's Index

Earlier, we stated that Laspeyre's Index tends to overstate and Paasche's Index tends to understate changes in prices or quantities. So we would expect Laspeyre's Index to exceed Paasche's Index, and if we examine the indexes of Al Coholic's expenditure, we find that this is indeed the case.

|            | *Volume* | *Price* | *Expenditure* |
|------------|----------|---------|---------------|
| Laspeyre's | 112.9    | 121.3   | 135.4         |
| Paasche's  | 111.7    | 120.0   |               |

However, you must not assume that Laspeyre's Index will always be greater than Paasche's Index. (In fact, you should consider what the implications would be if Paasche's Index is greater than Laspeyre's Index.) What is reasonable, however, is to conclude that the 'true' index lies somewhere between Laspeyre's Index and Paasche's Index, and Fisher has suggested that it is equivalent to the geometric mean of the two, i.e.

Fisher's Index $= \sqrt{\text{(Laspeyre's Index)} \times \text{(Paasche's Index)}}$.

Fisher's Price Index $= \sqrt{121.3 \times 120} = 120.6$

Fisher's Volume Index $= \sqrt{112.9 \times 111.7} = 112.3$

It is claimed that Fisher's is an 'ideal' index and it now remains to state in what sense it is ideal. At the beginning of this chapter, we stated that expenditure was made up of prices and quantities, so if we have a price index and a quantity index we should be able to correctly predict the expenditure index. Remembering that expenditure is price $\times$ quantities, the prediction for the expenditure index is as follows.

(a)   Using Laspeyre's data:

$$\frac{112.9 \times 121.3}{100} = 136.9$$

(which overstates the expenditure index)

(b)  Using Paasche's data:

$$\frac{111.7 \times 120.0}{100} = 134.0$$

(which understates the expenditure index)

(c)  Using Fisher's data:

$$\frac{120.6 \times 112.3}{100} = 135.4$$

Fisher's Index numbers are ideal in the sense that they are the only ones that correctly predict the expenditure index.

## Splicing index numbers

Sometimes we want to make historical comparisons over fairly long periods of time. Consider the following data taken from the *Annual Abstract of Statistics*, 1991.

**Index of Retail Prices**

| Year | Index |
|------|-------|
| 1984 | 351.8 |
| 1985 | 373.2 |
| 1986 | 385.9 |
| 1987 | 100.0 |
| 1988 | 106.9 |
| 1989 | 115.2 |
| 1990 | 126.1 |

Examine this data carefully and you will see that the series has undergone a change of base. The data for pre-1987 had 1974 as the base year, and a new base was introduced in 1987. However, if we wish to compare prices over the period then we require the entire series to have a common base. Fortunately, every time the base changes, the Central Statistical Office continues with the old base for a few periods. This enables us to give the entire series a common base: a technique known as *splicing*.

Again consulting the *Annual Abstract*, we see that the Index of Retail Prices for 1987 with 1974 as base was 394.5. Let us suppose that we wish to have 1987 as base for the entire series: we would recalculate the index numbers for the period 1984–86 by dividing each index number by 394.5

and multiplying by 100. So, for example, the index for 1984 with 1987 as base is:

$$\frac{351.8 \times 100}{394.5} = 89.2$$

The entire series would look like this:

**Index of Retail Prices (1987 = 100)**

| Year | Index |
|------|-------|
| 1984 | 89.2  |
| 1985 | 94.6  |
| 1986 | 97.8  |
| 1987 | 100.0 |
| 1988 | 106.9 |
| 1989 | 115.2 |
| 1990 | 126.1 |

You may now find it more convenient to express the series with 1984 as base. To do this, each number in the series would be divided by the old value for the new base (i.e. 89.2) and multiplied by 100. So the new value for 1985 would be:

$$\frac{94.6 \times 100}{89.2} = 106.1$$

The complete series would be:

**Index of Retail Prices (1984 = 100)**

| Year | Index |
|------|-------|
| 1984 | 100.0 |
| 1985 | 106.1 |
| 1986 | 109.7 |
| 1987 | 112.1 |
| 1988 | 119.9 |
| 1989 | 129.2 |
| 1990 | 141.4 |

A few words of warning about splicing index numbers. Remember that when the base changes, it is almost certain that the weights will change also, so had we, for example, continued with 1974 as the base period the index numbers generated would be somewhat different from those which we have calculated. You should always bear this in mind when making long period historical comparisons.

## Using an index to deflate a series

It is a well known fact that incomes in the United Kingdom have risen over recent years. Unfortunately, prices have also been rising, so income recipients have not been able to reap the full benefits of their income increases. Let us examine the facts for the male members of the working population.

**Average weekly earnings: all males, all industries**

| Year | Earnings (£) |
|------|------|
| 1984 | 178.8 |
| 1985 | 192.4 |
| 1986 | 207.5 |
| 1987 | 224.0 |
| 1988 | 245.8 |
| 1989 | 269.5 |
| 1990 | 295.6 |

Economists have coined the term *real income* which is a measure of income that takes into account price rises. Real income, then, is a better measure of changes in the wealth of a community. We shall now calculate average weekly earnings based on 1984 prices, and use this as a measure of real income. To do this, we multiply average weekly earnings by 100, and divide by the Retail Price Index for that year. We shall use the spliced Index of Retail Prices obtained in the last section as the basis for deflating average weekly earnings.

| Year | Average weekly earnings (£) | Retail Price Index 1984 = 100 |
|------|------|------|
| 1984 | 178.8 | 100.0 |
| 1985 | 192.4 | 106.1 |
| 1986 | 207.5 | 109.7 |
| 1987 | 224.0 | 112.1 |
| 1988 | 245.5 | 119.9 |
| 1989 | 269.5 | 129.2 |
| 1990 | 295.6 | 141.4 |

So, for example, income in 1986 based on 1984 prices is

$$\frac{£207.5 \times 100}{109.7} = £189.2$$

| Year | Average weekly earnings (£) | Retail Price Index 1984 = 100 | Real income (£) |
|------|------|------|------|
| 1984 | 178.8 | 100.0 | 178.8 |
| 1985 | 192.4 | 106.1 | 181.3 |
| 1986 | 207.5 | 109.7 | 189.2 |
| 1987 | 224.0 | 112.1 | 199.8 |
| 1988 | 245.8 | 119.9 | 205.0 |
| 1989 | 269.5 | 129.2 | 208.6 |
| 1990 | 295.6 | 141.4 | 209.1 |

If we look at average weekly earnings only, then we get the impression that incomes were rising rapidly over the period. However, if we examine real incomes, then a very different picture emerges. Standards of living were rising quite slowly, and in 1990 standards hardly rose at all. This situation is illustrated even more graphically if index numbers of average weekly earnings and real income are constructed. This has been done by taking 1984 as the base year, and to find real income index for any year we multiply that year's real income by 100 and divide by 1984's real income. So in 1986, for example, the real income index is:

$$\frac{189.2 \times 100}{178.8} = 105.8$$

Likewise, the index of average weekly earnings for 1986 is:

$$\frac{207.5 \times 100}{178.8} = 116.1$$

| Year | Index of real income | Index of average weekly earnings |
|------|------|------|
| 1984 | 100.0 | 100.0 |
| 1985 | 101.4 | 107.6 |
| 1986 | 105.8 | 116.1 |
| 1987 | 111.8 | 125.3 |
| 1988 | 114.7 | 137.5 |
| 1989 | 116.7 | 150.7 |
| 1990 | 116.9 | 165.3 |

We must conclude, then, that although average weekly earnings rose by 65.3% over the period, real income rose by a mere 16.9%! The comparison is illustrated in Fig 8.1.

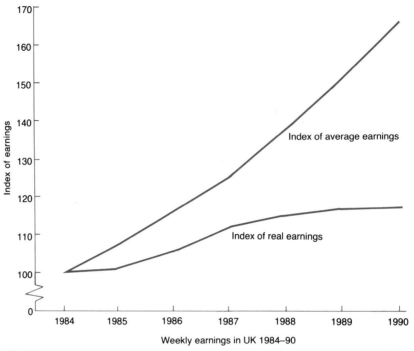

**Fig 8.1**

## Using the spreadsheet

The menu structure of the spreadsheet template to accompany this chapter is shown in Fig. 8.2.

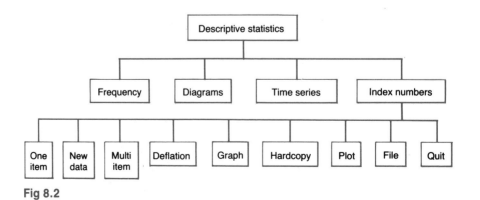

**Fig 8.2**

First, select 'One item' index and enter the following data:

| | A | B | C | D | E | F | G |
|---|---|---|---|---|---|---|---|
| 1 | | | | | | | |
| 2 | | | | | | | |
| 3 | | | | Index Numbers | | | |
| 4 | | | | ———————— | | | |
| 5 | | | | | | | |
| 6 | Period | Data | | | | | |
| 7 | | 155 | | | | | |
| 8 | | 143 | | | | | |
| 9 | | 144 | | | | | |
| 10 | | 139 | | Enter data | | | |
| 11 | | 140 | | | | | |
| 12 | | 131 | | Press ALT G when finished | | | |
| 13 | | | | | | | |
| 14 | | | | | | | |

This is the data on security prices considered in the chapter. Now press ALT G and the fixed-base and chain-base index numbers are calculated for this series. Select 'Graph' and the graph of both the fixed-base and chain-base index numbers is drawn. Press any key when you have finished with the graph.

Now suppose we wished to express the fixed-base series with a different base. Select 'Change base' and the cursor is positioned on cell A7 (that is, on period 1). Move the cursor to the new base (period 4, for example), press Enter and the fixed-base index is recalculated on the base that you have chosen. Select 'Graph' to view the effects of this change. Press any key when you have finished with the graph.

Now suppose we wished to use an index series to deflate data. Select 'Deflation'. If we wished to repeat the example on average and real income discussed in this chapter we would enter the data like this:

|   | A | B | C | D | E | F | G | H |
|---|---|---|---|---|---|---|---|---|
| 1 | | | | | | | | |
| 2 | | | | | | | | |
| 3 | | | | Index Numbers | | | | |
| 4 | | | | ———————— | | | | |
| 5 | | Data to | Index for | | | | | |
| 6 | Period | deflate | deflating | | | | | |
| 7 | | 178.8 | 100.0 | | | | | |
| 8 | | 192.4 | 106.1 | | | | | |
| 9 | | 207.5 | 109.7 | | | | | |
| 10 | | 224.0 | 112.1 | | Enter data to deflate and index | | | |
| 11 | | 245.8 | 119.9 | | for deflating. Press ALT C | | | |
| 12 | | 269.5 | 129.2 | | when finished | | | |
| 13 | | 295.6 | 141.4 | | | | | |
| 14 | | | | | | | | |
| 15 | | | | | | | | |
| 16 | | | | | | | | |
| 17 | | | | | | | | |

Press ALT C to see the deflated data, and select 'Graph' to draw the graph of the data and deflated data. Press any key when you have finished with the graph.

Finally, select 'Multi item' to find Laspeyre's, Paasche's and Fisher's Indexes for data over two years. The data for Al Coholic would be entered like this:

|   | A | B | C | D | E | F | G | H |
|---|---|---|---|---|---|---|---|---|
| 1 | | | | | | | | |
| 2 | | | | | | | | |
| 3 | | | | Index Numbers | | | | |
| 4 | | | | ———————— | | | | |
| 5 | | Base year | | Current year | | | | |
| 6 | | Price Quantity | | Price Quantity | | | | |
| 7 | | 1 | 40 | 1.15 | 50 | | | |
| 8 | | 0.2 | 100 | 0.27 | 90 | | | |
| 9 | | 2 | 1 | 2.2 | 1 | | | |
| 10 | | | | | | Enter data | | |
| 11 | | | | | | | | |
| 12 | | | | | | Press ALT I when finished | | |
| 13 | | | | | | | | |
| 14 | | | | | | | | |

Press ALT I to reveal the index numbers for the current year. You should move the cursor to display columns I to L if you wish to see the tabulations used in calculating these index numbers (if you are using Lotus, select 'Edit' to enable cursor movement, and ALT M to return to the menu).

Selecting 'Quit' at any time would save the current data and return you to the main menu.

QUESTIONS

**8.1** What considerations must be borne in mind when an index number is compiled? You should illustrate your answer by reference to any index number with which you are familiar.

**8.2** What is the purpose of an index number? Describe the main methods for constructing index numbers, indicating the advantages and disadvantages of each. Illustrate one of the methods by reference to any index number in current use.

CIPFA

**8.3** Why are weights used in the construction of index numbers? What is meant by:

(a)  base weighting

(b)  current weighting;

and what are the advantages and disadvantages of each?                    CIMA

**8.4** Define the following kinds of index numbers:

(a)  fixed base;

(b)  chain base;

(c)  base weighted;

(d)  current weighted.

Give an example of any published index with which you are familiar, briefly indicating how it is compiled and what the information it gives is intended to show.

**8.5** A company has reached an agreement with representatives of its employees that wages and salaries will in future be tied to a local cost of living index which the company will compile. Advise the company how they should gather information and compile this local cost of living index. What are the problems the company will encounter in completing this exercise?

**8.6** A certain company uses approximately six, two, five, and three thousand units of raw materials, A, B, C, D respectively. The average price (£) per unit of the raw materials in 19X1 and 19X9 is given in the following table:

| Raw material | Average price in 19X1 (£) | Average price in 19X9 (£) |
|---|---|---|
| A | 10 | 15 |
| B | 21 | 39 |
| C | 2 | 3 |
| D | 46 | 101 |

Calculate the simple aggregative index for the year 19X9 with 19X1 as base year. Calculate also a weighted aggregative index for the period 19X1–19X9 and explain why this may be considered preferable to the simple aggregative index.

**8.7** The average prices of four commodities for the years 19X1, 19X5 and 19X9 are shown in the following table:

| Commodity | Average Price per Unit (£) | | |
|---|---|---|---|
| | 19X1 | 19X5 | 19X9 |
| A | 8 | 15 | 14 |
| B | 54 | 70 | 72 |
| C | 15 | 22 | 29 |
| D | 75 | 84 | 78 |

(a) Calculate the simple aggregative index for each of the years 19X5 and 19X9 with 19X1 as base year.

(b) Write down *two* main disadvantages in the use of the simple aggregative index.

(c) The number of units used annually by a certain company is approximately 5000, 1000, 3000 and 8000 for commodities. A, B, C and D respectively. Calculate a weighted aggregative index for the period 19X1–19X9 and explain to what extent this Index overcomes the disadvantages you mentioned in part (b) of this question.

**8.8** **Index of average price of new houses**

| Year | Index |
|---|---|
| 1984 | 400.7 |
| 1985 | 452.3 |
| 1986 | 478.1 |
| 1987 | 103.3 |
| 1988 | 112.5 |
| 1989 | 135.2 |
| 1990 | 163.7 |

Source: *Annual Abstract of Statistics*, 1992

All index numbers refer to 1 January. On 13 January 1987, the base changed. On the old base, the index for 1987 was 494.5. Produce a complete index series based on 13 January 1987.

**8.9**  (a)  Describe the main features of the Index of Industrial Production.

(b)  The following table shows the US consumption (millions of pounds weight) and price (dollars per pound weight) of vegetable oil products.

|  | 19X3 | | 19X4 | | 19X5 | |
|---|---|---|---|---|---|---|
| Type of oil | Quantity | Price | Quantity | Price | Quantity | Price |
| Soybean | 322 | 0.13 | 368 | 0.12 | 367 | 0.13 |
| Cotton seed | 96 | 0.15 | 114 | 0.14 | 123 | 0.14 |
| Linseed | 32 | 0.13 | 31 | 0.13 | 19 | 0.12 |

Taking 19X3 as the base year, calculate Laspeyre's base-weighted index numbers for the general level of prices of these products for 19X4 and 19X5.

ACCA

**8.10**  Index of retail prices, October 1992 (1987 = 100)

| Group | Weight | Index |
|---|---|---|
| Food | 152 | 127.1 |
| Catering | 47 | 149.6 |
| Alcoholic drink | 80 | 150.1 |
| Tobacco | 36 | 145.9 |
| Housing, fuel and light | 219 | 154.7 |
| Household goods and services | 125 | 131.2 |
| Clothing and footwear | 59 | 120.0 |
| Personal goods and services | 40 | 143.9 |
| Motoring and travel | 163 | 140.0 |
| Leisure goods and services | $x$ | 134.2 |
| | 1000 | |

Find the missing weight $x$ and the all-items index.

**8.11**  The table below gives the weights and index numbers for a group of items used in calculating the index of retail prices in Ruritania.

| Group | Index | Weight |
|---|---|---|
| Food | 104 | 319 |
| Housing | 110 | 104 |
| Durable household goods | 100 | 64 |
| Miscellaneous goods | 108 | 63 |

(a) Calculate a price index for the above four groups.

(b) If the price index for all items (total weight = 100) was 104, calculate a price index for the remaining groups combined.

**8.12** Recalculate Laspeyre's index numbers for the data in Question 8.9 but this time use price relatives and make 19X4 the base year.

**8.13** A steel stockist notices that prices and values of sales for the main units of steel supply were:

|  | 19-4 | | 19-9 | |
|---|---|---|---|---|
|  | Price per tonne (£) | Sales (£m) | Price per tonne (£) | Sales (£m) |
| Ingots | 162 | 324 | 200 | 600 |
| Steel bars | 188 | 564 | 190 | 760 |
| Steel strip | 220 | 880 | 275 | 1100 |

Calculate a Paasche index number for 19-9 prices, taking 19-4 = 100.

Recalculate the Paasche Price Index using price relatives and the appropriate weights. ICSA

**8.14** A company employs three grades of male direct operators, M1, M2 and M3, and three grades of female direct operators, F1, F2, and F3. The following table gives the number of operators employed and the rates paid.

| Labour grade | 19-1 | | 19-3 | |
|---|---|---|---|---|
|  | Rate per hour (£) | No. of ops. | Rate per hour (£) | No. of ops. |
| M1 | 2.66 | 32 | 2.80 | 35 |
| M2 | 2.62 | 14 | 2.74 | 10 |
| M3 | 2.56 | 16 | 2.66 | 12 |
| F1 | 2.44 | 40 | 2.64 | 45 |
| F2 | 2.41 | 18 | 2.58 | 16 |
| F3 | 2.36 | 25 | 2.52 | 30 |

With 19-1 as base, calculate an index number for the average wage in 19-3 using

(a) base weighting, and

(b) current weighting.

Comment on the relationship between the two indices.

**8.15** The prices and sales by value of four commodities are shown below for 19X1 and 19X9. Calculate Laspeyre's and Paasche's index numbers for 19X9 taking 19X1 = 100. Would you expect the two answers to have the same value?

| | 19X1 | | 19X9 | |
|---|---|---|---|---|
| Commodity | Price (£) | Sales by value (£m) | Price (£) | Sales by value (£m) |
| A | 2.00 | 8.0 | 3.00 | 12.0 |
| B | 1.00 | 6.5 | 1.50 | 9.0 |
| C | 4.50 | 9.0 | 5.50 | 11.0 |
| D | 7.00 | 14.0 | 8.50 | 17.0 |

ICSA

**8.16** The following data shows the price index numbers of three groups of commodities for five years. Groups 1 and 2 have been prepared on the fixed-base principle, but Group 3 numbers are chain-based and unlinked.

| Year | 1 | 2 | 3 | 4 | 5 |
|---|---|---|---|---|---|
| Group 1 | 100 | 106 | 113 | 122 | 128 |
| Group 2 | 84 | 94 | 100 | 108 | 114 |
| Group 3 | 100 | 102 | 104 | 101 | 103 |

(a) Recalculate the Group 2 numbers to make them more easily comparable with the Group 1 numbers.

(b) Convert the Group 3 numbers into a series linked to the index number of 100 for Year 1.

(c) Tabulate the figures for Group 1 and the revised figures for Groups 2 and 3 and briefly comment on the situation revealed.

**8.17**

|  | Imports through certain UK ports | |
|---|---|---|
|  | Declared value (£m) | Value at 19-0 prices (£m) |
| 19-0 | 522 | 522 |
| 19-1 | 430 | 533 |
| 19-2 | 351 | 469 |

Construct index numbers for price and volume with 19-0 as base year.

**8.18**

|  | Laspeyre's | Paasche's | Fisher's |
|---|---|---|---|
| Price index | — | — | 107.4 |
| Volume index | — | 108.5 | — |

Find the missing data given that the expenditure index is 115.7, and given that base-year expenditure at base-year prices is £58 430m.

**8.19**

| Year | Index of producer prices |
|---|---|
| 1983 | 124.4 |
| 1984 | 132.1 |
| 1985 | 100.0 |
| 1986 | 104.3 |
| 1987 | 108.3 |
| 1988 | 113.2 |
| 1989 | 119.0 |
| 1990 | 126.0 |
| 1991 | 133.0 |

Source: *Monthly Digest of Statistics*

Given that the index of producer prices for 1985 on the old base is 139.4, obtain a single index series based on 1985.

**8.20** (a) From the information stated below construct a quantity index for the products made by Multiproducts Ltd for the period 19X6–19X9 weighted as to 19X6 prices, and

(b) explain the purpose of preparing a quantity index, state what the indices calculated in (a) above indicate about the production of Multiproducts Ltd for the years 19X6-19X9 and discuss the influence of individual products on the index.

**Multiproducts Ltd**

| Product | 19X6 average price (£) | 19X6 production (000s) | 19X7 production (000s) | 19X8 production (000s) | 19X9 production (000s) |
|---|---|---|---|---|---|
| Pliers | 2.00 | 62 | 65 | 66 | 90 |
| Wrenches | 3.00 | 138 | 120 | 110 | 80 |
| Bolts | 0.50 | 500 | 540 | 580 | 800 |
| Drills | 4.50 | 10 | 10 | 10 | 10 |

ACCA

**8.21** Given the following data, calculate an index of output of motor vehicles (passenger and commercial) taking 1989 as base year.

| Year | Passenger cars | | Commercial and light vehicles | |
|---|---|---|---|---|
| | Total | Value (£m) | Total | Value (£m) |
| 1989 | 1 299 082 | 8 188.2 | 267 135 | 2 752.9 |
| 1990 | 1 295 610 | 8 436.8 | 230 510 | 2 258.2 |
| 1991 | 1 236 900 | 8 441.6 | 184 005 | 2 206.4 |

**8.22** The profit earned by a particular firm (£000) was as follows:

| Year | Profit (£000) |
|---|---|
| 1983 | 1 412 |
| 1984 | 1 583 |
| 1985 | 1 898 |
| 1986 | 2 182 |
| 1987 | 2 488 |
| 1988 | 2 736 |
| 1989 | 2 933 |
| 1990 | 3 020 |
| 1991 | 3 216 |

Use the spliced index of producer prices from Question 8.19 to deflate profits. Find a deflated profit index with 1983 as the base year.

**8.23**    **The ABC Plc indices of production (19X0 = 100)**

| | | Indices | |
|---|---|---|---|
| Dept | Weights | 19X2 | 19X4 |
| A | 15 | 108 | 116 |
| B | 26 | 122 | 112 |
| C | 4 | 92 | 106 |
| D | 35 | 134 | 130 |

(a) Calculate for each of the two years 19X2 and 19X4 an index number of production for the whole firm.

(b) Calculate index numbers for each department and for the whole firm for 19X4 taking 19X2 as the base year.

**8.24**  **Purchases of and expenditure on frozen vegetables**

|  | *000 tonnes* | | *£m* |
|---|---|---|---|
|  | *19X2* | *19X9* | *19X2* |
| Peas | 160 | 150 | 124 |
| Beans | 44 | 42 | 42 |
| Potato products | 157 | 233 | 108 |
| Other | 104 | 135 | 99 |

With 19X2 as base, calculate a volume index for 19X9.

**8.25** (a) What are the main problems to be faced in the construction of an index number?

(b) Compute a cost and a quantity index number for 19X4 from the following figures (19X0 = 100).

| *Item* | *Quantity (00 tonnes)* | | *Cost (£000)* | |
|---|---|---|---|---|
|  | *19X0* | *19X4* | *19X0* | *19X4* |
| A | 172 | 197 | 154 | 185 |
| B | 34 | 47 | 128 | 151 |
| C | 49 | 42 | 277 | 248 |
| D | 64 | 66 | 219 | 206 |

# 9 Dispersion

In Chapter 5 we found it desirable to summarise data with a measure of central tendency and the main reason we did this was to enable us to compare sets of data or frequency distributions. We spent quite some time deciding how such measures could be truly representative of the data, and discussed the suitability of using the arithmetic mean (or average), the median and the mode. However, it is not sufficient to summarise data with a measure of central tendency only, we also need a measure of dispersion.

The problem with quoting a measure of central tendency only is that we can be led into drawing the wrong conclusions. Suppose, for example, we were examining income at two periods of time, and we find that there has been no change in average income. We might be tempted to conclude that economic welfare has not changed. However, although average income may not have changed, it is quite possible that welfare did increase through a more equal distribution of income. While our measure of central tendency will detect changes in average income, a measure of dispersion will detect changes in the spread of income. Clearly, both measures are desirable, so we shall now critically examine methods of measuring dispersion.

## Measures of the range

To measure dispersion, we could simply take the difference between the greatest and the least value in a series or distribution. We call this measure the *range*. To illustrate how the range is calculated, consider the data below which gives the average price of a certain security over a six-month period.

|        | *Average Price (p)* |
|--------|---------------------|
| Jan    | 155                 |
| Feb    | 143                 |
| March  | 144                 |
| April  | 139                 |
| May    | 140                 |
| June   | 141                 |

The highest price during the period was 155p and the lowest price was 139p, giving a range of 16p. Nothing, then, could be more simple both in concept and calculation. However, the range does have two great faults.

- It ignores the bulk of the data available to us, being concerned only with extreme values.

- Being concerned with the extreme values only, the range may be quite unrepresentative of the spread of items, especially as the extreme values are probably quite untypical of the data.

Suppose, for example, we were to use the range as a measure of dispersion of the heights of males in Liverpool. The range would be the difference between the tallest person (say 205 cm) and the smallest person (say 135 cm) – a range of 70 cm. However, we would probably find that by far the bulk of the population would be contained within the limits 165 to 185 cm – a range of 20 cm. Despite these criticisms, the range is used considerably – especially in statistical quality control. The reason is that in this field a measure of dispersion is often required quite quickly, and the range is eminently suited to this condition. However, it should be pointed out that, in these circumstances, the range will be found repeatedly from a large number of samples, and this does minimise the chances of obtaining untypical values at the extremes.

Because the range can be so misleading, statisticians have turned to alternative measures of dispersion. The one we shall now examine finds the range containing the central 50% of a distribution. Consider the data below which refer to the bonuses paid to the salesmen of a particular firm during a particular month.

| Monthly bonus (£) | Number of salesmen | Cumulative frequency |
|---|---|---|
| Under 60 | 8 | 8 |
| 60 and under 70 | 10 | 18 |
| 70 – | 16 | 34 |
| 80 – | 14 | 48 |
| 90 – | 10 | 58 |
| 100 and under 110 | 5 | 63 |
| 110 and over | 2 | 65 |
| | 65 | |

We want to find the range of bonuses earned by the central 50% of salesmen. We can do this by finding the bonus earned by the $\frac{65+1}{4} = 16.5$th salesman and the bonus earned by the $\frac{3(65+1)}{4} = 49.5$th salesman. Fig 9.1 shows the relevant part of the ogive from which we can read that 16.5 salesmen earn a bonus of less than £68.50 and 49.5 salesmen earn a bonus of less than £91.50. So the range earned by the central 50% of salesmen is £91.50 – £68.50 = £23. We call this range the *interquartile range* (it is the range of bonuses earned by the central two quarters of the distribution). We call the lower end of this range (£68.50) the *lower quartile* ($Q_1$) and 25% of salesmen earn less than this figure. Likewise, the upper end of the range is called the *upper quartile* ($Q_3$) and 25% of salesmen earn more than this figure. Calling the lower quartile $Q_1$ and the upper quartile $Q_3$ would naturally lead us to call the median $Q_2$. Notice also that although the median *salesman* lies midway between the upper-quartile salesman and the lower-quartile salesman, the median *bonus* is not at the centre of the interquartile range. Beware of this – many students fall into this trap.

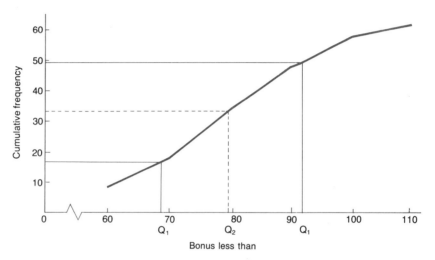

**Fig 9.1**

Sometimes you will come across the *quartile deviation* – this is merely half the interquartile range, i.e.:

$$\text{Quartile deviation} = \frac{Q_3 - Q_1}{2}$$

so the quartile deviation for monthly bonuses is $\frac{23}{2} = £11.50$.

Notice that in this example, we could not have calculated the range for bonuses, as we have no way of knowing the highest bonus nor the lowest bonus earned. The range cannot be used for open-ended distributions. This disadvantage will probably not apply to the interquartile range, as it is unlikely that the central 50% of frequencies will penetrate the open-ended class. However, the interquartile range does have the same disadvantage as the range – it uses only two values and ignores the rest. What we shall now examine are measures of dispersion that use all the data available to us.

## Measures of average deviation

So far, we have examined two predetermined points in a series or distribution and calculated the difference between them. We have fixed the points either at the ends of the distribution (the range) or about the central 50% (the quartile deviation). We could, of course, have fixed these two points anywhere we wished; for example, covering the central 40% or 60% of the items. But let us now consider dispersion in an entirely different way: we could choose some central value and calculate the deviation of the items from this value. What central value should we choose? Well, the arithmetic mean is one choice that automatically springs to mind. However, there is a snag with choosing the arithmetic mean – can you see what it is? Clearly, we are not going to be interested in the individual deviations themselves – we would still have a series of numbers rather than a single measure of dispersion. Surely, it would be more sensible to consider the average deviation from the mean. Now here's where the snag comes in. If you remember the definition of the arithmetic mean, then you will appreciate that the sum of the deviations from the mean is zero. Hence the average deviation from the mean must always be zero! Clearly, this will not do – we cannot use the average deviation from the mean as a measure of dispersion, because irrespective of the distribution under consideration our measure of dispersion will always be zero.

**Absolute deviations**

One way out of this problem is to find the *absolute deviations* from the mean, irrespective of whether they are positive or negative. Let us do this for the data on security prices considered earlier. The average price was:

$$\frac{155 + 143 + 144 + 139 + 140 + 141}{6} = \frac{862}{6} = 143\tfrac{2}{3}\mathrm{p}$$

and the deviations from this price are:

| Price (x) | Deviation $x - \hat{x}$ | Absolute deviation |
|---|---|---|
| 155 | $11\tfrac{1}{3}$ | $11\tfrac{1}{3}$ |
| 143 | $-\tfrac{2}{3}$ | $\tfrac{2}{3}$ |
| 144 | $\tfrac{1}{3}$ | $\tfrac{1}{3}$ |
| 139 | $-4\tfrac{2}{3}$ | $4\tfrac{2}{3}$ |
| 140 | $-3\tfrac{2}{3}$ | $3\tfrac{2}{3}$ |
| 141 | $-2\tfrac{2}{3}$ | $2\tfrac{2}{3}$ |
| | $0$ | $23\tfrac{1}{3}$ |

So the average absolute deviation from the mean is:

$$\frac{23\frac{1}{3}}{6} = 3.89$$

The measure of dispersion we have just calculated is called the *mean absolute deviation*, and using the $\Sigma$ notation we calculate it like this:

$$\text{Mean absolute deviation} = \frac{\Sigma \mid x - \bar{x} \mid}{N}$$

The vertical lines enclosing $x - \bar{x}$ simply means 'take the absolute deviations', whereas brackets would imply that we must take account of signs. Only a minor adjustment is needed to this formula if we are confronted with a frequency distribution:

$$\text{Mean absolute deviation} = \frac{\Sigma f \mid x - \bar{x} \mid}{\Sigma f}$$

where $f$ represents the frequencies and $x$ represents the centre point of the various classes.

The mean absolute deviation has a number of disadvantages.

- Because we have taken absolute deviations and ignored the signs, it is not capable of being manipulated mathematically in the ways that the statistician requires.

- It will be quite cumbersome to calculate when the mean is not a whole number.

- We cannot combine a number of mean absolute deviations to obtain an overall measure of dispersion. Suppose, for example, a number of samples will be made available to us over a period of time, and we intend to estimate dispersion in the population. We cannot calculate the mean deviation of each sample, and pool them, adjusting our estimate as more samples become available. We would have to pool all the samples, making one single sample.

We do not wish, however, to leave you with the impression that the mean absolute deviation is of little use – far from it. One thing it cannot be criticised for is its ability to be a *representative* measure of dispersion. Probably no other measure of dispersion does this quite so well. The advantage of the mean absolute deviation is that conceptually it is so easy to understand. So what advice can we give you about when to use it? If you are interested merely in representing dispersion, then you can do no better than to use the mean absolute deviation, but if further statistical analysis is required we must look to other measures.

## The standard deviation

The main problems surrounding the mean absolute deviation arise because we took all the deviations as being positive in order to prevent the sum of the deviations being zero. Is there any other course of action open to us? Well, we could square all the deviations – the square of a negative number is a positive number, so the pluses and minuses will no longer cancel each other out. If we find the average of the square of the deviations, then we have a measure called the *variance*:

$$\text{Variance} = \frac{\Sigma(x - \bar{x})^2}{n}$$

So we would calculate the variance of security prices as follows:

| Price $(x)$ | $(x - \bar{x})$ | $(x - \bar{x})^2$ |
|---|---|---|
| 155 | 11.33 | 128.44 |
| 143 | −0.67 | 0.44 |
| 144 | 0.33 | 0.11 |
| 139 | −4.67 | 21.78 |
| 140 | −3.67 | 13.44 |
| 141 | −2.67 | 7.11 |
| | | 171.32 |

$$\text{Variance} = \frac{171.32}{6} = 28.55\text{p}$$

The trouble with the variance is that (in this example) it is measured in units of the square of the price deviations. Strictly speaking, the variance of security prices is not 28.55p but 28.55 (pence)$^2$. It would seem more sensible, then, to take the square root of the variance. We give the name *standard deviation* $(\sigma)$* to this measure of dispersion, and of all the measures this is the one that is most commonly used:

$$\sigma = \sqrt{\frac{\Sigma(x - \bar{x})^2}{n}}$$

So the standard deviation of the price of securities is $\sqrt{28.55} = 5.34\text{p}$.

---

* This is the Greek small letter sigma. Do not confuse it with the capital letter sigma $(\Sigma)$ which we met earlier.

It is quite easy to show that an alternative form of the standard deviation is:

$$\sigma = \sqrt{\frac{\Sigma x^2}{n} - \left(\frac{\Sigma x}{n}\right)^2}$$

Notice that this expression does not ask us to calculate the deviations from the arithmetic mean – and this will be very useful when the mean is an awkward number. We do not intend to prove that the two expressions are the same (you can do this for yourself) but we shall demonstrate that both expressions give the same result by calculating the standard deviation of the price of securities this time using the second expression.

| $x$ | $x^2$ |
|-----|-------|
| 155 | 24 025 |
| 143 | 20 449 |
| 144 | 20 736 |
| 139 | 19 321 |
| 140 | 19 600 |
| 141 | 19 881 |
| 862 | 124 012 |

$$\sigma = \sqrt{\frac{124\ 012}{6} - \left(\frac{862}{6}\right)^2} = 5.34\text{p}$$

If we wish to find the standard deviation of a frequency distribution, we simply replace $x$ with $fx$ and $n$ with $f$:

$$\sigma = \sqrt{\frac{\Sigma fx^2}{\Sigma f} - \left(\frac{\Sigma fx}{\Sigma f}\right)^2}$$

where $x$ is the centre point of the class and $f$ is the frequency. Let us now look at an example.

**ABC Plc Debtors' Balances at 31 December 19-9**

| Balance outstanding (£) | Number of accounts |
|-------------------------|--------------------|
| 20 and under   40 | 1 |
| 40 and under   60 | 3 |
| 60 and under   80 | 6 |
| 80 and under 100 | 10 |
| 100 and under 120 | 5 |
| 120 and under 140 | 3 |
| 140 and under 160 | 2 |
| | 30 |

We need first to find the centre point of each class.

| Centre point (x) | f | fx | $fx^2 = fx \times x$ |
|---|---|---|---|
| 30 | 1 | 30 | 900 |
| 50 | 3 | 150 | 7 500 |
| 70 | 6 | 420 | 29 400 |
| 90 | 10 | 900 | 81 000 |
| 110 | 5 | 550 | 60 500 |
| 130 | 3 | 390 | 50 700 |
| 150 | 2 | 300 | 45 000 |
| | $\Sigma f = 30$ | $\Sigma fx = 2\ 740$ | $\Sigma fx^2 = 275\ 000$ |

$$\sigma = \sqrt{\frac{275\ 000}{30} - \left(\frac{2740}{30}\right)^2}$$

$$= £28.72$$

Notice that in constructing the table for calculating the standard deviation, we have also obtained all the information we need to calculate the arithmetic mean. It would make sense, then to calculate the mean as well as the standard deviation:

$$\bar{x} = \frac{\Sigma fx}{\Sigma f} = \frac{2740}{30} = £91.33$$

Unless you have a calculator at your disposal, it can be very tedious to calculate the standard deviation using this method. Fortunately, we can simplify the calculations (you will remember that we did this when calculating the arithmetic mean) by taking an assumed mean – in this case we will take £90. We then calculate the deviation of the centre points x from the assumed mean (column two). As all the deviations are divisible by 20, this is done in the column headed d. We can now use the column d to calculate the standard deviation.

| x | (x – 90) | d | f | fd | $fd^2$ |
|---|---|---|---|---|---|
| 30 | – 60 | – 3 | 1 | – 3 | 9 |
| 50 | – 40 | – 2 | 3 | – 6 | 12 |
| 70 | – 20 | – 1 | 6 | – 6 | 6 |
| 90 | 0 | 0 | 10 | 0 | 0 |
| 110 | 20 | 1 | 5 | 5 | 5 |
| 130 | 40 | 2 | 3 | 6 | 12 |
| 150 | 60 | 3 | 2 | 6 | 18 |
| | | | $\Sigma f = 30$ | $\Sigma fd = 2$ | $\Sigma fd^2 = 62$ |

Calculating the standard deviation as before, we have:

$$\sigma = \sqrt{\frac{62}{30} - \left(\frac{2}{30}\right)^2}$$

$$= £1.436$$

However, we divided all the deviations by 20, so we must multiply the standard deviation above by 20:

$$\sigma = £1.436 \times 20 = £28.72$$

which agrees exactly with our previous result. Let us see if we can write a formula which describes the above calculation. If $d$ is the deviation from an assumed mean $x_0$, and if $d$ is divided by a constant $c$, then:

$$\sigma = c \times \sqrt{\frac{\Sigma fd^2}{\Sigma f} - \left(\frac{\Sigma fd}{\Sigma f}\right)^2}$$

## Relative dispersion

So far, we have been trying to measure dispersion within a series or distribution. We shall now attempt to measure dispersion between distributions, and we shall find that the standard deviation cannot do this. Consider the two series below:

A = 8, 9, 10, 11, 12, 13, 14                   Mean 11
B = 1008, 1009, 1010, 1011, 1012, 1013, 1014     Mean 1011

Both A and B have the same standard deviation – can you see why? The deviations from the mean are identical in both series ($-3, -2, -1$, etc.) and both series have the same number of observations, so $\Sigma(x - \bar{x})^2$, and $n$ would be the same whichever series we examined. You should verify that the standard deviation is, in fact, two for both series. Now does this mean that both series show the same degree of spread? Surely not! An increase from the smallest to the largest value in A is an increase of:

$$\frac{14 - 8}{8} \times 100 = 75\%$$

but the same increase for series B is only:

$$\frac{1014 - 1008}{1008} \times 100 = 0.595\%!$$

Clearly, A has a much greater percentage spread than B, and if we are going to compare dispersion between series we must take into account not only dispersion within each series (i.e. the standard deviation) but also the mean of the series. We can do this by calculating the *coefficient of variation*:

$$V = \frac{100 \times \sigma}{\bar{x}} \%$$

For the series above, the coefficients of variation are:

$$\frac{100 \times 2}{11} = 18.18\% \text{ (for A)}$$

and

$$\frac{100 \times 2}{1011} = 0.198\% \text{ (for B)}$$

confirming our suspicion that A has a greater relative spread than B. Notice that the coefficient of variation is a percentage, and not a particular measurement (centimetre, dollar, kilogram, etc.) and so it can be used for comparing distributions which have different units.

Now we would like to issue a word of warning. If you attempt to quantify the differences in dispersion using the coefficient of variation, ask yourself whether the result you have obtained 'feels right'. Compare your result with a 'gut feeling' you have obtained by visually examining the histogram of each distribution. If your results do not feel right then you would be well advised to compare the distributions using the quartiles. Earlier, we defined the quartile deviation as $\frac{1}{2}(Q_3 - Q_1)$, and we could take the median $Q_2$ as a measure of central tendency, so an alternative measure of relative dispersion is:

$$\frac{100 \times \frac{1}{2}(Q_3 - Q_1)\%}{Q_2} = \frac{50(Q_3 - Q_1)\%}{Q_2}$$

and we shall call this measure the *quartile coefficient of variation*. We shall say no more about it now, but in the questions at the end of this chapter you will find an example where its use is obviously required.

Finally, do you remember that in Chapter 5 we introduced the concept of skewness? Now that we know how to measure dispersion, we can also measure skewness with the coefficient of skewness:

$$\text{Coefficient of skewness} = \frac{3 \text{ (mean} - \text{median)}}{\text{Standard deviation}}$$

If the distribution is symmetrical, then the mean and median are the same, so the coefficient would be zero. With negative skewness, the median exceeds the mean, and the coefficient is negative. With positive skewness, the mean exceeds the median and the coefficient is positive. By itself, the coefficient is of little use, but it is useful when we are trying to decide which of a number of distributions shows the greater degree of skewness.

## Using the spreadsheet

The spreadsheet template for this chapter is the same as the template used for Chapter 5. When the option 'Statistics' is chosen, in addition to the mean and median, the other statistical measures introduced in this chapter are calculated. Retrieve the main menu, select 'Descriptive statistics' then select 'Frequency'. Select 'New data' and enter the data on ABC Plc debtor's balances used in this chapter. Select 'Statistics', type 0 (because the frequencies are exact), press Enter and the following should be output:

|  | A | B | C | D | E | F | G |
|---|---|---|---|---|---|---|---|
| 1 |  |  |  |  |  |  |  |
| 2 | Input 0 if frequencies exact, 1 if frequencies rounded |  |  |  |  |  | 0 |
| 3 |  |  |  |  |  |  |  |
| 4 |  | Lower | Upper | Frequency |  |  |  |
| 5 |  | Bound | Bound |  |  |  |  |
| 6 |  | 20 | 40 | 1 |  |  |  |
| 7 |  | 40 | 60 | 3 |  |  |  |
| 8 |  | 60 | 80 | 6 |  |  |  |
| 9 |  | 80 | 100 | 10 |  |  |  |
| 10 |  | 100 | 120 | 5 |  |  |  |
| 11 |  | 120 | 140 | 3 |  |  |  |
| 12 |  | 140 | 160 | 2 |  |  |  |
| 13 | Total Frequency = |  | 30 |  |  |  |  |
| 14 |  |  |  |  |  |  |  |
| 15 |  | Mean | 91.33333 |  | Variance | 824.8888 |  |
| 16 |  | Q1 | 72.5 |  | Stdev | 28.72087 |  |
| 17 |  | Median | 91 |  | C of V | 31.44621 |  |
| 18 |  | Q3 | 113 |  |  |  |  |
| 19 |  |  |  |  |  |  |  |

If you want to see the tabulations, then move the cursor to reveal columns J to R. The values $fx$ are shown in column P starting at row 6. Cell P5 gives the value of $\Sigma fx^2$, and cell P3 gives the value of the variance. Columns Q and R are used to determine the lower and upper quartile respectively (the lower quartile is the value of the 7.75th account and the upper quartile is the value of the 23.25th account. The columns K to O were explained in Chapter 5.

**9.1** The monthly production in two factories in thousands of units is as follows:

A: 23, 30, 28, 31, 29, 26, 34, 36, 28, 32, 25, 26
B: 53, 65, 70, 50, 62, 58, 52, 63, 69, 72, 64, 54

(a) Compare the variability of production in the two factories by calculating the standard deviation in each case.

(b) Calculate the coefficient of variation in each case.

**9.2** From the figures below state what is:

(a) the range;

(b) the arithmetic mean;

(c) the median;

(d) the lower quartile;

(e) the upper quartile;

(f) the quartile deviation;

(g) the mean deviation.

Explain what is meant by the mean deviation and quartile deviation.

```
 8   35   45   50   60   68
13   37   46   52   61   70
26   40   47   55   65   71
29   41   48   58   67   75
33
```

**9.3** The table shows the age distribution of the estimated UK population.

| Age in years | Total UK population (millions) |
|---|---|
| 0 and under 5 | 4.4 |
| 5 and under 10 | 4.7 |
| 10 and under 15 | 4.3 |
| 15 and under 20 | 3.9 |
| 20 and under 25 | 4.1 |
| 25 and under 30 | 4.0 |
| 30 and under 35 | 3.3 |
| 35 and under 40 | 3.2 |
| 40 and under 45 | 3.3 |
| 45 and under 50 | 3.4 |
| 50 and under 55 | 3.4 |
| 55 and under 60 | 3.3 |
| 60 and under 65 | 3.2 |
| 65 and over | 7.5 |

Source: *Monthly Digest*

(a) Draw an appropriate graph and from it estimate the median and the upper and lower quartiles. Hence obtain the semi-interquartile range.

(b) Detail how the quartiles could be obtained other than by using the graph.

**9.4** Details of the monthly bonuses paid to sales staff employed by a large wallpaper manufacturer have recently been made available.

| Monthly bonus (£) | Number of bonuses |
|---|---|
| under 600 | 8 |
| 600 and under 700 | 10 |
| 700 and under 800 | 16 |
| 800 and under 900 | 14 |
| 900 and under 1000 | 10 |
| 1000 and under 1100 | 5 |
| over 1100 | 2 |

(a) Using graphical methods, estimate the median bonus paid and comment on the suitability of the median in interpreting this type of data. How many sales staff receive a monthly bonus of:

(i)   Less than £880?

(ii)  At least £630 but less than £750?

(iii) £960 or more?

(b) From the graph, estimate a measure of dispersion, using the quartiles. What is meant by dispersion?

**9.5**        **Estimated wealth of individuals in Great Britain**

| Wealth | Frequency (thousands) |
|---|---|
| Not over £25 000 | 5518 |
| £25 000– £50 000 | 3372 |
| £50 000– £100 000 | 4010 |
| £100 000– £200 000 | 1864 |
| £200 000– £500 000 | 576 |
| £500 000–£1 000 000 | 76 |
| over £1 000 000 | 22 |

Source: Inland Revenue, 1991

(a) Calculate: (i)  the median net wealth;

(ii)  the quartile deviation.

(b) How appropriate are these measures to this distribution?

(c) State briefly the advantages and disadvantages of using quartile deviation and standard deviation as measures of dispersion.

**9.6** Profits made by a sample of firms in a certain industry in a given year are as follows:

| Profits (£) | % of firms |
|---|---|
| Up to 20 000 | 6.8 |
| 20 001 – | 11.4 |
| 40 001 – | 14.1 |
| 60 001 – | 13.5 |
| 80 001 – | 11.5 |
| 100 001 – | 24.1 |
| 120 001 – | 6.4 |
| 130 001 or more | 5.8 |
| Showing a loss | 6.4 |
| All firms | 100% |
| Number of firms | 5231 |

Calculate the median and quartile deviation of the profits made by the 5231 firms included in the sample. Construct a block diagram to represent the distribution and discuss whether the mean is likely to be higher or lower than the median.

CIPFA

**9.7** The following data gives the weekly expenditure on advertising of the branches of Cosmetics Plc:

**Cosmetics Plc monthly advertising expenditure**

| £ | Number of branches |
|---|---|
| 800 and less than 1000 | 50 |
| 1000 and less than 1200 | 200 |
| 1200 and less than 1400 | 350 |
| 1400 and less than 1600 | 150 |
| 1600 and less than 1800 | 100 |
| 1800 and less than 2000 | 75 |
| 2000 and less than 2200 | 50 |
| 2200 and less than 2400 | 25 |

(a) From the above data calculate the median monthly expenditure, and explain what it indicates about the branches' advertising expenditure.

(b) Calculate the semi-interquartile range from the data and explain the purpose of this calculation.

ACCA

**9.8** **Deliveries of gravel from a quarry**

| Weight of load (tonnes) | No. of loads Week 1 | No. of loads Week 2 |
|---|---|---|
| 5 and under 10 | 84 | 45 |
| 10 and under 20 | 86 | 63 |
| 20 and under 30 | 122 | 140 |
| 30 and under 40 | 86 | 77 |
| 40 and under 60 | 16 | 21 |
| 60 and under 80 | 6 | 4 |
| | 400 | 350 |

(a) Express the frequencies as percentages of their respective totals and use those figures to draw, on the one graph, cumulative frequency curves for the loads of gravel delivered in Week 1 and Week 2.

(b) Use your graph to find the median weight and the semi-interquartile range for the two weeks.

(c) Comment briefly on your results.

**9.9**    **Local authorities with central purchasing organisations**

| Average % discount obtained | Number of authorities |
|---|---|
| 8 and under 12 | 0 |
| 12 and under 16 | 0 |
| 16 and under 20 | 2 |
| 20 and under 24 | 0 |
| 24 and under 28 | 3 |
| 28 and under 32 | 0 |
| 32 and under 36 | 6 |
| 36 and under 40 | 7 |
| 40 and under 44 | 2 |
| 44 and under 48 | 3 |

**Local authorities without central purchasing organisations**

| Average % discount obtained | Number of authorities |
|---|---|
| 8 and under 12 | 5 |
| 12 and under 16 | 16 |
| 16 and under 20 | 12 |
| 20 and under 24 | 8 |
| 24 and under 28 | 13 |
| 28 and under 32 | 1 |
| 32 and under 36 | 0 |
| 36 and under 40 | 1 |
| 40 and under 44 | 1 |
| 44 and under 48 | 0 |

Source: LGORU

For each of these distributions calculate:

(a) the arithmetic mean of the average % discount obtained;

(b) the standard deviation of the average % discount obtained.

Compare the arithmetic means and suggest what conclusions might be drawn from these statistics.

**9.10** The table below gives an analysis of the debtors' balances of Fuel Suppliers Ltd.

**Fuel Suppliers Ltd debtors' balances**

| Balance outstanding (£) | Number of accounts |
|---|---|
| 20– 39.9 | 1 |
| 40– 59.9 | 3 |
| 60– 79.9 | 6 |
| 80– 99.9 | 10 |
| 100–119.9 | 5 |
| 120–139.9 | 3 |
| 140–159.9 | 2 |

You are required to:

(a) calculate the mean balance and the standard deviation, and

(b) explain the value of knowing the standard deviation in respect of the outstanding balances due to Fuel Suppliers Ltd. ACCA

**9.11** The distribution shown below is the output of the factories of Quality Clothing Ltd, for a randomly chosen month. You are required to:

(a) calculate the standard deviation from these figures, and

(b) contrast the mean deviation and the standard deviation as measures of dispersion and indicate briefly what the standard deviation calculated in (a) means for the monthly output of Quality Clothing Ltd.

**Quality Clothing Ltd**

| Monthly output men's suits (000s) | Number of factories |
|---|---|
| 23 and under 28 | 10 |
| 28 and under 33 | 20 |
| 33 and under 38 | 20 |
| 38 and under 43 | 24 |
| 43 and under 48 | 20 |
| 48 and under 53 | 16 |
| 53 and under 58 | 8 |
| 58 and under 63 | 2 |

ACCA

**9.12** From the following frequency distribution of the weekly overtime earnings of the staff of Catering Ltd, you are required to:

(a) calculate (i) the mean and (ii) the standard deviation, and

(b) indicate what the value of the standard deviation tells you about the weekly overtime earnings of the staff of Catering Ltd.

Catering Ltd

| Weekly overtime earnings (pence) | Number of Staff | |
|---|---|---|
| 500– 749.99 | 2 | |
| 750– 999.99 | 5 | |
| 1000–1249.99 | 10 | |
| 1250–1499.99 | 17 | |
| 1500–1749.99 | 10 | |
| 1750–1999.99 | 4 | |
| 2000–2249.99 | 2 | ACCA |

**9.13** A furnace whose size is nominally 200 tonnes is used to cast steel ingots of 10 tonnes weight. The amount of steel in the furnace cannot be controlled accurately, so that an incomplete ingot is normally produced when ingots are cast. For example, a furnace load of 198 tonnes will produce 19 full ingots and one 8-tonne ingot. The following data show the weight of 100 furnace loads of steel.

| Weight of furnace load (tonnes) | Frequency |
|---|---|
| 190.0 and under 192.5 | 1 |
| 192.5 and under 195.0 | 4 |
| 195.0 and under 197.5 | 8 |
| 197.5 and under 200.0 | 19 |
| 200.0 and under 202.5 | 36 |
| 202.5 and under 205.0 | 20 |
| 205.0 and under 207.5 | 8 |
| 207.5 and under 210.0 | 4 |

Required: Compile a frequency distribution of the weight of incomplete ingots, and calculate its mean and standard deviation.                 ACCA

**9.14**       Total income before tax, 1988–89, UK

| Income range (£) | Number (thousands) |
|---|---|
| Less than  3 000 | 557 |
| 3 000–  5 000 | 3369 |
| 5 000–  7 000 | 3275 |
| 7 000–  10 000 | 4350 |
| 10 000–  15 000 | 5220 |
| 15 000–  20 000 | 2940 |
| 20 000–  50 000 | 3067 |
| 50 000–100 000 | 232 |
| 100 000 and over | 55 |

Source: Board of Inland Revenue, 1991

(a) Rewrite the number of incomes to the nearest hundred thousand.

(b) Using the rounded data, calculate the standard deviation.

**9.15** A survey of house prices in a local newspaper yielded the following information:

| Price of house (£000) | Number of houses for sale |
|---|---|
| below 50 | 16 |
| 50 and under 60 | 41 |
| 60 and under 70 | 39 |
| 70 and under 80 | 22 |
| 80 and under 90 | 10 |
| 90 and under 100 | 11 |
| 100 and under 110 | 4 |
| 110 and under 120 | 5 |
| 120 and under 130 | 1 |
| 130 and under 140 | 5 |
| 140 and under 150 | 4 |
| 150 and over | 2 |
| | 160 |

(a) Calculate the mean price of houses in the area and the standard deviation, stating clearly any assumptions you may make.

(b) For what reason may the mean and standard deviation be inappropriate for such a distribution? Suggest better alternatives.

**9.16** At a General Election the sizes of constituencies were distributed as shown in the table below:

| Number of voters (000s) | Number of constituencies |
|---|---|
| 20 and under 30 | 7 |
| 30 and under 40 | 17 |
| 40 and under 50 | 74 |
| 50 and under 60 | 176 |
| 60 and under 70 | 183 |
| 70 and under 80 | 115 |
| 80 and under 90 | 48 |
| 90 and under 100 | 13 |
| 100 and over | 2 |
| Total | 635 |

(a) Calculate the average number of voters per constituency and also the standard deviation.

(b) In order that constituencies may be kept to a roughly similar size, constituency boundaries are from time to time revised. From your results in (a) suggest a range of sizes outside which changes might be made, and give reasons for your suggestions.

**9.17** Electric lamps

| Hours of life (hundreds) | Number of lamps |
|---|---|
| 0– 5 | 5 |
| 5–10 | 10 |
| 10–20 | 38 |
| 20–40 | 36 |
| 40 and over | 15 |

(a) Calculate the mean and standard deviation of the life of the whole batch of lamps whose pattern of duration is given in the table above.

(b) Compare and contrast the standard deviation and the quartile deviation as measures of dispersion. CIPFA

**9.18** (a) Explain the meaning of absolute and relative measures of dispersion and compare their use.

(b) In Department A of a firm the average weekly earnings are £366 with a standard deviation of £28.2. Calculate the relative dispersion.

(c) In Department B the earnings in pounds in a certain week of the 10 members are as follows:

237  245  283  296  253  249  236  254  305  242

Calculate the mean and the standard deviation of this department. Compare this result with Department A and comment.

**9.19** Explain the use of the coefficient of variation.

A company has two factories A and B, situated in different parts of England. Labour turnover in factory B is much higher than in factory A. The consultant engaged by the firm to investigate the causes of labour turnover suggests that a possible cause of the higher turnover in factory B is a wider variation in the annual wages of workers in factory B than in factory A: he found that the standard deviation of wages of workers in factory B was £3000 compared with a standard deviation of £2500 for factory A. Given the information that the mean annual wage of workers in factory B is £10 000 and in factory A £7500, show how the consultant's suggestion may be tested by use of the coefficient of variation, and say whether he is right. ACCA

**9.20**     Projected population in Scotland (tens of thousands)

| Age group | Males | Females |
|---|---|---|
| 0–14 | 75 | 72 |
| 15–29 | 59 | 58 |
| 30–44 | 46 | 47 |
| 45–59 | 43 | 48 |
| 60–74 | 31 | 41 |
| 75 and over | 6 | 14 |
| All ages | 260 | 280 |

(a)  Calculate the standard deviation for each distribution.

(b)  Calculate the arithmetic mean of the male distribution and hence obtain a relative measure of dispersion.

**9.21**

| Monthly salary (£) | No. of trainee draughtsmen |
|---|---|
| Under 400 | 4 |
| 400 and under 425 | 9 |
| 425 and under 450 | 16 |
| 450 and under 475 | 28 |
| 475 and under 500 | 45 |
| 500 and under 525 | 66 |
| 525 and under 550 | 85 |
| 550 and under 575 | 72 |
| 575 and under 600 | 54 |
| 600 and under 625 | 38 |
| 625 and under 650 | 27 |
| 650 and under 675 | 18 |
| 675 and under 700 | 11 |
| 700 and under 725 | 5 |
| 725 and under 750 | 2 |

(a)  The above figures relate to the monthly salaries of the trainee draughtsmen of a local company. Calculate the arithmetic mean and the standard deviation.

(b)  Information relating to the trainees employed by a rival firm gives a coefficient of variation of 18%. Are they, or the local company's trainees, more variable with respect to salaries?

**9.22** A company selling a consumer product directly to retail outlets has collected the following information:

| Average number of orders taken per month by individual salesmen | Number of salesmen |
|---|---|
| 20 and under | 3 |
| 21–30 | 7 |
| 31–40 | 16 |
| 41–50 | 22 |
| 51–60 | 19 |
| 61–70 | 8 |
| 71 and over | 2 |

Calculate (a) the approximate range; (b) the standard deviation; (c) the coefficient of variation. All of these are measures of dispersion. Describe, with additional examples, when the use of each would be appropriate.

**9.23** The following table shows the distribution of weekly income for two towns.

| Weekly income (£) | Town A | | Town B | |
|---|---|---|---|---|
| | No. | Income (£) | No. | Income (£) |
| 0 and under 30 | 0 | 0 | 1 | 5 |
| 30 and under 60 | 4 | 60 | 5 | 75 |
| 60 and under 90 | 9 | 225 | 9 | 225 |
| 90 and under 120 | 17 | 595 | 13 | 455 |
| 120 and under 150 | 23 | 1035 | 19 | 855 |
| 150 and under 180 | 19 | 1045 | 23 | 1265 |
| 180 and under 210 | 13 | 845 | 17 | 1105 |
| 210 and under 240 | 9 | 675 | 9 | 675 |
| 240 and under 270 | 5 | 425 | 4 | 340 |
| 270 and under 300 | 1 | 95 | 0 | 0 |
| Totals | 100 | 5000 | 100 | 5000 |

(i) Show that the arithmetic mean income is the same in both towns. In the light of this result, do you feel that the arithmetic mean is a useful measure to use for comparison of the two towns' 'average' income? If not, derive an alternative measure that you consider better, giving reasons for your choice.

(ii) Show that the standard deviation of incomes is the same in both towns. In the light of this result do you feel that the standard deviation is a useful measure to use for comparison of the two towns' dispersion of income? If not, derive an alternative measure that you consider better, giving reasons for your choice.

(iii) Given your discussion of (i) and (ii) above, what do you consider to be the essential differences between the two towns' distributions of income? How *might* you express this by a statistical measure? CIPFA

**9.24**   The table below shows the salaries of the 600 employees of a certain company.

| Range of salary | No. of employees |
|---|---|
| Under £6000 | 0 |
| £6000 but under £6500 | 80 |
| £6500 but under £7000 | 170 |
| £7000 but under £7500 | 90 |
| £7500 but under £8000 | 80 |
| £8000 but under £8500 | 70 |
| £8500 but under £9000 | 50 |
| £9000 but under £9500 | 40 |
| £9500 but under £10 000 | 20 |
| £10 000 and over | 0 |

(a)   Calculate the mean and standard deviation of the salaries of the employees.

(b)   Obtain and comment on an arithmetical measure of the skewness of the salary distribution.

(c)   State the main reason for normally using the median salary as a measure of position rather than the arithmetic mean or average; illustrate your answer with reference to the above data.

**9.25**   The table shows the age distribution of those males receiving retirement pensions. Calculate the arithmetic mean and standard deviation for this distribution. If the median is 71.8 years, obtain a measure of skewness and comment on what this tells you about the shape of the frequency curve of the distribution.

| Age (years) | Number receiving pensions (thousands) |
|---|---|
| 65–69 | 1030 |
| 70–74 | 820 |
| 75–79 | 460 |
| 80–84 | 240 |
| 85–89 | 80 |
| 90 and over | 20 |

Source: Department of Social Security, 1992

# 10 The normal distribution

We have considered in detail measures of central tendency and measures of dispersion, and we have found that many such measures are available to us. So far, we have used such measures for descriptive purposes, and the time has now come to consider their analytical implications. To do this, we shall confine ourselves to two measures: we shall use the arithmetic mean as a measure of central tendency, and the standard deviation as a measure of dispersion. We shall start by analysing a simple problem involving comparison.

## Standard scores

Acme Plc is considering the profits that it made last year. Its Office Equipment Division earned a profit of £65 000 and its Domestic Appliance Division earned a profit of £55 000. At first sight, it seems that the Office Equipment Division had the more successful year. Suppose, however, that we were told that the average profit earned in the office equipment industry was £50 000, and that the average profit earned in the domestic appliance industry was £45 000. Seemingly, the profit opportunities in office equipment are greater. How, then, can we compare the performance of the two divisions? If we were told that the standard deviation of profits in the office equipment industry was £10 000, then a profit of £65 000 is:

$$\frac{65\ 000 - 50\ 000}{10\ 000}$$

= 1.5 standard deviations above the mean. Suppose also that we know the standard deviation of profit earned in the domestic appliance industry was £5000, then a profit of £55 000 is:

$$\frac{55\ 000 - 45\ 000}{5000}$$

= 2 standard deviations above the mean. So we see that in the domestic appliance industry the relative performance (i.e. the performance with respect to competitors) was better than in the office equipment industry. Data calculated in this way – in terms of standard deviations measured from the mean – are called *standard scores* or *Z scores*, and for any value of *x* drawn from a population with a mean $\mu$ and a standard deviation $\sigma$, we can calculate the Z score like this:

$$Z = \frac{x - \mu}{\sigma}$$

Notice that the Z score is in relative, not absolute units; so they can be used to compare values in distributions that do not use the same unit of measurement.

## The standard normal distribution

Now Z scores are very important to statisticians: under certain conditions Z scores can be used to predict the proportion of a distribution that is more than, or less than a certain measurement. Let us first examine the conditions necessary for us to be able to do this. The distribution must be continuous; it must be symmetrical and it must be bell-shaped. In other words, the distribution must be shaped like the one in Fig 10.1. We call such a distribution a *normal distribution*, and call its shape *mesokurtic*. Now you may (with some justification) think that these conditions are very stringent and will not often be met in practice. We will have more to say about this in later chapters and for the moment we will concentrate on learning how to make predictions based on the normal distribution.

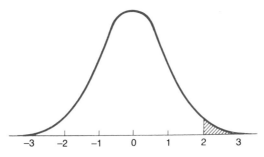

**Fig 10.1**

If you consult the tables at the end of this book you will find a table headed the normal distribution function. In the first column there is a list of Z scores ranging from 0.0 to 4.0. The second column gives the proportion of the normal distribution with a Z score greater than the corresponding figure in the first column. Suppose that we wanted to find the proportion in a normal distribution with a Z score greater than 2.0 (i.e. the proportion greater than two standard deviations above the mean). The shaded area in Fig 10.1 represents the proportion diagrammatically. Finding 2.0 in the first column, we read that the corresponding figure in the second column is 0.02275 (or 2.275%), so 2.275% of a normal distribution has a Z score greater than 2.0. This being so, it must follow that $100 - 2.275 = 97.725\%$ of a normal distribution has a Z score less than 2.0 (we imply here that a negligible proportion will have a Z score *exactly* equal to 2.0).

The remaining columns in the table enable us to take an extra place of decimals when calculating our Z score. Suppose we wanted to find the proportion in a normal distribution with a Z score greater than 2.12. We find the required proportion at the junction of the row with a Z score 2.1, and the column headed 0.02, i.e. the proportion required is 0.01700. The normal distribution tables, then, follow the standard format followed by other mathematical tables.

## Applications of the normal distribution

How can we apply this knowledge? Suppose we know that electric light bulbs have an average life of 2000 hours and a standard deviation of 60 hours. Furthermore, we know that the lives of bulbs are normally distributed (this would be a reasonable assumption) and we wish to know the proportion of bulbs failing after 2120 hours. We could represent the problem diagrammatically as in Fig 10.2.

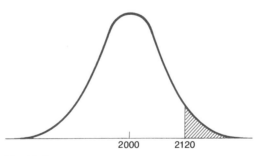

**Fig 10.2**

Notice that as the distribution is symmetrical, the mean bisects the distribution, and the mean, median and mode coincide. The shaded area will, of course, represent the proportion of bulbs failing after 2120 hours, and only a small proportion will do so. The first thing we do is calculate the Z score:

$$Z = \frac{2120 - 2000}{60} = 2 \text{ standard deviations.}$$

Now we already know that 2.275% of items in a normal distribution have a Z score more than 2, and in this particular normal distribution any bulb with a life above 2120 hours has a Z score more than 2. So it must follow that 2.275% of bulbs will fail after 2120 hours.

So far, we have considered cases where the Z score is positive, but it is perfectly possible for a Z score to be negative. This will occur when an item under consideration has a value less than the arithmetic mean. Suppose, for example, we wished to find the proportion of bulbs with lives more than 1850 hours. This involves finding the proportion of items with Z scores more than:

$$\frac{1850 - 2000}{60} = -2.5$$

If we consult the table, we notice that only positive Z scores are given – but the table can also be used for negative Z scores. A glance at Fig 10.3(a) and 10.3(b) will confirm that as the distribution is symmetrical, the proportion of items with Z scores more than $-2.5$ is the same as the proportion with Z scores less than 2.5. Reading from the table, we see that 0.621% of items have Z scores more than 2.5, so 99.379% have Z scores less than 2.5, and so 99.379% must have Z scores greater than $-2.5$. So we can see that 99.379% of bulbs can be expected to fail after 1850 hours.

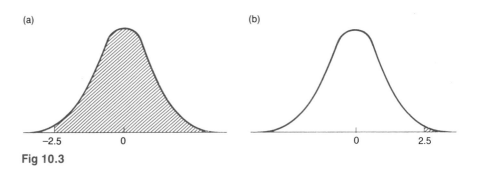

(a) (b)

−2.5　　0　　　　　　　　0　　2.5

**Fig 10.3**

Now you may find this all a bit confusing – sometimes the Z score is positive and sometimes it is negative; sometimes we read the percentage directly from the table, and sometimes we subtract it from 100. Can we offer some advice? When considering problems involving the normal distribution, *always* draw a sketch of the problem and shade the area under consideration. You can then see at a glance whether the area required is greater or less than 50%. If the area is less than 50%, then the proportion in the table is the one required. If the area required is greater than 50%, subtract from 100 the percentage obtained from the table.

Suppose we know that the weights of bags of flour are normally distributed with a standard deviation of 0.01 kilograms. The bags are marked 'weight not less than 1 kilogram', and the machine is set to fill bags to an average weight of 1.015 kilograms. We require to know the proportion of bags that satisfy the claim printed on the bag. First, let us draw a sketch of the problem (see Fig 10.4).

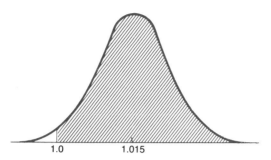

**Fig 10.4**

The Z score is:

$$\frac{1 - 1.015}{0.01} = -1.5$$

and looking up 1.5 in the table we obtain a proportion of 6.68%. Now the diagram tells us immediately that this cannot be the percentage we require – it obviously should be more than 50%. So the proportion of bags meeting the claim is $100 - 6.68 = 93.32\%$.

Sometimes it is necessary to use the normal distribution in reverse, i.e. given a proportion, we enter the tables to find the corresponding Z score, and so find a corresponding value in a given normal distribution.

EXAMPLE

Suppose that in order to satisfy legal requirements, a pork pie manufacturer may only produce 0.2% of pies below a weight of 75 grams. The pie-producing machine operates with a standard deviation of 0.5 grams. If the weights of pies are normally distributed, to what (mean) weight should the machine be set? Fig 10.5 illustrates the situation, and $\mu$ is the machine setting required.

Consulting the table we see that the nearest Z score to a proportion 0.2% is 2.88. Notice that the weight we are considering (75 grams) is *less than* the mean, so its Z score must be negative. In other words:

$$\frac{75 - \mu}{0.5} = -2.88$$

so the machine setting ($\mu$) is 76.44 grams (i.e. $2.88 \times 0.5 + 75$).

**Fig 10.5**

Let us take this example a stage further. The pie manufacturer's weekly output is 200 000 pies, and the pie contents cost 5p per 100 grams. Pies with weights in excess of 77 grams require additional packing at a cost of 0.5p per pie. Find the firm's weekly cost.

First, we are going to have to find the proportion of 'overweight' pies. This is illustrated in Fig 10.6. The Z score is:

$$\frac{77 - 76.44}{0.5} = 1.12$$

so 13.14% of output will need extra packaging.

**Fig 10.6**

We can now calculate the weekly cost like this:

Weekly pie content requirement is $200\,000 \times 76.44 = 15\,288\,000$ grams
Weekly cost of contents is $15\,288\,000 \times 0.05\text{p} = £7644$
Each week 13.14% of 200 000 = 26 280 pies need extra packing
Weekly cost of extra packing is $26\,280 \times 0.5\text{p} = £131.40$

Finally, let us suppose that a new pie producing machine is available; operating with a standard deviation of 0.2 grams, but costs an additional £225 per week to operate. Would you recommend that the pie manufacturer purchases the new machine? To answer this question, we must first determine the machine setting using the new machine, and determine the percentage of 'overweight' pies. To obtain the machine setting, we know that:

$$\frac{75 - \mu}{0.2} = -2.88$$

so the machine setting ($\mu$) must be 75.576 gms. (Notice that the lower standard deviation enables the machine setting to be lowered.) To obtain the percentage of 'overweight' pies, we know that:

$$Z = \frac{77 - 75.576}{0.2} = 7.12.$$

Now if you consult the normal distribution tables, you will see that the Z scores only go up to 4.0, and the proportion of a normal distribution with a Z score of more than 4 is only 0.003%. Clearly, then, it follows that as 77 grams has a Z score of 7.12, we would not expect to have any 'overweight' pies if the new machine is used.

We can now calculate the cost of using the new machine:

Weekly pie content requirement is $200\ 000 \times 75.576 = 15\ 115\ 200$ gms.
Weekly cost of contents is $15\ 115\ 200 \times 0.05p = £7557.60$

and as there are no 'overweight' pies, this is the total weekly cost of using the new machine. So the new machine involves a weekly cost saving of £7775.40 − £7557.60 = £217.80. However, as the new machine costs an extra £225 per week to operate, the manufacturer would be well advised to retain the use of the old machine.

Before ending this chapter, two points deserve attention. First, the normal distribution is of paramount importance in Statistics, and you would be well advised to master it before moving on to the following chapters. Second, you may be rather worried by the stringent conditions imposed before the normal distribution may be used. Well, there are many cases in which a population shows a very good approximation to the normal distribution, and any errors resulting from its application should not be too serious. More importantly, although populations may not approximate to the normal distribution, there are sound theoretical reasons for assuming that sampling statistics will do so. It is to this important truth that we shall shortly turn our attention.

## Using the spreadsheet

The spreadsheet that accompanies this chapter will calculate, amongst other things, proportions using the normal distribution. The menu structure for this template is shown in Fig 10.7.

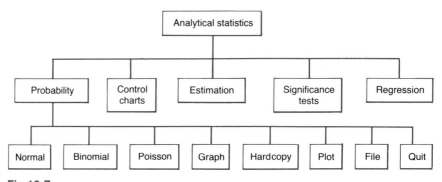

**Fig 10.7**

Retrieve this template from the main menu by selecting 'Analytical statistics' then selecting 'Probability'. Now select the 'Normal' option. The first thing to notice is that you are requested to input the mean. Input 200 and press Enter. You are now asked for the standard deviation, so input 12.65 and press Enter. Finally, you are requested to input the value. Input 220.5 and press Enter. The value of the Z score (1.62) is output, together with the percentage of items in the population with a mean 200 and a standard deviation 12.65 that exceeds 220.5. The answer generated by the spreadsheet is 5.24%, whereas the exact value is 5.26%. So the approximation used by this template generates quite acceptable results. If you want to change any of the values input, press Esc then simply move the cursor to the appropriate position and type in the new value. Pressing Alt and M together retrieves the menu.

**10.1**  (a)  What are the more important characteristics of the normal distribution?

(b)  Discuss the importance of the mean and standard deviation in the use of the normal distribution.

**10.2** The length of rods in a large batch is normally distributed with mean 120 mm and standard deviation 1.5 mm. What percentage of the rods would you expect to measure:

(i) over 122.5 mm;

(ii) between 116 mm and 124 mm?

**10.3** A random sample was taken of 200 candidates who had submitted scripts in a certain question paper at a public examination. The results obtained by the 200 candidates in the examination were as follows:

| Marks obtained out of a possible 100 | Number of candidates |
|---|---|
| Under 20 | 0 |
| 20–29 | 6 |
| 30–39 | 18 |
| 40–49 | 41 |
| 50–59 | 68 |
| 60–69 | 49 |
| 70–79 | 14 |
| 80–89 | 4 |
| 90 and over | 0 |
| Total | 200 |

(a) Calculate:

(i) the mean;

(ii) the standard deviation.

(b) (i) What does the standard deviation measure?

(ii) How does the standard deviation you have calculated differ from what might be expected if results were normally distributed? ICMA

**10.4** (a) What are the principal features of the normal distribution?

(b) Suppose that the distribution of women by size of feet is normal, with an arithmetic mean length of 8 inches and a standard deviation of 1 inch. A manufacturer of women's shoes has an output of 10 000 pairs per week and he wants to know how many pairs of shoes of each length to produce. How could a table of the area under a normal curve help him to plan his output? How many pairs per week should be (i) above $8\frac{1}{2}$ inches; (ii) below $6\frac{1}{2}$ inches; (iii) above $7\frac{1}{2}$ inches; (iv) below 9 inches? CIPFA

**10.5** (a) Sketch a normal distribution curve. On this sketch indicate the approximate proportions of the area under the curve which are contained within the following limits:

arithmetic mean ± 1 standard deviation,
arithmetic mean ± 2 standard deviations, and
arithmetic mean ± 3 standard deviations.

(b) A company packing spices knows that the weights of 500 packets form a normal distribution with a mean weight of 16 grams and a standard deviation of 0.2 grams. How many of these 500 packets can be expected to weigh:

(i) less than 15.6 g;

(ii) between 15.8 and 16.4 g;

(iii) at least 16.2 g?

**10.6** Describe a normal distribution, paying particular attention to precise definitions of its most important properties. Give examples of statistical data which might be expected to conform closely to a normal distribution.

An automatic machine produces packages whose weights are normally distributed with a standard deviation of 0.07 grams. To what weight should the machine be set so that at least $97\frac{1}{2}\%$ of the packages are over 16 grams in weight?

**10.7** (a) Illustrate graphically the relationship between the standard deviation and areas under the normal curve of distribution.

(b) Assuming that the hub thickness of a certain type of gear is normally distributed around a mean thickness of 2.00 cm, with a standard deviation of 0.04 cm, say:

(i) approximately how many gears will have a thickness between 1.96 and 2.04 cm in a production run of 5000 gears;

(ii) in a random selection of one gear from this production run of 5000, with what degree of confidence could it be predicted that its thickness would be between 1.92 and 2.08 cm? ACCA

**10.8** A manufacturer makes chocolate bars with a mean weight of 110 grams and a standard deviation of 2 grams. The weights are normally distributed. What proportion of the bars are likely to be less in weight than 106 grams? The manufacturer decides to make 'bigger' bars with a mean weight of 115 grams, with the same standard deviation as before. What proportion of the new bars is likely to be less in weight than the old ones? (The weights of the 'bigger' bars are also normally distributed.)

It is decided that the covers of these 'bigger' bars will be marked 'Minimum weight 115 grams'. What mean weight will have to be aimed at if no more than one bar in 100 is to be less than 115 grams in weight? ICSA

**10.9**   Components made by a certain process have a thickness which is normally distributed about a mean of 3.00 cm and a standard deviation of 0.03 cm. A component is classified as defective if its thickness lies outside the range 2.95 cm to 3.05 cm.

Required:

(1)   What is the proportion of defective components?

(2)   Find the change in the proportion of defective components if the mean thickness is increased to 3.01 cm, the variability remaining the same.     ACCA

**10.10**   (a)   Explain the meaning of the term normal distribution and illustrate with a simple diagram.

(b)   Records kept by the goods inwards department of a large factory show that the average number of lorries arriving each week is 248. It is known that the distribution approximates to the normal with a standard deviation of 26. If this pattern of arrivals continues, what percentage of weeks can be expected to have a number of arrivals of: (i) less than 229 per week; (ii) more than 280 per week?

**10.11**   The length of rods in a large batch is normally distributed with mean 120 mm and standard deviation 1.5 mm. What percentage of the rods would be expected to measure (i) over 122.5 mm; (ii) between 116 mm and 124 mm?

**10.12**   The mean weight of a consignment of 500 sacks of sugar is 151 kg and the standard deviation 15 kg. Assuming that the weights are normally distributed, find how many sacks weigh:

(a)   between 120 and 155 kg,

(b)   more than 185 kg, and

(c)   less than 12 kg.

**10.13**   The average number of newspapers purchased by a population of urban households in 1992 was 400, and the standard deviation was 100. Assuming that purchases were normally distributed, what is the probability that households bought:

(a)   between 250 and 500 papers;

(b)   less than 250 papers;

(c)   between 500 and 600 papers;

(d)   more than 500 papers?

**10.14** The thermal efficiency of electricity generating stations varied from below 10% to over 34% as shown in the table:

**Electricity: output and efficiency**
**Thermal efficiency of steam stations**

| Thermal efficiency of stations (%) | No. of stations with given efficiency |
|---|---|
| 34 and over | 7 |
| 32–34 | 17 |
| 30–32 | 12 |
| 28–30 | 17 |
| 26–28 | 21 |
| 24–26 | 22 |
| 22–24 | 27 |
| 20–22 | 27 |
| 18–20 | 15 |
| 16–18 | 15 |
| 14–16 | 12 |
| 12–14 | 4 |
| 10–12 | 4 |
| 10 and under | 3 |
| Total | 203 |

(a) Calculate (i) the average thermal efficiency, (ii) the standard deviations.

(b) Assuming the distribution to be nearly normal, what would you expect the range to be, observing that the end classes are 34 and over and 10 and under?

**10.15** A firm is considering the purchase of a machine to turn ball-bearings. A machine is borrowed for testing purposes, and it is found that 6.68% of ball-bearings have mean diameters greater than 5.03 mm. Assuming the machine to be set at 5 mm, find the standard deviation to which the machine operates. The firm wishes to produce ball-bearings to a design dimension of $5 \pm 0.05$ mm, and any ball-bearings outside this range would be rejected. Assuming the machine produces 1 million units per month, and each unit rejected costs the firm 1p, find the monthly cost of rejects.

A more accurate machine is available, which costs an additional £100 per month to purchase. If this machine is known to operate with a standard deviation of 0.016 mm, which machine should be purchased? **ICAEW**

**10.16** A manufacturer finds that although he promises delivery of a certain item in seven weeks, the time he takes to deliver to customers is approximately normally distributed with a mean of six weeks and a standard deviation of two weeks.

(a) What proportion of customers receive their deliveries late?

(b) What proportion of customers receive deliveries within four to seven weeks?

(c)  To what figure should his delivery promise be amended if it is required that only 20% of deliveries should be late?

(d)  What proportion of customers will receive deliveries within five weeks if the manufacturer reduces the standard deviation of delivery time to one week, keeping the mean time at six weeks?

**10.17**  The heights of 8585 adult males born in the British Isles were measured. The standard deviation and arithmetic mean for this sample were calculated and found to be 2.57 inches and 67.52 inches respectively. Use the area under the normal curve to find the proportion of men, during the year in which this operation was carried out, who would have been:

(i)  over 71 inches;

(ii)  less than 61 inches;

(iii)  either taller than 71 inches or shorter than 61 inches;

(iv)  between 71 inches and 61 inches.

**10.18**  A maintenance engineer has established that component XYZ has an operating life of 2500 hours and a standard deviation of 250 hours. Assuming a normal distribution, calculate the probability that any one component XYZ chosen at random would have an operating life of:

(a)  less than 2200 hours;

(b)  between 2300 and 2700 hours;

(c)  between 2300 and 2400 hours;

(d)  more than 3000 hours;

(e)  between 2000 and 3000 hours.

**10.19**  A machine is packaging nominal 800 gram packets and it has been found that over a long period the actual weight put in the packets has been normally distributed with a standard deviation of 5 grams. The company wishes to ensure that no more than 1% of the packets has a weight of less than 800 grams; at what mean weight should the machine be set?

The weekly output of packages averages 2 400 000 and the cost, in pence, of producing a packet of weight $w$ grams is given by the relationship $c = 6 + 0.5w$. If, by installation of new machinery, the standard deviation could be reduced to 2 grams, and the mean allowed to fall just far enough to give the same percentage below 800 grams as before, determine the average saving in pounds per week.

# 11 Probability

If you have read the previous chapters carefully, you will have realised by now that much of a statistician's time is spent measuring data and drawing conclusions based on these measurements. Sometimes, all the data is available to the statistician, and the measurements are bound to be accurate. In such circumstances, we can say that there is perfect knowledge of the population being investigated. Unfortunately, this will not be the usual situation. In most cases, the statistician will not have the details required about the entire population, and will be unable to collect all the desired information because of the cost and labour involved. To take an example: suppose it is required to find the average height of adult males in a particular country; it would not be possible to measure the height of every male. Instead, the statistician would have to make do with the average height of a sample. Now, if the statistician is careful about how the sample is drawn, and if the sample is not too small, then the sample average will give a good approximation to the population average. However, because the entire population has not been examined, the statistician can never be completely sure of results, so when quoting conclusions based on sample evidence it is usual to state just how confident we are of our results.

So you will often see the estimates which are based on sample results quoted 'with 95% confidence'. Now what, exactly, does this statement mean? Suppose that we are selecting a sample and calculating its average in order to provide an approximation of the population average. To say we are 95% confident cannot mean that the sample we have selected has a 95% probability of being a good or a satisfactory approximation. After all, once we have selected a sample it either gives a good approximation of the population mean or it does not. No, what we mean is that if we were to select a large number of all the possible samples, 95% of them would give us a good approximation. The 95% confidence refers to the probability of our selecting a sample which does this, not the probability that a sample which has already been selected will do so. You may argue, of course, that we are splitting hairs. The difference is not so great as all that. But it is important for sampling theory that you get the distinction clear in your own mind.

In order to understand the principles of sampling, then, we must first understand the meaning and theory of probability. Furthermore, the emphasis of this book will now undergo a change. Previously, we have been concerned with statistical measurement and representation, but from now on we will concentrate on *statistical analysis*. The basis for all statistical analysis is the theory of probability – something that must be mastered if we are to appreciate fully the work of the statistician.

## Some definitions

Let us suppose that we toss a coin. This experiment can have two outcomes: the coin can land with either heads showing or tails showing. The result of such an experiment is called an *event*. Notice that in this case the events are *mutually exclusive*, that is, if a head occurs, then a tail cannot occur at the same time. Now not all events are mutually exclusive, and we must be careful to recognise when events are mutually exclusive and when they are not. Suppose, for example, we are selecting a card from a pack; and the first event is that the card is red and the second event is that the card is an ace. If we draw the ace of hearts or the ace of diamonds, then both events have occurred simultaneously. Clearly, the events are *not* mutually exclusive. Usually, we use a capital $E$ with a suitable subscript to identify the events in an experiment. We could write the events in the coin-spinning experiment like this:

$E_1$ = the coin shows a head
$E_2$ = the coin shows a tail

Notice too that $E_1$ and $E_2$ are *collectively exhaustive*: that is, they account for all the logical possibilities (we treat with contempt the suggestion that the coin lands on its edge!).

Sometimes we will find it convenient to consider the situations when the event would not occur, and we can do this by placing a dash after the symbol for the event. So we could write:

$E_1'$ = the coin does not show a head

Can you see that in this case $E_1'$ and $E_2$ are equivalent events? If the coin does not show a head then it must show a tail. We can conclude that if $E_1' = E_2$, then $E_1$ and $E_2$ must be both mutually exclusive and collectively exhaustive.

## How we measure probability

Let us consider a certain experiment, and list all the possible events; that is, we will ensure that the events are collectively exhaustive. Events that are equally likely will be assigned the same 'weighting'. Suppose, for example, we again consider tossing a coin. We have:

$E_1$ = the coin shows a head
$E_2$ = the coin shows a tail

If we make the assumption that the coin is unbiased, then $E_1$ and $E_2$ must be equally likely. What we will now do is to assign 'weights' to the events in proportion to the likelihood that they will occur. So we have:

|  | *Weight* |
|---|---|
| $E_1$ | 1 |
| $E_2$ | 1 |

Now the probability that the event $E$ occurs is:

$$P(E) = \frac{\text{Weighting for event } E}{\text{Sum of the weights}}$$

So      $P(E_1) = \frac{1}{2}$ (or 0.5)
and     $P(E_2) = \frac{1}{2}$

So we can see that the probability of obtaining a head with a single throw of a coin is one half. Just what do we mean by this? Well, it is obvious that we cannot demonstrate probability with a single toss of a coin. In fact, the outcome of a single toss depends on the force we exert together with the way the coin was originally facing. It has nothing to do with probability! When we state that the probability of a head is a half, we are surely making some prediction as to the proportion of heads occurring if we repeat this experiment many times. The outcome of each *individual* toss is determined by the forces mentioned earlier, but the outcome of many tosses obeys a law of 'mass behaviour', and it is this 'mass behaviour' that our probability measure is trying to predict. So when we state that the probability of a head is a half, we mean that if the coin is tossed a large number of times, then we would expect heads to occur on 50% of occasions.

Let us now see if we can restate our measure of probability. If an experiment has $N$ *equally likely* outcomes, $n$ of which constitute event $E$, then we can state that:

$$P(E) = \frac{n}{N}$$

Suppose, then, we wished to find the probability of drawing an ace from a well-shuffled pack of cards. Here we have $N = 52$ (there are 52 cards in a pack, all of them having an equal chance of being drawn) and $n = 4$, so:

$$P(\text{ace}) = \tfrac{4}{52} = \tfrac{1}{13}$$

Easy, isn't it?

Now suppose that $n = N$. This implies that each and every outcome must constitute event $E$. In other words, if we perform the experiment we are absolutely certain that event $E$ will occur. Moreover, if $n = N$, then $P(E) = 1$, so we assign a probability measure of 1 to events that are absolutely certain to occur. If the event $E$ cannot possibly occur, then $n = 0$ and $P(E) = 0$, so we assign a zero probability measure to events that are absolutely impossible. As absolute certainty and absolute impossibility are at opposite ends of the spectrum, we have now obtained limits to our measure of probability, i.e. $P(E)$ must lie between zero and one. We can write this statement mathematically like this:

$$0 \leqslant P(E) \leqslant 1$$

So let this be a warning to you – if you are calculating the probability of an event, and your result is either negative, or greater than one, then you have made a mistake somewhere. We, as examiners, have frequently met solutions to probability problems in the form of (say) $P(E) = 1.5$. Now not only has the candidate obviously performed the calculations incorrectly, but also he has demonstrated that he does not know that $P(E)$ cannot exceed one – you cannot be more certain than absolute certainty! So if you obtain an answer like this in an examination, and you cannot discover where you have gone wrong, please do state that your answer is wrong, and state why it is wrong!

Earlier, we stated that an experiment has $N$ equally likely outcomes, $n$ of which constitute event $E$. Hence, it must follow that $N - n$ of the outcomes would not constitute event $E$. We can now formulate that:

$$P(E') = \frac{N - n}{N}$$

$$= 1 - \frac{n}{N}$$

So $\quad P(E') = 1 - P(E)$

We have already discovered that the probability of drawing an ace from a pack of cards is $\tfrac{1}{13}$, so it must follow that the probability of not drawing an ace is $1 - \tfrac{1}{13} = \tfrac{12}{13}$. Later, we will find this formula extremely useful.

## Three approaches to probability

Well, we have now seen how to measure probability. However, we have so far been making an assumption without actually spelling it out. We have assumed that we not only know all the possible outcomes of an experiment, but also that we can weight the probability of each outcome in proportion to its likelihood. More importantly, we have assumed we can do both of these things *before the experiment is performed*. In other words, we assume a prior knowledge of the outcomes – we have been using the so-called *a priori* approach to probability. Now although it is true that in many cases we will have the necessary information to use an *a priori* approach (it is true, for example, when considering games of chance), there are many cases in which an *a priori* approach cannot be used.

Suppose we have a large case of wood screws, and we wish to find the probability that one screw chosen at random is defective. Clearly, it is possible here to define all the events (the screw is either defective or it isn't) but it is not possible to weight the events in proportion to their likelihood. The only way we can determine probability in this case is to draw a sample of $N$ screws, and count the number of defectives (call this $n$). We can *estimate* the probability that a randomly chosen screw is defective is $n/N$.

This is the so-called *empirical approach* – there is just no way of estimating the probability without drawing that sample!

An appreciation of these two approaches to probability helps to explain a problem that confuses so many students. The problem runs something like this. If I spin a penny 100 times, and on 99 occasions the coin shows heads, what is the probability that it will show heads on the next spin? Some people would argue that the outcome can be either a head or a tail, and the coin has no memory of the 100 previous tosses. So the probability that the coin will show heads on the next spin must be $\frac{1}{2}$. Others would argue that the coin is more likely to show heads than tails, and would estimate the probability of obtaining a head on the next spin to be $\frac{99}{100}$. Well, which approach is the correct one? Surprisingly, the answer is both! In the first case, we are using an *a priori* approach, reasoning that the experiment has produced a fluke result which does not detract from the fact that the coin is unbiassed. In the second case, we are using an *empirical approach*, stating that the experimental evidence indicates that the coin is biassed in favour of heads. Now ask yourself this – if you were a gambler, which approach would you prefer to use.

There is a third approach to probability that we must now examine. Suppose we wished to find the probability that a particular horse wins the Derby – clearly we cannot use an *a priori* approach. Nor can we use an empirical approach, as this would demand that the same race be repeated many times under identical conditions! The only way we can obtain this probability is to give a personal, 'gut feeling' of the horse's chances. This is the so-called *subjective* approach to probability, and it is the method used by bookmakers when fixing odds for a particular horse to win a race. Initially, the odds will be determined by the personal view of the bookmaker, and will be modified as the race approaches according to the collective, subjective views of the punters.

These three distinct approaches to probability raise an interesting philosophical problem. We know that $P(E)$ can never exceed one, but does $P(E) = 1$ imply absolute certainty? It all depends on the approach used. If we use an *a priori* approach then $P(E) = 1$ means that $E$ *must always* occur. However, using an empirical approach $P(E) = 1$ means that $E$ *has always* occurred – which does not imply that it must occur in the future. Likewise, using a subjective approach $P(E) = 1$ means that *we think that E will occur* – which again does not imply that it must occur.

Without doubt, the empirical and subjective approaches are more interesting and more useful than the *a priori* approach. However, in an introductory book such as this, it is preferable to concentrate our attention on *a priori* probability, and, unless we state to the contrary, you should assume that an *a priori* approach is being used.

## The laws of probability

**The additional law**

Let us suppose that we cast two dice, and add the scores of the dice. We could represent all the outcomes in a table like this:

*Second die*

|  |  | 1 | 2 | 3 | 4 | 5 | 6 |
|--|--|---|---|---|---|---|---|
|  | 1 | 2 | 3 | 4 | 5 | 6 | 7 |
|  | 2 | 3 | 4 | 5 | 6 | 7 | 8 |
| *First* | 3 | 4 | 5 | 6 | 7 | 8 | 9 |
| *die* | 4 | 5 | 6 | 7 | 8 | 9 | 10 |
|  | 5 | 6 | 7 | 8 | 9 | 10 | 11 |
|  | 6 | 7 | 8 | 9 | 10 | 11 | 12 |

(Remember that die is the singular, and dice the plural.)

The number in front of each row represents the possible scores of the first die, and the number at the head of each column represents the possible scores of the second die. The numbers in the main body of the table represent the sums of the two possible scores. So we see that if we score a total of 11, we must have thrown either a six with the first die and a five with the second, or a five with the first die and a six with the second. We see, then, that there are 36 equally likely total scores ($N = 36$). Let us now define two events:

$E_1$ = the sum of the scores is 7
$E_2$ = the sum of the scores is 9

Now there are six ways of scoring a total of seven, so $P(E_1) = \frac{6}{36} = \frac{1}{6}$. Again, there are four ways of scoring a total of nine, so $P(E_2) = \frac{4}{36} = \frac{1}{9}$. Now suppose we wished to find the probability that the sum of the scores is *either* seven *or* nine. We can write the probability symbolically like this:

$P(E_1 \cup E_2)$

where $\cup$ is a shorthand way of writing 'either–or'. Consulting the table, we see that there are 10 ways of obtaining a total score of either seven or nine, so $P(E_1 \cup E_2) = \frac{10}{36} = \frac{5}{18}$. Notice that the 10 ways are obtained by adding the number of ways for $E_1$ and $E_2$. This gives us our first law of probability: the so-called additional law:

$P(E_1 \cup E_2) = P(E_1) + P(E_2)$

a law which is true only if $E_1$ and $E_2$ are mutually exclusive. If the events are not mutually exclusive, then using this law will not yield the correct probability. Suppose we draw a card from a pack, and $E_1$ is that the card is an ace. So $P(E_1) = \frac{4}{52}$. If $E_2$ is that the card is a heart, then $P(E_2)$ is $\frac{13}{52}$. If we want to find the probability that the card is either a heart or an ace, we notice that there are 52 equally likely outcomes, 16 of which would be either a heart or an ace (i.e. 13 hearts plus the three other aces). So the probability that the card is either a heart or an ace is $\frac{16}{52}$. Notice that if we had applied the addition law, we would have obtained $\frac{13}{52} + \frac{4}{52} = \frac{17}{52}$ – the wrong probability! So beware – before using this law make absolutely sure that the events are mutually exclusive!

**The
multiplication law**

Look again at the table we obtained earlier which refers to the sum of the possible scores from casting two dice. Notice that there are 36 equally likely total scores. We could deduce this as follows: there are six ways the first die can fall, each of which can combine with any one of the six ways that the second die can fall. So there are $6 \times 6 = 36$ ways that both dice can fall. Now suppose we have two piles of cards. The first pile contains the two red aces and the four kings, and the second pile contains the two red aces and the ace of spades and the four kings. Suppose we draw a card from each pile – as there are six cards in the first pile and seven cards in the second, there will be $6 \times 7 = 42$ ways of drawing a pair of cards, one from each pile. We could represent the situation in a table like this:

|  |  | Second card | | | | | | |
|---|---|---|---|---|---|---|---|---|
|  |  | A♡ | A♢ | A♠ | K♡ | K♢ | K♠ | K♣ |
|  | A♡ | 1 | 2 | 3 | 4 | 5 | 6 | 7 |
|  | A♢ | 8 | 9 | 10 | 11 | 12 | 13 | 14 |
| First | K♡ | 15 | 16 | 17 | 18 | 19 | 20 | 21 |
| card | K♢ | 22 | 23 | 24 | 25 | 26 | 27 | 28 |
|  | K♠ | 29 | 30 | 31 | 32 | 33 | 34 | 35 |
|  | K♣ | 36 | 37 | 38 | 39 | 40 | 41 | 42 |

In this table we have numbered all the possible 42 combinations of events $1, 2, 3, \ldots$ etc., so combination 25, for example, means drawing the king of diamonds with the first card and the king of hearts with the second. Let us now define two events:

$E_1 =$ the first card is an ace, so $P(E_1) = \frac{2}{6}$
$E_2 =$ the second card is an ace, so $P(E_2) = \frac{3}{7}$

Suppose we wanted to find the probability that both cards were aces: we could write it symbolically like this:

$$P(E_1 \cap E_2)$$

where the symbol $\cap$ is a shorthand form for 'both ... and'. Notice that there are six ways of obtaining two aces, so $P(E_1 \cap E_2) = \frac{6}{42}$. Now we could have obtained this result by multiplying $P(E_1)$ and $P(E_2)$ together $(\frac{2}{6} \times \frac{3}{7} = \frac{6}{42})$. This gives us the second law of probability: the so-called *multiplication law*:

$$P(E_1 \cap E_2) = P(E_1) \cdot P(E_2)$$

a law which applies only if $E_1$ and $E_2$ are *independent* (i.e. as long as the outcomes in no way affect each other). We will discuss this point more fully later, but it is worth noting now that independent events cannot be mutually exclusive, and mutually exclusive events cannot be independent.

**The general law of addition**

The second law of probability enables us to modify the first law to take account of events that are not mutually exclusive. A little earlier, we considered the case of drawing a card from a pack, calling $E_1$ that the event was a heart (so $P(E_1) = \frac{13}{52}$), and calling $E_2$ that the card is an ace (so $P(E_2) = \frac{4}{52}$). We stated that the probability that the card is either a heart or an ace $P(E_1 \cup E_2)$ is not $\frac{4}{52} + \frac{13}{52} = \frac{17}{52}$. Now why doesn't the addition law work? Surely the fault here is that the card we draw could be the ace of hearts *and we have counted this card twice* – once as a heart and once as an ace. So the probability that the card is either an ace or a heart is $\frac{17}{52}$ minus the probability that the card is the ace of hearts. Using the second law, the probability that the card is the ace of hearts is $P(E_1 \cap E_2) = \frac{4}{52} \times \frac{13}{52} = \frac{1}{52}$, so the probability that the card is either an ace or a heart is $\frac{17}{52} - \frac{1}{52} = \frac{16}{52}$ (which agrees precisely with the result we obtained from first principles). We can now restate the addition law to take account of situations when the events are not mutually exclusive:

$$P(E_1 \cup E_2) = P(E_1) + P(E_2) - P(E_1 \cap E_2)$$

This is the so-called *general law of addition*, and it works whether the events are mutually exclusive or not (if the events are mutually exclusive, then they cannot occur, so $P(E_1 \cap E_2)$ will be zero).

## Applications of the laws of probability

EXAMPLE 1

Two types of metal A and B, which have been treated with a special coating of paint have probabilities of $\frac{1}{4}$ and $\frac{1}{3}$ respectively of lasting four years without rusting.

If both types of metal are given the special coating on the same day, what is the probability that:

(i)   both last four years without rusting;
(ii)  at least one of them lasts four years without rusting.

For part (i), we can use the multiplication law to obtain a probability of $\frac{1}{4} \times \frac{1}{3} = \frac{1}{12}$ that both last for four years. Turning to the second part, we should first notice that four distinct outcomes are possible:

(a)   both last four years       (probability is $\frac{1}{4} \times \frac{1}{3} = \frac{1}{12}$)
(b)   A lasts, B doesn't         (probability is $\frac{1}{4} \times \frac{2}{3} = \frac{2}{12}$)
(c)   B lasts, A doesn't         (probability is $\frac{3}{4} \times \frac{1}{3} = \frac{3}{12}$)
(d)   neither lasts              (probability is $\frac{3}{4} \times \frac{2}{3} = \frac{6}{12}$)

Now any of the outcomes (a), (b) or (c) satisfies the condition that at least one lasts four years, so that probability we require is $\frac{1}{12} + \frac{2}{12} + \frac{3}{12} = \frac{6}{12} = \frac{1}{2}$. Notice that we could have calculated the probability more directly by using the fact that:

$$P(\text{at least one lasts}) = 1 - P(\text{neither lasts})$$

This second method can save quite a lot of time, and you should always use it in preference to writing out all the possible outcomes.

| EXAMPLE 2 | An item is made in three stages. At the first stage, it is formed on one of four machines, A, B, C or D, with equal probability. At the second stage it is trimmed on one of three machines, E, F or G, with equal probability. Finally, it is polished on one of two polishers, H and I, and is twice as likely to be polished on the former as this machine works twice as quickly as the other. Required: |

(1)  What is the probability that an item is:

  (i)    polished on H?

  (ii)   trimmed on either F or G?

  (iii)  formed on either A or B, trimmed on F and polished on H?

  (iv)  either formed on A and polished on I, or formed on B and polished on H?

  (v)   either formed on A or trimmed on F?

(2)  Suppose that items trimmed on E or F are susceptible to a particular defect. The defect rates on these machines are 10% and 20% respectively. What is the probability that an item found to have this defect was trimmed on F?                                        ACCA

First, we shall determine the probabilities for each machine. As the formation stage is equally likely to occur on any one of the four machines, we have:

$$P(A) = P(B) = P(C) = P(D) = \tfrac{1}{4}$$

Again, trimming is equally likely to occur on any one of the three machines, so:

$$P(E) = P(F) = P(G) = \tfrac{1}{3}$$

Polishing is twice as likely to occur on machine H as machine I, so:

$$P(H) = \tfrac{2}{3}, \quad P(I) = \tfrac{1}{3}$$

(i)    The probability that an item is polished on H $= P(H) = \tfrac{2}{3}$.

(ii)   The probability that an item is trimmed on either F or G

$$= P(F \cup G) = P(F) + P(G) = \tfrac{2}{3}.$$

(iii) Formed on either A or B, trimmed on F and polished on H:

$$= P(A \cup B) \cap F \cap H$$
$$= [P(A) + P(B)] \cdot P(F) \cdot P(H)$$
$$= (\tfrac{1}{4} + \tfrac{1}{4}) \times \tfrac{1}{3} \times \tfrac{2}{3} = \tfrac{1}{9}$$

(iv) Either formed on A and polished on I or formed on B and polished on H:

$$= P[(A \cap I) \cup (B \cap H)]$$
$$= [P(A) \cdot P(I)] + [P(B) \cdot P(H)]$$
$$= (\tfrac{1}{4} \times \tfrac{1}{3}) + (\tfrac{1}{4} \times \tfrac{2}{3})$$
$$= \tfrac{1}{4}$$

(v) Either formed on A or trimmed on F. These events are *not* mutually exclusive as it is possible to form on A *and* trim on F, so we need the general rule of addition, i.e.:

$$P(A \cup F) = P(A) + P(F) - P(A \cap F)$$
$$= \tfrac{1}{4} + \tfrac{1}{3} - (\tfrac{1}{4} \times \tfrac{1}{3})$$
$$= \tfrac{1}{2}$$

Dealing with the second part of this question, we notice that F is twice as likely to produce a defective item as is machine E. So, given that the item is defective, the probability that it was trimmed on F must be $\tfrac{2}{3}$.

---

| EXAMPLE 3 |

In the past, two building contractors, A and B, have competed for 20 building contracts of which 10 were awarded to A and six were awarded to B. The remaining four contracts were not awarded to either A or B. Three contracts for buildings of the kind in which they both specialise have been offered for tender.

Assuming that the market has not changed, find the probability that:

(a) A will obtain all three contracts;
(b) B will obtain at least one contract;
(c) Two contracts will not be awarded to either A or B;
(d) A will be awarded the first contract, B the second, and A will be awarded the third contract.                                      CIMA

The probability that A gets the contract is $P(A) = \tfrac{10}{20} = \tfrac{1}{2}$, the probability that B gets the contract is $P(\mathrm{B}) = \frac{6}{20} = \frac{3}{10}$, and the probability that neither A nor B gets the contract is $P(\mathrm{A} \cup \mathrm{B})' = \frac{4}{20} = \frac{1}{5}$.

(a) The probability that A will obtain all three contracts is $\frac{1}{2} \times \frac{1}{2} \times \frac{1}{2} = \frac{1}{8}$.

(b) The probability that B will obtain at least one contract:

$$= 1 - P(\mathrm{B} \text{ obtains no contracts})$$
$$= 1 - (\tfrac{7}{10} \times \tfrac{7}{10} \times \tfrac{7}{10}) = \tfrac{657}{1000}$$

(c) The probability that a contract is awarded to A or $\mathrm{B} = P(\mathrm{A} \cup \mathrm{B}) = \frac{4}{5}$. We require to know the probability that two contracts will not be awarded to either A or B: this is equivalent to finding the probability that one of the contracts is awarded to either A or B. But the contract awarded to either A or B could be either the first, second or third contract. So the probability we require is:

$$\frac{4}{5} \times \frac{1}{5} \times \frac{1}{5} \text{ (A or B wins the first contract)}$$
plus $\quad \frac{1}{5} \times \frac{4}{5} \times \frac{1}{5}$ (A or B wins the second contract)
plus $\quad \frac{1}{5} \times \frac{1}{5} \times \frac{4}{5}$ (A or B wins the third contract)
equals $\quad 3 \times \frac{4}{5} \times \frac{1}{5} \times \frac{1}{5} = \frac{12}{125}$

(d) The probability that A is awarded the first contract, B the second and A the third is $\frac{1}{2} \times \frac{3}{10} \times \frac{1}{2} = \frac{3}{40}$.

## Tree diagrams

One of the major problems that occur when dealing with probability is that of ensuring that all logical possibilities are considered. In fact, this is probably the most common student error when dealing with this topic. A tree diagram is a device to help us avoid such errors: it is a diagram which looks something like a tree, each branch of which represents one logical possibility. We shall illustrate tree diagrams by means of an example.

Buggsy Flynn owns 60% of protection rackets and 80% of illegal gambling in Chicago, and he is informed that the police are about to investigate both these activities. Police records show that 70% of investigations into the protection racket and 90% of investigations into gambling lead to court action. What is the probability that Buggsy will end up in court as a result of the investigations? (You may care to attempt to solve this problem before reading on.)

This problem involves an examination of whether Buggsy is investigated and whether he is charged. We can begin the tree diagram by calculating the probability of an investigation into Buggsy's protection rackets. Since he owns only 60% of the protection in Chicago there is a 0.6 probability that the police investigation will concern him, and the position is illustrated in Fig 11.1.

**Fig 11.1**

Notice that the probabilities have been inserted on to the diagram. We can now add the possibility of an investigation into illegal gambling on to the diagram (*see* Fig 11.2).

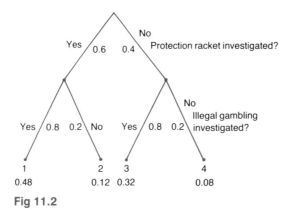

**Fig 11.2**

We now have four routes on our tree, and if we multiply the probabilities along each route, then we have deduced the probability of certain events occurring at each point. For example, Point 1 represents the situation where Buggsy is investigated on both activities and we find the probability of this happening is 0.48; Point 3 is the situation where Buggsy is not investigated on his protection racket but he is investigated on his illegal gambling, and the probability of this is 0.32. Notice that four points cover all the logical possibilities of investigations, so the probabilities must total 1 $(0.48 + 0.12 + 0.32 + 0.08 = 1.0)$.

We will now insert on to the diagram the possibilities of court action resulting from a protection racket investigation (*see* Fig 11.3).

**Fig 11.3**

**Fig 11.4**

Notice particularly points a and b on this tree diagram. Since on this branch the protection racket has not been investigated there can be no court action on that charge and hence the probabilities at points a and b remain at 0.32 and 0.08. Finally we can insert the possibility of court action on an illegal gambling charge and find the probability of each logical possibility (*see* Fig 11.4).

Notice again points a, b and c. In each of these branches there has been no investigation of illegal gambling. Hence there can be no court charge and the probabilities remain as they were at the previous junction.

In the diagram we have underlined every logical possibility that results in Buggsy landing up in court. The probability of his facing a court charge is the sum of the probabilities of all these, i.e.:

$$0.3024 + 0.0336 + 0.1296 + 0.084 + 0.288 = 0.8376$$

## Conditional probability

In the first section, we stated that events cannot be mutually exclusive and independent. This should not be taken to mean that if events are not mutually exclusive then they must be independent: there is a third category that we must now examine. When we state that events are independent, we mean that the outcome of the one event in no way affects the outcome of the other. Now there are many cases where this is not true: the outcome of the second event is *conditional* on the outcome of the first event. Two examples may clarify this point.

Suppose we draw a card from a well-shuffled pack, and this card happens to be an ace. We now draw a second card – what is the probability that this card is also an ace? Well, having removed one card already, there must be 51 equally likely outcomes left, three of which would yield an ace. So the probability of an ace with the second card is $\frac{3}{51}$. Suppose the first card was not an ace: there would be 51 equally likely outcomes of which four would yield an ace. In this case, the probability of an ace with the second card would be $\frac{4}{51}$. In the first case, we are drawing from a pack with a lower proportion of aces than originally, and in the second case, the pack has a higher proportion. Whichever way you consider this problem, the outcome of the first trial affects the outcome of the second.

Now this raises an interesting philosophical problem: we cannot predict the outcomes of the second event until we know the outcome of the first. If I deal a card to you, and you do not reveal it to me, the probability that I deal myself an ace must be $\frac{4}{52}$. Why is this so when a card has been removed from the pack? It is the *information* from the first card that is important, not the fact that it has been dealt. In this case, as you do not reveal the card it has a zero information value to me: from the information viewpoint, it is irrelevant to me whether the card is in your hand or in the pack. However, if your card is revealed to me, then I can use this information to calculate the probability that I deal myself an ace – the probability will be $\frac{4}{51}$ or $\frac{3}{51}$, depending on whether you have an ace or not.

We need a new notation to take into account the fact that events can be conditional upon each other. If we have two events $E_1$ and $E_2$ then $P(E_2 \mid E_1)$ is the probability that $E_2$ occurs given that $E_1$ has occurred. So we can now modify our multiplication law to take account of conditional probability:

$$P(E_1 \cap E_2) = P(E_1) \cdot P(E_2 \mid E_1)$$

If $E_1$ is draw an ace with the first card, then $P(E_1) = \frac{1}{13}$. If $E_2$ is draw an ace with the second card, then $P(E_2 \mid E_1) = \frac{3}{51}$. The probability of drawing an ace with both cards is $P(E_1 \cap E_2) = \frac{1}{13} \times \frac{3}{51} = \frac{1}{221}$.

Now let us consider a second example. Suppose we have a box of 10 machine parts, three of which are defective. From this we draw a sample of two parts – what is the probability they are both defective? If $E_1$ is that the first part is defective, and $E_2$ is the second part is defective, then the events are conditional. $P(E_1) = \frac{3}{10}$, $P(E_2 \mid E_1) = \frac{2}{9}$ and $P(E_1 \cap E_2) = \frac{3}{10} \times \frac{2}{9} = \frac{1}{15}$. Can you see that if we had replaced the first part before drawing the second then $E_2$ would not be conditional on $E_1$, and $P(E_2)$ would also be $\frac{3}{10}$? Using the statisticians' jargon, we would say that *sampling without replacement makes the events conditional*. Is this always true? We might have drawn two parts from a very large consignment indeed, and it would seem rather pedantic to state that the consignment is poorer in defectives if the first item drawn is defective. Moreover, the proportion of defectives in a very large consignment can only be an estimate. When sampling from a large population, then $E_1$ and $E_2$ can for all intents and purposes be considered independent.

The importance of conditional probability is that it enables us to modify our probability predictions in the light of any additional information that is made available to us.

| EXAMPLE 4 |
|---|

When exploration for oil occurs a test hole is drilled. If, as a result of this test drilling it seems likely that really large quantities of oil exist (a bonanza), then the well is said to have structure. Examination of past records reveals the following information:

| | |
|---|---|
| Probability (structure and bonanza) | 0.20 |
| Probability (structure but no bonanza) | 0.15 |
| Probability (no structure but a bonanza) | 0.05 |
| Probability (no structure and no bonanza) | 0.60 |

We can put this information into a table like this:

|  | Structure | No structure |  |
| --- | --- | --- | --- |
| Bonanza | 0.20 | 0.05 | 0.25 |
| No bonanza | 0.15 | 0.60 | 0.75 |
|  | 0.35 | 0.65 | 1.00 |

Calculating the row totals and the column totals (often called the marginal probabilities), we can deduce that:

Probability (bonanza) $= 0.25$

since a bonanza can occur either with or without structure. Similarly:

Probability (no bonanza) $= 0.75$
Probability (structure) $= 0.35$
Probability (no structure) $= 0.65$

Such probabilities are known as *prior probabilities* – they are obtained from past records. But suppose we are given some additional information – in particular, suppose we know that a well has been sunk and structure is revealed. The number of possible outcomes has been reduced to two. We can ignore the 'no structure' column of the table and conclude that the weighting for a 'bonanza' is 0.2 and the weighting for 'no bonanza' is 0.15. So Probability (bonanza | structure) $= \frac{0.2}{0.2 + 0.15} = 0.571$; and Probability (no bonanza | structure) $= \frac{0.15}{0.2 + 0.15} = 0.429$.

Now suppose we were given the information that the hole does not have structure. We can deduce that:

Probability (bonanza | no structure) $= \frac{0.05}{0.65} = 0.077$

and

Probability (no bonanza | no structure) $= \frac{0.6}{0.65} = 0.923$

The probabilities we have just calculated are called *posterior probabilities* – they cannot be established until after something has happened (i.e. the test hole drilled). The knowledge whether the test hole has structure or not is valuable. Without this knowledge we would estimate the probability of obtaining a bonanza at 0.25, but once the test hole is drilled we can revise our estimates. If the test hole reveals structure then the probability of a bonanza rises to 0.571; if it does not reveal structure the probability of a bonanza falls to 0.077.

Sometimes it is more useful to use tree diagrams to solve conditional probability problems.

**EXAMPLE 5**

Suppose we have 100 urns. Type 1 urn (of which there are 70) each contains five black and five white balls. Type 2 urn (of which there are 30) each contains eight black and two white balls. An urn is randomly selected and a ball is drawn from that urn. If the ball chosen was black, what is the probability that the ball came from a Type 1 urn?

First we notice that:

$P$  (urn type 1)   $= 0.7$        $P$  (White | type 1) $= 0.5$
$P$  (urn type 2)   $= 0.3$        $P$  (Black | type 2) $= 0.8$
$P$  (Black | type 1) $= 0.5$      $P$  (White | type 2) $= 0.2$

We can now draw the tree diagram and find the prior probabilities (*see* Fig 11.5).

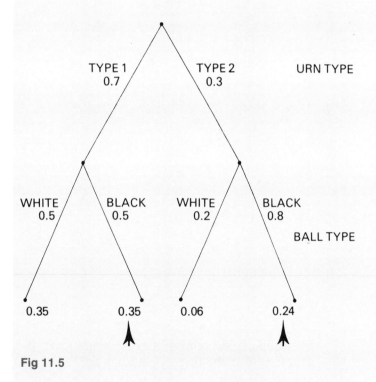

**Fig 11.5**

Now given that a black ball was drawn, the logical possibilities of the tree are reduced from four to the two arrowed. So the probability that the ball came from a Type 1 urn is $\frac{0.35}{0.35 + 0.24} = 0.593$.

One of the great difficulties of Statistics examiners is the problem of ensuring that the questions they set are not ambiguous. Consider this case.

**EXAMPLE 6**

Firm A is one of many firms competing for a contract to build a bridge. The probability that Firm A is the first choice is $\frac{1}{9}$; the probability that it is the second choice is $\frac{1}{3}$, and the probability that it is the third choice is $\frac{1}{2}$. What is the probability that Firm A will not be the first, second or third choice?

The ambiguity in this question arises from the precise meaning of the expression 'second choice' and 'third choice'. Are these probabilities joint probabilities, or are they conditional? Suppose we say that the probabilities are conditional – then the $\frac{1}{3}$ probability means that Firm A is the second choice, given that it is not the first choice. The question can then be approached as in the tree diagram in Fig 11.6.

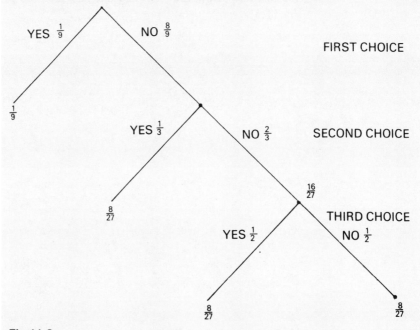

**Fig 11.6**

So, assuming the probabilities are conditional, the probability that the firm is neither the first, second nor third choice is $\frac{8}{27}$.

On the other hand, if the probabilities are joint probabilities, the probability of $\frac{1}{3}$ is the probability that the firm is not the first choice but is the second. Think carefully about this distinction. If the probabilities are conditional we say that the probability that the firm is the second choice given that it is not the first is $P$(not the first) $\times P$(it is the second) $= \frac{8}{9} \times \frac{1}{3} = \frac{8}{27}$. But if the probabilities are joint we are given the probability that the firm is not the first choice and the probability that it is (both not the first and is the second). That is we now say $\frac{8}{9} \times P$(it is the second) $= \frac{1}{3}$. The question would be approached like this.

We will calculate the conditional probability that Firm A is the government's second choice, given that it is not the first as follows:

$$P(\text{it is not the first}) \times P(\text{it is the second} \mid \text{not the first}) = $$
$$P(\text{it is both not the first and is the second})$$

that is $\frac{8}{9} \times$ Conditional probability $= \frac{1}{3}$

Conditional probability $= \frac{1}{3} \times \frac{9}{8} = \frac{3}{8}$

Thus we can build up our tree diagram (*see* Fig 11.7).

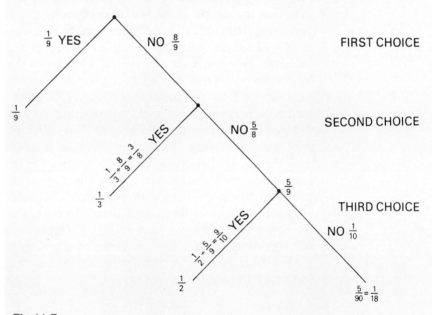

**Fig 11.7**

We could deduce the probability that the firm is not the first, second nor third choice by subtraction:

$$1 - (\tfrac{1}{9} + \tfrac{1}{3} + \tfrac{1}{2}) = \tfrac{1}{18}$$

But it is more informative to work through conditional probabilities that we can calculate. Thus the probability that the firm is not the first choice is $\frac{8}{9}$. So:

$P$(Firm A is second choice | not first choice) $= \frac{1}{3} \div \frac{8}{9} = \frac{3}{8}$

$P$(Firm A is not second choice | not first choice) $= 1 - \frac{3}{8} = \frac{5}{8}$

$P$(Firm A is neither first nor second choice) $= \frac{8}{9} \times \frac{5}{8} = \frac{5}{9}$

$P$(Firm A is third choice | not first or second choice) $= \frac{1}{2} \div \frac{5}{9} = \frac{9}{10}$

$P$(A is not third choice | neither first nor second) $= 1 - \frac{9}{10} = \frac{1}{10}$

$P$(Firm A is not first nor second nor third choice) $= \frac{1}{10} \times \frac{5}{9} = \frac{1}{18}$

the same answer as before.

Now a few words to conclude this chapter. The concepts underlying probability are extremely easy to understand, and there are very few rules that must be learnt. However, putting these rules (or combinations of these rules) into practice can be very tricky indeed. You would be well advised to re-read the section on the laws of probability to make absolutely sure that you understand them. Also, make certain that you understand the logic employed in the previous examples before you attempt the following exercises. Before you attempt any calculations on the exercises, you should be certain you know the way or ways the desired event can occur (for example, 'at least one' means one or more). Also, you should decide on the relationship between the events – whether they are mutually exclusive, independent, or conditional. Suppose that, after all this, you still cannot cope with probability – what then? Well, at least you can console yourself with the knowledge that although some students find probability a highly stimulating intellectual exercise, by far the bulk of students find probability problems the nearest thing to purgatory! Frequently you will find that although you can see that your answer is wrong, it is extremely difficult to see just where you have gone wrong! Fortunately, a lack of capability at solving probability problems need not hold you up in a Statistics course, as a knowledge of what probability means and how it is measured are the important things.

## QUESTIONS

**11.1**  Explain carefully what is meant by 'the probability of an event'.     ICAEW

**11.2**  A bag contains 19 balls, each of which is painted in two colours. Four are red and white, seven are white and black, and eight are black and red. A ball is chosen at random and seen to be partly white. What is the probability that its other colour is red?

**11.3** (a) Explain what is meant by the terms

(i) mutually exclusive;

(ii) independent.

(b) A manufacturer purchases two machines $A$ and $B$. The probability that $A$ will last five years is $\frac{4}{5}$ and the probability that $B$ will last five years is $\frac{3}{4}$. Find the probability that

(i) both machines will last five years;

(ii) only machine $A$ will last five years;

(iii) at least one machine will last five years.

**11.4** (a) Explain what you understand by

(i) independent events;

(ii) conditional probability.

(b) 8% of the items produced in a manufacturing process are known to be faulty. A sample of five items is drawn at random. Calculate the probability that the sample

(i) does not contain any faulty items;

(ii) only contains one faulty item.

(c) Two independent events A and B are such that $P(A) = 0.2$ and $P(B) = 0.4$. Find the values of (i) $P(AB)$, (ii) $P(A + B)$ and (iii) the probability of A occurring given that B has already occurred.

**11.5** (a) State the theorems of addition and multiplication of probabilities.

(b) An analysis of the national origins of the employees of a manufacturing company produced the following result:

| Nationality | Frequency |
|---|---|
| English | 488 |
| Scots | 230 |
| Irish | 112 |
| Welsh | 108 |
| American | 30 |
| Other European | 16 |

If two employees of this company are chosen at random, state the probability that:

    (i)    both will be other European

    (ii)   both will be English

    (iii)  both will be either Irish or Welsh

    (iv)  at least one of the two will be a Scot.

**11.6**  (a)  What is the chance of throwing a number greater than four with an ordinary die?

    (b)  If the probability of throwing a seven with a pair of dice is $\frac{1}{6}$, what is the probability of rolling two sevens in a row?

    (c)  If three dice are thrown together, what is the probability of obtaining at least one five?

    (d)  Out of 10 steel valve springs three are defective. Two springs are chosen at random for testing. What is the probability that both test specimens are

        (i)    not defective;

        (ii)   defective?

**11.7**  The following results were obtained from interviews with 500 people who changed their cars recently, cars being classified as large, medium or small in size, depending on their length.

| | Present car size | | | |
|---|---|---|---|---|
| *Previous car size* | *Large (>15')* | *Medium (13'–15')* | *Small (<13')* | *Total* |
| Large | 75 | 47 | 22 | 114 |
| Medium | 36 | 75 | 69 | 180 |
| Small | 11 | 63 | 102 | 176 |
| Total | 122 | 185 | 193 | 500 |

Required:

  (a)  What proportion of people in the survey changed to:

    (i)    a smaller car;

    (ii)   a larger car?

(b) What effect would such car-changing habits have generally on the size of car owned in the future?

(c) What is the probability that a person from the survey selected at random who bought a large car, previously had a small or medium car?

(d) Estimate the average length of car owned at present by the 500 people surveyed, if no owner has a car less than 9 feet or greater than 19 feet.

ACCA

**11.8** The probability that machine A will be performing a useful function in five years' time is $\frac{1}{4}$ while the probability that machine B will still be operating usefully at the end of the same period is $\frac{1}{3}$.

Find the probability that in five years' time:

(a) both machines will be performing a useful function;

(b) neither will be operating;

(c) only machine B will be operating;

(d) at least one of the machines will be operating.     CIMA

**11.9** The probability that a man now aged 59 years will be alive in 2010 is $\frac{5}{8}$ while the probability that his wife now aged 57 years will be alive in 2010 is $\frac{5}{6}$.

Determine the probability that in 2010:

(a) both will be alive;

(b) at least one of them will be alive;

(c) only the wife will be alive.     CIMA

**11.10** A sub-assembly consists of three components A, B and C. Tests have shown that failures of the sub-assembly were caused by faults in one, two and sometimes all three components. Analysis of 100 sub-assembly failures showed that there were 70 faulty components A, 50 faulty components B, and 30 faulty components C. Of the failures 44 were caused by faults in two components only (i.e. A and B, or A and C, or B and C) and 10 of the 44 faults were in B and C.

If a faulty component is randomly selected, find the probability that it has faults in:

(a) all three components;

(b) component A on its own.     CIMA

**11.11** (a) One bag contains four white balls and two black balls; another contains three white balls and five black balls. If one ball is drawn from each bag, find the probability that (i) both are white, (ii) both are black, (iii) one is white and one is black.

(b) A purse contains two silver coins and four copper coins, and a second purse contains four silver coins and three copper coins. A coin is selected at random from one of the two purses. What is the probability that it is a silver coin?

(c) A box contains M components of which N are defective. Selection occurs without replacement. Find the probability that:

(i) the first selection is defective;

(ii) the first two selections consist of one defective and one non-defective;

(iii) the second selection is defective. ICAEW

**11.12** An amplifier circuit is made up of three valves. The probabilities that the three valves are defective are $\frac{1}{20}$, $\frac{1}{25}$ and $\frac{1}{50}$ respectively. Calculate the probability that (a) the amplifier works, (b) that the amplifier has one defective valve.

A bag contains $r$ red balls and $w$ white balls, $r > w$. If they are drawn one by one, show that the chance of drawing first a red, then a white and so on alternately until only red balls are left is

$$\frac{r!w!}{(r+w)!}$$

ICAEW

*Note*: Do not attempt the second part of this question until you have read Chapter 14.

**11.13** In a particular factory, an automatic process identifies defective items produced. Defectives can be classified as lacking strength, incorrect weight or incorrect diameter. A random sample of 1000 items were checked and the following results recorded:

120 have a strength defect;
80 have a weight defect;
60 have a diameter defect;
22 have strength and weight defects;
16 have strength and diameter defects;
20 have weight and diameter defects;
8 have all three defects.

Find the probability that a randomly chosen item (i) is not defective; (ii) has exactly two defects. ICAEW

**11.14** A manufacturer supplies transistors in boxes of 100. A buyer takes a random sample of five transistors and if one of them is faulty he rejects the box; otherwise he accepts the box.

(i)   If there are 10 faulty transistors in the box, what is the probability that the buyer will accept it?

(ii)  What is the probability that he will reject a box which in fact only contains one faulty transistor?

**11.15** The table given below shows a frequency distribution of the lifetimes of 500 light bulbs made and tested by ABC Limited:

| Lifetime (hours) | Number of light bulbs |
|---|---|
| 400 and less than 500 | 10 |
| 500 and less than 600 | 16 |
| 600 and less than 700 | 38 |
| 700 and less than 800 | 56 |
| 800 and less than 900 | 63 |
| 900 and less than 1000 | 67 |
| 1000 and less than 1100 | 92 |
| 1100 and less than 1200 | 68 |
| 1200 and less than 1300 | 57 |
| 1300 and less than 1400 | 33 |
| | 500 |

(a)   Using the information in this table, construct an ogive.

(b)   Determine the percentage of light bulbs whose lifetimes are at least 700 hours but less than 1200 hours.

(c)   What risk is ABC Limited taking if it guarantees to replace any light bulb which lasts less than 1000 hours?

(d)   Instead of guaranteeing the life of the light bulb for 1000 hours, ABC Limited suggests introducing a 100-day money-back guarantee. What is the probability that refunds will be made, assuming the light bulb is in use:

(i)   seven hours per day;

(ii)  11 hours per day?                                                                                        ACCA

**11.16** A businessman estimates that the probability of gaining an important contract to build a factory is 0.65. If this contract is obtained he will certainly have a probability of gaining a further contract of building an associated computer block – he estimates that this probability is 0.8. If he fails to obtain the contract to build the factory, he will not be asked to deal with the computer block construction. As an alternative to the factory/block contract, there is a probability of 0.35 that the businessman could obtain the contract to build an office block – he could only deal with this if the first set of contracts was not obtained. What is the probability that both factory and computer block contracts will be gained? Also, what is the probability that the businessman will obtain either the computer block contract or the office block contract?                                                                                        ICSA

**11.17** A company in which the training period for apprentices is five years is considering its intake for the coming year. Information concerning apprentices recruited in previous years is given below:

| Year of intake | 1983 | 1984 | 1985 | 1986 |
|---|---|---|---|---|
| Number of apprentices recruited | 700 | 500 | 150 | 250 |
| Number of apprentices leaving in: | | | | |
| First year | 28 | 18 | 8 | 14 |
| Second year | 29 | 18 | 6 | 10 |
| Third year | 17 | 8 | 2 | 1 |
| Fourth year | 13 | 8 | 1 | 2 |
| Fifth year | 2 | 2 | 1 | 1 |

(a) What is the probability that an apprentice will qualify?

(b) What is the probability that an apprentice will stay for longer than two years?

(c) How many apprentices should be recruited in 1994 to provide the company with 300 qualified men in 1999? CIMA

**11.18** (a) Explain briefly the value of conditional probability calculations to the businessman.

(b) *Number of boxes of 100 units containing defective electron tubes*

| | No. of defective tubes | | | |
|---|---|---|---|---|
| *Firm* | *0* | *1* | *2* | *3 or more* |
| Supplier *A* | 500 | 200 | 200 | 100 |
| Supplier *B* | 320 | 160 | 80 | 40 |
| Supplier *C* | 600 | 100 | 50 | 50 |

From the data given in the above table, calculate the conditional probabilities for the following questions:

(i) If one box had been selected at random from this universe what are the probabilities that the box would have come from Supplier A; from Supplier B; from Supplier C?

(ii) If a box had been selected at random, what is the probability that it would contain two defective tubes?

(iii) If a box had been selected at random, what is the probability that it would have no defectives and would have come from Supplier A?

(iv) Given that a box selected at random came from Supplier B, what is the probability that it contained one or two defective tubes?

(v) If a box came from Supplier A, what is the probability that the box would have two or less defectives?

(vi)   It is known that a box selected at random has two defective tubes. What is the probability that it came from Supplier A; from Supplier B; from Supplier C?                                                      ACCA

**11.19**  Two companies A and B regularly bid against each other for building contracts. A has a probability of $\frac{2}{3}$ of winning any given contract while B has a probability of $\frac{1}{3}$. Assuming independence, calculate the probabilities that, of the next two contracts, (i) A wins both, (ii) B wins both, (iii) each company wins one.

**11.20**  (a)  If an 'event' is defined as an outcome of an experiment, explain what is meant by

   (i)    mutually exclusive events,

   (ii)   independent events, and

   (iii)  conditional events.

   Give examples of events that would fall into each category.

   (b)  To control the quality of output, a sample of 10 items is examined each hour and if no defective items are found the process continues, otherwise the process is stopped and adjustments are made. What is the probability that the process will be stopped after a sample is drawn if 10% of the items produced by this process is defective? How large a sample should be drawn to ensure that if 10% of items is defective, then the probability that the process is stopped is at least 99%?                                                                        ICAEW

**11.21**  A circuit is protected by two fuses, $F$ and $G$, so arranged that the correct operation of either of them is sufficient to stop the circuit being damaged. The reliability (i.e. the probability that the device operates successfully when required) of the fuses, $F$ and $G$, is 0.95 and 0.90 respectively. What is the probability that on a given occasion the circuit will not be protected?

**11.22**  In an experiment the probability of success is $\frac{1}{3}$. If it is performed six times, what is the probability of occurrence of (i) five successes, (ii) more than four successes?

**11.23**  (a)  Explain what are meant by mutually exclusive events, independent events and dependent events.

   (b)  A public company holds two accounts: an account A with a government department and an account B with a merchant bank. It has been established that on any given day there is a finite and distinct probability that each account will exceed its overdraft facilities. It may be assumed that the probability that either or both accounts exceed their overdraft facilities is 0.55 whilst the probability that account B exceeds its overdraft facility is 0.25.

(i)   If the fluctuations of the accounts are independent what is the probability that account A exceeds its overdraft facilities on any given day?

(ii)  Had the fluctuations of the accounts been dependent what would have been the probability that account A exceeded its overdraft facilities on any day in which account B also exceeded its overdraft facilities if the probability that both accounts exceeded their overdraft facilities had been 0.12?                                                                                            ICAEW

**11.24**  If three cards are withdrawn from a pack (without replacement) find the probability that they are

(a)  Jack, Queen, and King (in that order)

(b)  A Jack, a Queen and a King.

**11.25**  Look again at Example 4. Suppose $E_1$ is that oil is found in commercial quantities and $E_2$ is that the well has structure. Given that $P(E_1 \cap E_2) = 0.42$, $P(E_1 \cap E_2') = 0.18$, $P(E_1' \cap E_2) = 0.28$ and $P(E_1' \cap E_2') = 0.12$, what would you conclude?

**11.26**  A certain mass-produced article sometimes has a dimension defect and sometimes a surface defect. Let

$E_1$ = an article has a dimension defect
$E_2$ = an article has a surface defect
$E_3$ = an article is non-defective.

If $P(E_1) = 0.06$, $P(E_2) = 0.07$ and $P(E_3) = 0.9$, what would you conclude?

**11.27**  Tom, Dick and Harry are candidates for the post of works manager. The managing director will recommend a candidate and the recommendation must be ratified by the board of directors. The probability that the managing director recommends Harry is 60%, with 25% for Dick and 15% for Tom. The probabilities that the board ratifies are 40% for Harry, 35% for Tom, and 25% for Dick.

(a)  Find the probability that none of the candidates are appointed.

(b)  Find for each candidate the probability that he is appointed given that the board has ratified the managing director's recommendation.

*Note*: use a tree diagram to solve this problem.

# 12 Decision criteria

We are all experts in taking decisions. Does this surprise you? Well throughout your life you have had many decisions to take, and the fact that you are alive today, reading this book, indicates that you have taken many decisions correctly. Take a simple problem – the need to get to the other side of a busy road. You have to decide when it is safe to cross. The fact that you have so far taken the correct decision proves that you have carefully weighed up the evidence, and interpreted the evidence correctly. Sometimes the decision will be easy to take; the road might be completely empty and you can cross with safety; and at times the road will be so busy that to attempt to cross would be suicidal. In other words, we have all the necessary information available to make the correct decision every time. A cautious (and according to Road Safety Officers a sensible) person would obey the following decision rule: only cross the road when no traffic is in sight. If we obey this rule, then we will always cross the road safely (unless we fall down an uncovered manhole!) Unfortunately, however, it is not always possible to obey this rule, as there are many roads so busy that we could never cross. With normal city centre roads we will seldom find a situation where they are completely empty of traffic, and we must use our judgment to decide when it is safe to cross.

Now of course, the decision-taking problems faced by businessmen are much more complex than the decision whether to cross the road. Not only must the businessman decide between any alternatives, but also he often cannot be sure of the consequences of any decision he may make. In this chapter, we shall attempt to discover criteria that may aid the decision-taking process.

## Decision criteria

Guy Rope owns a camp site in the Dordogne, and he wishes to develop the site in order to increase his profits. He realises that three options are open to him: he could build a swimming pool and charge the campers for its use, he could build a tennis court (and charge for its use), or he could build a restaurant to supply the campers with simple hot meals. He has sufficient funds to undertake just one of the options – what should he do? Obviously, the decision taken by Guy will depend on the profitability of the options, and he realises that the profitability will depend upon the weather. If the summer is too hot, then tennis may prove to be too exhausting; also evening barbecues in the open air will be more popular than restaurant meals. Given a hot summer, then, the swimming pool would be the most profitable option. If the summer is poor, then Guy reckons that his campers would welcome somewhere where they could buy hot meals, and so the restaurant would be the most profitable. People seem to prefer playing tennis when the weather is neither too hot nor too cold, so the tennis court would prove to be the most profitable given an 'average' summer. Armed with these beliefs, Guy estimates the annual profitability of each course of action as follows (all figures in thousand francs).

|  |  | State of nature | | |
|  |  | Cool | Summer is Average | Hot |
| --- | --- | --- | --- | --- |
| Strategies | Swimming pool | 50 | 100 | 150 |
|  | Tennis court | 30 | 180 | 90 |
|  | Restaurant | 170 | 100 | 40 |

Notice that the options facing Guy are called *strategies*: a list of strategies is a list of courses of action facing the decision taker who has direct control over which course is chosen. However, Guy has no control whatsoever over the weather (if he had then there would be no problem!). The different types of summer that can occur are called *states of nature*; a list of events outside the control of the decision taker. The table above is usually called a *payoff matrix*. For each strategy it shows the payoff (in this case, the profit) that would result from each state of nature.

What should we advise Guy to do? Unfortunately, statistics alone cannot help us – we need to know something about Guy's character. What sort of person is he?

**The maximax criterion**

Is he a gambler, a risk taker who is supremely confident that lady luck is always on his side? If Guy is this type of person, then he would reason as follows: 'Lucky me, I am always right. If I build a swimming pool, then the summer will be hot and I will earn 150 000FF. If I build a tennis court, then the summer will be average and I will earn 180 000FF. If I open a restaurant, the summer will be cool and I will earn 170 000FF. The most logical thing for me to do is to go for the greatest profit, so I will build a tennis court'.

For each strategy, Guy notes the maximum payoff that can result. He then chooses the strategy with the greatest maximum payoff. If Guy acts in this way, then Guy is applying the *maximax criterion*: he is maximising his maximum possible payoff by gambling that the summer will be average. We can summarise Guy's reasoning as follows.

|  | Cool | Average | Hot | Maximum payoff |
|---|---|---|---|---|
| Swimming pool | 50 | 100 | 150 | 150 |
| Tennis court | 30 | 180 | 90 | 180← |
| Restaurant | 170 | 100 | 40 | 170 |

Decision takers who practise the maximax criterion must be very rare specimens. If maximax was widely practised, then although we would have a few more millionaires, we would certainly have many more bankruptcies! Lady luck smiles on very few of us indeed!

**The maximin criterion**

We shall now move to the other end of the spectrum and suppose that Guy is a born pessimist, who always assumes that the states of nature work against him. He would argue something like this: 'Suppose I build a swimming pool. Will the summer be hot or even average? No Chance! You can bet your bottom dollar that the summer will be cool! Likewise, one sure fire way to ensure a cool summer is for me to build a tennis court. Of course, if I open a restaurant then the summer will be the hottest for years and only a few campers will want feeding. The big money always avoids me. I might as well build a swimming pool as this at least guarantees me 50 000FF profit. If I build a tennis court I can only be sure of 30 000FF and opening a restaurant guarantees me no more than 40 000FF. A swimming pool it is, then.' We can summarise Guy's reasoning as follows:

|  | Cool | Average | Hot | Minimum payoff |
|---|---|---|---|---|
| Swimming Pool | 50 | 100 | 150 | 50← |
| Tennis Court | 30 | 180 | 90 | 30 |
| Restaurant | 170 | 100 | 40 | 40 |

For each strategy, he notes the minimum payoff that can result. He then selects the strategy that maximises his minimum payoff. Guy is applying the *maximin criterion*; he is maximising his minimum possible payoff.

So we see that the two criteria are fundamentally different, reflecting quite different states of mind. If Guy adopts the maximax criterion then he is pushing the ceiling on his profits to the highest level (180 000FF) by building a tennis court. No other strategy could earn this much. However, he is taking a risk: his profit would only be 30 000FF if the summer was cool. On the other hand, if Guy adopts the maximin criterion, then he is raising the floor on his profits to the highest level (50 000FF) by building a swimming pool. No other strategy could guarantee as much as this. However, by building a swimming pool he foregoes the possibility of really large profits (180 000FF from a tennis court or 170 000FF from a restaurant).

**The minimax criterion**

There is a third way of analysing the problem facing Guy – a way that neither assumes that Guy is ultra optimistic nor assumes that he is ultra pessimistic. The reasoning is something like this: suppose the summer turns out to be cool – if Guy had opened a restaurant then he would have made the right decision. He would have no 'regret' at all, and earn the maximum possible profit under the circumstances (170 000FF). But suppose he had built a swimming pool – he has made the wrong decision and would certainly regret it. His profit would be 50 000FF, 120 000FF less than it would have been had he made the correct decision. It would seem reasonable, then, to use the 120 000FF as a measure of the extent of his regret. In a similar fashion, if the summer was cool and Guy had built a tennis court, then he would regret the $170\,000 - 30\,000 = 140\,000$FF he had foregone. If we use similar reasoning and assume an average summer; then assume a hot summer; we can calculate Guy's regret under all possible circumstances. Our results are summarised in a *regret matrix* as follows:

|  | Cool | Average | Hot | Maximum regret |
|---|---|---|---|---|
| Swimming pool | 120 | 80 | 0 | 120 |
| Tennis court | 140 | 0 | 60 | 140 |
| Restaurant | 0 | 80 | 110 | 110← |

For each strategy, the maximum regret has been identified (for example, had he built a tennis court, then Guy's maximum regret would have been the 140 000FF in profit foregone during a cool summer). Examining the matrix we conclude that Guy should open a restaurant, as this is the strategy that minimises the maximum regret he could experience. If he uses this reasoning as a basis for decision making, then Guy is applying the *minimax criterion*.

## Summary

In this section, we have examined three quite distinct criteria for decision taking, and we shall now state a few simple rules to summarise them. The rules will assume that in the payoff matrix the rows refer to the strategies and the columns refer to states of nature.

*Rule 1*

For each row in the payoff matrix, find the maximum value. If we select the row with the greatest maximum value then we are applying the maximax criterion:

|  | *Cool* | *Average* | *Hot* | *Maximum* |
|---|---|---|---|---|
| Swimming pool | 50 | 100 | 150 | 150 |
| Tennis court | 30 | 180 | 90 | 180← |
| Restaurant | 170 | 100 | 40 | 170 |

*Rule 2*

For each row in the payoff matrix, find the minimum value. If we select the row with the greatest minimum value then we are applying the maximin criterion.

|  | *Cool* | *Average* | *Hot* | *Minimum* |
|---|---|---|---|---|
| Swimming pool | 50 | 100 | 150 | 50← |
| Tennis court | 30 | 180 | 90 | 30 |
| Restaurant | 170 | 100 | 40 | 40 |

*Rule 3*

Find the maximum value for each column in the payoff matrix, and subtract all the payoffs in each column from their corresponding maximum value. This gives the regret matrix.

*Rule 4*

For each row in the regret matrix, find the maximum value. If we select the row with the least maximum value, then we are applying the minimax criterion.

|  | Cool | Average | Hot |
|---|---|---|---|
| Swimming pool | 50 | 100 | 150 |
| Tennis court | 30 | 180 | 90 |
| Restaurant | 170 | 100 | 40 |
| Maximum | 170 | 180 | 150 |

|  | Cool | Average | Hot | Maximum regret |
|---|---|---|---|---|
| Swimming pool | 120 | 80 | 0 | 120 |
| Tennis court | 140 | 0 | 60 | 140 |
| Restaurant | 0 | 80 | 110 | 110← |

## Which criterion?

We have applied three different criteria to the problem facing Guy. The maximax criterion suggests he should build a tennis court. The maximin criterion suggests he should build a swimming pool. The minimax criterion suggests he should open a restaurant. Poor Guy must be utterly confused! Which criterion is appropriate to this problem? As we suggested earlier, this is an impossible question to answer as the strategy selected will depend upon Guy's character. However, it is possible to comment generally on the criteria.

1  For the problem facing Guy, each criterion suggested a different strategy, but it frequently happens that different criteria would suggest that we should select the same strategy. For example, if the payoff matrix was

|  | Cool | Average | Hot |
|---|---|---|---|
| Swimming pool | 30 | 100 | 170 |
| Tennis court | 50 | 180 | 90 |
| Restaurant | 170 | 100 | 40 |

then whatever criterion is applied the strategy selected would be the same – build a tennis court (you should verify for yourself that this is true). This strategy is said to be *dominant*, and no problem of strategy selection exists.

2   The minimax criterion minimises the decision taker's maximum regret, and so it attempts to minimise the consequences of taking the wrong decision. This is an intrinsically satisfying criterion – it seems to be a highly logical method of decision taking. Moreover, this criterion fits in well with economists' ideas of opportunity cost (if you do not know what opportunity cost is, talk to an economist).

3   If we examine the payoff matrix facing Guy, then we notice that whatever strategy he selects and whatever the state of nature, Guy always makes a profit. Because of this, Guy may be tempted to apply the maximax criterion – especially if Guy is what economists call a profit maximiser. He would be following the well quoted 'law' that you must speculate to accumulate. But suppose it was possible for losses to occur: this could well be the case if he opened a restaurant and the summer was hot, or he built a swimming pool and the summer was cool. Surely, Guy would then be strongly tempted to apply the maximin criterion, especially if the losses could threaten his survival as a camp site owner.

4   Guy has a problem selecting the appropriate strategy because he has no control over the states of nature, but if he has *more information* about the states of nature then his decision can be more soundly based. What additional information would help? Well, the states of nature will not be equally likely to occur, so if Guy can assign probabilities to the states of nature this should increase his insight into the problem.

## Expected monetary value

Suppose that Guy examines the Dordogne weather records over the last 100 years. On 20 occasions the summer was cool, on 70 occasions the summer was average and on 10 occasions the summer was hot. This information enables Guy to deduce the following empirical probabilities:

| State of nature | Probability |
| --- | --- |
| Cool | 0.2 |
| Average | 0.7 |
| Hot | 0.1 |

Suppose Guy thinks ahead over the next 10 years – using the probability distribution he would predict two cool, seven average and one hot summer. So if he was to build a swimming pool, he would estimate his earnings (in thousands francs) at:

$$2 \times 50 + 7 \times 100 + 1 \times 150 = 950$$

which is an average of $950 \div 10 = 95$ per year. This average earning is called the *expected monetary value* (EMV) of building a swimming pool, and we could calculate it more directly like this:

$$0.2 \times 50 + 0.7 \times 100 + 0.1 \times 150 = 95.0$$

In a similar fashion we could deduce that

$$\text{EMV (build tennis court)} = 0.2 \times 30 + 0.7 \times 180 + 0.1 \times 90 = 141$$
$$\text{EMV (open restaurant)} = 0.2 \times 170 + 0.7 \times 100 + 0.1 \times 40 = 108$$

We now have another criterion for selecting the appropriate strategy – *select the strategy with the greatest EMV* as this maximises the long-run average gains. Guy would be well advised to build a tennis court and earn an average of 141 000FF per year.

Of the four criteria we have examined, EMV has the soundest logical base. Maximising your average long-run profits certainly seems a sensible thing to do. However, the criterion does have its drawbacks. We have stated that Guy should build a tennis court because this has the greatest EMV (141 000FF) – but on any particular year he cannot earn this amount. He will earn either 30 000FF or 180 000FF or 90 000FF. Suppose one of these options was a loss, then we would have to enquire whether Guy is capable of shouldering the loss. Sooner or later, losses would be bound to occur, and if they could result in bankruptcy then Guy is clearly using the wrong criterion. The maximin criterion would be more appropriate.

The second problem with using the EMV criterion arises when the term 'long-run payoff' makes no sense. In particular, let us suppose that Guy intends to run the camp site for just one summer, obtain the maximum profit he can, then leave the industry (he would be what economists call a 'snatcher'). The EMV of building a tennis court cannot be his long-run average profit as there will be no long run! His average profit will be the profit for the year – either 30 000FF or 180 000FF or 90 000FF. But if he stays in the industry then as the years elapse, the closer will his average annual profit move towards 141 000FF. If Guy is a snatcher, must we conclude that the EMV criterion is inappropriate? Not necessarily. If Guy applies the EMV criterion to all the decision problems facing him, however diverse they may be, then he would be maximising his returns over the entire range of problems.

## The value of perfect information

For the rest of this problem, we will assume that Guy is a snatcher, basing his decisions on the EMV criterion. He decides to build a tennis court as this has the greatest EMV (141 000FF). Now suppose additional information is available to Guy – in particular, let us suppose that a peasant is prepared to predict the weather and that his predictions are always right. In the jargon, we would say that Guy has *perfect information* available to him. This will certainly help the decision-taking process. If the peasant predicts a cool summer (and there is a 20% chance that he will) then Guy will open a restaurant. If he predicts an average summer (and there is a 70% chance that he will) then Guy will build a tennis court. If he predicts a hot summer (and there is a 10% chance that he will) Guy will build a swimming pool. Given perfect information, then, Guy will earn either 170 000FF or 180 000FF or 150 000FF. His expected earnings, then, are:

$$0.2 \times 170 + 0.7 \times 180 + 0.1 \times 150 = 175\ 000\text{FF}$$

Without this information, Guy's expected earnings were 141 000FF. So the information has a value to Guy of 175 000 – 141 000 = 34 000FF. This 34 000FF is the *expected value of perfect information* (EVPI). Now it is highly likely that the peasant will charge for the information, but it would certainly be worth buying if its cost was less than EVPI. In other words, if the peasant charges less than 34 000FF for his predictions, then they are worth buying, but if the peasant charges more than 34 000FF, then Guy would be advised not to buy and simply apply the EMV criterion.

## Multi-stage decision analysis

We shall now examine a more complex problem, in which the decision-taking process is divided into stages. Flint McRae owns the oil prospecting and development rights for a plot of land in California, and a property development company has offered him $50 000 for the plot. Flint must now decide whether to sell the land or to exploit it as an oilfield. Suppose that Flint decides to exploit the land – he sinks the well but finds no oil. In the jargon of the oil industry, the well is said to be 'dry', and Flint would lose $20 000. However, the well might yield oil in commercial quantities – a so-called 'wet' well – and this would earn Flint $100 000 in total income. Exceptionally, Flint could obtain a real bonanza from his oilwell, a so-called 'soaking' well, and this would earn $500 000 in total net income. From past experience, Flint knows that there is a 70% chance that the well is 'dry', a 20% chance that it is 'wet' and a 10% chance that it is 'soaking'. If he wishes, Flint can engage a firm of geologists to undertake a seismic survey of the land, and this will cost him $30 000. The geologists supply the following information as to the reliability of such surveys (all figures are prior probabilities):

|  |  | *Survey report is* | | |
|---|---|---|---|---|
|  |  | *Bad* | *Good* |  |
|  | Dry | 0.44 | 0.26 | 0.7 |
| True state of the well | Wet | 0.05 | 0.15 | 0.2 |
|  | Soaking | 0.01 | 0.09 | 0.1 |
|  |  | 0.50 | 0.50 | 1.0 |

If Flint always uses the EMV criterion, what should he do? In this problem there are two sets of strategies facing Flint:

(a)  Should he engage the geologists' services?

(b)  Should he drill or should he sell?

Likewise, there are two sets of states of nature facing Flint:

(a)  The result of the survey (is the report good or bad?)

(b)  The true state of the well (is it dry, wet or soaking?).

Armed with this information, we can construct a tree diagram of the problem facing Flint (Fig 12.1). The boxes represent decision points and the circles represent states of nature. So we see that there are four distinct decision points facing Flint.

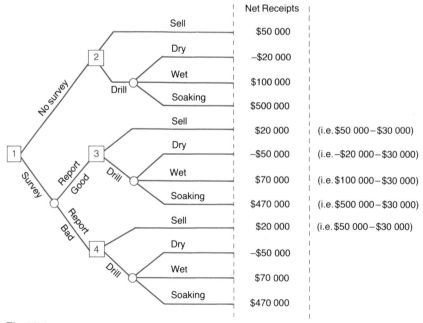

**Fig 12.1**

Now before Flint can decide on Decision Point 1, he must decide on Decision Points 2, 3 and 4. Hence we will analyse the tree diagram from right to left – a method called the *rollback principle*.

First we shall analyse Decision Point 2 (Fig 12.2). Assuming that Flint reaches Decision Point 2:

$$EMV \text{ (sell)} = \$50\ 000$$
$$EMV \text{ (drill)} = 0.7 \times -\$20\ 000 + 0.2 \times \$100\ 000 + 0.1 \times \$50\ 000$$
$$= \$56\ 000$$

**Fig 12.2**

So we see that if Decision Point 2 is reached, then Flint will drill. If we now turn to Decision Point 3 (*see* Fig 12.3), we will need conditional probabilities, i.e. the probabilities that the well is dry, wet or soaking given a good report from the geologist.

$$P(\text{dry well} \mid \text{good report}) = 0.26 \div 0.5 = 0.52$$
$$P(\text{wet well} \mid \text{good report}) = 0.15 \div 0.5 = 0.30$$
$$P(\text{soaking well} \mid \text{good report}) \qquad = 0.09 \div 0.5 = 0.18$$

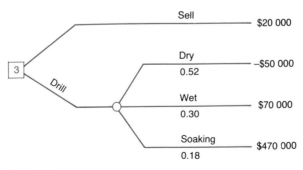

**Fig 12.3**

Assuming that Flint reaches Decision Point 3:

EMV(sell)  = $20 000
EMV(drill) = 0.52 × −$50 000 + 0.3 × $70 000 + 0.18 × $470 000
           = $79 000

So if Decision Point 3 is reached, Flint should drill. Turning now to Decision Point 4 (Fig 12.4):

$P$(dry well | bad report)      = 0.44 ÷ 0.5 = 0.88
$P$(wet well | bad report)      = 0.05 ÷ 0.5 = 0.10
$P$(soaking well | bad report) = 0.01 ÷ 0.5 = 0.2

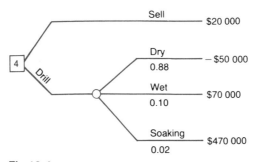

**Fig 12.4**

Assuming that Flint reaches Decision Point 4:

EMV(sell)  = $20 000
EMV(drill) = 0.88 × −$50 000 + 0.1 × $70 000 + 0.02 × $470 000
           = −$27 600

Clearly, then, if Decision Point 4 is reached, then Flint should sell.

Now that we have evaluated Decision Points 2, 3 and 4, we can evaluate Decision Point 1. Before we do this, however, it might be useful to summarise what we have concluded. If Flint does not employ the geologists' services, then his best course of action is to drill (EMV = $56 000). If he does employ the geologists' services, then his action will depend upon the geologists' report. If the report is good, then Flint should drill (EMV = $79 600) but if it is bad he should sell (EMV = $20 000).

Evaluating Decision Point 1 (Fig 12.5) we have:

EMV(no survey) = $56 000
EMV(survey)    = $79 600 × 0.5 + $20 000 × 0.5 = $49 800

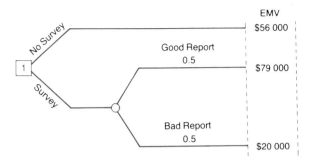

**Fig 12.5**

Finally, then, we conclude that Flint should not engage the services of the geologists and drill for oil. Before leaving this problem, you should notice that there is a chance (a 70% chance, in fact) that Flint faces a loss of $20 000 if he drills. Now if this loss is too great for Flint to shoulder, then he should sell to the property developer, i.e. apply the maximin criterion.

## Revising probabilities

In the last example, we were given all the necessary information to enable us to insert the probabilities directly on to the decision tree. Sometimes it is necessary to obtain the probabilities ourselves.

Consider the case of John Smith, who is taking a three-month holiday in the United States. He realises that his holiday would be more enjoyable if he had a car available to him, and a car rental firm quotes him a fee of $2500 to rent him a car for the duration of this stay. Alternatively, he could buy a used car of the same type for $3500, and sell it at the end of his holiday for $2000. So buying rather than renting would involve John Smith with a net outlay of $1500. The problem with buying a used car is that the car might break down, and while John is perfectly capable of undertaking minor repairs himself at a negligible outlay, he reckons that a major breakdown could involve him with repair charges of $1500. A friend advises John that the probability that a car of this age and type will break down over the next three months is 20%. There is a further alternative facing John Smith: he could persuade his friend to rent the used car for a day for $50. John and his friend could then examine the vehicle, and assess its likelihood of breaking down over the next three months. There is a 90% chance that any prediction they make will be right. What should John Smith do?

First we shall draw the decision tree of the problem, inserting the associated costs (Fig 12.6). We know that the probability of no major fault occurring is 0.8, so we can evaluate Decision Point 2:

$$\text{Cost if car rented} = \$2500$$
$$\text{Expected cost if car bought} = 1500 \times 0.8 + 3000 \times 0.2 = \$1800$$

So if Decision Point 2 is reached, John Smith would buy the car as this action has the lower expected cost.

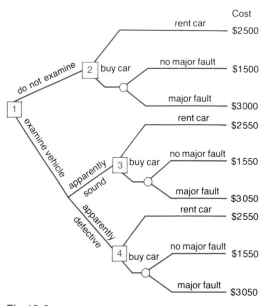

**Fig 12.6**

Evaluation of Decision Points 3 and 4 is not so straightforward. We need to know the probabilities that the car is apparently sound and apparently defective, and Fig 12.7 illustrates the problem.

The first branch of the tree diagram gives the true experience with the car: either a major fault occurs or it does not. Each of the branches now divide according to whether or not John and his friend made a correct prediction. The joint probabilities have been inserted at the end of each branch. Consider the part of the tree diagram marked ①: no major fault occurred and John was right, so he must have predicted that the car was apparently sound. Now consider the part marked ④: a major fault occurred and John was wrong, *so again he must have predicted that the car was apparently sound.* So, the probability that John predicts that the car is apparently sound is $0.72 + 0.02 = 0.74$, and the probability that he says that the car is apparently defective is $0.08 + 0.18 = 0.26$. We can now draw the tree diagram in

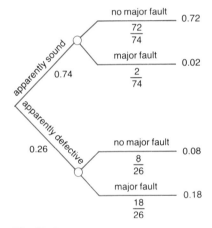

**Fig 12.7**

**Fig 12.8**

reverse, insert the probabilities we have deduced, and deduce the remaining probabilities (Fig 12.8).

Notice that it is necessary to alter the order of some of the probabilities. We can obtain the conditional probabilities by division – for example, the probability that no major fault occurs given that John thinks the car is sound is $0.72/0.74 = 72/74$. Likewise, the probability that no major fault occurs given that John thinks the car is defective is $0.08/0.26 = 8/26$. We can now evaluate the remaining decision points. Taking Decision Point 3 (Fig 12.9):

Cost of renting $\quad\quad\quad = \$2550$
Expected cost of buying $= 1550 \times \frac{72}{74} + 3050 \times \frac{2}{74} = \$1590.54$

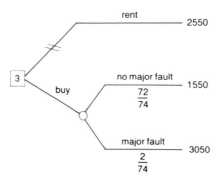

**Fig 12.9**

So if Decision Point 3 is reached, John should buy. Now evaluating Decision Point 4 (Fig 12.10):

Cost of renting $\qquad = \$2550$
Expected cost of buying $= 1550 \times \frac{8}{26} + 3050 \times \frac{18}{26} = \$2588.46$

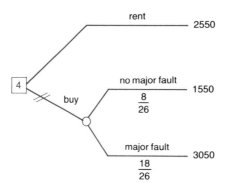

**Fig 12.10**

So if Decision Point 4 is reached, John should rent. Finally, we can evaluate Decision Point 1 (Fig 12.11):

Expected cost if vehicle not examined $= \$1800$
expected cost if vehicle examined $= 1590.54 \times 0.74 + 2550 \times 0.26$
$= \$1840$

We would advise John to go ahead and buy the vehicle outright, though the decision is very marginal. Should the cost of borrowing the car for a day be less than \$50, and/or should John and his friend be more accurate in their prediction, then the alternative course of action might well be chosen.

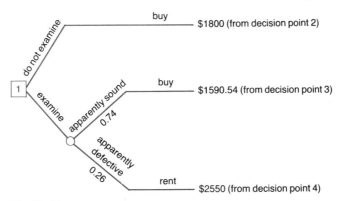

buy ——— $1800 (from decision point 2)

buy ——— $1590.54 (from decision point 3)

rent ——— $2550 (from decision point 4)

**Fig 12.11**

## QUESTIONS

**12.1** An investment trust manager wishes to buy a portfolio of shares and he has sufficient funds to buy either Portfolio A, Portfolio B or Portfolio C. The potential gains from the portfolios will depend upon the level of economic activity in the future, and the following estimates have been made (all figures in £000):

|  | State of nature | | |
| --- | --- | --- | --- |
| Portfolio | Expansion | Stability | Contraction |
| A | 100 | 50 | −50 |
| B | 50 | 100 | −25 |
| C | −50 | 0 | 180 |

Which portfolio should be selected if the manager applies:

(a)  The maximax criterion?

(b)  The maximin criterion?

(c)  The minimax criterion?

**12.2** Suppose that in Question 12.1 the investment manager makes the following probability estimates:

| Expansion | Stability | Contraction |
| --- | --- | --- |
| 0.1 | 0.4 | 0.5 |

Which portfolio should be selected if he uses the expected monetary value criterion?

**12.3** If perfect information is available to the investment manager in Questions 12.1 and 12.2, how much should he pay for it?

**12.4** Mr Wealthy has £50 000 invested at 10% per annum compound. He has been given the chance to buy the patent rights for an automatic rifle, and these rights will last for 10 years. All rifles made under this patent are sold to the Ministry of Defence, and the contract is worth £10 000 per year. Now it has been hinted that the government is contemplating an increase in defence expenditure, and should this happen the value of the contract would rise to £40 000 per year. Given that there is a 20% chance of an increase in defence expenditure, and that the patent rights would cost £50 000 per annum, should Mr Wealthy buy the patent rights, or should he leave his money invested? You should ignore the income-earning capacity on the income from royalties. (Hint: £50 000 invested at 10% per annum would grow to £129 687 in 10 years' time.)

**12.5** What would the increase in defence expenditure in Question 12.4 have to be to make it just worth while for Mr Wealthy to buy the patent rights?

**12.6** Suppose in Question 12.4 an official at the Ministry of Defence is prepared to reveal the government's intention on defence spending to Mr Wealthy for a bribe of £30 000. Is this information worth buying?

**12.7** International Conglomerates Plc is considering which of two firms it should purchase. It could buy Allied Dog Foods for £3m and this could be expected to yield £0.75m per year. However, parliament is considering legislation to restrict the number of dogs. The decision is not expected for two years, but if the number of dogs is restricted, then the annual receipts would fall to £0.1m. Alternatively, Guided Systems could be bought for £1m, and this would yield a cash flow of £0.5m per year. Within two years, the government must decide whether to replace the present early warning system, and Guided Systems must decide whether or not to expand at a cost of £2m and tender for the replacement system. If the tender is successful, Guided Systems' cash flow would increase to £0.8m per year, but if the tender is unsuccessful (or if no tender is made) then it would fall to £0.1m per year. Any decision taken now must last for the next ten years.

Draw a tree diagram of the alternative courses of action facing International Conglomerates. Insert the payoffs and decide on the best course of action under the maximax and maximin criteria.

**12.8** For question 12.7, find the best course of action according to the EMV criterion, given the following probabilities:

$P$(government restricts number of dogs) $= 0.4$
$P$(government replaces early warning system) $= 0.7$
$P$(Guided Systems' tender is successful) $= 0.9$

**12.9**  If in Question 12.8, an official at the Home Office is prepared to release information on the government's intention towards restricting the number of dogs, how much is this information worth to International Conglomerates?

**12.10**  A manufacturer has spent £20 000 on developing a product, and must now decide whether to manufacture on a small scale or a large scale. If the demand for the product is high, then the expected profit during the product's life would be £700 000 for a high manufacturing level and £150 000 for a low manufacturing level. If demand is low, then the expected profit is £100 000 for a high manufacturing level and £200 000 for a low manufacturing level. The initial indication is a 40% chance of a high demand, but a market research survey could predict the demand with 85% accuracy. How much can the manufacturer afford to spend on market research?

# 13 Simulation

Have you noticed how someone latches on to a particular word or phrase, and then it is picked up by the mass media and hammered at us? War 'escalates', people 'commute' to work, law enforcement officers avoid 'no go' areas. We no longer have spares; we have back-up systems. We no longer spoil the countryside; we pollute the environment. It would be easy to write a long list of such words and phrases. Nowadays, we are all familiar with the word 'simulation'. How did its popularity arise?

During World War II many raw materials were in short supply or not obtainable, and were produced artificially. Such goods were stamped 'imitation', and this proved to be a marketing disaster! 'Imitation' is a highly emotive word. It means made in the likeness of, but it did not mean this to potential purchasers! It meant a rather inferior substitute, to be avoided at all costs. If people were to buy such goods then the 'imitation' label would have to be dropped. Thus, 'imitation' silk became 'synthetic' silk, and sales were much healthier. Although the word synthetic was an improvement, it still did not produce the required product image. Now we have 'simulated' fur and 'simulated' suede. Why did the word 'simulated' succeed when 'imitation' and 'synthetic' failed? Probably because 'simulated' is more pleasant sounding, and almost certainly because fewer people knew what the word meant!

The exploration of space has certainly extended the popularity of the word 'simulation'. To most people, it means a cartoon of an orbital docking or the re-entry of the capsule into the Earth's atmosphere. To NASA, 'simulation' means a vital part of mission planning and mission control. At the Space Centre in Houston there is a mock-up of the space vehicles in which the astronauts familiarise themselves with layout and control systems. Clearly, it is better to learn in the simulator than to learn in the vehicle. The simulators were not merely used for astronaut training – if something goes wrong during the mission the failure can be reproduced on the simulators and experiments performed to rectify the fault. Again, it is better to experiment on the ground than in the vehicle.

The motives of simulation are clearly indicated by NASA. A problem is solved by simulation if it is too costly, too dangerous or just impractical to solve directly. For the rest of this chapter, we will consider problems that are difficult to solve directly because they contain random elements. However, we will assume that the random elements can be quantified in an empirical probability distribution. We will examine how to apply simulation to queuing problems later, but initially we will examine a supply and demand model.

## A supply and demand model

Suppose we take the case of a wholesale fishmonger selling boxes of fish. Daily demand will vary, but we will assume that the wholesaler has kept careful records of daily demand – records that can be summarised in an empirical probability distribution. Suppose he faces the following distribution of demand:

| No. of boxes demanded per day | Probability |
|:---:|:---:|
| 8 | $\frac{1}{4}$ |
| 9 | $\frac{1}{2}$ |
| 10 | $\frac{1}{4}$ |

The wholesaler, for some reason, wishes to predict a typical chain of demand over the next 12 days. How can he do this?

The essence of simulation techniques is to substitute for the actual probability distribution some other distribution with the same probabilities. We can then use this second distribution to simulate the actual situation. Suppose we spin two coins: the probability distribution below would result:

| Result | Probability |
|:---|:---:|
| Head Head | $\frac{1}{4}$ |
| Head Tail or Tail Head | $\frac{1}{2}$ |
| Tail Tail | $\frac{1}{4}$ |

Now as this second distribution matches perfectly the distribution of demand, we can simulate a chain of daily demand by spinning coins. We could let two heads simulate a demand of 8 boxes, two tails simulate a demand of 10 boxes, and a head and a tail simulate a demand of 9 boxes. A prediction of demand for the next 12 days might look something like this:

| Day | Result of spinning two coins | Simulated demand |
|:---:|:---:|:---:|
| 1 | H H | 8 |
| 2 | H H | 8 |
| 3 | H H | 8 |
| 4 | T T | 10 |
| 5 | H T | 9 |
| 6 | T H | 9 |
| 7 | H T | 9 |
| 8 | T T | 10 |
| 9 | H H | 8 |
| 10 | T T | 10 |
| 11 | H H | 8 |
| 12 | T H | 9 |

You should realise that it is necessary to resort to simulation to predict a sequence of demands because probability theory is a statement about long-run frequency. We can use probability theory to state that, in the long run, we will experience a daily demand for 8 boxes on 25% of occasions – we cannot use it to predict demand tomorrow, or on any particular day. Incidentally, you should notice that, using the probability distribution we would predict demand to be for 8 boxes on 25% of occasions, whereas in the simulated sequence we experienced a demand for 8 boxes on $5/12 = 41\%$ of occasions. This difference has arisen because we have taken a small sample of just 12 days. The longer the period over which we run the simulation, the closer would the simulated frequencies match the actual frequencies.

Clearly, it will not always be possible to spin coins and use the results as a basis for simulation. Suppose the pattern of demand facing the fishmonger was as follows.

| No. of boxes demanded | Probability (%) |
|:---:|:---:|
| 0 | 2 |
| 1 | 17 |
| 2 | 28 |
| 3 | 28 |
| 4 | 15 |
| 5 | 10 |
| | 100 |

Notice that in this case we have used percentage frequency as a measure of probability – it is often convenient to do this. We can use random numbers to obtain a frequency distribution that can form the basis of a simulation.

Originally, random numbers were generated by a device rather like a roulette wheel (which explains why simulation is sometimes called Monte Carlo methods). Nowadays, random numbers are generated by computers. If you ask a computer to generate a string of random numbers for you, then you should not be able to detect any pattern in the string (after all, 'random' means 'without pattern'). Moreover, we can ask a computer to generate random numbers within certain defined limits (for example, we would ask for random numbers in the range 1 to 10, or within the range 20 to 39).

Suppose we ask the computer to generate random numbers in the range 00 to 99 inclusive. As there are 100 possibilities for the number generated, then the probability that the computer generates any particular number in this range is 1%. The probability that the number is in the range 00–09 would be 10% (note that 00–09 inclusive is ten numbers, not nine). Likewise, the probability that the number generated is within the range 10–39 is 30%.

By grouping the random numbers in an appropriate fashion, we can obtain a distribution of random numbers that matches the distribution of demand.

We can then use this distribution of random numbers as the basis of our simulation. The probability that the computer generates a random number in the range 00–01 is 2% – the same as the probability that demand is zero. So if the computer generates a random number within the range 00–01, we will let this simulate a zero demand. The probability that the computer generates a random number in the range 02–18 is 17% – the same as the probability that demand is for one box. So if the computer generates a random number within the range 02–18, we will let this simulate a demand for one box. The probability that two boxes are demanded is 28%, and we can use the next 28 random numbers to stimulate this, i.e. if the number generated by the computer is in the range 19–46. The complete distribution would look like this:

| Random numbers | Frequency (%) | Simulates daily demand of |
|---|---|---|
| 00–01 | 2 | 0 |
| 02–18 | 17 | 1 |
| 19–46 | 28 | 2 |
| 47–74 | 28 | 3 |
| 75–89 | 15 | 4 |
| 90–99 | 10 | 5 |

Suppose the computer produces the following list of random numbers:

| 27 | 89 | 99 | 97 | 03 | 95 | 31 | 50 | 91 | 34 |
|---|---|---|---|---|---|---|---|---|---|

Then reading from the table above we see that this simulates the following demand sequence:

| 2 | 4 | 5 | 5 | 1 | 5 | 2 | 3 | 5 | 2 |
|---|---|---|---|---|---|---|---|---|---|

We shall now extend the example of the fishmonger to illustrate how simulation can be used. Suppose the supply of fish also varies randomly with the following probabilities:

| No. of boxes supplied | 0 | 1 | 2 | 3 | 4 | 5 |
|---|---|---|---|---|---|---|
| Probability (%) | 3 | 19 | 24 | 29 | 20 | 5 |

A box of fish costs the fishmonger £12, and the fishmonger sells a box for £23. Any box unsold at the end of the day is sold for cat food at £15 per box. If the fishmonger cannot supply a customer, then there is a loss of goodwill estimated at £5 per box. We will simulate 10 days' trading and estimate average daily profit.

We have already simulated 10 days' demand, so the first thing we must do is to simulate 10 days' supply. To do this, we need a distribution of random numbers corresponding to the supply frequencies.

| Random number | Frequency (%) | Simulates daily supply of |
|---|---|---|
| 01–02 | 3 | 0 |
| 03–21 | 19 | 1 |
| 22–45 | 24 | 2 |
| 46–74 | 29 | 3 |
| 75–94 | 20 | 4 |
| 95–99 | 5 | 5 |

If the computer produces the following list of random numbers:

72    94    52    78    12    21    25    20    34    93

then this simulates the following level of supply:

3    4    3    4    1    1    2    1    2    4

Summarising, we have used simulation to make the following predictions:

| Day | 1 | 2 | 3 | 4 | 5 | 6 | 7 | 8 | 9 | 10 |
|---|---|---|---|---|---|---|---|---|---|---|
| Boxes supplied | 3 | 4 | 3 | 4 | 1 | 1 | 2 | 1 | 2 | 4 |
| Boxes demanded | 2 | 4 | 5 | 5 | 1 | 5 | 2 | 3 | 5 | 2 |

Having simulated demand and supply, we have the necessary information to estimate average daily profit. You should notice the following rules must apply when estimating the numbers of unsold boxes and the levels of unsatisfied demand.

1  The number of boxes sold on any day is the number demanded or the number supplied, whichever is the smaller. After all, the fishmonger cannot sell more boxes than he has bought!
2  If on any one day, the number of boxes supplied exceeds the number demanded, then the difference represents the quantity unsold.
3  If on any particular day the number of boxes demanded exceeds the number supplied, then the difference represents the level of unsatisfied demand.

| Day | Boxes supplied | Boxes demanded | Boxes sold | Boxes unsold | Unsatisfied demand |
|---|---|---|---|---|---|
| 1 | 3 | 2 | 2 | 1 | 0 |
| 2 | 4 | 4 | 4 | 0 | 0 |
| 3 | 3 | 5 | 3 | 0 | 2 |
| 4 | 4 | 5 | 4 | 0 | 1 |
| 5 | 1 | 1 | 1 | 0 | 0 |
| 6 | 1 | 5 | 1 | 0 | 4 |
| 7 | 2 | 2 | 2 | 0 | 0 |
| 8 | 1 | 3 | 1 | 0 | 2 |
| 9 | 2 | 5 | 2 | 0 | 3 |
| 10 | 4 | 2 | 2 | 2 | 0 |
| | 25 | | 22 | 3 | 12 |

Using the totals, we can deduce that

| | | |
|---|---|---|
| Revenue from sales to customers = 22 × £23 = | £506 | |
| Revenue from sales for cat food = 3 × £15 = | £45 | |
| | £551 | |

Cost of boxes bought = 25 × £12 = £300
Loss of goodwill = 12 × £5 = £60
Total cost £360

Total profit earned £191
Average daily profit = 191/10 = £19.10

## A queuing model

The final stage in the manufacture of a certain product is inspection and rectification of faults. Previously, this was done by the distributor, but the firm making the product has decided that in future it will perform this operation itself. The production is scheduled such that one product leaves the production line every 20 minutes, but the actual time varies randomly like this:

| *Minutes late* | 3 | 4% |
|---|---|---|
| | 2 | 6% |
| | 1 | 18% |
| *On time* | | 36% |
| *Minutes early* | 1 | 21% |
| | 2 | 9% |
| | 3 | 6% |

Attempting to match production times, the inspector is supplied with sufficient mechanical aids to enable him to complete an inspection and to rectify any faults in 20 minutes, on average. Some products will be relatively free from defects and will pass through inspection in less than 20 minutes, while others will take longer. The following distribution of inspection times was obtained:

| *Time* | *Frequency* |
|---|---|
| 18 | 9% |
| 19 | 26% |
| 20 | 32% |
| 21 | 23% |
| 22 | 10% |

The factory operates for 8 hours each day, so 23 inspections are possible. The management wishes to derive various measures of performance for the proposed inspection system. In particular management wishes to know whether the 24 scheduled inspections can be completed on time. Management might also wish to know for how long during any day the inspector might be idle (which we will call idle time), and for how long products had to wait for inspection (which we will call waiting time). First, let us find the distribution of random numbers with the same frequencies as production times.

|  |  | Frequency | Random numbers |
|---|---|---|---|
| *Minutes late* | 3 | 4% | 00–03 |
|  | 2 | 6% | 04–09 |
|  | 1 | 18% | 10–27 |
| *On time* |  | 36% | 28–63 |
| *Minutes early* | 1 | 21% | 64–84 |
|  | 2 | 9% | 85–93 |
|  | 3 | 6% | 94–99 |

The production times give the times when the products arrive at the inspection shop. It will be logical to call them 'arrival times' and mark them with a minus when late, a plus when early, and zero when on time. Let us suppose that a product is waiting for inspection at the beginning of the day (it will be the last product produced on the previous day). This means we will require 23 arrival times. The following random numbers were obtained from a computer:

| 72 | 94 | 52 | 78 | 12 | 21 | 25 | 20 | 34 | 93 |
|---|---|---|---|---|---|---|---|---|---|
| 27 | 89 | 99 | 97 | 03 | 95 | 31 | 50 | 91 | 91 |
| 34 | 46 | 73 | | | | | | | |

These numbers simulate the following arrival times:

| +1 | +3 | 0 | +1 | −1 | −1 | −1 | −1 | 0 |
|---|---|---|---|---|---|---|---|---|
| +2 | −1 | +2 | +3 | +3 | −3 | +3 | 0 | 0 |
| +2 | +2 | 0 | 0 | +1 | | | | |

If we note that the first arrival time refers to the second item produced (the first product is awaiting inspection), and arrivals are scheduled at 20 minute intervals, actual arrival times are:

| 0 | 19 | 37 | 60 | 79 | 101 | 121 | 141 | 161 |
|---|---|---|---|---|---|---|---|---|
| 180 | 198 | 221 | 238 | 257 | 277 | 303 | 317 | 340 |
| 360 | 378 | 398 | 420 | 440 | 459 | | | |

Now we require a sequence of inspection times. The distribution of random numbers with the same frequency as the inspection times is:

| Time | Frequency | Random pairs |
|------|-----------|--------------|
| 18   | 9%        | 00–08        |
| 19   | 26%       | 09–34        |
| 20   | 32%       | 35–66        |
| 21   | 23%       | 67–89        |
| 22   | 10%       | 90–99        |

Obtaining 24 random numbers will give inspection times.

| 27 | 49 | 14 | 34 | 05 | 99 | 17 | 69 | 11 | 84 | 20 |
|----|----|----|----|----|----|----|----|----|----|----|
| 65 | 05 | 23 | 31 | 21 | 79 | 72 | 67 | 65 | 53 | 75 |
| 45 | 69 |    |    |    |    |    |    |    |    |    |

So the inspection times will be (in minutes):

| 19 | 20 | 19 | 19 | 18 | 22 | 19 | 21 | 19 | 21 | 19 |
|----|----|----|----|----|----|----|----|----|----|----|
| 20 | 18 | 19 | 19 | 19 | 21 | 21 | 21 | 20 | 20 | 21 |
| 20 | 21 |    |    |    |    |    |    |    |    |    |

There are four rules for this simulated system.

1  The starting time for any inspection will be determined by either the finishing time of the previous inspection or the arrival time of the product; whichever is the later.

2  The finishing time for any inspection will be the starting time plus the inspection time.

3  If the arrival time of any product exceeds the time the previous inspection was finished, then the difference represents the inspector's idle time.

4  If the time at which the inspection starts exceeds the arrival time, then the difference represents the product's waiting time.

The simulation shows that on this particular day, the inspector was idle for 11 minutes, and the 24 inspections took 7 minutes longer than scheduled. The average waiting time for products was $468/24 = 2.83$ mins. This is tolerable as a queue is not forming.

| Product number | Arrival time | Start | Inspection time | End | Idle time | Waiting time |
|---|---|---|---|---|---|---|
| 1 | 0 | 0 | 19 | 19 | 0 | 0 |
| 2 | 19 | 19 | 20 | 39 | 0 | 0 |
| 3 | 37 | 39 | 19 | 58 | 0 | 2 |
| 4 | 60 | 60 | 19 | 79 | 2 | 0 |
| 5 | 79 | 79 | 18 | 97 | 0 | 0 |
| 6 | 101 | 101 | 22 | 123 | 4 | 0 |
| 7 | 121 | 123 | 19 | 142 | 0 | 2 |
| 8 | 141 | 142 | 21 | 163 | 0 | 1 |
| 9 | 161 | 163 | 19 | 182 | 0 | 2 |
| 10 | 180 | 182 | 21 | 203 | 0 | 2 |
| 11 | 198 | 203 | 19 | 222 | 0 | 5 |
| 12 | 221 | 222 | 20 | 242 | 0 | 1 |
| 13 | 238 | 242 | 18 | 260 | 0 | 4 |
| 14 | 257 | 260 | 19 | 279 | 0 | 3 |
| 15 | 277 | 279 | 19 | 298 | 0 | 2 |
| 16 | 303 | 303 | 19 | 322 | 5 | 0 |
| 17 | 317 | 322 | 21 | 343 | 0 | 5 |
| 18 | 340 | 343 | 21 | 364 | 0 | 3 |
| 19 | 360 | 364 | 21 | 385 | 0 | 4 |
| 20 | 378 | 385 | 20 | 405 | 0 | 7 |
| 21 | 398 | 405 | 20 | 425 | 0 | 7 |
| 22 | 420 | 425 | 21 | 446 | 0 | 5 |
| 23 | 440 | 446 | 20 | 466 | 0 | 6 |
| 24 | 459 | 466 | 21 | 487 | 0 | 7 |
| | | | | | 11 | 68 |

## Simulating a cash flow

Given the probability distribution of the patterns of receipts and expenditures experienced by a firm, and given the opening balance, it is possible to stimulate the movement of cash into and out of the firm's bank account. This may be especially useful to the firm because even though on average the firm makes a profit, in a particular time period expenditures may exceed receipts and a negative bank balance would result.

Suppose we have the following data referring to the monthly movement of cash:

| Sales revenue (£000) | Frequency (%) |
|---|---|
| 30–34 | 10 |
| 34–38 | 30 |
| 38–42 | 40 |
| 42–46 | 20 |

| Wages and salaries (£000) | Frequency (%) | Raw materials (£000) | Frequency (%) |
|---|---|---|---|
| 10–12 | 30 | 6– 8 | 20 |
| 12–14 | 50 | 8–10 | 30 |
| 14–16 | 20 | 10–12 | 30 |
|  |  | 12–14 | 20 |

Fixed costs are £14 000 per month.

If we find the average monthly sales revenue, the average monthly wages and salaries and average monthly raw material costs it is possible to predict the average monthly profit.

Sales revenue

| x | f | fx |
|---|---|---|
| 32 | 10 | 320 |
| 36 | 30 | 1080 |
| 40 | 40 | 1600 |
| 44 | 20 | 880 |
|  | 100 | 3880 |

Average = 3880/100 = 38.8
            = £38 800

| Wages and salaries | | | | Raw materials | | |
|---|---|---|---|---|---|---|
| x | f | fx | | x | f | fx |
| 11 | 30 | 330 | | 7 | 20 | 140 |
| 13 | 50 | 650 | | 9 | 30 | 270 |
| 15 | 20 | 300 | | 11 | 30 | 330 |
|  | 100 | 1280 | | 13 | 20 | 260 |
|  |  |  | |  | 100 | 1000 |

Average = 1280/100 = 12.8          Average = 1000/100 = 10
            = £12 800                              = £10 000

Average monthly profit =
            average sales revenue – fixed costs – average variable costs.

Average monthly profit = £38 800 – £14 000 (fixed) – £12 800 (payroll) –
            £10 000 (materials)
            = £2000.

Hence, we would expect that on average the firm's cash balance would increase by £2000 per month. It would be interesting to run a twelve months' simulation and compare the movement of the firm's cash balance with that predicted from the averages.

Allocating random numbers to the distributions of sales revenue, wages and salaries and raw materials:

| Sales revenue (£000) | Prob (%) | Mid-point | Random numbers |
|---|---|---|---|
| 30–34 | 10 | 32 | 00–09 |
| 34–38 | 30 | 36 | 10–39 |
| 38–42 | 40 | 40 | 40–79 |
| 42–46 | 20 | 44 | 80–99 |

| Wages and salaries (£000) | Prob (%) | Mid-point | Random numbers |
|---|---|---|---|
| 10–12 | 30 | 11 | 00–29 |
| 12–14 | 50 | 13 | 30–79 |
| 14–16 | 20 | 15 | 80–99 |

| Raw materials (£000) | Prob (%) | Mid-point | Random numbers |
|---|---|---|---|
| 6– 8 | 20 | 7 | 00–19 |
| 8–10 | 30 | 9 | 20–49 |
| 10–12 | 30 | 11 | 50–79 |
| 12–14 | 20 | 13 | 80–99 |

Note that because we have grouped frequency distributions, the random numbers will predict the mid-point values.

Obtaining 36 random numbers will enable monthly predictions for each random variable:

| Random numbers | 97 | 20 | 52 | 13 | 87 | 02 | 48 | 95 | 32 | 77 | 69 | 88 |
|---|---|---|---|---|---|---|---|---|---|---|---|---|
| Sales revenue | 44 | 36 | 40 | 32 | 44 | 32 | 40 | 44 | 36 | 40 | 40 | 44 |

| Random numbers | 30 | 62 | 83 | 67 | 47 | 96 | 22 | 96 | 55 | 97 | 13 | 45 |
|---|---|---|---|---|---|---|---|---|---|---|---|---|
| Wages and salaries | 13 | 13 | 15 | 13 | 13 | 15 | 11 | 15 | 13 | 15 | 11 | 13 |

| Random numbers | 80 | 19 | 69 | 67 | 37 | 08 | 81 | 42 | 46 | 80 | 57 | 46 |
|---|---|---|---|---|---|---|---|---|---|---|---|---|
| Raw materials | 13 | 7 | 11 | 11 | 9 | 7 | 13 | 9 | 9 | 13 | 11 | 9 |

Given that fixed costs are £14 000 per month and assuming an opening balance of £5000, the closing balance would fluctuate like this:

| Month | Opening balance | Sales revenue | Wages and salaries | Raw materials | Fixed cost | Closing balance |
|---|---|---|---|---|---|---|
| 1 | 5 | 44 | 13 | 13 | 14 | 9 |
| 2 | 9 | 36 | 13 | 7 | 14 | 11 |
| 3 | 11 | 40 | 15 | 11 | 14 | 11 |
| 4 | 11 | 32 | 13 | 11 | 14 | 5 |
| 5 | 5 | 44 | 13 | 9 | 14 | 13 |
| 6 | 13 | 32 | 15 | 7 | 14 | 9 |
| 7 | 9 | 40 | 11 | 13 | 14 | 11 |

| Month | Opening balance | Sales revenue | Wages and salaries | Raw materials | Fixed cost | Closing balance |
|---|---|---|---|---|---|---|
| 8 | 11 | 44 | 15 | 9 | 14 | 17 |
| 9 | 17 | 36 | 13 | 9 | 14 | 17 |
| 10 | 17 | 40 | 15 | 13 | 14 | 15 |
| 11 | 15 | 40 | 11 | 11 | 14 | 19 |
| 12 | 19 | 44 | 13 | 9 | 14 | 27 |

Notice that although the closing balance sometimes moves downward, the overall trend is upward (this is what you would expect as the average monthly profit has been calculated to be £2000). The cash movement of the firm's bank account is illustrated in Fig 13.1. It would be perfectly possible to predict the average monthly profit from the simulation. The firm has earned a net revenue of £27 000 – £5000 = £22 000 over the twelve months. This represents an average monthly profit of 22 000/12 = £1833.33.

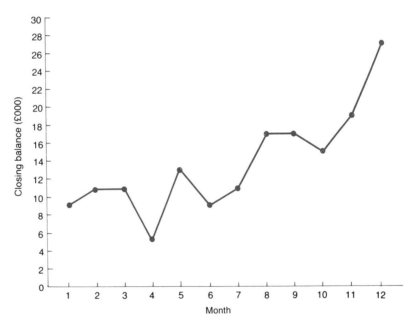

**Fig 13.1**

## QUESTIONS

**13.1** Look again at the fishmonger problem earlier in this chapter. Suppose that any boxes left over at the end of the day are put into cold storage for sale on the following day. Using the same data for supply and demand, find average daily profit and stock level at the end of the period.

**13.2** This question refers to the production model analysed in this chapter. Suppose that instead of giving a distribution of deviations from scheduled production times, the problem had given actual production times. If the actual production times were:

| Times (mins) | 17 | 18 | 19 | 20 | 21 | 22 | 23 |
|---|---|---|---|---|---|---|---|
| Frequency | 4 | 6 | 18 | 36 | 21 | 9 | 6 |

then very different results would have been obtained. Use the same random numbers as used in the text, and rework the simulation using actual production times.

**13.3** A doctor setting up a new general practice at a health centre wishes to set up an appointments system for daily consultations. A colleague supplies him with the following information as to patient punctuality.

| | | |
|---|---|---|
| Minutes early | 3 | 6% |
| | 2 | 29% |
| | 1 | 41% |
| On time | | 12% |
| Minutes late | 1 | 7% |
| | 2 | 5% |

The doctor times his consultations over a period, and derives the following distribution of expected consultation times:

| | |
|---|---|
| 12 minutes | 10% |
| 13 minutes | 15% |
| 14 minutes | 28% |
| 15 minutes | 34% |
| 16 minutes | 13% |

For convenience, he would like to issue appointments at 15-minute intervals. He wishes to have an idea of his idle time, the patients' waiting time, and whether he can complete his appointments on schedule. Simulate 16 consultations and derive the required information.

Random numbers for arrivals:
17 50 83 94 49 79 43 90 09 40 46 09 95 52 91 15

Random numbers for consultation:
14 40 13 08 98 51 74 24 21 12 91 05 44 79 53 16

**13.4** The distributions of arrivals and services at a supermarket checkout per time period are given below.

| Arrivals | Frequency | Services | Frequency |
|----------|-----------|----------|-----------|
| 8 | 8% | 7 | 9% |
| 9 | 22% | 8 | 19% |
| 10 | 38% | 9 | 42% |
| 11 | 26% | 10 | 25% |
| 12 | 6% | 11 | 5% |

Simulate 40 time periods and find the queue length.

Random numbers for arrivals

| | | | | | | | | | |
|---|---|---|---|---|---|---|---|---|---|
| 53 | 63 | 35 | 63 | 98 | 02 | 03 | 85 | 58 | 34 |
| 64 | 62 | 08 | 07 | 01 | 72 | 88 | 45 | 96 | 43 |
| 50 | 22 | 96 | 31 | 78 | 84 | 36 | 07 | 10 | 55 |
| 53 | 51 | 35 | 37 | 93 | 02 | 49 | 84 | 18 | 79 |

Random numbers for services

| | | | | | | | | | |
|---|---|---|---|---|---|---|---|---|---|
| 98 | 79 | 49 | 32 | 24 | 43 | 84 | 69 | 38 | 37 |
| 82 | 23 | 28 | 57 | 12 | 86 | 73 | 60 | 68 | 69 |
| 42 | 58 | 94 | 65 | 90 | 76 | 33 | 30 | 91 | 33 |
| 53 | 45 | 50 | 01 | 48 | 21 | 47 | 25 | 56 | 92 |

**13.5** In the previous example, the queue will become very long. If the queue is 10 or more, it spills over into the selling area. Under such conditions, it is necessary to open an extra checkout. Find the appropriate time periods when it is necessary to do this. You may allocate the random numbers 74, 24 and 21 for services at the second checkout.

**13.6** Items arriving per time period for servicing at a servicing shop have the following distribution:

| Arrivals | 0 | 1 | 2 | 3 | 4 | 5 | 6 | 7 | 8 | 9 |
|----------|---|---|---|---|---|---|---|---|---|---|
| Frequency (%) | 2 | 7 | 15 | 20 | 20 | 16 | 10 | 6 | 3 | 1 |

Servicing times vary with the complexity of the fault, and the distribution of the number of services completed in each time period is:

| Services | 1 | 2 | 3 | 4 | 5 | 6 | 7 | 8 | 9 | 10 |
|----------|---|---|---|---|---|---|---|---|---|----|
| Frequency (%) | 4 | 8 | 14 | 18 | 18 | 15 | 10 | 7 | 4 | 2 |

Simulate 25 time periods and assess the maximum queue length.

Random numbers for arrivals

| | | | | | | | | | |
|---|---|---|---|---|---|---|---|---|---|
| 09 | 35 | 63 | 35 | 90 | 98 | 47 | 73 | 25 | 35 |
| 67 | 39 | 92 | 15 | 46 | 45 | 03 | 66 | 08 | 65 |
| 85 | 15 | 26 | 69 | 45 | | | | | |

Random numbers for services

| | | | | | | | | | |
|---|---|---|---|---|---|---|---|---|---|
| 51 | 16 | 26 | 46 | 17 | 35 | 46 | 78 | 93 | 79 |
| 30 | 96 | 95 | 90 | 13 | 52 | 53 | 90 | 56 | 09 |
| 21 | 13 | 61 | 31 | 86 | | | | | |

**13.7** The time it takes a cashier to clear a customer at a supermarket checkout varies according to the number of items purchased. The manager times the cashier, and derives the following frequency distribution.

| Time taken to clear customer (seconds) | 40 | 45 | 50 | 55 | 60 | 65 | 70 |
|---|---|---|---|---|---|---|---|
| Frequency (%) | 5 | 8 | 20 | 31 | 22 | 10 | 4 |

He has only one cashier. The manager notices that during the busiest times, a long queue is forming and overspilling into the selling area. He fears that this is causing people to shop elsewhere. The distribution of 'inter-arrival times' of customers is:

| Inter-arrival time (seconds) | 30 | 35 | 40 | 45 | 50 |
|---|---|---|---|---|---|
| Frequency (%) | 12 | 21 | 29 | 28 | 10 |

Simulate 25 arrivals using random numbers and find the queue length after 25 arrivals.

Random numbers for arrivals

| | | | | | | | | | |
|---|---|---|---|---|---|---|---|---|---|
| 40 | 65 | 03 | 89 | 17 | 14 | 32 | 13 | 17 | 51 |
| 09 | 03 | 78 | 31 | 93 | 88 | 12 | 34 | 79 | 10 |
| 50 | 40 | 63 | 79 | 71 | | | | | |

Random numbers for services

| | | | | | | | | | |
|---|---|---|---|---|---|---|---|---|---|
| 11 | 36 | 46 | 21 | 15 | 16 | 12 | 74 | 20 | 17 |
| 45 | 46 | 61 | 30 | 41 | 02 | 65 | 65 | 21 | |

**13.8** In any one day, the price of stock traded on a certain stock exchange can rise, fall or remain unchanged. It is assumed that the direction of the change today depends upon what happened to the stock yesterday. The following probabilities are available:

| | | Today | | |
|---|---|---|---|---|
| | | Up | Unchanged | Down |
| | Up | .7 | .2 | .1 |
| Yesterday | Unchanged | .3 | .4 | .3 |
| | Down | .1 | .3 | .6 |

Moreover, if the price changes, it changes by the following amounts:

| Amount of change (p) | Probability |
|---|---|
| 0.5 | 0.30 |
| 1.0 | 0.40 |
| 1.5 | 0.20 |
| 2.0 | 0.05 |
| 2.5 | 0.05 |

Using the random digits below, simulate the next 10 days' trading on the assumption that the stock closed yesterday unchanged at 100:

Random numbers for direction of change

| 72 | 94 | 52 | 78 | 12 | 21 | 25 | 20 | 34 | 93 |
|---|---|---|---|---|---|---|---|---|---|

Random numbers for amount of change

| 27 | 49 | 14 | 34 | 05 | 99 | 17 | 69 | 11 | 84 |
|---|---|---|---|---|---|---|---|---|---|

**13.9** The following distributions of daily supply and demand for a particular component were recorded as follows:

| Daily demand | Frequency (%) | Daily supply | Frequency (%) |
|---|---|---|---|
| 8 | 30 | 7 | 5 |
| 9 | 40 | 8 | 30 |
| 10 | 20 | 9 | 40 |
| 11 | 5 | 10 | 20 |
| 12 | 5 | 11 | 5 |

Simulate 10 days' trading using the following random numbers:

| For demand | 21 | 52 | 68 | 33 | 31 | 99 | 91 | 72 | 56 | 90 |
|---|---|---|---|---|---|---|---|---|---|---|
| For supply | 94 | 95 | 66 | 78 | 91 | 08 | 52 | 26 | 47 | 01 |

Obtain a distribution of unsatisfied demand and find the stock level at the end of the period.

**13.10** A car hire firm has four cars to rent. The daily distribution of demand for cars is as follows:

| No. of cars demanded | Frequency (%) |
|---|---|
| 0 | 10 |
| 1 | 20 |
| 2 | 20 |
| 3 | 25 |
| 4 | 15 |
| 5 | 10 |

The distribution of the time for which the car is demanded is

| No. of days demanded | Frequency (%) |
|---|---|
| 1 | 15 |
| 2 | 25 |
| 3 | 30 |
| 4 | 20 |
| 5 | 10 |

Random numbers for number of cars demanded

| 38 | 53 | 29 | 32 | 91 | 52 | 48 | 89 | 70 | 24 | 06 | 31 |
|---|---|---|---|---|---|---|---|---|---|---|---|
| 48 | 09 | 06 | 60 | 24 | 42 | 08 | 08 | | | | |

Random numbers for number of days demanded

| 94 | 37 | 01 | 49 | 51 | 59 | 63 | 17 | 51 | 44 | 06 | 52 |
|---|---|---|---|---|---|---|---|---|---|---|---|
| 55 | 44 | 92 | 56 | 93 | 75 | | | | | | |

Using the random numbers above, simulate the demand for vehicles over 20 days.

**13.11** A study of monthly income and expenditure patterns for a certain firm revealed the following information:

| Monthly income (£) | Probability | Monthly expenditure (£) | Probability |
|---|---|---|---|
| 1000 | 0.2 | 800 | 0.2 |
| 1500 | 0.3 | 1000 | 0.4 |
| 2000 | 0.4 | 1400 | 0.3 |
| 2500 | 0.1 | 1900 | 0.1 |

The firm has a balance of £500 at the start of the year. Using the following random numbers, run a simulation and determine the balance at the end of the year:

| Income: | 72 | 94 | 52 | 78 | 12 | 21 | 25 | 20 | 34 | 93 | 27 | 89 |
|---|---|---|---|---|---|---|---|---|---|---|---|---|
| Expenditure: | 27 | 49 | 14 | 34 | 5 | 99 | 17 | 69 | 11 | 84 | 20 | 36 |

**13.12** A firm has noticed that the demand for a certain product has the following distribution.

| Daily demand | Frequency (%) |
|---|---|
| 4 | 7 |
| 5 | 12 |
| 6 | 14 |
| 7 | 19 |
| 8 | 28 |
| 9 | 3 |
| 10 | 9 |
| 11 | 7 |
| 12 | 1 |

At present, the firm has 60 units in stock. It is the policy of the firm to reorder a batch of 40 components when stock falls to 30 units. Additionally, the firm will order sufficient items to bring stock back up to the reorder level of 30 units.

The time interval between placing an order and receiving delivery is called the lead time. The lead time has the following distribution:

| Lead time (days) | Frequency (%) |
|:---:|:---:|
| 3 | 14 |
| 4 | 41 |
| 5 | 26 |
| 6 | 19 |

The firm is interested in knowing the number of occasions that stock levels will be insufficient to meet demand. Using the random numbers below, run a suitable simulation.

Random numbers for daily demand

| 03 | 97 | 16 | 12 | 55 | 16 | 84 | 63 | 33 | 57 | 18 | 26 |
|----|----|----|----|----|----|----|----|----|----|----|----|
| 23 | 52 | 37 | 70 | 56 | 99 | 16 | 31 | 68 | 74 | 27 | 00 |

Random numbers for lead time

| 47 | 56 | 76 |
|----|----|----|

# 14 Probability distributions

In Chapter 11, we examined the basic concepts of probability. We can now use our knowledge to examine aspects of probability under certain rigidly defined conditions. The main difficulty that you have probably experienced so far in dealing with probability problems is that there is no one, assured method of dealing with them. However, when the conditions underlying a problem match the conditions we shall examine in this chapter, there will be a well-defined route to the solution. So although the concepts explained here are probably more involved than in Chapter 11, you can rest assured that the applications of the concepts will be much simpler. Our first task will be to examine what is meant by a probability distribution.

## What is a probability distribution?

Suppose in an experiment we define all the outcomes, and choose one of the outcomes as an attribute. We could then form a frequency distribution by finding the probability that the attribute does not occur, occurs once, occurs twice – and so on. The distribution we have formed is called a *probability distribution*. An example will clarify what we mean by this. Suppose we spin a coin, and choose as our attribute the number of heads occurring. The probability distribution would look like this:

| Number of heads | Probability (frequency) |
|:---:|:---:|
| 0 | $\frac{1}{2}$ |
| 1 | $\frac{1}{2}$ |
| | $\underline{1}$ |

Notice that the sum of the frequencies is one – a feature of all probability distributions. This is because the number of times the attribute can occur (in this case zero or one), form mutually exclusive, collectively exhaustive events.

In forming the above probability distribution, we have been using *a priori* concepts: we calculated the probabilities *before* the experiment was performed. However, it is certainly possible to form a probability distribution using empirical evidence, i.e. after the experiment is performed. Suppose, for example, we know that in a large batch of components some will be defective. We decide to draw a sample of six items, so the sample could be free from defectives, or contain 1, 2, 3, 4, 5 or 6 defectives. We wish to find the probability of each outcome. Well, we could draw, say, 100 samples and count the number of defectives in each. Our result may look like this:

| Number of defectives | 0 | 1 | 2 | 3 | 4 | 5 | 6 |
|---|---|---|---|---|---|---|---|
| Frequency | 75 | 15 | 7 | 2 | 1 | 0 | 0 |

To form the probability distribution we divide each of the frequencies by 100 (the total frequency). So we have:

| Number of defectives | 0 | 1 | 2 | 3 | 4 |
|---|---|---|---|---|---|
| Probability | 0.75 | 0.15 | 0.07 | 0.02 | 0.01 |

In this chapter we will examine certain standard types of probability distributions and use them as a basis for calculating *a priori* probabilities. You may feel that we are devoting too much time to *a priori* probability and ignoring the other forms. However, if we *suspect* that the outcome of an experiment would conform to one of the standard types of probability distributions then we can make some very useful predictions. We can always check our assumptions by obtaining empirical probabilities and comparing them with *a priori* probabilities. Later, we will show you how to test how well an *a priori* distribution fits or corresponds to the empirical evidence.

## The binomial distribution

The first probability distribution we will examine is the so-called *binomial distribution*, and we shall examine how it arises by considering a very simple example. Let us suppose that three coins are tossed together and take as our attribute the number of heads occurring. Well, the probability that none of the coins is a head can be calculated very simply using the multiplication law:

$$P_{(0)} = \tfrac{1}{2} \times \tfrac{1}{2} \times \tfrac{1}{2} = \tfrac{1}{8}$$

Now let us calculate the probability that one of the coins shows a head. The problem here is that whereas there is only one event where no heads occur, there are a number of events where just one head occurs, namely HTT, THT, TTH (where H is a head occurring and T is a tail occurring). Fortunately, each of the events is equally likely ($\tfrac{1}{2} \times \tfrac{1}{2} \times \tfrac{1}{2}$), so:

$$P_{(1)} = 3 \times \tfrac{1}{2} \times \tfrac{1}{2} \times \tfrac{1}{2} = \tfrac{3}{8}$$

Two heads can occur in three equally likely ways (HHT, HTH, THH) so:

$$P_{(2)} = 3 \times \tfrac{1}{2} \times \tfrac{1}{2} \times \tfrac{1}{2} = \tfrac{3}{8}$$

but three heads can occur in one way only (HHH) so:

$$P_{(3)} = \tfrac{1}{2} \times \tfrac{1}{2} \times \tfrac{1}{2} = \tfrac{1}{8}$$

We have now calculated the full probability distribution, and we could represent it like this:

| No. of heads occurring | Probability | or Probability |
|:---:|:---:|:---:|
| 0 | $\tfrac{1}{8}$ | 0.125 |
| 1 | $\tfrac{3}{8}$ | 0.375 |
| 2 | $\tfrac{3}{8}$ | 0.375 |
| 3 | $\tfrac{1}{8}$ | 0.125 |
| | 1 | 1.000 |

A binomial distribution is concerned with two terms (hence its name) – the probability that the event we are considering occurs (we will call this $p$) and the probability that the event does not occur (we call this $1 - p = q$). We have just considered an example where $p = q$ (the probability of obtaining a head is identical to the probability of obtaining a tail), but we can use a very similar analysis for cases where $p$ and $q$ are unequal *as long as the experiment is performed three times*. Suppose we have a very large consignment of components, and we know from past experience that 10% of components are defective. We randomly select three components from the consignment – what is the probability distribution of the number of defectives in the sample? We let $p$ be the probability that an item in the sample is defective. Hence we have $q = 0.9$, $p = 0.1$:

$$P_{(0)} = q \times q \times q = q^3 = (0.9)^3 \qquad\qquad = 0.729$$
$$P_{(1)} = 3 \times q \times q \times p = 3q^2 p = 3 \times 0.9^2 \times 0.1 \qquad = 0.243$$
$$P_{(2)} = 3 \times q \times p \times p = 3qp^2 = 3 \times 0.9 \times 0.1^2 \qquad = 0.027$$
$$P_{(3)} = p \times p \times p = p^3 = 0.1^3 \qquad\qquad = 0.001$$
$$\overline{\phantom{xxxxxxxxxxxxxxxxxxxxxxxxxxxxxx} 1.000}$$

Notice that we are using the results of the previous example. There is only one way for the sample to contain no defectives, and only one way for it to contain three defectives. There are three equally likely ways that the sample can contain one defective, and three equally likely ways that the sample can contain two defectives.

Examining the above examples, we can see that to calculate the individual probabilities in a binomial distribution, we must find the number of equally likely events comprising the outcome we require, and multiply this by the probability of any one of the events. Suppose we increased the sample size in the question above to five items, and wished to find the probability that three of the items were defective. Now we know that this outcome can occur in a number of equally likely ways, and it is easy to calculate the probability of any one of these ways. For example:

$$q \times q \times p \times p \times p = q^2 p^3 = (0.9)^2 (0.1)^3 = 0.00081$$

is the probability that the first two items are non-defective and the last three are defective. We now need to know the number of equally likely ways of obtaining this outcome. We could write out all the events (as we did previously) but this would be very tedious – there are 10 equally likely events in this case. Also, we could never be sure that we have included all of the outcomes! How do you think we could go on writing out all the outcomes of drawing, say, two defectives if the sample contained 100 items?

## Pascal's Triangle

A very useful device for finding all the equally likely events in a binomial distribution is *Pascal's Triangle*, and an example of it is constructed below.

|   |   |   |   |   |   |   | $n =$ no. of items |
|---|---|---|---|---|---|---|---|
| 1 | 1 |   |   |   |   |   | 1  in the |
| 1 | 2 | 1 |   |   |   |   | 2  sample |
| 1 | 3 | 3 | 1 |   |   |   | 3 |
| 1 | 4 | 6 | 4 | 1 |   |   | 4 |
| 1 | 5 | 10 | 10 | 5 | 1 |   | 5 |
| 1 | 6 | 15 | 20 | 15 | 6 | 1 | 6 |

Number of defectives  0  1  2  3  4  5  6

Reading off from the triangle, we see that if we draw a sample of five items ($n = 5$) there is one way that a sample can contain no defectives, there are five equally likely ways that the sample can have one defective, 10 ways for it to have two defectives – and so on. Using this information we can calculate the complete binomial distribution.

| No. of Defectives | No. of equally likely events | Probability of one of these events | Required probability | |
|---|---|---|---|---|
| 0 | 1 | $(0.9)^5$ | $(0.9)^5$ | $= 0.59049$ |
| 1 | 5 | $(0.9)^4(0.1)$ | $5(0.9)^4(0.1)$ | $= 0.32805$ |
| 2 | 10 | $(0.9)^3(0.1)^2$ | $10(0.9)^3(0.1)^2$ | $= 0.0729$ |
| 3 | 10 | $(0.9)^2(0.1)^3$ | $10(0.9)^2(0.1)^3$ | $= 0.0081$ |
| 4 | 5 | $(0.9)(0.1)^4$ | $5(0.9)(0.1)^4$ | $= 0.00045$ |
| 5 | 1 | $(0.1)^5$ | $(0.1)^5$ | $= 0.00001$ |
| | | | | $1.00000$ |

So you can see that Pascal's Triangle is a useful way of finding the number of equally likely events. But if you are going to use Pascal's Triangle, it will be necessary for you to be able to construct it. The first thing you should notice is that the first and last number in any row is one. The rest of the numbers are obtained by adding the numbers in the previous row together in pairs. So the numbers for row six would be:

$$\begin{array}{ccccccc} 1 & 1+5 & 5+10 & 10+10 & 10+5 & 5+1 & 1 \\ =1 & 6 & 15 & 20 & 15 & 6 & 1 \end{array}$$

and the numbers in row seven would be:

$$\begin{array}{ccccccc} 1 & 1+6 & 6+15 & 15+20 & 20+15 & 15+6 & 6+1 & 1 \\ =1 & 7 & 21 & 35 & 35 & 21 & 7 & 1 \end{array}$$

The numbers that we are obtaining in the rows of Pascal's Triangle are called the *binomial coefficients*, and certainly it is easy to obtain them. But suppose we are drawing a sample of 20 items. If we don't have a copy of Pascal's Triangle available, it will be necessary to construct its first 20 rows, and this is going to be quite a task! It is possible, of course, but let us examine an alternative to Pascal's Triangle which we think that, in the long run, you will find easier.

## Combinations

Most gamblers are aware that if you want the bookmaker to choose a stated number of results (say, three) from a larger number of selections (say, six) he will do so. In fact, this is one of the most popular forms of betting both on the football pools and on the racetrack. So popular is it that many book-makers issue tables telling us how much it will cost to bet on any number of results chosen from a larger number. Such a table is a copy of Pascal's Triangle, but instead of reading off 'the number of defectives' we read off the 'number of correct results'. So gamblers can now look at the table and see that if they want to select six football teams and win the bet if any three of them draw, then they must make 20 bets. Bookmakers call these tables 'permutation tables', and instruct us to write our bets in the form 'Perm any three results from six selections = 20 bets'.

Now strictly, the bookmaker is wrong – when we are betting on three results from six we are dealing not with a permutation but with a combina-tion, and we will now show you how to calculate how many combinations of *r* results there are if you make *n* selections. We can write this problem symbolically like this:

$$^nC_r$$

and to calculate the number of combinations we apply the formula:

$$^nC_r = \frac{n(n-1)(n-2)\ldots[(n-r)+1]}{r(r-1)(r-2)\cdots\times 1}$$

This formula looks very fearsome, but in fact it is very easy to apply. If we examine Pascal's Triangle we see that if we select seven football teams to win then there are 35 equally likely ways of just three of them winning. Now let us check this by using the formula for combinations. Here we have $n = 7$, $r = 3$, so $(n - r) + 1 = (7 - 3) + 1 = 5$, and

$$^7C_3 = \frac{7\times 6\times 5}{3\times 2\times 1} = 35$$

We are now in a position to derive a general expression for a binomial distribution. Suppose that within a population a proportion $p$ has a certain attribute (call it 'defective') – it follows that $1 - p = q$ is the proportion of non-defectives. Now suppose we draw a sample of $n$ items.

- The probability that the sample is free from defective items $= P_{(0)} = q^n$.

- The probability that the sample has one defective item is $P_{(1)} = {}^nC_1 q^{n-1}p$ (if one item is defective then $n - 1$ must be non-defective).

- The probability that the sample has two defective items is $P_{(2)} = {}^nC_2 q^{n-2}p^2$.

We could continue in this way until we reach the probability that all the items in the sample are defective, which must be $P_{(n)} = p^n$. Now we know that all the probabilities must add up to one, so:

$$q^n + {}^nC_1 q^{n-1}p + {}^nC_2 q^{n-2}p^2 + {}^nC_3 q^{n-3}p^3 + \cdots + p^n = 1$$

We also know that $q + p = 1$, so $(q + p)^n$ must equal one. Now we can write:

$$(q + p)^n = q^n + {}^nC_1 q^{n-1}p + {}^nC_2 q^{n-2}p^2 + {}^nC_3 q^{n-3}p^3 + \cdots + p^n$$

and call the right-hand side of this expression the expansion of the binomial $(q + p)^n$. The individual terms of the right-hand side give the probabilities of $0, 1, 2 \ldots n$ defectives.

The great advantage of using the general expression for the binomial distribution is that we often do not wish to calculate the entire distribution, but just part of it. If we knew that a bag of seeds had a 95% germination rate, and we planted 10 of these seeds, we could quite easily calculate the probability that (say) 2 of the seeds fail to germinate. We have:

$$q = 0.95, \ p = 0.05, \ n = 10, \ r = 2, \ (n - r) + 1 = 9$$

$$P_{(2)} = \frac{10 \times 9}{1 \times 2} (0.95)^8 (0.05)^2 = 0.0746$$

We would like to point out that when we state that it is quite easy to calculate probabilities using the general expression for the binomial distribution, we really mean that it is easy to decide *what* to do. We are only too willing to admit that the actual arithmetic operations are most tedious.

## The mean and standard deviation of a binomial distribution

Let us begin by calculating the probabilities of the binomial distribution $(\frac{3}{4} + \frac{1}{4})^5$ (for example, sampling in groups of five from a population with 25% defectives). We shall use the general expression rather than Pascal's Triangle:

$$(\tfrac{3}{4} + \tfrac{1}{4})^5 = (\tfrac{3}{4})^5 + {}^5C_1(\tfrac{3}{4})^4(\tfrac{1}{4}) + {}^5C_2(\tfrac{3}{4})^3(\tfrac{1}{4})^2 + {}^5C_3(\tfrac{3}{4})^2(\tfrac{1}{4})^3$$
$$+ {}^5C_4(\tfrac{3}{4})(\tfrac{1}{4})^4 + (\tfrac{1}{4})^5$$

$$= (\tfrac{3}{4})^5 + 5(\tfrac{3}{4})^4(\tfrac{1}{4}) + \frac{5 \cdot 4}{2 \cdot 1} (\tfrac{3}{4})^3(\tfrac{1}{4})^2 + \frac{5 \cdot 4 \cdot 3}{3 \cdot 2 \cdot 1} (\tfrac{3}{4})^2(\tfrac{1}{4})^3$$

$$+ \frac{5 \cdot 4 \cdot 3 \cdot 2}{4 \cdot 3 \cdot 2 \cdot 1} (\tfrac{3}{4})(\tfrac{1}{4})^4 + (\tfrac{1}{4})^5$$

$$= 0.2373 + 0.3955 + 0.2637 + 0.0879 + 0.0146 + 0.001$$

We can now calculate the mean and standard deviation of the number of defectives in samples of five items.

| Number of defectives (x) | Probability (f) | fx | fx² |
|---|---|---|---|
| 0 | 0.2373 | 0 | 0 |
| 1 | 0.3955 | 0.3955 | 0.3955 |
| 2 | 0.2637 | 0.5274 | 1.0548 |
| 3 | 0.0879 | 0.2637 | 0.7911 |
| 4 | 0.0146 | 0.0584 | 0.2336 |
| 5 | 0.0010 | 0.0050 | 0.0250 |
| | 1.0000 | 1.2500 | 2.5000 |

$$\bar{x} = \frac{\Sigma fx}{\Sigma f} = \frac{1.25}{1} = 1.25 \text{ defectives per sample}$$

$$\sigma = \sqrt{\frac{\Sigma fx^2}{\Sigma f} - \left(\frac{\Sigma fx}{\Sigma f}\right)^2} = \sqrt{\frac{2.5}{1} - \left(\frac{1.25}{1}\right)^2}$$

$$= 0.968 \text{ defectives per sample}$$

In fact, there is no need to go through this procedure to obtain the mean and standard deviation. For any binomial distribution we know that:

$$\text{mean} = np$$
$$\text{standard deviation} = \sqrt{npq}$$

We have just been considering the distribution $(\frac{3}{4} + \frac{1}{4})^5$, in which $p = \frac{1}{4}$, $q = \frac{3}{4}$ and $n = 5$. The mean is $np = 5 \times \frac{1}{4} = 1.25$, and the standard deviation is $\sqrt{5 \times \frac{1}{4} \times \frac{3}{4}} = 0.968$.

## The normal approximation to the binomial distribution

Earlier, we considered the normal distribution, and used it to find the proportion in a distribution that was greater than or less than a given value. Now in fact, the normal distribution is another type of probability distribution. Earlier, we asked what *proportion* of electric lamps failed before (say) 1000 hours – but in fact we were also finding the probability that a lamp failed before 1000 hours. Can you see why? Surely, the proportion of lamps failing before 1000 hours can be taken as a measure of the probability that a particular lamp fails before this period. So when we are considering a normal distribution, *we can consider the words proportion and probability to be interchangeable*. The binomial distribution and the normal distribution, then, are two types of probability distributions. However, there is a subtle difference between them – the normal distribution is continuous in so far as the measurements considered can have any value (they are a continuous variable). The binomial distribution is discrete (we are concerned with integers only).

The greatest problem in using the binomial distribution is that it involves awkward arithmetic. Now if the sample size is very large, we can use the normal distribution as an approximation to the binomial distribution, and this will save a considerable amount of arithmetic. Suppose we draw a sample of 1000 packets of soap powder from a batch in which 20% of items are underweight, and we require to know the probability of obtaining more than 220 underweight packets in our sample. The appropriate binomial distribution is $(0.8 + 0.2)^{1000}$, and the probability we require is $P_{(221)} + P_{(222)} + P_{(223)} + \cdots + P_{(1000)}$. Obviously, this is going to be quite some task! Now the appropriate normal distribution to use is the one with the same mean and standard deviation as the binomial distribution. In this case, we have:

$$\bar{x} = np = 1000 \times 0.2 = 200$$
$$\sigma = \sqrt{npq} = \sqrt{1000 \times 0.2 \times 0.8} = 12.65$$

In Fig 14.1 we have drawn part of the histogram of the probability distribution $(0.8 + 0.2)^{1000}$ – it is not drawn to scale. If we want to find the probability of obtaining more than 220 packets, we must add the areas of the rectangles enclosing $221, 222, 223, \ldots 1000$.

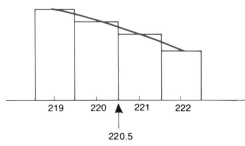

**Fig 14.1**

The line joining the mid-points at the top of each rectangle represents the normal distribution that we are using as an approximation. If we wish to use the normal distribution as an approximation, then the figure clearly shows that we require the proportion to the right of 220.5. This 0.5 adjustment is always used when we use the normal distribution as an approximation to a discrete distribution. So the situation looks like Fig 14.2.

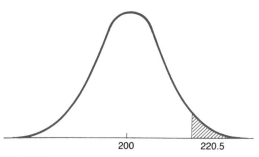

**Fig 14.2**

The Z score for 220.5 is:

$$\frac{220.5 - 200}{12.65} = 1.62$$

and consulting the normal distribution tables we see that the probability we require is $100 - 94.74 = 5.26\%$.

Before we leave the binomial distribution, one very important point must be emphasised (though it is hoped that many of you will have realised it already). A binomial distribution assumes that the events are independent, that is, when we are drawing the sample the outcome of the first item drawn in no way affects the outcome of the second item drawn. This is only true if we are drawing from a large population.

## The Poisson distribution

Suppose we draw samples of two items from a population with 50% of items defective, and samples of 100 from a population with 1% of items defective. In both cases the mean is the same (one defective per sample) – but we could not expect to get the same probability distribution. In the first case, the number of defectives per sample can range between zero and two, but in the second case it can range between zero and 100. But if we draw large samples from a population containing a small proportion of defectives, then a very remarkable thing happens. The probability distributions for such samples tend to become the same *as long as the mean is constant*. To illustrate this feature we consider three cases: drawing samples of 100 from a population containing 1% defectives, samples of 1000 from a 0.1% defective population and samples of 10 000 from a 0.01% defective population. In each case then the mean is the same (one defective per sample):

$$(0.99 + 0.01)^{100} = 0.366 + 0.370 + 0.185 + 0.061 + 0.014$$
$$+ 0.003 + 0.001 + \cdots$$
$$(0.999 + 0.001)^{1000} = 0.368 + 0.368 + 0.184 + 0.061 + 0.015$$
$$+ 0.003 + 0.001 + \cdots$$
$$(0.9999 + 0.0001)^{10000} = 0.368 + 0.368 + 0.184 + 0.061 + 0.015$$
$$+ 0.003 + 0.001 + \cdots$$

It would seem reasonable to suppose that we could discover the probability distribution for such samples as long as we knew the mean number of defectives per sample. A third probability distribution – the *Poisson distribution* – will enable us to do this.

Before we examine the Poisson distribution and discover how it works, let us examine another condition which calls for its use. So far, we have been considering a sample of known and determinable size, and counting the number of times that an event occurred. We could also count the number of times the event did not occur. However, there are many cases where we cannot count the number of times the event did not occur. Suppose, for example, we wished to investigate the incidence of industrial accidents in a particular trade. We could count the number of accidents within (say) one year and use this as an estimate of the mean number of accidents. But we cannot count the number of times the accident did not occur! For problems such as this, we would have to use the Poisson distribution, as we have no way of evaluating $p$, $q$ or $n$.

The Poisson distribution looks like this:

$$e^{-x}\left[1 + x + \frac{x^2}{2!} + \frac{x^3}{3!} + \frac{x^4}{4!} + \cdots\right]$$

Let us look at this distribution and examine certain features of it that you might not have met before. First, notice the numbers 2!, 3!, 4! (pronounce them '2 factorial, 3 factorial', etc.). This is just a convenient way of writing 'multiply the number $n$ by $(n - 1)$, then by $(n - 2)$ and so on until finally we multiply it by one'. So:

$2! = 2 \times 1$
$3! = 3 \times 2 \times 1$
$4! = 4 \times 3 \times 2 \times 1$
$5! = 5 \times 4 \times 3 \times 2 \times 1$

and so on. Second, there is the number $e$. This is a well-known constant and has a value 2.7183 (to four decimal places). In fact, most books of mathematical tables will have a table giving values of $e^{-x}$. Third, the expression contains $x$, which is the mean of the distribution. We obtain probabilities from the expression like this:

$$P_{(0)} = e^{-x} \times 1$$

$$P_{(1)} = e^{-x} \times x$$

$$P_{(2)} = e^{-x} \times \frac{x^2}{2!}$$

$$P_{(3)} = e^{-x} \times \frac{x^3}{3!}$$

and so on. Now as $e$ is a constant, the only variable in the expression is the mean $x$. So provided we know the mean of a distribution we should be able to calculate the probabilities. Let's try it and see.

| EXAMPLE |

In a particular industry, there are on average two fatal accidents per year. We want to find the probability that (a) the industry is free from fatal accidents and (b) the industry has three fatal accidents in a year.

In this case, we have $x = 2$, and the appropriate Poisson distribution is:

$$e^{-2}\left[1 + 2 + \frac{2^2}{2!} + \frac{2^3}{3!} + \cdots\right]$$

$$P_{(0)} = e^{-2} \times 1$$

$$P_{(3)} = e^{-2} \times \frac{2^3}{3!}$$

Consulting a book of mathematical tables, we see that $e^{-2} = 0.1353$. However, in some examinations you are asked to calculate $e^{-x}$ from first principles. To do this, we make use of the fact that:

$$\log e^{-x} = \log 1 - x \log e$$

Using logarithm tables, $\log e = 0.4343$.

so

$$\log e^{-2} = 0 - (2 \times 0.4343)$$
$$= \bar{1}.1314$$

and

$$e^{-2} = 0.1353$$

Returning to our example:

$$P_{(0)} = 0.1353$$

so the probability that the industry is free from fatal accidents is 0.1353, or 13.53%:

$$P_{(3)} = 0.1353 \times \frac{2^3}{3!}$$

$$= 0.1804$$

The probability that the industry has three fatal accidents in a year is 18.04%.

# Conditions necessary for using the Poisson distribution

We can calculate probabilities using the Poisson distribution provided that we know the arithmetic mean of the distribution, and provided that $p$ is small and $n$ is large. A further condition is that the mean must remain constant. However, perhaps the most important condition is that the occurrence of the event must be purely at random.

A good illustration of this is the flow of traffic along a highway. If we choose an isolated point on a highway and count the number of vehicles passing that point, then we would probably find a random flow of vehicles. However, if the point we choose is near a set of traffic lights, then we will not find a random flow – the flow will be 'bunched', i.e. the flow will be heavy when the lights show green. So we should be able to tell whether the occurrence of the event is random or not by using the Poisson distribution.

---

**EXAMPLE**

In fact, this distribution was used for an important piece of statistical investigation during the Second World War. In 1944, London was subjected to bombardment by German V1 rockets (called doodlebugs). This was a pilotless vehicle packed with high explosive and equipped with sufficient fuel to carry it to London. When the fuel ran out, the vehicle would fall out of the sky and explode on impact. The problem was to decide whether the V1 rockets were guided to particular targets with a great degree of precision, or whether they fell on London at random. In other words, were the V1 rockets falling in clusters to a greater degree than could be ascribed to chance? RD Clark divided an area of 144 square kilometres into 576 equal squares, and counted the number of rockets falling in each square.

| No. of bombs per square | 0 | 1 | 2 | 3 | 4 | 5 | Total |
|---|---|---|---|---|---|---|---|
| No. of squares | 229 | 211 | 93 | 35 | 7 | 1 | 576 |

Now if we divide the frequencies by 576, then we can find the empirical probability distribution of the number of bombs per square:

| No. of bombs per square | 0 | 1 | 2 | 3 | 4 | 5 |
|---|---|---|---|---|---|---|
| Probability | 0.3976 | 0.3663 | 0.1615 | 0.0608 | 0.0121 | 0.0017 |

If the bombs were falling at random, then we should be able to predict this probability distribution using the *a priori* Poisson distribution. To do this, we need to know the mean number of bombs per square.

| $x$ | $f$ | $fx$ | $fx^2$ |
|---|---|---|---|
| 0 | 0.3976 | 0.0000 | 0.0000 |
| 1 | 0.3663 | 0.3663 | 0.3663 |
| 2 | 0.1615 | 0.3230 | 0.6460 |
| 3 | 0.0608 | 0.1824 | 0.5472 |
| 4 | 0.0121 | 0.0484 | 0.1936 |
| 5 | 0.0017 | 0.0085 | 0.0425 |
| | 1.0000 | 0.9286 | 1.7956 |

For the moment, ignore the column headed $fx^2$. The mean is:

$$\frac{\Sigma fx}{\Sigma f} = \frac{0.9286}{1} = 0.93 \text{ bombs per square}$$

and the Poisson distribution we require is:

$$e^{-0.93}\left[1 + 0.93 + \frac{(0.93)^2}{2!} + \frac{(0.93)^3}{3!} + \frac{(0.93)^4}{4!} + \frac{(0.93)^5}{5!}\right]$$

Using the tables at the end of this book we find that:

$$e^{-0.93} = 0.3946 \quad \text{so}$$

$$P_{(0)} = 0.3946$$

$$P_{(1)} = 0.3946 \times 0.93 = 0.3670$$

$$P_{(2)} = 0.3946 \times \frac{(0.93)^2}{2!} \quad \text{or using the previous term}$$

$$P_{(2)} = 0.3670 \times \frac{0.93}{2} = 0.1706$$

$$P_{(3)} = 0.3946 \times \frac{(0.93)^3}{3!}$$

$$= 0.1706 \times \frac{0.93}{3} = 0.0529$$

$$P_{(4)} = 0.3946 \times \frac{(0.93)^4}{4!}$$

$$= 0.0529 \times \frac{0.93}{4} = 0.0123$$

$$P_{(5)} = 0.3946 \times \frac{(0.93)^5}{5!}$$

$$= 0.0123 \times \frac{0.93}{5} = 0.0023$$

Let us now write the empirical and Poisson probabilities adjacent to each other so that we can compare them:

| No. of bombs per square | 0 | 1 | 2 | 3 | 4 | 5 |
|---|---|---|---|---|---|---|
| Empirical probabilities | 0.3967 | 0.3663 | 0.1615 | 0.0608 | 0.0121 | 0.0017 |
| Poisson probabilities | 0.3946 | 0.3670 | 0.1706 | 0.0529 | 0.0123 | 0.0023 |

We feel sure that you will agree that there is a fantastically good agreement between the empirical and Poisson probabilities, and we must conclude that the V1 rockets were falling at random over the area.

Before we leave the Poisson distribution, we should note that its mean equals its variance (do you remember that the variance is the square of the standard deviation?). Now as the empirical and Poisson probabilities show such close agreement, we would expect the mean of the empirical probabilities to be approximately equal to the variance. We have already obtained the mean – it is 0.9286. The variance is:

$$\frac{\Sigma fx^2}{\Sigma f} - \left(\frac{\Sigma fx}{\Sigma f}\right)^2$$

$$= \frac{1.7956}{1} - \left(\frac{0.9286}{1}\right)^2$$

$$= 0.9333$$

Again, we find a very close agreement between the mean and variance.

Of the two discrete probability distributions we have examined in this chapter, the Poisson distribution is the most widely used. It has been found to describe 'accidents', traffic flows, and the arrivals into queuing situations, very well indeed. Without doubt, both distributions are very important. However, the probability distribution that is the most important in statistical analysis is the one we examined in an earlier chapter – the normal distribution.

## Using the spreadsheet

The spreadsheet that accompanies this chapter will calculate binomial, Poisson and normal probabilities. This template can be retrieved from the main menu by selecting 'Analytical statistics', then selecting 'Probability'.

Let us first select 'Binomial'. You are prompted to input the sample size, so type 5 and press Enter. You are now prompted to input the probability, so type 0.9 and press Enter. The output will look like this;

|    | A      | B      | C      | D    | E | F | G | H |
|----|--------|--------|--------|------|---|---|---|---|
| 1  |        |        |        |      |   |   |   |   |
| 2  |        | Sample size = |  | 5    |   |   |   |   |
| 3  |        | Probability = |   | 0.9  |   |   |   |   |
| 4  |        |        |        |      |   |   |   |   |
| 5  |        |        | Cum    |      |   |   |   |   |
| 6  | Trials | Prob   | Prob   |      |   |   |   |   |
| 7  | 0      | 0.0000 | 0.0000 |      |   |   |   |   |
| 8  | 1      | 0.0004 | 0.0005 |      |   |   |   |   |
| 9  | 2      | 0.0081 | 0.0086 |      |   |   |   |   |
| 10 | 3      | 0.0729 | 0.0815 |      |   |   |   |   |
| 11 | 4      | 0.3280 | 0.4095 |      |   |   |   |   |
| 12 | 5      | 0.5905 | 1.0000 |      |   |   |   |   |
| 13 |        |        |        |      |   |   |   |   |
| 14 |        |        |        |      |   |   |   |   |

Select 'Graph' to view the graph of the probabilities and cumulative probability.

Now select the Poisson option: you are requested to input the mean, so type 0.93 (the mean number of bombs per square as discussed in this chapter) and press Enter. Your output should look like this:

|    | A      | B      | C      | D    | E | F | G |
|----|--------|--------|--------|------|---|---|---|
| 1  |        |        |        |      |   |   |   |
| 2  |        |        |        |      |   |   |   |
| 3  |        | Mean = |        | 0.9  |   |   |   |
| 4  |        |        |        |      |   |   |   |
| 5  |        |        | Cum    |      |   |   |   |
| 6  | Trials | Prob   | Prob   |      |   |   |   |
| 7  | 0      | 0.3946 | 0.3946 |      |   |   |   |
| 8  | 1      | 0.3669 | 0.7615 |      |   |   |   |
| 9  | 2      | 0.1706 | 0.9321 |      |   |   |   |
| 10 | 3      | 0.0529 | 0.9850 |      |   |   |   |
| 11 | 4      | 0.0123 | 0.9973 |      |   |   |   |
| 12 | 5      | 0.0023 | 0.9996 |      |   |   |   |
| 13 | 6      | 0.0004 | 0.9999 |      |   |   |   |
| 14 |        |        |        |      |   |   |   |
| 15 |        |        |        |      |   |   |   |

In other words, the probabilities are calculated until the cumulative probability exceeds 0.9999. Again, select 'Graph' to view the graph of the probabilities and cumulative probabilities.

## QUESTIONS

**14.1** A chain is made of 10 links, and the strength of each link is equally likely to have any value between 50 and 60 kilos. What is the probability that the chain will break under a load of (a) 51 kilos; (b) 54 kilos?

**14.2** If half the electorate are supposed to vote Tory, and 100 investigators each ask 10 people their voting intentions, how many will report three or less voting Tory in their sample?

**14.3** A large company's records show that they have an average of 6% of their employees off work on any one day. They employ six van drivers. You may assume that the probability of absence from work of a van driver on any one day is the same as that for any other employee.

(i) What is the probability that all their van drivers will be at work on a given day?

(ii) What is the probability that at least five of their van drivers will be at work on a given day?

**14.4** (a) The probability of a missile hitting a warship is $\frac{3}{5}$, and three hits are needed to put the warship out of action. If a salvo of six missiles is fired, show that the probability of putting the ship out of action is:

$$\frac{19 \times 3^3}{5^4}$$

and evaluate to four decimal places.

(b) Razor blades are sold in packets of five. The distribution below shows the number of faulty blades in 100 packets.

| No. of faulty blades | 0 | 1 | 2 | 3 | 4 | 5 |
|---|---|---|---|---|---|---|
| No. of packets | 84 | 10 | 3 | 2 | 1 | 0 |

Calculate the mean number of faulty blades per packet. Assuming the distribution is binomial, estimate the probability that a blade taken at random from a packet will be faulty. (Hint: mean $= np$.) ICAEW

**14.5** It is expected that 10% of the production from a continuous process will be defective and scrapped. Determine the probability that in a sample of ten units chosen at random:

(a) exactly two will be defective; and

(b) at the most two will be defective, using in each case both: (i) the binomial distribution; and (ii) the Poisson approximation to the binomial distribution. (It is given that the value of $e = 2.718$.) CIPFA

**14.6** A buying department is considering an acceptance sampling scheme for incoming lots of a manufactured item that can be classified as either good or defective. The plan calls for a random sample of 50 items from each lot. If there is one or less defectives in the sample the lot is accepted, otherwise it is rejected.

(a) Find (i) from the binomial distribution, the probability of rejecting a lot that is 1% defective, and (ii) accepting a lot that is 10% defective.

(b) Find, using the Poisson distribution, the Poisson approximations to the above probabilities.

Comment on your results. ICAEW

**14.7** 10% of males suffer from a certain disease. Use the normal approximation to the binomial distribution to find the probability that more than 60 men in a randomly selected group of 500 will suffer from the disease.

**14.8** (a) The mean inside diameter of a sample of 400 washers produced by a machine is 8.92 mm and the standard deviation is 0.12 mm. Washers with inside diameters within the range of 8.74 to 9.10 mm are acceptable. Calculate the percentage of defective washers produced by the machine, assuming the diameters are normally distributed.

(b) 5% of the units produced in the manufacturing process turn out to be defective. Find the probability that in a sample of 10 units chosen at random exactly two will be defective using:

(i) the binomial distribution,

(ii) the Poisson approximation to the binomial distribution. CIMA

**14.9** An insurance salesman sells policies to five men, all of identical age and in good health. The probability that a man of this age will be alive in 30 years is $\frac{2}{3}$. Show that the probability of at least 3 men surviving the 30 years is:

$$\frac{2^3 \times 8}{3^4}$$

The probability that an individual suffers a bad reaction from an infection of a given serum is 0.001. Use the Poisson distribution to determine the probability that out of 2000 individuals, more than two will suffer a bad reaction. ICAEW

**14.10**    A manufacturer uses high-speed weighing and packing machines with an accuracy adequate to ensure that only one bag in 20 is likely to be underweight when the machines are set to weigh a given weight. A customer receives a consignment of 60 bags. What are the chances that four or more will be underweight? (It is given that $e = 2.718$.)                CIMA

**14.11**    At a certain time of day, the number of telephone calls coming in to a particular switchboard follows a Poisson distribution with a mean of two calls per minute. Calculate the probability of more than four calls in a minute.

**14.12**    The number of failures per week, of a certain type of machine, has been found to follow a Poisson distribution with mean 0.5. What is the probability that a given machine has three or more failures in a given week?

A firm owns five of these machines. What is the distribution of the total number of failures per week?

**14.13**    The demand for a component is two per month, and forms a Poisson distribution. Stock is made up at the beginning of each month. What should be the stock level at the beginning of each month so that the probability of a stockout is less than 5%? $(e^{-2} = 0.1353.)$           ICAEW

**14.14**    In a particular industry, one worker in 500 is fatally injured per year. What is the probability that a firm in the industry has not more than one fatal accident in a given year, given that the firm has a labour force of 300 men?

**14.15**    Suppose samples of 200 are drawn from a population with 0.5% of items defective. Use the Poisson distribution to find the probability distribution for the number of defectives per sample. What percentage of samples contains a greater number of defectives than the mean plus $3 \times$ standard deviation?

**14.16**    

| Number of defectives per sample | 0 | 1 | 2 | 3 | 4 | 5 |
|---|---|---|---|---|---|---|
| Number of samples | 20 | 30 | 25 | 15 | 5 | 5 |

Fit a Poisson distribution to this data.

**14.17**    For mean values of 10 or more the Poisson distribution can be approximated by the normal distribution with the same mean and variance. The number of red blood cells per unit volume for a particular animal has the Poisson distribution with mean 15. Find the probability that the number of red cells in a given unit volume exceeds 20.

**14.18** A complex television component has 1000 joints soldered by a machine which is known to produce, on average, one defective joint in 40. The components are examined, and faulty soldering corrected by hand. If components requiring more than 35 corrections are discarded, what proportion of the components will be thrown away? CIMA

**14.19** In a certain company after long years of experience the following information is known about 'debtor' accounts. Accounts have a mean value of £2500 and a standard deviation of £300. With regard to collection on time, 5% of the accounts can be classified as 'doubtful'. Stating carefully any assumptions you might make, answer the following questions.

(i) If an account is randomly chosen, what is the probability that its value will be between £2600 and £2850?

(ii) If five accounts are randomly chosen, what is the probability that there would be exactly two doubtful accounts?

(iii) One account is randomly chosen and it is learnt that its value is less than a certain amount with a 0.12 probability. What is that specific amount?

BA(Business Studies)

**14.20** Among the products of a certain lumber company are beadings of mean length 80 cm and standard deviation 2 cm. The production process is estimated to produce 10% 'misshaped' beadings. It is specified also that the average number of knots per 100 cm of beading is 1.5. Stating carefully any assumptions you might make, answer the following questions:

(i) If one beading is chosen, what is the chance that its length is between 83 cm and 85 cm?

(ii) If a sample of five beadings are selected, what is the probability that there are three misshapes?

(iii) What is the probability that one beading of mean length will contain two or less knots?

BA(Business Studies)

# 15 Sample design

You will probably be aware that most statistical information is obtained, not by examining the whole population, but by obtaining a sample and arguing that the characteristics of the sample are the same as those of the population as a whole. The sample result, obviously, will differ from that we obtain by taking a complete census, and later chapters will be concerned with the reliability of the sample results. Our objective here is not to discuss the results of a sample survey, but to explain to you how to select a sample which is truly representative of the population. You would not, for example, expect to obtain a reliable estimate of the heights of men in the United Kingdom if you chose your sample only from men in the Guards' regiments; you could not possibly estimate the number of miles people travel by taxi each week if your sample consisted only of taxi-drivers.

Such statements as this are, we think, obvious, but they only tell us how not to select a sample; they give no information about how we should select one. So let us proceed step by step. The basic principle underlying any selection of a sample is that it should be a *random* selection – that is, that every single unit within the population should have an equal chance (or the same probability) of being chosen as a member of the sample. This is, of course, very difficult to achieve.

Consider the simple case of drawing a raffle ticket to select the winners of five prizes. Why do you think that after each ticket is drawn the drum containing them is turned? It is, as you will know, to mix up the tickets once again. But would it make any difference if the drum were not turned? In our opinion, it would make a great deal of difference. The person drawing the ticket can easily introduce *bias* into the selection. Consider carefully how you yourself would select the winning tickets. Our observation shows that few people will choose tickets from the top of the drum. They tend rather to plunge into the pile of tickets and select one from near the bottom. Can you see that this sort of behaviour means that tickets near the top of the pile do not have an equal chance of selection with those nearer the bottom? The drum is turned after each ticket is selected in order to offset this type of bias. We cannot change human behaviour, but we can change the position of the tickets so as to give each one an equal chance of selection.

To return to sampling proper, in selecting a sample to determine the average number of miles travelled by taxi each week, the person who never takes a taxi must have just as much chance of being selected as have those who use taxis regularly – but no greater chance. In order to ensure this, statisticians have devised various methods of selection which, as far as possible, eliminate bias.

If we are able to list the population in some sort of order and number them, we could determine the members of our sample by drawing numbers at random, drawing sufficient numbers to include, say, 5% of the total population. Better still, we could use a table of *random numbers* to determine who should be included in our sample. This table is so constructed that if you select any point at which to start and move through the table consistently in one direction, horizontally, vertically or diagonally, the digits you read off are randomly chosen and every number has the same probability of being selected. Suppose that the total population consisted of 1000 units. These can be numbered from 0 to 999 and you could select those to be included in the sample by reading off digits from the table of random numbers in groups of three. If, for example, the first three digits were 294, we would select the unit numbered 294 as a part of our sample. Similarly if the first three digits were 004, we would select the unit numbered four.

If, on the other hand, we were examining industrial output for faulty units, we could use a form of pseudo-random sampling, by examining and checking the unit coming off the production line at predetermined time intervals. Alternatively, we could examine, say, five units, chosen at random from every carton of output. One way or another, however, we must ensure that our selection of the sample is random.

## The sampling frame

Before we can draw a truly random sample we must be able to define the total population. The Electoral Register contains the names of all those entitled to vote in the United Kingdom; enrolment forms will list the names of all students in your college; business files will contain all the orders placed in a given financial year. Such lists, files or card indexes form what is known as a *sampling frame*. They will give basic details about every member of the population you are concerned with. Now, before drawing a sample, you must carefully examine the sampling frame to ensure that it is adequate for your purpose. If it is deficient in that a number of units are not included, those units have no chance of being selected and your sample cannot be truly random. Let us illustrate such deficiencies by looking at a very real problem.

It is the habit in Britain for public opinion polls to try to predict the results of government elections by interviewing a relatively small number of voters. The sampling frame for such a survey is the Electoral Roll, a list of all those eligible to vote who lived in the area last November. The list is produced in March each year, so when it is published it is already four months out of date. By the following February then, just before a new list is published, it is 16 months out of date. Since about 0.5% of the population move into and out of the district each month (according to a Social Survey report) this would mean that about 8% of those who are on the Roll no longer live in the area, while about 8% of those living in the area are not on the Roll. Add to this the fact that about 4% of those who should be on the register are omitted because they do not return the necessary forms, and we find that the Electoral Roll is only about 88% accurate – not a good situation for a sampling frame. It is for this reason that investigators interview only those who actually go to the polling booth, or say that they intend to do so.

## Systematic sampling

In practice true random sampling is not possible unless there is a good sampling frame and the population is fairly small. So, for most practical work, investigators resort to methods of selection which are *quasi-random*, or not truly random. One of the most popular is to choose as a member of the sample every $n$th item on a list, the first sample unit being selected by some random method. If, for example, we wanted a sample consisting of $2\frac{1}{2}$% of the population we would firstly select at random the first unit, say the 29th invoice in a file, and then every 40th invoice after that – the 69th, 109th and so on. Can you see why this type of sampling is not truly random? While the first item is chosen by random methods, every other item is then preselected. Nevertheless, this method of selection (called *systematic sampling*) approximates to random sampling sufficiently well to justify its widespread use.

Once again we need a reasonably good sampling frame, but, in our opinion, having accepted that the sample is not truly random, it need not be 100% accurate. However, if we are to use systematic sampling, we must ensure that there are no 'cyclical' patterns in the sampling frame that match our choice of items. If, for example, we are taking a survey on a housing estate to assess the opinion of the residents about the 'open plan' layout, and every tenth house is a corner house, then a 10% systematic sample either always, or never, includes a corner house. Such a pattern as this could substantially affect the results we get.

Now, systematic sampling is useful so long as the population is homogeneous. It is suitable, for example, if accountants are selecting a sample of invoices to check for errors; or if the police are taking a sample of motorists passing a certain point to check that they have a valid driving licence. But you will appreciate that in much statistical work the population is heterogeneous. This is especially true if we are investigating opinions, because in many cases a person's opinions are formed by, or result from, the social class to which he belongs. If we are asking the simple question, 'Do you think that people earning over £30 000 a year pay too much in taxes?' the answer we get will often depend on the income of the person being questioned. Inevitably the rich will answer 'yes', while the poor are more likely to say 'no'.

## Stratified sampling

When the response we get to our questions is likely to depend in this way on the social group to which the person being questioned belongs, we will get far better results if we adopt *stratified sampling*. If we are investigating the social evils of traffic on the roads, it is quite possible that systematic sampling would result in a sample which contained only those who owned cars. The opinions of those who do not own cars would not be represented, and to that extent the sample results will be biased. Stratified sampling has been designed to ensure that all important views are represented in the sample. In this type of sample each social group is represented in the sample in proportion to the size of that group in the population as a whole.

Let us take a simple example to show how stratified samples are constructed. Suppose we are investigating opinions on education of those who are still at school or college. We may decide that these opinions will depend on whether the student is at university, state school, or private school. We know that 20% of students are at university, 10% at private school and 70% at a state school. If we are selecting a sample of 2000 students, our first step is to say that 20% of the sample, or 400 students, must be university students, 200 (10%) from private schools, and 1400 (70%) from state schools. We may now additionally decide that men and women have markedly different opinions, so we will now divide our three groups (or strata) into two sub-groups. If, for example, we know that 15% of university students are women, we would include 60 women among our sample of 400 university students. Each of these sub-groups can be further subdivided, perhaps in relation to age or to parents' social class.

It does not matter how far groups are subdivided, provided that we are stratifying according to a characteristic which is relevant to the survey. If, for example, we are investigating television viewing habits there is little point in stratifying the sample according to political affiliations. It is probably completely irrelevant. On the other hand, our viewing habits might well be affected by the size of our family, or whether we live in a rural or urban area and we would stratify according to these criteria.

Once we have decided on the number of people in each stratum of our sample, the persons to be included must, of course, now be chosen by some random method.

Now, one peculiarity can arise with this type of sampling. If our strata are many, it may be that an important sub-group of the population is entitled to be represented by only one or two members. It may be that we feel that we cannot obtain an adequate representation of the opinion of this group if we question one person only, and, if so, we should include more representatives of the group, say four or five. While this may seem reasonable, it means, of course, that members of this group have a far higher probability of being chosen as a part of the sample than have people in other strata. This type of sampling is known as sampling with a *variable sampling fraction*, and in assessing our final results we must make allowance for the difference in the representation of such strata.

In many surveys, when samples are drawn from a markedly heterogeneous population the sampling fraction is variable rather than uniform. This principle finds its most important application in the evaluation of stock value by sampling methods. We can afford to take a very small sample of items costing only a few pence, since, if our sample is inaccurate it will make little difference to the total value of stock. But if the items of stock cost a great deal, even a small error may significantly affect our total stock valuation. Thus, in determining total stock value from a sample valuation of stock, accountants almost invariably ensure that high-value items have a greater probability of being selected than do low-value items.

Once again, with stratified sampling, we need a sampling frame which will give us a great deal of information about the social structure. Fortunately nowadays governments undertake so many social surveys and publish so many statistics that there is little difficulty in obtaining the necessary information. Hence stratified sampling is becoming increasingly popular whenever the objective is to assess people's attitudes or opinions.

## Multi-stage sampling

One of the problems of simple random sampling is that if the sample selected is widely scattered over the country the interviewer may spend more time in travelling than he does in actually interviewing. Often, then, the cost of taking such a sample can be prohibitive. This is especially true in countries in which urbanisation has not yet developed. You can imagine the problems involved if you were to take a sample of people scattered all over central Canada, Malaysia or West Africa. Interviewers might have to spend weeks in travelling.

It is to overcome this problem that multi-stage sampling has been developed. Rather than spending time in travelling to interview 2000 people scattered all over Malaysia, is it not more convenient to interview say 100 people in each of 20 selected areas? Provided that we can ensure that the sample ultimately selected is representative, a great deal of time and expense can be saved.

In many ways the selection of a multi-stage sample is similar to the selection of a stratified sample, but we select primary groups and sub-groups geographically rather than on the basis of social characteristics. Typically, the first stage is to break down the area under survey into a number of standard regions. These may be areas such as the English county, the Canadian province or any other easily defined administrative area. The sample is then divided among these regions according to their population. The second stage is to select at random a small number of districts, say towns and villages, within the primary region. Once again it is necessary to allocate to each of these districts a number of interviews proportional to its population. Almost certainly at this stage, an element of stratification must appear if the sample is to be representative. Let us suppose that we are selecting six towns at random within each region. If $\frac{1}{3}$ of the population live in cities of over 200 000 people, a further $\frac{1}{3}$ in towns with a population of from 20 000 to 200 000 and the remainder in small towns and villages of under 20 000 inhabitants, it would be desirable to select two areas of each type.

Finally, having selected our towns and villages within each region, the sample in each town or village is chosen by some random method. Again, it may be felt to be desirable to choose a stratified sample within each town. How far this stratification is carried depends, of course, on the purpose of the survey and the homogeneity of the population. If we are examining housing conditions, and the type of housing ranges from one-roomed flats to 25-roomed mansions, some degree of stratification will be necessary. But if all the housing in the area is of an essentially similar type, as it may be in a small village, stratification is probably not necessary.

Every type of sampling discussed so far depends on the existence of a sampling frame. If no such frame exists, random sampling is not possible, and to undertake a census to derive a sampling frame is a very expensive process indeed. Unfortunately, in most underdeveloped countries, satisfactory sampling frames do not yet exist. Sometimes too, the very cost of conducting a survey may make it necessary to use a different type of sampling. To overcome these problems statisticians have designed two further sampling methods – *cluster sampling* and *quota sampling*.

## Cluster sampling

Cluster sampling was devised in the United States of America to try to overcome the problems of cost and the lack of a satisfactory sampling frame. Instead of selecting a random sample scattered over a wide area, it is a few geographical areas that are selected at random and every single household in each area is interviewed. Obviously the areas chosen must be relatively small. It is not possible to interview every household in cities like London and Singapore. The typical area selected might be three or four streets in a town, or perhaps an apartment block. The great advantage of this type of sampling is the saving in time and cost. Many interviews can take place within a short space of time with a minimum of travelling. Moreover it does not require any knowledge of the population before the survey is undertaken, i.e. no sampling frame is necessary.

On the other hand, there is a basic problem with this type of sample. Whilst the population is heterogeneous, those who live in a small area or the same block of flats will tend to be homogeneous. They will tend to have the same opinions, the same characteristics, the same life style. Naturally one cannot be certain of this, but it seems to be highly probable, and since the statistician is selecting only a few such areas there is a great danger that the sample will be biassed. One way of trying to offset this tendency to bias is to increase the number of clusters in the hope that you will then include in your sample every important strata, but every increase in the number of clusters raises the cost of the survey. There comes a time when you will have to weigh the risk of selecting a biassed sample against the cost of avoiding the danger of bias. It is, however, a useful type of sample when you have no sampling frame, or when the cost of taking a random sample is too high.

## Quota sampling

There can be few people who have not been stopped in the street by an interviewer holding a questionnaire, or who at least know someone who has been so stopped. And the immediate reaction seems to be, 'why did they choose me?'

The essence of this type of sample is that it is not preselected, but is chosen by the interviewer on the spot. He, or more usually she, is given a certain number (a quota) of questionnaires which it is her job to have completed during the course of the week, or month. She has a free choice of whom she asks to answer the questions. This choice, naturally, is subject to some general restrictions. One can imagine a young male interviewer stopping only girls at about his own age whom he thought to be pretty. Free choice does not extend as far as this. The interviewer is told that the completed quota of questionnaires must include a certain number of males and of females; a certain number from specified age groups such as, under 18, 18 to 40, 40 to 65. Controls such as this are easy to implement, but often the quota has to be further subdivided by social class or occupation. This can make quota sampling very difficult as there is no real definition of what constitutes, say, the upper middle class, and certainly you can seldom tell a person's social class by looking at him. Such a requirement necessitates the interviewer being given detailed definitions and descriptions of what the survey body means by each term it uses. Subject, however, to controls such as this, the sample is chosen by the interviewer from people who pass in the street.

Now, obviously, such a technique of sampling can be open to a great deal of abuse and bias. When it was first introduced, many cases were reported of interviewers sitting at home filling in their own questionnaires without ever interviewing anyone. Of course this was soon remedied by the questionnaire asking for names and addresses, and the survey body makes a spot check to ensure that such people had actually been interviewed. Deliberate fraud of this nature is very rare now.

Much more important is the bias to which the quota survey may be subject. If the interviewer does not start work until, say, 10.00 a.m., the majority of people she can stop must of necessity be housewives or the unemployed; if she starts at, say 9.00 a.m., the vast majority will be clerical or managerial workers; to start even earlier means that she will probably meet largely manual workers. Thus, the interviewer must be prepared to spread her work throughout the day. It is little use trying to have all the questionnaires completed before the morning coffee-break.

A further source of bias is that the people you meet in the street are either going somewhere or doing something; they resent being interrupted and their answers may be hurried and slapdash, given without serious thought. These problems necessitate further controls and advice being given to the interviewer. She may be told at what times to conduct the interviews or even where to conduct them. We would not wish to imply that interviewers are rascals or rogues – far from it – but we must point out that the success of such a survey depends very much on their following their instructions to the letter.

Since the quota sample has these weaknesses, why is it becoming increasingly common? Well, for one thing, it is cheap. It eliminates repeated calls to interview a person who may not be in at home on the first two or three occasions. In fact, it is estimated that each interview in a quota sample costs only about half as much as each interview in a random sample. Then, too, we have in every survey a number of people who do not respond. In a quota sample it does not matter. They are ignored and we pass straight on to the next person with no loss of time and no cost. In other types of sample, a substitute has to be found for each person who does not respond.

It might, in fact, be argued that this itself introduces bias into the sample. It may be that the man who is prepared to fill in questionnaires is some kind of extrovert, and we may be getting the views of only one type of individual.

Nevertheless, given the existence of the controls and checks we have mentioned, all the evidence points to the fact that in skilled hands quota sampling gives reasonably satisfactory results. Statisticans generally accept that it is not a substitute for random sampling statistically, but it is so quick and so cheap a method of carrying out surveys that it is not likely to be replaced for a very long time.

Finally, we must stress that the effectiveness of any sample survey, whatever the method of sampling used, depends to a very large extent on the questions which are asked. If they are ambiguous, the answers will be; if the interviewer puts the question with a bias, our results will be biassed. No survey result can be better than the questionnaire on which it is based, and the design of questionnaires is something we must now take up in the next chapter.

## QUESTIONS

The questions to Chapter 15 can be found with those to Chapter 16.

# 16 Planning a sample survey

During every general election newspapers are full of public opinion polls, all of which claim to tell us which way the electors are going to cast their votes. So dogmatic are some of the statements they make that one sometimes wonders if it is really necessary for us to go to the polling booth at all! Then on voting day, most of those forecasters who were wrong rapidly disappear, leaving the field to those few who have been reasonably successful. Yet those who have failed need not be ashamed. No statistician will ever dare hope that his sample results will ever be 100% accurate, and hours of time are devoted to every sample survey merely to reduce the error to the irreducible minimum. Before we can explain how we do try to avoid errors and bias in our results, we must first look at the possible ways in which the sampling error may arise.

You will have appreciated already that one of the most important factors in any sample survey is the questionnaire – the form which poses the questions which give us the information we want. It is a highly flexible instrument. It can be filled in by the interviewer after a series of oral questions; it can be completed by the person being interviewed in the privacy of his own home; it can be completed on the doorstep; or by telephone; or it can be sent by mail. But in spite of this tremendous flexibility, it lends itself readily to bias and error.

## Potential sources of error

Even before an interview takes place, error may have crept into the survey design. In constructing our questionnaire we may have failed to ask questions which ultimately turn out to be relevant. The field of sampling is littered by experienced researchers who cry 'if only I had asked that question!'

Once we pose our questions sources of error become far more numerous. Questions we ask may be misleading or not easily understood; they may mean different things to different people. A question on wages earned last week will be understood by some people to mean gross wages; by others to mean net wages; some will include overtime and bonus payments; others will merely state the basic wage; workers paid monthly may merely divide the monthly wage by four, ignoring the fact that in any month apart from

February, there are more than four weeks, and that he really ought to divide his annual salary by 52.

Then too there may arise a great deal of bias from the fact that the interviewee does not like to admit to things which he feels may put him in a bad light. If we were to ask, 'How often do you take a shower?', how many people do you think would have the courage to say 'Seldom', or 'Never'? We have a suspicion that the reaction would be something like this: 'Most people shower at least once a day or more. If I admit to less than this I am classifying myself as a dirty person. The investigator will never know anyway, so I will say once or twice a day'. Here, the response is adjusted to present a particular image which the respondent feels is necessary for his own self-esteem.

In the very nature of things, many questions posed in a survey must be personal or intimate questions. Some women never seem to pass the age of 39; a man who is a junior clerk in a professional office may well give his occupation as an accountant or lawyer; an unmarried mother may be reluctant to admit that she has children; a man who has not told his wife how much he earns may not be willing to state his true salary. Every one of us has something to hide – something we may not be willing to admit publicly.

Thus, however careful we are, it is not likely that our questionnaire will give us a completely true picture of our sample, and it is always as well to regard the results of a sample survey as, at best, an approximation to reality. Nevertheless, an understanding of the possible sources of error is the first step in reducing the error that may arise in a survey.

## Stages in a sample survey

Although surveys are designed for an infinite variety of purposes, the basic pattern is the same in every case. The preparation of a sample survey can be divided into the following stages:

- Defining objectives;
- Deciding how the information is to be obtained;
- Preparing the questionnaire;
- Selecting the sample;
- Undertaking a pilot survey;
- Briefing the interviewers.

Each of these stages will be discussed in the next sections. The quality of the data we derive depends particularly on three of the stages we will outline. The first is the selection of the sample, since, if this is not representative of the population, no reliable conclusions can be drawn. Second, as we have seen, the drafting of the questions to be asked demands very careful thought. Third, there is the all-important task of interviewing, since more errors will creep in at this stage than at any other. Most of our discussion in this chapter will centre around these three points.

## Defining objectives

It should be merely common sense to ask right at the beginning what we are trying to find out and how the survey can help us. Yet, all too often, this trite and obvious point is ignored, and as a result the questionnaire deviates from its objectives, asking questions which are irrelevant to the survey, and failing to ask questions which are essential. It is often useful initially to make a study of any already published statistics to see if it will simplify the survey (or perhaps make it unnecessary). Above all, a study of secondary data will help you to clarify your mind as to the type of information which will or will not be useful to you. Beyond this, the best advice we can give you is to bear in mind constantly *why* you are undertaking the survey. Ask yourself constantly in what way any given piece of information is going to help you to meet your survey objectives. You may still fail to get all the information which, with hindsight, is necessary; but you will be sure that what you do get is relevant.

## Deciding how the information is to be obtained

Here you have a choice of two main methods – the postal enquiry, and the survey using personal interviews.

**The postal enquiry**

The great advantage of the *postal enquiry* is the relatively low cost. It can be sent to a very large number of people relatively cheaply, and so the sample size can be increased considerably without overspending. Additionally, there is no risk of bias or mistakes which may occur if the interviewer influences the respondent to give particular answers.

But when you get down to it, these apparent advantages are often fictitious. The great weakness of the postal enquiry is that very few people bother to complete and return the questionnaire. On average a response rate of 20% of questionnaires returned without reminders is considered satisfactory, while 40% is exceptionally good. Now, missing data due to non-response can be a major source of error. Unfortunately we cannot ignore those who do not reply and assume that they have the same characteristics as those who do reply. It is very likely that a group who do not bother to return the questionnaire will differ in some important way from those who do take the time and trouble to fill it in. Almost inevitably a postal survey will necessitate sending several reminders, and even then a very high response rate is seldom achieved. Thus, in the final analysis, the cost per completed questionnaire can be quite high.

Often, the response rate can be increased substantially by writing a letter to members of the sample explaining the importance of the survey, what it is hoped may result from it, and requesting their co-operation. Sometimes the promise of a copy of the results might do the trick, especially in business surveys, while, in the case of very important enquiries, it may be necessary to offer a small gift, or even a nominal cash payment. But whatever we do, we are not likely to get a response rate as high as we would like.

WA Hendricks, in his book *The Mathematical Theory of Sampling*, suggests that it is legitimate to make adjustments to the results of a postal survey to allow for missing data. He quotes a survey undertaken to discover the average number of fruit trees on a particular type of farm. The original questionnaire was mailed, and followed up by two reminders to those who had not yet replied. The response at each stage was noted, and the average number of trees per farm was calculated at each stage. The results were as follows:

| No. of mailings | Response (%) | Avge. no. of trees per farm |
|---|---|---|
| 1 | 13 | 456 |
| 1 + 2 | 26 | 408 |
| 1 + 2 + 3 | 39.4 | 385 |

It is obvious that those who replied late were those who had the fewer numbers of trees, and it could be argued that those who had not replied at all would have fewer trees still on their farms. One way of dealing with this data would be to construct a fully logarithmic graph, showing the relationship between the response rate and the average number of trees per farm. We could then project the trend shown and estimate the average number of trees for a 100% response rate. If we convert all our figures into logarithms, we get the following table:

| *Logarithm of* | |
|---|---|
| *Response rate* | *Avge. no. of trees* |
| 1.1139 | 2.6590 |
| 1.4150 | 2.6107 |
| 1.5995 | 2.5855 |

These figures can now be graphed and the trend shown projected (*see* Fig 16.1).

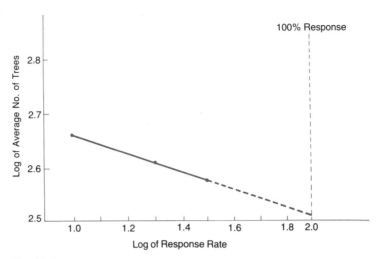

**Fig 16.1**

On our diagram the log of the estimated number of fruit trees for a response rate of 100% (log 2.0000) is 2.525, which converts to an estimated average number of fruit trees per farm of 335. In fact the true value was known to be 329. Our estimate is not completely accurate (in fact it is almost 2% in error), but it is still very, very much better than our sample result with a response rate of only 39.4%. The assumption we made here was, in fact, that those who did not respond were similar to those who replied late, and in many surveys replies are divided into groups according to the date of reply in an effort to discover the main characteristics of non-respondents.

There is little doubt, however, that non-response is a major source of weakness of the postal survey, and the best strategy of all is to arouse and maintain interest in the survey so as to secure as high an initial response as possible. The experience of the British Social Survey points to the fact that response rates of 80% *can* be achieved, if the respondent's co-operation is secured, if the idea can be put over that the survey is of importance to him personally, and if the questionnaire is short and simple. But in spite of their limited success, the hard fact of the matter is that a self-selecting group who decide to return the questionnaire is not representative of the population as a whole. The only way in which non-response can be completely overcome is to make the return of the forms compulsory, and even then there is no guarantee that they are filled in accurately. Since only the government can exercise compulsion, they are the main users of this type of survey.

**The personal interview**

Perhaps the most widely used method of conducting the sample survey is the *personal interview*. Here a third party, the interviewer, acts as a communications link between the investigator and the members of the sample. He, or she, is responsible for contacting the respondent, for asking questions and for recording the responses. So important is the interviewer that it can well be argued that the representativeness of the sample depends on their ability to persuade their subject to co-operate in filling in the questionnaire, and the accuracy of the sample depends on their skill in extracting and recording information.

Unfortunately, it is all too easy for the interviewer to introduce bias. His tone of voice, even facial expression, and any tendency for him to indicate his own views may all lead to the interviewee expressing opinions which are those of the interviewer and not his own. There are times when, however simply a question is worded, it will be misunderstood and will have to be 'interpreted' by the interviewer. In this interpretation the precise meaning that was intended may well be lost. Then too, faced with a hesitant or tongue-tied member of the public, even the skilled interviewer may prompt, or even put answers into her mouth. Shortly before writing this, one of your authors was stopped, in a quota sample, and asked if he had recently seen a television advertisement for a particular brand of after-shave lotion. Since he was preoccupied thinking about this chapter he hesitated to collect his thoughts; to his horror, before he could speak, the young interviewer said, 'Perhaps you haven't seen it,' and underlined that phrase on the questionnaire. Can you see what went wrong? Busy people, stopped on their way to work, need a few minutes to collect their thoughts before questions are put; the interviewer suggested the response instead of waiting; and worst of all, she then accepted her own suggestion. In fact, your author not only *has* seen the advertisement in question, but actually uses that brand of after-shave lotion. We hate to think of the bias that will appear in that particular survey and can only hope that it was a practice survey carried out by students of statistics.

In spite of these problems, the personal interview does have a large number of advantages over the postal questionnaire.

- Non-response is minimised. In fact a response rate as high as 80% is not at all unusual. Inevitably, there will be some non-response as a few people may be out every single time the interviewer calls; they may be on holiday, or have left the district, or merely refuse to answer. We would distrust any interviewer who claimed to have a 100% response, but would not dispute a claim of 90% from a trained investigator.

- More questions (and more complicated ones) can be asked in an interview than can be asked in a postal questionnaire.

- Questions can be asked of people who could not complete a written questionnaire – the very young, the very old, or the illiterates.

- Often mere visual observation will enable the interviewer to check whether the answers are likely to be correct.

- In a personal interview, the order in which the questions are put is under control, whereas in a postal survey there is no control over the order in which they are answered. As we will see later, this can be a crucial factor in eliminating bias.

Nevertheless, some surprising things occur. Just after the Second World War, in a survey to ascertain how many people would claim campaign medals, it was found that the age of the female interviewer affected the response of the ex-servicemen. The younger, and perhaps prettier, the interviewer was, the greater was the percentage of her interviewees who denied that they would claim their medals.

Obviously training can do a great deal to eliminate interviewer bias. But, however well your team may be trained, mistakes will still occur. It is not the obvious mistakes that matter. When we edit the schedules we will soon pick up the fact that John William Smith is a man, and not a woman as marked on his form. It is the small mistakes which we cannot detect which are important. It is very easy to misunderstand an answer, especially if it cannot be answered by a simple 'yes' or 'no'. It is just as easy to classify an answer wrongly, underlining *Never* for example, instead of *Infrequently*. The only way in which mistakes of this nature can be detected is if a sub-sample of an interviewer's respondents are interviewed a second time by the most highly skilled interviewers available. In fact, many bodies do this to check the potential accuracy of the completed questionnaires as a matter of course. It is, however, expensive, and in the long run the best solution may well be to give each interviewer as detailed instructions as are possible, and as much training and experience as can be afforded. Some investigators argue that tests have shown that on a normal sample survey, the trained interviewer is no more accurate than the amateur; but there is little doubt that in the modern 'in-depth' surveys the trained interviewer can elicit responses that the amateur can never hope to elicit.

## Preparing the questionnaire

We have stressed repeatedly that a badly designed questionnaire may ruin an otherwise well-planned survey. Essentially, questions and answers are the means of communication between the investigator and his subject. If you think about it, in this process there are five possible sources of error for every question.

- The question itself may not be phrased to enquire about what the investigator wishes to know.

- The question may not be heard correctly.

- What is heard may be misunderstood.

- The reply may be misheard by the interviewer.

- The reply may be misunderstood by the interviewer.

Is it not obvious that what we need are short, unambiguous questions which allow for a limited number of unambiguous replies? Unfortunately, this is not always possible. If we desire questions which allow the simple answer 'yes' or 'no', there can be no misunderstanding of the answer, even if the question itself is ambiguous. But there is always the need for the third alternative answer, 'Don't know', and such questions are difficult to devise.

Suppose we asked the simple question, 'Do you think that garages should give vouchers and free gifts with sales of petrol?' Let us consider just how 'simple' this question is. Apart from the obvious replies, 'yes', 'no', and 'I don't know', some people may think that it depends on the number of vouchers given with each gallon or on the nature of the free gift. Others may wish to say 'yes' to gifts and 'no' to vouchers or vice versa. Are we to assume in our answer that if the garages cease to give gifts or vouchers that the price of petrol will be reduced, or will it remain the same? So you see, the question is not so simple, and considerable skill is called for in constructing questions to which the answer is a categorical 'yes' or 'no'. Usually this kind of question is confined to purely factual matters such as, 'Do you own a car?'

The second type of question is what we have come to know as a multiple-choice question. Here the respondent is asked a question such as, 'Why did you take your holiday in Spain last year?', and the question is followed by a number of possible reasons, one of which is to be underlined. The problem with this type of question is that the list of reasons must be limited, and of necessity we must conclude with a category 'other reasons', leaving the respondent to reply as he wishes. Once again we have opened the door to ambiguity. A further problem is the implication in such a question that only one of the reasons given is important. Two or three, or perhaps all, the reasons may be equally important, or perhaps none are of importance. Here the order of the alternatives can be of importance. Experiments in varying their order show that there is a marked tendency to choose alternatives at the top and bottom of the list, ignoring those in the middle.

The final type of question is open-ended, leaving the reply entirely to the respondent: 'Why do you drink this particular brand of beer?' This is a very useful kind of question to obtain qualitative information, but it is the most open of all to ambiguity. If it is summarised by the interviewer what we are recording is what the interviewer thought the respondent meant. If the reply is quoted in full it may be rambling, incoherent and open to many interpretations, and this is just as dangerous.

In order to help us get over this problem of communicating with our sample, there are a number of rules we must follow when we are constructing the questions to ask. The problem is to devise questions which everyone understands, which mean the same thing to everyone, and which ask what they are meant to ask.

1   *Keep the questions short.* Not only is a short question easier to understand, but also there is nothing more confusing to a person being interviewed than to forget the beginning of a question before the end is reached. The ideal type of question from this point of view is the extremely simple, 'What is your age?' As a general rule it is better to break down a more complicated question into two or three shorter ones. Consider the following question which you could be asked if you were filling in a car accident report form for an insurance company. 'If you were driving your own car give the reference number of your insurance policy; if not, state the owner's name, whether his insurance cover is comprehensive or third party only, and give the name of his insurance company.'

Such an example is of course grossly exaggerated. No one but an amateur (or perhaps a civil servant) would produce such a question, and in practice it would appear in this form:

(i)   (a)   Were you driving your own car?     Yes/No
      (b)   What is the number of your insurance policy?   7K/..........

(ii)   If your answer to question (i)(a) is NO:

      (a)   Give the name of the owner.     Mr/Mrs/Miss
      (b)   What type of insurance cover does he/she have?
                                      Comprehensive/Third Party
      (c)   What is the name of his/her insurance company?     ..........

You will see that each of these short questions concentrates on one thing at a time and it is not likely to confuse the person filling in the form.

2   *Use simple language.* In any sample there is likely to be a very wide variety of ability in the use of language, and we must make sure that everyone understands what we mean. It is not a question of underrating the intelligence of the members of the sample but of trying to ensure that the interviewer does not have to explain the question in his own words which may introduce some bias into the answer. In any case we feel it is better to say, 'Are you telling a lie?', rather than, 'Are you perpetrating a terminological inexactitude?' Simplicity has been the keynote of every great speech in history, from Julius Caesar's 'I came, I saw, I conquered', to Winston Churchill's great wartime speeches. They were great because everyone understood them. Follow the same policy in drafting your own questions.

3 *Avoid questions which lead to a particular answer.* It is far better to ask, 'What do you consider to be the best brand of toothpaste?', than to ask 'Do you consider White Shine to be the best brand of toothpaste?' The mere mention of a name is often enough to cause a particular response. Equally we must try to avoid emotive words. Socialist and Tory arouse more passion than do Conservative and Labour. Try at all costs to avoid implying in your question that you would like a particular answer.

4 *Make sure that the respondent has the information.* It is of little use asking people in Central Africa what type of central heating they prefer. Even if the question is a simple one, the informant may not know the answer. The respondent may have forgotten when he last bought chocolates. Often he has to be led up to such things step by step. First he should be asked if he has ever bought Brand X chocolates. If he replies 'yes', he can be asked if he has bought them in the last year, then the last month, then in the last fortnight and so on until he remembers clearly. The approach may seem cumbersome, but experience has taught us that we should not rely too much on people's memory.

5 *Consider if a respondent would be willing to tell the truth.* He may know the answer, but be unwilling to reveal it, since certain answers may appear (to him) to lower his prestige in the eyes of the interviewer. Television viewers may claim to prefer the more serious programmes to the more frivolous ones; readers may claim to read classical novels when in fact they read cowboy stories. We can, of course, always insert test questions to check if these answers are truthful. We could, for example, ask them to summarise the content of two serious television programmes they have seen in the last week, or give the author and title of a couple of serious novels they have read. In 1960, when one of your authors was helping to undertake a survey, one housewife gave her age as 41, and then when asked for her date of birth, gave it as 1911, which, of course, made her age 49. Such a situation calls for a great deal of tact on the part of the interviewer. More interesting is a further American survey in which the following questions were asked:

|  |  | % Replying Yes |
|---|---|---|
| (a) | Have you ever heard of the word 'afrohetin'? | 8 |
| (b) | Do you recall voting last December in the special election for your state representatives? | 33 |
| (c) | Have you ever heard of the famous writer John Voolson? | 16 |

   (d)  Have you heard of the *Midwestern Life*
       *Magazine?*                                      25

   (e)  Have you heard of the Taft-Johnson-Pepper
       Bill on veterans' housing?                  53

The interesting thing about this survey is that none of the things mentioned in fact ever existed, yet so many people said they had heard of them. Those who said 'yes' probably did so because they felt that if they had taken more interest in current affairs they *would* have heard of them.

6  *Consider the order of the questions.* Here, two things are important. The persons being interviewed must not feel that the questionnaire is going to be too difficult to complete, or pry too much into their private lives. The early questions should be easy and general, and only as confidence builds up should searching questions be introduced. Equally, wait until the interviewer has been able to build up some sort of rapport with the respondent before you introduce, slowly and carefully, questions on his private life. And if your questions are really personal, such as, 'Have you ever been unfaithful to your partner?', do stress that the survey is absolutely confidential. A question such as this would, of course, have been preceded by more general questions as to whether the respondent believed that fidelity in a relationship was of great importance, or usual.

7  *Finally, try to ensure that the answers given are capable of being interpreted in one way only.* A very common category of answer is 'Don't know'. This, however, could mean, 'I do not understand the question', or 'I do not have the information', or 'I have the information, but cannot decide between alternatives', or 'I have the information, but am not going to tell you'.

It is important that interviewers should indicate which of these alternatives is meant, rather than lumping together such diverse information under one general heading.

## Selecting the sample

Since we have already dealt with many different types of sampling in the last chapter, we will merely stress here that the sample must be chosen to be of such a size and composition that it will yield the best possible results consistent with the expenditure you are permitted.

## Undertaking a pilot survey

However careful we have been so far, what we have done still remains to be tested in the field. It may be that the questionnaire we have designed will be unsatisfactory in practice. To test what we have done so far, we usually undertake a small pilot survey. How many people we interview does not matter so long as they are chosen at random; the results themselves are not as important as the lessons we learn. We may find, for example, that a question we thought to be simple and self-explanatory is misunderstood by most people, and will have to be altered. It may be that one section of the questionnaire results in replies so vague that it becomes obvious that we are asking questions about which few of our respondents have any knowledge. It would be better to leave it out altogether.

At this stage it is our work we are testing, and experience of the pilot survey will yield valuable information about the difficulties we are likely to meet in the field, and will save us from making serious mistakes in the much more costly survey proper.

## Briefing the interviewers

Before the fieldwork proper starts, all interviewers should hold a final meeting. They will already have a copy of their instructions, and great care should be taken to ensure that they understand them. The lessons learned, and the difficulties met within the pilot survey should be carefully examined and a course of action determined to meet circumstances that may arise. We will never be able to foresee all the difficulties of every single interviewer, but we must ensure that every single one of them has every scrap of information which is available and knows exactly what he is about to do.

Now, finally, we do not pretend that if you follow all the above advice and rules you will produce the perfect sample survey. There will still be mistakes, but we hope that you will have avoided the worst. Nor will we claim that your sample results will be 100% accurate. Such a sample has yet to be devised. But you will have avoided some of the major sources of error.

Error there will be, however. If you have done your job well, it will be small. Later chapters will show you how to estimate the magnitude of the error that may remain: those that follow will show you how to assess the significance of your sample results and take decisions on them.

**QUESTIONS**     (Chapters 15 and 16)

**16.1**   Statistical data may be collected by sample or census inquiry. Describe both methods and explain why sample inquiry is more frequently used than census inquiry.                                                                    ACCA

**16.2**   Identify the relative advantages and disadvantages of different techniques of sampling such as random, systematic, stratified, multi-stage and quota. Select the technique which you think would be most appropriate for a motorcar manufacturing company seeking information from car owners to enable the company to design 'the most popular family saloon car'. Support your selection with a reasoned argument.

**16.3**   (a)  What is meant by the term 'sampling frame'? Give two examples of a sampling frame from which a human population could be sampled.

    (b)  Define each of the following and describe the advantages of each type of sample:

       (i)    stratified;

       (ii)   multi-stage;

       (iii)  quota.

**16.4**   (a)  An inquiry is to be carried out among a population which has the following characteristics:

| | |
|---|---|
| Proportion of bus travellers to travellers by other means | 4 : 8 |
| Proportion travelling less than five miles to that travelling five miles and over: | |

       (i)    bus travellers                                                                          7 : 3

       (ii)   travellers by other means                                                  2 : 3

    If each interviewer is to question a quota of sixty people, how many of each class of person should be selected per quota?

    (b)  What chief advantage has the quota method of sample selection when compared with other methods? What are its disadvantages?

    (c)  What advantages are derived from the use of statistical samples?

**16.5**   Discuss the sampling methods which you consider should be used to obtain the following information:

    (a)  Public opinion on the European Community;

    (b)  Weights of workers (male, female and juvenile) employed in a very large factory;

    (c)  Heights of Canadian-born persons resident in the UK;

    (d)  Health details relating to office workers employed by local authorities in the UK.

**16.6**  (a)  Postal questionnaires and interviews are two methods of collecting data. List the advantages of each method.

    (b)  One of the main defects of surveys by interview is the problem of interview bias. What is interviewer bias and how can the problem be minimised?

    (c)  What are the main points to be considered in the design of a postal questionnaire?                                CIMA

**16.7**  (a)  What rules should be observed in constructing a questionnaire for collecting statistical information?

    (b)  What are the advantages and disadvantages of using questionnaires for collecting data?

**16.8**  Describe briefly the ways in which bias may arise in response to each of the following questions when directed by an interviewer at members of the class of people indicated.

    (a)  Do you sympathise with Communism? (general public)

    (b)  Do you use 'X' (a washing-up liquid)? (housewives)

    (c)  How many people are there in your family? (general public)

**16.9**  Describe carefully the way in which you would select a sample for an investigation into:

    (a)  the journeys made by car and lorry drivers through a town;

    (b)  the brands of scotch whisky drunk by men in a particular residential suburb.

**16.10**  As the Personnel Officer of a factory employing 10 000 workers at three locations of approximately equal labour strength, you wish to carry out an inquiry among all the employees to find their views on a rearrangement of holidays. It has already been agreed that the present 14 days per annum with six additional days at bank holidays should be increased to a total of 27 days per annum. The inquiry is to find out how the workers prefer the new total to be distributed through the year.

Draft in general outline a questionnaire to be used with the method upon which you have decided.

**16.11**  A large local authority with approximately 100 000 residents proposes to conduct a survey to obtain some idea of the expected use of a proposed new sports centre. Explain briefly:

(a)  the advantages of employing random sampling methods instead of non-random sampling methods;

(b)  the principal factors affecting sample size;

(c)  how you would deal with the problem of non-respondents;

(d)  how you would stratify the population if it was decided to employ a stratified random sample.

**16.12**  You have been asked to conduct a survey on wages within a large company. Explain in detail how you would go about the designing, carrying out and reporting on the results of your survey.

**16.13**  (a)  Outline the principles of questionnaire design.

(b)  Draw up a questionnaire of about eight questions either

(i)  to discover from part-time students in a technical college information relating to the course they are pursuing and its relevance to their future job prospects, or

(ii)  to test public opinion on a proposal to set up a Welsh parliament.

**16.14**  (a)  Describe how bias occurs in a statistical investigation. Which sampling technique would be used to obtain an unbiassed sample of:

(i)  ages of West Indian-born males, resident in the United Kingdom;

(ii)  health details of councillors in English district councils?

(b)  Explain briefly the following: (i) sampling frame; (ii) quota sampling; (iii) systematic sampling.

# 17 Sampling theory

You will have realised by now that the art of sampling is central to the study of statistics, and that we sample to learn something about the population from which the sample was drawn. As the sample we draw is likely to form only a fraction of the population, it is evident that any conclusion we draw about the population is subject to error, and, as we have seen, we can minimise the scale of such errors by using sound sampling methods. However, despite all the care we may take in designing a sample, the chance of making errors still exists, and we shall now turn our attention to attempts to quantify the scale of such errors.

Before we start, it must be stated that our analysis of sampling errors will be limited in three ways. First, we will confine our attention to large samples, as small samples create problems of their own which we shall examine later. This naturally begs the question as to what constitutes a large sample, and we will state now (without any attempt at justification) that *a large sample is a sample with more than 30 items.* The second limitation that we will place on our analysis of sampling is that we will confine our attention to simple random samples. Thirdly, we shall (for the present) either confine our attentions to infinitely large populations or, what amounts to the same thing, if we sample from finite populations then we will replace each item before drawing the next.

It is a fundamental truth about statistical theory that if we have prior knowledge of the population, we can make predictions about the behaviour of samples drawn from that population. Now you may object that this is of little use: we want to draw conclusions about the population from a sample. However, before we can assess the validity of such conclusions, it is necessary to understand thoroughly the theory of sample behaviour.

## The sampling distribution of sample means

Let us start by assuming that we have a population with a known mean $\mu$ and a known standard deviation $\sigma$. From this population we will draw many samples of $n$ items, and for each sample we will find the mean $\bar{x}$. Clearly, each time we draw a sample, we are not going to obtain the same value for the sample mean, so it would be sensible to arrange our sample means into a frequency distribution. We call this frequency distribution a *sampling distribution of sample means*, and we shall now attempt to make some predictions about this sampling distribution.

Suppose you were asked to guess the value of one of these sample means, what would your guess be? As we know that the population mean is $\mu$, it would surely be sensible to guess that the sample mean would also be $\mu$. For example, if we know that the average heights of all male adults in a certain town is 175 cm, then it would be sensible to guess that a sample of 100 men from this town would also have an average height of 175 cm. Now of course, in practice any *individual* sample mean cannot be expected to be exactly the same as $\mu$; some sample means will be more than $\mu$ and some less than $\mu$. So perhaps it would be more sensible to generalise, with a statement about all sample means like this:

*The average value of $\bar{x}$ (the sample mean) is $\mu$ (the population mean).*

We can expect, then, that the sample means will be clustered about the population mean, and it would be sensible to measure the degree of spread with a measure of dispersion. The measure we will use is the standard deviation, but you should note that to distinguish the fact that we are considering a sampling distribution rather than a sample or a population, we call the standard deviation the *standard error* (s.e.).

Now the size of the standard error will depend on the size of the sample drawn, and will lie within limits that we can define precisely. Let us consider the largest sample we can possibly draw: this would occur if we selected every item in the population. The sample mean would be exactly equal to the population mean, and we would obviously obtain the same value for the sample mean in every sample we selected. So the sample means would not show any spread, and the standard error of the mean would be zero. Now suppose we selected the smallest samples possible, i.e. samples of one item only. The sample means would show exactly the same spread as the individual items in the population and the standard error of the mean would be $\sigma$ – the population standard deviation. We can conclude, then, that the standard error of the mean must be at least zero, and at most $\sigma$. Moreover, as the sample size is increased, then the standard error decreases. In fact it can be shown that:

*The standard error of the sample mean* $= \dfrac{\sigma}{\sqrt{n}}$

We do not intend to prove this formally, but you can satisfy yourself that it is true by undertaking the following experiment.

EXPERIMENT 1 | Let the population consist of the digits 1, 2 and 3, so:

$$\text{The population mean} = \frac{1 + 2 + 3}{3} = 2, \text{ and}$$

$$\text{The population standard deviation} = \sqrt{\frac{(1-2)^2 + (2-2)^2 + (3-2)^2}{3}}$$

$$= \sqrt{\frac{2}{3}}$$

If we drew samples of two items from this population then we would predict that:

$$\text{The average value of the sample means} = \mu = 2, \text{ and}$$

$$\text{The standard error of the sample means} = \frac{\sigma}{\sqrt{n}} = \frac{\sqrt{\frac{2}{3}}}{\sqrt{2}} = \frac{\sqrt{2}}{\sqrt{3}} \times \frac{1}{\sqrt{2}} = \frac{1}{\sqrt{3}}$$

(a) List all the samples of two items that can be drawn (there are nine of them) and find the mean of each sample. (Remember you are sampling with replacement.)

(b) Find the average value of the sample means and verify that it is 2.

(c) Find the standard deviation of the sample means (i.e. the standard error of the mean) and verify that it is $\frac{1}{\sqrt{3}}$.

## The central limit theorem

Let us summarise what we have learnt so far. If we draw samples of $n$ items from a population with a known mean $\mu$ and a known standard deviation $\sigma$, then we can make predictions about the sampling distribution of the sample mean. We can predict that the average value of the sample mean is $\mu$, and that the standard error of the sample mean is $\frac{\sigma}{\sqrt{n}}$. Now if the population itself is normally distributed, you would expect the sample means to be normally distributed, but what is rather curious is that even if the population is not normally distributed the sample means still turn out to be normally distributed *as long as the sample is reasonably large*. This strange feature of the sample mean is called the *central limit theorem* and explains why we spend so much time considering the normal distribution.

Again, the algebraic proof of the central limit theorem is rather complicated, but a simple experiment will demonstrate its truth. Suppose we take as our population the ten digits 0 to 9, and select single items from this population. Each digit has an equal probability of being selected, the distribution is by no means normal – it is a rectangular distribution as shown in Fig 17.1.

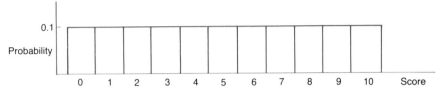

**Fig 17.1**

Now let us suppose that samples of two digits are drawn (the first digit is replaced before the second is drawn), then 100 different samples are possible. For each sample we could add together the two digits drawn. The smallest sample total would be $0 + 0 = 0$, and the largest $9 + 9 = 18$. All the sample totals must fall within the range 0 to 18, so the sample means must be in the range 0 to 9. We must now find the number of ways of obtaining each sample total. A sample total of zero can be obtained in one way only – if both the digits drawn are zero. A sample total of one can be obtained in two ways $(0 + 1$ or $1 + 0)$. A sample total of 2 can be obtained in three ways $(0 + 2, 2 + 0$ or $1 + 1)$. Continuing in this way we can obtain the sampling distribution of sample means:

| Sample total | Sample mean | No. of ways | Probability |
|---|---|---|---|
| 0 | 0 | 1 | 0.01 |
| 1 | 0.5 | 2 | 0.02 |
| 2 | 1.0 | 3 | 0.03 |
| 3 | 1.5 | 4 | 0.04 |
| 4 | 2.0 | 5 | 0.05 |
| 5 | 2.5 | 6 | 0.06 |
| 6 | 3.0 | 7 | 0.07 |
| 7 | 3.5 | 8 | 0.08 |
| 8 | 4.0 | 9 | 0.09 |
| 9 | 4.5 | 10 | 0.10 |
| 10 | 5.0 | 9 | 0.09 |
| 11 | 5.5 | 8 | 0.08 |
| 12 | 6.0 | 7 | 0.07 |
| 13 | 6.5 | 6 | 0.06 |
| 14 | 7.0 | 5 | 0.05 |
| 15 | 7.5 | 4 | 0.04 |
| 16 | 8.0 | 3 | 0.03 |
| 17 | 8.5 | 2 | 0.02 |
| 18 | 9.0 | 1 | 0.01 |

The sampling distribution of the sample means has been drawn in Fig 17.2. We can conclude that if samples of two items are drawn from a rectangular distribution, then the distribution of the sample means will be triangular.

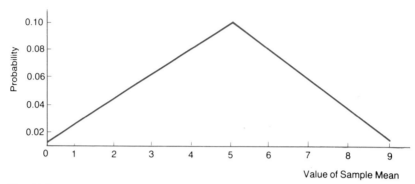

**Fig 17.2**

If we increase the sample size to three, then the distribution of sample means would look like the curve in Fig 17.3.

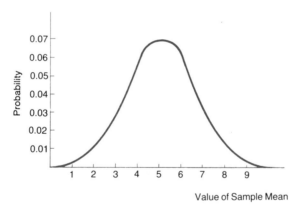

**Fig 17.3**

We see, then, that as the sample size increases from one to two to three, then the distribution of sample means changes from rectangular to triangular to bell-shaped. In fact, it is not difficult to imagine that the greater the sample size, the closer will the distribution of sample means move to a normal distribution. So as long as we confine our attention to large samples then, we can use normal distribution tables to make predictions about sample means.

**EXAMPLE 1**

What proportion of samples of 100 items drawn from a population, mean 100 and standard deviation 20, would have a mean greater than 105? We would predict that the average value of the sample mean would be 100, and the standard error of the sample mean would be $\frac{20}{\sqrt{100}} = 2$. The diagram in Fig 17.4 illustrates the proportion we require.

**Fig 17.4**

The Z score for 105 is:

$$\frac{105 - 100}{2} = 2.5$$

and consulting the normal distribution tables we can expect only 0.621% of sample means to exceed 105.

**EXAMPLE 2**

A confectioner produces cakes which he packs in cartons of 100 for the catering trade. He prints on the carton 'average weight per cake not less than 95.5 grams'. If cakes have a mean weight of 100 grams and a standard deviation of 20 grams, what proportion of batches contravenes the Trade Descriptions Act?

Every time the confectioner packs a carton, this is equivalent to selecting a sample of 100 cakes. We can consider, then, that the average weight of cakes in the cartons forms a sampling distribution of sample means, with a standard error $\frac{20}{\sqrt{100}} = 2$. As we wish to know the proportion of cartons with mean weight of cakes less than 95.5 grams, the problem can be illustrated as in Fig 17.5.

The Z score for 95.5 is

$$\frac{95.5 - 100}{2} = -2.25$$

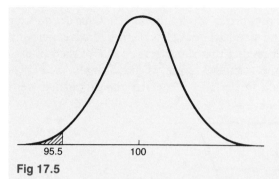

**Fig 17.5**

and consulting the tables we find that only 1.222% of cartons would contravene the Act.

## The sampling distribution of sums and differences

We shall now discuss sampling distributions formed by taking sums or differences. To understand just what this means, consider modern industry; a considerable part of industrial activity is based, not on making something but on assembling components that have been made in a number of different factories. This is especially true of the motor industry. Let us take a very simple case and imagine that we are joining end-to-end two straight metal bars produced in two workshops. The first workshop aims to produce bars with lengths of 20 cm, but of course there will be variation in the actual lengths. We will assume that the length of bars are normally distributed with a mean of 20 cm, and a standard deviation of 0.05 cm. Bars produced in the second workshop we will again assume to be normally distributed, this time with a mean length of 10 cm and a standard deviation of 0.04 cm.

When a workman picks up two bars for joining he is, in fact, sampling. He is drawing samples of two items; one from the first workshop and one from the second. Almost certainly, the length of the assembled bars will be important and this is the sampling statistic. It is obtained by taking the sum of the lengths of the two individual bars. Now as the length of the individual bars varies, then so will the lengths of the assembled bars. We could form a frequency distribution of the lengths of the assembled bars. As the bars have been obtained by *sampling*, and as their lengths have been obtained by *adding*, the frequency distribution of the lengths of assembled bars is called *a sampling distribution of sums*. What can we conclude about this sampling distribution? Well, as the lengths of the individual bars are normally distributed it would seem reasonable to assume that the lengths of the assembled bars will also be normally distributed. It is true that:

*If the populations are normally distributed so will be the distribution of sample sums formed from the populations.*

Suppose you were asked to guess the mean length of the assembled bars – it is probable that you would argue something like this: as bars produced in the first workshop have a mean length of 20 cm and bars produced in the second workshop have a mean length of 10 cm, then the mean length of the joined bars would be $20 + 10 = 30$ cm:

*The mean of the sample sums is the sum of the means of the populations from which they were formed, i.e. mean of sample sums $\bar{x} = \mu_1 + \mu_2 + \cdots + \mu_n$.*

What can we conclude about the dispersion of the lengths of the assembled bars? Suppose we take $\bar{x} \pm 4\sigma$ as covering the effective limits of any normal distribution (consult the table and you will see that it covers all but 0.06%). The longest bar produced in the first workshop would be $20 + 4 \times 0.05 = 20.2$ cm, and the shortest would be $20 - 4 \times 0.05 = 19.8$ cm. This gives a range of lengths of $20.2 - 19.8 = 0.4$. Bars produced in the second workshop would have a maximum length of $10 + 4 \times 0.04 = 10.16$ cm, and a minimum length of $10 - 4 \times 0.04 = 9.84$ cm. This gives a range of $10.16 - 9.84 = 0.32$ cm. When a workman picks up two rods for joining he could pick the two longest bars and produce an assembled bar of $20.2 + 10.16 = 30.36$ cm. He could choose the two shortest bars and produce an assembled bar of $19.8 + 9.84 = 29.64$ cm. So the range of assembled bars is $30.36 - 29.64 = 0.72$ cm. *Notice that this is the sum of the ranges of the two populations $(0.4 + 0.32 = 0.72)$.*

However, we do not usually measure dispersion with the range – we prefer to use the standard deviation (as we are dealing with a sample we should call this measure the standard error). Unfortunately, what is true of the range is not true of the standard error. We cannot add the two populations' standard deviations and conclude that the standard error of the sample sums is $0.04 + 0.05 = 0.09$ cm. But although we cannot add the standard deviations we can add the variances:

*The variance of the sample sums is the sum of the variances of the populations from which they were formed.*

This additive property explains why statisticians often prefer to use the variance to the standard deviation. We can now conclude that:

*Standard error of the sample sums $= \sqrt{\sigma^2_1 + \sigma^2_2 + \cdots + \sigma^2_n}$.*

The standard error of the lengths of the assembled bars would be:

$$\sqrt{0.04^2 + 0.05^2} = 0.064$$

**EXPERIMENT 2**

This experiment is designed to verify the statements we have just made about the mean and the standard error of sample sums. Let the population A be the digits 1, 2, and 3, which we know from Experiment 1 has a mean 2 and a standard deviation $\sqrt{\frac{2}{3}}$. Let the population B be the digits 5, 7 and 9 which has a mean of 7 and a standard deviation of:

$$\sqrt{\frac{(5-7)^2 + (7-7)^2 + (9-7)^2}{3}} = \sqrt{\frac{8}{3}}$$

Now suppose we form all possible samples by drawing one digit from each population. If we find the sample sums then we would predict their average value to be $2 + 7 = 9$, and the standard error to be:

$$\sqrt{\sigma^2_A + \sigma^2_B}$$

$$= \sqrt{\frac{2}{3} + \frac{8}{3}} = \sqrt{\frac{10}{3}}$$

1  List all the samples that can be formed by drawing one item from each population.

2  Find all the sample sums, verify that their average is 9 and their standard error is $\sqrt{\frac{10}{3}}$.

**EXAMPLE 3**

A manufacturer produces two types of metal rods. Type A has a mean length of 3.5 cm and a standard deviation of 0.03 cm. Type B has a mean length of 4.5 cm and a standard deviation of 0.04 cm. A rod of each type is selected, joined together, and the joined rods are then placed in a slot 8.1 cm long. What proportion of joined rods will not fit the slot?

Mean length of joined rods $= 3.5 + 4.5 = 8$ cm

Standard error of the lengths of joined rods $= \sqrt{0.03^2 + 0.04^2}$
$$= 0.05 \text{ cm}$$

The shaded area in Fig 17.6 illustrates the proportion of assemblies that will not fit. To find this proportion we must first find the Z score for 8.1 cm:

$$Z = \frac{8.1 - 8}{0.05} = 2.$$

Consulting the tables we would expect 2.275% of assembled rods not to fit the slot.

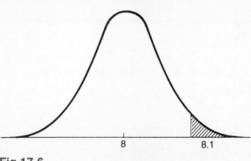

**Fig 17.6**

We shall now turn our attention to considering the sampling distribution of sample differences, and we shall do this by developing Example 3. Let us suppose that part of the assembly process of a certain machine involves placing a metal bar into a slot. The bars have lengths that are normally distributed with a mean of 8 cm and a standard deviation of 0.03 cm. You should check for yourselves that all but 0.06% of bars will have lengths within the limits 7.88 cm to 8.12 cm – a range of 0.24 cm. Slots have lengths that are normally distributed with a mean 8.3 cm and a standard deviation of 0.04 cm, so slots will have lengths within the limits 8.14 cm to 8.46 cm – a range of 0.32 cm. Now there will be a gap between the slot and the bar – it is measured by subtracting the bar length from the slot length. The gaps then form a sampling distribution of sample differences. Now as you would imagine, the mean gap would be 8.3 – 8.0 = 0.3 cm:

*The mean of the sample differences is the difference between the means of the populations from which they were formed, i.e. mean of sample differences $\bar{x} = \mu_1 - \mu_2$.*

Turning now to the range of the gap, the largest gap will be obtained by taking the largest slot with the smallest bar, so the largest gap is 8.46 – 7.88 = 0.58 cm. The smallest gap is obtained by taking the smallest slot with the largest bar, so the smallest gap is 8.14 – 8.12 = 0.02 cm. So the range of gaps is 0.58 – 0.02 = 0.56 cm. This is the sum of the ranges of the two populations (0.24 + 0.32 = 0.56). As variances are additive we can conclude that:

*Standard error of sample differences $= \sqrt{\sigma_1^2 + \sigma_1^2}$.*

| EXPERIMENT 3 | This experiment is designed to verify the statements we have made about the mean and standard error of sample differences. Find your results of Experiment 2. If we form sample differences by subtracting the digit drawn from population A from the digit drawn from population B, then we would predict the mean difference to be $7 - 2 = 5$, and the standard error of the difference to be: |

$$\sqrt{\frac{2}{3} + \frac{8}{3}} = \sqrt{\frac{10}{3}}$$

Form all the sample differences, verify that their mean is 5 and their standard error is $\sqrt{\frac{10}{3}}$.

| EXAMPLE 4 | Full boxes of rice have weights that are normally distributed with a mean of 225 grams and a standard deviation 1.5 grams. The empty boxes have weights that are normally distributed with a mean 7 grams and a standard deviation 0.05 grams. Printed on the packet is the claim that the minimum net weight of the contents is 214 grams. What proportion of packets fail to meet this claim? |

Mean weight of contents = $225 - 7 = 218$ grams

Standard error of the weights of contents = $\sqrt{1.5^2 + 0.05^2}$

$= \sqrt{2.2525}$ grams

The shaded area in Fig 17.7 represents the proportion we require. The Z score is:

$$\frac{214 - 218}{\sqrt{2.2525}} = -2.665$$

**Fig 17.7**

The table tells us that a very low proportion – only 0.385% of packets – are below the specified minimum weight.

## The sampling distribution of sample proportions

There has been an increasing tendency in recent years to give the results of sample surveys in percentage form. A manufacturer may claim that not more than 3% of his output develops faults in the first year of use or public opinion surveys may report that 38.2% of the population can be expected to vote Labour at the next general election. But most statisticians prefer to use proportions rather than percentages; they would report that the proportion that can be expected to vote Labour is 0.382.

Let us suppose that we are considering a population, some members of which possess a certain attribute. For example, the population we are considering might be the female population of the United Kingdom, and the attribute might be blue-eyed blondes. Again, the population might be a very large batch of manufactured goods and the attribute might be that the good is defective. If we draw many samples from this population, calculate the proportion in each sample that has the attribute and record our results in a frequency distribution, then we will have formed a sampling distribution of sample proportions. Now if we know the proportion in the population which has the attribute (call this proportion $\pi$), then we can make the following predictions about the sampling distribution:

*The mean proportion in the sampling distribution will be $\pi$ – the same as the proportion in the population.*

*If the samples all contain n items, then the standard error of the proportions is*

$$\sqrt{\frac{\pi(1-\pi)}{n}}$$

Notice that, just like the standard error of sample mean, the larger the sample size the smaller will be the standard error.

EXPERIMENT 4

This experiment is designed to enable you to verify the statements we have just made about the sampling distribution of sample proportions. Suppose we have a population consisting of the items A, A, and B, where A means that the item is perfect and B means that the item is defective. So we have a proportion of defective items in the population of $\pi = \frac{1}{3}$. If we draw samples of two items from the population, then we could predict that:

The mean proportion defective in the sample $= \pi = \frac{1}{3}$
The standard error of the proportion defective

$$= \sqrt{\frac{\pi(1-\pi)}{n}} = \sqrt{\frac{\frac{1}{3} \times \frac{2}{3}}{2}} = \sqrt{\frac{1}{9}} = \frac{1}{3}$$

(a)  List all the possible samples of two items and find the proportion defective in each.

(b)  Verify that the mean proportion defective is $\frac{1}{3}$ and that the standard error of the proportions is $\frac{1}{3}$.

**EXAMPLE 5**

Suppose we know from past experience that 5% of a certain output is defective. We intend to draw samples of 800 items and find the proportion defective in each. In this case, we have $\pi = 0.05$, so:

The mean proportion defective in the samples $= \pi = 0.05$

The standard error of proportions $= \sqrt{\frac{0.05(1-0.05)}{800}} = 0.0077$

If we wish to know the proportion of samples that can be expected to contain more than 6% defective items then, as the sample is large, we can use the normal distribution:

$$Z = \frac{0.06 - 0.05}{0.0077} = 1.3$$

The table tells us that 9.68% of samples would have more than 6% defectives. *See* Fig 17.8.

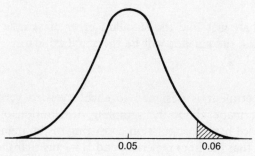

0.05          0.06

**Fig 17.8**

## Confidence limits

Let us return to the population we consider in Example 1, i.e. the population with a mean of 100 and a standard deviation 20. If we draw samples of 100 from this population, then their means will be normally distributed with a standard error $\frac{20}{\sqrt{100}} = 2$. Let us now ask ourselves between what limits we would expect the central 95% of sample means to lie. Fig 17.9 illustrates the problem. We are excluding the 2.5% of means at the extreme right of the distribution and the 2.5% at the extreme left, and we require the Z scores for the points $a$ and $b$. Now $b$ has a Z score that is exceeded only on 2.5% of occasions, so consulting our table we find that $b$ must have a Z score of 1.96. In other words:

$$\frac{b - 100}{2} = 1.96$$

so   $b = 103.92$

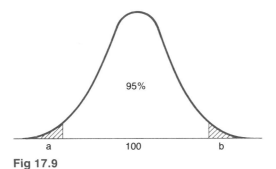

**Fig 17.9**

As $a$ and $b$ are symmetrical about the mean, $a$ must have a Z score of $-1.96$, so:

$$\frac{a - 100}{2} = -1.96$$

so   $a = 96.08$

Thus, 95% of sample means can be expected to fall within the range 96.08 to 103.92. Such limits are known as *confidence limits*, and the one we have calculated is the 95% confidence limit. Now let us generalise. If we draw samples of $n$ items from a population with a mean $\mu$ and a standard error $\sigma$:

$$95\% \text{ confidence limits for sample means} = \mu \pm 1.96 \, \frac{\sigma}{\sqrt{n}}$$

Beware in your interpretation of 95% confidence limits. The concept does not mean that we are 95% sure that a single sample mean lies within these limits – all that we can say about a single sample mean is that either it will lie within the limits or it will not. *The 95% confidence limits mean that if we draw many samples, and find the mean for each, then we can expect 95% of sample means to lie within the stated limits.* Now of course, you may not be satisfied with 95% confidence limits, and you may want to be more sure than this. We could, for example, use:

$$99\% \text{ confidence limits for sample means} = \mu \pm 2.576 \frac{\sigma}{\sqrt{n}}$$

So for our example, we can expect 99% of sample means to lie within the range:

$$100 \pm 2.576 \times \frac{20}{\sqrt{100}}$$

i.e. 94.848 to 105.152. So we notice that if we wish to increase the level of confidence, we must widen the range for the sample means.

So far, we have been taking the central range of sample means, but occasions might arise when we wish to assess how confident we are that sample means will not be greater than a certain value. In medicine, for example, it is often important that a dose of medicine does not contain more than a certain amount of drug. No harmful effects occur if the patient takes less, but he must not take more. Suppose that in a distribution of sample means, we wish to know the value below which we would expect 95% of sample means to lie. Here, of course, we are still considering 95% of the possible sample means, but here we are excluding the 5% at the top rather than the $2\frac{1}{2}\%$ at each end (Fig 17.10). Reference to our table tells us that a Z score of 1.645 is the value below which 95% of sample means will lie. So an alternative 95% confidence limit can be expressed as:

$$\mu + 1.645 \frac{\sigma}{\sqrt{n}}$$

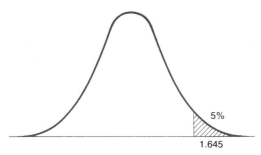

5%

1.645

**Fig 17.10**

Likewise, an alternative form for the 99% confidence limit is:

$$\mu + 2.326 \, \frac{\sigma}{\sqrt{n}}$$

So we see that confidence limits can take two forms. On the one hand, we can state a central range for sample means – this is called a *two-sided confidence limit*. On the other hand, we can state a confidence limit that will be exceeded by a certain percentage of sample means – this is called a *one-sided confidence limit*. Perhaps an example will clarify the difference.

<table>
<tr><td>EXAMPLE 6</td></tr>
</table>

Samples of 100 items are drawn from a population with a mean 1000 and a standard deviation 200. Set up 95% confidence limits for the sample means. Dealing first with the two-sided confidence limit:

$$\mu \pm 1.96 \, \frac{\sigma}{\sqrt{n}}$$

$$1000 \pm 1.96 \times \frac{200}{\sqrt{100}}$$

$$= 1000 \pm 39.2$$

This is illustrated in Fig 17.11, showing the range within which the central 95% of sample means will lie.

**Fig 17.11**

The one-sided confidence limit could be expressed as an upper limit (see Fig 17.12, which shows the value above which only 5% of sample means will lie):

$$\mu + 1.645 \times \frac{\sigma}{\sqrt{n}}$$

$$1000 + 1.645 \times \frac{200}{\sqrt{100}} = 1032.9$$

Alternatively, the one-sided confidence limit could be expressed as a

**Fig 17.12**

lower limit (see Fig 17.13, which shows the value below which only 5% of sample means will lie):

$$\mu - 1.645 \times \frac{\sigma}{\sqrt{n}}$$

$$1000 - 1.645 \times \frac{200}{\sqrt{100}} = 967.1$$

**Fig 17.13**

The differences between one-sided and two-sided confidence limits are important – and we will meet them again in later chapters. However, it must be stated that *when a statistician talks of a confidence limit he usually means the two-sided case.* Although we have examined confidence limits for sample means, they could be applied to sample proportions or sums and differences. For example, the 95% two-sided confidence limits for sample proportions is:

$$\pi \pm 1.96 \times \sqrt{\frac{\pi(1 - \pi)}{n}}$$

## Summary

In this chapter, we have introduced concepts that are of fundamental importance in Statistics, and it would be useful to summarise what we have learned. If we draw samples and derive some statistic (for example, the sample mean or the sample proportion) and record our results in a frequency distribution, then we have formed a *sampling distribution*. The *standard error* measures the variation in our sample statistics, and we met three standard errors:

1  Standard error of the mean $= \dfrac{\sigma}{\sqrt{n}}$

2  Standard error of the proportion $= \sqrt{\dfrac{\pi(1-\pi)}{n}}$

3  Standard error of the sum (or difference) $= \sqrt{\sigma_1{}^2 + \sigma_2{}^2}$

A *confidence limit* is a prediction about sample results, and two types are possible. A *two-sided* confidence limit gives the central limits for sample results, so

$$95\% \text{ two-sided confidence limits} = \pm 1.96 \times \text{s.e.}$$
$$99\% \text{ two-sided confidence limits} = \pm 2.576 \times \text{s.e.}$$

where s.e. is the standard error.

A *one-sided* confidence limit gives a limit that will be exceeded by a certain percentage of samples:

95% one-sided confidence limit is either
$$+1.645 \times \text{s.e.} \text{ or } -1.645 \times \text{s.e.}$$
99% one-sided confidence limit is either
$$+2.326 \times \text{s.e.} \text{ or } -2.326 \times \text{s.e.}$$

In the next chapter, we will consider an important application of these concepts.

## QUESTIONS

**17.1**  Write brief notes on each of the following:

(a)  a sampling distribution;

(b)  standard error and sampling errors;

(c)  the central limit theorem;

(d)  sampling sums and sampling differences.

**17.2** Suppose samples of 100 items were drawn from a population with a mean 200 and a standard deviation of 30. What proportion of samples will have means:

(a) greater than 202;

(b) less than 199;

(c) between 198.5 and 203?

**17.3** Set up 90%, 95% and 99% two-sided confidence intervals for the sample means in question 17.2.

**17.4** Set up 90%, 95% and 99% one-sided confidence intervals for the sample means in question 17.2.

**17.5** A manufacturer produces metal rods which have a mean breaking strength of 60 kg, and a standard deviation of 5 kg. He wishes to pack the rods in bundles and guarantee that the average breaking strength of rods exceeds 59 kg. How many rods should he pack in each bundle if he wishes no more than 5% of bundles to violate the guarantee?

**17.6** A machine cuts rods to a specified length of 2 cm and it is known that the machine operates with a standard deviation of 0.02 cm. If a sample of 100 rods has a mean length of 2.005 cm, what would you conclude?

**17.7** There are three distinct stages in the servicing of a particular machine:

| Stage | Mean time | s.d. of times |
|---|---|---|
| Cleaning | 18 mins | 1.0 mins |
| Greasing | 12 mins | 0.5 mins |
| Setting | 10 mins | 0.5 mins |

Assuming that the times are independent and normally distributed, find the proportion of machines serviced in less than 37.5 mins.

**17.8** Now you will have to think about this one! Part of the assembly of a machine involves placing a metal rod into a slot. Both the rods and the slots have lengths that are normally distributed with the following parameters:

| | Mean | Standard Deviation |
|---|---|---|
| Rods | 16 cm | 0.03 cm |
| Slots | 16.1 cm | 0.04 cm |

Find the distribution of the clearance between the bars and the slots. If a clearance of under 0.2 cm is satisfactory, find the proportion of assemblies that fail to meet this requirement.

**17.9** Paddy Flynn has won a contract with an industrial estates corporation to erect a number of single-storey industrial units. He won the contract because he promised to complete each unit within 82 days of starting. Paddy's quantity surveyor produced the following estimates for each unit:

|  | Mean time | Standard deviation |
|---|---|---|
| Foundation work | 10 days | 2 days |
| Brickwork | 40 days | 5 days |
| Roofing | 20 days | 3 days |

The corporation has imposed a penalty of £100 000 for each unit that is completed after the 82 days promised. An insurance company will insure Paddy against exceeding the 82 days' completion time for a premium of £5000 per unit. Advise Paddy as to whether the insurance policy should be taken up.

**17.10** In a certain country, men have a mean height of 5 feet 6 inches, standard deviation 3 inches, and women have a mean height of 5 feet 3 inches, standard deviation 2 inches. In a random sample of 100 married couples, the average height difference between husband and wife was 2 inches. What might you conclude from the result of this sample?

**17.11** It is known that some 8% of components produced are defective. If components are packed in batches of 1000, what proportion of batches contain more than 8.5% defective items?

**17.12** Set up 95% and 99% confidence intervals for the proportion defective in samples of 500 drawn from a population that contains 7% defective items.

**17.13** The Ruritanian Ministry of Agriculture has set a standard 94% germination rate for grain seed, and only 2% of batches of seed must have germination rates less than the standard. If a certain crop of grain seed is known to have a 95% germination rate, how many seeds should be in each batch in order to meet the minimum requirement?

**17.14** The Blotto Distillery has in the past maintained a 30% share of the market for gin in a certain country. The company wishes to monitor its market share by sampling 1000 gin buyers at weekly intervals. In a particular week, 290 buyers in the sample bought Blotto's gin – what would you conclude?

**17.15** The Lightning Spark Plug Company has a contract to supply the Ministry of Defence with 100 000 spark plugs per week. If more than 1075 plugs are defective, then the company must pay a £1000 penalty to the Ministry. On average, 1% of plugs produced by the company are defective. The company can employ an inspection scheme to ensure that the Ministry's specifications will be met, but this will cost £150 per week. Advise the company.

# 18 Quality control

In this chapter we shall consider a particular application of sampling theory. We will examine how sampling theory might be used to help in the control of quality. You should note, however, that the purpose of this chapter is to illustrate examples of applied sampling, and it is not intended to emulate established practices.

If you conducted a 'popularity poll' of all the jobs in a factory, it is an odds on bet that the inspector would be low down the list. The factory operatives dislike the inspector because they see him or her as the person who rejects part of their output, and so reduces bonus earnings. Management all too often (although incorrectly) sees the inspector as a necessary evil – a cost that they would dearly like to dispense with! Some managers even call inspectors 'unproductive labour'. Fortunately, rational people recognise that inspectors perform a most important function. After all, quality *does* matter. Mass production has meant that goods are available to us as consumers at prices we can, on the whole, manage to afford. Unfortunately, mass production can also mean that a proportion of the goods produced will inevitably be of inferior quality. We have all had experience of annoying faults developing in the goods we buy. The inspector can, and should, be the guardian of quality.

Now we do not wish to give you the impression that inspectors should solely be seen as fulfilling an important social function – they also serve the firm well (despite the cynical attitude of some sectors of management). Quality also matters to the firm – for the firm that produces shoddy goods will eventually find its sales falling, and will find an unacceptable part of its output returned as rejects. The efficient inspector is a positive asset to the firm.

Having recognised the need for inspection, we must now decide on the form that the inspection will take. Some firms inspect finished goods in special inspection shops. The fault with this method is that as faults are found after the goods have been made, it is possible that the firm has produced large batches of defective items that have not been discovered until it is too late to do much about it. The purpose of inspection is not merely to identify defective items, but also to stop further defectives occurring. Inspection should occur as near to the point of production as possible, and inspection should be frequent. A fairly common, and commendable, system of inspection is the 'patrolling inspector'. The 'patrolling inspector' visits each machine as frequently as possible and inspects items produced by that machine, so if lapses from quality are occurring the trouble can be rectified before too many defectives have been produced. Also, the inspector who works to a sensible system will keep good records of how each machine is performing. This often enables him to spot the lapses from accepted standards *before* they occur.

In very few cases would there be 100% inspection – not only would this be costly, but in many cases the machines can produce faster than the inspectors can inspect! Quality control, then, in the main depends upon sampling theory. The actual inspection system used will depend on the nature of the possible faults that can occur.

## Control system for variate sampling

Industry abounds with examples of goods and components that must be within certain measurable dimensions (or tolerance limits) and we will examine a quality control system for such goods. We shall consider the case of a manufacturer producing metal rods, which must have diameters within the tolerance limits 1 cm to 1.01 cm, i.e. $1.005 \pm 0.005$. When we dealt with the standard deviation we found it convenient to take an arbitrary origin, and remove the decimal point by taking a different unit of measurement. We shall resort to this method again. Taking 1 cm as an origin, and one ten thousandth of a cm as unit, the tolerance limit becomes $50 \pm 50$. How can we set up a suitable quality control system for this manufacturer?

Step 1

Before we can set up any quality control system, we must have some idea of the mean and standard deviation of the diameters of the rods produced by the machinery. Suppose we measure a large number of rods, and obtain the following information:

Mean diameter $= \mu = 52$
Standard deviation of diameters $= \sigma = 13.76$

Step 2

We now check that the machinery is capable of meeting the tolerances, because if it cannot, then there is little point in continuing. To do this, we will assume (quite reasonably) that the diameters of rods are normally distributed. If you consult the table at the end of this book you will learn that 99.8% of items in any normal distribution can be expected to lie within the range:

$\mu \pm 3.09\sigma$

In this case, then, we can expect 99.8% of rods to have diameters within the range:

$$\pm\,3.09 \times 13.76 = \pm\,43$$

Now to meet the tolerances, the diameters must be within the limits $\pm\,50$, so we can conclude that the machinery is capable of meeting the tolerances.

**Step 3**

We must now decide on just how the inspection will take place. Of course, there is nothing to stop the inspector randomly selecting a rod, measuring its diameter, and making some judgement as to the performance of the machinery. However, we have learnt enough about sampling to realise that it is most unwise to draw conclusions based on a sample of one item. It is far safer to draw a sample of a number of rods, and form judgements on the basis of the mean diameter. We will assume that the inspector will base his conclusions on the mean diameters of samples of five rods.

**Step 4**

In the previous chapter, we saw that if samples of $n$ items were drawn from a population with a mean $\mu$ and a standard deviation $\sigma$, then the 95% confidence limit for sample means is:

$$\mu \pm \frac{1.96\sigma}{\sqrt{n}}$$

Now strictly speaking, this will not apply to the system we are considering as the sample size we have chosen can hardly be considered large. However, it is the normal practice in quality control to assume that the central limit theorem does apply to small samples. The justification for this is that many samples will be drawn, and these many small samples can be considered as equivalent to a large sample. In the case of rods, then, 95% of sample means will be within the range:

$$52 \pm \frac{1.96 \times 13.76}{\sqrt{5}} = 40 \text{ to } 64$$

In other words, we can expect 19 out of 20 sample means to be within the range 40 to 64. We call this range the *warning limits* for sample means.

In a similar fashion, we can deduce that 99.8% of sample means will lie in the range:

$$\mu \pm \frac{3.09\sigma}{\sqrt{n}}$$

or in the case of our example:

$$52 \pm \frac{3.09 \times 13.76}{\sqrt{5}} = 33 \text{ to } 71$$

So we can expect 499 out of 500 sample means to fall within the range 33 to 71 and we call these limits the *action limits*.

We now have a basis for controlling the quality of output. As long as only one sample mean in 20 lies outside the warning limits, and one sample mean in 500 lies outside the action limits, we are producing a uniform quality and the process is said to be under control. We will consider later what action should be taken if these limits are violated.

**Step 5**
In Step 2 we verified that the machinery was capable of meeting the tolerances. However, it is also necessary to ensure that the control system is capable of detecting any lapses from the tolerance limits. We might get this situation if the machine setting (i.e. the mean) was rather high. Suppose that the mean was 60. Now we already know that individual items have a range of $\pm 43$, so if the mean was 60 then the individual diameters could be as high as 103, and the upper tolerance limit would be exceeded.

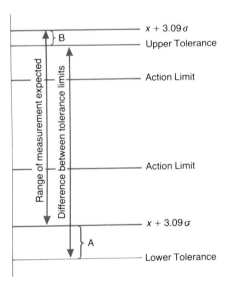

**Fig 18.1**

If we look carefully at Fig 18.1 the first thing we notice is that the upper tolerance limit minus the lower tolerance limit exceeds the range of measurement expected ($A > B$). According to the test conducted in Step 2, we can conclude that the machinery is capable of meeting the tolerances.

However, the upper tolerance limit is below the upper range for individual items, so it is possible that the upper tolerance limit will be exceeded (i.e. individual lengths can penetrate into area *B*). If we were now to use the action limits as our quality control system, i.e. check that the means of samples do not fall outside these limits, then the samples could indicate that the production was under control and *lapses from the upper tolerance limit would go undetected.*

Can you see that if the tolerances are outside one of the limits $\mu \pm 3.09\sigma$, then no undetected lapses from tolerances will occur? More formally, we can state that the tolerance limits must be at least:

$$3.09\sigma - \frac{3.09\sigma}{\sqrt{n}}$$

outside the action limits if no undetected lapses from tolerance are to occur. Putting it another way, the upper action limit must be at least this amount below the upper tolerance limit, and the lower action limit at least this amount above the lower tolerance. This is called the *allowable width of the control lines* (AWCL). Writing $T_U$ for the upper tolerance limit and $T_L$ for the lower tolerance limit, we have:

$$\text{AWCL} = T_L + \left[3.09\sigma - \frac{3.09\sigma}{\sqrt{n}}\right] \quad \text{to} \quad T_U - \left[3.09\sigma - \frac{3.09\sigma}{\sqrt{n}}\right]$$

Substituting, we have:

$$0 + \left[3.09 \times 13.76 - \frac{3.09 \times 13.76}{\sqrt{5}}\right]$$

$$\text{to} \quad 100 - \left[3.09 \times 13.76 - \frac{3.09 \times 13.76}{\sqrt{5}}\right]$$

i.e.   24 to 76

As the action limits (33 to 71) lie well within this range, we conclude that no undetected lapses from tolerance will occur.

**Step 6**

We can now set up the *control chart for sample means*. In Fig 18.2 the action and warning limits have been inserted. We have assumed that the inspection system is under way; that twenty samples of five items have been drawn; and their means plotted on the control chart. All of the samples are well within the action limits. Notice that two sample means fall outside the warning limits – but we would have expected only one to do so. Is this significant? Probably not – it is quite likely that all of the means of the next 20 samples will be within the warning limits.

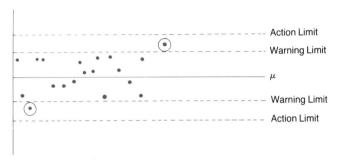

**Fig 18.2**

Suppose we use the means chart as our basis for controlling quality. We draw samples of five items every (say) 15 minutes, and plot the means on the chart. Our results may look something like Fig 18.3.

**Fig 18.3**

Carefully compare the last two diagrams. In Fig 18.2, the sample means are clustered fairly evenly about the mean. In Fig 18.3, the means are clustering about the upper warning limit. What does this second case signify? It would appear that the mean diameter has increased – the setting of the machinery has drifted upwards. Would we be justified in halting production and lowering the setting of the machine? Now breaks in production are expensive, and we must be sure that drifting has occurred before a resetting is justified. Common sense tells us that in the first diagram there is insufficient evidence of a drift.

Suppose we now reset the machine and continue to draw samples. The first sample drawn has a mean less than the lower action limit. What shall we do? We expect only one sample in 500 to be outside these limits – yet the first sample drawn is outside the lower action limit. It is possible that the first sample drawn is that one sample in 500–the rogue sample is just as likely to be the first as any other. However, exceeding the action limits by definition demands that we take some action. The appropriate action is to draw more samples immediately – we certainly would not be justified in waiting

15 minutes to draw the next sample. If their means are clustered about $\mu$, then it seems likely that we have indeed met the odd 1 in 500 case. However, if the means are clustered about the lower warning limit, then trouble is indicated.

## Estimating the standard deviation

In the previous example, we assumed that the standard deviation was carefully calculated. In practice, this is seldom done: instead the standard deviation is estimated from the sample range. To see how this is achieved, let us consider another example.

EXAMPLE

Suppose again that we wish to set up a control system to check the diameters of metal rods. Twenty samples, each of five items were drawn, and their diameters measured and recorded in 10 000ths of a centimetre above 1 cm. The results were as follows.

| | Sample no. | | | | | | | | | |
|---|---|---|---|---|---|---|---|---|---|---|
| | 1 | 2 | 3 | 4 | 5 | 6 | 7 | 8 | 9 | 10 |
| | 59 | 24 | 58 | 58 | 54 | 67 | 55 | 22 | 68 | 53 |
| | 57 | 28 | 52 | 67 | 45 | 43 | 44 | 54 | 59 | 74 |
| | 44 | 66 | 32 | 46 | 79 | 33 | 45 | 62 | 49 | 39 |
| | 53 | 53 | 35 | 76 | 46 | 39 | 40 | 35 | 42 | 58 |
| | 82 | 43 | 11 | 46 | 69 | 53 | 74 | 69 | 44 | 67 |
| Sample total | 295 | 214 | 188 | 293 | 293 | 235 | 258 | 242 | 252 | 291 |
| Sample mean | 59 | 43 | 38 | 59 | 59 | 47 | 52 | 48 | 50 | 58 |
| Sample range | 38 | 42 | 47 | 30 | 34 | 34 | 34 | 47 | 26 | 35 |

| | Sample no. | | | | | | | | | |
|---|---|---|---|---|---|---|---|---|---|---|
| | 11 | 12 | 13 | 14 | 15 | 16 | 17 | 18 | 19 | 20 |
| | 52 | 66 | 42 | 46 | 63 | 71 | 43 | 34 | 47 | 53 |
| | 73 | 63 | 58 | 53 | 65 | 67 | 66 | 36 | 45 | 48 |
| | 48 | 30 | 44 | 40 | 70 | 55 | 52 | 41 | 78 | 64 |
| | 37 | 68 | 65 | 31 | 51 | 36 | 49 | 31 | 55 | 46 |
| | 62 | 49 | 50 | 33 | 58 | 52 | 40 | 47 | 77 | 53 |
| Sample total | 272 | 276 | 259 | 203 | 307 | 281 | 250 | 189 | 302 | 264 |
| Sample mean | ·54 | 55 | 60 | 41 | 61 | 56 | 50 | 38 | 60 | 53 |
| Sample range | 36 | 38 | 23 | 22 | 19 | 35 | 26 | 16 | 33 | 18 |

To estimate the mean diameter of all the rods, we calculate the mean of the sample means ($\bar{\bar{x}}$ – pronounced '$x$ double-bar'):

$$\bar{\bar{x}} = \frac{59 + 43 + 38 + \cdots}{20} = \frac{1041}{20} = 52$$

You should realise that in the original units this represents 1.0052 correct to the nearest $\frac{1}{10\,000}$ inch.

The next stage is to calculate the range within each sample (in case you have forgotten, the range is the difference between the greatest and the smallest item. So the range of the first sample is $82 - 44 = 38$). Then we calculate the mean range $\bar{R}$:

$$\bar{R} = \frac{38 + 42 + 47 + \cdots}{20} = \frac{633}{20} = 32$$

(or 0.0032 in original units).

We estimate the standard deviation by multiplying the mean range by an amount $A_n$. Now $A_n$ is a statistical constant that varies according to the sample size. Unfortunately, the derivation of the distribution of the constant $A_n$ is beyond the scope of this book, but tables are available, and an extract is printed below:

**The distribution of $A_n$ for samples of $n$ items**

| Sample size n | $A_n$ | Sample size n | $A_n$ |
|---|---|---|---|
| 2 | 0.8862 | 7 | 0.3698 |
| 3 | 0.5908 | 8 | 0.3512 |
| 4 | 0.4857 | 9 | 0.3367 |
| 5 | 0.4299 | 10 | 0.3249 |
| 6 | 0.3946 | | |

We have drawn samples of five items, so the estimated standard deviation is:

$$0.4299 \times 32 = 13.76$$

(or 0.001376 in original units).

We will now use $\bar{\bar{x}}$ as an estimate of the mean diameter of all metal rods, and 13.76 as an estimate of their standard deviation (we will examine the validity of these estimates in the next chapter). Armed with these estimates, we can now proceed to set up a control system, starting at Step 2 of the previous section.

## Control system for attribute sampling

We shall now examine a quality control system for goods that are classified as either defective or non-defective. Much of what we have said for the first system also applies here – the warning limits and the action limits will be fixed at the same confidence intervals, and records will be kept in a similar fashion. The difference in this system is the lack of tolerance limits and so there will be no AWCL.

Suppose electric light bulbs are packed in consignments of 500 and periodically a batch is exhaustively examined for defectives. So far, 50 batches have been examined, and have yielded the following number of defectives:

| 10 | 8 | 7 | 6 | 6 | 6 | 8 | 8 | 6 | 6 |
|----|---|---|---|---|---|---|---|---|---|
| 8 | 6 | 6 | 7 | 5 | 8 | 8 | 7 | 8 | 8 |
| 6 | 7 | 9 | 8 | 8 | 6 | 6 | 9 | 6 | 7 |
| 6 | 7 | 3 | 7 | 5 | 7 | 6 | 7 | 9 | 8 |
| 6 | 8 | 7 | 6 | 6 | 6 | 8 | 8 | 6 | 6 |

We will use this information to set up a quality control system. First we put the data into the form of a frequency distribution, and calculate the mean and the standard deviation:

| No. of defectives per sample $x$ | No. of samples $f$ | $fx$ | $fx^2$ |
|---|---|---|---|
| 3 | 1 | 3 | 9 |
| 4 | 0 | 0 | 0 |
| 5 | 2 | 10 | 50 |
| 6 | 19 | 114 | 684 |
| 7 | 10 | 70 | 490 |
| 8 | 14 | 112 | 896 |
| 9 | 3 | 27 | 243 |
| 10 | 1 | 10 | 100 |
| | 50 | 346 | 2472 |

$$\bar{x} = \frac{346}{50} = 6.92$$

$$\sigma = \sqrt{\frac{2472}{50} - (6.92)^2} = 1.245$$

Now, in fact, a distribution of defectives is typically binomial, but it is more usual to assume that a normal distribution is a good approximation. So, we have the warning limits at:

$$6.92 \pm (1.96 \times 1.245) = 4.48 \text{ to } 9.36 \text{ defectives}$$

Only one sample in 20 can be expected to have defectives outside these limits. The action limits are:

$$6.92 \pm (3.09 \times 1.245) = 3.07 \text{ to } 10.77$$

Only one sample in 500 can be expected to have defectives outside these limits.

On the chart (*see* Fig 18.4) the results of the first 50 samples have been recorded. As you can see, the process is well under control.

**Fig 18.4**

You may be wondering why we have bothered with lower warning and action limits: after all, if samples contain defectives less than those limits, then surely this is indicative of good performance. However, as we can expect one sample in 40 to fall below the lower warning limit, and one in a thousand to fall below the lower action limit, this acts as a good check on whether or not the samples drawn are truly random.

## Using the spreadsheet

The spreadsheet to accompany this chapter produces control charts for the sample mean. The menu structure for this template is illustrated in Fig 18.5.

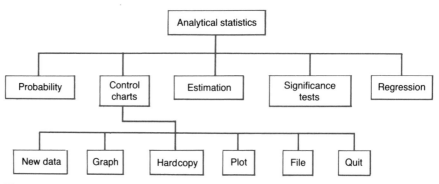

**Fig 18.5**

Select 'Analytical statistics' from the main menu and then select 'Control charts'. Now select the 'New data' option and your opening screen should look like this:

```
        A      B      C      D      E      F      G      H
 1                     Control Chart for Sample Means
 2
 3    Grand mean =                                 Upper   Lower
 4    Stand dev =                  Warning limits
 5                                 Action limits
 6
 7
 8
 9
10
11             Insert sample values. Press ALT B when finished
12    Sample Number
13          1      2      3      4      5      6      7      8
14
15
16
```

The cursor is positioned at cell A14. You should now enter the sample values for each sample in columns, starting with sample number 1. You can enter data for up to 25 samples. When you have finished entering the sample data, press ALT B. The grand mean and standard deviation is output, together with the values for the action and warning limits.

Select the 'Graph' option and the control chart is output. When you have finished with the graph, you can either enter new data, or exit and save the current data. If you wish, you can add more sample details (up to a maximum of 25 samples) and press ALT B to see the effects of this. Before adding more samples, however, you must press Esc. Press ALT B when you have finished entering more samples.

## QUESTIONS

When attempting these questions, use the distribution of $A_n$ to estimate the standard deviation.

**18.1**   A machine produces and gaps spark plugs to tolerance limits of 25 thousandths of an inch $\pm 2$ thousandths. Plugs outside this range would give erratic running of the engine. It is decided to set up a control chart for the machine. Records reveal that the average range for samples of five items is 1.05, and the mean of the sample means is 25.1. Set up a control chart, conducting a check that the tolerances are being met.

**18.2**   In Step 2 (*see* page 347) we implied that:

Tolerance limits $> 3.09\sigma$,

and as $\sigma = \bar{R}A_n$

Tolerance limits $> 3.09 A_n\bar{R}$

If we put $R = 3.09 A_n$, then tolerance limits $> R\, \bar{R}$.

Evaluate R when $n = 5$, calculate the value of $R\bar{R}$ for Question 18.1, and compare with the result in Question 18.1.

**18.3**   The warning limits for sample means are:

$$\mu \pm \frac{1.96\sigma}{\sqrt{n}}$$

or $\mu \pm \dfrac{1.96\, \bar{R}A_n}{\sqrt{n}}$

If $\dfrac{1.96 A_n}{\sqrt{n}} = W$, then

Warning limits $= \bar{\bar{x}} \pm W\bar{R}$

Evaluate W when $n = 5$. Use the expression above to agree the warning limits obtained in Question 18.1.

**18.4**   If the action limits for sample means are

$$\mu \pm A\bar{R}$$

write an expression for $A$ and evaluate when $n = 5$. Agree the action limits obtained in Question 18.1 using the constant $A$.

**18.5**   If AWCL is

$$T_L + C\bar{R} \text{ to } T_U - C\bar{R}$$

write an expression for $C_1$ and evaluate $C$ when $n = 5$. Agree the AWCL found in Question 18.1 using the constant $C$. You can now complete the following table and use it for the other exercises you will be asked to work.

| $A_n$ | $R$ | $W$ | $A$ | $C$ |
|--------|-----|-----|-----|-----|
| 0.4299 |     |     |     |     |

**18.6**   A machine is filling bags of fertiliser automatically. Samples of five were drawn, the grand mean weight being 25.02 kg, and the mean range 0.06 kg. Set up a quality control system. The firm receives an order on the understanding that bags will not contain less than 25 kg. What conclusions would you draw?

**18.7**   Samples of five items are drawn at periodic intervals from the output of spark plugs. On a particular day, the first 10 samples were:

|      |      |      |      | Sample no. |      |      |      |      |      |
|------|------|------|------|------|------|------|------|------|------|
| *1*  | *2*  | *3*  | *4*  | *5*  | *6*  | *7*  | *8*  | *9*  | *10* |
| 24.8 | 26.0 | 26.1 | 25.6 | 25.7 | 25.2 | 25.3 | 25.5 | 25.1 | 25.9 |
| 25.6 | 25.4 | 25.0 | 25.5 | 25.8 | 26.1 | 25.9 | 25.6 | 25.8 | 25.7 |
| 25.5 | 24.9 | 25.0 | 25.0 | 25.9 | 25.6 | 25.7 | 26.2 | 26.3 | 25.1 |
| 25.8 | 24.8 | 25.4 | 26.0 | 25.5 | 25.4 | 26.0 | 25.1 | 25.2 | 25.8 |
| 24.8 | 24.9 | 25.5 | 24.9 | 25.1 | 25.2 | 25.1 | 26.1 | 25.1 | 25.5 |

Plot these samples on a control chart. What action would you recommend?

**18.8**   A particular component is produced to a design dimension of $20 \pm 12$ (in some convenient units). A large number of samples of five items are drawn, giving $\bar{x} = 22.5$ and $\bar{R} = 8$. Calculate the action limits and the AWCL. What do you notice? What action would you recommend?

**18.9** For the machine quoted in Question 18.1, find the minimum tolerance to which it can operate.

**18.10** Again for the machine in Question 18.1, find the maximum shift that could occur in the mean before there was a danger of exceeding the tolerances.

**18.11** A manufacturer knows that a supplier of components produces one defective item in 100. He instructs his quality control department to open each batch delivered and randomly select 100 items. If more than one defective item is found, the batch is returned to the supplier. The manager of the quality control department criticises this instruction – why?

**18.12** A manufacturer makes metal washers, and a large number of samples of five items have been kept. The mean range of washers is 0.0002 cm. The firm receives an order for washers within the tolerance limits of $1 \pm 0.0003$ cm. Should the order be accepted?

**18.13** Show that the warning limits for samples of two items are in approximately the same position as the action limits for samples of five items. (Assume the same population is used for both types of samples.)

**18.14** The diameter of cable is specified as 0.75 cm $\pm$ 0.025 cm. A pilot production run is undertaken and 20 groups of five measurements were taken, all the individual results satisfying the specifications. The following results (in units of 0.001 cm) were obtained.

| Sample | 1 | 2 | 3 | 4 | 5 | 6 | 7 | 8 | 9 | 10 |
|--------|-----|-----|-----|-----|-----|-----|-----|-----|-----|-----|
| Mean | 756 | 763 | 751 | 756 | 748 | 752 | 757 | 755 | 759 | 752 |
| Range | 30 | 12 | 13 | 16 | 24 | 17 | 21 | 15 | 24 | 21 |

| Sample | 11 | 12 | 13 | 14 | 15 | 16 | 17 | 18 | 19 | 20 |
|--------|-----|-----|-----|-----|-----|-----|-----|-----|-----|-----|
| Mean | 762 | 746 | 753 | 756 | 761 | 753 | 758 | 754 | 748 | 764 |
| Range | 15 | 12 | 11 | 22 | 17 | 15 | 23 | 10 | 12 | 14 |

(a) Set up a control chart for sample means.

(b) Does the pilot run indicate satisfactory performance of the plant?

**18.15** A machine is programmed to produce ball-bearings having a mean diameter of 17.5 mm and a standard deviation of 0.06 mm.

(a) Set up a control chart for the means of samples of nine items.

(b) Calculate the minimum tolerance limits that the machine can meet.

(c)   The first nine samples yielded the following results

| Sample | 1 | 2 | 3 | 4 | 5 | 6 | 7 | 8 | 9 |
|--------|---|---|---|---|---|---|---|---|---|
| Mean | 17.47 | 17.50 | 17.49 | 17.52 | 17.54 | 17.57 | 17.51 | 17.52 | 17.50 |

Plot the results on the control chart and comment.

**18.16**   A chemical plant shows the following production levels over a ten-hour period.

| Hour | 1 | 2 | 3 | 4 | 5 | 6 | 7 | 8 | 9 | 10 |
|------|---|---|---|---|---|---|---|---|---|----|
| Production | 140 | 131 | 142 | 121 | 134 | 145 | 131 | 148 | 132 | 136 |

Set up a suitable control system.

**18.17**   In order to set up a quality control system, 50 samples were exhaustively examined for the number of defectives. The results were:

| No. of defectives | 5 | 6 | 7 | 8 | 9 | 10 | 11 | 12 | 13 |
|-------------------|---|---|---|---|---|----|----|----|----|
| No. of samples | 2 | 0 | 8 | 12 | 16 | 8 | 0 | 3 | 1 |

Set up a quality control system for the number of defectives per sample.

**18.18**   (a)   In a sample of 1000 items produced, 42 were rejected. It was decided that control samples of 200 would be taken at frequent intervals. Find the warning limits and action limits.

(b)   The first 15 control samples yielded the following results

| Sample no. | No. of rejects |
|------------|----------------|
| 1 | 8 |
| 2 | 11 |
| 3 | 9 |
| 4 | 6 |
| 5 | 12 |
| 6 | 8 |
| 7 | 13 |
| 8 | 11 |
| 9 | 14 |
| 10 | 15 |
| 11 | 18 |
| 12 | 10 |
| 13 | 8 |
| 14 | 12 |
| 15 | 7 |

Plot the results of these samples onto a control chart. What would you conclude?

**18.19** From a particular productive process 20 samples, each of 20 items were selected. The following number of defectives were recorded: 3, 1, 0, 2, 1, 0, 0, 1, 1, 2, 0, 0, 4, 1, 0, 3, 0, 0, 1, 0. Set up a control chart for the number of defectives in a sample. *Note:* The mean number of defectives per sample is too small to be able to use a normal approximation, so the Poisson distribution must be used. Find the appropriate Poisson distribution, and use this to find the number of defectives that will be exceeded on only 5% of occasions (this gives the warning limit) and the number of defectives that will be exceeded on just 1% of occasions (this gives the action limit).

**18.20** Motor vehicle bodies are produced by a spot welding operation, and some joints will need rewelding. The table below gives the number of defective welds found on vehicles which were selected at hourly intervals during a three-day period. The number of defects can be assumed to form a Poisson distribution.

| 1st day | 2nd day | 3rd day |
|---------|---------|---------|
| 2 | 5 | 6 |
| 4 | 3 | 4 |
| 7 | 7 | 3 |
| 3 | 11 | 9 |
| 1 | 6 | 7 |
| 4 | 4 | 4 |
| 8 | 9 | 7 |
| 9 | 9 | 12 |

The results are those of one welder, and for each day the first four refer to morning work and the second four to afternoon work.

(a) What is the mean number of defectives?

(b) Find the action and warning limits for the number of defective welds. (*Hint:* as the mean is high we can use a normal approximation. Remember that for a Poisson distribution mean = variance.)

(c) Make any comments you consider relevant.

# 19 Estimation

In Chapter 17 we concerned ourselves with making predictions about sample behaviour and we did this by introducing the idea of sampling distributions and confidence limits. In order to form sampling distributions, we required knowledge of the appropriate population parameters. If we were variate sampling then we needed to know the population mean and variance, and if we were attribute sampling then we needed to know the population proportion. Now in this chapter, we will reverse the process: we will assume that the population parameters are unknown to us and that we want to predict them from sample evidence. We will use the technique known as *statistical estimation*. It goes without saying that we require any estimate made to be a 'good' one – an estimate that a statistician would call unbiassed. Before we start, then, we need to define precisely what is meant by an unbiassed estimate. *An unbiassed estimate is one that is just as likely to be too great as it is to be too small.* In other words, if we drew all possible samples size $n$ and made an estimate of the population parameter from each, then the average value of our estimate would be equal to the true value of the population parameter. Obviously this is a sensible definition – the more data that we have then the more accurate would be our estimate.

## Estimating a population mean

Let us suppose that we draw a sample of $n$ items, and we use the sample to estimate the population mean. We can use the symbol $\wedge$ to mean 'an estimate of', so the estimated population mean is denoted by $\hat{\mu}$. Think back to Experiment 1 in Chapter 17 – here we drew all possible samples from an infinite population, and found that the average value of the sample mean was the same as the population mean. The sample mean, then, fits our criterion for an unbiassed estimate precisely, so we can state that:

$$\hat{\mu} = \bar{x}$$

The single estimate of $\mu$ is called a *point estimate*, and we are going to be extremely lucky if our estimate is bang on target. It would seem reasonable to adopt the policy of Chapter 17 and state a confidence interval, or *interval estimate* of the population mean.

To set up this confidence interval, we must decide on how sure we want to be that our interval estimate does include the true value of the population mean and as we saw in Chapter 17, it is usual to apply a 95% level of confidence. To see how the method works, let us suppose we know that a population has a mean 100 and a standard deviation 20, though we keep this information to ourselves. We now ask a statistician to estimate the mean of this population by sampling. If the statistician decides to draw 100 items for his samples we can use confidence limits to predict that 95% of the means of such samples would be in the range:

$$100 \pm 1.96 \times \frac{20}{\sqrt{100}}$$

or (roughly) within the range 96 to 104.

The statistician now draws his samples, and sets up a 95% interval estimate from each sample. Suppose his first sample had a mean of 99.5, then his interval estimate for the population mean would be:

$$\hat{\mu} = 99.5 \pm 19.6 \times \frac{20}{\sqrt{100}},$$

or between 95.5 and 103.5 – an interval estimate that does in fact bracket the true value of the population mean. If his second sample had a mean of 102.5, then his interval estimate would be:

$$\hat{\mu} = 102.5 \pm 1.96 \times \frac{20}{\sqrt{100}}$$

or between 98.5 and 106.5 – which again brackets the true value of the population mean. Fig 19.1 illustrates the situation, and a glance at the diagram will show that provided the sample mean lies between 96 and 104, then the interval estimate will bracket the true value of the population mean. Now sampling theory tells us that we can indeed expect 95% of sample means to lie within these limits, so we can expect 95% of interval estimates to bracket the true value of the mean. This is what is meant, then, when we talk of a 95% interval estimate for the population mean. If we draw many samples from a population, and set up interval estimates for the population mean, then 95% of our interval estimates will include the true value of the population mean.

Now if you think carefully about what we have learnt so far, you will realise that there are two snags with this analysis. First, we have used the true value of the population standard deviation to set up interval estimates for the population mean – but in practice we will not know the true value of the population standard deviation, and we will have to use the sample standard deviation ($s$). Our interval estimate is, then:

$$\hat{\mu} = \bar{x} \pm \frac{1.96s}{\sqrt{n}}$$

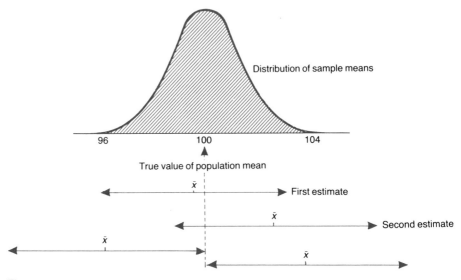

**Fig 19.1**

Now as $s$ is only an estimate of $\sigma$, to retain 95% confidence, we really should widen our estimate a little. However, you can rest assured that as long as our sample is large (greater than 30), the amount by which we would have to widen our estimate is insignificantly small. We will examine this more closely later.

Second, we have assumed that the statistician has drawn many samples to estimate the population mean – but in practice he will draw just one. Once the estimate has been made, then the statistician is either right or wrong – there is no way he can be right on 95% of occasions. What, then, would an interval estimate mean in this case? The statistician is using a method that has a 95% chance of success in the long run – he knows that if he uses this method every time he is asked to estimate a population mean, then 95% of his interval estimates will bracket the true value of the population mean. He will be right on 95% of occasions.

## Estimating a population proportion

Quite often, we will find it useful to use a sample to estimate the proportion of a population with a certain characteristic ($\hat{\pi}$). For example, we might wish to estimate the proportion in the population who intend to buy a certain product, or the proportion of defective items in a large batch. To do this, we can use a method essentially similar to estimating a population mean – i.e. we can set up a 95% interval estimate. Now the point estimate of the population proportion is the sample proportion (which we shall call $p$), so:

$$\hat{\pi} = p$$

Moreover, Experiment 4 in Chapter 17 demonstrates that $p$ satisfies the criterion for an unbiassed estimate. The experiment demonstrated that if samples of $n$ items are drawn from a population with a proportion 'defective', $\hat{\pi}$, and if the proportion 'defective' $p$ is calculated for each sample, then the average value of $p$ will be $\hat{\pi}$. To calculate an interval estimate, we will need the standard error of the proportion. Using the sample proportion, this is:

$$\sqrt{\frac{p(1-p)}{n}}$$

So our 95% interval estimate for the population proportion is:

$$\hat{\pi} = p \pm 1.96\sqrt{\frac{p(1-p)}{n}}$$

EXAMPLE 1

In order to estimate its share of the market, a detergent manufacturer randomly selects 500 women and asks them whether they use the manufacturer's products. Two hundred and sixty report that they do so. Estimate the manufacturer's market share:

$$\hat{\pi} = p = \frac{260}{500} = 0.52$$

95% interval estimate for market share =

$$0.52 \pm 1.96\sqrt{\frac{0.52(1-0.52)}{500}}$$

$$= 0.52 \pm 0.0437$$

or, using percentages

$$52\% \pm 4.37\%$$

## Determining the sample size

We have seen that we can give a 95% interval estimate for a population parameter by calculating:

sample statistic $\pm$ 1.96 $\times$ standard error

and the quantity $\pm 1.96 \times$ standard error is called the *sampling error*. Now clearly, the smaller is the size of the sampling error, the more precise will our interval estimate be. We shall now ask what determines the size of the sampling error, and see what we can do to reduce its size. If we multiply the standard error by a constant smaller than 1.96 then we will reduce the sampling error – but we will no longer have the interval estimate we require as our level of confidence would be less than 95%. If, then, we are to reduce the size of the sampling error we must turn our attention to the standard error.

Let us turn our attention first to estimating the population mean. In this case, the standard error is $s/\sqrt{n}$, and if we reduce the size of $s$ or increase the size of $n$, then the standard error (and so the sampling error) will be reduced. Now although we cannot reduce the size of $s$ (after all, the sample standard deviation is quite outside our control) we can increase the size of $n$. This will improve the precision of our estimate. Think about this for a minute and you will realise that it makes sense, because after all we should have more confidence in large sample results than in small sample results.

Suppose a sample of 100 items has a mean of 50 and a standard deviation of 20. Our interval estimate (with 95% confidence) for the population mean is:

$$\hat{\mu} = 50 \pm 1.96 \times \frac{20}{\sqrt{100}}$$

i.e. $50 \pm 4$ (approximately)

If this was not sufficiently precise, we could draw a larger sample and reduce the sampling error. If we wanted the sampling error to be two rather than four, then

$$2 = 1.96 \times \frac{20}{\sqrt{n}}$$

so $\quad \dfrac{2}{1.96} = \dfrac{20}{\sqrt{n}}$

and $\quad n = \left(\dfrac{20 \times 1.96}{2}\right)^2$

$\qquad\quad = 384$

If we now draw another sample of 384 items, this should give us the degree of precision we require for our interval estimate. We can see then, that if we are prepared to state in advance the size of the sampling error that would satisfy us (call this $r$) and then undertake a pilot sample to determine the size of the sample standard deviation ($s$), then the sample size $n$ that will give the required sampling error is:

$$n = \left(\dfrac{1.96s}{r}\right)^2$$

with 95% confidence, or:

$$n = \left(\dfrac{2.576s}{r}\right)^2$$

with 99% confidence.

We can use a similar analysis to find the sample size necessary to obtain a sampling error of $\pm r$ when estimating a population proportion. This is:

$$n = \dfrac{(1.96)^2 p(1-p)}{r^2}$$

with 95% confidence or:

$$n = \dfrac{(2.576)^2 p(1-p)}{r^2}$$

with 99% confidence.

---

**EXAMPLE 2**

A sales manager has conducted a survey, and found that 5% of his competitors intend to switch to his product on their next purchase. He urges the board to sanction a capacity expansion. Before doing this, the board want to be 99% certain that the sales manager's estimate is correct to within $\pm\frac{1}{2}\%$. What size sample should be examined to check the sales manager's claim?

$$n = \dfrac{(2.576)^2 \times 0.05(1-0.05)}{(0.005)^2} = 12\ 608$$

Obviously, such an exceptionally large sample would cost a lot of money!

## Estimating a population variance

Let us turn our attention to estimating a population variance. From what we have learnt in this chapter you would expect that the unbiassed estimate of the population variance ($\hat{\sigma}^2$) is the sample variance $s^2$, but unfortunately this is not so. This can be demonstrated with a simple experiment.

| EXPERIMENT 5 | Find your results of Experiment 1 in Chapter 17, where you drew samples of two items from the population 1, 2, 3:

$$\mu = \frac{1+2+3}{3} = 2$$

$$\sigma^2 = \frac{(1-2)^2 + (2-2)^2 + (3-2)^2}{3} = \frac{2}{3}$$

(a)  For each sample, find the variance $s^2$.

(b)  Show that the average value of the sample variance is $\frac{1}{3}$.

So we see from this experiment that we must not use the sample variance as an estimate of the population variance – the sample variance is a *biassed* estimate as it *underestimates* the population variance. To obtain an unbiassed estimate of the population variance, we must increase the sample variance, and we do this by applying *Bessel's correction*: multiply the sample variance by $\frac{n}{n-1}$, i.e.:

$$\hat{\sigma}^2 = s^2 \times \frac{n}{n-1}$$

or what amounts to the same thing:

$$\hat{\sigma}^2 = \frac{\Sigma (x - \bar{x})^2}{n-1}$$

| EXPERIMENT 6 | Suppose we have a population comprising the digits 5, 9:

$$\hat{\mu} = \frac{5+9}{2} = 7$$

$$\sigma^2 = \frac{(5-7)^2 + (9-7)^2}{2} = 4$$

(a) Draw all possible samples of three items from this population (there are eight) and find the variance of each sample.

(b) Show that the average value of the sample variance underestimates the population variance.

(c) Multiply each sample variance by $\frac{n}{n-1}$ and show that the average value of the adjusted sample variance is 4 (the same as the population variance).

Let us examine again the expression for estimating the population variance:

$$\hat{\sigma}^2 = s^2 \times \frac{n}{n-1}$$

Now the adjustment we must make to the sample variance to get an unbiassed estimate of the population variance will depend on the size of the sample we draw. The larger the value of $n$, the smaller the adjustment we must make. This is clearly illustrated in the table below:

| $n$ | $\dfrac{n}{n-1}$ |
|-----|------------------|
| 2 | 2.000000 |
| 5 | 1.250000 |
| 10 | 1.111111 |
| 50 | 1.020408 |
| 100 | 1.010101 |
| 1000 | 1.001001 |

So we can see that when the sample size is two, we must increase the sample variance by 100% in order to obtain an unbiassed estimate of the population variance. If the sample size increases to 50 items, then the size of the adjustment falls to 2%, but if we increase the sample size to 1000 then the adjustment necessary is only 0.1%.

We have applied Bessel's correction to variate sampling, but it applies equally to attribute sampling. If the sample is large, then the variance of the sample proportion is a good approximation to the population proportion –

but if the sample is small then Bessel's correction must be applied, i.e.:

$$\hat{\sigma}^2 = \frac{p(1-p)}{n} \times \frac{n}{n-1}$$

$$= \frac{p(1-p)}{n-1}$$

Now the importance of Bessel's correction is the implications it has when we either predict sample behaviour, or make estimates of the population mean or proportion. So far, we have used Z scores for the normal distribution when we set up confidence intervals or made interval estimates, but this is only justified as long as the population standard deviation is known or can be estimated with great precision, i.e. if the sample is large. However, if the sample is small then the normal distribution will not apply: we will have no justification at all for using Z scores for the calculation of confidence intervals. Suppose we have a sample of $n$ items with a mean $\bar{x}$ and a standard deviation $s$, then:

$$\hat{\mu} = \bar{x}$$

$$\hat{\sigma}^2 = s^2 \times \frac{n}{n-1}$$

$$\hat{\sigma} = s \times \sqrt{\frac{n}{n-1}}$$

The estimated standard error of the mean will be:

$$\frac{\hat{\sigma}}{\sqrt{n}} = s \times \sqrt{\frac{n}{n-1}} \times \frac{1}{\sqrt{n}}$$

$$= \frac{s}{\sqrt{n-1}}$$

Now if the sample is large, we can make a 95% interval estimate like this:

$$\hat{\mu} + \bar{x} \pm 1.96 \frac{s}{\sqrt{n-1}}$$

but suppose the sample is small – then the constant 1.96 cannot be used. You see, the problem is that by using small samples we have introduced further sampling errors into our estimates. In estimating the population mean we have also had to estimate the population variance – an estimate which itself is subject to error. The error we quote in our interval estimate, then, is too small and we should increase it; we must multiply the standard error by a constant *greater than* 1.96. Just how much greater than 1.96 should be our constant depends on the accuracy of our estimate of the population variance – which in turn depends on the sample size.

This problem of the size of the constant to use was investigated by WS Gosset in 1908, who published his results under the pseudonym 'A Student' (his employers would not allow him to use his real name). He realised that standard normal Z scores would not apply to small samples, so he replaced them with a statistic he called $t$. Gosset discovered the sampling distribution of $t$, which takes into account the variations in $s$ as well as the variations in $\bar{x}$. For each sample size, then, there is a different $t$ distribution, so it is vitally important that we use the right one. Now Gosset did not tabulate the $t$ distribution against the sample size – instead he tabulated it against the number of *degrees of freedom* in the sample. Don't worry about what this means just yet – for the moment just accept that the number of degrees of freedom is the denominator in Bessel's correction, i.e. one less than the sample size.

Turn to the tables at the end of this book and you will find some values of the $t$ distribution (reasonably complete tables as we gave for the normal distribution would fill an entire book). Tabulated in the first column is the number of degrees of freedom, and in the first row are the varying probability levels. To see how to use these tables, let us consider an example.

---

| EXAMPLE 3 |
|---|

A sample of 10 items has a mean 35 and a standard deviation 10. Estimate the mean of the population from which the sample was drawn.

First, let us make the point estimate:

$$\hat{\mu} = \bar{x} = 35$$

To obtain an interval estimate, we must estimate the standard error of the mean:

$$\text{s.e. of sample mean} = \frac{s}{\sqrt{n-1}} = \frac{10}{\sqrt{10-1}} = 3.333$$

The interval estimate of the population mean is:

$$\hat{\mu} = 35 \pm t \times 3.33$$

The appropriate value of $t$ depends upon the degrees of freedom in the sample, and the level of confidence we require for the interval estimate. In this case, the sample has nine degrees of freedom, so the $t$ value we require will be given in the ninth row of the table.

Suppose we wished to set up a 95% interval estimate: the $t$ value we require will be in the column headed Pr. = 0.025 not Pr. = 0.05 because, like the normal distribution table the $t$ table is concerned with the area in the right-hand tail (*see* Fig 19.2).

**Fig 19.2**

So the appropriate $t$ value for this interval estimate is 2.262, and the 95% interval estimate of the population mean is:

$$\hat{\mu} = 35 \pm 2.262 \times 3.333$$
$$= 35 \pm 7.54$$

Likewise, the $t$ value for a 99% interval estimate would be found in the column headed Pr. = 0.005, i.e.:

$$\hat{\mu} = 35 \pm 3.250 \times 3.333$$
$$= 35 \pm 10.833$$

As the sample size increases, the $t$ distribution becomes closer to the normal distribution. In fact, if the sample has 120 degrees of freedom (i.e. a sample of 121 items) then the 95% interval estimates for the population mean is:

$$\hat{\mu} = \bar{x} \pm 1.98 \text{s.e.}$$

whereas for a 'large' sample it would be:

$$\hat{\mu} = \bar{x} \pm 1.96 \text{s.e.}$$

– hardly any difference. In fact, most statisticians argue that if the sample has at least 30 items, it makes little difference whether the normal distribution or the $t$ distribution is used. This is the reason why statisticians call samples greater than 30 'large' samples.

# Degrees of freedom

The time has now arrived to examine what is meant by degrees of freedom – a concept that creates problems for most students of Statistics. The concept arises because sample results vary: if we use samples to estimate (say) a population mean, then we will not obtain the same estimate from each sample. Moreover, the smaller the sample size chosen, then the greater will be the variation in our estimates. Suppose we drew samples of five items from a certain population and found that the sample mean $\bar{x} = 20$. Of course, another, different, sample of five items could also yield the same estimate, and we will now examine the values that this sample could contain. If the sample is to contain five items and have a mean of 20, then the sample total ($\Sigma x$) must be $5 \times 20 = 100$. In fact, we are perfectly 'free' to assign arbitrary values to any four of the five items in the sample. Suppose the first four items sampled are 10, 25, 30 and 18: then the last item must be $100 - (10 + 25 + 30 + 18) = 17$. It couldn't possibly be any other value. So we see that if we 'fix' the sample mean at $\bar{x}$ in a sample of $n$ items, we can arbitrarily assign values to $n - 1$ items in the samples. We have $n - 1$ degrees of freedom left in the sample after fixing the sample mean.

A similar analysis can be applied to the sample variance. Suppose a sample of four items has a variance 62.5. Again we have $4 - 1 = 3$ degrees of freedom in constructing a similar size sample with the same variance. Suppose three of the items sampled are 90, 95 and 105 (and the last is $x$), then the sample mean is:

$$\bar{x} = \frac{90 + 95 + 105 + x}{4} = \frac{290 + x}{4}$$

$$s^2 = \frac{\Sigma (x - \bar{x})^2}{n}$$

so $\Sigma (x - \bar{x})^2 = ns^2$

$$\left(90 - \frac{290 + x}{4}\right)^2 + \left(95 - \frac{290 + x}{4}\right)^2 + \left(105 - \frac{290 + x}{4}\right)^2 + \left(x - \frac{290 + x}{4}\right)^2$$

$$= 4 \times 62.5$$

$$(70 - x)^2 + (90 - x)^2 + (130 - x)^2 + (3x - 290)^2 = 4000$$

$$12x^2 - 2320x + 110\,000 = 0$$

which solves to give $x = 110$ or $83\frac{1}{3}$.

If we wish to fix both the mean and variance, then we will have less choice in arbitrarily assigning values to a sample. We will have $n - 2$ degrees of freedom. Suppose we want a sample of four items to have a mean 20 and a variance 10. We can fix any two of the items in the sample. Suppose we fix the first two items at 16 and 18:

$$\bar{x} = 20, \text{ so } \Sigma x = 4 \times 20 = 80$$

If we call the first item $x$, then the fourth must be:

$$80 - (x + 16 + 18) = 46 - x$$

The formula for the sample variance is:

$$s^2 = \frac{\Sigma x^2}{n} - \left(\frac{\Sigma x}{n}\right)^2$$

so $\dfrac{\Sigma x^2}{4} - (20)^2 = 10$

which gives $\Sigma x^2 = 1640$

so $16^2 + 18^2 + x^2 + (46 - x)^2 = 1640$

which reduces to:

$$x^2 - 46x + 528 = 0$$

and solves to give either $x = 22$ or $x = 24$

So the sample must be $16, 18, 22, 24$.

Generalising, if we fix $m$ statistics (for example the mean, variance, etc.) in a sample of $n$ items, then we will have $n - m$ degrees of freedom in fixing the values in the sample.

## 'Pooled' estimates of the population variance

If we draw two samples from the same population we may find that the first sample of $n_1$ items has a variance $s_1{}^2$. From this sample we would estimate the population variance to be:

$$\frac{s_1{}^2 n_1}{n_1 - 1}$$

Suppose that we draw a second sample of $n_2$ items with a variance $s_2^2$ the estimated population variance from this sample is:

$$\frac{s_2^2 n_2}{n_2 - 1}$$

Now it would seem logical to argue that we can get a better estimate of the population variance by pooling the results of both samples than we could from either sample alone. We pool the variances like this:

$$\hat{\sigma}^2 = \frac{s_1^2 n_1 + s_2^2 n_2}{n_1 + n_2 - 2} \quad \text{and} \quad \hat{\sigma} = \sqrt{\frac{s_1^2 n_1 + s_2^2 n_2}{n_1 + n_2 - 2}}$$

In this case, we have $n_1 + n_2 - 2$ degrees of freedom associated with our estimate.

If the samples were large then there would be no need to include the correction factor $(-2)$ in the denominator as the difference in our results would be negligible. Suppose we draw a sample of 1000 items with a variance of 90, and a second sample of 1200 with a variance of 84, then our estimates of the population variance are:

$$\hat{\sigma}^2 = \frac{90 \times 1000 + 84 \times 1200}{1000 + 1200 - 2} = 86.806, \text{ which incorporates the adjustment}$$

or

$$\hat{\sigma}^2 = \frac{90 \times 1000 + 84 \times 1200}{1000 + 1200} = 86.72, \text{ without the adjustment}$$

The difference in our estimates is extremely small. But if the samples were small, say 10 and 16 items respectively:

$$\hat{\sigma}^2 = \frac{90 \times 10 + 84 \times 16}{10 + 16 - 2} = 93.5, \text{ which incorporates the adjustment}$$

or

$$\hat{\sigma}^2 = \frac{90 \times 10 + 84 \times 16}{10 + 16} = 86.31, \text{ without the adjustment}$$

The difference is alarming and serves as a warning not to ignore the adjustment when dealing with small samples.

EXPERIMENT 7

This experiment is designed to verify that the unbiassed estimate of the population variance from two samples is given by:

$$\hat{\sigma}^2 = \frac{n_1 s_1^2 + n_2 s_2^2}{n_1 + n_2 - 2}$$

Let the population be the digits, 1, 2. We could draw samples of two items from this population, and the values of $n_1 s_1^2$ would be $0, \frac{1}{2}, \frac{1}{2}$, and 0. We could draw eight samples of three items from this population and the values of $n_2 s_2^2$ would be $0, \frac{2}{3}, \frac{2}{3}, \frac{2}{3}, \frac{2}{3}, \frac{2}{3}, \frac{2}{3}$ and 0. Now suppose we estimate the population variance by pooling a sample of two items with a sample of three items, then four different estimates could be obtained

(i) $\quad \dfrac{0 + 0}{3 + 2 - 2} = 0$

(ii) $\quad \dfrac{0 + \frac{2}{3}}{3 + 2 - 2} = \dfrac{2}{9}$

(iii) $\quad \dfrac{\frac{1}{2} + \frac{2}{3}}{3 + 2 - 2} = \dfrac{7}{18}$

(iv) $\quad \dfrac{\frac{1}{2} + 0}{3 + 2 - 2} = \dfrac{1}{6}$

Find the number of ways it is possible to make each estimate; find the average value of the estimate and verify that it is equal to the population variance.

Just as we can pool two sample variances to estimate the population variance, we can also pool two sample means to estimate the population mean. If a sample of $n_1$ items has a mean $\bar{x}_1$, and a sample of $n_2$ has a mean $\bar{x}_2$, then we would estimate the population mean like this:

$$\hat{\mu} = \frac{n_1 \bar{x}_1 + n_2 \bar{x}_2}{n_1 + n_2}$$

EXPERIMENT 8

If we draw samples of two items from the population 1, 2, then the possible sample totals $n_1 \bar{x}_1 = 2, 3, 3$ and 4. If we draw samples of three items, then the possible samples totals $n_2 \bar{x}_2 = 3, 4, 4, 4, 5, 5, 5$, and 6. Find all the possible estimates of the population mean by pooling samples of two items with samples of three items. Find the average value of the estimates and verify that it is equal to the population mean.

## Finite population adjustments

So far, we have been assuming that we sample from an infinite population, or (what amounts to the same thing) if we sample from a finite population then we sample with replacement. This is not a realistic assumption: although populations under consideration may be very large, they will still be finite, and it is difficult to imagine why a statistician would practise replacement sampling. We must now examine the effect of finite populations on sampling distributions. Well, the first thing to notice is that if the population is finite and we use the formulas developed so far, then we will be *overstating* the situation. For example, if we are variate sampling, drawing a sample of $n$ items from a population of $N$ items, then the expression $\frac{\sigma}{\sqrt{n}}$ would overstate the standard error of the mean. This can be demonstrated with a simple experiment.

| EXPERIMENT 9 |

Suppose we have a population comprising the digits 4, 5 and 6:

$$\mu = \frac{4 + 5 + 6}{3} = 5$$

$$\sigma = \sqrt{\frac{(4 - 5)^2 + (5 - 5)^2 + (6 - 5)^2}{3}} = \sqrt{\frac{2}{3}}$$

If we draw samples of two from this population then:

$$\text{standard error of sample mean} = \frac{\sigma}{\sqrt{n}} = \sqrt{\frac{2}{3}} \times \frac{1}{\sqrt{2}} = \frac{1}{\sqrt{3}}$$

(1)  Draw all possible samples of two items, but, this time, sample without replacement (there are six possible samples).

(2)  Find the sample mean and the standard error of the mean.

Now if you have performed this experiment correctly, then your calculated value for the standard error of the sample mean will be less than $\frac{\sigma}{\sqrt{n}}$. Can you see why $\frac{\sigma}{\sqrt{n}}$ must overstate the standard error? If we practise replacement sampling then the smallest sample mean will be $\frac{4+4}{2} = 4$, and the largest sample mean will be $\frac{6+6}{2} = 6$. But if we practise sampling without replacement then the smallest sample mean will be $\frac{4+5}{2} = 4.5$, and the largest sample mean will be $\frac{5+6}{2} = 5.5$. So sampling without replacement reduces the range of sample means. The correct value for the standard error or the mean can be obtained using the formula:

$$\frac{\sigma}{\sqrt{n}} \times \sqrt{\frac{N-n}{N-1}}$$

where $N$ is the population size. So we would predict the standard error of the sample mean to be:

$$\frac{1}{\sqrt{3}} \times \sqrt{\frac{3-2}{3-1}} = \frac{1}{\sqrt{3}} \times \sqrt{\frac{1}{2}} = \frac{1}{\sqrt{6}}$$

which should agree exactly with the standard error calculated from the samples in Experiment 9.

The quantity $\sqrt{\frac{N-n}{N-1}}$ is called the *finite population adjustment factor* and it must also be applied to the standard error of proportions, i.e.:

$$\sqrt{\frac{\pi(1-\pi)}{n}} \times \sqrt{\frac{N-n}{N-1}}$$

Sometimes, it makes sense to ignore the finite population adjustment factor. Suppose that $N$ is very large in comparison to $n$, then the adjustment factor will be very close to one, and it will not be worthwhile using the adjustment factor. For example, if we draw samples of 100 from a population of 1000 then the size of the adjustment would be:

$$\sqrt{\frac{1000-100}{1000-1}} = 0.949$$

but if we draw samples of 100 from a population of 100 000 then the adjustment would be:

$$\sqrt{\frac{100\ 000-100}{100\ 000-1}} = 0.9995$$

We can use the finite population adjustment factor to show that it is the absolute size of the sample that is important and not its size relative to the size of the population. Let us suppose that a firm receives components in batches, and it wishes to verify that the proportion of defectives in the batches is remaining constant. The method used is to take a 5% sample, and use this to estimate the proportion in the batch. We know that the standard error is a measure of the accuracy of the estimate: the smaller the standard error then the better is the estimate. Suppose that a batch of 2000 items is received, then a sample of 100 would be examined to give a standard error:

$$\sqrt{\frac{p(1-p)}{100}} \times \sqrt{\frac{2000-100}{2000-1}}$$

The next batch to arrive contains 10 000 items: according to our sampling scheme we would have to examine 500 items – a very large sample indeed.

Is it really necessary to examine such a large sample? Suppose that the standard error obtained from the previous batch gave a satisfactory degree of accuracy – what size sample from a batch of 10 000 would give the same degree of accuracy? If this sample has $n$ items, then the standard error is:

$$\sqrt{\frac{p(1-p)}{n}} \times \sqrt{\frac{10\,000-n}{10\,000-1}}$$

and if this standard error is to be the same as previously then:

$$\sqrt{\frac{p(1-p)}{n}} \times \sqrt{\frac{10\,000-n}{10\,000-1}} = \sqrt{\frac{p(1-p)}{100}} \times \sqrt{\frac{2000-100}{2000-1}}$$

Squaring both sides of this expression and cancelling:

$$\frac{p(1-p)}{n} \times \frac{10\,000-n}{9999} = \frac{p(1-p)}{100} \times \frac{1900}{1999}$$

$$\frac{10\,000-n}{9999n} = \frac{19}{1999}$$

$$n \simeq 104.$$

In other words, a sample of 104 items from a population containing 10 000 items can be expected to yield the same degree of accuracy as a sample of 100 from a population of 2000. If the population size increases by 500% then we need only increase the sample size by 4%! Sampling schemes that rely on drawing a fixed percentage from the population are wasteful and inefficient – you should concentrate on the absolute size of the sample and not its size relative to the population.

## Conclusion

In this chapter, we have examined the principles of statistical estimation. We have distinguished between biassed and unbiassed estimates, and have seen that interval estimates are more useful than point estimates. Finally, we have introduced the idea of finite population adjustments, and have seen that as long as the population size is large in comparison to the sample size, then such adjustments are not really necessary.

## Using the spreadsheet

The spreadsheet to accompany this chapter is concerned with estimating a population mean or proportion using sample data. The menu structure for this template is illustrated in Fig 19.3.

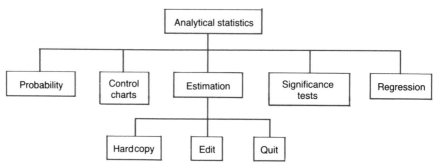

**Fig 19.3**

Retrieve the main menu, select 'Analytical statistics' first, and then select 'Estimation' and finally select 'Edit'. The screen should now look like this:

| | A | B | C | D | E | F | G |
|---|---|---|---|---|---|---|---|
| 1 | | | Statistical Estimation | | | | |
| 2 | | # # # # # # ALT M for menu # # # # # # | | | | | |
| 3 | # # # # Mean # # # # | | | | # # # # Proportion # # # # | | |
| 4 | Sample details: | | | | Sample details: | | |
| 5 | ** Size | | 100 | | ** Size | | 100 |
| 6 | ** Std deviation | | 20 | | ** Proportion | | 0.05 |
| 7 | Std error | | 2 | | Std error | | 0.021794 |
| 8 | | | | | | | |
| 9 | Population details | | | | Population details | | |
| 10 | ** Size | | 1.0E + 20 | | ** Size | | 1.0E + 20 |
| 11 | Adj factor | | 1.0000 | | Adj factor | | 1.0000 |
| 12 | | | | | | | |
| 13 | Sampling error | | | | Sampling error | | |
| 14 | 95% conf | | 3.92 | | 95% conf | | 0.042717 |
| 15 | 99% conf | | 5.152 | | 99% conf | | 0.056142 |
| 16 | | | | | | | |
| 17 | Sample size | | | | Sample size | | |
| 18 | ** Desired s.e. | | 2 | | ** Desired s.e. | | 0.005 |
| 19 | 95% conf | | 384.16 | | 95% conf | | 7299.04 |
| 20 | 99% conf | | 663.5776 | | 99% conf | | 12607.97 |
| 21 | | | | | | | |

The left-hand side of the screen is concerned with estimating a population mean and the right-hand side is concerned with estimating a population proportion. This template runs completely interactively: as you change the sample data, so the population estimates change. The data that you are free to change is marked thus: ★★.

Let us now change some of the data, and note its effects. Move the cursor to cell C5 and change the sample size to 150 and the sample standard deviation to 15. Notice that the standard error changes to 1.224744. Looking at the block marked 'Sampling error' we can conclude that if we attempt to estimate a population mean from a sample of 150 items, with a standard error of 15, then our estimate will have a sampling error of ±2.400499 (with 95% confidence) and ±3.154942 (with 99% confidence).

Now look down to the block marked sample size. This enables us to find the sample size necessary to give a desired sampling error. Move the cursor to cell C18 and enter 1.5 (to show that we consider a sampling error of 1.5 to be satisfactory). We can deduce that, to be 95% confident of our estimate, we would have to draw a sample of 385 items, and to be 99% confident of our estimate we would have to draw a sample of 664 items.

The block marked 'Population details' enables you to apply the finite population adjustment factor should you know the size of the population. The population size is entered in cell C10. If you do not know the population size, then you should enter a very large number in order to give an adjustment factor equal to 1. As the template stands now, the very large number 1E20 has been entered (this is another way of writing 100 000 000 000 000 000 000). If you do not know the population size, then you should always enter 1.OE + 20 in cell C10. Try changing the population size to 10 000. The sampling errors (in block 3), and the sample sizes (in block 4) all decline.

Now try altering the starred values in the second column. The sample proportion must lie between zero and one. Again, if the population size is unknown, then the very large number 1.OE + 20 should be entered into cell G10 to ensure an adjustment factor of 1.

## QUESTIONS

**19.1**   Write brief notes on each of the following:

(a)  Point estimates and interval estimates;

(b)  A sampling error;

(c)  Biassed and unbiassed estimates;

(d)  Degrees of freedom.

**19.2** A simple random sample of 100 sales invoices was taken from a very large population of sales invoices. The average value was found to be £18.50 with a standard deviation of £6.00. Obtain a 95% interval estimate for the true average value per sale.

**19.3** A population of sales invoices is to be sampled so that the mean value per sale can be estimated. One hundred sales invoices are selected at random from this population and classified by value as shown in the following frequency distribution.

| Value (£) | No. of sales invoices |
|---|---|
| 0– 50 | 10 |
| 50–100 | 9 |
| 100–150 | 15 |
| 150–200 | 22 |
| 200–250 | 13 |
| 250–300 | 7 |
| 300–350 | 9 |
| 350–400 | 5 |
| 400–450 | 6 |
| 450–500 | 4 |

Use the sample information to construct interval estimates for the population mean at the 95% and 99% levels of confidence.

**19.4** An auditor randomly selects 100 invoices and checks for error in calculation. Errors in the firm's favour he marks with a plus and errors in the supplier's favour he marks with a minus. He tabulates his results as follows:

| Error (£) | Frequency |
|---|---|
| −40 to −30 | 1 |
| −30 to −20 | 2 |
| −20 to −10 | 16 |
| −10 to   0 | 49 |
| 0 to  10 | 23 |
| 10 to  20 | 6 |
| 20 to  30 | 2 |
| 30 to  40 | 1 |

Find the mean and standard deviation.

Assuming a normal distribution, estimate limits within which you would expect the mean error of all invoices to be. Assuming the firm handles 10 000 invoices per annum, estimate the most likely, most favourable and least favourable errors for one year.

**19.5**   A manufacturer wishes to estimate the mean weight of sacks of carbon black. He would be satisfied if his estimate was within $\pm 5$ lbs of the true mean weight and be 99% sure of his estimate. An initial sample gives a standard deviation of 15 lbs. What size sample yields the required estimate?

**19.6**   From a random sample taken over the period of a year a shopkeeper calculated his average daily sales to be £218 and the standard deviation of the sample to be £18. The number of days' sales in the sample was 60.

(i)   Estimate the mean daily sales for the year at the 99.8% level of confidence.

(ii)   On the assumption that the shopkeeper would be unable to obtain any further stock for another 24 hours, estimate the value of stock he should hold in order to be 95% sure that his stock would last for 24 hours. State any other assumptions you would find necessary to make in order to calculate your estimate.

**19.7**   Ordit and Partners are carrying out a study of three independent magazine retail firms that each have a large number of shops around the country. From samples taken from shops of each firm, the following information was determined:

| Firm | Sample size | Sample average selling price (£) | Sample standard deviation selling price (£) |
|------|-------------|----------------------------------|---------------------------------------------|
| A | 81 | 0.85 | 0.20 |
| B | 49 | 0.76 | 0.18 |
| C | 36 | 0.87 | 0.08 |

(a)   Ordit wish to estimate the average selling price of magazines for each of the three firms. Use the data given to set up a confidence interval estimate for the true average magazine selling price of each of the three firms, using a confidence level of 90%. Comment on your results.

(b)   If, for all three firms, Ordit wished to be within £0.05 of the true average price of magazines with 90% confidence, what size of sample should they have taken from the shops of each firm?

(c)   In the light of your answer to (b) comment on the appropriateness of the data originally collected for the purpose as given in (a).

**19.8**   A local election is being held and there are two candidates, Smith and Jones, for one vacancy. A random sample of the electorate reveals that 55% of them will vote for Smith. How confident can you be that Smith will be elected if the sample size was 100? How large a sample would be needed for the 55% sample results for Smith to make you 99% confident of a win for him?

**19.9** Your sales manager excitedly informs you that he has conducted a survey of competitors' customers, and he has discovered that 5% intend to switch to your product at the next purchase. He advises you to invest now to take advantage of this increase. The sales manager interviewed 100 people. What would you tell him? To be sure that it is worthwhile to expand capacity, you must be convinced within $\frac{1}{2}$% of your sales increase. What size sample should be examined? What would you conclude?

**19.10** In a random sample of 200 garages it was found that 79 sold car batteries at prices below that recommended by the manufacturer.

(i) What is a random sample? Describe briefly how one can be selected.

(ii) Estimate the proportion of all garages selling below the list price.

(iii) Calculate 95% and 99% confidence limits for this estimate and explain what these mean.

(iv) What size sample would have to be taken in order to be 95% certain that the population parameter could be estimated to within 2%?

(v) What size sample is necessary in order to be completely certain that the percentage could be estimated to within 2%. Explain your answer.

**19.11** Nine bags of sugar were randomly selected and carefully weighed. The mean weight was 1.004 kg and the standard deviation 0.0002 kg. Find the 95% interval estimate for the mean weight of all bags.

**19.12** A sample of 10 items has a mean 20 and a standard deviation 0.5. A second sample of 15 items has a mean 19.5 and a standard deviation 0.4. Assuming that both samples came from the same population, estimate the population mean and standard deviation.

**19.13** Show that the maximum value for the standard error of the proportion is:

$$\sqrt{\frac{0.25}{n}}$$

*Note*: You will need calculus to show this.

**19.14** A sample of five items has values 12, 13, 17, 23 and $x$. Find $x$ given that the sample mean is 18.

**19.15** For the sample quoted in Question 19.14, find $x$ given that the sample variance is 21.2.

**19.16**   A sample of five items has values 15, 18, 24, $x$ and $y$. Find $x$ and $y$ given that:

$$\bar{x} = 20 \text{ and } s^2 = 18.$$

**19.17**   A civil engineering contractor buys a job lot of 10 000 pipes which have a nominal length of 10 metres each. A random sample of 100 pipes were chosen and their lengths were carefully measured. The mean length was 9.59 metres and the standard deviation 0.01 metres. Give a 95% interval estimate for the total length of piping in the job lot.

**19.18**   For the job lot of pipes quoted in Question 19.17, find the sample size necessary to predict the total length of piping within $\pm 15$ metres, with 95% confidence.

**19.19**   A by-election has been declared at Anytown, which has 40 000 voters. A random sample of 100 voters reported that 53% can be expected to vote Democrat. Assuming that 70% of registered voters do actually vote, give a 95% interval estimate for the proportion voting Democrat at the election. What size sample should be examined to be 95% sure of a Democrat victory?

**19.20**   Suppose we are sampling to estimate a population proportion. If the population contains 500 items then a sample of 50 gives a satisfactory degree of accuracy to the estimate. What size sample should be examined if the population contains 5000 items?

# 20 Hypothesis testing

In Chapter 12 we developed criteria that were intended to help us in the decision-taking process. We assumed that all the information we needed to apply the criteria was available to us. But how often will this happen in the real world? It is likely that in many cases we will have to resort to sampling to give us some idea of the information we need. Now as you already know, we cannot be completely sure of sample results, so if we base our decisions on sample evidence, it is quite conceivable that we make the wrong choice. It is a major task of statistics to evaluate the probability of making an incorrect decision, and to keep this probability to a minimum.

## Type I errors

We will now return to a problem that faces many manufacturers: how to control the quality of the output. Let us suppose that the manufacturer produces woodscrews by a completely automatic process. One of the problems with the automatic process is that occasionally a screw misses the threading stage, so such screws should be rejected. Now there is little that can be done about this, and the manufacturer has installed machinery that would automatically remove such rejects. From past experience it is known that about 5% of output would be rejected by this machine. Now, although there is not much chance of bettering this rate, machine malfunction can cause the rate to worsen considerably. The problem experienced so far is that it has been difficult to detect just when the rate of rejects has increased because the quantity of output is so great. Obviously, the manufacturer wants to keep the rate as near to 5% as possible – after all, rejects cost money! What he decides to do is to install an automatic sampling device which randomly selects 1000 screws per hour, sorts them, and counts the number of rejects.

The purpose of drawing these samples is, of course, to detect when the reject rate has worsened, and do something about it. Taking remedial action involves stopping the process, and this will be expensive as output will be lost. So if remedial action is to be taken, the manufacturer wants to be pretty sure that the reject rate has worsened. What he wants is some *decision rule* to determine when to stop the process and make the necessary adjustments. Now as 5% of the output is rejected, the manufacturer can expect, on average, 50 rejects in each sample. Suppose he errs on the cautious side, and takes as his decision rule: 'stop the process if the number of defectives exceeds 60'.

Unfortunately, this rule does not exclude the possibility of taking the wrong decision, i.e. stopping the machine when the reject rate has not increased. Using our knowledge of the binomial distribution, we should be able to calculate the probability of taking the wrong decision. It will be the wrong decision if the number of defectives exceeds 60, but the reject rate is still 5%. The appropriate binomial distribution is $(0.95 + 0.05)^{1000}$ and the probability we require is $P_{(61)} + P_{(62)} + P_{(63)} + \cdots + P_{(1000)}$. Now obviously it would be advisable to use the normal approximation to the binomial distribution. First, we require the standard deviation:

$$\sigma = \sqrt{npq}$$
$$n = 1000, \ p = 0.05, \ q = 0.95$$
$$\sigma = \sqrt{1000 \times 0.05 \times 0.95}$$
$$= 6.89$$

The probability that the sample contains more than 60 defects is shown in Fig 20.1 by the shaded area (remember that we must make a 0.5 adjustment when using a normal approximation to the binomial distribution). The Z score is:

$$\frac{60.5 - 50}{6.89} = 1.52$$

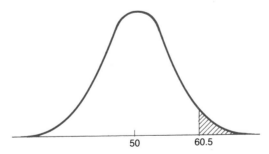

**Fig 20.1**

Consulting the normal distribution tables, the probability we require is 6.43%. So if the manufacturer decides to stop the process if the number of defectives in the sample exceeds 60 on the assumption that the reject rate has risen above 5%, then the probability that he has made the wrong decision is 6.43%.

Is this, then, an acceptable risk? Well, this is really a decision that only the manufacturer can take. To decide whether this risk is too high, he must weigh up what is at stake. Can you see how the manufacturer can reduce the risk of taking the wrong decision? All that he need do is to alter his decision rule, taking a number of defectives greater than 60 as the borderline. If, for example, his decision rule was to stop the process if the number of rejects in the sample exceeds 65, then the Z score would be:

$$\frac{65.5 - 50}{6.89} = 2.25$$

and the probability of making the wrong decision would be 1.22%.

The relationship between the probability of taking the wrong decision and the number of defectives in the decision rule is something we will examine in more detail later. What we shall now do is express the problem in statistical jargon. The manufacturer formulates the *hypothesis* that the overall number of rejects is 5%. He uses the following decision rule: if the number of rejects in a sample exceeds 60, reject the hypothesis and stop the process, otherwise accept the hypothesis. Notice that we have not altered the philosophy of his decision rule – all that we have done is to introduce the word 'hypothesis'. Now we have seen that there is a danger of making the wrong decision and needlessly stopping the process. Using statistical jargon, there is a danger of *rejecting the hypothesis when it should be accepted*. Statisticians refer to the risk as a *Type I error*. We have seen that the risk of a Type I error will vary according to the number of rejects quoted in the decision rule. We can quantify this risk by calculating the Z score for each number of rejects quoted in the decision rule:

| No. of rejects quoted in the decision rule | Z score | Probability of a Type I error |
|---|---|---|
| 52 | 0.36 | 0.3594 |
| 54 | 0.65 | 0.2578 |
| 56 | 0.94 | 0.1736 |
| 58 | 1.23 | 0.1093 |
| 60 | 1.52 | 0.0643 |
| 62 | 1.81 | 0.0351 |
| 64 | 2.10 | 0.0179 |
| 66 | 2.39 | 0.0084 |
| 68 | 2.69 | 0.0036 |
| 70 | 2.98 | 0.0014 |

It is useful to draw a graph of this data, and this is done in Fig 20.2. The manufacturer can see at a glance the risk of incurring a Type I error as he varies the number of defectives in the decision rule. Of course, it is quite possible to state the degree of risk of a Type I error that would be acceptable, and read off from the graph the number of defectives in the decision rule that would yield this degree of risk. Suppose, for example, he would consider as acceptable a 5% chance of a Type I error, then consulting the graph we see that the decision rule should be 'stop the process if the number of defectives exceeds 61'. Using statistical jargon, we say that the graph is the *performance chart* for Type I errors in our decision rule. Notice that as we increase the number of defectives in our decision rule, the probability of a Type I error decreases.

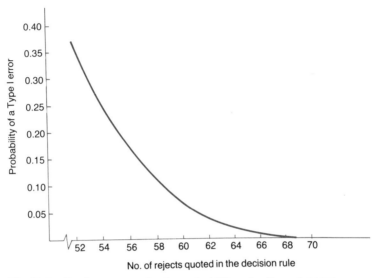

**Fig 20.2    Performance chart: probability of a Type I error**

Let us summarise what we have done so far. We have formulated the hypothesis that the number of rejects is 5%, and we use as a decision rule that if the number of defectives in a sample exceeds a certain number $n$, then we would reject the hypothesis and stop the process, otherwise we accept the hypothesis and allow the process to continue. We have seen that in operating this decision rule there is a danger of rejecting the hypothesis when it should be accepted – so we would needlessly stop the process. This is because it may be possible that the number of rejects in the sample exceeds $n$ even though the overall number of defectives is still 5%. We call this a Type I error, and the performance chart shows how the risk of a Type I error varies with the size of $n$ in our decision rule.

## Type II errors

Now the Type I error is not the only risk the manufacturer runs when operating the decision rule. Originally, he operated the rule: stop the process if the number of defectives exceeds 60, otherwise allow the process to continue. The philosophy underlying this rule is that if the number of defectives is 60 or less, then the overall number of defectives produced is 5%. Now it is quite possible for the overall rate of defectives to rise above 5%, but the sample he draws will contain 60 defectives or less. Should this be the case, then he will be allowing the process to continue when really he should stop the process and make the necessary adjustments. Returning to statistical jargon, there is a danger of *accepting a hypothesis that should be rejected*. Such risks are referred to as *Type II errors*, and we should be able to calculate the probability of such errors.

Suppose the overall rate of rejects produced rose to 7%. For samples of 1000, we have $n = 1000$, $p = 0.07$ and $q = 0.93$. So the appropriate binomial distribution is $(0.93 + 0.07)^{1000}$.

$$\text{Mean} = np = 1000 \times 0.07 = 70$$

$$\text{Standard deviation} = \sqrt{npq} = \sqrt{1000 \times 0.07 \times 0.93} = 8.07$$

We can now use the normal approximation to the binomial distribution to obtain the probability of obtaining 60 or less defectives in a sample of 1000 items. (*See* Fig 20.3.)

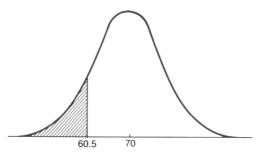

**Fig 20.3**

The Z score is

$$\frac{60.5 - 70}{8.07} = -1.18$$

and consulting the normal tables we see that the probability of a Type II error is 0.119. In other words, there is an 11.9% chance that the decision rule will fail to detect a rise in the overall rate of defectives to 7%, i.e. there is an 11.9% chance that the manufacturer makes the wrong decision.

The probability of making a Type II error will depend on the actual rate of defectives produced by the process. So if we list some possible reject rates, we can calculate the appropriate probabilities of Type II errors:

| Proportion of rejects produced by the process | Mean (np) | s.d. $\sqrt{(npq)}$ | Z score | Probability of Type II error |
|---|---|---|---|---|
| 0.055 | 55 | 7.21 | 0.76 | 0.7764 |
| 0.060 | 60 | 7.51 | 0.07 | 0.5279 |
| 0.065 | 65 | 7.80 | −0.58 | 0.2810 |
| 0.070 | 70 | 8.07 | −1.18 | 0.1190 |
| 0.075 | 75 | 8.33 | −1.74 | 0.0409 |
| 0.080 | 80 | 8.58 | −2.27 | 0.0116 |
| 0.085 | 85 | 8.82 | −2.78 | 0.0027 |
| 0.090 | 90 | 9.05 | −3.26 | 0.0004 |
| 0.095 | 95 | 9.27 | −3.72 | 0.0001 |
| 0.100 | 100 | 9.49 | −4.16 | 0.0000 |

Fig 20.4 shows this information graphically. Notice as the percentage of defectives produced by the process increases, the smaller is the probability of making a Type II error. Notice also that to calculate the probability of making a Type II error we must make an assumption about the value of the

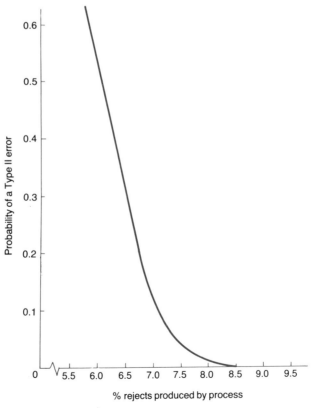

Fig 20.4   **Performance chart: probability of a Type II error**

overall rate of defectives produced by the system. For Type I errors, this was not necessary, so it is easier to calculate the performance chart for Type I errors. Also, the performance chart for Type II errors is not in a very convenient form – it does not show the manufacturer how he can lessen the probability of a Type II error.

Earlier, we calculated that if the overall rate of defectives produced by the process was 7%, then the probability of a Type II error, given our decision rule, is 11.9%. Suppose we changed the decision rule to read: 'stop the process if a sample contains more than 55 defectives'. Now if the overall rate of defectives is 7% and a sample contains 55 defectives or less, then the process will not be stopped when it should be, and the probability of this happening can again be calculated:

$$Z = \frac{55.5 - 70}{8.07} = -1.80$$

and from the normal tables, the probability of taking the wrong decision is 3.59%. So if we reduce the number of defectives in our decision rule, this decreases the probability of a Type II error. Unfortunately, this action would automatically increase the probability of a Type I error!

Summarising then, a Type I error occurs when we reject a hypothesis that should be accepted, and a Type II error occurs when we accept a hypothesis that should be rejected. Many statisticians summarise the distinction in a table like this:

|  |  | *Decision* | |
|  |  | *Accept* | *Reject* |
|  | *True* | Correct decision | Type I error |
| *Hypothesis is* |  |  |  |
|  | *False* | Type II error | Correct decision |

If we state our hypothesis and decision rule, we can immediately calculate the probability of a Type I error, but we cannot calculate the probability of a Type II error without introducing other assumptions. In other words, to calculate the probability of Type I errors, we keep the hypothesis constant and vary the decision rule; but to calculate the probability of Type II errors, we keep the decision rule constant and vary the hypothesis. We can reduce the probability of a Type I error by increasing the number of rejects in our decision rule, but unfortunately this would increase the probability of a Type II error. Now this is quite a problem, and in the next section we will try to reconcile this problem.

## Significance testing

In the last section we found no difficulty at all in calculating the probability of a Type I error. The reason for this was the form taken by our hypothesis: that the overall rate of rejects was 5%. So we could put $p = 0.05$ into the binomial distribution and calculate the probability of a Type I error with ease. Notice that in applying this hypothesis, we are assuming that the reject rate found in the past has continued, i.e. that the reject rate has not changed. We have done this despite the fact that the purpose of our investigation is to detect when the reject rate worsens. Because our hypothesis assumes that 'nothing has happened', it is called a *null hypothesis* and we use the symbol $H_0$ to stand for a null hypothesis. Now you may object that this seems rather strange – the purpose of sampling is to detect when the reject rate worsens, so we should be testing the hypothesis that the reject rate is greater than 5%. Now this is all very well, but it will mean that we are unable to calculate the probability of a Type I error without stating by *how much* the reject rate has worsened. In other words, stating that $p > 0.05$ means that we do not have a value for $p$ to insert in the binomial distribution, and so we will be unable to calculate the probability of a Type I error. It is for this reason that we will ensure that from now on all the hypotheses we test will be null hypotheses.

The testing of null hypotheses has two implications that we must now examine. First, the null hypothesis involves stating the complete opposite to what you are trying to detect. In the example we have been considering so far, we were trying to detect whether the reject rate had worsened, but the null hypothesis is that the reject rate is still 5%. Again, suppose we are trying to test for bias in a coin – the appropriate null hypothesis would be that the coin is unbiassed. It would follow from this that the probability of a head is 0.5, so we could then calculate the probability of a Type I error. We can now state a rule for formulating null hypotheses – if you are trying to detect change, then the appropriate null hypothesis is that no change has occurred.

The second implication of formulating a null hypothesis is that it is no help to us whatsoever, in calculating the probability of a Type II error. To do this we must state an *alternative hypothesis*. This is precisely what we did when calculating the probabilities of a Type II error in the last section. In fact, we stated a number of alternative hypotheses ($p = 5.5\%$, $p = 6\%$, $p = 6.5\%$, etc.). Now obviously there is a problem here: if we reject the null hypothesis it would seem reasonable to accept the alternative hypothesis: but which alternative hypothesis should we accept?

Let us now see if we can find a way round this problem. We incur Type II errors if we accept a hypothesis that should be rejected – so if we never accept a hypothesis we cannot make a Type II error! Let us restate the problem we have so far been considering in order to investigate this situation more closely.

We know from past experience that the process is, on average, rejecting 5% of all screws produced. Now suppose we know that this reject rate can change either way; i.e. improve or get worse, and we wish to sample to detect such changes. The reason for this is that perhaps we can then account for fluctuations in reject rates – they may depend on the quality of steel used, or which shift is operating the machinery. In any case, we will adopt the null hypothesis that the reject rate is 5%, and operate the decision rule 'reject the null hypothesis if the number of defectives in the sample is greater than 60 or less than 40, otherwise *reserve judgment*'. Notice that we never accept the null hypothesis, and in many statistics textbooks you will come across the conclusion 'no reason to reject the null hypothesis' – which of course doesn't mean that it should be accepted! The philosophy behind this argument is that samples which contain between 40 and 60 defectives do not show a *significant* departure from the expected 50 defectives. In other words, the range 40–60 can be attributed to chance or sampling fluctuations. However, defectives outside this range cannot be attributed to chance, the *sample result is significant* and we must reject the null hypothesis. Notice the use of the word 'significant' – many statisticians give the title *significance testing* to the methods we have been describing.

So you see it is possible to avoid making Type II errors altogether. However, you may complain that the reasoning behind this is very suspect. Initially, we were trying to detect when the overall reject rate rose so that we could do something about it. Our null hypothesis was that the overall reject rate was 5%, and our decision rule was 'stop the process if the number of defectives exceeds 60', i.e. reject the null hypothesis. Now suppose that the number of rejects was 60 or less, and that this would induce us to conclude that there is no reason to reject the null hypothesis. Now think carefully about this! If the number of defectives in the sample exceeds 60, we stop the process; if the number does not exceed 60 we reserve judgment. But can we reserve judgment? If we try to do this, we will allow the process to continue – which is tantamount to accepting the null hypothesis! In such circumstances, then, we cannot avoid the risk of a Type II error!

Let us now see if we can devise an acceptable methodology for significance testing. First, we will formulate a null hypothesis $(H_0)$ in such a way that we can calculate the probability of a Type I error. Also, we will formulate an alternative hypothesis $(H_1)$ so that rejection of $H_0$ automatically involves the acceptance of $H_1$. We will then specify the probability of a Type I error that we would be prepared to consider an acceptable risk. We call this probability the *level of significance*, and it is usual to specify probabilities of 5% and 1%. We then construct a decision rule based on the hypothesis and level of significance we have chosen. Whenever possible we word the alternative hypothesis in such a way that if we do not reject the null hypothesis we reserve judgment. If this is not possible, then the wording of the alternative hypothesis is such that the alternative to rejecting the null hypothesis is accepting it. In this latter case, we keep our fingers crossed that the probability of a Type II error is not too large. If Type II errors would be really serious, then we must examine the performance chart to see how likely they are.

## One-sided and two-sided tests

We will now apply this methodology to the problem we have so far been considering. First, we specify the hypotheses:

$H_0$: $\pi = 0.05$, i.e. the overall reject rate is 5%
$H_1$: $\pi > 0.05$, i.e. the overall reject rate is greater than 5%
Level of significance = 0.05, i.e. the risk of a Type I error is 5%.

Consulting the performance chart for Type I errors, we see that for a 5% probability we must quote 61 defectives in our decision rule, so our decision rule is 'reject $H_0$ if the number of defectives in the sample exceeds 61, otherwise accept $H_0$'. We could represent this situation diagrammatically as in Fig 20.5.

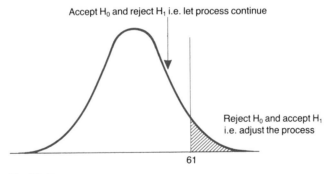

Accept $H_0$ and reject $H_1$ i.e. let process continue

Reject $H_0$ and accept $H_1$
i.e. adjust the process

61

**Fig 20.5**

Summarising this situation, then, we can say that on the basis of our null hypothesis we expect, on average, 50 defectives in samples of 1000. If the number of defectives is 61 or less, then we can say that the deviation from 50 can be attributed to chance. But if the number of defectives exceeds 61 we cannot attribute this to chance, i.e. the result is significant, and we reject the null hypothesis concluding that the reject rate is greater than 5%. We realise that in using this decision rule we run a 5% risk of making a Type I error.

In this example, we are interested in detecting shifts in the reject rate in one direction only. If the reject rate increases, then we must take some action. But if it decreases – so much the better. Tests to detect changes in one direction only are called *one-sided tests* or *one-tail tests*, and a glance at Fig 20.5 will explain why this is so. However, there will be many cases when it will be more meaningful to detect changes in either direction.

To take an example, suppose we know that 40% of the electorate vote Labour, and we wish to detect changes in the Labour vote by sampling. It will be of equal interest to know whether the Labour vote has increased or decreased. The appropriate hypotheses here would be:

$H_0$: $\pi = 0.4$
$H_1$: $\pi \neq 0.4$

Notice that in this case the alternative hypothesis is stated in a 'not equal to' form. Without going into the mechanics of this problem (we will do this in the next chapter) suppose the decision rule was: 'in a sample of 1000, if the number voting Labour is between 370 and 430 accept $H_0$ and reject $H_1$, otherwise accept $H_1$ and reject $H_0$'. Diagrammatically, the decision rule could be represented as in Fig 20.6.

**Fig 20.6**

Tests such as this are called *two-sided* or *two-tail tests*, again for obvious reasons. So if you wish to test for a change in an *unspecified direction* you should use a two-sided test, but if you wish to test for a change in a *specified direction* you would use a one-sided test. The type of test used will be reflected in the formation of the alternative hypothesis. Which type of test is appropriate will depend on the problem under consideration. There is no hard-and-fast rule to follow: as we shall see in the next chapter the choice is really a matter of common sense.

## QUESTIONS

The questions to Chapter 20 can be found with those to Chapter 21.

# 21 Statistical significance

In the last chapter, we indicated how statistics can help us come to the right decision. The methodology we used was as follows. We formulated two hypotheses: a null hypothesis and an alternative hypothesis, in such a way that rejecting one meant accepting the other. The wording we chose for the null hypothesis enabled us to calculate the probability of a Type I error. We then stated a decision rule, for example 'reject the null hypothesis and accept the alternative hypothesis if the number of defectives in the sample exceeds $x$'. If we rejected the null hypothesis, we then calculated the probability of a Type I error, and we called this probability the level of significance. This, then, is the methodology of the statistical technique called *significance testing*. In this chapter, we will move from methodology to the technique itself. In particular, we will be dealing with tests involving sample means and sample proportions. Before we do this, however, we must examine the choice of an appropriate level of significance.

We saw in the last chapter that when we altered our decision rule in such a way that we reject the null hypothesis only if the number of defectives is greater than previously stated, we then reduced the probability of a Type I error. We must now decide on the risk of a Type I error that we could consider acceptable. Now, of course, the acceptable level of risk is a personal choice, and it will vary with the problem we are considering. We would want, for example, a lower level of risk if we were testing the efficacy of a new drug than we would want if we were testing a marksman for bias in shooting. Despite this essentially subjective nature of the level of risk, statisticians do apply conventions. They consider a 5% probability of a Type I error as being acceptable, and construct their decision rules accordingly. If the hypothesis is rejected on the basis of this decision rule, we state that the sample result is *significant at the 5% level*. In other words, we do not think that the sample result can be attributed to chance, and our probability of making a Type I error is 5%. Also, it is usual to construct a second decision rule based on the probability of a Type I error being 1%, so if the null hypothesis is rejected on the basis of this rule, we state that the sample result is *significant at the 1% level*. So applying our decision rules to sample results, there are four possible conclusions we could reach:

1   Accept the null hypothesis and reject the alternative hypothesis. In this case, we are saying that the sample results can be attributed to chance. However, as we saw in the last chapter, reaching this conclusion leaves

us wide open to Type II errors, and the only way to avoid them is to conclude that:

2 There is insufficient reason to reject the null hypothesis – a conclusion that does not conclude anything and suggests the necessity for further sampling. However, if anything useful is to be achieved, then sooner or later we must risk the possibility of a Type II error and come to some definite conclusion.

3 Reject the null hypothesis and accept the alternative hypothesis at the 5% level, but not at the 1% level. Here we are stating that the occurrence of the sample results cannot be attributed to chance, and the probability of a Type I error is less than 5% but greater than 1%.

4 Reject the null hypothesis (and so accept the alternative hypothesis) at the 1% level. In this situation we are taking a less than 1% chance of incurring a Type I error.

Now let us look at the actual wording of the decision rule. We have implied that the decision rule will be stated in terms of the sample statistic, for example 'reject the null hypothesis if the proportion defective exceeds $x$'. How can we find the value of $x$? To do this, we must state the level of significance (which we will assume to be 5%), the sample size (call this $n$) and the null hypothesis about the population proportion (call this $\pi$). The value of $x$, then, is the proportion that would be exceeded in our samples on only 5% of occasions, and we can obtain the value from a one-sided confidence interval, i.e.:

$$x = \pi + 1.645 \sqrt{\frac{\pi(1-\pi)}{n}}$$

(If you cannot see that $x$ is obtained from the one-sided confidence interval, then you should read the chapter on Sampling Theory again.) Alternatively, we may be testing for a change in the population proportion – a movement in either direction. Here, a two-sided decision rule would be appropriate, for example, 'accept the null hypothesis if the proportion defective in the sample is outside the range $x_1$ to $x_2$, otherwise reject it'. Keeping the same level of significance, this range can be obtained from the two-sided confidence interval:

$$\pi \pm 1.96 \times \sqrt{\frac{\pi(1-\pi)}{n}}$$

So we see that the decision rule is merely a confidence interval. In fact, if you think about it you will realise that a confidence interval is a prediction about the sample statistic on the assumption that the null hypothesis is true.

Now although there is absolutely nothing wrong with using decision rules to test hypotheses, statisticians do not, in fact, use them. Taking a one-sided test, a statistician would argue something like this; the null hypothesis would be rejected if:

$$p > \pi + 1.645 \times \sqrt{\frac{\pi(1-\pi)}{n}}$$

where $p$ is the sample proportion. Rearranging this condition, the null hypothesis would be rejected if:

$$\frac{p - \pi}{\sqrt{\dfrac{\pi(1-\pi)}{n}}} > 1.645$$

You should recognise the left-hand side of this condition: it is the Z score of the sample proportion, and because it is being used to test the null hypothesis we call the Z score a *test statistic*. The right-hand side of the condition is the value for the Z score that would be exceeded only on 5% of occasions: if it is exceeded by the test statistic then we would reject the null hypothesis. So the right-hand side of this expression is a kind of a *critical value* for our test statistic.

This, then, is how we shall undertake significance testing. We will set up a null hypothesis and an alternative hypothesis. If we assume that the null hypothesis is true, then we can calculate a test statistic (which basically is the standard score of our sample statistic), and compare the test statistic with its critical value. If the test statistic is greater than its critical value, then we would reject the null hypothesis and accept the alternative hypothesis. However, if the test statistic is less than its critical value, we would accept the null hypothesis and reject the alternative hypothesis.

## Tests of population means using large samples

When we discussed sampling theory, we saw that if we drew large samples from a population with a known mean and standard deviation, then the sample means will be normally distributed. So, if we use large samples to test hypothesis about a population mean, then the test statistic would be the Z score of the sample mean, i.e.:

$$\text{Test statistic } Z = \frac{|\bar{x} - \mu|}{\text{standard error}}$$

Notice that the test statistic is always taken as positive. We can use our knowledge of confidence intervals to state the critical values for Z. The critical value will depend upon the level of significance and on whether the test is one-sided or two-sided:

| | Critical values for Z 5% level | 1% level |
|---|---|---|
| One-sided test | 1.645 | 2.323 |
| Two-sided test | 1.96 | 2.576 |

Can you see why we always take the absolute value of the test statistic? If we did not, then we would have to state *two* critical values for each level of significance for a two-sided test – for example at the 5% level the critical values would be 'greater than 1.96' and 'less than −1.96'. Now as, say, a test statistic of 2 and −2 are equally significant, it makes sense to take the absolute value of the Z score.

---

**EXAMPLE 1**

A sugar refiner packs sugar into bags weighing, on average, 1 kg. Now the setting of the machine tends to 'drift', i.e. the average weight of bags filled by the machine sometimes increases and sometimes decreases. If the mean weight of bags increases, then in effect he is actually giving away some sugar. If the mean weight decreases then he may find himself in trouble with the Weights and Measures Inspector. So it is really important that he controls the average weight of bags of sugar. He wishes to detect shifts in the mean weight of bags as quickly as possible, and reset the machine. In order to detect shifts in the mean weight, he will periodically select a sample of 100 bags, weigh them, and calculate the sample mean.

In effect, the refiner is performing a significance test, adopting as his null hypothesis that the population mean is 1, i.e.

$H_0$: $\mu = 1$.

Now shifts in $\mu$ in either direction are important, so the test is two-sided and the appropriate alternative hypothesis is:

$H_1$: $\mu \neq 1$.

What other information do we need to know? Clearly, we need to know the variance of the weight of bags of sugar – suppose this is 0.01 kg. We can now calculate the standard error of the mean for samples of 100 bags:

$$\frac{\sigma}{\sqrt{n}} = \frac{0.1}{\sqrt{100}} = 0.01 \text{ kg}$$

and if we drew a sample of 100 bags and use the sample mean $\bar{x}$ to test the null hypothesis, then the test statistic Z would be:

$$\frac{|\bar{x} - \mu|}{\text{s.e.}} = \frac{|\bar{x} - 1|}{0.01}$$

so the test is two-sided, we would compare the test statistic with the critical values 1.96 and 2.576:

Suppose the sample mean was 1.03 kg, then:

$$\text{Test statistic } Z = \frac{|1.03 - 1|}{0.01} = 3$$

and as this exceeds the critical value we would reject the null hypothesis and accept the alternative hypothesis at the 1% level of significance. We would conclude that the overall mean weight was no longer 1 kg, and run a less than 1% chance of a Type I error.

---

**EXAMPLE 2**

A certain highway in a city centre has been investigated in the past for noise pollution by vehicles. As a result of many measurements it has been found that between 4.30 p.m. and 5.30 p.m. on any weekday the average noise level is 130 decibels, with a standard deviation of 20 decibels. The residents are convinced that the noise level is getting worse, and having taken 50 readings, obtain an average of 134 decibels. Is their claim justified?

Clearly, this is a one-sided test, so we can formulate:

$H_0$: $\mu = 130$
$H_1$: $\mu > 130$

$$\text{Test statistic } Z = \frac{|\bar{x} - \mu|}{\text{s.e.}} = \frac{|134 - 130|}{20/\sqrt{50}} = 1.41$$

As this is a one-sided test, the critical values for Z are 1.645 (at the 5% level) and 2.326 (at the 1% level). So we see that the difference between the population mean and the sample mean is not significant – it can be accounted for by sampling fluctuations. We would accept the null hypothesis and reject the alternative hypothesis, and we cannot conclude that noise levels have increased.

The two examples we have considered so far assume that we have a prior knowledge of the population – in particular they assume that the population mean and standard deviation are known. Had we not known the population standard deviation, we could have estimated it using $s$, the sample standard deviation. No adjustment to $s^2$ would have been necessary because in both cases we had large samples. Now of course, it will not always be the case that we know the population mean, and if we cannot compare a sample with a population then we must compare a sample with a sample. Tests of this nature come under the general heading of the *significance of the difference between the means of two samples*. Let us see how this test works by considering an example.

---

**EXAMPLE 3**

The authors of this book agree on most matters, be they academic, social or cultural. They are both keen supporters of association football. However, on one thing they will never agree – which is the best team in the English Football League. One of the authors (the misguided one) is convinced that the finest team is Manchester United, but the other author (the one you must agree with) is, of course, a Liverpool supporter. To settle this argument once and for all, the authors agreed to apply statistical analysis to this problem. They will examine a sample of football matches, count up the number of attacking moves made per match, and so obtain a mean and standard deviation of the number of attacking moves made per match for both teams. Now we have a real problem here – is this test one-sided or two-sided? Suppose that $\bar{x}_1$ is the mean number of attacking moves made by Manchester United, and $\bar{x}_2$ is the mean number of attacking moves made by Liverpool. We can take $\bar{x}_1$ as the mean of a sample drawn from a population with a mean $\mu_1$ (the long-run mean number of attacking moves made by Manchester United). Likewise, we can take $\mu_2$ as the long-run mean number of attacking moves made by Liverpool. The appropriate null hypothesis is that there is no difference in the mean number of attacking moves, i.e.:

$H_0$: $\mu_1 = \mu_2$ or
$H_0$: $\mu_1 - \mu_2 = 0$.

Now the Manchester United supporter is convinced that his team is the better, so the alternative hypothesis that he wishes to test is:

$H_1$: $\mu_1 > \mu_2$

i.e. a one-sided test. Likewise, the Liverpool supporter would wish to test the alternative hypothesis:

$H_1$: $\mu_2 > \mu_1$

Again a one-sided test. But what of you, the unbiassed reader (at least, we will assume that you are unbiassed). You really don't know what to expect, so the appropriate alternative hypothesis from your viewpoint would be:

$$H_1: \mu_1 \neq \mu_2$$

i.e. a two-sided test! For the purpose of this problem we will adopt the two-sided alternative hypothesis.

Let us suppose that sampling from the matches played we have:

| | Number of attacking moves | | Number of matches |
|---|---|---|---|
| | Mean | Standard deviation | |
| Manchester United | $30 = \bar{x}_1$ | $6 = s_1$ | $50 = n_1$ |
| Liverpool | $32 = \bar{x}_2$ | $5 = s_2$ | $60 = n_2$ |

Now the standard error of the mean for Manchester United is:

$$\frac{s_1}{\sqrt{n_1}} = \frac{6}{\sqrt{50}} = 0.849$$

and the standard error of the mean for Liverpool is:

$$\frac{s_2}{\sqrt{n_2}} = \frac{5}{\sqrt{60}} = 0.645$$

In making these calculations, we assume that the sample results for Manchester United come from a population with a standard deviation of six, and the sample results for Liverpool come from a population with a standard deviation of five. (This assumption is reasonable: the samples are large so the sample variance is a legitimate estimate of the population variance.) We can now use the sample difference theorem to calculate the standard error of the difference between the means, i.e.:

$$\text{Standard error of the difference} = \sqrt{\left(\frac{s_1}{\sqrt{n_1}}\right)^2 + \left(\frac{s_2}{\sqrt{n_2}}\right)^2}$$

$$= \sqrt{\frac{s_1^2}{n_1} + \frac{s_2^2}{n_2}}$$

$$= \sqrt{(0.849)^2 + (0.645)^2}$$

$$= 1.066$$

Now the actual difference between the means is $|\bar{x}_1 - \bar{x}_2| = 2$, but if the null hypothesis is correct, then the difference does not deviate significantly from zero. In other words, we can consider the difference of 2 as coming from a population of sample mean differences, with a mean zero and a standard error 1.066. We now have all the information necessary to undertake a significance test.

Test statistic $Z = \frac{2-0}{1.066} = 1.876$. As we are conducting a two-sided test, the critical values for $Z$ are 1.96 (at the 5% level) and 2.576 (at the 1% level). So we must accept the null hypothesis: the samples do not provide evidence that there is a difference in the long-run mean number of attacking moves made by the two football clubs.

We must state, though, that to use this method of significance testing, the samples must be *independent*, i.e. both samples are assumed to have come from the same population, and the selection of the first sample in no way affects the selection of the second. This method, then, could not be used for 'before and after' types of experiments, i.e. when the same sample is considered under different conditions. Later we will show you how to deal with samples that are not independent (statisticians call them *paired samples*).

In this section, we have introduced two types of significance tests and it would be useful to introduce general expressions for the test statistic $Z$. In Examples 1 and 2, we tested a hypothesis about a population mean $\mu$ using a sample mean $\bar{x}$. The test statistic in this case was:

$$Z = \frac{|\bar{x} - \mu|\sqrt{n}}{\sigma}$$

In Example 3 we tested for a difference in population means $\mu_1$ and $\mu_2$ using sample means $\bar{x}_1$ and $\bar{x}_2$, and sample standard deviations $s_1$ and $s_2$. The test statistic in this case was:

$$Z = \frac{|\bar{x}_1 - \bar{x}_2| - 0}{\sqrt{\dfrac{s_1^2}{n_1} + \dfrac{s_2^2}{n_2}}}$$

## Tests of population means using small samples

Let us now suppose that we use small samples to test hypotheses about population means. Now if we use the methods of the last section, we will run into trouble on two accounts. First, our small sample will underestimate the population variance, so our test statistic will be wrong. Secondly, the means of small samples are not normally distributed, so our critical values will be wrong. We have learnt that the means of small samples have a *t*-distribution, and the appropriate *t*-distribution will depend on the number of degrees of freedom in estimating the population variance. If we use large samples to test a hypothesis, then the critical values we use will depend upon the type of test (i.e. one-sided or two-sided). But if we use small samples, then the critical values will depend upon the degrees of freedom in the sample as well as the type of test. Fortunately, we already know how to use tables of the *t*-distribution (if you have forgotten, then refresh your memory by re-reading Estimation, Chapter 19). Using small samples, then, both the test statistic and the critical values will be *t*-scores.

| |
|---|
| **EXAMPLE 4** |

The expected lifetime of electric light bulbs produced by a given process was 1500 hours. To test a new batch a sample of 10 was taken which showed a mean lifetime of 1410 hours. The standard deviation is 90 hours. Test the hypothesis that the mean lifetime of the electric light bulbs has not changed, using a level of significance of:

    (a)   0.05;

    (b)   0.01.

This question asks us to test that the mean has not changed, so we must employ a two-sided test:

    $H_0$: $\mu = 1500$
    $H_1$: $\mu \neq 1500$

In this example, we do not know the population standard deviation, so we must estimate it using the sample standard deviation. In an earlier chapter we saw that:

$$\sigma^2 = \frac{ns^2}{n-1}$$

So the estimated population variance is:

$$\frac{10 \times 90^2}{9} = 9000$$

and the estimated standard deviation is:

$$\sqrt{9000} = 94.87$$

So the test statistic *t* for our sample mean is:

$$t = \frac{|\,1410 - 1500\,|\,\sqrt{10}}{94.87} = 2.999. \ (=3)$$

Now for the critical values of $t$, we enter the $t$-table with $10 - 1 = 9$ degrees of freedom, remembering that this is a two-sided test. The critical values are 2.262 (at the 5% level) and 3.25 (at the 1% level). Our test statistic is significant at the 5% level but not at the 1% level. We reject $H_0$ and accept $H_1$, and conclude that there is some evidence to suggest that the mean lifetime of all bulbs has changed.

In fact, we can find the test statistic $t$ directly without first estimating the population variance if we use the expression:

$$\text{Test statistic } t = \frac{|\bar{x} - \mu| \sqrt{(n - 1)}}{s}$$

In the last example, this would give:

$$t = \frac{|1410 - 1500| \sqrt{10 - 1}}{90} = 3, \text{ as before.}$$

---

**EXAMPLE 5**

After treatment with a standard fertiliser, the average yield per hectare is 4.2 tonnes of wheat. A super fertiliser is developed and administered to 10 hectares. The yields from the 10 hectares were 4.3, 6.0, 4.9, 6.1, 6.2, 5.4, 4.1, 4.2, 3.8 and 3.9 tonnes. Does this fertiliser give a higher yield?

First, we should notice that in this case a one-sided test is appropriate, so we have:

$H_0$: $\mu = 4.2$
$H_1$: $\mu > 4.2$

We now need the sample mean and variance:

| $x$ | $x^2$ |
|------|--------|
| 4.3 | 18.49 |
| 6.0 | 36.00 |
| 4.9 | 24.01 |
| 6.1 | 37.21 |
| 6.2 | 38.44 |
| 5.4 | 29.16 |
| 4.1 | 16.81 |
| 4.2 | 17.64 |
| 3.8 | 14.44 |
| 3.9 | 15.21 |
| 48.9 | 247.41 |

$$\bar{x} = \frac{\Sigma fx}{\Sigma f} = \frac{48.9}{10} = 4.89$$

$$s^2 = \frac{\Sigma x^2}{n} - \left(\frac{\Sigma x}{n}\right)^2$$

$$= \frac{247.41}{10} - (4.89)^2$$

$$= 0.8289$$

$$s = 0.9104.$$

$$\text{Test statistic } t = \frac{|4.89 - 4.2|\sqrt{10-1}}{0.9104} = 2.27$$

For a one-sided test with nine degrees of freedom, the critical values of $t$ are 1.833 (at the 5% level) and 2.821 (at the 1% level), so the sample mean is significant at the 5% level but not at the 1% level. We reject $H_0$ and accept $H_1$, concluding that there is evidence to suggest that the super fertilizer is effective.

When we dealt with large samples, we found it was possible to test the significance of the difference between the means of two populations. Using the $t$-distribution, we can also do this for small samples. In some cases, it is necessary to test the mean difference by calculating the difference between the items in the sample. For us to be able to do this, the samples must be 'paired', i.e. the same item must appear in both samples, though treated under different conditions. We would use this method for the 'before and after' type of statistics so favoured by advertising agencies (i.e. the samples are not independent).

**EXAMPLE 6**

Before coaching, five candidates scored 38, 41, 52, 27 and 18% respectively in a Statistics examination. After coaching, they scored 40, 45, 49, 30 and 24% respectively. Does this evidence suggest that coaching is effective?

Although this problem appears similar to Example 3, we cannot use the same method as that method requires independent samples. In this case, we are looking at the same sample but under different conditions. What should we do?

Subtracting the scores, we obtain the change following coaching:

$$x = 2, 4, -3, 3, 6 \qquad \bar{x} = 2.4, \ s = 3.007$$

Suppose we adopt as our null hypothesis that coaching is ineffective: then the mean difference $\bar{x}$ could well be zero:

$$H_0: \mu = 0$$

We are asked to test whether coaching is effective, i.e. increases the marks gained by students, so a one-sided test is appropriate and the alternative hypothesis is:

$$H_1: \mu > 0$$

Test statistic $t = \dfrac{|2.4 - 0| \sqrt{5 - 1}}{3.007} = 1.596$

For a one-sided test with four degrees of freedom, the critical values for $t$ are 2.132 (at the 5% level) and 3.747 (at the 1% level). We must conclude that the test statistic is not significant, we accept the null hypothesis and reject the alternative hypothesis. There is insufficient evidence to suggest that coaching is effective.

In most cases, samples will be independent rather than paired, and if we want to test the significance of the difference between their means, we must use the method employed earlier in this chapter. Suppose we have two samples, the details of which are as follows:

|  | Sample size | Mean | Variance |
|---|---|---|---|
| First sample | $n_1$ | $\bar{x}_1$ | $s_1^2$ |
| Second sample | $n_2$ | $\bar{x}_2$ | $s_2^2$ |

We will assume that the first sample comes from a population with a mean $\mu_1$, and the second sample comes from a population with a mean $\mu_2$. We can now formulate the null hypothesis:

$$H_0: \mu_1 = \mu_2 \text{ or}$$
$$H_0: \mu_1 - \mu_2 = 0.$$

We have a variance for each sample, and using the methods of the chapter on estimation we can pool the variances of the samples to estimate the variance of the population, i.e.:

$$\hat{\sigma}^2 = \frac{n_1 s_1^2 + n_2 s_2^2}{n_1 + n_2 - 2}$$

Having estimated the variance of the population, we can now estimate the standard error of the difference between two independent means to be:

$$\sqrt{\frac{\hat{\sigma}^2}{n_1} + \frac{\hat{\sigma}^2}{n_2}}$$

For samples, then:

$$\text{Test statistic } t = \frac{|\bar{x}_1 - \bar{x}_2| - 0}{\sqrt{\frac{\hat{\sigma}^2}{n_1} + \frac{\hat{\sigma}^2}{n_2}}}$$

Before examining an example, we must now ask how many degrees of freedom are associated with this test. There are $(n_1 - 1)$ degrees of freedom associated with the first sample, and $(n_2 - 1)$ associated with the second sample. Now as we are pooling both samples, there are $n_1 + n_2 - 2$ degrees of freedom associated with estimating the population variance.

---

**EXAMPLE 7**

Lumo Plc manufacture electric light bulbs, and claim that on average their lamps last longer than the lamps of their competitor Brighto Plc. A random sample of 10 lamps made by Lumo had the following lives (in hours) before failing:

$$x_1 = 200 \quad 210 \quad 190 \quad 200 \quad 190 \quad 200 \quad 180 \quad 200 \quad 200 \quad 210$$

and a random sample of eight lamps made by Brighto yielded:

$$x_2 = 190 \quad 200 \quad 210 \quad 190 \quad 180 \quad 190 \quad 200 \quad 190$$

Does this evidence substantiate Lumo's claim?

First, we use suitable short-cut methods to calculate the mean and variance for each sample:

| $x_1$ | $\dfrac{x_1 - 200}{10}$ | $\left(\dfrac{x_1 - 200}{10}\right)^2$ |
|---|---|---|
| 200 | 0 | 0 |
| 210 | 1 | 1 |
| 190 | −1 | 1 |
| 200 | 0 | 0 |
| 190 | −1 | 1 |
| 200 | 0 | 0 |
| 180 | −2 | 4 |
| 200 | 0 | 0 |
| 200 | 0 | 0 |
| 210 | 1 | 1 |
|  | −2 | 8 |

| $x_2$ | $\dfrac{x_2 - 200}{10}$ | $\left(\dfrac{x_2 - 200}{10}\right)^2$ |
|---|---|---|
| 190 | −1 | 1 |
| 200 | 0 | 0 |
| 210 | 1 | 1 |
| 190 | −1 | 1 |
| 180 | −2 | 4 |
| 190 | −1 | 1 |
| 200 | 0 | 0 |
| 190 | −1 | 1 |
|  | −5 | 9 |

$$\bar{x}_1 = 200 + \frac{-2 \times 10}{10} = 198 \text{ hrs} \qquad \bar{x}_2 = 200 + \frac{-5 \times 10}{8} = 193.75 \text{ hrs}$$

$$s_1^{\,2} = 100 \times \left[\frac{8}{10} - \left(\frac{-2}{10}\right)^2\right] \qquad s_2^{\,2} = 100 \times \left[\frac{9}{8} - \left(\frac{-5}{8}\right)^2\right]$$

$$= 76 \text{ hrs} \qquad\qquad\qquad = 73.44 \text{ hrs}$$

We will test the null hypothesis that there is no difference between the mean lengths of lives of lamps, against the alternative hypothesis that Lumo's lamps last longer than Brighto's lamps, i.e.:

$$H_0: \mu_1 = \mu_2 \quad \text{and} \quad H_1: \mu_1 > \mu_2$$

As we are in fact assuming that both samples could have been drawn from the same population, the estimated variance of this population is:

$$\hat{\sigma}^2 = \frac{n_1 s_1^{\,2} + n_2 s_2^{\,2}}{n_1 + n_2 - 2}$$

$$= \frac{10 \times 76 + 8 \times 73.44}{10 + 8 - 2}$$

$$= 84.22 \text{ hrs, with 16 degrees of freedom.}$$

So the test statistic $t$ is:

$$t = \frac{\mid 198 - 193.75 \mid - 0}{\sqrt{\dfrac{84.22}{10} + \dfrac{84.22}{8}}} = 0.976$$

For a one-sided test with 16 degrees of freedom, the critical values of $t$ are 1.746 (at the 5% level) and 2.583 (at the 1% level).

So we see that the difference between the means is not significant. We accept the null hypothesis: there is insufficient evidence to suggest that Lumo's lamps last longer.

## Tests of proportions

Tests involving sample proportions are extremely important in practice. In the last chapter, we saw the basis of such a test applied to quality control. Again, many market researchers express their results in terms of proportions, for example, '40% of the population clean their teeth with Gritto'. It will be useful to design tests that will detect changes in proportions. As you can imagine, the binomial distribution forms the basis of such tests. Let us first examine how we can test the significance of the proportion of a small sample.

EXAMPLE 8

Suppose it is claimed that in a very large batch of components, about 10% of items contain some form of defect. It is proposed to check whether this proportion has increased, and this will be done by drawing a sample of 20 components. Adopting our null hypothesis in the usual way we have:

$H_0$: $\pi = 0.1$
$H_1$: $\pi > 0.1$

Assuming that $H_0$ is true, then we can calculate the probability distribution for samples of 20 components like this:

$$(0.9)^{20} + {}^{20}C_1(0.9)^{19}(0.1) + {}^{20}C_2(0.9)^{18}(0.1)^2 + {}^{20}C_3(0.9)^{17}(0.1)^3 + \cdots$$

Evaluating this expression, we have:

| No. of defectives | Probability | Cumulative probability |
|---|---|---|
| 0 | 0.1215 | 0.1215 |
| 1 | 0.2700 | 0.3915 |
| 2 | 0.2850 | 0.6765 |
| 3 | 0.1900 | 0.8665 |
| 4 | 0.0897 | 0.9562 |
| 5 | 0.0319 | 0.9881 |
| 6 | 0.0089 | 0.9970 |
| 7 | 0.0020 | 0.9990 |
| 8 | 0.0004 | 0.9994 |
| 9 | 0.0001 | 0.9995 |

Examining this table, we see that the probability of obtaining more than four defectives is $1 - 0.9562 = 4.38\%$, and the probability of obtaining more than six defectives is $1 - 0.9970 = 0.3\%$. So if we obtain more than four defectives in a sample, we can reject the null hypothesis at the 4.38% level of significance, and if it contains more than six defectives we can reject at the 0.3% level of significance.

Now calculations involving the binomial distribution are very tedious. The way to avoid them is to draw a large sample, and we can then use the normal approximation. Suppose that in the last example a sample of 150 contained 20 defectives – would this indicate that the proportion defective had increased? Again, we have:

$H_0$: $\pi = 0.1$
$H_1$: $\pi > 0.1$

And on the basis of our null hypothesis:

$$\text{Mean} = n\pi = 0.1 \times 150 = 15 \text{ defectives per sample}$$
$$\sigma = \sqrt{n\pi(1 - \pi)} = \sqrt{150 \times 0.1 \times 0.9} = 3.67$$

As the sample is large, our test statistic is the Z score:

$$\frac{20.5 - 15}{3.67} = 1.4986$$

(Remember to make the 0.5 adjustment when using the normal approximation to the binomial distribution.) For a one-sided test, the critical values for Z are 1.645 (at the 5% level) and 2.326 (at the 1% level), so we could conclude that the proportion defective in the sample is not significant. We would accept the null hypothesis that the proportion defective is 0.1.

**EXAMPLE 9**

Finally, let us examine how we could investigate the significance of the difference between two proportions in two samples. Suppose that in a sample of 300 people from Liverpool, 220 cleaned their teeth with Gritto, and in Manchester 240 out of 350 use Gritto. We wish to determine whether there is any difference between the proportion using Gritto. Clearly, this is a two-sided test, so we have:

$H_0$: $\pi_1 = \pi_2$ (or $\pi_1 - \pi_2 = 0$)
$H_1$: $\pi_1 \neq \pi_2$

The proportion using Gritto in Liverpool is $\frac{220}{300} = 0.733$, and the proportion using Gritto in Manchester is $\frac{240}{350} = 0.686$. If the null hypothesis is true, then we can regard both samples as coming from the same population. The best estimate we have of the proportion using Gritto in this population is:

$$\hat{\pi} = \frac{220 + 240}{300 + 350} = \frac{460}{650} = 0.708$$

In an earlier chapter, we saw that the variance of the proportion of a sample of $n$ items is:

$$\frac{\hat{\pi}(1 - \hat{\pi})}{n}$$

So the variance of the proportion of samples of 300 is:

$$\frac{0.708 \times 0.292}{300}$$

and the variance of the proportion of samples of 350 is:

$$\frac{0.708 \times 0.292}{350}$$

Using the theorem of sample differences, the variance of the differences between these proportions is:

$$\frac{0.708 \times 0.292}{300} + \frac{0.708 \times 0.292}{350}$$

$$= 0.708 \times 0.292 \left( \frac{1}{300} + \frac{1}{350} \right)$$

$$= 0.00128$$

and the standard error of the difference is $\sqrt{0.00128} = 0.0358$. Now if the null hypothesis is true, then the difference between the proportions in the sample could well be zero. The test statistic Z is:

$$\frac{|\,0.733 - 0.686\,| - 0}{0.0358} = 1.31$$

For a two-sided test, the critical values of Z are 1.96 (at the 5% level) and 2.576 (at the 1% level), so we would accept the null hypothesis that the proportion using Gritto in Liverpool and Manchester could well be the same.

As you can see, there are a wide variety of significance tests for testing means and proportions. Certainly, there are more than those mentioned in this chapter – there are tests, for example, for testing several means and proportions. However, the tests covered in this chapter will take you quite a long way in statistical analysis. Before we finish this chapter, let us stress again the importance of the sample size. You will have noticed that large samples impose fewer restrictions on testing, and their results will be much more reliable. It is for this reason that you should use large samples wherever possible.

## Using the spreadsheet

The template to accompany this chapter deals with a number of significance tests. The menu structure for this template is illustrated in Fig 21.1.

In this exercise we will be looking at a number of different tests covered in this chapter. For large samples, we will perform significance tests on:

- a single mean

- the difference between means; and

- the difference between proportions.

For small samples, we will perform significance tests on:

- a single mean

- paired samples; and

- independent samples.

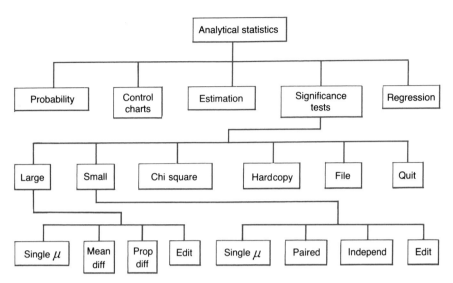

**Fig 21.1**

Retrieve the main menu 'Analytical statistics' and then select 'Significance tests'. First, we will perform a significance test using the mean of a large sample. Select 'Large samples' and then select 'Single mean'. The screen should now look like this:

|    | A | B | C | D | E | F | G | H |
|----|---|---|---|---|---|---|---|---|
| 1  |   |   |   |   |   |   |   |   |
| 2  |   |   |   |   |   |   |   |   |
| 3  |   |   | Testing a sample mean |   |   |   |   |   |
| 4  |   |   |   |   |   |   |   |   |
| 5  | Sample mean | = |   |   |   |   |   |   |
| 6  | Sample Size | = |   |   |   |   |   |   |
| 7  | Population mean | = |   |   |   |   |   |   |
| 8  | Population s.d. | = |   |   |   |   |   |   |
| 9  |   |   |   |   |   |   |   |   |
| 10 |   |   |   |   |   |   |   |   |

You should now enter details of the sample and population, pressing Enter after each entry. The cursor will automatically jump to the next position after you have pressed Enter. The output is the test statistic Z together with its critical values. So, for example, if you were to input the data referring to road noise (Example 2 in this chapter) the output would look like this:

| | A | B | C | D | E | F | G | H |
|---|---|---|---|---|---|---|---|---|
| 1 | | | | | | | | |
| 2 | | | | | | | | |
| 3 | | | Testing a sample mean | | | | | |
| 4 | | | | | | | | |
| 5 | Sample mean | = | 134 | | | | | |
| 6 | Sample Size | = | 50 | | | | | |
| 7 | Population mean = | | 130 | | | | | |
| 8 | Population s.d. | = | 20 | | | | | |
| 9 | | | | | | | | |
| 10 | Test statistic Z | | 1.414213 | | | | | |
| 11 | | | | | | | | |
| 12 | Critical values of Z | | | | | | | |
| 13 | | | 5% level 1% level | | | | | |
| 14 | One sided 1.645 | | 2.326 | | | | | |
| 15 | Two sided 1.96 | | 2.576 | | | | | |
| 16 | | | | | | | | |
| 17 | | | | | | | | |
| 18 | | | | | | | | |

Now let us look at the test for the difference between means. Select 'Large samples' and then select 'Mean diff'. The screen should now look like this:

| | A | B | C | D | E | F | G |
|---|---|---|---|---|---|---|---|
| 1 | | | | | | | |
| 2 | | | | | | | |
| 3 | | | Testing the difference between means | | | | |
| 4 | | | | | | | |
| 5 | | | Sample 1 Sample 2 | | | | |
| 6 | Mean | | | | | | |
| 7 | Standard deviation | | | | | | |
| 8 | Size | | | | | | |
| 9 | | | | | | | |
| 10 | | | | | | | |

You should input data for Samples 1 and 2, pressing Enter after each entry. Again the cursor will automatically jump to the next position each time Enter is pressed. The standard error of the difference is output, together with the test statistic Z and its critical values. So, for example, if you were to input details on the two football teams (Example 3 in this chapter), then the output would look like this:

|  | A | B | C | D | E | F | G |
|---|---|---|---|---|---|---|---|
| 1 |  |  |  |  |  |  |  |
| 2 |  |  |  |  |  |  |  |
| 3 |  |  | Testing the difference between means |  |  |  |  |
| 4 |  |  |  |  |  |  |  |
| 5 |  |  | Sample 1 | Sample 2 |  |  |  |
| 6 | Mean |  | 30 | 32 |  |  |  |
| 7 | Standard deviation |  | 6 | 5 |  |  |  |
| 8 | Size |  | 50 | 60 |  |  |  |
| 9 |  |  |  |  |  |  |  |
| 10 | S.E. of difference |  |  | 1.066145 |  |  |  |
| 11 | Test statistic Z |  |  | 1.875916 |  |  |  |
| 12 |  |  |  |  |  |  |  |
| 13 | Critical values of Z |  |  |  |  |  |  |
| 14 |  |  | 5% level | 1% level |  |  |  |
| 15 | One sided | 1.645 | 2.326 |  |  |  |  |
| 16 | Two sided | 1.96 | 2.576 |  |  |  |  |
| 17 |  |  |  |  |  |  |  |
| 18 |  |  |  |  |  |  |  |

Finally for large samples, let us examine the difference between proportions. Select 'Large samples' and then select 'Prop diff'. The screen looks like this:

|  | A | B | C | D | E | F | G | H |
|---|---|---|---|---|---|---|---|---|
| 1 |  |  |  |  |  |  |  |  |
| 2 |  |  |  |  |  |  |  |  |
| 3 |  |  | Testing the difference between proportions |  |  |  |  |  |
| 4 |  |  |  |  |  |  |  |  |
| 5 |  |  | Sample 1 | Sample 2 |  |  |  |  |
| 6 | No. in sample |  |  |  |  |  |  |  |
| 7 | Size |  |  |  |  |  |  |  |
| 8 |  |  |  |  |  |  |  |  |
| 9 |  |  |  |  |  |  |  |  |
| 10 |  |  |  |  |  |  |  |  |

For each sample, you should enter the number in the sample with the attribute under consideration, and the sample size. Again, press Enter after entry and the cursor will move automatically to the next position. The output is the estimated population proportion, standard error of the difference and the test statistic Z together with the critical values. If you were to enter the data on the people using Gritto in Liverpool and Manchester (Example 8 in this chapter) then the output would look like this:

|  | A | B | C | D | E | F | G |
|---|---|---|---|---|---|---|---|
| 1 | | | | | | | |
| 2 | | | | | | | |
| 3 | | | Testing the difference between proportions | | | | |
| 4 | | | | | | | |
| 5 | | | Sample 1 | Sample 2 | | | |
| 6 | No. in sample | | 220 | 240 | | | |
| 7 | Size | | 300 | 350 | | | |
| 8 | | | | | | | |
| 9 | | | | | | | |
| 10 | Est. pop proportion | | | 0.707692 | | | |
| 11 | | | | | | | |
| 12 | S.E. of difference | | | 0.035785 | | | |
| 13 | | | | | | | |
| 14 | Test statistic Z | | | 1.330688 | | | |
| 15 | | | | | | | |
| 16 | Critical values of Z | | | | | | |
| 17 | | | 5% level | 1% level | | | |
| 18 | One sided | 1.645 | 2.326 | | | | |
| 19 | Two sided | 1.96 | 2.576 | | | | |
| 20 | | | | | | | |

Now let us examine significance tests using a small sample. Select 'Small samples' and then select 'Single mean'. This test caters for two types of data entry: you can either enter the individual sample observations in the column starting from the cursor position, or enter the sample details directly starting in cell E5. Whichever method you use, press ALT E when you have finished entering the data. You will then be asked to enter the population mean. Input this value and press Enter. The degrees of freedom are output, together with the test statistic $t$ with its corresponding critical values. Entering the details directly on the length of lives of electric light bulbs (Example 4 in this chapter) would result in the following:

|   | A | B | C | D | E | F | G |
|---|---|---|---|---|---|---|---|
| 1 | | | | | | | |
| 2 | | | | | | | |
| 3 | | | Population mean = | | 1500 | | |
| 4 | | | | | | | |
| 5 | | | Sample size = | | 10 | | |
| 6 | | | Sample mean = | | 1410 | | |
| 7 | | | Sample st dev = | | 90 | | |
| 8 | | | | | | | |
| 9 | | | Deg of freedom = | | 9 | | |
| 10 | | | | | | | |
| 11 | | | Test statistic t = | | 3 | | |
| 12 | | | | | | | |
| 13 | | | Critical values of t | | | | |
| 14 | | | | 5% level | 1% level | | |
| 15 | | | One sided | 1.833 | 2.821 | | |
| 16 | | | Two sided | 2.262 | 3.25 | | |

If you entered the individual observations on wheat yield (Example 5 in this chapter), then the output would look like this:

|   | A | B | C | D | E | F | G | H |
|---|---|---|---|---|---|---|---|---|
| 1 | 4.3 | | | | | | | |
| 2 | 6 | | | | | | | |
| 3 | 4.9 | | Population mean = | | 4.2 | | | |
| 4 | 6.1 | | | | | | | |
| 5 | 6.2 | | Sample size = | | 10 | | | |
| 6 | 5.4 | | Sample mean = | | 4.89 | | | |
| 7 | 4.1 | | Sample st dev = | 0.910439 | | | | |
| 8 | 4.2 | | | | | | | |
| 9 | 3.8 | | Deg of freedom = | | 9 | | | |
| 10 | 3.9 | | | | | | | |
| 11 | | | Test statistic t = | 2.273627 | | | | |
| 12 | | | | | | | | |
| 13 | | | Critical values of t | | | | | |
| 14 | | | | 5% level | 1% level | | | |
| 15 | | | One sided | 1.833 | 2.821 | | | |
| 16 | | | Two sided | 2.262 | 3.25 | | | |
| 17 | | | | | | | | |
| 18 | | | | | | | | |

Now let us examine a test involving paired samples. Select 'Small samples' and then select 'Paired samples'. The screen looks like this:

| | A | B | C | D | E | F | G | H |
|---|---|---|---|---|---|---|---|---|
| 1 | | | \*\*\*\*\*\* Paired samples \*\*\*\*\*\* | | | | | |
| 2 | | | | | | | | |
| 3 | | | Enter sample details. Press ALT G when finished | | | | | |
| 4 | | | | | | | | |
| 5 | Sample 1 | Sample 2 | | | | | | |
| 6 | | | | | | | | |
| 7 | | | | | | | | |
| 8 | | | | | | | | |
| 9 | | | | | | | | |
| 10 | | | | | | | | |

You should enter the details for Sample 1 in the column A starting at the cursor position. Details for Sample 2 should be entered in column B starting at cell B6. You should press ALT G when you have finished entering the data. If you enter the details of the two samples which attempt to measure the effectiveness of coaching (Example 6 in this chapter), then the output would look like this:

| | A | B | C | D | E | F | G |
|---|---|---|---|---|---|---|---|
| 1 | | | \*\*\*\*\*\* Paired samples \*\*\*\*\*\* | | | | |
| 2 | | | | | | | |
| 3 | | | | | | | |
| 4 | | | | | | | |
| 5 | Sample 1 | Sample 2 | Difference | | | | |
| 6 | 38 | 40 | − 2 | | Mean difference | | − 2.4 |
| 7 | 41 | 45 | − 4 | | | | |
| 8 | 52 | 49 | 3 | | Std deviation | | 3.006659 |
| 9 | 27 | 30 | − 3 | | | | |
| 10 | 18 | 24 | − 6 | | Deg of Freedom | | 4 |
| 11 | | | | | | | |
| 12 | | | | | Test statistic t | | 1.596456 |
| 13 | | | | | | | |
| 14 | | | | | Critical values of t | | |
| 15 | | | | | | 5% level | 1% level |
| 16 | | | | | One sided | 2.132 | 3.747 |
| 17 | | | | | Two sided | 2.776 | 4.604 |
| 18 | | | | | | | |
| 19 | | | | | | | |

Finally, let us perform a test using independent samples. Select 'Small samples' followed by 'Independent samples'. The screen now displays the following:

| | A | B | C | D | E | F | G | H |
|---|---|---|---|---|---|---|---|---|
| 1 | | | ****** Independent samples ****** | | | | | |
| 2 | | | | | | | | |
| 3 | | | Enter sample details. Press ALT I when finished | | | | | |
| 4 | | | | | | | | |
| 5 | Sample 1 Sample 2 | | | | | | | |
| 6 | | | | | | | | |
| 7 | | | | | | | | |

Data is entered in exactly the same way as in the previous example, and ALT I is pressed when you have finished entering the data. Entering the data for Lumo's lamps and Brighto's lamps (Example 7 in this chapter) would result in the following output:

| | A | B | C | D | E | F | G | H |
|---|---|---|---|---|---|---|---|---|
| 1 | | | ****** Independent samples ****** | | | | | |
| 2 | | | | | | | | |
| 3 | | | | | | | | |
| 4 | | | | | | | | |
| 5 | Sample 1 | Sample 2 | | **** Sample 1 ***** | | | | |
| 6 | 200 | 190 | | Size | | 10 | | |
| 7 | 210 | 200 | | Mean | | 198 | | |
| 8 | 190 | 210 | | Variance | | 76 | | |
| 9 | 200 | 190 | | ***** Sample 2 ***** | | | | |
| 10 | 190 | 180 | | Size | | 8 | | |
| 11 | 200 | 190 | | Mean | 193.75 | | | |
| 12 | 180 | 200 | | Variance | 73.4375 | | | |
| 13 | 200 | 190 | | | | | | |
| 14 | 200 | | | Degrees of freedom | | 16 | | |
| 15 | 210 | | | | | | | |
| 16 | | | | Est pop variance | 84.21875 | | | |
| 17 | | | | | | | | |
| 18 | | | | Test statistic t | 0.976322 | | | |
| 19 | | | | | | | | |
| 20 | | | | Critical values of t | | | | |
| 21 | | | | | 5% level | 1% level | | |
| 22 | | | | One sided | 1.746 | 2.583 | | |
| 23 | | | | Two sided | 2.12 | 2.921 | | |
| 24 | | | | | | | | |

Finally, you may have noticed that another test called 'Chi-square' is included in the menu. We will examine this test in the next chapter.

21.1 Discuss briefly the following statements:

    (i)  In hypothesis testing it is more important to minimise the Type I error than to worry about the Type II error;

    (ii)  In hypothesis testing it is essential that the decision to use either a one- or a two-tailed test should be taken before the sample is drawn.

21.2 From past experience it has been found that 5% of a certain output is rejected. To test the null hypothesis $H_0$: $\pi = 5\%$, a sample of 400 items is drawn. Form decision rules for testing $H_0$ at the 1% level if (a) the alternative hypothesis is one-sided; and (b) the alternative hypothesis is two-sided.

21.3 Suppose that in Question 21.2 we adopt the one-sided alternative hypothesis, and the true reject rate rises to 7%. What is the probability of a Type II error?

21.4 Metal plugs are turned to a mean diameter of 5 cm, standard deviation 0.01 cm. We wish to test for change in the mean diameter at the 5% level of significance by drawing a sample of 100 plugs. Devise an appropriate decision rule. What would your decision rule have been if we wished to detect increases in the mean diameter?

21.5 A manufacturer produces cables with a mean breaking strength of 2000 lbs and a standard deviation of 100 lbs. By using a new technique the manufacturer claims that the breaking strength can be increased. To test this claim, a sample of 50 cables produced by the new technique is tested, and the mean breaking strength found to be 2050 lbs. Can the manufacturer's claim be supported at a 0.01 level of significance?                                                         CIMA

21.6 If the sample quoted in Question 21.5 had contained nine cables, could the claim be justified?

21.7 What is the minimum sample size for the sample in Question 21.5 that would justify the manufacturer's claim (assume a sample mean of 2050 lbs)?

21.8 In a certain country, men have a mean height of 168 cm, standard deviation 8 cm, and women have a mean height of 160 cm, standard deviation 5 cm. In a random sample of 100 married couples, the average height difference between husband and wife was 5 cm. Does this suggest that height of partner affects the decision to propose marriage?

**21.9**   A survey has provided data on the television watching habits of ten-year-old children of different social classes. A sample of 220 children in social class five were found to watch for a mean period of 3.8 hours per day with a standard deviation of 0.5 hours, while a sample of 63 children in social classes one/two watched for a mean period of 3.2 hours with a standard deviation of 0.42 hours. Test, at the 1% level, whether children in social class five spend more time watching television than do those in one/two.

**21.10**   Two drugs, $A$ and $B$, were tested for a certain effect on laboratory mice. Two samples, each of 50 mice, were chosen randomly, one drug administered to each, and a measure, $x$, of the effect, obtained. The results were as follows:

Drug A   $\Sigma x = 1750$   $\Sigma x^2 = 62\ 520$
Drug B   $\Sigma x = 1980$   $\Sigma x^2 = 85\ 610$

Test, at the 1% level of significance, the hypothesis that the two drugs have the same mean effect against the alternative hypothesis that drug $B$ has a higher mean effect. You may assume that the effect on mice, of each drug, is normally distributed.

**21.11**   What is meant by 'standardising' a normal distribution and how is it done? A company samples the products of two suppliers of light bulbs. The 80 bulbs in the batch from supplier A are shown to have a mean life of 503 hours with a standard deviation of 43 hours, the 110 bulbs from supplier B have a mean life of 488 hours with a standard deviation of 39 hours. Test the hypothesis that there is no difference between the mean lives of bulbs from the two suppliers at the 10%, 5% and 1% levels of significance.

**21.12**   Suppose that a survey of a number of firms in two regions of a country shows that their investment in a given year was as follows:

|  | 24– | 28– | 32– | 36– | 40– | 44–48 |
|---|---|---|---|---|---|---|
| Region A | 8 | 41 | 77 | 90 | 58 | 26 |
| Region B | 19 | 36 | 47 | 58 | 27 | 13 |

*Investment (£000)*

*Number of firms*

Is there any evidence of a difference in average investment between the two regions?

**21.13**   The table below gives distributions of earnings for samples of workers taken from two firms:

|  | 200– | 220– | 240– | 260– | 280– | 300–320 |
|---|---|---|---|---|---|---|
| Number of workers in Firm A | 11 | 23 | 42 | 40 | 28 | 14 |
| Number of workers in Firm B | 12 | 36 | 54 | 62 | 44 | 38 |

*Earnings (£)*

What evidence is there of a difference between average earnings in the two firms?

**21.14**    **Permanent houses completed** (including flats, each flat being counted as one unit)

| Year | For private owners (thousands) | For local housing authorities (thousands) |
|------|-------------------------------|-------------------------------------------|
| 1 | 177.8 | 123.9 |
| 2 | 221.3 | 154.7 |
| 3 | 217.2 | 165.0 |
| 4 | 208.6 | 176.9 |
| 5 | 204.2 | 199.7 |
| 6 | 226.0 | 188.0 |
| 7 | 186.0 | 180.9 |
| 8 | 174.3 | 177.0 |
| 9 | 196.3 | 154.8 |
| 10 | 200.6 | 120.4 |
| 11 | 190.6 | 102.6 |

Is there a significant difference in the average number of permanent houses completed in the two groups over the period?

**21.15**    In conducting a survey of food prices, two samples of prices of a given food item were collected. Sample A came from a congested city area, and Sample B was obtained in the suburbs. The results were as follows:

| | Sample A | Sample B |
|---|----------|----------|
| $n$ | 14 | 18 |
| $\sum_{i=1}^{n} p_i$ | 12.60 | 14.96 |
| $\sum_{i=1}^{n} (p_i - \bar{p})^2$ | 1.68 | 1.96 |

where $p_i$ = price recorded in the $i$th store. Test the hypothesis that there is no difference between the mean price of the particular food item in the two areas. (Use 5% level of significance.)

**21.16**    A machine has been operating at 60% efficiency. After adjustment, nine test runs produced the following efficiencies:

64,  59,  71,  63,  68,  61,  62,  61,  63

Test, at the 5% level, whether efficiency has improved.

**21.17**   In order to test the effectiveness of a drying agent in paint, the following experiment was carried out. Each of six samples of material was cut in two halves. One half of each was covered with paint containing the agent and the other half with paint without the agent. Then all 12 samples were left to dry. The time taken to dry was as follows:

| | *Drying time (hours)* | | | | | |
|---|---|---|---|---|---|---|
| | *1* | *2* | *3* | *4* | *5* | *6* |
| Paint with the agent | 3.4 | 3.8 | 4.2 | 4.1 | 3.5 | 4.7 |
| Paint without the agent | 3.6 | 3.8 | 4.3 | 4.3 | 3.6 | 4.6 |

Carry out a '$t$'-test to determine whether the drying agent is effective, giving your reasons for choosing a one-tailed or two-tailed test. Carefully explain your conclusion.

**21.18**   Ten pairs of identical twins had the following birthweights in kilograms:

| *Pair* | *1* | *2* | *3* | *4* | *5* | *6* | *7* | *8* | *9* | *10* |
|---|---|---|---|---|---|---|---|---|---|---|
| First-born | 3.95 | 3.41 | 3.73 | 4.13 | 3.48 | 4.28 | 3.98 | 4.18 | 4.04 | 3.73 |
| Second-born | 3.93 | 3.35 | 3.72 | 4.18 | 3.44 | 4.15 | 3.89 | 4.20 | 4.00 | 3.72 |

(i)   Stating any assumptions which you make, test, at the 5% significance level, the hypothesis that there is no difference in weight between first-born and second-born twins.

(ii)   If the data had been collected to test the hypothesis that the first-born are heavier, what conclusion would you reach?

**21.19**   A group of 10 students scored the following marks in a test:

| Candidate | A | B | C | D | E | F | G | H | I | J |
|---|---|---|---|---|---|---|---|---|---|---|
| Score | 53 | 60 | 61 | 47 | 40 | 56 | 75 | 46 | 82 | 61 |

After coaching, their marks were

| Candidate | A | B | C | D | E | F | G | H | I | J |
|---|---|---|---|---|---|---|---|---|---|---|
| Score | 60 | 58 | 67 | 51 | 60 | 72 | 71 | 48 | 94 | 76 |

Did coaching improve their marks?

**21.20**   Define the standard error of a mean of samples of $n$ observations and use the concept to explain briefly why one has more confidence in the mean of a large sample than in the mean of a small one.

Show why it is unlikely that a sample of 64 observations with a mean of 5.2 was drawn from a population with a mean of 5.5 and a standard deviation of 0.8. Would your answer be the same if the sample contained 16 items?

**21.21**  Suppose samples of 10 items are to be drawn from a population with 5% of items defective. Find the 5% and 1% critical values for the alternative hypothesis that the percentage defective has increased.

**21.22**  The internal auditor of your company has reported to you as management accountant as follows:

'From 1000 sample postings made before lunch 210 errors were discovered whereas 250 errors were found in 1000 sample postings made after lunch. It would appear that although the staff has not changed, the postings before lunch were more accurate than they are after. Special steps should be taken to achieve a consistent level of accuracy.'

(a)  What statistical hypothesis does this statement imply?

(b)  Evaluate this hypothesis and state if it should influence you as management accountant in your decision on whether to take special action.

**21.23**  A market research company, wishing to determine whether it is more usual in the North for working men to come home to a midday meal than in the South, interviews two random samples each of 500 men. In the sample from the North, 330 men come home midday compared with 280 in the sample from the South. Is the difference significant?

**21.24**  Two groups, A and B, each consist of 100 people who have a disease. A serum is given to group A but not to group B; otherwise, the two groups are treated identically. It is found that in groups A and B, 75 and 65 people, respectively, recover from the disease. Does this result support the hypothesis that the serum helps to cure the disease?

**21.25**  A company selling a prestige product carries out market research surveys in two consecutive years on heads of households with income in excess of £10 000 per year. The survey results were:

|                              | *1991* | *1992* |
| ---------------------------- | ------ | ------ |
| Sample Size                  | 1300   | 1000   |
| Number possessing product    | 351    | 240    |

Assuming the rejection area to be outside 2.33 s.d., does the 1992 survey suggest that the product's sales are declining?

**21.26**    Family Expenditure Survey: household expenditure on commodities and services

| | North (£ per week) | South-west (£ per week) |
|---|---|---|
| Housing, etc. | 37.70 | 48.60 |
| Food | 61.70 | 61.80 |
| Drink and tobacco | 24.60 | 18.70 |
| Clothing and footwear | 20.70 | 17.90 |
| Durables and other goods | 27.90 | 35.00 |
| Transport and services | 45.40 | 55.30 |
| Total | 218.00 | 237.30 |
| Number of households in sample | 1000 | 1000 |

Do households in the North spend a significantly greater proportion of their total expenditure on drink and tobacco than those in the South-west? Explain fully the theoretical basis for the test you have applied.

**21.27**    A motor-car manufacturer purchases gear assemblies from a sub-contractor who undertakes to ensure that not more than 5% of his supplies will be defective. In order to provide a check on the quality of incoming supplies a random sample of 200 assemblies is selected of which 17 are found to be defective.

(a)    Does the sample evidence indicate that the sub-contractor is not maintaining the quality of his supplies at the agreed level? Use the significance levels of 0.05 and 0.01.

(b)    Construct an interval estimate for the proportion of all the sub-contractor's supplies that are defective. Use a confidence level of 95%.

(c)    What is the minimum sample size required to estimate the proportion in (b) of the question to within $\pm 0.5\%$ at the 95% confidence level.

(d)    As the result of a board decision the firm now purchases gear assemblies from a second sub-contractor. A random sample of 500 gear assemblies from this supplier reveals that 20 units are defective. Test the hypothesis that there is a significant difference in quality between the two sub-contractors' supplies. Use significance levels of 0.01 and 0.05.

**21.28**    In a public opinion poll of 500 people, 70% favoured a certain policy. In another district 60% of the 500 interviewed favoured the policy. Is there a significant difference of opinion?

**21.29**    For Question 21.28, what is the minimum sample size that would make a difference between 60% and 70% significant?

# 22 The chi square test

We will now pick up and develop a point we made in the last chapter: that in all the tests we have so far studied we have assumed that the population from which the sample was drawn was normally distributed and that the sample we drew was truly random. Even if the population was not normally distributed, we learned from the central limit theorem that the sampling distribution of sample means would be normally distributed. You will realise that for much of the work we do it is this latter population (a population of sample means) from which we draw our individual sample. Thus whether we are considering a population known to be normally distributed or are considering a sample drawn from a population with unknown characteristics we have based our tests and our estimations on the normal distribution curve. Even when we discussed small samples and used the *t* test we were making an implicit assumption that, provided our population distribution does not depart too far from normal, the *t* test will yield valuable results. All the empirical evidence we have tends to support the view that the *t* test is insensitive to movements away from the normal distribution when we are testing null hypotheses of sample means.

Now, why do we make this assumption of a normally distributed population which we would find very hard to prove if we were asked? The point is, all the tests we have looked at involve the use of parameters such as the population mean, the population proportion and the variance. If we assume that the population is normally distributed we can infer a great deal from these parameters. You will remember, for example, that the variance of the sampling distribution of sample means (the standard error)$^2$ is taken as being equal to $\sigma^2/n$; or that 95% of the normally distributed population will fall within the range $\mu \pm 1.96\sigma$.

Suppose, however, that we do not know, and are unwilling to assume, the precise form of the population distribution. We can not now make any assumptions about the value of a parameter. Yet often a statistical test would appear to be useful. In such circumstances we would have to use a distribution free, or *non-parametric*, test technique. You will understand of course, that even if we could confidently make presumptions about the population distributions or parameters, we need not do so. We could always make our test using non-parametric methods. Thus for every parametric test there is a corresponding non-parametric test.

The methodology we use for non-parametric tests is identical to that which we have already used for both $Z$ and $t$ tests. First, on the basis of a null hypothesis a sampling distribution of some sample characteristic is derived. Then having prescribed an acceptable level for a Type I error a decision criterion can be fixed. If the sample characteristic exceeds the critical value it is deemed significant at the level you have chosen; if it does not fall into the region of rejection the null hypothesis is accepted, subject always to the possibility that a Type II error may have been committed. And this is the point. For samples of the same size, non-parametric tests always leave a higher possibility of a Type II error than do parametric tests. We can always offset this, of course, by taking a large sample size. In any case non-parametric tests make up in generality what they lack in power. The conclusions we reach do not depend on assumptions which may only apply to the situation we are studying, and so they tend to be of universal application.

## The chi square test

Probably the most widely used of all non-parametric tests is the *chi square test* (pronounce it 'kye' and use the symbol $\chi^2$), and certainly it has a wider range of applications than most other tests. But first, let us consider the nature of the chi square distribution.

In fact, there is not merely one distribution. Like the $t$ distribution there are many chi square distributions – one for each degree of freedom. Three such distributions are shown in Fig 22.1. Notice that as the degrees of freedom become fewer, the distribution becomes positively skewed more and more. Conversely, as the number of degrees of freedom is increased, the distribution becomes approximately normal.

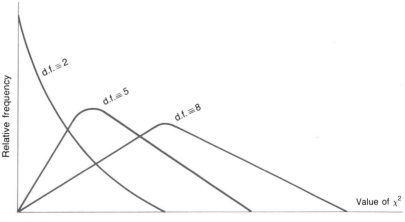

**Fig 22.1**

## Observed and expected frequencies

Suppose you have been given the task of assessing consumer preference with respect to five washing powders – Zip, Whito, Acme, Blanco and Bleacho. You supply a small quantity of each powder in boxes marked A, B, C, D and E to 1000 consumers, and ask them to test the powders and state which powder they prefer. The result of your enquiry is as follows:

| Washing powder | Zip | Whito | Acme | Blanco | Bleacho |
|---|---|---|---|---|---|
| No. preferring that powder | 187 | 221 | 193 | 204 | 195 |

Now you suspect that consumers are unable to distinguish between washing powders. Any preference that they have will be influenced not by the powder's characteristics, but by the persuasive powers of the advertisements promoting the powder, and by the attractiveness of the packet. For this reason, the consumers do not know which powder they are using (remember they are labelled A, B, C, D and E, and each powder is packed in a plain white box). Returning to statistical jargon, we have formulated the null hypothesis that consumers are unable to distinguish between the powders, and we will use the sample evidence to test the validity of this hypothesis. Of course, the appropriate alternative hypothesis is that consumers can distinguish between the powders.

Earlier in this book, we implied that the null hypothesis to be tested should always be formulated in such a fashion that we would know what to expect if it was true. Assuming that our null hypothesis is correct, then, we expect that an equal number would report that they prefer each of the powders. In other words, the results expected from our sample would be:

| Washing powder | Zip | Whito | Acme | Blanco | Bleacho |
|---|---|---|---|---|---|
| No. expected to prefer that powder | 200 | 200 | 200 | 200 | 200 |

The frequencies that we obtain in our sample we will call the *observed frequencies*, and the frequencies we expect on the basis of our null hypothesis we will call the *expected frequencies*. We shall now devise a significance test on whether there is a significant difference between the observed (O) and expected (E) frequencies.

The method we shall apply for testing the null hypothesis is to measure the total deviation of the observed from the expected frequencies, i.e. $\Sigma(O - E)$:

| Product | Observed | Expected | (O – E) |
|---|---|---|---|
| Zip | 187 | 200 | – 13 |
| Whito | 221 | 200 | 21 |
| Acme | 193 | 200 | –7 |
| Blanco | 204 | 200 | 4 |
| Bleacho | 195 | 200 | –5 |

As you would expect $\Sigma(O - E) = 0$, so we are faced with a similar problem to when we were attempting to measure dispersion. If $\Sigma(O - E)$ always equals zero, then we cannot use it as a measure of testing our null hypothesis. When considering the standard deviation, we got round this problem by squaring the deviations, and we can use the same method in this context, i.e. calculate $\Sigma(O - E)^2$. However, a further adjustment is necessary: we divide the $(O - E)^2$ values by E. Now why do we do this? Well, the reason is not apparent in this example, so let us consider another case:

| Observed | Expected | (O − E) | (O − E)² |
|---|---|---|---|
| 150 | 200 | − 50 | 2500 |
| 150 | 100 | 50 | 2500 |

Clearly the deviation of 50 is twice as significant on an expected value of 100 as it is on an expected value of 200, and to take this into account we can weight the $(O - E)^2$ values by dividing by E. So we have

| Observed | Expected | (O − E) | (O − E)² | $\dfrac{(O-E)^2}{E}$ |
|---|---|---|---|---|
| 150 | 200 | − 50 | 2500 | 12.5 |
| 150 | 100 | 50 | 2500 | 25 |

which shows precisely the information required. Now if we calculate the sum of the:

$$\frac{(O - E)^2}{E}$$

values, we have a weighted sum of the deviations of the observed and expected values, and we call this statistic $\chi^2$:

$$\chi^2 = \Sigma \frac{(O - E)^2}{E}$$

Calculating the value of $\chi^2$ for our washing powder example we have:

| Observed | Expected | (O − E) | (O − E)² | $\dfrac{(O-E)^2}{E}$ |
|---|---|---|---|---|
| 187 | 200 | − 13 | 169 | 0.845 |
| 221 | 200 | 21 | 441 | 2.205 |
| 193 | 200 | − 7 | 49 | 0.245 |
| 204 | 200 | 4 | 16 | 0.080 |
| 195 | 200 | − 5 | 25 | 0.125 |
|  |  | 0 |  | 3.500 |

If our null hypothesis is true, then our expected value for $\chi^2$ is zero, as we would expect our observed and expected values to have the same value. But as we are sampling, the actual values of $\chi^2$ will fluctuate from sample to sample. Now $\chi^2$ is like Z in so far as it is just another kind of standard score – so to test our null hypothesis we can use the same method as we did in the last chapter. We will compare our value for chi square with certain critical values that we would not expect to be exceeded. However, there are two problems involved in obtaining these critical values.

When we examined sampling distributions, we learnt that as long as the sample size is sufficiently large then we can expect the sample statistic to be normally distributed. We could use normal distribution tables to obtain critical values, and compare them with the Z score of the sample statistic. Now here is where the first problem occurs: $\chi^2$ is not normally distributed, so the normal distribution tables are of no help to us. We must obtain our critical values from $\chi^2$ tables. Now there are many $\chi^2$ distributions, but only one standard normal distribution – so here is where our second problem arises: which $\chi^2$ distribution should we use?

Just as with the $t$ distribution there are many chi square distributions – one for each degree of freedom. The distribution applicable in this case is the one with four degrees of freedom, and this is illustrated in Fig 22.2. Can you see why there are four degrees of freedom in this case? Clearly, when we assigned expected values to the numbers buying each detergent, we were not completely free to assign any values that we wished. In order that we could compare expected values with observed values, the total of the expected values had to be 1000. This means that any hypothesis we adopt leaves us free to assign expected values to any four of the five brands. For example, we could assign an expected frequency of 150 to Whito, 300 to Acme, 200 to Blanco and 150 to Bleacho – then the expected frequency for Zip *must* be $1000 - (150 + 300 + 200 + 200 + 150) = 300$, otherwise we would not have a total frequency of 1000. So we have just four degrees of freedom when fixing expected values (generalising for problems like this, if we have $n$ observed values, then we will have $(n - 1)$ degrees of freedom in calculating the expected values).

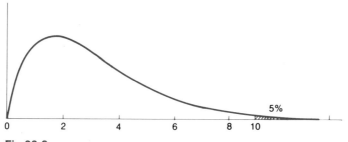

**Fig 22.2**

Consulting the $\chi^2$ tables with 4 degrees of freedom, we see that the critical values are 9.49 at the 5% level, and 13.3 at the 1% level. As our value of $\chi^2$ is 3.5 (much less than both of the critical values), we would accept the hypothesis that consumers are unable to distinguish between the washing powders.

## Errors resulting from the use of $\chi^2$

Before we go any further, it is worth considering the errors that can occur if we use $\chi^2$. A glance at Fig 22.1 shows that the distribution is continuous, and we have used it to test discrete data. Clearly, then, this is a possible source of error. Now this error is not really serious *unless there is only one degree of freedom*, and when $\nu = 1$ we compensate for this error by applying *Yates' correction*. All that is involved in this correction is that we subtract $\frac{1}{2}$ from the *absolute* difference between the observed and expected values. Let us examine an example to see how we apply the correction.

EXAMPLE

In a sample of 1000 people, 452 said they would vote Labour at the next election. We wish to test the hypothesis that 50% of the electorate vote Labour. On the basis of this hypothesis, then, we have:

|  | Observed | Expected |
|---|---|---|
| Labour | 452 | 500 |
| Not Labour | 548 | 500 |

In this case, we have only one degree of freedom, so our critical values are 3.84 (at the 5% level) and 6.63 (at the 1% level).

Also, as $\nu = 1$ we must apply Yates' correction:

| Observed | Expected | $(O-E)$ | $\lvert O-E \rvert - \frac{1}{2}$ | $(\lvert O-E \rvert - \frac{1}{2})^2$ | $\dfrac{(\lvert O-E \rvert - \frac{1}{2})^2}{E}$ |
|---|---|---|---|---|---|
| 452 | 500 | $-48$ | 47.5 | 2256.25 | 4.5125 |
| 548 | 500 | 48 | 47.5 | 2256.25 | 4.5125 |
| | | | | | $\chi^2 = 9.0250$ |

So we can see that the sample result is significant at the 1% level. We reject the null hypothesis and conclude that less than 50% of the electorate vote Labour.

There is a second type of error that can arise from using the $\chi^2$ distribution. If the expected frequency in any cell is unusually small, the use of the $\chi^2$ test might lead to erroneous conclusions. Two general rules concerning small cell frequencies are:

1  If there are only two cells the expected frequencies in each cell should be five or more. We could, then, use the $\chi^2$ test in the following case:

|  | *Observed* | *Expected* |
|---|---|---|
| Agreeing | 643 | 642 |
| Disagreeing | 4 | 5 |

We could not, however, use it in this case:

|  | *Observed* | *Expected* |
|---|---|---|
| Agreeing | 643 | 644 |
| Disagreeing | 4 | 3 |

2  If there are more than two cells, $\chi^2$ should not be used if more than 20% of the expected frequencies are less than five.

According to this rule we could use the $\chi^2$ test for the examination data on the left in the following table. Only one cell out of six has a frequency less than five, i.e. only 16.67% of the cells.

| *No. of students* | | | *No. of students* | |
|---|---|---|---|---|
| *Observed* | *Expected* | *Grade* | *Observed* | *Expected* |
| 18 | 16 | A | 30 | 32 |
| 39 | 37 | B | 110 | 113 |
| 8 | 13 | C | 86 | 87 |
| 6 | 4 | D | 23 | 24 |
| 82 | 78 | E | 5 | 2 |
| 10 | 15 | F | 5 | 4 |
| — | — | U | 4 | 1 |
| 163 | 163 | | 263 | 263 |

The $\chi^2$ test should not, however, be used for data on the right, since three of the seven cells have an expected frequency of less than five, i.e. 43%.

The reasoning behind this rule can be seen if we examine the data carefully. You will see that there is a very close relationship between the observed and the expected frequencies. The maximum difference is three. It would be commonsense to assume that there is not significant difference between the observed and the expected frequencies. Yet if you compute the value of $\chi^2$, you will find it to be 14.01, greater than the critical value at the 0.05 level. Contrary to commonsense, we would reject the null hypothesis. The dilemma can be resolved if we combine the last three classes into a single class:

| Grade | Observed | Expected |
|-------|----------|----------|
| E and below | 14 | 7 |

Using these revised frequencies the computed value of $\chi^2$ is 7.26, less than the critical value for 4 degrees of freedom at the 0.05 level which is 9.49. The null hypothesis would be accepted, and we would argue that there is no difference between the observed and the expected frequencies. This is, of course, a much more logical conclusion.

## Testing goodness of fit to a probability distribution

Do you remember that in the chapter on probability distributions we investigated the pattern of V1 rockets falling on London during World War II? We divided an area of 144 square kilometres into 576 equal squares, and counted the number of bombs per square. We wanted to find if the bombs were falling at random, or were 'clustered' to a greater degree than could be ascribed to chance. If the bombs did fall randomly, then we should be able to predict the frequency distribution of bombs per square by using the Poisson distribution. The observed distribution was:

| No. of bombs per square | 0 | 1 | 2 | 3 | 4 | 5 |
|-------------------------|-----|-----|----|----|---|---|
| Frequency | 229 | 211 | 93 | 35 | 7 | 1 |

This distribution forms our observed frequencies, and has a mean of 0.93 bombs per square. We now formulate the null hypothesis that the bombing pattern could be predicted by the Poisson distribution with a mean 0.93. (This may not sound like a null hypothesis, but it would if we restated it slightly – there is no difference between the bombing pattern and the Poisson distribution with a mean of 0.93.) On the basis of our null hypothesis, we can calculate the expected frequencies like this:

$$576e^{-0.93}\left[1 + 0.93 + \frac{0.93^2}{2!} + \frac{0.93^3}{3!} + \frac{0.93^4}{4!} + \frac{0.93^5}{5!}\right]$$

$$= 576\,[0.3946 + 0.3670 + 0.1706 + 0.0529 + 0.0123 + 0.0023]$$

$$= 227.3 + 221.4 + 98.3 + 30.5 + 7.1 + 1.3$$

When we dealt with the Poisson distribution previously, we were content to deal with probabilities. Here we are more interested in expected values, and we can obtain these by multiplying the probabilities by 576 – the total frequency. Notice that the sum of the expected frequencies is 575.9 –

implying that we expect 0.1 squares to have more than five bombs. It would seem sensible, then, to combine this 0.1 into the five bombs per square class. We can now calculate a value for $\chi^2$ to see how well the observed data fits the expected data:

| Observed | Expected | $(O-E)$ | $(O-E)^2$ | $\dfrac{(O-E)^2}{E}$ |
|----------|----------|---------|-----------|----------------------|
| 229 | 227.3 | 1.7 | 2.89 | 0.0127 |
| 211 | 211.4 | $-0.4$ | 0.16 | 0.0008 |
| 93 | 98.3 | $-5.3$ | 28.09 | 0.2858 |
| 35 | 30.5 | 4.5 | 20.25 | 0.6639 |
| $\left.\begin{array}{c}7\\1\end{array}\right\}$ | $\left.\begin{array}{c}7.1\\1.4\end{array}\right\}$ | $-0.5$ | 0.25 | 0.0294 |

$$\chi^2 = \overline{0.9926}$$

We must now investigate the number of degrees of freedom in calculating the expected values. The first thing to notice is that after combining the last two classes we have five classes in total. We used up one degree of freedom in making both sets of frequencies have the same total, and we used up another degree of freedom by making both sets of frequencies have the same mean. So we must have had $5 - 2 = 3$ degrees of freedom when calculating the expected values. Generalising, for a Poisson distribution with $n$ classes, there will be $\nu = n - 2$ degrees of freedom in calculating the expected frequencies.

Consulting the $\chi^2$ table, with $\nu = 3$ we would reject the null hypothesis at the 5% level if $\chi^2$ exceeds 7.81, and at the 1% level if $\chi^2$ exceeds 11.34. Now, as our value of $\chi^2$ is far less than these critical values, we must accept the null hypothesis and conclude that the observed frequencies fit the Poisson frequencies excellently. The differences between the observed and expected values could well be accounted for by sampling fluctuations.

Now let us see if the data would fit a binomial distribution. First, we must find the probability that a particular square is bombed. Now we know that in any binomial distribution, the mean is $np$. In this case the mean is 0.93, and we can take $n$ to be 5. So:

$$0.93 = 5p$$

$$p = 0.186$$

and $q = 1 - 0.186 = 0.814$. So for examples of five squares, the probability distribution would be given by $(0.814 + 0.186)^5$:

$$= (0.814)^5 + 5(0.814)^4(0.186) + 10(0.814)^3(0.186)^2$$
$$+ 10(0.814)^2(0.186)^3 + 5(0.814)(0.186)^4 + (0.816)^5$$

$$= 0.3574 + 0.4083 + 0.1866 + 0.0426 + 0.0049 + 0.0002$$

Multiplying the probabilities by 576 would give the expected frequencies:

| Observed | Expected | $(O - E)$ | $(O - E)^2$ | $\dfrac{(O - E)^2}{E}$ |
|---|---|---|---|---|
| 229 | 205.9 | 23.1 | 533.61 | 2.59 |
| 211 | 235.2 | −24.2 | 585.64 | 2.49 |
| 93 | 107.5 | −14.5 | 210.25 | 1.96 |
| 35 | 24.5 | 10.5 | 110.25 | 4.50 |
| 7⎱<br>1⎰ | 2.8⎱<br>0.1⎰ | 5.1 | 26.01 | 8.97 |
| | | | | ‾‾‾‾‾ |
| | | | | 20.51 |

The null hypothesis we have used here is that the observed frequencies could be described by the binomial distribution $(0.814 + 0.186)^5$. To test the goodness of fit, we now need to know the degrees of freedom in calculating the expected values. As with the Poisson distribution, we used up two degrees of freedom – one to make the totals agree and one to make the means agree. Again, we have $5 - 2 = 3$ degrees of freedom, and so we can use the critical values of the last example. Applying these rules, we must reject the null hypothesis at the 1% level. The observed data could not be described by a binomial distribution.

We shall not give an example of testing goodness of fit to a normal distribution, as the method is essentially similar, but it would be as well to investigate the number of degrees of freedom involved in such tests. To fit a normal distribution to observed data, we will use up three degrees of freedom, as the distributions must have the same mean, standard deviation and total. Assuming we have $n$ classes in our expected frequencies, then, to test goodness of fit to a normal distribution would involve $n - 3$ degrees of freedom.

## Contingency tables

To illustrate a further application of $\chi^2$ testing, let us now examine a question set by the ACCA.

**EXAMPLE**

Using the $\chi^2$ distribution as a test of significance, test the statement that the number of defective items produced by two machines, as shown in the following table, is independent of the machine on which they were made.

| | Machine output | | |
|---|---|---|---|
| | *Defective articles* | *Effective articles* | *Total* |
| Machine A | 25 | 375 | 400 |
| Machine B | 42 | 558 | 600 |
| | 67 | 993 | 1000 |

We are asked to test the statement that the number of defective items is independent of the machines on which they were made, and we adopt this as our null hypothesis. Now if the statement is not true, then the number of defectives will depend on the machine on which they were made, and the table will enable us to calculate the degree of dependence. A table constructed in this way (to indicate dependence or association) is called a *contingency table*. 'Contingency' means dependence. Many of you, for example, will be familiar with the terms 'contingency planning', i.e. plans that will be put into operation *if* certain things happen.

As usual, let us suppose that our null hypothesis is true. Given this assumption, then we are only interested in the totals in the table, i.e. that out of 1000 articles, 67 were defective, and that out of 1000 articles 400 were produced on machine A. Using only this information, we can now predict the expected number of defectives produced by the two machines. We have:

$$\frac{400}{1000} = \frac{4}{10}$$

of the total output is produced on machine A, and as 67 items are defective, then we would expect:

$$67 \times \frac{4}{10} = 26.8$$

of them to have been produced by machine A. Now as machine A produces 400 items, then $400 - 26.8 = 373.2$ items can be expected to be non-defective. Likewise, it follows that as we can expect 67 defective items, $67 - 26.8 = 40.2$ of them can be expected to be produced by machine B. Finally, as we can expect B to produce 600 items, we can expect $600 - 40.2 = 559.8$ of the items to be non-defective. The expected table, then, would look like this:

|  | Machine output | | |
|---|---|---|---|
|  | *Defective articles* | *Non-defective articles* | *Total* |
| Machine A | 26.8 | 373.2 | 400 |
| Machine B | 40.2 | 559.8 | 600 |
|  | 67.0 | 933.0 | 1000 |

Notice that after we have calculated just one of the values in the table, the remainder will be fixed by subtraction. So we have $\nu = 1$ degree of freedom in calculating the expected values for a $2 \times 2$ contingency table and we must apply Yates' correction:

| *Observed* | *Expected* | *(O − E)* | $\mid O - E \mid - \frac{1}{2}$ | $\frac{(\mid O - E \mid - \frac{1}{2})^2}{E}$ |
|---|---|---|---|---|
| 25 | 26.8 | −1.8 | 1.3 | 0.063 |
| 375 | 373.2 | 1.8 | 1.3 | 0.005 |
| 42 | 40.2 | 1.8 | 1.3 | 0.042 |
| 558 | 559.8 | −1.8 | 1.3 | 0.003 |
|  |  |  | | $\chi^2 = 0.113$ |

With $\nu = 1$ we would reject the null hypothesis if $\chi^2 > 6.64$ (1% level). Now as our value is much less than this, there is no reason to reject the null hypothesis – the number of defective items is independent of the machine on which they were produced.

If you are going to use the above technique, then make absolutely sure that the samples are *independent*. We could not use it if the same sample is being tested under different conditions (i.e. 'before and after' investigations). It could not be used in the following case: a sample of 100 people were given a standard washing powder to test and report whether the powder was satisfactory or unsatisfactory. The same people were then asked to test a new super powder. The results were:

|  |  | *New powder* | |
|---|---|---|---|
|  |  | Satisfactory | Unsatisfactory |
| *Old powder* | Satisfactory | 20 | 10 |
|  | Unsatisfactory | 50 | 20 |

Examining this table, we see that 60 people 'changed their minds', i.e. 50 changed from unsatisfactory to satisfactory and 10 changed from satisfactory to unsatisfactory. Now suppose we formulate the null hypothesis that the type of powder had no effect on their response (i.e. they could not distinguish between them), then we would expect an equal number to change their minds in either direction. So we would expect 30 to change from unsatisfactory to satisfactory and 30 to change from satisfactory to unsatisfactory. This now enables us to calculate $\chi^2$:

| Observed | Expected | $(O-E)$ | $\|O-E\|-\frac{1}{2}$ | $\frac{(\|O-E\|-\frac{1}{2})^2}{E}$ |
|----------|----------|---------|----------------------|-------------------------------------|
| 50 | 30 | 20 | 19.5 | 12.675 |
| 10 | 30 | −20 | 19.5 | 12.675 |
| | | | | 25.350 |

Using the critical values for $\nu = 1$, we must reject the null hypothesis at the 1% level. The difference between the observed and expected values cannot be attributed to chance and we must conclude that association between response and type of powder is established.

If we were to test for association for tables larger than a $2 \times 2$, then we could use a very similar analysis.

---

**EXAMPLE**

Let us consider a $2 \times 3$ table comprising independent samples. Suppose that a random sample of men and women indicated their view on a certain proposal as follows:

| | In favour | Opposed | Undecided | |
|---|-----------|---------|-----------|-----|
| Women | 118 | 62 | 25 | 205 |
| Men | 84 | 78 | 37 | 199 |
| | 202 | 140 | 62 | 404 |

At a level of significance of (a) 0.01 and (b) 0.05, test the hypothesis that there is no difference in opinion between men and women in so far as this proposal is concerned.                                   CIPFA

We adopt the null hypothesis that there is no association between the response and the sex of the person interviewed. On this basis we may deduce that the proportion of the sample who are female is $\frac{205}{404}$, and as 202 people are in favour of the proposal, the expected number of women in favour of the proposal is:

$$\frac{205}{404} \times 202 = 102.5$$

Also, as 140 people are against the proposal, the expected number of women against the proposal is:

$$\frac{205}{404} \times 140 = 71$$

We can obtain the remaining expected values by subtraction, i.e.:

Expected number of undecided women $= 205 - (102.5 + 71) = 31.5$
Expected number of men in favour $\quad = 202 - 102.5 = 99.5$
Expected number of men opposed $\quad = 140 - 71 = 69$
Expected number undecided men $\quad = 62 - 31.5 = 30.5$

So the expected table looks like this:

|  | In favour | Opposed | Undecided |
|---|---|---|---|
| Women | 102.5 | 71 | 31.5 |
| Men | 99.5 | 69 | 30.5 |

| Observed | Expected | (O − E) | $\frac{(O-E)^2}{E}$ |
|---|---|---|---|
| 118 | 102.5 | 15.5 | 2.34 |
| 62 | 71 | −9 | 1.14 |
| 25 | 31.5 | −6.5 | 1.34 |
| 84 | 99.5 | −15.5 | 2.41 |
| 78 | 69 | 9 | 1.17 |
| 37 | 30.5 | 6.5 | 1.38 |

$$\chi^2 = 9.78$$

In this example, we have two degrees of freedom in calculating the expected values. Consulting the table, we see that the critical values for $\chi^2$ are 5.99 at the 5% level and 9.21 at the 1% level, hence we would reject the null hypothesis accepting the alternative hypothesis (that men and women think differently) with 99% confidence.

## Summary of degrees of freedom

We see then, that the $\chi^2$ test is very versatile, and it might be useful here to summarise the number of degrees of freedom.

(a)  For goodness of fit tests with $n$ classes, $v = n - 1$.

(b)  For goodness of fit tests to a binomial or Poisson distribution with $n$ classes, $v = n - 2$.

(c) For goodness of fit tests to a normal distribution with $n$ classes, $v = n - 3$.[*]

(d) For tests of association for a contingency table with $m$ rows and $n$ columns $v = (n - 1)(m - 1)$.

In conclusion, it should be noted that of all significance tests, $\chi^2$ is probably the most widely used. However, many statisticians are highly critical of $\chi^2$ testing, reasoning that there are other tests available which are far more suitable. We do not consider this book to be aimed at a level sufficient to discuss the criticisms in detail, but we will leave you one point to ponder. None of the null hypotheses we have considered with respect to goodness of fit can be *exactly* true, so if we increase the sample size (and hence the value of $\chi^2$) we would ultimately reach the point when all null hypotheses would be rejected. All that the $\chi^2$ test can tell us, then, is that the sample size is too small to reject the null hypothesis!

## Using the spreadsheet

The menu structure of the template that will perform the chi square test is shown in Fig. 22.3.

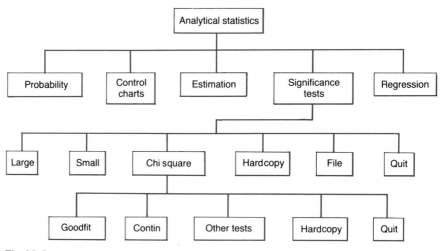

**Fig 22.3**

---

[*]When calculating expected normal distribution frequencies we use up three degrees of freedom, one to make the totals agree, one to make the means agree and one to make the standard deviations agree.

Select 'Analytical statistics' from the main menu, then select 'Significance tests' and finally select 'Chi square'. Two tests are available: goodness of fit and association. Select 'Goodfit' and the screen will now look like this:

|   | A | B | C | D | E | F |
|---|---|---|---|---|---|---|
| 1 | | | | | | |
| 2 | Enter observed and expected values | | | | | |
| 3 | | | | | | |
| 4 | Press ALT A when finished | | | | | |
| 5 | | | | | | |
| 6 | Observed Expected | | | | | |
| 7 | | | | | | |
| 8 | | | | | | |
| 9 | | | | | | |
| 10 | | | | | | |

Enter the observed values in column A from cell A7 downward, and the expected values in column B from cell B7 downward. Press ALT A when you have finished entering the data. If you entered the data for the washing powder example considered in the chapter, then the following would be output:

|    | A | B | C | D | E | F | G | H |
|----|---|---|---|---|---|---|---|---|
| 1 | | | | | | | | |
| 2 | Enter observed and expected values | | | | | | | |
| 3 | | | | | | | | |
| 4 | Press ALT A when finished | | | | | | | |
| 5 | | | | | | | | |
| 6 | Observed | Expected | $(O-E)\hat{\ }2/E$ | | | | | |
| 7 | 187 | 200 | 0.845 | | | | | |
| 8 | 221 | 200 | 2.205 | | | | | |
| 9 | 193 | 200 | 0.245 | | | | | |
| 10 | 204 | 200 | 0.08 | | | Test statistic chi-square = | | 3.5 |
| 11 | 195 | 200 | 0.125 | | | | | |
| 12 | | | | | | Degrees of freedom = | | 4 |
| 13 | | | | | | | | |
| 14 | | | | | | Critical values: | 5% | 1% |
| 15 | | | | | | | 9.488 | 13.277 |
| 16 | | | | | | | | |
| 17 | | | | | | | | |

The assumption undertaken in constructing this template was that for goodness of fit tests, there are $(n-1)$ degrees of freedom in calculating the expected values. Now as you know, this will not always be the case. It will not be true if we are testing for goodness of fit to one of the three standard probability distributions. However, the facility exists for you to alter the number of degrees of freedom as appropriate. Press the Esc key, move the cursor to cell H12, reduce the number of degrees of freedom and notice the effect on the critical values. Press ALT M to retrieve the chi square menu.

The goodness of fit tests will apply Yates' correction for one degree of freedom, but will not make adjustments for a low expected value frequency. You must make such adjustments manually before entering the data.

Now let us examine the test of association. Select 'Contingency' from the chi square menu and the following screen appears:

```
        A        B        C        D        E        F
1
2     Enter observed values       Press ALT G when finished
3
4     * * * * * * * * * * * * * * * * * * * * * * * * * *
5                                                       *
6                                                       *
7                                                       *
8                                                       *
9                                                       *
10                                                      *
11    * * * * * * * * * * * * * * * * * * * * * * * * * *
12
```

The template is designed to cope with contingency tables with at most six rows and at most six columns. In other words, the table should be within the limits imposed by the stars. After entering the data, you should press ALT G. If you entered the data on the differences in male and female opinion considered in this chapter then the following would be output:

|   | A | B | C | D | E | F | G | H |
|---|---|---|---|---|---|---|---|---|
| 1 | | | | | | | | |
| 2 | | | | | | | | |
| 3 | | | | | | | | |
| 4 | * * * * * * * * * * * * * * * * * * * * * * * * * * * * * * * | | | | | | | |
| 5 | 118 | 62 | 25 | | | * | | |
| 6 | 84 | 78 | 37 | | | * | | |
| 7 | | | | | | * | | |
| 8 | | | | | | * | | |
| 9 | | | | | | * | | |
| 10 | | | | | | * | | |
| 11 | * * * * * * * * * * * * * * * * * * * * * * * * * * * * * * * | | | | | | | |
| 12 | | | | Test statistic chi square = 9.786974 | | | | |
| 13 | | | | | | | | |
| 14 | | | | Degrees of freedom = | | 2 | | |
| 15 | | | | | | | | |
| 16 | | | | Critical values | 5% | 1% | | |
| 17 | | | | | 5.991 | 9.21 | | |
| 18 | | | | | | | | |
| 19 | | | | | | | | |
| 20 | | | | | | | | |

The option 'Other tests' will return you to the template for $Z$ and $t$ tests, 'Quit' will save the current data and return you to the main menu.

## QUESTIONS

**22.1** (a) What does the $\chi^2$ test test?

(b) The number of rejects in six batches of equal size were:

| Batch | Number of rejects |
|---|---|
| A | 270 |
| B | 308 |
| C | 290 |
| D | 312 |
| E | 300 |
| F | 320 |

Test the hypothesis that the difference between them is due to chance using a level of significance of 0.05.

**22.2** The number of breakdowns that have occurred during the last 100 shifts is as follows:

| Number of breakdowns per shift | 0 | 1 | 2 | 3 | 4 | 5 |
|---|---|---|---|---|---|---|
| Frequency: | | | | | | |
| Expected number of shifts | 14 | 27 | 27 | 18 | 9 | 5 |
| Actual number of shifts | 10 | 23 | 25 | 22 | 10 | 10 |

Show whether the manager is justified in his claim that the difference between the number of actual and expected breakdowns is due to chance. It has been customary to use a significance level of 0.05.

**22.3** A manufacturer of fashion garments for the younger age groups suspects that the market for his product has changed recently. Sales records for previous years showed that 14% of buyers were below 16 years of age, 38% were 16 to 20 years of age, 26% were 21 to 25 years and 22% were over 25. A random sample of 200 recent buyers, however, showed the following results:

| Age | Under 16 | 16–20 | 21–25 | Above 25 |
|---|---|---|---|---|
| Frequency | 22 | 62 | 60 | 56 |

(a) Compare the results of the sample with those expected from previous records.

(b) What null hypothesis should be tested using these data?

(c) Carry out a chi square ($\chi^2$) test of significance.

(d) Express your conclusions in terms meaningful to management.

**22.4** The quality control department of a certain firm randomly selects 200 components and tests them for surface defects. The results were as follows:

| Number of surface defects | 0 | 1 | 2 | 3 | 4 | 5 | 6 and over |
|---|---|---|---|---|---|---|---|
| Number of components | 90 | 62 | 31 | 13 | 3 | 1 | 0 |

Fit a Poisson distribution to this data, and test for goodness of fit.

**22.5** Assuming that a component never contains more than five defects, fit a binomial distribution to the data in Question 22.4, and test for goodness of fit.

**22.6** The following experiment was performed 64 times: a coin was tossed until it came up heads and $x$, the number of tosses to achieve a head, was recorded. The following data were obtained:

| $x$ | Frequency |
|---|---|
| 1 | 24 |
| 2 | 17 |
| 3 | 16 |
| 4 | 3 |
| Greater than 4 | 4 |
| Total | 64 |

Is the data consistent with the hypothesis that the coin was fair?

**22.7**   An examination of the purchase department's records for a random sample of 100 orders for a certain commodity reveals the following distribution of lead times, that is, delays between placing an order and receiving the consignment.

| Lead times | Orders |
|---|---|
| Under 14 days | 28 |
| 14 and under 21 days | 52 |
| 21 days and over | 20 |

If it is assumed that the lead times are normally distributed with mean 16 days and standard deviation five days, what frequencies of orders would be expected for each category of lead time?

Apply the chi square test at a 10% significance level to check whether the observed data contradicts the assumptions of normality.

**22.8**   (a)   An association between two characteristics, which is apparent from some data, is found to be of borderline statistical significance. Explain this conclusion and say what action should be taken in order to reach a clearer decision.

   (b)   Three types of machine A, B and C, are used by a company to produce items which are very prone to a certain type of imperfection. A random sample of 100 items from each machine showed the number of perfect and imperfect items to be as follows:

|  |  | Perfect | Imperfect |
|---|---|---|---|
|  | A | 33 | 67 |
| Machine | B | 39 | 61 |
|  | C | 48 | 52 |

Use the chi square $(\chi^2)$ test to examine at the 0.05 level of significance whether there is any association between machine type and proneness to imperfection.

**22.9** Suppose that a random sample of men and women indicated their view on a certain proposal as follows:

|  | In favour | Opposed | Undecided |
|---|---|---|---|
| Women | 118 | 62 | 25 |
| Men | 84 | 78 | 37 |

At a level of significance of (a) 0.01, (b) 0.05, test the hypothesis that there is no difference in opinion between men and women in so far as this proposal is concerned.

**22.10** Two factories using materials purchased from the same supplier and closely controlled to an agreed specification produce output for a given period classified into three quality grades, A, B and C, as follows:

|  | Output in tonnes | | | |
|---|---|---|---|---|
|  | A | B | C | Total |
| Factory: | | | | |
| X | 42 | 13 | 33 | 88 |
| Y | 20 | 8 | 25 | 53 |
| Total | 62 | 21 | 58 | 141 |

(a) Do these output figures show a significant difference at the 5% level?

(b) What hypothesis have you tested?

**22.11** Suppose that a random sample of men and women indicated their view on a proposal of public importance as follows:

|  | Opposed | Undecided | In favour |
|---|---|---|---|
| Men | 156 | 74 | 170 |
| Women | 122 | 50 | 236 |

At levels of significance of (a) 0.01 and (b) 0.05, test the hypothesis that there is no difference between the views of men and women on this issue.

**22.12** A certain drug was administered to 100 volunteers with common colds, and 35 reported that the drug brought some relief. The next winter, a new improved drug was given to the same group, and this time 43 reported that the drug brought some relief. Are we justified in assuming that the second drug is more likely to bring relief?

**22.13** Pharmaceuticals Plc have developed three new respiratory drugs. They submitted the drugs to clinical trials, the results of which are given in the table below. Determine whether or not these figures indicate a real difference in response of the diseases to the drugs, and explain your conclusion. Use the chi-square $(\chi^2)$ distribution as a test of significance at the 0.01 level.

| Drug | Percentage of patients recovered | Percentage of patients not recovered |
|------|------|------|
| A | 65 | 35 |
| B | 90 | 10 |
| C | 85 | 15 |

**22.14**  (a)  A marketing information firm has kept records on a random sample of 144 drivers who bought new cars last year. Drivers were classified according to their age last year, and records kept include data on how many other new cars each driver has bought in the last 10 years. This information is tabulated below:

| Additional new cars bought | Age of driver | | | Total |
|------|------|------|------|------|
| | 20 and under 30 | 30 and under 40 | 40 and over | |
| 0 | 19 | 5 | 12 | 36 |
| 1 | 23 | 13 | 12 | 48 |
| 2 | 11 | 18 | 7 | 36 |
| More than 2 | 7 | 12 | 5 | 24 |
| Total | 60 | 48 | 36 | |

Determine whether there is any evidence that there is a relationship between propensity to buy new cars and age of drivers in UK.

(b)  How useful might your conclusion be for a car assembly firm which is investigating the problem of advertising directed at specific age groups?

**22.15**  A market research agency has been commissioned to report on the smoking habits of men and women in a particular area. Two samples were taken, one of 200 men and the other of 200 women. The findings are shown in the following table:

| | Smokers | Non-Smokers | Total |
|------|------|------|------|
| Men | 110 | 90 | 200 |
| Women | 104 | 96 | 200 |

(a)  Test the hypothesis that differences in sex has no effect on the number of smokers in the two samples; and

(b)  Explain your conclusion in (a).

Use the Chi Square $(\chi^2)$ distribution as a test of significance, at the 0.05 level.

**22.16**  Acca Plc tests all components built into its products to ensure that they have attained the standard of quality required. There are three checkers, A, B and C, who undertake this work. The table below shows the number of components accepted and rejected by the checkers when they tested three batches of component 1703 recently delivered to the factory. You are required to test the hypothesis that the proportions of components rejected by the three are equal and explain the significance of your conclusion. Use the chi square $(\chi^2)$ distribution as a test of significance, at the 0.05 level of significance.

**Acca Plc Components Quality Test**

|          | Checker A | Checker B | Checker C | Total |
|----------|-----------|-----------|-----------|-------|
| Accepted | 44        | 56        | 50        | 150   |
| Rejected | 16        | 24        | 10        | 50    |

**22.17**  The number of students passed and failed by three examiners in a certain examination were as follows:

|        | Mr X | Mr Y | Mr Z |
|--------|------|------|------|
| Passed | 50   | 47   | 56   |
| Failed | 5    | 14   | 8    |

Test the hypothesis that the proportions of students failed by the three examiners are equal.

**22.18**  The following data is based on a random sample of 1000 businessmen:

|                        | Profit maximisers | Revenue maximisers | Total |
|------------------------|-------------------|--------------------|-------|
| Studied economics      | 200               | 100                | 300   |
| Did not study economics| 200               | 500                | 700   |
| Total                  | 400               | 600                | 1000  |

Test using two different statistical techniques whether the above information suggests any association between education in economics and the objectives of businessmen.

**22.19**  Samples of students with varying educational backgrounds obtained the following results in their final degree examinations:

|                    | Third class | Second class (lower) | Upper second/ first |
|--------------------|-------------|----------------------|---------------------|
| Secondary          | 24          | 58                   | 18                  |
| Comprehensive      | 36          | 112                  | 52                  |
| Grammar            | 80          | 230                  | 90                  |
| Public/Direct grant| 60          | 200                  | 40                  |

Test whether there is any association between pre-university education and the class of degree.

# 23 Regression and correlation

If you have listened carefully to news bulletins, or read the business pages of a responsible newspaper you will probably have come across the phrase 'economic indicator' or 'business indicator'. Such an indicator is an event which, although it may be important in its own right, is of even more importance in helping us to predict what is going to happen to some other variable in the future. It is commonly believed, for example, that government expenditure will affect the level of employment. What is important, of course, is knowledge of how much extra expenditure is needed to create, say, one thousand new jobs, and what is the time lag before the unemployed actually start work. Surely a man who can identify and quantify relationships such as this is worth his weight in gold to any company.

No text books can teach you to identify every relationship which may be important in a particular set of circumstances, but you should have a good idea of those relationships which are relevant to your own work. You will know, for example, that next month's sales figures are influenced by this month's advertising, or that the major influence on your departmental budget is the behaviour of labour costs. What you have to learn is how a knowledge of such relationships can be used to enable you to make predictions (or estimates). After all, in forecasting sales figures or preparing a departmental budget you *are* being asked to make predictions.

## Bivariate distributions

At some time, every businessman must have faced the problem as to whether or not he should advertise. Some believe that their sales depend on the amount of advertising they undertake; others hold equally firmly to the view that the key to increasing their sales lies in providing service, in offering a wide selection of goods, or in giving an unconditional guarantee of satisfaction. The only way of settling this sort of argument for any individual firm is to examine the facts.

Brown's Department Store has recently hired a consultant to help boost its sales and thereby the morale of its management (and hopefully its employees). The consultant, a marketing specialist, has reasoned that sales are a function of advertising expenditure. Thus he has decided to try to relate sales to the amount spent on advertising. The data from the company's records are produced for him by the accountant and he is presented with the following information:

| Year | Advertising X (£000) | Sales Y (£m) |
|---|---|---|
| 1 | 100 | 9 |
| 2 | 105 | 8 |
| 3 | 90 | 5 |
| 4 | 80 | 2 |
| 5 | 80 | 4 |
| 6 | 85 | 6 |
| 7 | 87 | 4 |
| 8 | 92 | 7 |
| 9 | 90 | 6 |
| 10 | 95 | 7 |
| 11 | 93 | 5 |
| 12 | 85 | 5 |
| 13 | 85 | 4 |
| 14 | 70 | 3 |
| 15 | 85 | 3 |

Now this series is rather different from others we have considered. Whereas in the series we have so far studied each item has had a single value, in this series there are two items associated with each value. We call distributions like this *bivariate distributions*.

We cannot, of course, draw any meaningful conclusions from the data as it stands. Possibly it would help if we were to present the information in the form of a diagram – in this case, the scatter diagram.

Before we get too involved with the scatter diagram itself, let us consider the variables which are the subject of analysis. First, what is the nature of the data which comprises the two variables? Can it be treated as an enumeration of the population; or must we treat it as a sample? The answer may seem very simple, but there are serious implications underlying it. We shall be calculating measures which contain constants. If we treat the data as a population we will treat the constants we calculate, $\alpha$ and $\beta$ (alpha and beta), as population parameters, absolutely accurate and unchanging. If the data, however, is treated as a sample, the constants we calculate will be $a$ and $b$, which are no more than estimates of $\alpha$ and $\beta$. As such they might be wrong and will certainly be subject to some sampling error.

Second, which is the dependent and which the independent variable? In terms of the analysis we shall assume one variable to be a function of the other. But in terms of the actual data, the analysis itself cannot determine which is which. This determination can be made only on the basis of your own knowledge of the subject matter. In so far as Brown's Department

Store is concerned there is little doubt that most people would agree that advertising expenditure is the independent variable and sales the dependent. We shall proceed to analyse on this assumption, even if one or two of you disagree.

## The scatter diagram

The purpose of the scatter diagram, as you know, is to illustrate diagrammatically any relationship that may exist between the dependent and independent variables. To the extent that it succeeds it can help the analyst in three ways:

1   It indicates generally whether or not there appears to be a relationship between the two variables.

2   If there is a relationship it may indicate whether it is linear or non-linear.

3   If the relationship is linear, the scatter diagram will show whether it is negative or positive.

If you look at Fig 23.1 you will see that the data does provide some evidence that the higher the level of advertising, the higher the level of sales achieved. Certainly the same level of advertising is associated occasionally with differing levels of sales, just as the same level of sales is associated with

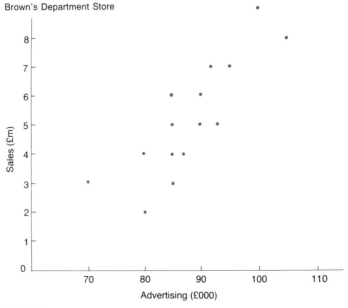

Fig 23.1

differing levels of advertising. But as you can see, the general trend of the points on this diagram is an upward slope from left to right. It is indicated that there is a relationship, that it is linear and that it is a positive relationship in the sense that as one variable rises so does the other.

The scatter diagram, then, is the graph of a bivariate distribution and is used to obtain an indication of whether association exists between the two variables. Having discovered that in this case an association is indicated, we shall now try to discover the nature of the relationship and the degree of association between the variables. If we can do that, we can use our knowledge to estimate what the value of sales will be for any given level of advertising.

## Regression

First we will attempt to discover the nature of the relationship by calculating an equation enabling us to estimate the value of one variable given that we know the value of the other. The variable we are trying to predict is the dependent variable (the one plotted conventionally on the y axis) while the variable we are using as a basis for prediction is the independent variable (plotted on the x axis). In this book we will confine ourselves to an analysis of the simple linear case; *simple* implying two variables only, such that y depends on the value of x and not on another variable; *linear* implying that the relationship between x and y is a straight line relationship. In this simple case the equation which best fits the data is an equation of the form:

$$\hat{Y} = a + bX$$

where $\hat{Y}$ is an estimate of the average value of $Y$ corresponding to a given value of $X$;

$X$ is the actual value of the independent variable;
$a$ is a constant – an estimate of $\alpha$, the y intercept of the regression line; and
$b$ is an estimate of $\beta$, the slope of the regression line – also a constant.

You will notice that we are distinguishing between the value of $Y$, which is the *actual* value of the sales resulting from a given level of advertising expenditure, and $\hat{Y}$ which is an *estimate* of what the sales will be. Our estimate in fact corresponds to the average value of the differing level of sales resulting from the same value of advertising expenditure.

The accuracy of an estimate of this nature naturally depends on the extent to which the regression equation $\hat{Y} = a + bX$ and its graph actually fits the data. Thus we must try to ensure that the regression line is the line of best fit.

## The regression line

One way of obtaining the line of best fit would be to place a ruler across the scatter diagram and draw in the line which 'looks right'. We could then find where this line cuts the y axis to give us the value of the constant $a$, and calculate the gradient of the line to give us the value of the constant $b$. But guessing the line of best fit is just not good enough, especially if decisions are to be taken on the basis of our estimates. What we need is some criterion by which we can determine what we mean by 'best fit'.

One criterion we could adopt would be to minimise the magnitude of the error involved, that is, the differences between the value of the points on the diagram $(Y)$ and the value of the points on the regression line we have drawn $(\hat{Y})$. We could, that is, minimise the value of $\Sigma(Y - \hat{Y})$. Problems arise with this criterion however. In Fig 23.2(a) three errors are shown, one positive and two negative. They offset each other and the net error is zero. In this case, by minimising the error we have obtained what seems to be quite a good fit. Look now at Fig 23.2(b).

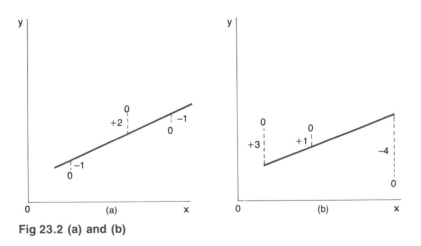

**Fig 23.2 (a) and (b)**

This regression line, too, reduces the error to zero, yet quite clearly in this case the fit is bad. Reducing the error to a minimum then, is no criterion for positioning the line of best fit. It may give a good fit, but it is just as likely to give a bad one.

What, then, if we were to minimise the absolute error, ignoring the sign? Once again this will not guarantee a line of best fit. In Fig 23.3, the line in (a) is clearly a better fit than the line in (b), yet line (b) minimises the absolute error. Statisticians reject both of these criteria as unsatisfactory.

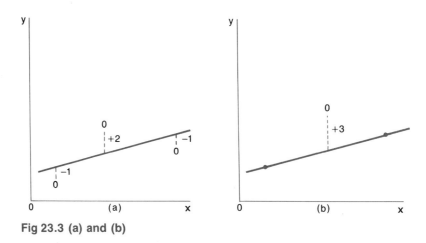

**Fig 23.3 (a) and (b)**

## The least squares regression line

Statisticians have defined the line of best fit as 'that line which minimises the sum of the squares of the errors – the *least squares regression line*'. The use of this criterion has several advantages.

- By squaring the errors we remove all negative signs and so avoid negative errors cancelling out the positive ones;

- Squaring tends to emphasise the larger errors and the minimising criterion means that we are trying to avoid the larger errors;

- All points are taken into account so the criterion avoids lines such as that in Fig 23.3(b).

How can we fit a line to our data which minimises the sum of the squares of the errors? We know that the equation of the line we need is:

$$\hat{Y} = a + bX$$

and we can obtain this if we can solve the so called normal equations, which will enable us to calculate the values of $a$ and $b$.

These equations are:

$$\Sigma Y = na + b\Sigma X$$

$$\Sigma XY = a\Sigma X + b\Sigma X^2$$

If you examine these equations you will see that we need to know five quantities, $\Sigma X$, $\Sigma Y$, $\Sigma XY$, $\Sigma X^2$ and $n$ (the number of observations). It will also be useful if, at the same time, we were to calculate the value of $\Sigma Y^2$, which we shall be using very shortly. We will calculate these values for advertising expenditure $(X)$ and the resultant sales $(Y)$, and obtain the regression equation connecting the two.

| $X$ ($£000$) | $Y$ ($£m$) | $XY$ | $X^2$ | $Y^2$ |
|---|---|---|---|---|
| 100 | 9 | 900 | 10 000 | 81 |
| 105 | 8 | 840 | 11 025 | 64 |
| 90 | 5 | 450 | 8 100 | 25 |
| 80 | 2 | 160 | 6 400 | 4 |
| 80 | 4 | 320 | 6 400 | 16 |
| 85 | 6 | 510 | 7 225 | 36 |
| 87 | 4 | 348 | 7 569 | 16 |
| 92 | 7 | 644 | 8 464 | 49 |
| 90 | 6 | 540 | 8 100 | 36 |
| 95 | 7 | 665 | 9 025 | 49 |
| 93 | 5 | 465 | 8 649 | 25 |
| 85 | 5 | 425 | 7 225 | 25 |
| 85 | 4 | 340 | 7 225 | 16 |
| 70 | 3 | 210 | 4 900 | 9 |
| 85 | 3 | 255 | 7 225 | 9 |
| 1322 | 78 | 7072 | 117 532 | 460 |

We can now insert these figures in the normal equations and calculate the value of $a$ and $b$:

$$78 = 15a + 1322b$$
$$7072 = 1322a + 117\ 532b$$

Now these equations look fearsome, but they can be solved as normal simultaneous equations. If we multiply the first equation by 1322 – the coefficient of $a$ in the second equation we get:

$$103\ 116 = 19\ 830a + 1\ 747\ 684b$$

Now multiply the second equation by 15, i.e. the coefficient of $a$ in the first equation and we get:

$$106\ 080 = 19\ 830a + 1\ 762\ 980b$$

We now have a pair of simultaneous equations in which the coefficient of the term $a$ is the same. If we subtract one of these equations from the other we will have an equation not containing the term $a$:

$$106\ 080 = 19\ 830a + 1\ 762\ 980b$$
$$103\ 116 = 19\ 830a + 1\ 747\ 684b$$
$$2\ 964 = 15\ 296b$$
$$b = 0.193776$$

Now, given the value of $b$, we can insert this value in the first equation and so find the value of $a$:

$$78 = 15a + (0.193776 \times 1322)$$
$$78 = 15a + 256.1721$$
$$-178.1721 = 15a$$
$$a = -11.8781$$

We have calculated the values of both $a$ and $b$ and can insert them in the regression equation $\hat{Y} = a + bX$.

Thus the regression equation connecting sales and advertising expenditure is:

$$\hat{Y} = -11.8781 + 0.19378X$$

or more simply

$$\hat{Y} = -11.9 + 0.19X$$

You will agree that, even with calculators, solving simultaneous equations with figures of this magnitude is cumbersome and productive of errors. We can however solve the normal equation using only symbols and so obtain expressions which enable us to obtain the value of $a$ and $b$ more directly and this is infinitely preferable.

The statistics necessary to find $a$ and $b$ are the variance of $X$, and what we call the *covariance* of $X$ and $Y$. The variance of $X$ we will symbolise as $S^2_x$, and as you know this is calculated as:

$$S^2_x = \frac{\Sigma x^2}{n} - \left(\frac{\Sigma x}{n}\right)^2$$

The covariance is symbolised as $S^2_{xy}$ and it is calculated as:

$$S^2_{xy} = \frac{\Sigma XY}{n} - \frac{\Sigma X \Sigma Y}{n.n}$$

The expression from which you can calculate the value of $b$ is:

$$b = \frac{\text{Covariance}}{\text{Variance}} = \frac{S^2_{xy}}{S^2_x}$$

and the expression for $a$ is:

$$a = \frac{1}{n} (\Sigma Y - b\Sigma X)$$

We have already calculated all the totals necessary for these expressions. Substituting we find:

$$S_{xy}^2 = \frac{\Sigma XY}{n} - \frac{\Sigma X \Sigma Y}{n.n} = \frac{7072}{15} - \frac{1322 \times 78}{15 \times 15} = 13.17333$$

$$S_x^2 = \frac{\Sigma X^2}{n} - \left(\frac{\Sigma X}{n}\right)^2 = \frac{117\,532}{15} - \left(\frac{1322}{15}\right)^2 = 67.98222$$

Hence $\quad b = \dfrac{13.17333}{67.98222} = 0.193776$

and $\qquad a = \dfrac{1}{15}(78 - 1322 \times 0.193776) = -11.8781$

As you can see, the values of $a$ and $b$ are exactly the same as when calculated from the normal equations, but with the aid of calculators, a great deal of tedious work is taken out of obtaining the regression equation.

How well does this equation fit the original data? Let us calculate what our estimate of the value of $Y$ would be for the various values of $X$, and then compare them with the observed values.

Using the regression equation:

$$\hat{Y} = -11.8781 + 0.1938X$$

we find that:

| For a value of X | Observed Y | Estimated $\hat{Y}$ |
|---|---|---|
| 100 | 9 | 7.5019 |
| 105 | 8 | 8.4709 |
| 90 | 5 | 5.5639 |
| 80 | 2 | 3.6259 |
| 80 | 4 | 3.6259 |
| 85 | 6 | 4.5949 |
| 87 | 4 | 4.9825 |
| 92 | 7 | 5.9515 |
| 90 | 6 | 5.5639 |
| 95 | 7 | 6.5329 |
| 93 | 5 | 6.1453 |
| 85 | 5 | 4.5949 |
| 85 | 4 | 4.5949 |
| 70 | 3 | 1.6879 |
| 85 | 3 | 4.5949 |

Well, as you can see the estimation of the value of $Y$ is not perfect, but on the whole, we think you will agree, it is pretty good.

The equation we have calculated is known as the equation of the regression line of y on x because we are estimating the value of $Y$ given the value of $X$. Thus if we had spent £75 000 on advertising we would estimate a sales figure by putting $X = 75$ (thousand) in the regression equation, i.e.:

$$\hat{Y} = -11.8781 + (75 \times 0.1938) = 2.6569 = £2\ 656\ 900$$

What does this prediction mean? Obviously it cannot mean that every time we spend £75 000 on advertising we would have sales of exactly £2 656 900. Conditions could never be quite the same on each occasion, and the fact that we spent some money last month would, of itself, influence the effect of spending more this month, since advertising has a cumulative effect. In fact, actual sales would fluctuate, even if advertising expenditure did not. The figure we estimate for sales is, in fact, an average figure.

We calculated the regression equation from observed values of $X$ ranging from £70 000 to £105 000 and used that equation to estimate the level of sales resulting from advertising expenditure of £75 000. When we take a value of the independent variable within the range of the observed values we call the process *interpolation* (placing between). We might have asked, however, for the estimated value of sales from advertising expenditure of £120 000:

$$\hat{Y} = -11.8781 + (0.1938 \times 120) = £1\ 137\ 790$$

Here we used a value of $X$ outside the range of observed values. We call this process *extrapolation* (placing outside). Both estimates are subject to error, but an extrapolated estimate is less reliable than an interpolated

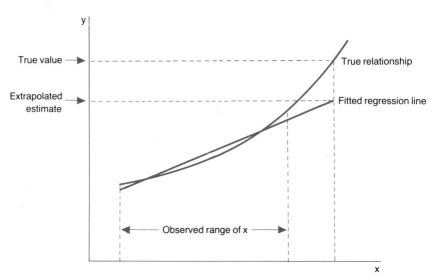

**Fig 23.4**

estimate. Can you see why? Within the observed range of $X$ we know how the data behaves, and how well the straight line fits. Outside the observed range we do not know how the data behaves, and the straight line may no longer be a good fit for these values of $X$. This is illustrated in Fig 23.4 and we can see that great caution is needed when making extrapolated estimates.

## Linear regression and the time series

We saw in an earlier chapter that the trend of many time series is linear and we learned to calculate that trend using a moving average. Now although a time series is not strictly a bivariate series, we can obtain the linear trend by using regression analysis.

Suppose we are examining the figures of quarterly profit made by a firm. If the data appears to demand a linear trend we can assume that profits depend on time and convert time into an independent variable by numbering successive quarters $1, 2, 3, 4, 5$ and so on.

Profits have varied over the last four years quarter by quarter, but have been generally rising. The figures, in thousands of pounds, are:

|  | Quarter | | | |
|---|---|---|---|---|
| Year | 1 | 2 | 3 | 4 |
| 19-5 | 40 | 60 | 90 | 70 |
| 19-6 | 50 | 70 | 110 | 80 |
| 19-7 | 70 | 80 | 120 | 90 |
| 19-8 | 80 | 100 | 130 | 100 |

If we number the quarters from 1 to 16 and use this as the independent variable, we can convert the time series into a bivariate distribution.

| Year | Quarter | $X$ | $Y$ | $X^2$ | $XY$ |
|---|---|---|---|---|---|
| 19-5 | 1 | 1 | 40 | 1 | 40 |
|  | 2 | 2 | 60 | 4 | 120 |
|  | 3 | 3 | 90 | 9 | 270 |
|  | 4 | 4 | 70 | 16 | 280 |
| 19-6 | 1 | 5 | 50 | 25 | 250 |
|  | 2 | 6 | 70 | 36 | 420 |
|  | 3 | 7 | 110 | 49 | 770 |
|  | 4 | 8 | 80 | 64 | 640 |
| 19-7 | 1 | 9 | 70 | 81 | 630 |
|  | 2 | 10 | 80 | 100 | 800 |
|  | 3 | 11 | 120 | 121 | 1 320 |
|  | 4 | 12 | 90 | 144 | 1 080 |
| 19-8 | 1 | 13 | 80 | 169 | 1 040 |
|  | 2 | 14 | 100 | 196 | 1 400 |
|  | 3 | 15 | 130 | 225 | 1 950 |
|  | 4 | 16 | 100 | 256 | 1 600 |
|  |  | 136 | 1340 | 1496 | 12 610 |

$$b = \frac{12\,610 - \dfrac{136 - 1340}{16}}{1496 - \dfrac{(136)^2}{16}} = 3.59$$

$$a = \frac{1}{16}\,(1340 - 136 \times 3.59) = 53.235$$

Thus the equation of our trend line for this series is:

$$\hat{Y} = 53.235 + 3.59\,X$$

We can obtain trend values by inserting into this equation $X = 1, 2, 3 \ldots 16$. Having thus obtained the trend we could use it to calculate the deviations from the trend and to calculate the average seasonal variation. The original data and the trend are plotted in Fig 23.5. As you know, only two points are needed to plot a straight line, and we have chosen $X = 1$ and $X = 10$:

When $X = 1$, $\hat{Y} = 56.825$ and when $X = 10$, $\hat{Y} = 89.135$

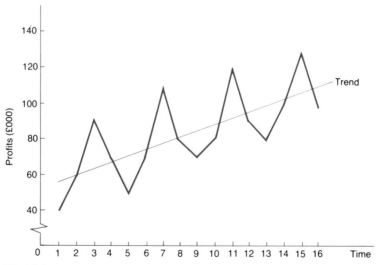

**Fig 23.5**

So far in this chapter we have been concentrating on the nature of the relationship between two variables but we must also pay attention to the degree of relationship. We will now turn our attention to measuring the extent to which two variables are related when that relationship is less than perfect.

## Correlation

Our analysis of regression has shown us that it is possible to obtain an expression showing the relationship between two variables such that for any value of $X$ it is possible for us to estimate the value of $Y$ associated with it. Sometimes the estimate we make is consistently good and there seems to be a very close relationship between the two variables. At other times the estimate is very poor indeed and we are led to think that the relationship is weak. Naturally we would like to know more about this relationship and in particular we would like to be able to measure its strength. Statisticians have designed a measure, the coefficient of correlation, which measures the relationship between the variables by asking the question, 'how much of the variation in the value of $Y$ can be explained by variations in the value of $X$?'

Suppose we take an extreme case. Having calculated the regression equation we find that the regression line is such that every point in the scatter diagram falls exactly on the line. The whole of the variation in $Y$ is explained by variations in the value of $X$. We have here a case of what we call *perfect correlation*. Now this definition has one great drawback. Fig 23.6 illustrates two cases of perfect correlation, though we can see that they are of quite different types. In case (a) we notice that $y$ increases as $x$ increases, and call this *positive correlation*. In case (b), however, $y$ decreases as $x$ increases and we call this a *negative correlation*. It would seem sensible, then, not merely to measure correlation, but also to state whether it is positive or negative.

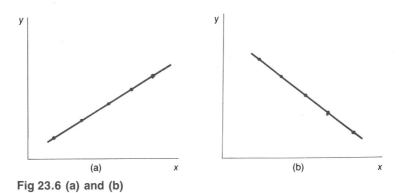

**Fig 23.6 (a) and (b)**

There is a second problem too, though it is not quite so obvious. We always tend to assume that if the correlation between two variables is high that variations in one are caused by variations in the other. Now association has no causal implications. There is a very high association between admissions into mental institutions and the number of TV licences issued. But it would be a bold man who maintained that we have proved that watching television causes insanity. We have here a case of spurious or nonsense correlation and we must always beware of this. In using the correlation coefficient we must be sure in our own mind that association between two variables is likely, or at least possible.

Bearing in mind this warning how will we go about measuring correlation?

## Concepts of variation

So important is the idea of variation in the analysis of correlation that it would be as well to look at it more closely. First, we will draw a scatter diagram of our data and superimpose on the diagram a line representing the mean value of $Y(\bar{Y})$ (Fig 23.7). This line will, of course be a horizontal straight line since the mean value of $Y$ is the same for all values of $X$. As you can see there is a great deal of variation of the values of $Y$ about $\bar{Y}$, and we will measure the total variation by totalling the squares of the individual deviations. Can you see why we must square the deviations? Obviously if we have calculated the value of $\bar{Y}$ correctly, the sum of the deviations must be equal to zero. Thus, as a measure of total variation we have:

Sum of the squares of the deviations from $Y = \Sigma(Y - \bar{Y})^2$

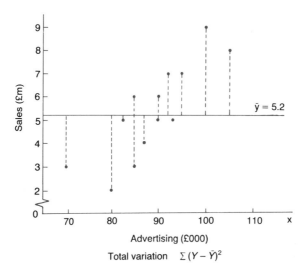

Total variation $\Sigma(Y - \bar{Y})^2$

**Fig 23.7**

You will have realised already that if we take the average of the deviations squared we will have the variance of $Y$:

$$S_y^2 = \frac{\Sigma(Y - \bar{Y})^2}{n} = \frac{\Sigma Y^2}{n} - \left(\frac{\Sigma Y}{n}\right)^2$$

If you turn now to Fig 23.8, here we have inserted on the scatter diagram not $\bar{Y}$, but the regression line. Here we have quite a different concept of variation. Each point on the regression line differs from the value of $\bar{Y}$, and we could consider this variation $(\hat{Y} - \bar{Y})$. Again we will take the sum of the squares of the deviations, $\Sigma(\hat{Y} - \bar{Y})^2$. Now there is an important characteristic of this variation. The value of $\hat{Y}$ is in each case calculated from the regression equation and hence is determined by the value we give to $X$. Thus we can say that this variation is entirely explained by the regression equation.

Fig 23.8

Finally you will notice that there is yet another variation we might consider – the variation of the points on the scatter diagram around the regression line. As you will remember, in constructing the regression line we made the square of these deviations as small as possible. We minimised $\Sigma(Y - \hat{Y})^2$. Think about these variations for a minute. The value of $Y$ is an established fact; sales reached a particular level and this we must accept. The value of $\hat{Y}$ we calculated from the regression equation and we have argued that the variation of $\hat{Y}$ from $\bar{Y}$ is fully explained by the equation. But there remains a part of the variation of $Y$ (equal to $Y - \hat{Y}$) which is unaccounted for. It is a part of the total variation which is not explained by the regression equation. It is, then, an unexplained variation. This variation is shown in Fig 23.9.

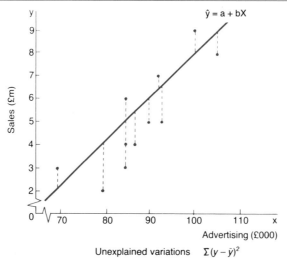

Unexplained variations  $\Sigma(y - \hat{y})^2$

**Fig 23.9**

Summarising then, we have:

$$\text{Total variation squared} = \Sigma(Y - \overline{Y})^2$$
$$\text{Explained variation squared} = \Sigma(\hat{Y} - \overline{Y})^2$$
$$\text{Unexplained variation squared} = \Sigma(Y - \hat{Y})^2$$

Suppose we had spent £85 000 on advertising and as a result actual sales had been £6 000 000. From our regression equation we would have estimated that sales $(Y)$ would be £4 594 900. The total variation is the actual value of sales $(Y)$ less the average value of sales (£5 200 000) which is equal to £800 000. Of this total variation an amount equal to $\hat{Y} - \overline{Y}$ is explained by the regression equation equal to £4 594 900 − £5 200 000, i.e. −£605 100. We would have expected sales to be £605 100 below the average, whereas in fact they were £800 000 above the average. There is then a variation of £1 405 100 which we have not explained.

What we have done in fact is to divide total variation into two – that part which we can explain, and that part which remains unexplained:

$$\text{Total variation} = \text{Explained variation} + \text{Unexplained variation}$$

Let us now calculate these three variations from the data for Brown's Department Store.

| | | | *Total* | | *Unexplained* | | *Explained* | |
|---|---|---|---|---|---|---|---|---|
| $X$ | $Y$ | $\hat{Y}$ | $Y - \bar{Y}$ | $(Y - \bar{Y})^2$ | $Y - \hat{Y}$ | $(Y - \hat{Y})^2$ | $\hat{Y} - \bar{Y}$ | $(\hat{Y} - \bar{Y})^2$ |
| 100 | 9 | 7.5019 | 3.8 | 14.44 | 1.4981 | 2.2443 | 2.3019 | 5.299 |
| 105 | 8 | 8.4709 | 2.8 | 7.84 | −0.4709 | 0.2217 | 3.2709 | 10.699 |
| 90 | 5 | 5.5639 | −0.2 | 0.04 | −0.5639 | 0.3180 | 0.3639 | 0.132 |
| 80 | 2 | 3.6259 | −3.2 | 10.24 | −1.6259 | 2.6436 | −1.5741 | 2.478 |
| 80 | 4 | 3.6259 | −1.2 | 1.44 | 0.3741 | 0.1400 | −1.5741 | 2.478 |
| 85 | 6 | 4.5949 | 0.8 | 0.64 | 1.4051 | 1.9743 | −0.6051 | 0.366 |
| 87 | 4 | 4.9825 | −1.2 | 1.44 | −0.9825 | 0.9653 | −0.2175 | 0.047 |
| 92 | 7 | 5.9515 | 1.8 | 3.24 | 1.0485 | 1.0994 | 0.7515 | 0.565 |
| 90 | 6 | 5.5639 | 0.8 | 0.64 | 0.4361 | 0.1902 | 0.3639 | 0.132 |
| 95 | 7 | 6.5329 | 1.8 | 3.24 | 0.4671 | 0.2182 | 1.3329 | 1.777 |
| 93 | 5 | 6.1453 | −0.2 | 0.04 | −1.1453 | 1.3117 | 0.9453 | 0.894 |
| 85 | 5 | 4.5949 | −0.2 | 0.04 | 0.4051 | 0.1641 | −0.6051 | 0.366 |
| 85 | 4 | 4.5949 | −1.2 | 1.44 | −0.5949 | 0.3540 | −0.6051 | 0.366 |
| 70 | 3 | 1.6879 | −2.2 | 4.84 | 1.3121 | 1.7216 | −3.5121 | 12.335 |
| 85 | 3 | 4.5949 | −2.2 | 4.84 | −1.5949 | 2.5437 | −0.6051 | 0.366 |
| $\bar{Y} = 5.2$ | | | | 54.40 | | 16.1101 | | 38.3 |

Rounding errors cause the sum of explained plus unexplained variation to differ from total variation by 0.01.

## Measuring the relationship

Armed with our knowledge of variation we can now go ahead to devise a measure of the degree of relationship between $X$ and $Y$. Suppose that the whole of the variation in $Y$ were explained by the regression equation. We could then argue that the relationship was perfect – that we have perfect correlation. But if only a part of the variation was explained, the correlation between $X$ and $Y$ would be less than perfect. As a first approach then we could use as a measure of the relationship between the two variables that proportion of the variation in the values of the dependent variable which is explained. Thus, we have calculated the total variation squared to be 54.4 and the explained variations squared to be 38.3. As a first measure we have:

$$\frac{\Sigma(\hat{Y} - \bar{Y})^2}{\Sigma(Y - \bar{Y})^2} = 0.704$$

We call this measure the *coefficient of determination*, symbolised as $r^2$. It is not, perhaps, as well known as the *coefficient of correlation* but it is, in fact, far more meaningful. The value of the coefficient of determination cannot, of course, be greater than one since we cannot explain a greater proportion of total variation than the whole; nor can it be less than zero since we cannot have less than no variation explained.

Since we measured variation by taking the sum of the squares of the individual variations, it would seem logical to take the square root of the coefficient of determination. This we define as the coefficient of correlation:

$$r = \sqrt{\frac{\text{Explained variation}}{\text{Total variation}}} = \sqrt{\frac{\Sigma(\hat{Y} - \bar{Y})^2}{\Sigma(Y - \bar{Y})^2}} = \sqrt{\frac{38.3}{54.4}} = 0.839$$

Thus the coefficient is an abstract measure of the relationship between variables based on a scale ranging between $+1$ and $-1$.[*] Whether $r$ is positive or negative depends on the nature of the relationship between $X$ and $Y$. If the sign of $b$ in the regression equation is $+$, as $X$ increases so does $Y$, and we have positive correlation. On the other hand, if the sign of $b$ is negative, you will find that as $X$ increases the value of $Y$ decreases and we have negative correlation.

Now there is nothing wrong in calculating the coefficient of correlation in this way, but it is, you must agree, a most cumbersome way of doing it. Not only have you to calculate the regression equation first, you have then to use that equation to obtain the values of $\hat{Y}$, obtain $\Sigma(\hat{Y} - \bar{Y})^2$ and then express this as a proportion of total variation squared. Like all such methods, it has its uses, and explains precisely what we are doing. But what we need is a method of calculating the coefficient of correlation directly without calculating the regression equation first.

## Pearson's product moment correlation coefficient

We can calculate the value of the coefficient of correlation far more simply if we use the formula:

$$r = \frac{\text{Covariance}(XY)}{\sqrt{\sigma_x^2 \times \sigma_y^2}} = \frac{S_{xy}^2}{\sqrt{S_x^2 \times S_y^2}}$$

As you will remember, the covariance $(XY)$ is:

$$\frac{\Sigma XY}{n} - \frac{\Sigma X \cdot \Sigma Y}{n \cdot n}$$

The variance of $X$ is:

$$\frac{\Sigma X^2}{n} - \left(\frac{\Sigma X}{n}\right)^2$$

---

[*] Remember that $\sqrt{1} = \pm 1$.

The variance of $Y$ is:

$$\frac{\Sigma Y^2}{n} - \left(\frac{\Sigma Y}{n}\right)^2$$

You will notice the similarity between this formula and the formula we used earlier to calculate the value of $b$ in the regression equation. In fact the numerator is the same and one term in the denominator is the same.

Let us now confirm that, in fact, this formula will yield the same coefficient of correlation as our previous calculations:

$$S_{xy}^2 = \frac{\Sigma XY}{n} - \frac{\Sigma X \cdot \Sigma Y}{n \cdot n} = \frac{7072}{15} - \frac{1322 \times 78}{15 \times 15} = 13.17333$$

$$S_x^2 = \frac{\Sigma X^2}{n} - \left(\frac{\Sigma X}{n}\right)^2 = \frac{117\,532}{15} - \left(\frac{1322}{15}\right)^2 = 67.98222$$

$$S_y^2 = \frac{\Sigma Y^2}{n} - \left(\frac{\Sigma Y}{n}\right)^2 = \frac{460}{15} - \left(\frac{78}{15}\right)^2 = 3.62667$$

$$r = \frac{13.17333}{\sqrt{67.98222 \times 3.62667}} = 0.839$$

## The interpretation of $r$

One disturbing feature of many students' work is that although they can calculate the value of the coefficient of correlation in a perfectly efficient manner they completely ignore any effort to interpret what their results mean.

What is the point of calculating a statistic if you cannot interpret it? We have calculated that $r$ is $+0.839$ for the data we were working with. Thus it is clear that a strong positive correlation exists. But what does $+0.839$ mean? If we had another bivariate distribution for which $r = +0.42$, clearly our first coefficient implies a stronger correlation than the second. But is it twice as strong? In fact it is far more meaningful to consider the coefficient of determination. Do you remember that this measures the proportion of total variation that can be explained by the regression equation? When $r = 0.839$, $r^2 = 0.704$ and we can conclude that 70.4% of the variations in $Y$ can be explained by the regression equation, leaving less than 30% to be explained by other factors. But if we consider a coefficient of correlation of 0.42, we have a coefficient of determination of $0.42^2 = 0.1764$, which implies that only 17.64% of the variations in $Y$ are explained by the regression equation.

Thus a coefficient of correlation of 0.839 is four times as strong as one of 0.42.

We would like, however, to issue a few words of warning about the interpretation of even a high coefficient. Even though analysis indicates that correlation exists we are not justified in assuming that there is therefore a cause and effect relationship. We must never fall into the trap of assuming that cause and effect exists when it is nonsense to do so. Sometimes a high correlation is obviously nonsensical. There is, as noted earlier, a high positive correlation between the annual issue of television licences and the annual admissions into mental institutions. It would be ludicrous to suggest that cause and effect exists here. The only logical conclusion that one can draw is that, quite by chance, both statistics were increasing at the same rate. In this case it is quite obvious that cause and effect is not proved by a high correlation coefficient – but sometimes things are not quite so clear cut. The high correlation between infant mortality and the extent of overcrowding that was found in Bethnal Green between the First and Second World Wars does seem to suggest that overcrowding causes high infant mortality. In fact, however, both are probably a result of low income levels.

If, then, we can never use correlation analysis to prove a cause and effect relationship you may wonder if it is worth study. Well, we think it is. Correlation can give added weight to a relationship that theory suggests exists. We could use it, for example, to verify the economic theory that consumption depends on income. Again, correlation can sometimes suggest that causal relationships exist in areas that were not previously suspected – a technique much used in medical research. Here correlation can often point to promising avenues of investigation.

Finally we would like to point out that a low correlation coefficient does not necessarily mean a low degree of association. After all, the coefficient we have calculated measures the strength of a linear relationship. The relationship may be very high, but curvilinear, and our coefficient would not indicate this.

## Significance test for $r$

Let us now return to Brown's problem. We have calculated a regression equation which indicates the nature of the relationship between sales and advertising expenditure and our correlation coefficient seems to be fairly high. But our results are obtained from a sample and we must now face up to the question as to whether the evidence we have justifies the conclusion that there is some correlation. After all, we know that conclusions based on a small sample can be very wide of the truth. The obvious way of testing our conclusions is to undertake a significance test on our correlation coefficient.

We will assume that our sample has been drawn from a population with a zero correlation coefficient.

Thus:

$H_0$: $r = 0$
$H_1$: $r \neq 0$

If $H_0$ is true we would expect $r$ to be distributed about zero with a standard error:

$$S_r = \sqrt{\frac{1 - r^2}{n - 2}} = \sqrt{\frac{1 - 0.704}{15 - 2}} = \sqrt{0.022769} = 0.15089$$

This estimate is made with 13 degrees of freedom:

$$\text{The test statistic } t = \frac{0.839 - 0}{0.15089} = 5.56$$

For a two-sided test with 13 degrees of freedom the critical value for $t$ is 2.160 (at the 5% level) and 3.012 (at the 1% level).

We will accept $H_0$ and conclude that our correlation coefficient is highly significant. We must still remember, however, that we have not proved a cause and effect relationship and that in making the test we assume that our sample was drawn from a normally distributed population.

## Rank correlation

Positive correlation implies that large values of $x$ are associated with large values of $y$ and small values of $x$ with small values of $y$. The converse is true, of course, of negative correlation. A useful method of assessing whether the data shows any correlation would be to *rank* them, i.e. list the values of the variables as first, second, third and so on, the lowest rank being assigned to the lowest value of the variable.

**EXAMPLE**

The following data refers to gross investment as a percentage of National Income and the percentage growth in National Income in nine selected countries. We are trying to assess if the level of investment is associated with the growth in National Income. In order to make an initial judgement the data has been ranked and the difference in the ranks of the two series listed in the column headed D.

| | Gross investment (%) | National Income growth (%) | Ranked | | | |
|---|---|---|---|---|---|---|
| | x | y | x | y | D | D² |
| Belgium | 19.2 | 3.4 | 4 | 2 | 2 | 4 |
| Denmark | 18.8 | 3.6 | 3 | 4 | −1 | 1 |
| France | 19.5 | 4.9 | 5 | 6.5 | −1.5 | 2.25 |
| Germany | 25.9 | 7.1 | 7 | 9 | −2 | 4 |
| Italy | 21.8 | 5.6 | 6 | 8 | −2 | 4 |
| Netherlands | 26.0 | 4.9 | 8 | 6.5 | 1.5 | 2.25 |
| Norway | 28.1 | 3.8 | 9 | 5 | 4 | 16 |
| United Kingdom | 16.4 | 2.6 | 1 | 1 | 0 | 0 |
| United States | 18.4 | 3.5 | 2 | 3 | −1 | 1 |
| | | | | | | 34.5 |

You will notice that in ranking the growth of National Income two countries have a growth rate of 4.9%. We cannot rank them sixth and seventh, nor even equal seventh. Since the two countries are equal and between them occupy both the sixth and seventh ranks we rank them equal at $6.5 = \frac{(6+7)}{2}$. Now, looking at the ranks it does seem that there is some positive correlation here. While only the United Kingdom has the same rank in both series, only in the case of Norway is there any marked difference in the ranks. Generally countries with a higher level of gross investment tend to have the higher growth rate.

We can in fact get a very good approximation on the correlation coefficient using ranks rather than the original data. Moreover the calculations are easy as the formula simplifies to:

$$P = 1 - \frac{6 \Sigma D^2}{n(n^2 - 1)}$$

where $D$ is the difference in ranks and $n$ the number of observations. This is known as *Spearman's rank correlation coefficient* and in this case:

$$P = 1 - \frac{6 \times 34.5}{(9.81 - 1)} = 1 - \frac{207}{720} = 0.7125.$$

Thus there is a positive correlation, but since $P^2 = 0.5076$, only about 50% of the variation of $y$ is explained. Correlation is not strong. Our knowledge of economics leads us to think that possibly we are examining the wrong variables. It may be net investment rather than gross that affects growth. This too could account for the difference in ranks in the case of Norway. Possibly much of the high level of investment here is replacement of worn out equipment, or possibly it is investment which does not lead directly to growth.

One great advantage of rank correlation is that it can be used to rank *attributes* which cannot be given a numerical value. Thus we could assess the consistency with which different panels of judges assess the contestants in beauty contests such as Miss World. In the same way we could assess whether different methods of selecting applicants for employment are likely to lead to the same results. Do we for example end up with the same ranking from a personal interview as we would from a written test or a psychological test? Thus we can use rank correlation in many cases where Pearson's correlation coefficient is not applicable.

Finally, notice that in the table $\Sigma D = 0$. This must be so (do you see why?), and provides a useful check on our initial calculations.

## Using the spreadsheet

The template to accompany this chapter will perform all the calculations on bivariate distributions. The menu structure for this template is shown in Fig 23.10.

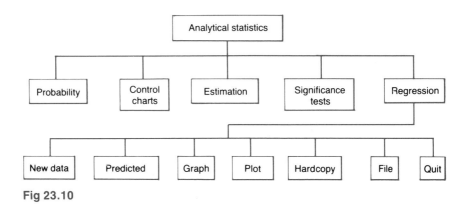

**Fig 23.10**

From the main menu select 'Analytical statistics' followed by 'Regression' and 'New data'. The opening screen looks like this:

|   | A | B | C | D | E | F | G | H |
|---|---|---|---|---|---|---|---|---|
| 1 | | | | | | | | |
| 2 | Sum X | | Cov(X, Y) | | | Correl coeff = | | |
| 3 | Sum Y | | Var(X) | | | Test stat t  = | | |
| 4 | Sum XX | | Var(Y) | | | Deg of free = | | |
| 5 | SUM YY | | | | | Crit values | | |
| 6 | SUM XY | | Gradient = | | | 5% | | |
| 7 | N | | Intercept = | | | 1% | | |
| 8 | | | | | | | | |
| 9 | X-value  Y-value | | | | | | | |
| 10 | | | | | | | | |
| 11 | | | | | | | | |
| 12 | | | | | | | | |
| 13 | | | | | | | | |
| 14 | Enter data | | | | | | | |
| 15 | | | | | | | | |
| 16 | Press ALT B when finished | | | | | | | |

As you can see, quite a lot of data is output using this spreadsheet. In addition to the totals of the tabulations, the variances and covariance are output. The values of the constants in the regression equation are computed. The correlation coefficient is computed and a test of significance is performed. Enter the pairs of values in columns A and B starting at line 10. The screen will scroll if more than 11 pair of items are entered. Try entering the data on advertising and sales used in this chapter. Press ALT B when you have finished entering the data. Your screen should now look like this:

|   | A | B | C | D | E | F | G | H |
|---|---|---|---|---|---|---|---|---|
| 1 | | | *** Regression and Correlation *** | | | | | |
| 2 | Sum X | 1322 | Cov(X, Y) | | 13.17333 | Correl coeff = 0.838965 | | |
| 3 | Sum Y | 78 | Var(X) | | 67.98222 | Test stat t  = 5.558655 | | |
| 4 | Sum XX | 117532 | Var(Y) | | 3.626666 | Deg of free = | | 13 |
| 5 | SUM YY | 460 | | | | Crit values | | |
| 6 | SUM XY | 7072 | Gradient = | | 0.193776 | 5% | | 2.16 |
| 7 | N | 15 | Intercept = | | − 11.8781 | 1% | | 3.012 |
| 8 | | | | | | | | |
| 9 | X-value | Y-value | | | | | | |
| 10 | 100 | 9 | | | | | | |
| 11 | 105 | 8 | | | | | | |
| 12 | 90 | 5 | | | | | | |
| 13 | 80 | 2 | | | | | | |
| 14 | 80 | 4 | | | | | | |
| 15 | 85 | 6 | | | | | | |
| 16 | 87 | 4 | | | | | | |
| 17 | 92 | 7 | | | | | | |
| 18 | 90 | 6 | | | | | | |
| 19 | 95 | 7 | | | | | | |
| 20 | 93 | 5 | | | | | | |

If you now select 'Predicted values', then the regression equation is used to predict the value of $Y$ for each corresponding value of $X$. Try it and see! Now select 'Graph' and the scatter diagram is drawn, together with the fitted regression line. The option 'Quit' will exit and save the current data, returning you to the main menu. You can change any of the values that you have input, but you must press Esc first. When you have changed the values, press F9 to see the effects of your changes. Pressing ALT M will return to the regression menu.

This template can be used to find the rank correlation coefficient, but you must rank the data manually before it is entered into the template.

## QUESTIONS

**23.1**  (a)  What is meant when two series of recorded figures such as expenditure on advertising and volume of sales are said to be linearly correlated?

(b)  If, in such a case, a regression line can be established what practical use does it have?

(c)  With the aid of scatter diagrams distinguish between positive and negative correlation.

**23.2**  Describe the construction of a scatter diagram and a line of best fit. Illustrate by means of scatter diagrams the following three types of relationship between two variables:

(a)  strong positive relationship;

(b)  weak negative relationship;

(c)  absence of relationship.

**23.3**  A company has found that the number of private cars with current licences can be used as a basis for estimating its production requirements. The following data has been collected over the last nine years:

| Year | No. of private cars (000s) |
|------|------------------|
| 1    | 8 247            |
| 2    | 8 917            |
| 3    | 9 513            |
| 4    | 10 303           |
| 5    | 10 816           |
| 6    | 11 228           |
| 7    | 11 515           |
| 8    | 12 059           |
| 9    | 12 717           |

Using the method of least squares, you are required to:

(a) estimate the number of private cars with current licences in Year 11.

(b) provide an estimate for Year 11 but assuming that because of other factors, for example labour unrest, only 60% of the normal annual increase will be realised in Year 11.

Answers should be submitted in millions correct to one decimal place of a million.

**23.4** The rate of growth of National Income per head of population and the percentage of National Income taken by the government in taxation in a number of countries is shown in the table:

| Country | Taxation as percentage of National Income $x$ | Growth rate per head (%) $y$ |
|---|---|---|
| United Kingdom | 35.5 | 1.8 |
| France | 39.4 | 4.2 |
| West Germany | 37.5 | 3.5 |
| Netherlands | 40.0 | 4.3 |
| Norway | 41.0 | 3.0 |
| Sweden | 46.3 | 3.2 |
| Switzerland | 25.4 | 2.2 |
| USA | 28.3 | 2.8 |

Source: OECD Statistics

Plot the points on a scatter diagram and, using the least squares method, draw the line of regression of $y$ on $x$. Comment on your result.

Explain briefly how you would calculate the line of regression of $x$ on $y$.

**23.5** **General knowledge test of 100 questions given to 20 students of different ages**

| Student | Age Years | Months | Number of questions answered correctly |
|---|---|---|---|
| A | 16 | 8 | 39 |
| B | 16 | 2 | 40 |
| C | 17 | 9 | 45 |
| D | 17 | 1 | 47 |
| E | 18 | 6 | 46 |
| F | 18 | 7 | 67 |
| G | 19 | 10 | 45 |
| H | 20 | 4 | 53 |

| Student | Age Years | Months | Number of questions answered correctly |
|---------|-----------|--------|----------------------------------------|
| I | 19 | 8 | 49 |
| J | 20 | 7 | 46 |
| K | 20 | 10 | 54 |
| L | 20 | 8 | 52 |
| M | 22 | 0 | 57 |
| N | 22 | 2 | 53 |
| O | 21 | 11 | 61 |
| P | 21 | 5 | 56 |
| Q | 19 | 11 | 48 |
| R | 21 | 8 | 56 |
| S | 18 | 11 | 52 |
| T | 21 | 10 | 64 |

(a) What is meant by a regression line?

(b) Draw a scatter diagram to illustrate the above results.

(c) Sketch in a line of best fit.

(d) Estimate, using this line of best fit, the number of questions likely to be answered (correctly) by a 17-year-old student.

**23.6** (a) Write a short note on regression lines.

(b) Calculate the product moment correlation coefficient between the following sets of figures:

| Intelligence test scores | Weekly income at age 23 (in £10s) |
|--------------------------|-----------------------------------|
| 121 | 16 |
| 84 | 6 |
| 105 | 19 |
| 93 | 18 |
| 126 | 18 |
| 109 | 17 |
| 97 | 22 |
| 112 | 13 |
| 116 | 14 |
| 86 | 9 |
| 97 | 20 |
| 103 | 21 |

**23.7** The following table gives the annual turnover and annual expenditure on advertising for 15 mail order firms.

|  Monthly turnover (£100 000) (Y) | Monthly expenditure on advertising (£1000) (X) |
| --- | --- |
| 4.5 | 22 |
| 5.1 | 28 |
| 5.3 | 31 |
| 5.4 | 31 |
| 5.9 | 35 |
| 6.0 | 43 |
| 6.5 | 43 |
| 6.6 | 48 |
| 6.6 | 43 |
| 6.8 | 49 |
| 6.9 | 56 |
| 7.0 | 52 |
| 7.0 | 57 |
| 7.5 | 58 |
| 8.7 | 61 |

Plot these figures on a scatter diagram and calculate a regression line by use of the least squares method. Draw this regression line on the scatter diagram. Describe how this line can be used to estimate the likely turnover for a given expenditure on advertising. Comment on the accuracy of such an estimate.

**23.8** Sales of groggets for each of the past five years have been as follows:

| Year ended 31 May 19X1 | 12 500 |
| Year ended 31 May 19X2 | 15 480 |
| Year ended 31 May 19X3 | 18 640 |
| Year ended 31 May 19X4 | 21 480 |
| Year ended 31 May 19X5 | 24 400 |

The seasonal pattern of sales is represented by the quarterly indices $70, 90, 160, 80$. You are required to use the least squares method to determine the trend line of the company's sales, project the trend line into the following year and calculate the expected sales for each quarter of that year.

**23.9** (a) From the following information draw a scatter diagram and by the method of least squares draw the regression line of best fit.

| Volume of sales (in thousands of units) | 5 | 6 | 7 | 8 | 9 | 10 |
| Total expenses (£000) | 74 | 77 | 82 | 86 | 92 | 95 |

(b) What will be the expected total expenses when the volume of sales is 7500 units?

(c) If the selling price per unit is £11, at what volume of sales will the total income from sales equal the total expenses?

**23.10**  The following data has been collected over eight periods:

| Period | Units of output | Total cost (£) |
|--------|-----------------|----------------|
| 1 | 10 000 | 32 000 |
| 2 | 20 000 | 39 000 |
| 3 | 40 000 | 58 000 |
| 4 | 25 000 | 44 000 |
| 5 | 30 000 | 52 000 |
| 6 | 40 000 | 61 000 |
| 7 | 50 000 | 70 000 |
| 8 | 45 000 | 64 000 |

Draw a scatter diagram and by the method of least squares draw a straight line which best fits the data.

Give the equation of the line and estimate the cost likely to be incurred at the output levels of 26 000 units and 48 750 units.

**23.11**  A machine will run at different speeds but the higher the speed the sooner a certain part has to be replaced. Trial observation gives the following data:

| Speed (revolutions per minute) | Life of drill-head (hours) |
|-------------------------------|----------------------------|
| 18 | 162 |
| 20 | 154 |
| 20 | 171 |
| 21 | 165 |
| 23 | 128 |
| 26 | 138 |
| 26 | 140 |
| 28 | 129 |
| 31 | 125 |
| 32 | 106 |
| 32 | 97 |
| 40 | 95 |
| 41 | 103 |
| 42 | 109 |
| 43 | 69 |

Plot the figures on a scatter diagram. Determine the equation of the regression line. Plot the line on the scatter diagram and estimate the life of the drill-head if the machine operates at 30 revolutions per minute.

**23.12**    Personal saving

| Quarter/Year | A (£m) | B (£m) | C (£m) | D (£m) |
|---|---|---|---|---|
| I | 673 | 684 | 918 | 923 |
| II | 569 | 582 | 555 | 662 |
| III | 570 | 533 | 549 | 658 |
| IV | 391 | 412 | 477 | 647 |

Fit a straight line trend to the above data, and find the seasonal components. Compare the actual figures for year D with those predicted using this trend and seasonal components approach. Consider the possible reasons for the divergences, paying particular attention to the quarter with the largest divergence.

**22.13**    Annual percentage change in manufacturing in a number of countries

| | Annual percentage change | |
|---|---|---|
| Country | Total output | Output per man-hour |
| Germany | 10.0 | 5.6 |
| Italy | 8.9 | 6.7 |
| Austria | 6.8 | 5.3 |
| France | 6.5 | 5.9 |
| Netherlands | 6.1 | 4.6 |
| Belgium | 3.8 | 3.5 |
| USA | 3.7 | 3.2 |
| Canada | 3.5 | 3.0 |
| UK | 3.4 | 2.6 |
| Denmark | 3.3 | 2.3 |
| Sweden | 3.3 | 3.2 |
| Ireland | 2.8 | 2.1 |

Source: CT Saunders: *Journal of the Royal Statistical Society, A*

Calculate the regression equation for total output on output per man-hour. Estimate the percentage change in total output corresponding to a 4% change in output per man-hour. How would you estimate the percentage change in output per man-hour corresponding to a 4% change in total output?

**23.14**    The advertising expenditure and product sales of a company for eight consecutive months are as follows:

| Month | 1 | 2 | 3 | 4 | 5 | 6 | 7 | 8 |
|---|---|---|---|---|---|---|---|---|
| Advertising expenditure (£000) | 26 | 52 | 18 | 47 | 51 | 36 | 18 | 26 |
| Sales (hundreds) | 102 | 142 | 135 | 115 | 156 | 171 | 127 | 110 |

The company has developed a relationship predicting the sales in each month from the amount of advertising expenditure in that and the previous months as:

$$s_i = 85 + 0.6a_i + 0.9a_{i-1}$$

where $s_i$ are the predicted sales in month $i$, in hundreds, and $a_i$ is the advertising expenditure in month $i$, in thousands of pounds.

1  Calculate the estimated sales in months 2 to 8 using the formula and comment on the results.

2  What is:

    (i)   the maximum discrepancy in any month between actual sales and expected sales?

    (ii)  the maximum percentage discrepancy, when the discrepancy is expressed as a percentage of actual sales?

3  What would be the effect on sales if advertising expenditure were reduced by £5000 per month?

## 23.15

### Advertising and related sales of two companies

| Company A | | Company B | |
|---|---|---|---|
| Sales (£000) | Advertising (£000) | Sales (£000) | Advertising (£000) |
| 190 | 9.0 | 439 | 51.4 |
| 100 | 14.5 | 632 | 58.8 |
| 279 | 18.3 | 856 | 82.2 |
| 241 | 11.4 | 896 | 86.8 |
| 176 | 20.8 | 626 | 73.6 |
| 314 | 23.1 | 717 | 78.8 |
| 223 | 29.6 | 749 | 67.4 |
| 120 | 25.1 | 605 | 64.1 |
| 156 | 34.6 | 468 | 66.4 |
| 73 | 38.2 | 513 | 58.9 |
| 104 | 18.7 | 803 | 74.6 |
| 71 | 30.9 | 484 | 54.5 |
| 184 | 38.6 | 726 | 71.9 |
| 101 | 42.6 | 771 | 81.0 |
| 253 | 36.9 | 664 | 72.1 |

(a)  What is meant by (i) positive correlation, (ii) zero correlation?

(b)  Describe briefly the limitations of scatter diagrams.

(c)  Draw *one* scatter diagram on which both companies' results are illustrated.

(d)  Interpret the results of the diagram.

**23.16**  (a)  Calculate the coefficient of correlation for the following data:

**Domestic Manufacturing Ltd. payroll and value of product × output**

| Month | Total payroll (£000) | Total Value of product × output (£000) |
|---|---|---|
| Jan | 5 | 8 |
| Feb | 6 | 9 |
| March | 7 | 9 |
| April | 9 | 11 |
| May | 8 | 13 |

(b)  What is the purpose of finding the correlation coefficient in respect of the above data, and what does the value of the coefficient indicate?

**23.17**  **Television licences current (thousands)**

| | Monochrome | Colour |
|---|---|---|
| 1984 | 3014 | 15 667 |
| 1985 | 2733 | 15 887 |
| 1986 | 2497 | 16 408 |
| 1987 | 2283 | 16 902 |
| 1988 | 2012 | 17 310 |
| 1989 | 1762 | 17 846 |
| 1990 | 1518 | 18 086 |
| 1991 | 1259 | 18 149 |

Source: *Monthly Digest of Statistics*

(a)  Prepare a scatter diagram based on the data given above, mark in the mean point and briefly comment on what is revealed.

(b)  Explain the difference between the product moment coefficient of correlation and the rank correlation coefficient, mentioning any advantages either might have over the other.

(c)  What is the association between correlation and regression?

**23.18**  Explain what is meant by the term 'product moment correlation coefficient'.

| Age (in years) | 18 | 20 | 21 | 27 | 23 | 34 | 24 | 42 | 38 | 44 |
|---|---|---|---|---|---|---|---|---|---|---|
| Length of training required (in days) | 8 | 5 | 6 | 8 | 7 | 11 | 8 | 10 | 6 | 8 |

The length of training required by operatives to be able to carry out a routine task is shown in the above table along with the age of the trainees. By calculating the product moment correlation coefficient determine whether the length of training required correlates with age.

**23.19**  (a)  Explain what is meant by 'product moment correlation coefficients' and 'rank correlation coefficients' and give examples where each one has advantages over the other.

(b)

| $x$ | 24 | 26 | 21 | 23 | 22 | 19 | 18 | 17 | 15 | 16 |
|---|---|---|---|---|---|---|---|---|---|---|
| $y$ | 35 | 33 | 31 | 29 | 25 | 24 | 23 | 21 | 20 | 19 |

Calculate the product moment correlation coefficient between the variables $x$ and $y$.

**23.20**  (a)  Measurements on two variables are found to yield a correlation coefficient of 0.35. Give two reasons why it cannot necessarily be inferred that the two variables are causally related.

(b)  The following table gives the mean daily temperature and the amount of electricity consumed on eight consecutive Mondays during a year.

| Temperature ($^\circ F$) | 37 | 32 | 35 | 40 | 40 | 44 | 42 | 48 |
|---|---|---|---|---|---|---|---|---|
| Electricity consumption (megawatt hours) | 3.7 | 3.8 | 3.7 | 3.6 | 3.7 | 3.4 | 3.4 | 3.3 |

Code the data about the assumed means of 40 and 3.5 so that $x = $ temperature $(-40)$; $y = $ electricity consumption $(-3.5)$, and calculate the coefficient of correlation between temperature and electricity consumption. Comment on your result.

**23.21**  The following data taken from a manufacturing company's budget relates to volume of sales and the corresponding expenses. Obtain the product moment correlation coefficient and comment, in the light of your result, on the relationship between volume of sales and the total expenses.

| Volume of sales (thousands of units) | 5 | 6 | 7 | 8 | 9 | 10 |
|---|---|---|---|---|---|---|
| Total expenses (£000) | 74 | 77 | 82 | 86 | 92 | 95 |

**23.22**  It is often suggested that unemployment and the rate of wage inflation are inversely related. Examine the evidence below and discuss whether it supports the above contention, producing where necessary relevant statistical measures:

| Year | Unemployment (%) | Change of wages (%) |
|---|---|---|
| 1 | 11.6 | 5.0 |
| 2 | 12.2 | 3.2 |
| 3 | 12.3 | 2.7 |
| 4 | 11.7 | 2.1 |
| 5 | 11.6 | 4.1 |
| 6 | 12.1 | 2.7 |
| 7 | 12.6 | 2.9 |
| 8 | 11.7 | 4.6 |
| 9 | 11.5 | 3.5 |
| 10 | 11.6 | 4.4 |

Does the inclusion of more recent experience agree with your conclusion above?

| | | |
|---|---|---|
| 11 | 12.5 | 4.0 |
| 12 | 12.5 | 7.7 |
| 13 | 12.5 | 5.7 |
| 14 | 12.7 | 9.5 |

**23.23**   Describe, with examples, what the coefficient of correlation measures and state the maximum and minimum values that $r$ can take.

An applicant for a certain post has to take five intelligence tests; he obtains the following results:

| Intelligence test (x) | Score obtained (y) |
|---|---|
| 1 | +2 |
| 2 | +2 |
| 3 | −3 |
| 4 | +1 |
| 5 | +3 |

Calculate the value of the product moment correlation coefficient $r$. Comment on the view that his score increases as he progresses from one test to the next.

**23.24**   (a)  Explain the value of a scatter diagram in investigating the association between two sets of figures. Illustrate the scatter diagrams associated with different values of the correlation coefficient.

(b)  The following table records annual rainfall and sunshine in a British coastal resort:

| Period | 1 | 2 | 3 | 4 | 5 | 6 | 7 | 8 | 9 | 10 | 11 |
|---|---|---|---|---|---|---|---|---|---|---|---|
| Rainfall (in) | 15.1 | 15.8 | 14.9 | 16.6 | 12.6 | 17.4 | 16.1 | 13.7 | 15.5 | 17.8 | 13.2 |
| Sunshine (hr) | 1692 | 1634 | 1835 | 1741 | 1876 | 1561 | 1921 | 1942 | 1822 | 1542 | 1874 |

Calculate the rank correlation coefficient between rainfall and sunshine.

**23.25**   (i)  Ten students enter for two papers in the final examination of a professional body. The marks obtained by each student are:

|                            |       | Paper 1 | Paper 2 |
|----------------------------|-------|---------|---------|
| Total marks awarded for paper |    | 100     | 10      |
| Marks obtained by student  | A     | 58      | 7       |
|                            | B     | 56      | 5       |
|                            | C     | 54      | 8       |
|                            | D     | 65      | 10      |
|                            | E     | 58      | 5       |
|                            | F     | 60      | 7       |
|                            | G     | 59      | 6       |
|                            | H     | 51      | 2       |
|                            | I     | 53      | 4       |
|                            | J     | 56      | 6       |

Calculate the product moment correlation coefficient $r$ between the two sets of marks and give a clear explanation of the meaning of your result.

(ii) Without doing any further calculations show the effect, if any, on $r$, of increasing all the marks by 15%.

**23.26**

|       | Finished output (thousand tonnes) | Expenditure on electricity (£000s) |
|-------|-----------------------------------|------------------------------------|
| Jan   | 20                                | 106                                |
| Feb   | 22                                | 138                                |
| March | 25                                | 158                                |
| April | 26                                | 172                                |
| May   | 21                                | 120                                |
| June  | 23                                | 142                                |
| July  | 28                                | 184                                |
| Aug   | 20                                | 102                                |
| Sept  | 25                                | 164                                |
| Oct   | 29                                | 192                                |

Express the relationship between the finished output and the expenditure on electricity during the period January to October in the form of the product moment coefficient of correlation and comment on the meaning of the figure obtained.

**23.27** (a) Explain what is meant by the terms 'correlation coefficients' and 'scatter diagrams' and comment on their use.

(b) Two instructors assess the apprentices in a course they are running and give them the following placings:

| Apprentice | A  | B  | C  | D  | E | F  | G  | H | I | J  | K   | L   |
|------------|----|----|----|----|---|----|----|---|---|----|-----|-----|
| 1st Instructor | 1 | 2= | 2= | 4 | 5 | 6= | 6= | 8 | 9 | 10 | 11= | 11= |
| 2nd Instructor | 1= | 3 | 5 | 1= | 4 | 6 | 10 | 7 | 8 | 11 | 9 | 12 |

Calculate the correlation between the two sets of placings.

Using the correlation you have just calculated comment on the agreement between the two instructors.

**23.28** The personnel department of a large company is investigating the possibility of assessing the suitability of applicants by using psychological tests instead of normal interview procedures. A comparative test of seven applicants was carried out using both methods. The results were as follows:

| Applicant | Ranking by interview procedure | Ranking by psychological tests |
|---|---|---|
| A | 4 | 5 |
| B | 1 | 2 |
| C | 7 | 7 |
| D | 6 | 4 |
| E | 2 | 1 |
| F | 3 | 3 |
| G | 5 | 6 |

(a) Calculate the rank coefficient of correlation.

(b) Interpret the result established.

**23.29** Retail Price Index and Index of Producer Prices, 1991

| | Retail Price Index all items | Index of Producer Prices manufacturing industries |
|---|---|---|
| January | 130.2 | 104.4 |
| February | 130.9 | 102.3 |
| March | 131.4 | 102.4 |
| April | 133.1 | 103.6 |
| May | 133.5 | 103.2 |
| June | 134.1 | 102.5 |
| July | 133.8 | 101.1 |
| August | 134.1 | 101.0 |
| September | 134.6 | 101.5 |
| October | 135.1 | 102.6 |
| November | 135.6 | 103.4 |

For the above data, calculate the product moment correlation coefficient. Comment on your result.

**23.30** (i)   Describe, with examples, what is meant by a scatter diagram.

(ii)   Describe, with examples, what the coefficient of rank correlation measures. Give the range of values that this coefficient can take. Two personnel managers each interview eight applicants for a vacant post. After the interviews each manager awards each applicant a mark, as given below:

| | | | | Candidate | | | | |
|---|---|---|---|---|---|---|---|---|
| | A | B | C | D | E | F | G | H |
| Manager X | 12 | 17 | 14 | 7 | 10 | 12 | 6 | 3 |
| Manager Y | 16 | 15 | 18 | 5 | 13 | 10 | 7 | 4 |

Convert the marks into ranks and then calculate and interpret the coefficient of rank correlation.

**23.31** (a)   Explain what is meant by a scatter diagram and coefficient of rank correlation.

(b)   Two personnel managers each interview the same five candidates for a vacant post. After the interviews the managers rank the candidates according to suitability for the post.

| | | | Candidate | | |
|---|---|---|---|---|---|
| | A | B | C | D | E |
| Manager X | 2 | 1 | 5 | 3 | 4 |
| Manager Y | 3 | 5 | 4 | 1 | 2 |

Obtain and interpret a coefficient of rank correlation for the two sets of rankings.

**23.32** (a)   Explain the connection between correlation and regression and briefly indicate how the latter may be measured.

(b)   The table given below shows the ranking obtained by ten typists who were first given speed tests and then subjected to speed checks as they worked in normal conditions. Using the rank coefficient of correlation determine whether the speed tests are a reliable guide to the speed likely to be attained by a typist working in normal conditions.

| | Ranking | |
|---|---|---|
| Typist | In Tests | In Normal Conditions |
| A | 1 | 3 |
| B | 2 | 4 |
| C | 3 | 6 |
| D | 4 | 1 |
| E | 5 | 2 |
| F | 6 | 8 |
| G | 7 | 9 |
| H | 8 | 10 |
| I | 9 | 7 |
| J | 10 | 5 |

(c) State which method of measuring correlation would give a more accurate result for (b) than the rank coefficient. What information would you have needed to have been able to use this more accurate method?

**23.33**   A group of redundant employees accepted for a re-training scheme are given an aptitude test, and six months after completion of their training period they are ranked according to the quality of their output. The following are the rankings:

| Employee | Aptitude test | Work quality |
|---|---|---|
| A | 2 | 1 |
| B | 3 | 2 |
| C | 1 | 3 |
| D | 6 | 4 |
| E | 7 | 5 |
| F | 4 | 6 |
| G | 8 | 7 |
| H | 5 | 8 |
| I | 12 | 9 |
| J | 11 | 10 |
| K | 9 | 11 |
| L | 10 | 12 |

You are required to use an appropriate statistical technique to determine whether the aptitude test is a reliable predictor of a worker's ability to perform quality work.

# 24 Statistical sources

There is little doubt that the second half of the twentieth century is the age when the data bank has come into its own. Data is collected on a large scale, not only by the government, but also by firms specialising in making market surveys and taking public opinion polls and by industrial firms and international organisations such as the United Nations or European Community. This data is stored and made available to investigators through data retrieval systems. At one extreme we may be seeking data from a highly sophisticated computer system; at the other we will be painstakingly searching through the files in a filing cabinet.

It is small wonder that in the last half-century the nature of the problem facing the statistical investigator has changed. As recently as 1920 the main problem was that data on many important problems was just not available, and the statistician had to find some means of organising his own survey to obtain primary data. Today the problem is often one of choice; of knowing where data is stored and selecting that which is most suited to immediate needs. There is still a great deal of primary data collected, of course, particularly when we are concerned with marketing a product or with assessing public opinion which, at best, is fickle. Yet modern sophisticated methods of sampling still have to be based on secondary data. Even so simple a task as assessing which way the electorate will vote will require not only the register of electors, but also information on the age structure and the social structure of the areas to be sampled. The survey itself is in fact very often only the tip of the iceberg. Where then are we to look for the data which may be essential to us?

Before we start hunting through the mass of published information we must realise that much of the data we need may already be held in the records of our own firm or trade organisation. A survey into market trends could well begin with an analysis of salesmen's performance and their opinion of how the market will develop, analysed by both product and area. We may not get all we require, but it will give us a good start. In the same way, a great deal of useful information is held in wages books, petty cash records, ledgers, personnel records and even in the published final accounts of the firm. One of the greatest advantages of using such internal data is that it is still possible to ask questions of those who originally recorded the data, to clarify definitions, to discuss problems and possibly even to extend the data. It is just not possible to obtain this supplementary information when we are using data produced by an outside body.

At the same time, we must remember that internal data is, by its very nature, narrowly based. It will relate to a single firm, or at best to a single industry. If we look at the sales analysis of a firm of seedsmen we will certainly get a very clear picture of sales trends for that firm. We may be able to extend the picture and argue that these trends are typical of the seed industry as a whole. What we cannot do is to pretend that the figures we have tell us anything about any other industry or about British industry in general.

Only when we have exhausted such internal sources should we turn to published data. No matter how narrow or specific our enquiry, however, we will still have to turn to secondary data because, if we are to put our results into perspective, there is still a mass of background information that we need; and often this data can be obtained only from published sources. Unemployment within our own industry becomes more meaningful when we can put it into the context of the unemployment rate within the region or within the United Kingdom; the rate of inflation means little until we compare it with the rate of increase in salaries and the rate of inflation in other countries. Much of the data we need will already have been produced by independent survey bodies such as Gallup Poll, or by research units within firms or universities, but by far the most important source of such secondary statistics is the Central Statistical Office, responsible for publishing data collected by the wide range of government departments. Whether you want to know the average July temperature at London Airport, the number of children in primary schools last year, or the balance of payments in 1992, you will find it tucked away among the government statistics published by the Central Statistical Office.[*]

## The *Annual Abstract of Statistics*

In the United Kingdom, possibly the best source of this official data is the *Annual Abstract of Statistics* published by the Central Statistical Office. It collates and summarises information relating to the United Kingdom produced by government departments (such as the Department for Education) and obtained from national surveys (such as the census of distribution or the census of population). As you might expect, it tends to give information for the United Kingdom as a whole rather than individual towns. If we need more detail we may have to refer to far more comprehensive reports issued by the appropriate government departments.

---

[*] Students are urged to obtain a copy of the Stationery Office publication, 'Government Statistics – a brief guide to sources' published by and issued free by The Press and Information Services, Central Statistical Office, Government Buildings, Cardiff Road, Newport, Gwent, NP9 1XG.

Population statistics, for example, comprise 29 tables in the *Annual Abstract*, but the Office of Population Census alone publishes comprehensive and detailed reports on each individual county, together with a Preliminary Report, and a general report. Additionally, the Registrar General's *Annual Review* and *Quarterly Reviews* supplement the census reports.

The *Annual Abstract* is precisely what its name implies – an abstract – but it is a good starting point for any investigation. Not only does its 15 sections cover such diverse topics as weather, output, finance, education and transport, but in most cases information is given on a comparative basis for at least ten years so that any marked trend can be spotted easily. For more recent years, most data is given monthly. Additionally, the Central Statistical Office publishes the *Monthly Digest of Statistics*, bringing the information in selected fields up-to-date month by month.

## Population and vital statistics

Not every statistician will agree, but we tend to think that of all the data produced by the government, that relating to population is the most useful. General knowledge of the population and its age–sex distribution is, of course, necessary for efficient administration, but think of what else is needed. We need age distribution to plan schools for the next generation, to assess the effect of changes in (say) child benefit, or to plan a policy for pensions. We need a knowledge of the causes of death to allocate funds for medical research. Information on housing is the first step in planning a housing policy. Questions on educational qualifications help the formulation of an educational policy – and so on. Information on all these topics, and many more, can be found in the reports on the census of population and the Annual Reports of the Registrar General. There is little doubt that the census of population is one of the most useful sources of data, and certainly, along with its necessary accompaniment – the compulsory registration of births, deaths and marriages – it is the most useful single source of information relating to vital statistics.

The census consists of a complete enumeration of the persons in a country on a given night together with questions on age, sex, marital status, occupation and the industry in which they work. In addition, the modern census collects information on social conditions such as the housing of the population or the educational standards reached. In the United Kingdom the first census was taken in 1801 and, apart from 1941, one has been taken every 10 years since that date. The government now have, in fact, the powers to take a census every five years if they so wish, and one such was taken in 1966.

Obviously, every census must ask certain questions which are never changed – such as name, sex, age, etc. – but the opportunity is usually taken to ask additional questions to throw light on social problems that rear their head from time to time. In 1921, for example, questions were asked relating to widows and orphans in view of the manpower losses between 1914 and 1918; in 1961 a 10% sample was asked to answer additional questions relating to educational attainment; and in 1966 questions were asked relating to the mobility of the population, on car ownership and garage space, and on the journey to work.

While such statistics are essential, in many developing countries a complete census is not possible, probably because of the distances involved, the lack of administrative machinery for collection and analysis of data, possibly because of the literacy rate, or the knowledge that the population would not willingly give the information required. In such cases, a limited census or even a sample survey may well be the only way to obtain the information about the population and its living conditions.

It would be foolish to pretend, however, that even in the United Kingdom the census information is completely accurate. There are sources of error at every stage. The distribution and collection of forms is in the hands of part-time enumerators who are each responsible for an area. We can never be absolutely sure that every house has received a form or that every form is returned. It is not likely, of course, but it is at least possible that an enumerator may not know where a house is, and may not bother to find out, particularly if the weather is very bad, as it was on census day in 1951. A much more probable source of error, however, lies in completing the questionnaire. Some people may misunderstand the question, others may only be able to guess the answer; others will believe that the answer they give is correct when, in fact, it is not. Educational standards in the UK vary tremendously and the quality of the completed questionnaires is bound to vary – some mistakes will inevitably occur. Admittedly some mistakes will be picked up by the enumerator on the doorstep; others will be spotted during the process of tabulation. But some will remain. How can any enumerator know that John Smith is not in fact married to the woman living in his house if he claims that he is married?

The census office itself is a fruitful source of error – such as those arising in transferring information from the forms to bulk storage media. That errors do exist has been shown by special post-census sample surveys designed to check accuracy, and by such techniques as comparing the death certificates of people who die shortly after the census with information given in their completed questionnaires. Yet errors are relatively few and the census office is able to claim a remarkably high degree of accuracy for most of the data obtained.

Information of this nature is supplemented annually by the reports of the Registrar General in respect of births, deaths, marriages, divorces, etc., while figures for immigration and emigration can be brought up-to-date from Home Office statistics. In the UK such figures are highly reliable since there are legal pressures to ensure that registration takes place. It is not possible to bury a corpse without a death certificate; to obtain a passport without a birth certificate: doctors and hospitals notify the Registrar of all births to ensure that parents ultimately register their children. Not all countries, however, have these same pressures, and in some the births of female children are regularly not notified, while in others deaths are not registered. Sometimes, of course, the discrepancy becomes obvious when the rate of male and female births (which stays remarkably stable) begins to change, or when the death rate differs markedly from a neighbouring country with very similar social conditions. Nor must we think that the information required is confined to the mere fact of the birth or marriage. The Population (Statistics) Acts require that informants also give such information as the age of parents, their occupation, the duration of the marriage and so on. So much information is available, in fact, that the analysis of the data has given rise to a whole new branch of Statistics – demography, the analysis of vital statistics.

## Economic statistics

Since the time of the Domesday Book in the eleventh century, governments have been interested in data on how the economy is progressing. In the very early days it was, of course, merely a question of listing manpower for military purposes and personal wealth for taxation purposes. It is interesting to remember that in many parts of the developing world people are still averse to giving information for fear that it might be used to assess them for taxes. By the sixteenth century, interest had developed in statistics of overseas trade since the philosophy of Mercantilism demanded a balance of payments surplus as a criterion of success. But the twentieth century is, after all, the century of economic planning, and for successful planning a mass of wide-ranging information is needed. Today, government departments produce statistical data on almost every aspect of economic life: on prices and incomes, on employment and productivity, on production and distribution, on trade and finance. Once again you will find information on all these in the *Annual Abstract*, but let us take one or two of the major fields and look behind the statistical tables.

## Price indexes

It is commonplace that whenever a body of workers ask for an increase in wages, one of the points that they make strongly is that the increase is designed to compensate for the rise in the level of prices, and they usually quote in evidence changes in the Index of Retail Prices. In Britain this index, introduced in 1947 to replace the old cost of living index, is probably the best method of measuring the changes in the standard of living. Constructed monthly, it is used not only as a measure of inflationary trends, but also has been used as the foundation of incomes policy.

If you think back to Chapter 8 you will recall that there are three main elements in the construction of a price index: the selection of commodities to be included, the determination of weight for each commodity or group of commodities, and obtaining the appropriate prices at the relevant point of time.

The present index originated in 1953 with the Household Expenditure Survey conducted by the then Ministry of Labour. This was an effort to discover the precise pattern of household expenditure in the United Kingdom. A sample of 20 000 households was selected and each person over 16 in the sample was asked to keep a detailed record of what he/she spent over a three-week period. The survey produced a 65 per cent response, some 13 000 forms being returned. In the event it was found that low-income families, and particularly those living mainly on state pensions, had an expenditure pattern so different from the majority of households that they could not be regarded as typical and so were ignored. Thus the usable sample was cut down to 11 600 household budgets. It was felt that this sample reflected the spending habits of over 90% of the public and was sufficiently accurate to form the basis of a new index of retail prices. The weights to be used were determined by the percentage of income spent on individual commodities, and the survey also indicated the commodities that should be included in the index. Thus with a total weight of 1000, the weight for food was 350 and alcoholic drink 71, indicating that the average consumer spent 35% of his/her income on food and 7.1% of his/her income on alcoholic drink. On this basis a new index was introduced based on 17 January 1956 = 100. This index remained in existence for six years only, until January 1962. The present index is based on 1987.

Now as you know, if an index is to be really useful, the base should not be changed too frequently. Why, then, was this index dropped after only six years? It was soon realised that as wages and prices rose in the post-war world, people's consumption patterns changed fairly rapidly. Three cases in particular are outstanding: people in the UK were spending a far higher proportion of income on such things as houses and motor vehicles, but spending a much lower proportion on food. Hence it was decided that the weights used in the construction of the index should be changed year by year. This annual revision was based on a smaller Family Expenditure Survey covering a sample of 5000 households each year.

Nowadays, it is a continuing survey covering some 12 500 households, from which an effective sample of about 10 500 households is obtained of which around 70% cooperate. Results of the survey are published in annual Family Expenditure Survey Reports.

These surveys are continuous throughout the year and each member of the household is required to keep a detailed account of his spending for a fortnight. It is not, of course, possible to use a single year's survey as a basis for revising the weights. Some items such as cars, carpets and washing machines are bought only infrequently, and this is likely to cause a large sampling error. So the weights are determined by the average of the previous three years' expenditure patterns disclosed by the survey. A study of the way the weights have changed over the years tells us a great deal about the way our expenditure patterns have changed.

|  | | | | | *Weight used in construction of IRP* | | | | | |
| *Group* | *1914* | *1952* | *1956* | *1962* | *1966* | *1970* | *1974* | *1983* | *1986* | *1992* |
| --- | --- | --- | --- | --- | --- | --- | --- | --- | --- | --- |
| Food | 600 | 399 | 350 | 319 | 298 | 255 | 253 | 203 | 185 | 152 |
| Alcoholic drink | | 78 | 71 | 64 | 67 | 66 | 70 | 78 | 82 | 80 |
| Tobacco | | 90 | 80 | 79 | 77 | 64 | 43 | 39 | 40 | 36 |
| Housing | 160 | 72 | 87 | 102 | 113 | 119 | 124 | 137 | 153 | 172 |
| Fuel and light | 80 | 66 | 55 | 62 | 64 | 61 | 52 | 69 | 62 | 47 |
| Durable household goods | | 62 | 66 | 64 | 57 | 60 | 64 | 64 | 63 | 77 |
| Clothing and footwear | 120 | 98 | 106 | 98 | 91 | 86 | 91 | 74 | 75 | 59 |
| Transport and vehicles | | | 68 | 92 | 116 | 126 | 135 | 159 | 157 | 163 |
| Services | | 91 | 58 | 56 | 56 | 55 | 54 | 63 | 58 | 61 |
| Meals consumed away from home | | | | | | | 43 | 51 | 39 | 44 | 47 |
| Miscellaneous | | 44 | 59 | 64 | 61 | 65 | 63 | 75 | 81 | 106 |
| Others | 40 | | | | | | | | | |
| Total | 1000 | 1000 | 1000 | 1000 | 1000 | 1000 | 1000 | 1000 | 1000 | 1000 |

You can see how over the years the percentage of income spent on food has fallen from 60% in 1914 to 15.2% in 1992. Since the bulk of residents in the UK were well fed in 1992, this fall is indicative of a rise in the standard of living. We can see also signs of the revolution in power. Coal and gas, the major fuels in 1914 absorbed 8% of income, whereas the proportion spent on coal, gas and electricity in 1992 was only 4.7%. The percentage of income spent on tobacco has also fallen rapidly. Most important of all in indicating the change in the quality of life is that, if we take the four basic necessities – food, clothing, housing and fuel and light – we find that in 1914, 90% of income was spent on these and in 1992, only 37.1% of income was spent on the four necessities. A study of these weights reveals a great deal about society.

Having solved the problem of obtaining a satisfactory weighting, and having made sure that the commodities covered by the index are those actually bought by the person in the street, we are still left with the crucial problem of what prices to use. Everyone knows that even in a small town or village, prices vary widely from shop to shop. Hypermarkets and supermarkets sell goods at prices which smaller shops cannot possibly hope to match. Prices differ according to the brand of the commodity we buy and, of course, from area to area, reflecting partly the degree of competition in the area and partly the costs of distribution. Motorists know that even in their own area there may be as much as 6p difference in the price of a litre of petrol. If they travel long distances, they will also see that as they move away from the vicinity of the oil refineries, the *general* level of prices tends to rise. The result is that while some people are paying $x$p for a litre of petrol, others may have to pay as much as 10p more. Which of these prices are we to use when constructing a retail price index? The Central Statistical Office uses an interesting technique to try to ensure that the prices they use are representative.

On the Tuesday nearest to the 15th of the month, prices are collected by visiting several shops selling the sample type of good, care being taken that the types of shop visited are those that handle the bulk of household spending. This is done in several areas of different types ranging from London and the cities to small townships with a population under 5000. Thus, both different types of retail outlets and different geographical areas are represented.

Price relatives are now calculated for each item in each town. Let us take bread as an example. The price relatives for a particular city where five shops have been visited are 182.3, 181.9, 183.1, 182.5 and 182.4. These price relatives are combined with those for other cities to give a simple unweighted average. Thus we have a price relative for cities. The same analysis is now carried out for the other population groups, and the resultant price relatives averaged to give a price relative for bread for the country as a whole. In the same way we get price relatives for every commodity covered by the index.

So far, weighting has not mattered, but now we begin to combine the items to obtain an index for each of the major classes, and the question of weights becomes important. Although we know that in 1992 the class 'food' was given a weighting of 152, in order to obtain the index of food prices this total weight has to be broken down into its constituent parts. We might, for example, apply weights of 19 to milk and cheese products, 21 to bread and cereals and so on. Once this has been done it is a simple matter to obtain an index for food, and having done the same for all other groups, to obtain an overall index of retail prices.

Can you see now why so many individuals cannot believe what the retail price index tells us? As individuals, we buy only a selection, and often only a small selection of the items included in the index. The items we buy may have gone up in price more than others that we do not buy, and it seems to us that the index understates the price rises. Or we may buy from a grocer whose prices have been steady when others are charging more. The index will then seem to overstate the rise in prices. Like many statistical measures, the index of retail prices is a good and useful measure when applied to large numbers. It is not so useful when applied to the individual.

## Manpower, production and distribution

If you ask any economist for a 'short list' of aims for economic policy, it is almost certain that among the items listed will be 'to promote economic growth'. At the risk of annoying our economist friends, we will interpret this to mean simply that we are trying to increase the volume of output. Equally surely we would guess that another aim would be 'to eliminate unemployment', and a third to 'raise the standard of living'. So long as such things as these are accepted as aims of economic policy, it is little wonder that modern governments devote a great deal of time to the collection of statistics of manpower, production and distribution.

**Manpower**

It might seem strange, but in spite of the twentieth century being the age of manpower planning, it was not until 1945 that we had any reliable detailed information from the Ministry of Labour* about the size and distribution of the working population. Before 1939 there was highly reliable data relating to unemployment, but so far as the working population was concerned, all we had were estimates based on the census of population, the census of production and the Ministry of Labour's annual estimate. The war changed all that. It is impossible for a country to wage total war without detailed knowledge of the manpower available, and of industry's need for manpower. So the UK emerged from the war in 1945 with more information about manpower than ever before – but as you will appreciate, it is not possible to rely on pre-war and post-war comparisons.

Just as the wartime planning necessitated the collection of manpower statistics, so post-war planning demanded not only knowledge of the size of the working population, but also its age and sex structure, its occupational skills, etc. Collection of such statistics was facilitated in 1948 by the passing of the National Insurance Act and the introduction of the Standard Industrial Classifications. The former required every gainfully employed person to register and in theory should have obtained a complete census of all those in employment. Unfortunately, there are some omissions resulting from the failure of some individuals to register – particularly married women and the self-employed. The Standard Industrial Classification was designed to provide a standard pattern of classification by industry which could be used by

---

*Now the Department of Employment.

all industrial statistics, and so facilitate comparison. Unfortunately from this point of view, there were major revisions in the classification in 1958 and 1968, and there have been many minor changes since. The effect of the major changes was to reclassify some industries as distributive and service industries which had previously been classed as manufacturing.

Originally, estimates of employees in employment were obtained from a count of National Insurance Cards. The first Census of Employment was undertaken in 1971, and a card count was simultaneously taken to provide a link between the data. Further censuses were taken in 1978, 1984, 1987. The latest census occurred in 1990. Estimates for years in which no census took place were made by interpolating and extrapolating data obtained in the last census using trends derived from sample surveys.

The Central Statistical Office considers that the workforce comprises five components:

(a) Employees in employment.

(b) Self-employed persons, though second occupations classified as self-employed are not included.

(c) Members of HM forces.

(d) Participants in work-related government training programmes.

(e) Claimants for unemployment benefit.

We would not wish to leave you with the impression that manpower statistics are concerned only with totals. Statistics are also produced relating to unemployment, unemployment rates, temporary lay-offs, days lost through strike action, average salaries and wages in the different industrial groups, holiday entitlement, etc.

## Production

Without doubt, one of the most important sources for data on industrial production is the census of production, the results of which are published by the Business Statistics Office. The full census is a massive document, but you will find a first-class summary of the relevant information in the *Annual Abstract of Statistics*. Although the expression 'census' is used, we must not imagine that it covers every firm in the UK. First, there is a rather narrow definition of production. The census covers extractive, manufacturing and building industries. So important sectors of the economy such as agriculture and fisheries, distribution and the service industries are excluded. Second, even within this limited field, not every firm is included. The small firm is only required to give the nature of the trade and the size of its labour force. However, in some industries where a significant proportion of total output is produced by small firms, the full census requires them to make a simplified return.

In spite of its limited scope, the census of production provides a great deal of information. It shows the way in which national industrial output is divided between different industries, and the study of this data over time brings out the trend and relative importance of individual industries. Central planning would be difficult without data like this, especially in respect of the distribution of labour and the allocation of capital resources. It is particularly important for the information it gives relating to changes in stocks of raw materials and finished goods, to capital expenditure on plant and machinery, and to building work undertaken. Without information such as this, national income statistics would be much less reliable, and the index of industrial production subject to major errors.

Naturally, much of the information contained in the census report can be obtained elsewhere. The Department of Trade and Industry publishes much information on the coal industry and all forms of fuel production; British Steel produces data on steel production; the building industry is covered by reports from the Department of the Environment. If you are interested in the details of a particular industry, say the tonnage of herrings landed at Hull, you would turn to the very comprehensive reports of the government departments, extracts from which appear in the *Annual Abstract of Statistics*. But the only place all this information is brought together is in the report on the census of production. Without this we would find it very difficult to estimate the total value of industrial production in the country.

In the UK, the first census of production was undertaken in 1907, and between the wars four more were taken. From 1948 it was intended to take a full census every year, but in fact the cost both to the state and to industry was heavy, and in the event a full census has been taken only every five years, while in the intervening years a sample survey is undertaken, or a limited survey in which fewer questions are asked.

The first annual census of production was undertaken in 1970 by the Business Statistics Office. The census collects information on working proprietors; employment; wages and salaries; stocks; capital expenditure; cost of industrial and non-industrial services; purchases of materials and fuel; sales, work done and services rendered; and indirect taxes.

A separate report is published for each industry in the *Business Monitor* series. The reports provide data on output and costs, capital expenditure, stocks and work in progress, the size of establishments, the regional distribution, the composition of the labour force and operating ratios.

## Distribution

Although Napoleon called England a nation of shopkeepers, it was not until 1951 that any official enquiry attempted to determine how many retail establishments there were in the UK, what kind of shops (multiples, independents) they were, what they sold or what was their turnover. The effort to obtain such information well illustrates the problems faced when attempting to take a census in a completely new field. Before any information could be obtained, the government had to build up a sampling frame. This was done from May to October 1950, enumerators all over the country listing names and addresses of traders who fell within the scope of the census, 'as far as could be judged from the outside of the premises'. They were not allowed to enter the shop and talk to the owner or his employees, but were asked to distinguish between shops, stalls, depots and other kinds of premises. So thorough was the initial enumeration that the shops omitted must be negligible.

Having established a sampling frame, the next step was to draft the questionnaire. This was the first time such a census had been undertaken, and a careful examination of objectives was necessary. It was decided that the census should provide information about:

(a) the number and size of retail and wholesale outlets;

(b) the value of services provided by the distributive sector;

(c) the relative efficiency of distribution in different areas, i.e. the number of shops per head of the population.

Although the first census was a complete survey obtaining a 91% response rate to the questionnaire, a committee on the census of distribution and production (the Vernon Smith Committee) recommended in 1954 that sample surveys be undertaken between the dates of the full census. It was decided to take a 12% sample and a most interesting thing about it was the way it was selected.

First, every distributive outlet with a turnover in excess of £100 000 was to be included. This covered all the multiple stores, department stores and the majority of the co-operative societies. But once again there was no up-to-date sampling frame for the smaller independent retailers, so as in 1950 an enumeration had to be made in the relevant sample areas. These areas were chosen as follows:

(a) Certain areas existed in which it was believed that important changes had taken place since 1950, for example, the new towns and central London. In these areas a complete enumeration of distributive outlets was undertaken and a 20% sample selected.

(b) In Greater London a sample of electoral wards stratified by size and distinguishing between mainly residential and mainly commercial was selected, and every shop in the selected wards was included in the survey.

(c) In the large towns (over 100 000 population) a sample of streets stratified by the number of shops there had been in 1950 was taken.

(d) Other towns were sampled by taking a cross-section of local authority areas stratified by population by sales in 1950, and by population changes since 1950.

(e) In rural districts, a regional sample stratified by population density or population changes was selected.

The survey was undertaken by post with a very energetic follow-up. In the end the response rates were a remarkable 96% for larger traders, 89% for independent traders, and even 75% for street traders, hawkers, etc. It was estimated that the error was no more than 0.5% of the overall totals.

Following the census in 1950, further censuses were taken in 1957, 1961, 1966 and 1971, after which they were abandoned. The main source of information is now a regular sample enquiry into retailing introduced in 1976. The enquiries were conducted annually between 1976 and 1980, after which they were conducted every other year. The enquiries cover businesses which operate as retailers and are taken as a sample from the Business Statistics Office's *Register of Businesses*. The core topics covered at each enquiry include turnover, capital expenditure, stocks, purchases for resale, employment and VAT on sales. Occasional topics covered include an analysis of earnings, detailed analysis of employment and questions on credit sales, charges and debts outstanding.

Monthly retail sales estimates, expressed as index numbers, cover the retail trade (except motor trades) in Great Britain. The statistics are based on voluntary returns from a panel of retailers representing all types and sizes of establishments. The panel consists of about 3250 small retailers (turnover less than £2 million) and about 350 large retailers who account for over 80% of the total sales for all large retailers. Detailed statistics are published each month in *Business Monitor*, SDM28 Retail Sales.

## National Income statistics

All of the data that we have discussed in the last few paragraphs is still sectional data, no matter how widely the net is spread. It is concerned with only one aspect of the economy. What we must now do is turn our attention to the performance of the economy as a whole. This is seen only when we bring together the various parts of the economy in the statistics of national income. We find these statistics in the book *National Income and Expenditure* published by HMSO. This is not the place to go into details of what the expression 'national income' means. However, we should note that all production is intended to satisfy consumer wants, and the more that is produced the greater can the consumption be. Thus what the national income statistics are measuring is basically the way our standard of living is changing.

Now any economist will tell you that national income can be measured in three ways – by aggregating expenditure, by aggregating income, or by aggregating output. In theory, whichever method is used should give the same totals, but in practice there is always a difference which appears in the tables as 'residual error'. This has at times been as much as £700 million. Obviously, we have not reached perfection!

To the extent that the data we have is accurate, overall planning is facilitated, but we must admit that despite a quarter of a century's experience in producing these figures, and despite many improvements that have taken place, several of the more important aggregates are little more than approximations. It is for this reason that each successive edition of *National Income and Expenditure* (called the 'Blue Book') amends the figures for the previous years.

There are differences in opinion as to what should be included in national income calculations, and this makes international comparison very difficult. For example, in the peasant economies of the developing countries food grown by the farmers and eaten themselves is a very important part of the national income and can be justifiably included. But in the UK such consumption is not included. In fact in this country only such goods and services as are exchanged for money are included; and this cuts out a host of services which contribute to our welfare. If your wife or mother washes your shirt, it does not affect the national income statistics, but if you send it to a laundry the national income is affected. Thus any change in social habits whereby people begin to pay for things they previously did for themselves will raise the national income – even though the goods and services available have not increased.

One further point to be borne in mind is that the national income is necessarily measured in money terms – and the value of money changes. Thus we may find that the national income has risen by 10% since the last year, but if inflation is at the rate of 15% can we really say we are better off?

In spite of these criticisms, however, the annual Blue Book on national income and expenditure contains a mass of information vital to the planners in society and to the students of society.

Beginning with the national income measured by the expenditure method, the Blue Book reconciles this figure with the national income measured by the income of the various factors of production (wages, profits, interest and rent). This is far more than an academic exercise. The first table indicates the changing pattern of people's consumption. Here we can see, for example, the changing expenditure on health, defence or education, the switch of expenditure to the service industries and the rise of the consumer durable industry. The second part of the table indicates the distribution of income in society; the proportion of income earned by the performance of work as compared with the proportion received from rents. Here we can trace the increasing share of the national income going to the 'working class'.

The third reconciliation indicates the gross national product by industry. Thus we can assess the contribution of each industrial group to the national income. Other tables in the Blue Book take many of these points and in turn analyse them in much more detail.

This type of data is obtained from three main sources: the statistics assembled by the Inland Revenue, the census of production and distribution, and the accounts of central and local government. But these are supplemented by a wide range of other sources. Unfortunately, the coverage is far from complete, and in many cases the accuracy is impaired by the fact that the data used has been compiled for purposes other than national income estimates.

The data we have discussed in this chapter is very important, but please remember that it is only a fraction of the data published each year. Much of this is a result of the day-to-day work of the government departments, some is an offspring of special surveys, and a great deal more is the result of the work of the statistical departments of banks, insurance companies, finance houses and the like. Overlooking and co-ordinating the work of the government departments is the Central Statistical Office producing the *Annual Abstract of Statistics*, the most important of all sources, and the starting point for a knowledge of what is available.

## QUESTIONS

**24.1**   Outline the procedures which are employed when a census of population is undertaken in the UK, or in a country of your choice.

**24.2**   Which statistics, published in the UK, are available relating to population? Mention the main publications in which they are to be found and write a summary of the details given in each.

**24.3**   Describe the statistical information which is obtained from the census of production.

**24.4**   Write an essay on the construction and use of *two* official index numbers published by the government.

**24.5** Explain how and by whom the General Index of Retail Prices is prepared, where it is published and what purpose it serves.

**24.6** (a) Describe the construction of the Official Retail Prices Index used in the UK; and

(b) explain how it could be used by:

(i) businessmen;

(ii) consumers; and

(iii) trade unions.

**24.7** Discuss the statistical material available on National Income and Expenditure in the UK.

**24.8** As a trade union official, you have been given the task of submitting a well-documented wage claim on behalf of your members.

(a) What kind of problems would you expect to encounter in making your case?

(b) What sources of economic statistics would you consult?

(c) What kind of information would you seek from those sources to justify your claim?

**24.9** Describe *two* of the main summary sources of statistics published regularly by government departments.

**24.10** Write briefly on four of the following sources of economic statistics. You should comment on the breadth and detail of the information in the publications you choose.

(a) *Economic Trends*;

(b) *Annual Abstract of Statistics*;

(c) *The Family Expenditure Survey*;

(d) *The Monthly Digest of Statistics*;

(e) *National Income and Expenditure* (the Blue Book);

(f) *The Business Monitor*.

**24.11**  (a)  If your employer wished to gain information on the following, suggest which publications would provide this:

    (i)  Wage rates and average earnings;

    (ii)  Retail and wholesale prices;

    (iii)  Industrial production;

    (iv)  Regional and national unemployment;

    (v)  Value and volume of monthly and annual imports and exports of goods.

(b)  Give examples of the purpose for which he may wish to use this information.

# Answers to questions

**Chapter 1**

**1.12** Taking classes as 650–659, 660–669, etc., frequencies are:

2  5  6  14  26  18  13  10  3  3 = 100

**1.14** Frequencies are:

0  5  13  7  9  27  19  19  10  7  4 = 120

**1.16** Suggested classes 10–19, 20–29, etc., frequencies are:

2  6  10  10  14  10  6  6  2 = 66

**Chapter 4**

**4.2** (b)  18.588 ± 0.056, i.e. ±0.3013%
(c)  341 ± 8, i.e. ±2.64%.

**4.3** Estimated profit is £440 000.
Minimum profit is £259 800.
Maximum profit is £610 600.

**4.6** (a)  Deposits = 10 969 ± 40.7 (million $)
(b)  Cash     = 1360 ± 10.6 (million $)

**4.8** (a)  (i)  5720 ± 0.96%, (ii)  5480 ± 1.004%
(b)  (i)  0.865  (ii)  395

**4.10** (b)  (i)   ± 43 000 tonnes
(ii)  Assuming series discrete, max. error = +85 914 tonnes, but if continuous, max. error is 86 000 tonnes.
(c)  (i)  135.92 ± 2.77 tonnes
(ii)  468 000 grams ± 11.43%

**4.12** (a)  £176 000 ± £32 802.5
(b)  ± 18.64%

**4.15** (a)  Net profit = £60 000 ± 42 000
(b)  Net profit = 24 ± 21.3%
(c)  £60 000

**4.16** (b)  (i)  Output = 2000 ± 65.5
Unit profit = £1 ± 0.1
Weekly profit = £2000 ± 272.05
(ii)  50% ± 6.5

**Chapter 5**

**5.2**  211

**5.4**  Median = 2    Mean = 2.48

**5.6**  Mean = £1448.14

**5.8**  Assuming employment starts at 18, and retirement age is 65, $\bar{x}$ = 43.61 years.

**5.10**  Assuming average age of those over 80 is 84.5, mean = 31.9 years.

**5.12**  Frequencies are: 7, 16, 12, 11, 10, 4, $\Sigma f$ = 60
If assumed mean is 549.5, and if $c$ = 20, then $\Sigma fd$ = 13
$\bar{x}$ = 553.83 miles.

**5.14**  Factory A: 27.23 years, Factory B: 37.09 years.

**5.18**  Median = 540p
Mean   = 565p
Mode   = 469p.

**5.20**  Frequencies are 3, 13, 23, 25, 22, 9, 4, 1, $\Sigma f$ = 100
Mode = 17 years $8\frac{1}{2}$ months

**5.22**  Taking an assumed mean of 6.5, $\Sigma fd$ = 212. $\bar{x}$ = 7.26 hours.
Median = 7.41 hours

**5.24**  Taking an assumed mean of 250, and $c$ = 100, $\Sigma f$ = 460, $\Sigma fd$ = -6,
$\bar{x}$ = £248.7
Total value of orders = £114 400
Mode = £205

**5.26**  Mean   = £12 814.22
Median = £9987.241

**5.28**  49 839 882

**Chapter 6**

**6.4**  Trend: 1347.5, 1382.5, 1440, 1532.5, 1608.75, 1658.75, 1717.5, 1800.0, 1878.75, 1926.25, 1997.5

**6.6**  Seven-day moving average:
1137.1, 1145.7, 1148.6, 1148.6, 1148.6, 1150, 1148.6, 1155.7, 1168.6, 1174.3, 1172.9, 1168.6, 1171.4, 1172.9, 1181.4, 1202.9, 1207.1, 1205.7

**6.8**  Trend:
2.55, 2.725, 2.95, 3.21, 3.475, 3.64, 3.675, 3.61, 3.41, 3.16, 2.9, 2.61, 2.425, 2.36

**6.9** Exponentially smoothed data for 6.5 = 70.0, 64.2, 61.8, 66, 68.4, 63.5, 60.4, 65.3, 68.9, 65.9, 62.9, 69.5, 72.6, 67.9, 65.1, 69.9

**Chapter 7**

**7.2** Trend: 14.875, 16.0, 16.75, 16.875, 17.5, 18.625, 19.375, 19.5, 19.625, 20.75, 22.5, 23.625
Seasonal variation $= -3, 14, -1, -10$

**7.4** Trend: 350.75, 350.625, 347.75, 341.625, 334.125, 325.875, 313.125, 299.125, 290.125
Seasonal variation: 0.9695, 0.9336, 0.9826, 1.1143

**7.6** Trend: 505.625, 515.875, 515.25, 510, 507.625, 507.625, 514.625, 523.875
Deviations: $-39.625$, 10.125, 25.75, 31, $-67.625$, 2.375, 23.375, 20.125
Seasonal variation: $+24, +25, -54, +6$
Deseasonalised series: 456, 495, 520, 520, 517, 516, 494, 504, 514, 519, 547, 525

**7.8** Trend: 180.125, 183.75, 205.125, 238, 251.625, 261.875, 259.25, 252.25, 254.125, 249, 245.625, 245.625, 242.375
Seasonal variation: 0.8609, 0.9377, 0.9819, 1.2195

**7.10** Trend: 13.125, 13.5, 13.875, 14.375, 15.125, 15.75, 16.375, 16.875
Actual/Trend: 1.219, 0.6667, 1.009, 1.113, 1.124, 0.7619, 1.0382, 1.0667
Seasonal variation: 1.09, 1.1717, 0.7144, 1.0238
Deseasonalised data: 13, 13, 14, 13, 14, 15, 15, 17, 17, 17, 17, 18

**Chapter 8**

**8.6** Simple index $= 200$. Weighted index $= 194.4$

**8.8** Spliced index  81.0    91.5    96.7   103.3
                  112.5   135.2   163.7

**8.10** $x = 79$, Index $= 140.1$

**8.12** Price index $19X4 = \dfrac{5624}{60.42} = 93.1$

$$19X5 = \frac{5914.000}{60.42} = 97.9$$

**8.14** Base weighting (Laspeyre's) $= \dfrac{9556}{7274} \times 100 = 131.4$

Current weighting (Paasche's) $= \dfrac{9700}{7318} \times 100 = 132.5$

**8.16**

| Group 1 | 100 | 106 | 113 | 122 | 128 |
|---------|-----|-----|-----|-----|-----|
| Group 2 | 100 | 112 | 119 | 129 | 136 |
| Group 3 | 100 | 102 | 106 | 107 | 110 |

**8.18**

|  | *Laspeyre's* | *Paasche's* | *Fisher's* |
|--|-----------|-----------|----------|
| Price index | 106.6 | 108.2 | 107.4 |
| Volume index | 106.9 | 108.5 | 107.7 |

**8.20** $\Sigma p_0 q_0 = 833$ $\Sigma p_0 q_1 = 805$ $\Sigma p_0 q_2 = 797$ $\Sigma p_0 q_3 = 865$
Index of production $19X7 = 96.6$, $19X8 = 95.7$, $19X9 = 103.8$

**8.22** 100.0, 105.4, 119.8, 132.0, 145.0, 152.5, 155.5, 151.2, 152.6.

**8.24** Laspeyre's volume index $= 119.3$

**Chapter 9**

**9.2** Range $= 67$; $\bar{x} = 48$; Median $= 48$; $Q_1 = 36$; $Q_3 = 63$;
Quartile deviation $= 27$; Mean deviation $= 14.08$

**9.4** Median $= £795$  Under £880 $\qquad = 45$
$\qquad\qquad\qquad\qquad$ £630 but under £750 $= 14$
$\qquad\qquad\qquad\qquad$ Over £960 $\qquad\quad = 11$
Quartile deviation $= £230$

**9.6** $Q_1 = £40\ 570$ $\qquad Q_2 = £76\ 740$ $\qquad Q_3 = £109\ 380$
$QD = £68\ 810$

**9.8**

|  | Median | SQR |
|--|--------|-----|
| Week 1 | 22.5 tonnes | 9.5 tonnes |
| Week 2 | 25 tonnes | 7.5 tonnes |

**9.10** $\bar{x} = £91.28$ $\sigma = £28.72$
Using mid-points £29.95, £49.95, etc.

**9.12** $\bar{x} = 1365p$, $\sigma = 339p$

**9.14** $\sigma = £11\ 248.53$

**9.16** Taking upper limit as 110:

$\qquad \bar{x} = 62.72$ thousand $\sigma = 13.52$ thousand

Reasonable rule might be to keep constituencies within the range $\bar{x} \pm \sigma$

**9.18** $\bar{x} = £260$ $\sigma = £23.9$ $cv = 9.19\%$

**9.20** Taking upper limit as 80 years

|  | $\bar{x}$ | $\sigma$ | $cv$ |
|--|-----------|----------|------|
| Males | 32.42 | 21.6 | 66.6% |
| Females | 35.77 | 23.14 | 64.7% |

**9.22** Taking lower limit as 11 and upper limit as 80
Range = 69; $\bar{x} = 45.76$; $\sigma = 13.48$; cv = 29.46%

**9.24** $\bar{x} = £7500$ $\sigma = £977$ Median = £7277.78
Coefficient of Skewness = 0.675

**Chapter 10**

**10.2** (i) 4.75% (ii) 99.242%

**10.4** (i) 3085 (ii) 668 (iii) 6915 (iv) 8413

**10.6** 16.1372 grams

**10.8** 0.023, 0.006, 120 grams

**10.10** N.B. this distribution is discrete, so if we wish to find percentage less than 229 we require area to left of 228.5. Likewise, percentage greater than 280 given by area to right of 280.5
(i) 22.66% (ii) 10.56%

**10.12** (a) 294 (b) 6 (c) 32

**10.14** Taking mid-point of first group to be 35, and of last group to be 9, $\bar{x} = 23.74$, $\sigma = 6.127$
Taking range as $\bar{x} \pm 3\sigma$, range = 5 to 43%

**10.16** (1) 30.8% (2) 53.3% (3) 7.68 weeks (4) 15.9%

**10.18** (a) 11.51% (b) 57.62% (c) 13.27% (d) 2.28% (e) 95.45%

**Chapter 11**

**11.2** $\frac{4}{11}$

**11.4** (b) (i) 0.6591 (ii) 0.2866
(c) (i) 0.08 (ii) 0.52 (iii) 0.2

**11.6** (2) (i) $\frac{1}{3}$ (ii) $\frac{1}{36}$ (iii) $\frac{91}{216}$
(iv) (a) $\frac{7}{15}$ (b) $\frac{1}{15}$

**11.8** (a) $\frac{1}{12}$ (b) $\frac{1}{2}$ (c) $\frac{1}{4}$ (d) $\frac{1}{2}$

**11.10** (a) 0.03 (b) 0.33

**11.12** (a) 0.8938 (b) 0.1025

**11.14** (i) 0.5838 (ii) 0.05

**11.16** 0.52 0.6425

**11.18** (b) (i) $\frac{5}{12}, \frac{1}{4}, \frac{1}{3}$
(ii) $\frac{11}{80}$
(iii) $\frac{5}{24}$
(iv) $\frac{2}{5}$
(v) $\frac{9}{10}$
(vi) $\frac{20}{33}, \frac{8}{33}, \frac{5}{33}$

**11.20** (b) 0.6513, 44

**11.22** (i) 0.0165 (ii) 0.0179

**11.24** (a) $\frac{64}{132600}$ (b) $\frac{16}{5525}$

**11.26** P (article has both defects)
= 0.03

**Chapter 12**    **12.2**   EMV(A) = £5000; EMV(B) = £32 500; EMV(C) = £85 000 so buy C.

**12.4**   EMV(Buy patent) = £110 000; so leave money invested.

**12.6**   EMV(information) = £143 749
EMV(no information) = £129 687

**12.8**   EMV(expand) = £3.84m
EMV(no expansion) = £0.8m

**12.10**   Buy market research if cost is less than £18 005.

**Chapter 13**    **13.1**   Average daily profit = £17.40

**13.3**   Idle time: 0, 1, 2, 3, 1, 0, 0, 2, 0, 2, 2, 0, 5, 0, 0, 0
Waiting time: $-2$, 0, 0, 0, 0, 0, 0, 0, 1, 0, 0, 2, 0, 2, 0, 3

**13.5**   Second checkout opened in periods 18, 26 and 36.

**13.8**   Price at end of simulation is 100.5.

**13.9**   Stock: 2, 4, 4, 5, 6, 2, 0, 0, 0, 0
Unsatisfied demand: 0, 0, 0, 0, 0, 0, 0, 2, 0, 4

**13.11**   Closing balance = £7300

**Chapter 14**    **14.2**   $100((\frac{1}{2})^{10} + {}^{10}C_1(\frac{1}{2})^9(\frac{1}{2}) + {}^{10}C_2(\frac{1}{2})^8(\frac{1}{2})^2 + {}^{10}C_3(\frac{1}{2})^7(\frac{1}{2})^3) = 17$

**14.4**   0.8208. $\bar{x} = 0.26$ $p = 0.052$

**14.6**   (a) (i) 0.0894 (ii) 0.0338 (b) (i) 0.0902 (b) (ii) 0.0402

**14.8**   (a) 0.1336 (b) (i) 0.0746 (ii) 0.0758

**14.10**  0.3526

**14.12**  0.0144
$$e^{-2.5}\left(1 + 2.5 + \frac{(2.5)^2}{2!} + \frac{(2.5)^3}{3!} + \cdots\right)$$

**14.14**  88%

**14.16**
| No. of defectives | 0 | 1 | 2 | 3 | 4 | 5 |
|---|---|---|---|---|---|---|
| No. of samples | 18.3 | 31 | 26.4 | 15 | 6.4 | 2.1 |

**14.18**  $\bar{x} = 25$, $\sigma = 4.937$, Proportion = 0.01659

**14.20**  (i) 6.059% (ii) 0.81% (iii) 87.95%

**Chapter 17**    **17.2**    (a) 25.14% (b) 37.07% (c) 53.28%

**17.4**    90% limits either $100 + 3.84$ or $100 - 3.84$
95% limits either $100 + 4.935$ or $100 - 4.935$
99% limits either $100 + 6.99$ or $100 - 6.99$

**17.6**    95% limits: $2 \pm 0.00392$
99% limits: $2 \pm 0.005152$
Sample mean (2.005) met infrequently, so machine probably needs resetting.

**17.8**    4.55% (2.275% have too large a clearance and 2.275% will not fit).

**17.10**   95% limits for sample means $= 3 \pm 0.707$
99% limits for samples means $= 3 \pm 0.929$
Limits calculated on assumption that men and women pair randomly. Actual mean difference outside 99% limits – this casts doubts on assumption.

**17.12**   95% limits $= 0.07 \pm 0.0224$, 99% limits $= 0.07 \pm 0.0294$

**17.14**   95% limits $= 0.3 \pm 0.02842$, sample proportion well within limits, so proportion buying Blotto's Gin could well be 0.3.

**Chapter 18**    **18.1**    Warning limits $= 25.1 \pm 0.396$
Action limits $= 25.1 \pm 0.624$
Minimum tolerances $\pm 1.395$
AWCL $= 23.771$ to $26.229$.

**18.5**

| $A_n$ | R | W | A | C |
|---|---|---|---|---|
| 0.4299 | 1.328 | 0.377 | 0.594 | 0.734 |

**18.6**    Warning limits $= 25.02 \pm 0.0226$
Action limits $= 25.02 \pm 0.356$
Firm cannot meet specifications.

**18.8**    Action limits $= 17.748$ to $27.252$
AWCL $= 13.872$ to $26.128$
Reset machine to 20.

**18.10**   0.505

**18.12**   Range for washers $= \pm 0.00027$, so accept order.

**18.14** $\bar{\bar{x}} = 755.2$, $\bar{R} = 17.2$, min tolerance $= \pm 22.84$
Warning limits $= 755.2 \pm 6.48$ Action limits $= 755.2 \pm 10.22$
AWCL $= 737.62$ to $762.38$
Samples, 2, 5, 11, 12, 20 outside warning limits.

**18.16** $\bar{x} = 136$, $\sigma$ 7.563
Warning limits $= 136 \pm 14.82$ Action limits $= 136 \pm 23.37$

**18.18** Proportion rejected $= 0.042$, standard error $= 0.0142$
Warning limits $= 2.8$ to 14
Action limits $= 0$ to 17.18
It appears that proportion rejected has increased.

**18.20** Warning limits $= 1.2$ to 10.8
Action limits $= 0$ to 13.5

**Chapter 19**      **19.2**   £18.50 $\pm$ £1.176

**19.4** $\bar{x} = -£2.80$, $\sigma = £10.45$
95% interval estimate $= -£2.80 \pm 2.0482$
Least favourable $= -£48\ 482$; most likely $= -£28\ 000$
Most favourable $= -£7518$

**19.6** (i) 99.8% interval estimate $= £218 \pm 6.57$ (ii) £245.10
*Note*: answers assume finite population adjustment made, as the estimate refers to the 365 days in the current year.

**19.8** 95% interval estimate $= 0.55 \pm 0.0976$. $n > 537$
*Note*: second part of question is one-sided.

**19.10** (ii) 0.395 (iii) $0.395 \pm 0.0677$, $0.395 \pm 0.08905$
(iv) 2295 (v) taking $\pm 3$ standard deviations as covering entire normal distribution, $n = 7320$

**19.12** $\hat{\mu} = 19.7$ $\hat{\sigma} = 0.46$

**19.14** 25

**19.16** 17 and 26

**19.18** $n \geqslant 168$

**19.20** $n \geqslant 55$

**Chapter 21**

**21.2** (i) Reject if number of defectives greater than 30.
(ii) Reject if number of defectives less than nine or greater than 31.

**21.4** For two-sided test, reject if sample means outside range 4.99804 to 5.00196 cm. For one-sided test, reject if sample mean greater than 5.001645.

**21.6** Test statistic $t = 1.41$. Sample does not substantiate claim.

**21.8** Test statistic $Z = 3.18$. This suggests choice of marriage partner is affected by height.

**21.10** Test statistic $Z = 2.5$. Difference is significant at 1% level.

**21.12** Test statistic $Z = 3.12$, difference significant at 1% level.

**21.14**

|          | Mean   | Variance |
|----------|--------|----------|
| Private  | 200.26 | 271.3    |
| LA       | 158.54 | 871.04   |

1 If data treated as two samples, test statistic $t = 3.9$, difference significant at 1% level.
2 If data considered as two populations:
Minimum mean for private = 200 214
Maximum mean for LA = 158 586
Average for private sector is greater.

**21.16** Test statistic $t = 2.85$, difference significant at 5% but not at 1% level.

**21.18** Assuming that the samples are paired, test statistic $t = 2.004$. Differences not significant.

**21.20** For samples of 64, test statistic $Z = 3$. Significant at 1% level.
For samples of 16, test statistic $t = 1.452$. Not significant.

**21.22** Test statistic $Z = 2.125$. Significant at 5% but not at 1% level.

**21.24** Test statistic $Z = 1.543$. Difference not significant.

**21.28** Test statistic $Z = 3.315$. Significant at 1% level.

**21.29** $n > 174$

**Chapter 22**

**22.2** $\chi^2 = 7.884$, $v = 5$, not significant.

**22.4** $\bar{x} = 0.9$. Expected values: 81.3, 73.2, 32.9, 12.6
$v = 2$, $\chi^2 = 4.292$, not significant.

**22.6**  Expected values: 32, 16, 8, 8
$v = 3$, $\chi^2 = 10.188$
Significant at 5% but not at 1% level.

**22.8**  $v = 2$, $\chi^2 = 4.751$, no association.

**22.10**  $v = 2$, $\chi^2 = 1.502$, no association.

**22.12**  Insufficient information given – need to know the number who 'changed their minds'.

**22.14**  $v = 6$, $\chi^2 = 14.741$, association established at 5% level.

**22.16**  $v = 2$, $\chi^2 = 3.379$, no difference in proportion.

**22.18**  $v = 1$, $\chi^2 = 125.4$, most highly significant.
Using difference between proportions, $Z = 11.2$

**Chapter 23**

**23.3**  $y = 537.25x + 7904.3$
(a) 13.8 m
(b) 13.6 m

**23.6**  $r = 0.33$

**23.8**

| Quarter | 1 | 2 | 3 | 4 |
|---------|------|------|--------|------|
| Sales | 4802 | 6174 | 10 976 | 5488 |

**23.10**  $y = 0.96x + 21\,250$
46 210, 68 050

**23.12**  $y = 543.625 + 8.125x$
Seasonal variation 199, $-16.625$, $-39.25$, $-143.125$

**23.14**  (1) 139.6, 142.6, 129.4, 157.9, 152.5, 128.2, 116.8
(2) (i) 1850 (ii) 10.82%
(3) total decline per month $= 750$

**23.16**  $r = 0.79$

**23.18**  $r = 0.46$

**23.20**  $r = -0.93$

**23.22**  $r = -0.56$, $r = 0.4026$

**23.24**  $p = -0.7$

**23.26** $p = 0.986$

**23.28** $p = 0.857$

**23.30** $p = 0.85$

**23.32** $p = 0.54$

# Tables

## 1 The Normal Distribution – areas in the right-hand tail of the Normal Distribution

| Z | .00 | .01 | .02 | .03 | .04 | .05 | .06 | .07 | .08 | .09 |
|-----|-------|-------|-------|-------|-------|-------|-------|-------|-------|-------|
| 0.0 | .5000 | .4960 | .4920 | .4880 | .4840 | .4801 | .4761 | .4721 | .4681 | .4641 |
| 0.1 | .4602 | .4562 | .4522 | .4483 | .4443 | .4404 | .4364 | .4325 | .4286 | .4247 |
| 0.2 | .4207 | .4168 | .4129 | .4090 | .4052 | .4013 | .3974 | .3936 | .3897 | .3859 |
| 0.3 | .3821 | .3783 | .3745 | .3707 | .3669 | .3632 | .3594 | .3557 | .3520 | .3483 |
| 0.4 | .3446 | .3409 | .3372 | .3336 | .3300 | .3264 | .3228 | .3192 | .3156 | .3121 |
| 0.5 | .3085 | .3050 | .3015 | .2981 | .2946 | .2912 | .2877 | .2843 | .2810 | .2776 |
| 0.6 | .2743 | .2709 | .2676 | .2643 | .2611 | .2578 | .2546 | .2514 | .2483 | .2451 |
| 0.7 | .2420 | .2389 | .2358 | .2327 | .2296 | .2266 | .2236 | .2206 | .2177 | .2148 |
| 0.8 | .2119 | .2090 | .2061 | .2033 | .2005 | .1977 | .1949 | .1922 | .1894 | .1867 |
| 0.9 | .1841 | .1814 | .1788 | .1762 | .1736 | .1711 | .1685 | .1660 | .1635 | .1611 |
| 1.0 | .1587 | .1562 | .1539 | .1515 | .1492 | .1469 | .1446 | .1423 | .1401 | .1379 |
| 1.1 | .1357 | .1335 | .1314 | .1292 | .1271 | .1251 | .1230 | .1210 | .1190 | .1170 |
| 1.2 | .1151 | .1131 | .1112 | .1093 | .1075 | .1056 | .1038 | .1020 | .1003 | .0985 |
| 1.3 | .0968 | .0951 | .0934 | .0918 | .0901 | .0885 | .0869 | .0853 | .0838 | .0823 |
| 1.4 | .0808 | .0793 | .0778 | .0764 | .0749 | .0735 | .0721 | .0708 | .0694 | .0681 |
| 1.5 | .0668 | .0655 | .0643 | .0630 | .0618 | .0606 | .0594 | .0582 | .0571 | .0559 |
| 1.6 | .0548 | .0537 | .0526 | .0516 | .0505 | .0495 | .0485 | .0475 | .0456 | .0455 |
| 1.7 | .0446 | .0436 | .0427 | .0418 | .0409 | .0401 | .0392 | .0384 | .0375 | .0367 |
| 1.8 | .0359 | .0351 | .0344 | .0336 | .0329 | .0322 | .0314 | .0307 | .0301 | .0294 |
| 1.9 | .0287 | .0281 | .0274 | .0268 | .0262 | .0256 | .0250 | .0244 | .0239 | .0233 |
| 2.0 | .02275 | .02222 | .02169 | .02118 | .02068 | .02018 | .01970 | .01923 | .01876 | .01831 |
| 2.1 | .01786 | .01743 | .01700 | .01659 | .01618 | .01578 | .01539 | .01500 | .01463 | .01426 |
| 2.2 | .01390 | .01355 | .01321 | .01287 | .01255 | .01222 | .01191 | .01160 | .01130 | .01101 |
| 2.3 | .01072 | .01044 | .01017 | .00990 | .00964 | .00939 | .00914 | .00889 | .00866 | .00842 |
| 2.4 | .00820 | .00798 | .00776 | .00755 | .00734 | .00714 | .00695 | .00676 | .00657 | .00639 |
| 2.5 | .00621 | .00604 | .00587 | .00570 | .00554 | .00539 | .00523 | .00508 | .00494 | .00480 |
| 2.6 | .00466 | .00453 | .00440 | .00427 | .00415 | .00402 | .00391 | .00379 | .00368 | .00357 |
| 2.7 | .00347 | .00336 | .00326 | .00317 | .00307 | .00298 | .00289 | .00280 | .00272 | .00264 |
| 2.8 | .00256 | .00248 | .00240 | .00233 | .00226 | .00219 | .00212 | .00205 | .00199 | .00193 |
| 2.9 | .00187 | .00181 | .00175 | .00169 | .00164 | .00159 | .00154 | .00149 | .00144 | .00139 |
| 3.0 | .00315 | | | | | | | | | |
| 3.1 | .00097 | | | | | | | | | |
| 3.2 | .00069 | | | | | | | | | |
| 3.3 | .00048 | | | | | | | | | |
| 3.4 | .00034 | | | | | | | | | |
| 3.5 | .00023 | | | | | | | | | |
| 3.6 | .00016 | | | | | | | | | |
| 3.7 | .00011 | | | | | | | | | |
| 3.8 | .00007 | | | | | | | | | |
| 3.9 | .00005 | | | | | | | | | |
| 4.0 | .00003 | | | | | | | | | |

## 2 Values of $e^{-x}$ (for use with Poisson distribution)

| $x$ | .00 | .01 | .02 | .03 | .04 | .05 | .06 | .07 | .08 | .09 |
|-----|-----|-----|-----|-----|-----|-----|-----|-----|-----|-----|
| 0.0 | 1.0000 | .9900 | .9802 | .9704 | .9608 | .9512 | .9418 | .9324 | .9231 | .9139 |
| 0.1 | .9048 | .8958 | .8869 | .8781 | .8694 | .8607 | .8521 | .8437 | .8353 | .8270 |
| 0.2 | .8187 | .8106 | .8025 | .7945 | .7866 | .7788 | .7711 | .7634 | .7558 | .7483 |
| 0.3 | .7408 | .7334 | .7261 | .7189 | .7118 | .7047 | .6977 | .6907 | .6839 | .6771 |
| 0.4 | .6703 | .6637 | .6570 | .6505 | .6440 | .6376 | .6313 | .6250 | .6188 | .6126 |
| 0.5 | .6065 | .6005 | .5945 | .5886 | .5827 | .5769 | .5712 | .5655 | .5599 | .5543 |
| 0.6 | .5488 | .5434 | .5379 | .5326 | .5273 | .5220 | .5169 | .5117 | .5066 | .5016 |
| 0.7 | .4966 | .4916 | .4868 | .4819 | .4771 | .4724 | .4677 | .4630 | .4584 | .4538 |
| 0.8 | .4493 | .4449 | .4404 | .4360 | .4317 | .4274 | .4232 | .4190 | .4148 | .4107 |
| 0.9 | .4066 | .4025 | .3985 | .3946 | .3906 | .3867 | .3829 | .3791 | .3753 | .3716 |
| 1.0 | .3679 | .3642 | .3606 | .3570 | .3535 | .3499 | .3465 | .3430 | .3396 | .3362 |
| 1.1 | .3329 | .3296 | .3263 | .3230 | .3198 | .3166 | .3135 | .3140 | .3073 | .3042 |
| 1.2 | .3012 | .2982 | .2952 | .2923 | .2894 | .2865 | .2837 | .2808 | .2780 | .2753 |
| 1.3 | .2725 | .2698 | .2671 | .2645 | .2618 | .2592 | .2567 | .2541 | .2516 | .2491 |
| 1.4 | .2466 | .2441 | .2417 | .2393 | .2369 | .2346 | .2322 | .2299 | .2276 | .2254 |
| 1.5 | .2231 | .2209 | .2187 | .2165 | .2144 | .2122 | .2101 | .2080 | .2060 | .2039 |
| 1.6 | .2019 | .1999 | .1979 | :1959 | .1940 | .1920 | .1901 | .1882 | .1864 | .1845 |
| 1.7 | .1827 | .1809 | .1791 | .1773 | .1755 | .1738 | .1720 | .1703 | .1686 | .1670 |
| 1.8 | .1653 | .1637 | .1620 | .1604 | .1588 | .1572 | .1557 | .1541 | .1526 | .1511 |
| 1.9 | .1496 | .1481 | .1466 | .1451 | .1437 | .1423 | .1409 | .1395 | .1381 | .1367 |
| 2.0 | .1353 | .1340 | .1327 | .1313 | .1300 | .1287 | .1275 | .1262 | .1249 | .1237 |
| 2.1 | .1225 | .1212 | .1200 | .1188 | .1177 | .1165 | .1153 | .1142 | .1130 | .1119 |
| 2.2 | .1108 | .1097 | .1086 | .1075 | .1065 | .1054 | .1044 | .1033 | .1023 | .1013 |
| 2.3 | .1003 | .0993 | .0983 | .0973 | .0963 | .0954 | .0944 | .0935 | .0925 | .0916 |
| 2.4 | .0907 | .0898 | .0889 | .0880 | .0872 | .0863 | .0854 | .0846 | .0837 | .0829 |
| 2.5 | .0821 | .0813 | .0805 | .0797 | .0789 | .0781 | .0773 | .0765 | .0758 | .0750 |
| 2.6 | .0743 | .0735 | .0728 | .0721 | .0714 | .0707 | .0699 | .0693 | .0686 | .0679 |
| 2.7 | .0672 | .0665 | .0659 | .0652 | .0646 | .0639 | .0633 | .0627 | .0620 | .0614 |
| 2.8 | .0608 | .0602 | .0596 | .0590 | .0584 | .0578 | .0573 | .0567 | .0561 | .0556 |
| 2.9 | .0550 | .0545 | .0539 | .0534 | .0529 | .0523 | .0518 | .0513 | .0508 | .0503 |
| 3.0 | .0498 | .0493 | .0488 | .0483 | .0478 | .0474 | .0469 | .0464 | .0460 | .0455 |
| 3.1 | .0450 | .0446 | .0442 | .0437 | .0433 | .0429 | .0424 | .0420 | .0416 | .0412 |
| 3.2 | .0408 | .0404 | .0400 | .0396 | .0392 | .0388 | .0384 | .0380 | .0376 | .0373 |
| 3.3 | .0369 | .0365 | .0362 | .0358 | .0354 | .0351 | .0347 | .0344 | .0340 | .0337 |
| 3.4 | .0334 | .0330 | .0327 | .0324 | .0321 | .0317 | .0314 | .0311 | .0308 | .0305 |
| 3.5 | .0302 | .0299 | .0296 | .0293 | .0290 | .0287 | .0284 | .0282 | .0279 | .0276 |
| 3.6 | .0273 | .0271 | .0268 | .0265 | .0260 | .0257 | .0257 | .0255 | .0252 | .0250 |
| 3.7 | .0247 | .0245 | .0242 | .0240 | .0238 | .0235 | .0233 | .0231 | .0228 | .0226 |
| 3.8 | .0224 | .0221 | .0219 | .0217 | .0215 | .0213 | .0211 | .0209 | .0207 | .0204 |
| 3.9 | .0202 | .0200 | .0198 | .0196 | .0194 | .0193 | .0191 | .0189 | .0187 | .0185 |
| 4.0 | 0.0183 | | | | | | | | | |
| $x$ | .00 | .01 | .02 | .03 | .04 | .05 | .06 | .07 | .08 | .09 |

### 3 Student's *t* critical points

Critical point

| Pr d.f. | .25 | .10 | .05 | .025 | .010 | .005 | .001 |
|---|---|---|---|---|---|---|---|
| 1 | 1.000 | 3.078 | 6.314 | 12.706 | 31.821 | 43.657 | 318.31 |
| 2 | .816 | 1.886 | 2.920 | 4.303 | 6.965 | 9.925 | 22.326 |
| 3 | .765 | 1.638 | 2.353 | 3.182 | 4.541 | 5.841 | 10.213 |
| 4 | .741 | 1.533 | 2.132 | 2.776 | 3.747 | 4.604 | 7.173 |
| 5 | .727 | 1.476 | 2.015 | 2.571 | 3.365 | 4.032 | 5.893 |
| 6 | .718 | 1.440 | 1.943 | 2.447 | 3.143 | 3.707 | 5.208 |
| 7 | .711 | 1.415 | 1.895 | 2.365 | 2.998 | 3.499 | 4.785 |
| 8 | .706 | 1.397 | 1.860 | 2.306 | 2.896 | 3.355 | 4.501 |
| 9 | .703 | 1.383 | 1.833 | 2.262 | 2.821 | 3.250 | 4.297 |
| 10 | .700 | 1.372 | 1.812 | 2.228 | 2.764 | 3.169 | 4.144 |
| 11 | .697 | 1.363 | 1.796 | 2.201 | 2.718 | 3.106 | 4.025 |
| 12 | .695 | 1.356 | 1.782 | 2.179 | 2.681 | 3.055 | 3.930 |
| 13 | .694 | 1.350 | 1.771 | 2.160 | 2.650 | 3.012 | 3.852 |
| 14 | .692 | 1.345 | 1.761 | 2.145 | 2.624 | 2.977 | 3.787 |
| 15 | .691 | 1.341 | 1.753 | 2.131 | 2.602 | 2.947 | 3.733 |
| 16 | .690 | 1.337 | 1.746 | 2.120 | 2.583 | 2.921 | 3.686 |
| 17 | .689 | 1.333 | 1.740 | 2.110 | 2.567 | 2.898 | 3.646 |
| 18 | .688 | 1.330 | 1.734 | 2.101 | 2.552 | 2.878 | 3.610 |
| 19 | .688 | 1.328 | 1.729 | 2.093 | 2.539 | 2.861 | 3.579 |
| 20 | .687 | 1.325 | 1.725 | 2.086 | 2.528 | 2.845 | 3.552 |
| 21 | .686 | 1.323 | 1.721 | 2.080 | 2.518 | 2.831 | 2.527 |
| 22 | .686 | 1.321 | 1.717 | 2.074 | 2.508 | 2.819 | 3.505 |
| 23 | .685 | 1.319 | 1.714 | 2.069 | 2.500 | 2.807 | 3.485 |
| 24 | .685 | 1.318 | 1.711 | 2.064 | 2.492 | 2.797 | 3.467 |
| 25 | .684 | 1.316 | 1.708 | 2.060 | 2.485 | 2.787 | 3.450 |
| 26 | .684 | 1.315 | 1.706 | 2.056 | 2.479 | 2.779 | 3.435 |
| 27 | .684 | 1.314 | 1.703 | 2.052 | 2.473 | 2.771 | 3.421 |
| 28 | .683 | 1.313 | 1.701 | 2.048 | 2.467 | 2.763 | 3.408 |
| 29 | .683 | 1.311 | 1.699 | 2.045 | 2.462 | 2.756 | 3.396 |
| 30 | .683 | 1.310 | 1.697 | 2.042 | 2.457 | 2.750 | 3.385 |
| 40 | .681 | 1.303 | 1.684 | 2.021 | 2.423 | 2.704 | 3.307 |
| 60 | .679 | 1.296 | 1.671 | 2.000 | 2.390 | 2.660 | 3.232 |
| 120 | .677 | 1.289 | 1.658 | 1.980 | 2.358 | 2.617 | 3.160 |
| ∞ | .674 | 1.282 | 1.645 | 1.960 | 2.326 | 2.576 | 3.090 |

## 4 Critical values of $\chi^2$

Critical value

| Pr<br>d.f. | .250 | .100 | .050 | .025 | .010 | .005 | .001 |
|------|------|------|------|------|------|------|------|
| 1 | 1.32 | 2.71 | 3.84 | 5.02 | 6.63 | 7.88 | 10.8 |
| 2 | 2.77 | 4.61 | 5.99 | 7.38 | 9.21 | 10.6 | 13.8 |
| 3 | 4.11 | 6.25 | 7.81 | 9.35 | 11.3 | 12.8 | 16.3 |
| 4 | 5.39 | 7.78 | 9.49 | 11.1 | 13.3 | 14.9 | 18.5 |
| 5 | 6.63 | 9.24 | 11.1 | 12.8 | 15.1 | 16.7 | 20.5 |
| 6 | 7.84 | 10.6 | 12.6 | 14.4 | 16.8 | 18.5 | 22.5 |
| 7 | 9.04 | 12.0 | 14.1 | 16.0 | 18.5 | 20.3 | 24.3 |
| 8 | 10.2 | 13.4 | 15.5 | 17.5 | 20.1 | 22.0 | 26.1 |
| 9 | 11.4 | 14.7 | 16.9 | 19.0 | 21.7 | 23.6 | 27.9 |
| 10 | 12.5 | 16.0 | 18.3 | 20.5 | 23.2 | 25.2 | 29.6 |
| 11 | 13.7 | 17.3 | 19.7 | 21.9 | 24.7 | 26.8 | 31.3 |
| 12 | 14.8 | 18.5 | 21.0 | 23.3 | 26.2 | 28.3 | 32.9 |
| 13 | 16.0 | 19.8 | 22.4 | 24.7 | 27.7 | 29.8 | 34.5 |
| 14 | 17.1 | 21.1 | 23.7 | 26.1 | 29.1 | 31.3 | 36.1 |
| 15 | 18.2 | 22.3 | 25.0 | 27.5 | 30.6 | 32.8 | 37.7 |
| 16 | 19.4 | 23.5 | 26.3 | 28.8 | 32.0 | 34.3 | 39.3 |
| 17 | 20.5 | 24.8 | 27.6 | 30.2 | 33.4 | 35.7 | 40.8 |
| 18 | 21.6 | 26.0 | 28.9 | 31.5 | 34.8 | 37.2 | 42.3 |
| 19 | 22.7 | 27.2 | 30.1 | 32.9 | 36.2 | 38.6 | 43.8 |
| 20 | 23.8 | 28.4 | 31.4 | 34.2 | 37.6 | 40.0 | 45.3 |
| 21 | 24.9 | 29.6 | 32.7 | 35.5 | 38.9 | 41.4 | 46.8 |
| 22 | 26.0 | 30.8 | 33.9 | 36.8 | 40.3 | 42.8 | 48.3 |
| 23 | 27.1 | 32.0 | 35.2 | 38.1 | 41.6 | 44.2 | 49.7 |
| 24 | 28.2 | 33.2 | 36.4 | 39.4 | 43.0 | 45.6 | 51.2 |
| 25 | 29.3 | 34.4 | 37.7 | 40.6 | 44.3 | 46.9 | 52.6 |
| 26 | 30.4 | 35.6 | 38.9 | 41.9 | 45.6 | 48.3 | 54.1 |
| 27 | 31.5 | 36.7 | 40.1 | 43.2 | 47.0 | 49.6 | 55.5 |
| 28 | 32.6 | 37.9 | 41.3 | 44.5 | 48.3 | 51.0 | 56.9 |
| 29 | 33.7 | 39.1 | 42.6 | 45.7 | 49.6 | 52.3 | 58.3 |
| 30 | 34.8 | 40.3 | 43.8 | 47.0 | 50.9 | 53.7 | 59.7 |
| 40 | 45.6 | 51.8 | 55.8 | 59.3 | 63.7 | 66.8 | 73.4 |
| 50 | 56.3 | 63.2 | 67.5 | 71.4 | 76.2 | 79.5 | 86.7 |
| 60 | 67.0 | 74.4 | 79.1 | 83.3 | 88.4 | 92.0 | 99.6 |
| 70 | 77.6 | 85.5 | 90.5 | 95.0 | 100 | 104 | 112 |
| 80 | 88.1 | 96.6 | 102 | 107 | 112 | 116 | 125 |
| 90 | 98.6 | 108 | 113 | 118 | 124 | 128 | 137 |
| 100 | 109 | 118 | 124 | 130 | 136 | 140 | 149 |

# Index

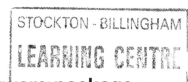
# Workbook and software package

Ron Jones has written a Workbook, which is available with or without a disk, to accompany the 4th edition of this book. It should be emphasised that the book can be used independently of the disk. The Workbook offers an additional learning resource, and includes further examination questions.

The disk package provides a number of pre-written spreadsheet templates. These templates automate much of the graphics drawing procedures of the spreadsheet and extend the statistical functions to cover the main concepts introduced in the book. The templates mirror as closely as possible the procedures used within the text.

### Specifications of the software

The software is presented on a 3.5 inch or 5.25 inch floppy disk which can be found inside the Workbook. The disk can be used on an IBM or compatible personal computer. It is run in Lotus 1-2-3 version 3, or Borland Quattro configured to run in Lotus mode, or ASEASYAS version 4.

*The Workbook costs £15.99.*

*The Workbook with the disk costs £15.99 inclusive of VAT.*

*Also available*
***Statistics*** with disk (ISBN 0 273 60569 0) £22.99 including VAT.
(*Note*: This is the same disk as that available with the *Workbook*.)

To obtain your Workbook or Workbook and software package

Complete this form and return it to: Financial Times Management, 12–14 Slaidburn Crescent, Fylde Road, Southport, PR9 9YF, United Kingdom.

---------------------------------------------------------------------------------------------

Please send me _____ copy(ies) of the *Workbook and software package* to accompany Statistics, 4th edition by Ron Jones (0 273 60322 1, £15.99 including VAT). Please specify disk size required: 3.5 inch _____ 5.25 inch _____. Please send me _____ copy(ies) of the *Workbook* (without disk) (0 273 60570 4, £15.99).

NB Postage and packing £3.00 per order in the UK
Payment must be made in £ sterling.

I enclose a cheque (payable to Financial Times Management) for £ _____

PLEASE USE CAPITALS

Name _____

Address _____

_____

_____ Postcode _____